FORTRESS AGAINST THE SUN

The B-17 Flying Fortress in the Pacific

FORTRESS AGAINST THE SUN

The B-17 Flying Fortress in the Pacific

Gene Eric Salecker

To Art Curren,
I hope that you enjoy learn
this book and that you learn
a little something about the
forgotten B-17s of the
Pacific War.

Gene Eric Salecker
Dec 2001

DA CAPO PRESS

Originally published by Combined Publishing in 2001.

Cataloging-in-Publication Data is available from the Library of Congress.

ISBN 1-58097-049-4

Printed in the United States of America.

First Da Capo Edition 2001.

EBA   01 02 03   10 9 8 7 6 5 4 3 2

To my father and mother—
Roy and Charlene,
and to my wife—
Susan.

CONTENTS

Introduction

By the Fall of 1944 it was commonplace to see 900-1000 B-17 Flying Fortresses in the air over England, winging their way towards Adolf Hitler's Nazi Germany. Two years earlier, however, in the far-off Pacific Theater, it took almost every available ounce of energy to get 10 B-17s off of an island runway at the same time. Although the B-17 fought in every theater of World War II, it won immortality with the Eighth Air Force (Eighth AF) in England. Yet, by the time the first Eighth Air Force heavy bomber raid took place on August 17, 1942, when 12 B-17s bombed Rouen, France, the Pacific B-17s had been battling the Japanese for more than nine months. Because of their use in the Pacific Theater, most of the major deficiencies and manufacturing flaws associated with the Flying Fortresses had been eliminated or had at least been recognized by the time the planes made their way to England. Likewise, lifesaving tactics and techniques had already been tried and tested by the Pacific aircrews before any Eighth Air Force crewman climbed into the belly of a B-17. Yet, when anyone happens to mention the Boeing B-17 Flying Fortress, it generally conjures up images of the war in Europe and the great daylight raids against Nazi Germany.

For all intents and purposes the Pacific Fortress crews started the war flying B-17C and D model planes. Neither model sported a tail gun and it soon became painfully evident that such a weapon was sorely needed. Likewise, both the B-17C and the B-17D lacked sufficient belly coverage. Through combat in the Pacific Theater against the highly maneuverable and highly effective Japanese Zero fighter, among others, it was shown that both models were already obsolete. Neither model would be used by the Americans in Europe[1] yet the Pacific aircrews were forced to use these obsolete planes for the first three months of the war against a Japanese juggernaut that was at its zenith.

Furthermore, although the better armed B-17E, the first model used in Europe, was already in production and actually flew into the Japanese surprise attack on Pearl Harbor, it was soon discovered that the unmanned, remote-controlled belly turret of the first 112 B-17Es built was useless. By the time the B-17E reached England, the ineffective turret had been replaced by the highly effective manned Sperry ball turret. And, when the Japanese changed tactics and began attacking the big bombers from head-on, the Pacific air and ground crews strengthened the weakly armed nose with improvised forward-firing machine guns. Although cheek guns and chin turrets would become standard equipment in Europe, the

---

[1]   Twenty B-17C models had been used by the British in mid-1942. They were disappointed in the plane's performance.

Pacific B-17s had none of these. The air and ground crews had been forced to improvise through trial and error.

Although the Flying Fortress gained its widest fame by bringing Hitler's Nazi Germany to its knees, taking great punishment while crippling Germany's strained war economy, the B-17 played an often overlooked crucial role in the Pacific. The Flying Fortress spent almost three years in combat in the Pacific Theater, battling in the skies over the Philippines, the Netherlands East Indies, New Guinea, and the Solomon Islands before being replaced by the longer range B-24. Flying over desolate stretches of open water, or through violent unpredictable tropical storms, the Pacific B-17 aircrews faced obstacles just as fearsome as their brethren in Europe. Moreover, the Japanese Zero fighter proved to be just as lethal as the German Messerschmitt, and the Japanese pilot, despite all of the pre-war propaganda, proved to be just as effective as the German pilot. Fresh from air victories in Manchuria and China, the early-war, experienced Japanese pilots were highly skilled individuals who gave the Fortress crews more than a few gray hairs.

This book is the most detailed and comprehensive account of the five Pacific B-17 bombardment groups and the hundreds of men who fought in the B-17 and/or serviced the plane. When compared to the 28 bomb groups that flew B-17s with the Eighth Air Force, the five Pacific groups might be considered a drop in the bucket. The trials and tribulations of the aircrews, who fought an enemy equally, if not more, tenacious than the Germans, and the many grounds crew mechanics who worked miracles without proper equipment or tools, make up the heart and soul of this book. While America fought a "Europe First" war, employing a total of 28 bomb groups against Nazi Germany, the men in the Pacific were forced to do whatever they could, with whatever they had, to stop the onrushing Japanese tide. The Pacific B-17s played a significant role in almost every major action in the Pacific during the first two years of the war, from the battles of the Bismarck Sea and the Coral Sea, to the battle of Midway and the actions around Guadalcanal. It should be an inspiration to everyone that the B-17 aircrews and mechanics were able to hang on in spite of all the hardships and setbacks, and never once thought of giving up.

I

Into the Valley of Death

EARLY ON THE morning of December 7, 1941, two very loose flights of four-engine Boeing B-17 Flying Fortress heavy bombers, six planes in each flight, flew high above the waters of the Pacific homing in on the Hawaiian radio stations KGMB or KGU.[1] As was becoming customary, whenever a flight of planes flew to Hickam Field, near Pearl Harbor on the island of Oahu, the Army Air Force (AAF) paid the stations to play music all night long to give the planes something to home in on. As long as the Army was willing to pay, KGMB and KGU, which normally did not broadcast 24 hours a day, were willing to stay on the air.[2]

The 12 B-17s had departed Hamilton Field near San Francisco, California, on the night of December 6, destined for Clark Field in the Philippines. Originally 16 planes, eight each from the 38th and the 88th Reconnaissance Squadrons (RS), had been scheduled to leave Hamilton but at the last minute two planes from each squadron had aborted.[3] The 38th RS was the reconnaissance component of the 19th Bombardment Group (BG) (Heavy), which was already at Clark Field, while the 88th RS belonged to the 7th BG, which was being sent to the Philippines to reinforce the 19th BG.[4] Before departing, the crews had been warned by Maj. Gen. Henry H. "Hap" Arnold, AAF Chief that, "War is imminent. You may run into a war during your flight."[5]

More than a bit concerned, Maj. Truman H. Landon, commanding the 38th BS, had voiced his anxiety. "If we might face a war situation on our trip, why don't we have the bomb sights and machine guns for our aircraft aboard, instead of having them shipped by surface vessel?"[6]

To get the most out of the B-17's limited fuel supply for the 2,400 mile flight to Hawaii, each plane had been stripped of all "non-essential items" and two long-range fuel tanks had been installed in the bomb bay. Reconsidering the possibilities, General Arnold decided to allow the crews to take their bomb sights and

11

machine guns.[7] Still, when the crews asked for 200 rounds of ammunition for each gun, they were told ". . . you'll get all of your ammunition in Hawaii."[8]

Generally, it is believed that the machine guns were still in their crates. However, this is wrong since the loaded crates would have added considerable weight to each aircraft. S/Sgt. Joseph Angelini (38th RS), flight engineer aboard 1st Lt. Robert Richards' B-17C (40-2049, *Skipper*), distinctly remembered that the guns "were in position to fire . . . [but] we had no ammunition."[9]

Additionally, it has been written that each B-17 flew with only a skeleton crew.[10] Again, this is wrong. Each plane carried a full crew while Lt. Richards carried an extra passenger—the six week old puppy of Sgt. Angelini. Described as "a Scotch terrier mixed with other durable alloys . . ." the puppy, named "Skipper," had been taken on all of the shakedown flights prior to the trip to Hawaii. In honor of the puppy, B-17C (40-2049) had been christened *Skipper*.[11]

Before the crews left the United States, Maj. Gen. Jacob E. Fickel, commanding general of 4th Air Force assigned to the protection of the western United States, had added, "Good luck and good shooting. It looks as if you might get to do some of that." As 2nd Lt. Walter H. Johnson (88th RS), bombardier on 1st Lt. Harold N. Chaffin's B-17E (41-2430, *Naughty But Nice*) wrote, "Maj. Gen. Fickle [sic] came closer to the truth than either he or we realized. If he had known what was actually [going to happen] he would have seen to it that we carried a goodly load of ammunition. As it was we carried none."[12]

The decision to send the planes without ammunition came from Gen. Arnold. He wrote, "Somebody had to weigh . . . the certainty of arriving there by providing sufficient gasoline against the probability of their using their machine guns and not getting there by carrying extra ammunition." Arnold fully believed that the airmen would run into trouble "somewhere on the other side of Hawaii."[13] Still, as a precaution, the planes, which were usually a shiny, natural aluminum had all been painted with the new AAF color scheme of olive drab top and sides over neutral gray undersides.[14]

In reality, the heavy bombers were lucky to be around at all. In August 1938 the Army General Staff in Washington, adhering to the isolationist feelings of the times, had prohibited the purchase of any more B-17s and had ruled out the development of any bomber bigger than the B-17 on the grounds that it was a weapon of aggression. However, as the war in Europe escalated and Japan expanded her control southward, people outside of the General Staff, mainly Chief of Staff Gen. George C. Marshall and Gen. Arnold, would not let the B-17 die. They knew the potential of the Flying Fortress and had fought tooth and nail to keep it alive.[15]

Near 9:00 P.M. on December 6, the B-17s from the 38th RS had begun taking off.[16] Maj. Landon's B-17E (41-2413) was the first to leave with the other planes of the squadron, four B-17Cs and one more B-17E, following close behind.[17] At 10:10 P.M., Capt. Richard Carmichael's lead plane from the 88th RS, B-17E (41-2429, *Why Don't We Do This More Often*), took off. The remaining planes of the squadron, all brand new B-17Es, soon followed.[18] 1st Lt. Robert E. Thacker (88th RS), B-17E (41-

THE ISLAND OF OAHU
TERRITORY OF HAWAII

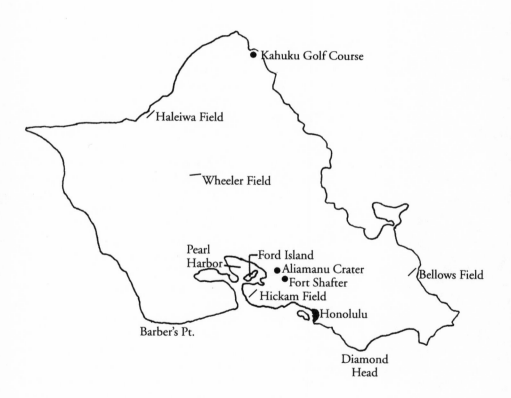

2432, *The Last Straw*), recalled, "We roared down the runway of Hamilton towards the lights of San Francisco and over the Golden Gate bridge and into the starry night, flying over a sea of overcast clouds . . ."[19]

The flight to Hawaii had been uneventful as each B-17 flew alone through the night. "Each crew was on its own," Lt. Johnson wrote. "A thirteen hour trip is a long one, particularly over water. We seldom saw the surface of the ocean, for we flew at 8 thousand feet and over the overcast. . . The navigators shot the stars, kept track of position, [and] estimated the time of arrival. Everything ran smoothly. . ."[20]

Many people believe that the Navy had stationed ships across the Pacific to serve as directional indicators. Sgt. Angelini disagreed. "We navigated by the stars. There was no place that we could check along the way that I know of."[21] Lt. Thacker saw no Navy ships. "We saw one [other plane] during the night," he recalled, "it's green and red and white lights bringing joy to our hearts, for we knew if anyone was lost there were two of us . . ." 1st Lt. David G. Rawls (88th RS), B-17E (41-2434), reported, "At dawn we saw another B-17 twenty miles to our left and leading us. That was a welcome sight after the solitude of the night."[22]

As day dawned and the individual planes drew closer to Hawaii, they picked up the music from either KGMB or KGU. "A thousand miles out we could hear KGN [sic], Honolulu," penned Lt. Johnson. "That gave us confidence. We were coming closer, closer . . . [but] the gas became less and less . . . If we were not exactly on course we might pass to one side of the island of Oahu and never know it . . ."[23] In fact, two planes were out of position. On B-17E (41-2408), flown by 1st Lt. Karl T. Barthelmess (38th RS), someone had accidentally flipped a switch, throwing off the navigation so that the plane was actually far north of Oahu. When Barthelmess realized the mistake, he quickly turned due south, homed in on KGMB and hoped that he had enough gas to reach Hickam Field.[24]

At about the same time, Maj. Landon also found out that he was off course. Throughout the night, an inexperienced navigator had plotted the course. Around daybreak the navigator informed Landon that they were still 100 miles from Hickam but that he did not know if they were north or south of Oahu. Being a skilled navigator himself, Landon listened to the radio station signals and determined that Hawaii lay to the south. So, like Barthelmess, he made a quick turn and kept an eye on his depleting gas.[25]

Near 7:15 A.M., with the individual B-17s nearing Hawaii, a portable Army radar unit detected a large "blip" approaching from the north. When the operators reported the contact to a central plotting station the officer in charge, knowing that the B-17s were coming in from California and certain that the blip was the incoming bombers, told the men, "Well, don't worry about it."[26] In reality, the radar had picked up a fast approaching flight of Japanese attack planes.

A few minutes later, Lt. Richards spotted Oahu and Bellows Field, a short fighter plane field near the northeast tip of the island. The 38th RS B-17C was the first of the 12 B-17s to reach Hawaii. "[W]e homed in on the radio and we hit Bellows Field on the nose," Sgt. Angelini recalled. Turning south, Richards headed towards Hickam and Pearl Harbor. The time was about 7:55 A.M. "We came around Diamond Head," Angelini continued, "and we saw some smoke . . . just starting to come up from Pearl Harbor."[27]

Richards and his crew had no way of knowing that they were flying into the start of a war. At precisely 7:55 A.M., carrier-based Japanese planes unexpectedly hit the American fleet at anchor in Pearl Harbor, causing considerable damage. At the same time, the Japanese struck Hickam Field, due east of the harbor.[28]

"[T]he radio was still playing in town," Sgt. Angelini recalled, indicating that everything seemed all right. "So we got over Hickam and looked and then [a Japanese plane] came up alongside flying formation with us." The crew of *Skipper* did not know what to make of the strange looking plane. "[W]e didn't know what the hell it was and he didn't know who we were either for that matter," Angelini said. For a few minutes the two planes flew side by side and then suddenly the Japanese pilot fired at the B-17.

Caught by surprise, Angelini shouted, "What the hell are they shooting at!"

Bombardier S/Sgt. Lawrence B. Velarde thought that the attack was part of an army exercise and that the plane was firing wax bullets.

"Wax bullets hell!" Angelini exclaimed. "We got goddamn holes in our wings!"[29]

Lt. Richards raced for the safety of a cloud and was able to lose the Zero but when he emerged on the other side, he was jumped by three more enemy planes. Once again the B-17 sustained damage. The No. 2 engine, the inboard engine on the left side, began smoking and the left aileron was torn apart, leaving it practically useless. Afraid of landing at Hickam while it was under attack, Richards turned back towards Bellows Field.[30]

Next to reach Hawaii was 1st Lt. Bruce G. Allen's (38th RS) B-17C (40-2063). Nearing Pearl Harbor, Allen saw thick columns of smoke above the area and thought it was the result of burning sugarcane. In spite of the attack on Pearl Harbor and Hickam Field, and the large amount of antiaircraft fire that was beginning to fill the air, Lt. Allen landed his B-17 at Hickam without any trouble.[31]

Following hot on the heels of Allen's plane was B-17C (40-2074) flown by Capt. Raymond T. Swenson (38th RS). As the plane approached Hickam, copilot 2nd Lt. Ernest L. Reid saw a few black bursts of antiaircraft fire and thought that some artillery unit was having gunnery practice. At almost the same instant he saw a flight of six fighter planes fly through the fire. "I recall thinking," Reid wrote, "that somebody on the ground was getting a little careless about where he was shooting."

As the B-17 drew closer to Hickam, things did not look right. "I noticed a great deal of black smoke coming up from Pearl Harbor," Lt. Reid wrote. "There was too much ack-ack [antiaircraft fire] around, and I began to feel that something was wrong . . ."

When Capt. Swenson attempted to contact the Hickam control tower he got no response. Closer to the airfield and down to only 600 feet, Reid finally saw what was causing the oily, black smoke. "At least six planes were burning fiercely on the ground," Reid wrote. "Gone was any doubt in my mind as to what had happened." As if to punctuate the thought, two Japanese Zeros suddenly swept in from behind and stitched the B-17 with bullets.

Responding instantly, copilot Reid shoved the throttles forward, giving full power to the four engines. "It seemed only logical," he later recalled, "to get quickly into some nearby clouds . . . since we had no way of fighting back."[32]

1st Lt. William R. Schick, a flight surgeon only recently assigned to the 38th RS, was standing between Lts. Swenson and Reid and called out, "They are shooting at us from the ground."

As Reid shouted back that the fire was coming from behind, Schick suddenly grabbed his leg. "Damn it! Those are real bullets they're shooting. I am hit in the leg."

The plane was heading for the clouds when smoke suddenly began filling the flight deck. Tracer bullets from one of the Zeros had ignited a box of magnesium flares stored in the radio compartment. With the center of the aircraft on fire, Swenson and Reid turned the bomber back towards Hickam. Unable to see clearly because of the smoke, the pilots made a hard, bouncing landing and as the tail came down, the middle of the fuselage buckled and collapsed, splitting the plane in two. "When that happened we stopped very quickly," Reid noted.[33]

High above Hickam, Japanese pilot Lt. Comdr. Shigeru Itaya watched the B-17C come apart and later claimed credit for shooting down the first B-17 in the Pacific war.[34] At the same time, Lt. Masanobu Ibusuki was radioing his carrier that he had shot down a B-17. Perhaps both pilots deserve credit for the kill since Lt. Reid distinctly recalled that two enemy fighters made a run at the bomber. Even Lt. Ibusuki reported, "With other planes, I shot down a flying B-17."[35]

When the plane split, the nine crewmen ran for safety. Those in the rear half sought protection in Hickam's large hangars, while those in the front ran for the high grass alongside the runway. Although the bomber was cut in two, Lts. Swenson and Reid could not overcome the habit of shutting down the engines and locking the parking brakes. As the men scrambled for safety, a Zero strafed the crowd, mortally wounding Lt. Schick in the head and slightly wounding four other crewmen.[36]

While the two parts of B-17C (40-2074) sat burning beside the runway, 1st Lt. Earl J. Cooper (38th RS), B-17C (40-2054), landed without mishap. Flying through enemy fighters and antiaircraft fire from the ground, the bombers were finally being guided into Hickam Field by a "calm voice" from the control tower. Capt. Gordon A. Blake, Hickam's base operations officer, had been waiting at the control tower to greet the B-17s, when the first bombs struck. After the initial shock, Blake's professionalism kicked in and he began giving the pilots the information they needed to land.[37]

Not too far behind Cooper was the B-17E of Lt. Barthelmess. Having corrected his navigational error, Barthelmess was coming in from the north at about 8:00 A.M. when about 15 Japanese dive-bombers suddenly overtook him from behind. Thinking that the planes were out to escort them in, the crew began waving to the "friendly" planes. Only then did they notice the big red circles on the wings.

Unsure of what was going on, S/Sgt. Lee Embree pointed a camera at the "escort" and took a picture. Only then did the Japanese pilots break away and fly ahead without further incident.[38]

The crew still did not know what was going on as the Fortress drew closer to Hickam Field and they saw the thick black smoke rising from the airfield and Pearl Harbor. 2nd Lt. Charles E. Bergdoll thought it was the most realistic drill he had ever seen, complete with smoke pots and fake bombs. However, when the plane landed and Bergdoll saw the smoking remains of a wrecked B-24 Liberator heavy bomber, the only one in Hawaii, he suddenly realized that the attack was real. The Army would never destroy such an expensive plane for a drill.[39]

Also coming in from the north was the B-17E of Maj. Landon. Sometime before, as he flew south, he had spotted a flight of nine small aircraft coming straight towards him. Expecting them to be Army escort planes sent out to guide him to Hickam, he was shocked when they suddenly opened fire. After reaching the safety of a nearby cloud, Landon continued south and tried to figure out what had just happened while the smaller planes continued north.

When Landon's B-17 drew closer to Hickam, it was suddenly jumped by three trailing Zeros and shot at by friendly ground troops. Braving both the Japanese fighters and the American antiaircraft fire, Landon came into Hickam and touched down at 8:20 A.M., the last of the 38th RS planes to land at Hickam.[40]

Only one plane from the squadron had failed to land at Hickam. Lt. Richards' B-17C had been the first to reach Hickam but had fled towards Bellows Field after sustaining considerable damage. Upon reaching Bellows, Richards ran into more trouble. As he made his landing approach on the short fighter airstrip he was suddenly forced to pull up. "When we got to Bellows they were towing a P-40 across the runway and we couldn't run into it, land, so we had to . . . come around," Sgt. Angelini recalled. "So we went around and jumped on the ground and went off the end of the runway and crashed . . ."[41]

A P-40 crew chief stationed at Bellows witnessed the second approach and landing:

> No one was aware of the flight of bombers arriving from the states, and to see that approaching monster trailing smoke from its right [sic] engines . . . was mind boggling. Our asphalt landing strip at Bellows was hardly long enough to accommodate our P-40's, much less a B-17; and when he made an approach from the ocean downwind, we knew we were in for a breathtaking crash landing. Even though his wheels were down, he flared out and touched down halfway on the strip . . . slid off the runway over a ditch and into a cane field bordering the air strip.[42]

"And then the people came running up," Sgt. Angelini recalled. "[T]hey came up and said, 'What the hell are you trying to land here for?' They knew nothing about [the Japanese attacks.]"[43]

All of that changed in an instant however, when nine enemy planes suddenly appeared. "Then fifteen [sic] of them started to strafe us there, trying to set the plane on fire," Angelini stated. Since Richard's bombardier had been wounded over Hickam, Sgt. Angelini took his puppy with him and scrambled into the nose section to remove the top-secret Norden bombsight. "One big problem was getting that damn Norden bombsight out," he recalled. "I tried, I had it loose except for one damn rod and I couldn't get it loose and they were strafing so . . . I left, picked up my dog and went up to the supply room to get a rifle."[44]

The fighters strafed the plane repeatedly, trying to set it on fire. Later, when the attack was over, base personnel counted 73 bullet holes in the plane. Almost completely out of fuel the B-17C never did catch fire.[45]

All of the planes from the 38th RS were now on the ground. Five were at Hickam and one at Bellows. Four were slightly damaged but still in commission. Capt. Swenson's B-17C (40-2074) had been burned in half and was a total loss and Lt. Richard's B-17C (40-2049, *Skipper*), at Bellows, was heavily damaged but thought to be repairable. (It was not.) Shortly after the arrival of the 38th RS, the B-17s of the 88th RS began to arrive.

Capt. Carmichael, commanding officer (CO) of the 88th RS, was the first pilot of the squadron to reach Oahu. "We rounded Diamond Head and first noticed moderately severe antiaircraft fire, a huge oil fire in Pearl Harbor, 3 to 5 ships on fire, the hangars at the west end of Hickam in flames and a large amount of smoke in the Wheeler Field area," he wrote.

After seeing a number of unidentified planes flying through the antiaircraft fire and "several bombs burst in the channel and harbor," the crew of *Why Don't We Do This More Often* realized that "a real war was in progress." Deciding not to land at Hickam, Carmichael headed for Bellows Field but arrived there while that airstrip was under fire. Unable to land at Bellows and running low on fuel, Carmichael headed towards Wheeler Field, a small fighter strip in the center of Oahu.[46]

Following close on the heels of Carmichael's plane was Lt. Chaffin, B-17E (41-2430, *Naughty But Nice*). "We saw the antiaircraft fire, the burning Hickam hangars and barracks, the burning ships in the harbor . . . a burning B-17E plane on the ground, and realizing that a war was on and swung away . . ." Unfamiliar with Oahu, Chaffin flew north, and finally landed at Haleiwa Field, a short emergency airstrip along the northern coast of Oahu.[47]

About five minutes later, Capt. Carmichael also landed at Haleiwa. After having spotted a Zero near Wheeler Field, Carmichael had assumed that Wheeler was under attack and flew to Haleiwa. "Lt. Chaffin had previously landed at Haleva [sic]," Carmichael reported, "and so, after dispersing the ship, we checked in by telephone with the Hawaiian department, and were ordered to Hickam Field." Quickly the two crews started refueling their planes.[48]

1st Lt. Frank P. Bostrom's (88th RS), B-17E (41-2416, *San Antonio Rose*), had been the last plane to leave California but was among the first of the squadron to reach Hawaii. As he neared Hickam Field, he contacted the control tower but was never informed of the Japanese attack. Unknowingly, Bostrom circled above Pearl Harbor and saw a ship burning in the water. An instant later, an antiaircraft shell exploded just beyond his right wing. "I grabbed my mike," Bostrom reported, "and asked the tower what the hell was going on and they finally told us that we were being attacked by enemy aircraft."

He was down to 700 feet when a few American ships opened fire on the unidentified bomber. Bostrom headed for the safety of the clouds. He recalled, "We flew in and out of broken cumulous clouds hoping not to be observed for we had no means of defense, but two minutes later we were attacked by a Jap pursuit coming from the rear." Although the B-17 was able to outmaneuver the lone Zero, three more fighters quickly pounced on the unprotected bomber and riddled it with fire.

"We had bullet holes in our tail, wings, a hole in the fuel transfer line, flap rod and electrical wiring," Bostrom noted. Using full power, Bostrom was able to outrun his pursuers but found that he was now nearly out of gas. "We knew we'd better land or we never would and after spotting a golf course succeeded in landing in the fairway." The badly damaged B-17E made a successful, if somewhat undignified, landing at Kahuku Golf Course on the northeast tip of Oahu.

Although no one was wounded on the plane, Bostrom was understandably furious with the officers in charge of Hickam. "I think that someone should be courtmarshalled [sic] for telling the tower operator to tell us to land without telling us what we were up against," he wrote in his official report. "Only by pure luck are we alive today."[49]

As Lt. Rawls, B-17E (41-2434), arrived over Hickam Field he saw a burning B-17 beside the runway and instantly knew that something was wrong. While following another B-17, perhaps Bostrom's, he ran into antiaircraft fire from the American warships. "The air was rough," he wrote, "and when we realized that we were being fired upon by antiaircraft, we made a quick 180 degree turn and began to climb."

Rawls flew towards Wheeler Field but "found it burning as badly as Hickam." Low on fuel, he headed back to Hickam and was almost on the ground when his Fortress was suddenly strafed by an enemy fighter. "One bullet hit [the] No. 2 propeller and another went through the main spar of the left wing," reported Rawls. "Numerous hits were scored but we got in." Having no ammunition for their machine guns, Sgt. Robert K. Palmer fired his .45 caliber automatic pistol at the attacker. As the crew ran from the plane they were strafed by three Japanese planes. "How we all got through I don't know," Rawls wondered.[50]

Lt. Thacker's crew in B-17E (41-2432, *The Last Straw*) had no knowledge of the Japanese attack until they neared Pearl Harbor and Hickam Field. "We saw a big oil fire in the harbor and a ship [i.e. plane] like the one we were flying burning on the ramp so we headed back towards Honolulu . . ." wrote Thacker. Coming back during a lull in the attacks, Thacker landed hard and fast and blew a tire. In order to stop the plane he had to do "a fancy ground loop at the end of the runway," actually spinning the plane around 180 degrees in order to break his speed. The quick maneuver caused the blown tire to catch fire but the crew managed to put it out in spite of two strafing attacks by Japanese planes.[51]

A few seconds later, 1st Lt. Harry N. Brandon, B-17E (41-2433), spotted the antiaircraft fire over Pearl Harbor which his copilot attributed to some sort of celebration. Contacting the Hickam control tower to see what was going on, Brandon was given landing instructions. "No mention was made of the situation at Pearl Harbor . . .," he wrote. As Brandon circled to avoid the antiaircraft fire a Japanese Zero fired a few shots at his B-17. Calling the tower again, Brandon demanded to know what was going on. In an understatement he wrote, "The operator reported that we had been attacked by enemy aircraft, and we were rather convinced of that by then."

Lt. Brandon turned for Wheeler Field but was called back to Hickam. However, just as he was about to land, someone pulled a burning plane in front of him and he was forced to circle again. Finally, on his third try, Brandon landed the B-17 safely and the crew quickly ran for cover.[52]

At Haleiwa emergency field, the two aircrews of Capt. Carmichael and Lt. Chaffin had managed to remove the empty bomb bay gas tanks and put 200 gallons of gasoline into the wing tanks of their Fortresses. After securing ammunition for their machine guns, the crews climbed back aboard their respective bombers and flew unmolested into Hickam.[53]

All of the 88th RS B-17s were now accounted for. Five were at Hickam and one was on Kahuku Golf Course. All 12 of the B-17s from the States had made it to Hawaii although one had been burned in half and destroyed, and two, Lt. Richards' at Bellows and Lt. Bostrom's at Kahuku, were heavily damaged.[54] While none of the pilots reported landing at Wheeler Field, someone obviously did.

Sometime during the attack on Wheeler, a lone B-17 touched down on the grass runway. Somehow the pilot managed to avoid the burning P-40 fighters strewn about the field and ground looped his plane to avoid crashing into a hangar. Rifle fire from the troops at Wheeler greeted the B-17 as it landed but, in the words of one soldier, "Fortunately, our people were notoriously poor marksmen and I don't think any of the crew was hit by the hostile welcome."[55]

Among those that witnessed the landing of the unidentified B-17 was Brig. Gen. Howard C. Davidson, commander of the 14th Pursuit Wing based at Wheeler, and Col. William J. Flood, in command at Wheeler. Once the Fortress landed, Col. Flood raced over to the pilot and told him to get back into the air and look for the Japanese fleet.

"You know, Colonel," the unidentified pilot replied, "we just came over from California."

"I know, but, son, there's a war on."

"Okay," said the pilot, "if I can get a cup of coffee, we're off."[56]

Although one author believes that Col. Flood may have been joking, apparently the pilot did not think so. When the attacks on Wheeler were finally over, an inventory was taken and no B-17 was present. Evidently, the unidentified pilot took Col. Flood's words to heart and left Wheeler, apparently flying on to Hickam Field.[57]

Hickam Field was the home of a number of air force groups and squadrons in December, 1941, but only two of the groups were designated as "Heavy" and flew B-17s. The 5th and 11th Bombardment Groups (Heavy) constituted the 18th Bombardment Wing (Heavy). The 5th BG consisted of a Headquarters and Headquarters Squadron (HqS), the 23rd, 31st and 72nd Bombardment Squadrons (BS) and the 4th RS (all Heavy). The 11th BG was made up of a HqS, the 26th, 42nd and 98th BSs, and the 50th RS (all Heavy). Twelve B-17Ds, were dispersed among the two groups, six with the 5th BG and six with the 11th.[58]

On December 7, 1941, most of Hickam's B-17s were lined up, wing tip to wing tip, beside the smaller bombers and fighter planes, on the concrete apron in front of Hickam's massive hangars. However, two or three of the Fortresses were inside the hangars awaiting maintenance. Prior to December 7, with the threat of war looming on the horizon, the planes had been armed with machine guns, loaded with bombs and dispersed about the field, but when it was reported that Japanese dignitaries might be stopping in Hawaii on their way to Washington for a last minute peace conference, the planes had been unloaded and placed side by side in a more friendly manner.[59]

The first wave of Japanese planes hit Hickam Field at approximately 7:55 A.M. and stayed for about 10 minutes. Nine dive-bombers came out of the west and hit the base buildings and hangar line. The large Hawaiian Air Depot, on the far west end of the field, was almost completely destroyed, and bombs hit the new million dollar Hale Makai consolidated barracks. Hickam's 10 huge strangely numbered hangars were set up in pairs, side-by-side, with each set connected by a short hallway. Each hangar took various amounts of damage. Hangar #11, home of the 5th BG, was completely wrecked but Hangar #13, home of the 11th BG, received only a few bomb hits.

At the same time that the first Japanese planes struck from the west, seven dive-bombers came out of the east, bombing the hangars and the parked planes on the apron, and three more bombers flew in from the northwest to hit the base buildings. Minutes later, nine Zeros appeared from the south, strafing the parked planes and anything and anyone that moved.[60]

Most of the personnel from the 11th BG were asleep in the huge consolidated barracks building, located just north of the flight line and hangars, when the Japanese struck.

The first bomb detonated in the kitchen, killing 35 men instantly. PFC Hiram Jenkins (50th RS) was still asleep when the Japanese attacked. "When the bomb hit the kitchen, the concussion threw me out of bed," Jenkins wrote. As he sat on the floor wondering what had just happened, a piece of hot shrapnel ripped through his empty bunk. Suddenly wide awake, Jenkins pulled on some clothes and made a dash for the squadron hangar.[61]

Pvt. Seymour Blutt (HqS/11th BG) was in the kitchen prior to the attack. Having heard the "rumbling of explosions," Blutt looked out a large window and saw the approaching planes. "They had large red circles on their wings," he remembered, "and they were bombing and strafing. I instinctively yelled, 'Take cover!'" His first thought was to seek cover inside the big walk-in freezer but for some unknown reason, he ran the other way, out onto the parade ground. After the attack it was found that all of the Chinese cooks had sought refuge inside the walk-in freezer and had been killed by the concussion of the falling bombs. "I don't know what made me dash the other way for the open ground," Blutt wondered, "but I'm glad I did."[62]

Already out on the flight line was Pvt. Thomas E. Bradshaw (50th RS), who had drawn guard duty from midnight until 8:00 A.M. Nearing the end of his shift, he heard low-flying aircraft approaching and watched in amazement as one of the planes dropped a bomb on Pearl Harbor. In an instant, "all hell broke loose," he wrote. As the Japanese fighters began strafing Hickam, Bradshaw assisted a wounded comrade over to the base hospital, while all the time firing his .45 caliber automatic at the low-flying planes.[63]

The personnel from the 5th BG were equally surprised by the unexpected attack. Pvt. Earl M. Schaeffer, Jr. (72nd BS) had taken a friend's assignment as switchboard operator from midnight to 8:00 A.M. for $2.00. He was in the communications shack between two hangars when he heard muffled explosions and a few minutes later experienced a "shaking and rattling and parts of the ceiling coming down . . ." Rushing out to the flight line, he saw three planes making a low level strafing run on the parked aircraft on the apron. "As they passed by, I saw the big red balls on the sides of their aircraft," Schaeffer wrote. "The awful truth came home with a jolt and nausea in my gut. I knew from the aircraft identification classes we had that I was looking at three Japanese Zero Fighter Planes." Not knowing "where else to go or what to do," Schaeffer returned to the switchboard.[64]

At 8:00 A.M. Phil Klingensmith (HqS/5th BG), who was planning to celebrate his 25th birthday later that evening at the Royal Hawaiian Hotel, should have been at nearby John Rodgers civilian airport. He was running late for his early morning flying lesson with flying instructor Bob Tyce. As Klingensmith wrote years later, ". . . I had to have been the luckiest, or one of the luckiest GI['s] on the seventh of Dec. . . ." While Bob Tyce was readying his private plane, a lone Zero made one strafing pass and killed Tyce instantly.[65]

Capt. Brooke E. Allen (5th BG) arrived at the flight line during the attack and instantly went into Hangar #11 to save his B-17D. Although only three of the four engines started, he taxied the plane out of the hangar and moved it away from the burning parked planes. As he continued to try and start the dead engine, he saw a large bomber fly over the runway. "Where did the Japs get four-engined bombers?" he thought, mistaking one of the California B-17s for an enemy plane.[66]

Squadron instructor pilot 1st Lt. James Latham (26th BS) reached Hangar #13 and found a group of mechanics frantically trying to put a wheel on a B-17D. A second later, two bombs hit the hangar roof and blew everyone "around inside the hangar." His eardrums damaged, Latham, along with the others, ran for the flight line, only to become targets for the strafing fighters. "[T]he Japs would come by strafing, and we would turn and run back to the hangar," he wrote, "I don't know how many times it happened." Finally Latham found refuge in the hangar latrine. "I was down there with my arms around the crapper, hanging on for dear life," he admitted.[67]

1st Lt. James V. Edmundson (HqS/5th BG) unlocked the gun room in Hangar #11 and passed out weapons to everyone. "As I recall," he wrote, "we had 3 old Lewis air-cooled 30 Caliber machine guns, World War I vintage, which I ordered passed out, too."[68] One of the men who got a machine gun was Phil Klingensmith who quickly set the gun up on the parade ground. Klingensmith wrote, "Sometimes I had the 30 cal. machine gun and two men, sometimes one man, and sometimes just me and the gun." Firing the gun by himself was difficult. "[Y]ep," he admitted, "I jammed it." When a bomb landed close by and blew Klingensmith off his feet, he moved the gun to the lip of the shell hole. "A place to dive into when needed," he figured.[69]

A short lull occurred after the first attack before the Japanese struck again at 8:25.[70] During the lull, a number of men were able to reach their squadron hangars. Pvt. Carlton Belz (50th RS) reached Hangar #13 and found a mass of men "all milling about in confusion" and demanding firearms. Incredibly, the armament sergeant refused to hand them out without orders. "Then some guy just ups and cold cocks him and opens the [armament] shack," wrote Belz. Joining a group of men with a .30 caliber machine gun, they improvised a tripod from a floodlight stand. "The hole in the light standard was larger than the swivel post of the gun so the gun had to be steadied by hand," Belz wrote, "[but we] did manage to get off a few rounds when a wave of Jap planes came over the runway."[71]

Capt. Allen was still trying to get the No. 1 engine started on his B-17D when he saw "ammunition bomb trucks being pulled out of the ammunition storage area loaded with bombs." He wrote, "The thought occurred to me to try to load the bombs so that I could attack any enemy ships in the vicinity." Gathering a few men, Allen had three bombs almost loaded when the Japanese returned, forcing the men to seek cover. As Allen helplessly watched, the Zeros disabled his B-17. "One engine was completely shot up and one wheel was shot from under it."[72]

After helping his friend to the hospital, Pvt. Bradshaw returned to Hangar #11 just as a flight of enemy bombers dropped their bombs on the building. Diving under a solid table with a "butcher block type surface" Bradshaw was one of the few survivors inside the hangar. Still, he suffered shrapnel wounds to his face, neck, and hands, lost a few teeth and had his tongue "half-severed on the lower part." Afraid of bleeding to death, Bradshaw headed back to the base hospital.[73]

Pvt. Jenkins was cutting through the hallway between Hangar #11 and Hangar #13 when the bombs exploded on Hangar #11. "The concussion ricocheted me through that hall, out into the middle of 13," Jenkins wrote. Uninjured, he was ordered to the flight line to get a machine gun from one of the parked planes but when a Zero appeared, he took cover under a tractor used to tow planes. Unfortunately, somebody jumped onto the tractor and drove it away, leaving him "completely exposed." As Jenkins recalled, "Those bullets came down on both sides of me . . . It scared me out of my wits."[74]

When Pvt. Schaeffer finally left the switchboard, he was grabbed "by someone in charge" and told to help disperse the planes on the flight line. "I ended up helping move our B-17[D], which was the older type without tailguns," he recalled. Once the plane was away from the flight line, he was ordered to set up a .50 caliber machine gun in the side blister of the plane. "This was fine," Schaeffer wrote, "except I had never seen a .50 caliber before and what they dumped off the armament truck weren't even completely assembled." As he and a friend tried to assemble the guns, the Zeros repeatedly strafed the B-17. "The Good Lord or Lady Luck was with me that morning," he wrote, "[I] came through unscathed."[75]

The third, and last, enemy attack came around 9:00, when two waves of Japanese planes swept in from the northwest and southwest. As the planes darted about, Pvt. Jenkins helped fire a .50 caliber air-cooled machine gun from the window of the Base Operations building. "I fired away until we ran out of ammunition," he remembered. Having no tripod, one of Jenkins' friends, Casey Jones, held the gun in his hands while Jenkins fired. "If anyone says he can hold a .50 caliber in his hands and fire it, he's nuts," Jenkins stated. "It burned Casey's hands something fierce."[76]

Capt. Frank H. Lane, acting hospital commander, was at Hickam's base hospital attending to the wounded when he spotted a soldier dressed in a dark winter uniform, which was unusual for Hawaii. The soldier was wounded in the head and wore the insignia of a medical officer. When Lane approached, the wounded man waved him off and pointed to the other casualties. "Take care of them," the man insisted. Turning away, Lane told the officer that the next ambulance would take him to Tripler Hospital, at Fort Shafter, a bit inland from Hickam. The wounded man was Flight Surgeon Lt. Schick, who had arrived from California and had been hit while escaping from Capt. Swenson's broken B-17. Although taken to Tripler, Schick died from his wounds shortly after arrival.[77]

When the third attack ended around 9:10, Lt. Latham and a scratchwork crew immediately began loading 500-lb. bombs into B-17D (40-3060), which had somehow survived the attack. "We got aboard, and I cranked this thing up and got to the runway," Latham recalled. Before he could take off however, a staff officer ordered Latham back to headquarters. The staff officer then climbed into the B-17 to find the Japanese fleet himself. "On a B-17 we had elevator locks," Latham wrote. "If you pull up the handle, it locks the elevators." As Latham watched, the B-17 started down the runway. "But then," Latham continued, "[the staff officer] grabbed the wrong lever and locked the elevators. The tail naturally came up and the nose went down and they swung off to the side in a cloud of dust." Fortunately, no one was injured but with four bent propellers, another B-17 was out of commission.[78]

Capt. Allen was still hoping to go after the Japanese fleet and located an undamaged B-17. With his scratch crew he managed to load it with bombs but as he was about to take off, orders came for him to wait for an escort of Army fighters. Almost two hours later, near 11:30 A.M., Allen was finally allowed to take off. However, instead of being escorted by a flight of fighters, he went out with a second B-17, this one piloted by Maj. La Verne G. "Blondie" Saunders (23rd BS/5th BG), whose thinning hair was actually jet-black.[79]

Despite a feeling that the enemy carriers were to the north, the two pilots were ordered "to attack two enemy carriers reported about 35 miles south of Barber's Point." In fact, Maj. Landon, from California, had rushed to headquarters after landing to inform someone that he had run into a flight of Japanese planes to the north of Oahu, apparently heading back to their carriers. Instead of finding a receptive audience, he had found almost everyone preoccupied with trying to fit their helmet liners into their steel helmets.[80]

As the two B-17s flew south, Capt. Allen found that his plane was not altogether undamaged. Two life vests were riddled with bullet holes and his radio connection with Hawaii was out, although he still had interplane communications with Maj. Saunders.[81]

Unable to find the Japanese fleet off Barber's Point, the two planes continued south for about two hours until Maj. Saunders turned back with engine trouble. Out on his own, Capt. Allen continued flying south for a few hours and thought that he had finally hit pay dirt when he suddenly spotted a "beautiful carrier." He started his bomb run and although the "enemy" ship fired at him, he suddenly pulled up. "God had a hand on me," Allen wrote, "because I knew this was not a Jap carrier." The ship was the United States carrier *Enterprise*. Apprised of the Japanese attack on Pearl Harbor the jumpy antiaircraft gunners had opened fire on the unidentified bomber.

Turning away, Capt. Allen continued his search and somehow happened upon the *Enterprise* again. This time however, two Navy fighters came up to look at the big B-17. With night descending and no radio communication with Hawaii, Allen decided to end his search and return to Hickam.[82]

The surprise attack on Hickam Field cost the 5th BG 21 killed and 44 wounded while the 11th BG lost 44 killed and 84 wounded. Besides the loss of life, the two groups suffered heavily in the loss of their B-17Ds. The 5th BG had two of their six B-17s destroyed and another two badly damaged while the 11th lost the use of all six of their planes with three destroyed, one badly shot up, one with four bent propellers, and one still awaiting repairs needed prior to the attacks. When the day was over, the two groups had only two B-17s still in commission.[83]

The first day of war for America had been a bad one for the Pacific B-17s. It would only get worse.

II

The First Line of Defense

ALMOST 5,000 MILES west of Hawaii was the Commonwealth of the Philippines, an archipelago of over 7,100 islands, of which Luzon was the largest. In December 1941, the Philippines was an American protectorate, scheduled to gain full independence in 1944. In mid-1941, as diplomatic relations with Japan broke down, the Army Air Corps (AAC) (soon to become the Army Air Force) had decided that it was time to beef up its first line of defense in the Philippines, hoping to deter Japan from expanding southward. One of the main articles of this strong defense was the B-17 Flying Fortress. Gen. Douglas MacArthur, commander of the United States Army Forces in the Far East (USAFFE), in command of all land and air forces in the Philippines, had no doubt that the Japanese would attack the Philippines but thought that they would not attack until April of 1942. He reasoned that he had enough time to build up his force of heavy bombers. By March 1942, he intended to have 163 B-17s in the Philippines, enough to deter or at least severely cripple a Japanese invasion.[1]

By December 1941, MacArthur had 35 B-17s of the 19th BG at Clark Field, 65 miles northwest of Manila, on the island of Luzon. The 19th BG was one of the original heavy bomber units in the AAC and was composed of, on paper at least, the 14th, 28th, 30th and 93d BSs (Heavy), and the HqS (Heavy).

In September 1941, the US Command had selected the 19th BG, originally consisting of only the HqS, and 30th and 93rd BSs, to go to the Philippines. However, when the 19th BG was delayed from leaving the United States while their older model B-17Cs were modified to B-17D standards, the decision was made to forward nine B-17s from the Hawaiian Air Force to MacArthur instead. The crisis in the Philippines was deemed too urgent to wait.

On September 5, 1941, nine B-17Ds belonging to the 14th Provisional Squadron (made up of crews and planes from the 5th and 11th BGs), left

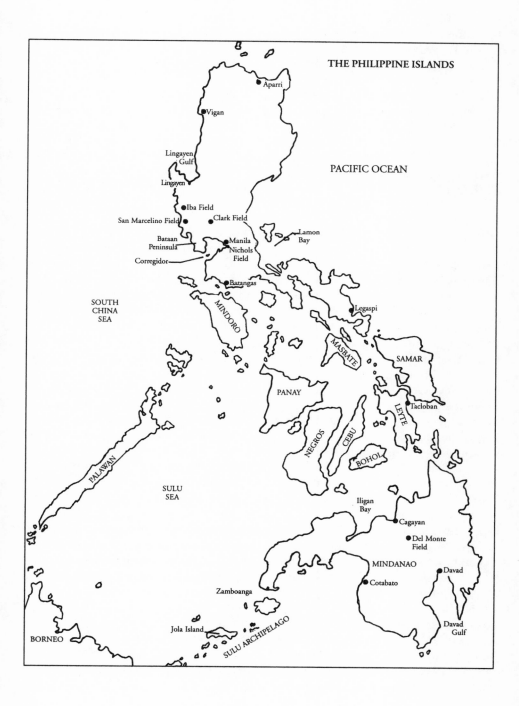

THE PHILIPPINE ISLANDS

PACIFIC OCEAN

Aparri

Vigan

Lingayen
Gulf

Lingayen

Iba Field

San Marcelino Field

Clark Field

Bataan
Peninsula

Manila

Nichols
Field

Lamon
Bay

Corregidor

Barangas

Legaspi

SOUTH
CHINA
SEA

MINDORO

MASBATE

SAMAR

PANAY

LEYTE

Tacloban

NEGROS

CEBU

BOHOL

PALAWAN

SULU
SEA

Iligan
Bay

Cagayan

Del Monte
Field

MINDANAO

Davad

Cotabato

Zamboanga

Jola Island

SULU ARCHIPELAGO

Davad
Gulf

BORNEO

27

Hickam Field under the overall command of Maj. Emmett C. "Rosie" O'Donnell Jr.[2] One of the pilots was 1st Lt. Edward C. Teats flying B-17D (40-3078). He recalled, "We had an advance agent who went to New Guinea and Australia, checking on the availability of high-octane gas, servicing facilities, usability of fields, all that sort of thing—all in preparation for the flight." Following the advance agent, the planes staged through Midway Island, Wake Island and Port Moresby, New Guinea. "Our course was so mapped as to detour Ponape—one of the main Jap bases in the eastern Carolines—at night and at high altitude," Teats wrote. "We made hourly position reports except on the third leg of the flight, that from Wake to Port Moresby. On it, we observed radio silence until we were well clear of [Ponape]." 1st Lt. Henry C. Godman, piloting B-17D (40-3097, *Ole Betsy*), recalled, "At Wake Island machine guns were loaded, test fired, and readied to ward off an attack should there be one over the Japanese Mandate Islands."[3]

Maj. William P. Fisher, B-17D (40-3093), leading the second element of three planes, took off from Wake but broke an oil line and was forced to turn back for repairs. Consequently, he was about two hours behind the others when they passed over Ponape. Once the others were past Ponape, Maj. O'Donnell broke radio silence to ask for status reports, unaware that Fisher was so far behind. As Teats recalled, "Each [pilot] reported except the No. 1 plane of the second flight. Finally, O'Donnell asked Fisher, 'What's your position?' Bill promptly came back with: 'I'd hate to tell you!'" Reported Teats, "We knew instantly that Bill was sitting right on top of Ponape at high altitude that very minute in broad daylight!"[4]

At New Guinea, native tribesmen refueled the planes from 50-gallon drums using hand-cranked pumps taking an average of four hours for each plane. Early the next morning, September 10, after losing a day by crossing the International Date Line, the nine B-17s flew on to Darwin, Australia, and two days later, headed north for the long flight to Clark Field. Near the Philippine island of Mindoro, about 300 miles south of Clark, the planes ran into a typhoon. "Our weather briefing had not indicated to us that a typhoon was passing Manila," wrote Godman. "Now that seems incredible to me that we would be allowed to fly into a typhoon."

Lt. Teats remembered, "We let down to within 100 feet of the water and bored right through with rain drops as big as goose eggs slamming the windows." Lt. Godman added, "At times we could see maybe two or three miles ahead of us, and as an island would loom up, we would veer to the left or to the right—talk about frightening!! We were flying under the typhoon."[5]

In spite of the weather, the planes reached Clark Field without incident and began to land. After flying a total of 7,000 nautical miles without incident, the flight suffered its only casualty when the last bomber to land was taxiing off the field and tore off its tail section when it accidentally hooked a derelict airplane that had been left beside the runway. Nevertheless, the successful completion of the longest overseas flight yet attempted by the AAC had earned universal praise for Maj. O'Donnell and his men. Each man was awarded a Distinguished Flying Cross.[6]

One month later, the 20 B-17Ds and six revamped B-17Cs of the 19th BG were finally ready to leave Hamilton Field, California. The bomber crews were no strangers to the long overseas flight to Hawaii. In May they had ferried 21 B-17s to the 5th and 11th BGs at Hickam Field, nine of which were soon flown to the Philippines by the 14th Provisional Squadron and 12 which were caught on the ground on December 7.[7]

On October 16, nine planes from the 30th BS under the command of Maj. David R. Gibbs, had left Hamilton Field for Hickam. Four days later, the 93d BS and the HqS, under the overall command of Lt. Col. Eugene L. Eubank, commanding officer of the 19th BG, left the States and flew the remaining 17 B-17s to Hawaii. Assembling at Hickam, all 26 shiny aluminum planes had been issued 100 rounds of ammunition for each gun. "In the event of contact in the air with planes of a possibly belligerent nation," their orders had read, "do not hesitate to bring them under immediate and accurate fire."[8]

Fully fueled and ever so lightly armed, the 26 planes were split into two flights of 13 planes each to help ease the strain on the small servicing facilities at Midway and Wake Islands. On October 24, the first flight, consisting of nine B-17s from the 30th BS and four from the HqS left Hawaii. Three days later, the second flight, consisting of nine planes of the 93rd BS and the remaining four bombers of the HqS followed.

On October 31, the first 13 planes reached Port Moresby. Having run into extremely bad weather, the flight was pretty well strung out. In fact, three planes had been forced to land at Rabaul on New Britain Island to refuel before continuing on to New Guinea. Avoiding the bad weather, the second group arrived at Port Moresby late in the afternoon of November 1 with their wing and bomb bay gas tanks practically empty.

Upon landing in New Guinea, the crews of the second flight had learned that the first echelon had gone on to Darwin the day before. On November 2, the second flight took off for Australia and finally caught up to the first flight. Now fully assembled, the combined group began leaving for Clark Field on the night of November 2, landing there throughout the day of November 3. One plane was delayed in Darwin after losing two engines on the short hop from New Guinea and did not reach Clark Field until November 20. Like the flight crews that had preceded them, all 26 crews were awarded the Distinguished Flying Cross for this unprecedented mass flight.[9]

When the aircrews from the 19th BG arrived at Clark they were greeted by their own ground crew personnel. Having left San Francisco on the transport *William H. Holbrook* on October 5 they had gone directly to the Philippines, arriving on October 23.[10]

Upon its arrival at Clark, the 19th BG absorbed "Rosie" O'Donnell's nine B-17Ds of the 14th Provisional Squadron. Although officially still a part of the 11th BG, the squadron was redesignated the 14th Bombardment Squadron and attached to the 19th BG. By the end of November, a total of 35 B-17s were in the Philippines, the largest collection of heavy bombers outside of the continental United States.[11]

In the autumn of 1941, Clark Field was the only airfield in the Philippines capable of handling a B-17 bomber. Located on the southwestern portion of a vast plain, Clark Field was 12 miles west of an unmistakable landmark, Mount Arayat, a 4,000 foot extinct volcano. The main landing strip at Clark was a hard-packed sod runway measuring 6,700 feet long with a hump in the middle that made it hard for someone standing at one end to see planes parked at the other. The land surrounding the airstrip was too soft to bear the weight of a B-17 so the planes had to be parked alongside the runway itself. To help deter sabotage, Clark Field personnel began constructing tall sandbag revetments around each plane, but by the end of November only two had been completed and these did little to conceal the shiny aluminum planes from being viewed from above.

When the 19th BG moved to Clark Field, the base suddenly found itself short of housing. Although some men were quartered at Fort Stotsenburg, an old military facility near the southwest corner of Clark Field, most of the men lived in small interwoven grass mat buildings west of the main runway.[12]

South of the runways were the hangars and machine shops, while large tents, used by engineering and operations, were set up beside the road leading to Fort Stotsenburg. In preparation for an attack, slit trenches had been dug behind the different buildings and near the runway itself. Although only one artillery unit provided antiaircraft fire for Clark Field, additional protection was provided by a number of sandbag machine gun emplacements set up around the field.[13]

The main air warning system for Clark came from Filipino air watchers stationed around the island of Luzon. Although there were seven radar sets in the Philippines, only the set at Iba Field, a fighter base northwest of Clark, was operational. Should enemy planes approach, the natives were to telephone Air Headquarters at Manila, which in turn would notify Clark Field. Unfortunately, the native watchers were poorly trained in plane identification. In a practice test in November, it was 46 minutes between the time the "enemy" planes were sighted and the information reached Clark Field.[14]

Morale at Clark was very high. Wholeheartedly, the personnel of the 19th BG felt that American airplanes were far superior to anything Japan had. 2nd Lt. Edgar D. Whitcomb (HqS) recalled:

> The feeling of American superiority had a strong hold on each of us. Since childhood we had been taught that American machines, American planes, American equipment, and American men were superior in quality to all others on the face of the earth . . . Why, then, should any of us doubt that we would be able to crush the Japanese in a very short time if they were foolish enough to attack us?
>
> We had been told that the Japs, by the very nature of their physical makeup, were poor pilots. Their vision and balance were poor,

and their aircraft were vastly inferior to our own. On the other hand, our B-17s could fly so high that they were beyond the reach of the Jap's antiaircraft and planes, and with our secret [Norden] bombsight we could pinpoint targets and destroy them with miraculous accuracy.[15]

Almost everyone was of the opinion that they had nothing to fear from the Japanese. M/Sgt. Benjamin F. Kimmerle (30th BS) wrote, "Everyone felt that if war did come we were strong enough to take care of ourselves." Boasted Lt. Godman, "The feel of war was in our veins, and we wanted some action." Lt. Teats admitted, however, "We had complete faith in our military dispositions and were confident that no matter what their force, they couldn't take the place overnight; but we also realized that unless we got a hell of a lot of help from the outside, the going would be plenty tough." Generally, the 19th BG personnel felt that when war finally came, the B-17s could keep the Japanese at bay while the Americans mounted an offensive of their own.[16]

Gen. Marshall, in Washington, was equally confident. In early November, he had told reporters that the B-17s in the Philippines could easily fend off any Japanese attack and set the "paper cities of Japan" ablaze. Likewise, Gen. MacArthur firmly believed that the present strength of the American fighters and bombers in the Philippines was enough to threaten the sea-lanes needed by Japan to expand southward or move raw materials back to her home islands.[17]

On November 3, Maj. Gen. Lewis H. Brereton the newly designated Air Commander of the Philippine air forces, Far East Air Force (FEAF), arrived in Manila and immediately broke his command into three subsidiary commands. The fighters were placed under the 5th Interceptor Command, the service personnel under the Far East Air Service Command and the bombers under the 5th Bomber Command. The bomber command was headed by Col. Eubank, who also retained command of the 19th BG.[18]

After inspecting the Luzon airbases, Brereton concluded, "Conditions were disappointing." He wrote, "Work hours, training schedules, and operating procedure were still based on the good old days of peace conditions in the tropics." On November 6, Brereton implemented orders to get his command in shape. A new training schedule was drawn up and one squadron of bombers and one squadron of fighters was placed on "constant readiness."[19] However, because of a lack of parts, ammunition and gasoline, the airmen could only do so much. 2nd Lt. Edward M. Jacquet Jr. (93rd BS) recalled, "We had to conserve the hours on our engines because there were no more [engines] in the Philippines. We would consolidate several training missions into one flight . . ."[20]

Additionally, Brereton realized that having only one airfield in the Philippines capable of handling his B-17s was courting disaster. Another bomber field on the island of Mindanao, 600 miles south of Luzon, was already under construction but progressing very slowly. The new B-17 airbase was being built on a natural meadow on the Del Monte Pineapple Corporation plantation in central Mindanao and although the runway was almost completed there were still no buildings or equipment. Around November 9, Brereton sent a detachment of airbase ground troops to Del Monte to hurry construction and a few days later sent down a load of gasoline, ammunition, and bombs.[21]

The work on Del Monte was sped up for a number of reasons. In addition to having a second bomber field in the Philippines, another B-17 group, the 7th BG, was scheduled to move to the Philippines in early December and since Clark Field was already overcrowded, Brereton was hoping to base the new arrivals at Del Monte. Additionally, any B-17 flying to Clark Field from Australia that was low on gas could land at Del Monte to refuel. And finally, although the Japanese fighters and bombers on Formosa could reach anywhere on Luzon, Del Monte would be out of the reach of any land based planes the enemy possessed.[22]

In an attempt to combine all of the Philippine bomb squadrons into one group, Gen. Brereton transferred the 28th BS, a medium bombardment squadron that had been in the Philippines since 1922, to the 19th BG and redesignated it a heavy bombardment squadron. The 19th BG, still under the command of Col. Eubank, and now consisting of the 14th, 28th, 30th, and 93rd BSs, and the necessary HqS, continued its training until it had progressed from "disorganized" to "an advanced level."[23]

Upon joining the group, the 28th BS discarded their obsolete B-18 and B-10 medium bombers and sought to replace them with B-17s from the other squadrons. However, the replacements never came. Maj. Cecil E. Combs, commanding officer of the 93rd BS, remembered that the 28th never operated as a heavy bombardment squadron while in the Philippines and the 28th BS historian reported that the 28th moved to Clark Field "without any ships at all." Since the 28th BS pilots had been flying medium bombers prior to joining the 19th BG, none of the pilots were qualified to fly B-17s.[24]

On November 28, Gen. Brereton placed all his air units, including the 19th BG, on an immediate war footing. Brereton had been informed that negotiations between the U.S. and Japan had broken down. Blackouts were ordered at all airfields and a 24-hour alert was established for half of the bombardment force and half of the fighter units. At Clark Field, Col. Eubank canceled all leaves and restricted almost every man to base. Lt. Whitcomb remembered, "[W]e were ordered to wear our forty-five's, a bulky gas mask on our left sides, and a steel helmet. This was the old-fashioned World War I type that our doughboys had worn in France."[25]

Flight training now included reconnaissance flights towards Formosa. Each day, at least two planes flew pie-shaped wedges north towards the Japanese island. Although the Army lacked recent reconnaissance photos of the Formosa airfields and desperately wanted to know what was going on, the B-17s were forbidden to fly over the island. The War Department had issued specific instructions "to avoid any overt act." The pilots were limited to "two-thirds of the distance between North Luzon and Southern Formosa" (later changed to the International Boundary of Formosa).[26]

In spite of orders, a few pilots ended up over Formosa. 1st Lt. Frank Kurtz (30th BS) was on a routine high-altitude test north of Luzon in B-17D (40-3099) when he happened to look down. "[M]y God!" he wrote. "[W]e were over, not the blue sea, but the big Japanese base on the island of Formosa! A big black ugly hunk of something that was forbidden." Recalled Kurtz, "I didn't want *Old 99* to become the first international incident, so I got out of there quick."[27]

Later, Maj. Gibbs, in another B-17, flew across the southern tip of Formosa in spotty weather at a height of only 2,000 feet and admitted seeing "landing fields literally stacked with Japanese bombers." Whether Gibbs flew over Formosa by accident or on purpose has never been determined. The information he brought back however was discounted. Noted 1st Lt. Earl R. Tash (93rd BS), "Gen. MacArthur was of the opinion that these Japanese preparations were not being gathered for a strike against us but that they were to make what moves they would against Indochina, or maybe Thailand." The men of the 19th BG thought differently.[28]

On the night of December 2, an unidentified airplane flew over Clark Field. Unknowingly, base personnel correctly identified it as a Japanese reconnaissance plane. After the war, Japanese fighter pilot Saburo Sakai admitted, "On the second of December . . . [we] sent the first reconnaissance planes over the Philippine Islands." A few nights later the plane returned and took aerial photographs of Clark Field. Wrote Sakai, "The photographs of Clark Field shown to us revealed thirty-two B-17 bombers . . ."[29] Japanese Intelligence was almost perfect. Although there were 35 B-17s at Clark Field, one was in the repair hangar, still awaiting repairs on its torn tail, and two were probably inside the hangars awaiting a camouflaging coat of paint. In an attempt to make the shiny aluminum bombers less visible, the B-17s were being spray painted with an olive-drab coat of paint.[30]

On December 4, Gen. Brereton decided to move some of his B-17s down to Del Monte, figuring that the Japanese had no knowledge of this new field. As Brereton wrote, "The overcrowding at Clark Field invited attack, and I directed that steps be taken immediately to move two squadrons of Flying Fortresses, 16 aircraft . . . to Del Monte." Brereton presented his decision to Gen. MacArthur's chief of staff, Brig. Gen. Richard Sutherland who disliked basing any of the bombers on Mindanao. The war plan for the defense of the Philippines did not call for any ground troops to be stationed on Mindanao and Sutherland felt that any B-17s based at Del Monte would be in jeopardy. According to Brereton, although Sutherland consented to the move, he stipulated that the two squadrons come back as soon as additional bomber fields could be built on Luzon.[31]

Actually, Gen. Brereton had intended to move all 35 of his B-17s down to Del Monte but rejected the idea for a couple of reasons. First, the sparse facilities at Del Monte could not handle all of the planes and personnel of the 19th BG. Second, the 7th BG was expected to arrive at Del Monte any day now. In fact, the ground personnel of the 7th BG were already en route by water. As Gen. Brereton explained, "It was planned to base the 7th Group at Del Monte, where two more landing fields were to be constructed." When the 7th BG arrived, the two 19th BG squadrons at Del Monte would have to return to Clark.[32]

On the night of December 5, the eight B-17s of the 14th BS under Maj. O'Donnell, and the eight B-17s of the 93rd BS under Maj. Combs began taking off for Mindanao. Since the facilities at Del Monte were far from complete, the men took their tents, cots, blankets and rations with them. "The 93rd felt that it always 'got it in the neck'," complained Lt. Jacquet. "Here we had to . . . fly to a remote field with no facilities. Gee, that was terrible to look forward to—field conditions for an infinite time." Lt. Teats added, "The men of the squadrons took with them only what they needed—tooth brush, razor, personal items of that sort and three or four changes of uniform. I don't think anyone had more than 25 pounds of luggage, and many had only cross-country bags."[33]

Although all 16 planes were suppose to clear Clark Field by midnight and fly en masse to Del Monte, troubles with some of the planes forced a delay of almost three hours. Then, even though Del Monte was only 600 miles away and only four hours flying time from Clark Field, the flight circled over the island of Panay for a couple of hours while they waited for daylight. Since most of the pilots had never been to Del Monte, they wanted to wait for daylight and avoid a hazardous night landing.[34]

At first light on December 6, the 16 planes turned towards Del Monte and landed without incident. Although Lt. John W. Carpenter III (93rd BS) was suppose to take B-17D (40-3063) down to Del Monte, the plane was out of commission with persistent generator trouble so he was replaced in the move by Capt. Elmer L. Parsel (93rd BS) in B-17D (40-3074). The only other trouble occurred when Lt. Tash's B-17 developed a gas leak during the flight due to the decomposition of the self-sealing material in one of the wing tanks. Since there was no repair shop at Del Monte, Tash was scheduled to fly back to Clark Field on the morning of Monday, December 8.[35]

Upon arrival at Del Monte, Lt. Teats was unimpressed. "In reality, it was just a big cow pasture backed up against some mountains . . .," he wrote. "There were . . . no shops, no hangars, no adequate servicing facilities, and the upper end of the runway slanted downhill like a ski-run." On the other hand, Lt. Jacquet, who had been expecting the worst, was pleasantly surprised. "Contrary to our expectations, the Del Monte Canning Company had a country club nearby with golf, tennis and a swimming pool. But," he added, "we still had to live in our tents."[36]

Although Del Monte airfield was "primitive" in comparison to the well equipped airfield at Clark, work was still being done to improve the facility. On December 1, two boatloads of men and equipment from the 5th Air Base Group, commanded by Maj. Raymond T. Elsmore, had arrived with orders to turn Del Monte into a top-rated airfield for the 7th BG. The ranking officer at Del Monte, Maj. Elsmore had quickly contracted with the manager of the Del Monte Corporation to start construction on a number of barracks buildings.[37]

When the 19th BG B-17s arrived, Maj. Elsmore immediately began camouflaging the shiny aluminum skinned bombers. The "one and only spray gun on Mindanao" was operated day and night to give the planes a coat of olive drab paint while newly hired Filipino workers, and a few base personnel, climbed aboard an odd assortment of trucks and drove 17 miles down to the beach to gather large coconut leaves. "It required ten truckloads to cover each Fortress," Elsmore admitted, but it was worth the effort to secure the safety of the B-17s on the wide open field.[38]

That same day, Gen. Brereton flew to Clark Field to confer with Col. Eubank about a bombing mission against Formosa should war break out. Since they were sorely lacking information on the disposition of Japanese troops on Formosa, it was decided that the first strike would be against Takao Harbor, thought to be full of Japanese transports and warships. In preparation, it was decided to hold a field exercise on Monday, December 8, with the entire 19th BG, which would require the 14th and 93rd BSs to come back from Del Monte.

One night later however, on December 7, Brereton was informed that, "in the opinion of the War and Navy departments hostilities might break out at any time." Immediately, he contacted his airbases and told them to go on full "combat alert" at first light on December 8. All fighters were to be ready to takeoff in a little under one hour while the bombers were expected to be bombed up, and the crews briefed and ready for takeoff in just over an hour. In light of the extremely dangerous situation, the field exercises involving the entire 19th BG were canceled and the 14th and 93rd BSs were told to stay at Del Monte.[39]

The attack on Pearl Harbor came at 7:55 A.M. Sunday, December 7, 1941, but because of the different time zones and the International Date Line, it was 2:55 A.M. Monday, December 8, 1941, in the Philippines. Near 4:00 A.M., Gen. MacArthur was notified of the attack and although lacking official confirmation, immediately contacted his staff.[40]

When Gen. Brereton heard the news, he admitted that it "came as a surprise to no one." After instructing his staff to notify all of his air bases about the attack, Brereton called Col. Eubank at Clark Field and instructed him to load his B-17s for the strike against Takao Harbor. Instead, however, Eubank wanted to leave the bombers empty and put them on standby. Then, if there was a change in target, and different size bombs were needed, time would be saved in changing the bomb loads. The ground crews would have ample time to load the planes while the aircrews were being briefed. And, just in case the Japanese struck first, it would be better if the bombers were not fully loaded. Brereton readily agreed.[41]

When the conversation was over, Col. Eubank ordered his bomb squadron commanders to report to base headquarters to inform them about Pearl Harbor and brief them on the attack against Formosa.[42] Being the only pilot from the 93rd BS still at Clark Field, Lt. Carpenter found himself as "the CO of the Sq[uadron] at Clark" and was awakened at 5:30 A.M. and ordered to report to headquarters as soon as possible. Once everyone was assembled, Eubank informed his commanders to "get their boys together and tell them that hostilities had started and that Hickam Field had been attacked." As Carpenter reported, "No one . . . was very downhearted about the news and some of the boys were pretty eager."[43] The long awaited news had finally arrived.

Although the commanders were told to inform their men about the Japanese raid on Oahu, most of the men heard the news from a commercial radio. "I got up at seven as usual," said Lt. Kurtz, "and, stumbling in sleepily to shave, snapped on my portable as I always did to get the morning news broadcast by Don Bell in Manila . . . In even more rapid-fire style than usual he told us the big news—that the Japs had hit Hawaii."[44]

Lt. Whitcomb heard a rumor at a little after 7:00 A.M. while he was on his way to the mess hall. "In general, we concluded that it was just a rumor and changed the subject to something else," he recalled. "It did not make sense to us that the Japanese should attack Pearl Harbor and leave Clark Field unharmed. With the B-17s and equipment we had at Clark, we felt certain that even the Japanese would not be foolish enough to commit such a blunder."

After leaving the mess hall, Whitcomb suddenly heard the familiar voice of Don Bell on a radio: "Japanese aircraft have attacked Pearl Harbor. There is no report of the damage at this time. Further information will be broadcast as soon as it is available." Realizing that the rumors were true, Whitcomb rushed down to headquarters but found everybody "going about their duties in the usual fashion." As Whitcomb remembered, "It was all so ordinary that it was almost mysterious."[45]

Sometime between 6:30 and 7:00 A.M. a radiogram came into Del Monte from Clark Field telling of the attack and informing the men "to take necessary precautions."[46] Like the men at Clark Field, those at Del Monte quickly turned on commercial radios to learn more. "I heard the news on the radio when I woke up that morning," bombardier T/Sgt. Durwood W. Fesmire (93rd BS) said, "but a lot of the fellows wouldn't believe it . . ."[47]

Maj. O'Donnell immediately ordered two B-17s from his 14th BS to fly reconnaissance patrols around Mindanao in opposite directions. Within a short time Lts. Teats and Godman were airborne.[48] A short time later, Lt. Tash asked Maj. O'Donnell if he should take his B-17 back to Clark Field for the scheduled repair of the gas leak. Since O'Donnell felt that "every plane [should] be perfectly fit and ready to go," Tash was instructed to carry on with his orders. Near 8:30 A.M., Lt. Tash took off from Del Monte for the four hour flight to Clark. As soon as they reached altitude, his crew summarily test fired their fully loaded machine guns.[49]

Shortly after talking with Gen. Brereton, Col. Eubank was ordered to report to Air Headquarters in Manila for an emergency staff meeting. Upon arrival, he discovered that Gen. Brereton had gone to see Gen. MacArthur concerning the planned strike on Formosa. The entire staff was of the opinion that the B-17s should strike Formosa as soon as possible, but when Brereton finally arrived, near 8:00 A.M., he said that the strike was on hold. Apparently, Gen. MacArthur and his staff felt that although the Japanese had committed an overt act of war against the United States, there had been no such move against the Philippines.[50]

Wrote Brereton:

Neither Gen. MacArthur nor Gen. Sutherland ever told me why authority was withheld to attack Formosa after the Japs had attacked Pearl Harbor. I have always felt that Gen. MacArthur may possibly have been under orders from Washington not to attack unless attacked . . . Owing to the political relationship between the Philippine Commonwealth and the United States it is entirely possible that the Pearl Harbor attack might not have been construed as an overt act against the Philippines.[51]

Later, however, MacArthur recalled that "he had not the slightest doubt that he would be attacked," and denied ever knowing about Brereton's request to send his bombers against Formosa. Army records, however, clearly show that MacArthur was informed.[52]

On the other hand, Gen. Sutherland insisted that it was Brereton, and not MacArthur, that delayed the bombers. Sutherland recalled "that there was some plan to bomb Formosa but Brereton said that he had to have photos first. That there was no sense in going up there to bomb without knowing what they were going after."[53]

The only concrete fact in the matter was that there was much discord between General Headquarters and Air Headquarters. Incredible as it seemed, no matter who initiated the orders, the B-17 Flying Fortresses, MacArthur's best offensive weapons, were not used. Told that he could obtain aerial photos of Formosa, Brereton instructed Col. Eubank to send three planes out on a photo reconnaissance mission and have his other planes stand by to takeoff at a moment's notice.[54]

Unknown to the Americans, only bad weather had prevented the Japanese on Formosa from already striking Clark Field. A 4:00 A.M. takeoff for a strike against the Philippines had been planned but a thick fog had rolled in at 3:00 A.M., preventing the scheduled takeoff. "Three hours passed this way, and still the fog had not abated," Saburo Sakai wrote. "If anything, it had thickened."

At 6:00, while the Japanese pilots were still waiting for the fog to lift, they were told of the successful attack on Pearl Harbor. "The attack created a factor which we must consider," Sakai noted. "The Americans were now warned of our attack plan, and it was incredible that they would not be waiting for us in strength in the Philippines." As Sakai saw it, the fog would "allow the Americans to send their bombers from Luzon and catch our planes on the ground the moment the fog lifted." Little did Sakai know that politics, and not fog, were keeping the B-17s on the ground.[55]

Near 8:15 A.M., Gen. Brereton got a call from Gen. Arnold in Washington who warned him not to get caught in a repetition of Hickam, with his bombers on the ground like sitting ducks. Once again Brereton called MacArthur's headquarters and asked for permission to strike Formosa. Permission was denied, "for the present."[56]

At 9:00 A.M., the fog began to lift over Formosa and the Japanese fighters and bombers were ordered into the air. At exactly 10:00 the "signal lights flickered through the last wisp of fog" and the planes began to take off. "By 10:45, all planes were airborne," recalled Sakai, "fifty-three bombers and forty-five Zero fighters." Their destination: Clark Field.[57]

Shortly after 9:00 A.M., Gen. Brereton received word that Japanese bombers, in spite of the weather, had bombed two American airfields on northern Luzon. Believing this was clearly an "overt act," Brereton called General Headquarters for permission to send his B-17s against Formosa. Unbelievably, permission was once again denied. It would take almost another hour before Gen. MacArthur himself called Brereton to say that he could send the B-17s on a raid in the afternoon if the aerial photos identified likely targets.[58]

By the time Clark Field heard the news, Maj. Gibbs, who had been left in charge of the 19th BG, already had a reconnaissance plane in the air. Shortly after Col. Eubank left for the staff meeting Maj. Gibbs had sent 1st Lt. Hewitt T. "Shorty" Wheless (30th BS) to photograph Formosa. Then, near 10:00 A.M., after being warned that a flight of enemy planes was heading his way, Gibbs ordered every bomber into the air, all without bombs. Told to maintain contact with the control tower the bombers took off and began circling Mount Arayat.[59]

Only three bombers failed to take off with the others. The plane missing the tail was still awaiting repairs, while Lt. Kurtz's plane was receiving a coat of camouflage paint, and Lt. Carpenter's B-17 was still grounded by generator trouble. Finally, at 10:30, Lt. Carpenter got his plane airborne and headed towards the northeast corner of Luzon, his previously assigned patrol area.[60]

Near 11:00 A.M., Col. Eubank returned to Clark Field and recalled his bombers when the expected enemy air raid did not materialize. Per instructions, he was prepared to send out three reconnaissance planes but minutes later, as the first of the Flying Forts began to trickle in, Eubank received word from Brereton that the bombing mission was on. Gen. Sutherland had finally given him the green light. The B-17s were to be loaded and sent against the "known airfields in southwest Formosa." At the same time, the two squadrons at Del Monte were instructed to come back to Clark Field tomorrow morning for "offensive action."[61]

As the B-17s landed they were disbursed beside the runway and the crews immediately began servicing the planes. "All activities were stopped on the field to get the planes back in the air as soon as possible," Sgt. Kimmerle wrote. "Food was brought to the field in containers for the combat crews and everyone was busy getting the planes serviced and their final instructions. Some of the officers were at hq., some on the field with their planes and some getting a bite to eat."[62]

While the planes were being refueled and loaded with bombs, the pilots and navigators were ordered to get a bite to eat and then head over to the Operations Tent for a briefing. Recalled Lt. Kurtz, whose B-17 was finally done being camouflaged, he was ordered to "eat fast, and get over to the operations tent quick and find out what plans they had lined up for us." By 12:20 P.M., he was at the scheduled briefing.[63]

"The operations tent was crowded with about forty pilots and navigators waiting for [the] briefing to begin," Kurtz remembered. "As we waited, I snapped on my radio and we all listened to Manila." As the men listened they heard announcer Don Bell say that Clark Field had been bombed and that he could see big plumes of smoke rising up from the burning bombers. "We all smiled at this," Kurtz recalled. "We didn't know that he, from Manila, could see around the little hill over in the direction of Iba Field, and that these plumes of smoke were burning P-40's there."[64]

Iba Field, with the only fully operational radar unit, was hit by the Japanese around noon. Besides destroying a large number of fighter planes, the Japanese also destroyed the radar set. With the radar at Iba knocked out, Clark Field had to rely on the primitive system of Filipino air watchers telephoning a warning of approaching planes to Air Headquarters, which in turn would relay the warning to Clark. Unexpectedly however, the telephone lines suddenly went dead and any warnings were subsequently cut off. Although Air Headquarters was still linked to Clark via radio, with no warnings coming in, there was nothing to report.[65] Fifth Column saboteurs had done their work well.

At Clark Field, the pilots and navigators were sitting in the operations tent waiting for the briefing to begin when a private spotted an approaching formation of planes.

"Oh, gee! Look at the pretty Navy formation," he said.

Looking at the planes 1st Lt. Lee Coats (30th BS) shouted, "Navy, hell! Here they come!"

An instant later the tent was empty as the airmen scrambled to find safety in a nearby drainage ditch.[66]

The Japanese bombers flew at about 17,000 feet altitude in two perfect V of Vs, like a flight of geese, one behind the other, 27 planes in the first, and 26 in the second. The time was 12:40 P.M. and unbelievably, they had arrived without detection.[67]

Japanese fighter pilot Sakai was astounded by what he saw:

> The sight which met us was unbelievable. Instead of encountering a swarm of American fighters diving at us in attack, we looked down and saw some sixty enemy bombers and fighters neatly parked along the airfield runways. They squatted there like sitting ducks . . . We failed utterly to comprehend the enemy's attitude. Pearl Harbor had been hit more than five hours before; surely [the Americans] had received word of the attack and expected one against these critical fields![68]

Unfortunately, through miscommunication, a flight of P-40s that should have been covering Clark Field had been sent elsewhere while the fighter planes based at Clark were on the ground refueling. Everything that could go wrong, was.[69]

At almost the exact moment that the Japanese appeared, Lt. Tash's B-17 from Del Monte arrived over Clark Field. It was exactly 12:40 A.M. and Tash was already on his landing approach with his wheels down when the first bomb exploded on Clark Field. Ordering wheels up, Tash immediately applied full throttle and raced for a "mildly dense cloud bank." Figuring that he had 35 minutes of fuel to spare before deciding whether to try a landing at Clark Field or return to Del Monte he remained inside the cloud as the Japanese pounded Clark Field.[70]

"The attack came without warning and so suddenly that no one had time to get under cover," wrote Sgt. Kimmerle. "As the apex of the [first] V approached the field the bombs started falling and as the V widened out the area of the bombs widened out. As the last of the first formation of bombers left the far end of the field the first of the second group started." The bombers came in from the northwest and flew towards the southeast, dropping their bombs as the went.[71]

Lt. Carlisle was inside his barracks room with four of his roommates when the bombs struck. As he recalled, "There was no whistles, no air raid alarm; the first [I] knew of the attack was when the bombs began screaming down, and then, the first thunderous, earthquaking explosion." An instant later the beams and ceiling rafters crashed down around the five. Wrote Carlisle, "It was a minute and a half of celestial upheaval." When the bombs finally stopped falling, Carlisle found that two of his roommates were dead, one was wounded and the other, like himself, was unhurt.[72]

As the bombs began to fall Lt. Whitcomb ran to a nearby slit trench. "The air was charged with a loud crack like that of dry boards being broken," he wrote. "Then, as I hit the bottom of the trench, there was a terrible explosion followed by another, another and another. The earth rocked and rolled . . . ." Lt. Kurtz, who was lying in the drainage ditch behind the Operations Tent, remembered, "We could think of nothing then except this earthquaking roar and grinding and the whistling of a mighty storm moving down the field." He tried to describe the feel of the explosions. "[A]t its mildest, the hard dirt quivered like a steel-tired truck thundering over cobblestones, and at its worst bucked and pitched like a bronco."[73]

Saburo Sakai saw the attack from a different perspective. "The attack was perfect," he wrote. "Long strings of bombs tumbled from the bays and dropped towards the targets . . . it was, in fact, the most accurate bombing I ever witnessed by our own planes throughout the war. The entire air base seemed to be rising into the air with the explosions. Pieces of airplanes, hangars, and other ground installations scattered wildly. Great fires erupted and smoke boiled upward."[74]

The enemy bombers completely patterned the field. Base personnel could not walk more than 30 feet in any direction without finding a bomb crater. Almost all of the buildings were hit and many were set on fire. An oil dump behind the hangars received a direct hit and burst into flames, sending a huge plume of thick black smoke skyward. Clark's P-40 fighters, which had been recalled with the B-17s, were caught on the ground. Only four got into the air, but the rest became flaming wrecks in front of the burning hangars.[75]

After only a few minutes, the bombers flew on, never deviating from their diagonal flight, and the personnel of Clark Field slowly pulled themselves out of their hiding spots. "When I was finally able to stand up I wiped the sand out of my eyes and ran over to the end of the headquarters building to see what had happened," Lt. Whitcomb wrote. "There, across the field, we could see our beautiful silver Flying Fortresses burning and exploding right before our eyes. . . ." As a hangar with a B-17 awaiting camouflage painting began to burn, 1st Lt. Fred T. Crimmins, Jr. (30th BS) hurried into the smoky building to save the plane.[76]

After a lull of about 10 minutes, Japanese fighter planes suddenly appeared. "We had started coming out of our foxholes," Lt. Kurtz recalled, "but now we ran back—we were in the rat stage now, the whole idea being to get the hell out of the target area . . ." Lt. Whitcomb agreed. "Like rabbits we pounced back into the trenches as a wave of strafing planes swept across the field, spraying their deadly machine gun fire as they went."[77]

Lt. Crimmins was just taxiing the unpainted B-17 out of the burning hangar when the fighters struck. Instinctively, he swung the tail of the big bomber between himself and the attackers. Bullets ricocheted off the armor plating on the back of the pilot's seat and a 20-mm shell exploded on the instrument panel, setting it on fire. As Crimmins reached over to shut down the engines, a machine-gun bullet tore through his right wrist.

Shutting down the engines, Crimmins took two slugs in the right shoulder and was creased across the top of his head by another as he squirmed out of the pilot seat. As Crimmins crawled for the side entrance door, flying shell fragments and pieces of the bombers' aluminum skin ripped into his head, neck, legs and arm. Finally exiting the plane, he ran over to an antiaircraft battery alongside the runway and gave assistance to the gun crew by advising them when and where to fire at the strafing planes. For his unselfish act of heroism Lt. Crimmins was awarded a Distinguished Service Cross (DSC).[78]

The other B-17 awaiting the camouflage paint job was also taxied out of the hangar during the attack. 1st Lt. Ray L. Cox and 2nd Lt. Austin W. Stitt jumped into the bomber and taxied her out as hostile bullets tore into the building. Once outside the Fortress became an instant target and while both men fled unharmed to safety, the big plane erupted in a ball of flames.[79]

From inside a ditch, Lt. Kurtz watched a fighter work over one of the B-17s. "Again and again the Jap comes in—making his approach . . . as low as fifteen feet above the Fortress's wings . . . [F]irst his small .25-caliber wing guns open up with a rattle . . . [then] we hear him open up with his 20-millimeter cannon . . ." As the men hunkered down inside the slit trenches, they could hear the sounds of the exploding bombers. "You'd hear a rising, hissing p-p-pf-f-f-o-O-OFFF!," Kurtz wrote, "which means a tracer has gone sizzling into the gas tank of one of our dear old Fortresses—followed quickly by a great roar (everything letting loose at once), which means that the burning gasoline has exploded her bombs."[80]

Fighting valiantly to defend his B-17, 37-year-old T/Sgt. Anthony Holub jumped into the bomber and manned the twin .50 caliber machine guns located in the radio compartment roof. According to his DSC citation: "After exhausting his supply of ammunition he ran through heavy strafing fire to a nearby damaged plane, removed therefrom as many ammunition cans as he could carry and returned to his guns where he continued to fire on attacking aircraft." Born in Bohemia, Holub had yet to receive his final citizenship papers.[81]

While the Zero fighters were strafing the field, the B-17 flown by Lt. Carpenter, which had had a late takeoff due to generator trouble, suddenly showed up. Looking down from above, Carpenter said it "looked like a thunderstorm over the field—a cloud of darkness." Spotting Lieutenat Tash's circling B-17 from Del Monte, Carpenter hesitated to go near it until he saw Tash lower his landing gear and begin another landing approach on Clark. Following suit, Carpenter lower his gear and lined up behind Tash.[82]

Tash had reached the limit of his 35-minute fuel buffer and had decided to land at Clark but before he could set down, a damaged P-40 flew past him and slammed into the ground, "crashing itself all over the countryside." Thinking it was still too dangerous to land at Clark, Tash started back to Del Monte but was suddenly jumped by three Zeros. With the first burst of enemy gunfire, bombardier S/Sgt. Michael Bibbin, manning the right waist gun, was hit in both shoulders. Raking the B-17 from tail to nose, the Zeros damaged the superchargers, tore away the aileron control cables, chewed away at the wing roots and put holes in the propellers.

As each Zero passed over the Fortress, Pvt. Arthur E. Norgaard fired at them with the twin .50 caliber radio compartment guns. Although he missed the first two, he raked the last plane from "prop spinner to tail wheel" and sent it spinning down trailing a plume of smoke. Through this act, Pvt. Norgaard became the first American to shoot down an enemy aircraft from a American bomber in World War II. Having one wounded man and a badly damaged plane, Tash headed back to Del Monte.[83]

After witnessing the attack on Tash's B-17, Lt. Carpenter decided to seek shelter in the clouds but was soon called by the Clark Field control tower and told to proceed to Del Monte. Low on fuel, he decided to try another approach on Clark and although a number of Japanese planes pumped his bomber full of holes, no one was injured and he touched down safely. As he climbed from the plane, Col. Eubank met him and shook his hand.

"That was a mighty nice landing, Carpenter," Eubank said. At 2:00 P.M. Carpenter's B-17 was the only heavy bomber still in commission at Clark Field.[84]

The Japanese fighters carried on their deadly work for approximately 45 minutes. When they finally flew away they left a shattered airbase behind them. "The field was covered with a pall of smoke," Sgt. Kimmerle wrote, "and there was an unearthly mixture of sounds, the moans of the dying . . . the crackling flames . . . the boom and flash of exploding gas tanks, the cries of the wounded and [the] shouts of the work crews braving the shrappnel [sic] to help the wounded and to fight fires." He admitted that the entire scene reminded him of "a horrible nightmare . . ."[85]

Slowly but surely the shocked airmen began climbing out of their slit trenches. "After a long time the strafing ceased as abruptly as it had started, and we climbed out to have another look at the wreckage," wrote Lt. Whitcomb. "Across the field there did not seem to be a plane that had not been hit. . . . Crews standing by their planes were destroyed along with the ships. Four bodies were found beside our own ship, number 87, charred beyond recognition . . ."[86]

Since Lt. Kurtz's B-17D (40-3099, *Old 99*) had been parked beyond the hump in the runway, he was hoping that it had been missed by the attacking planes. Unfortunately, like the rest, the *Old 99* had been thoroughly worked over by the enemy.

Kurtz described what he found:

> Her poor old ribs black, twisted now; and with the aluminum skin melted off them so her carcass is naked, and you can see right through into the pilot's compartment, and the seats where I sat . . . And my control wheel, and my two sets of pedals, and the duplicate set for [my copilot] only all melted or twisted with the heat—even the wall bracket where the coffee thermos used to hang is still there, only twisted. And her four motors tumbled forward out of their nacelles in her crumpled wings onto the ground—everything about Old 99 still there, only melted and bent and ruined and her back sagging and broken . . .

Beside the plane, Kurtz found the bodies of his eight crewmen. "There they were, lying so very still . . . my eight boys of *Old 99*'s crew in a senseless, irregular line . . ." The crew had been running from the plane when it exploded and killed them. Some of the bodies were found entirely naked, having lost their clothing by the blast.[87]

In only a short time, men were on the field filling bomb craters, extinguishing fires and removing demolished planes. Every available vehicle was turned into an ambulance but few could be found intact. The Japanese had done a thorough job. Still, working tirelessly, the runway was repaired and ready for use in three hours. At 5:00 P.M., Lt. Wheless returned from his photo reconnaissance mission to Formosa. With the return of Wheless's B-17D (40-3096), Col. Eubank now had two operational Flying Fortresses at Clark Field.[88]

The crews at Del Monte had been in the dark since early morning. Listening to a commercial radio, they had heard various reports of Japanese attacks and around noon had heard the unsubstantiated report that Clark Field was under attack. Because of the loss of communications at Clark and elsewhere, the men at Del Monte could not get a confirmed report that Clark had been hit.[89]

Late in the afternoon, Del Monte finally received a clearly worded message to load every bomber and set out to bomb enemy shipping north of Luzon. However, because the messsage was not in code, Maj. O'Donnell refused to follow it. Noted Gen. Brereton, "About 4:00 P.M. a message was received [from] Maj. O'Donnell at Del Monte refusing to move his squadrons because the order had been sent in the clear and he feared fifth columnisn." Although a coded message was sent back almost immediately, "the difficulties and delay in encoding, transmitting, and decoding" the second order delayed acknowledgment of the message until well after midnight. By then it was too late for the crews at Del Monte to do anything.[90]

In the meantime, near 5:00 P.M., Del Monte suddenly heard from Lt. Tash, who was returning from Clark Field and was asking for an ambulance. Their curiosity aroused, the men from the 14th and 93rd BSs went out to the runway as Tash's bomber approached. Recalled Lt. Jacquet, "It seemed to wobble all over the sky and make awful big circles to get onto the field." Unknown to all, Tash was forced to land his plane with severed aileron cables.

When Tash finally touched down, the men gathered around the plane. "Here and there sunlight could be seen through the side of the ship—'bullet holes!'" recalled Jacquet. Looking closer, Jacquet saw something "drip out of the bottom of the ship: 'blood!'" When Sgt. Bibbin was brought out with "almost all of his right shoulder blown off," the reality of the situation hit home. "Suddenly it dawned on us," Jacquet admitted. "We were at war!" Added Lt. Teats, "Our force in Mindanao had an abrupt christening in combat—by proxy, you might say."[91]

When the sun finally set on December 8, 1941, MacArthur's "first line of defense," his B-17 bomber force, had been decimated. Seventeen of the 19 Fortresses at Clark Field had been destroyed, leaving only two in commission, and one of the 16 planes at Del Monte had been badly damaged. All told, after starting the day with 35 B-17s, the 19th BG had only 17 operational bombers when darkness fell. The only weapon in the Philippines capable of hitting the Japanese airfields on Formosa had been greatly misused. Ineptitude at all levels had caused their strength to be cut in half. Wrote Lt. Whitcomb, "It cannot be denied that our generals and leaders committed one of the greatest errors possible to military men—that of letting themselves be taken by surprise."[92]

The Americans at both Hawaii and in the Philippines had underestimated the Japanese and had been caught with their pants down. America's first day of the war had not been a good one for the B-17 Flying Fortress.

III

The Boeing B-17 Flying Fortress

IN AUGUST, 1934, the Army Air Corps announced an open competition to aircraft manufacturers for the design of a new multi-engined bomber. The announcement stipulated that, among other things, the new plane must be able to fly 250 miles per hour at 10,000 feet altitude, have a service ceiling of 25,000 feet, and be able to stay airborne for six to ten hours. Among the competing manufacturers was the Boeing Airplane Company of Seattle, Washington.

Having already designed and produced several successful commercial and military aircraft throughout the early 1930s, Boeing set about to design a revolutionary new aircraft. The new plane would benefit from many of Boeings earlier improvements and inventions, including aluminum skin, a single low wing supported from within by a bridge-like truss structure, and streamlined retractable landing gear that disappeared into the wing during flight. Other improvements included the movement of the flight deck ahead of the wing and away from the engines, which had improved the visibility of the crew, and Boeing's special patented "control trim tabs" on the elevators and rudder which allowed the pilot to trim the balance of the plane while in flight.[1]

Boeing was already at work on a behemoth four-engine very long range bomber, the XB-15, with a wingspan of 150 feet when the Army issued their call for a new multi-engined heavy bomber. Engineers at Boeing realized that the term "multi-engined" meant that the Army was looking for a new twin-engine aircraft but upon investigation, found that the Army had no objection to a four-engine bomber. By combining the best features from their other aircraft and the

XB-15, Boeing began work on a new four-engine heavy bomber, giving it the company designation of Model 299.[2]

On July 17, 1935, Boeing unveiled Model 299, even before the first XB-15 was finished. Gleaming bright silver in its aluminum skin, the plane carried a crew of eight and had a wingspan of 103 feet 9 inches, and a length of 68 feet 9 inches. The new design was powered by four 750 horsepower Pratt and Whitney "Hornet" R-1690 radial engines fed by internal fuel tanks installed in each massive wing. To give the bomber a streamlined appearance and cut down on wind resistance, all bombs were brought inside, into an internal bomb bay situated between the wings. Adding to the unique design, a tall vertical tail rose majestically above an extremely tapered tail.[3]

For the first time in history all of the gunners were brought inside. Built to defend itself, the Model 299 bristled with protective machine guns fired through five stream-lined cupolas. One cupola was positioned on the nose, one was midway down the top of the plane at the rear of a "humped" radio compartment, one was underneath the plane just behind the wings, and two more were on either side of the rear fuselage. All positions could fire either a single .30 or .50 caliber machine gun. Although Boeing officials referred to the Model 299 as an "aerial battle-cruiser," it was quickly dubbed the "flying fortress."

Three theories exist as to how the Model 299 got its famous sobriquet. A book initiated by Boeing in 1943 reported that a workman looked at the bomber while it was being built and commented, "It's as big as a fortress." In turn, another worker stated, "Sure it is. It can fight like a fortress. You might say it's a flying fortress."[4] The second theory contends that when a newsman looked at all of the gun cupolas he quickly called it a "veritable flying fortress."[5] And finally, since 1930s America was only interested in protecting her shores and was not interested in an offensive machine, the plane was thought to be a "flying fortress" that could patrol America's coastlines and help defend her shores.[6] No matter the origin, "Flying Fortress" described the plane exactly and the name stuck.

When Model 299 was flown to Wright Field, near Dayton, Ohio for the competition testing it made the non-stop flight in just over nine hours, at an unheard of speed of 233 mph. When the plane landed, no one was there to greet it since it was not expected for at least two more hours.[7] When compared to the other entries—a twin-engined modified Martin B-10 bomber and a twin-engined Douglas DB-1, a bomber version of the successful Douglas DC-2 airliner—it was apparent who would win the competition.

From the outset the Model 299 outperformed the other two aircraft, flying faster, higher, carrying a larger bomb load, and staying aloft longer than the other planes. The government contract was almost in hand when tragedy suddenly struck. On October 30, 1935, two Army pilots, aided by the Boeing test pilot, started the big bomber down the runway. Seconds after take off, Model 299 went into an uncontrollable climb, stalled and then slammed back to earth, bursting into flames. Although the blaze was quickly extinguished, one Army pilot and the Boeing test pilot had suffered extensive injuries. The Army pilot died shortly after the crash while the Boeing man died several days later.

The unexpected end of Model 299 came not as a result of mechanical failure but because of pilot error. Model 299 was the largest plane ever built. To prevent the control surfaces, i.e. flaps, rudder, ailerons, etc., from being damaged by gusting winds while the plane was parked on the ground Boeing had designed special locking controls. Before takeoff, the pilot had to release these locks. On October 30, the Army pilot had failed to do so, resulting in the end of Model 299 and the Army contract.

From the beginning many of the old-time Army officers felt that the Air Corps needed nothing larger than a speedy twin-engine medium bomber. They felt a bomber's speed could make up for its lack of armament. They also felt that they could purchase twice as many medium bombers for the cost of one heavy. Additionally, the old-timers had believed that Model 299 was "too much airplane for any but super-pilots; that it could not be operated except from mammoth airdromes and under perfect conditions; that it couldn't be kept in flying condition and that it would have a high accident rate." They insisted that the crash of Model 299 proved this. Instead of Boeing getting the new contract, the Army gave it to Douglas.[8]

However, in January 1936, still impressed by the performance of Model 299, the Army placed a small "Service Test" order with Boeing for 14 Flying Fortresses for evaluation and testing. The new bomber was given the Army designation: YB-17.[9]

Boeing began production on the YB-17 immediately, changing the name to Y1B-17 when the Army changed the funding. The only major change between the Y1B-17 and Model 299 was the use of more powerful 850 horsepower military Wright R-1820-39 "Cyclone" engines instead of the Pratt and Whitney's. Minor changes included improved landing struts to facilitate changing tires; the use of fabric instead of metal covered flaps; rubber de-icer boots on the leading edges of the wings; a modified oxygen system; and the reduction of the crewmen to six. Of the 14 planes ordered, 12 were flown to the 2nd BG, America's first heavy bomber group, at Langley Field, Virginia and two were flown to Wright Field for testing.[10]

In early December 1936, when an Army test pilot skidded one of the new planes down the runway on its nose when he accidentally fused the brakes to the rotors, the old-time Army officers once again complained that the four-engine bomber was too much for anyone to control.[11] However, Gen. Frank Andrews, commanding General Headquarters Air Force, refused to listen. In the late 1930s, the idea of strategic bombing had reached the forefront of the Army way of thinking. Instead of destroying the enemy in the air, strategic bombing called for the destruction of his industrial bases. Gen. Andrews viewed the Y1B-17 as the perfect instrument for high level strategic bombing.[12]

The 2nd BG received their first Y1B-17 in January 1937 and the last in August. Knowing that the critics were watching, Lt. Col. Robert C. Olds, commander of the 2nd BG, put his men through extensive training with the new planes. To prevent the kind of accident that occurred with Model 299, Olds, developed a preflight check list. With the proper training, the Y1B-17 began earning speed and endurance records. Fully impressed, the Army ordered 10 more Fortresses in August and another 29 in November.

In 1938, to show off the extremely long range of their Y1B-17s, the 2nd BG took their planes on a good-will flight to Argentina. That same year three planes intercepted the Italian oceanliner *Rex* while it was still 725 miles out to sea. Although labeled a navigational exercise, in reality the flight was a way to show everybody, friends and critics alike, that heavy bombers could be used to attack an enemy fleet far from America's shores.[13]

Unfortunately, the meeting with the *Rex* had negative results. The Navy immediately sent a formal protest to Washington declaring that it was responsible for protecting the high seas. In response, the AAC was told to restrict all flights to no more than 100 miles from the coast, anything beyond that would be handled by the Navy.[14]

The thirteenth Y1B-17, intended for engineering tests and loaded with various flight recording instruments, was on a long range flight when it ran into a violent thunderstorm. Thrown back and forth and flipped over onto its back, the plane went into a violent downward spin before the pilot regained control. Once back on the ground it was found that the wings were twisted a bit and that the plane had lost a few rivets but the flight recording instruments showed that the airframe had held up under extreme conditions. Since the fourteenth Y1B-17 had been slated for stress and destruction tests, the Army felt that there was no longer any need for these tests and slated Number 14 for a different experiment.[15]

Equipped with General Electric turbo-superchargers, Number 14 was used for high altitude performance tests and re-designated Y1B-17A. To increase power, the engines were changed to four Wright R-1820-51 Cyclone engines. Equipped with turbo-superchargers, which increased the performance of the engines at high altitude, the newest Flying Fortress was capable of reaching a height of 38,000 feet and attaining a speed of 295 mph.

The Y1B-17A completely revolutionized military aircraft design. The new Fortress could now bomb from the substratosphere, almost unmolested by anti-aircraft fire, and could outclimb and outspeed almost all of the fighter planes then in production. Not only did the Y1B-17A usher in a new era of heavy bombers it also sent the fighter plane manufacturers scrambling for new designs. The use of turbo-superchargers was a complete success and the AAC immediately ordered all subsequent Flying Fortresses equipped with the device.[16]

The 39 Fortresses that had been ordered in late 1937 were upgraded with turbo-superchargers and redesignated the B-17B (the "Y" prefix designating a Service Test model was finally dropped.) The overall look of the Flying Fortress was changed somewhat with the appearance of a larger rudder, an aircraft commander's observation bubble above the flight deck, and a new nose. The earlier planes had a "kink" in the bottom of the forward fuselage where the bombardier/navigator sighted. In the B-17B, the bombing and navigating became separate jobs. The bombardier sat in the very front of the plane and sighted through a flat panel in the bottom of a new multipiece Plexiglas nose while the navigator was given a station directly behind the bombardier. The nose gun-cupola was eliminated and replaced with several ball and socket mountings fitted for a .30 caliber machine gun.[17]

By October 1939 all 39 B-17Bs had been delivered to the Army. The 2nd BG received a few of the B-17Bs while a brand new heavy bomber outfit, the 7th BG (Heavy), based at Hamilton Field, received the rest.[18] While the two groups were getting familiar with their new planes, Germany suddenly attacked Poland, prompting England to declare war on Germany. Almost immediately the 2nd and 7th BGs began practicing high altitude bombing.[19]

Instrumental in acquiring accuracy in high altitude bombing was the M-7 Norden bombsight. Actually a rudimentary computer, the bombsight was linked to the plane's automatic pilot which allowed the bombardier to literally fly the plane during the bomb run. When the altitude and speed of the aircraft were entered into the sight, a small mechanical calculator automatically adjusted the flight of the plane towards the target, and when the crosshairs inside the eyepiece came over the target, the bombardier released the bombs. Invented in 1931, the Norden bombsight was considered top secret and meticulously guarded.[20] Combined with the turbo-supercharged B-17, the AAC suddenly had a first rate warplane on their hands and in the autumn of 1939, contracted for 38 more B-17s, now improved and designated the B-17C.[21]

The B-17C was the first model fully designed for combat. Notable changes were the elimination of the limited-vision gun cupolas. The cupola above the radio compartment was replaced by a Plexiglas fairing that slid back so that a machine gun could fire backward over the tail. The two side cupolas in the waist were removed and changed to teardrop-shaped windows, each holding a single machine gun. The change gave the gunners a better field of vision and a better field of fire. The lower bottom cupola was replaced with a lower gun position, resembling a bathtub, with a single gun firing down and to the rear. To use the gun, a crewman had to face backwards and fire from a kneeling position.[22]

Other revisions were less visible. The four engines were changed once again, this time to new Wright R-1820-65 radials which increased the speed of the B-17C to 323 mph at 25,000 feet. To further protect the plane and crew, armor plating was installed around vital areas and around each crew position.[23]

However, due to a squabble between Boeing and the AAC over the price of the planes, the B-17C almost died a quick death. Fearful of losing his heavy bombers when another world war was just around the corner, Gen. Arnold came to the rescue and sent in a mediator. With each side making a few concessions the B-17 program continued and the Army quickly ordered another 42 planes, now incorporating even more improvements and designated the B-17D.[24]

The first B-17C was delivered to the Army on July 21, 1940, five weeks after the fall of Paris. With the English seemingly facing Hitler all by themselves, they turned to the United States and under the new Lend-Lease Program purchased 20 of the 38 B-17Cs for themselves. However, the British insisted that the light .30 caliber machine guns be upgraded to heavier .50 caliber guns, and that the plane be equipped with self-sealing fuel tanks.[25]

The principle behind the self-sealing tank was simple. Built of rubber and a layer of foam, the rubber closed up around a bullet hole, preventing a fuel leak, and the foam extinguished the "spark." Although simple, it increased the weight of a plane and some manufacturers, especially foreign, refused to compromise speed and maneuverability for safety.[26]

All 20 B-17Cs, called Fortress Is by the British, reached England by the third week in May. Overburdened and tactically misused, the combat debut of the Flying Fortress was far from impressive. The British complained that among other things, the guns tended to freeze in the cold, thin air at 30,000 feet; that the bombs tended to hang-up; and that the armor plating was inadequate. Discouraged, the British dismissed the B-17 and relegated the survivors to anti-shipping and submarine patrols.[27]

By the end of April 1941, all 42 B-17Ds had been delivered to the USAAF. Learning from the British, self-sealing fuel tanks and .50 caliber machine guns were now standard equipment. Wanting to increase the defensive firepower of the B-17D, a second .50 caliber machine gun was added to the top of the radio compartment, and to the belly bathtub. Cowling flaps were added to the engines to regulate heat, a new low-pressure oxygen system was installed, and the bomb racks were totally redesigned. Alarmed by the disastrous performance of the B-17C in Europe, all B-17Cs in the United States were brought up to B-17D standards.[28]

The next Fortress model, the B-17E, had a completely redesigned rear fuselage and tail section. Due to the need to protect the tail of the plane, the rear fuselage aft of the radio compartment was widened and a new tail gun position was installed. Sitting on something resembling a bicycle seat, the new tail gunner faced to the rear and fired two .50 caliber machine guns. Additionally, the firepower of the B-17 was increased with the addition of two powered gun turrets, each capable of traversing 360 degrees and carrying twin .50 caliber machine guns.[29]

The Sperry top turret replaced the aircraft commander's observation bubble atop the flight deck. To fire the guns, a crewman, usually the engineer, stepped onto a pedestal and looked between the two guns, sighting through a Plexiglas dome. The lower turret, a remote-controlled Bendix gun turret, replaced the bathtub gun position and required the gunner to lay on his stomach and sight through a periscopic sight fitted inside a small Plexiglas bubble located a few feet behind the turret.

With the addition of the new gun positions, the B-17E bristled with 10 machine guns, including the .30 caliber gun in the nose and the single .50 caliber gun in the radio compartment roof. (The radio armament had been reduced to a single gun again with the addition of the top turret.) Although the earlier models had been dubbed the "Flying Fortress," the B-17E actually lived up to the name.[30]

With the widening of the fuselage the B-17 lost its sleek, streamlined appearance, yet, the most noticeable change came from a sweeping dorsal fin that started just behind the radio compartment and ran down the spine of the bomber, culminating in a huge tail and rudder. With this new look, the B-17E was sometimes called the "Big Ass Bird."[31]

Though heavier and slightly longer than its predecessors, the giant tail, sweeping dorsal fin, and a larger horizontal stabilizer made the B-17E a more stable plane. Through practice and training a bombardier could now place a bomb within a few yards of a target from a height of 20,000 feet.[32] The B-17E, accurate and defensible, was now truly a fighting plane. Wrote an unknown pilot, "We built the early models of the Flying Fortresses, from old 299 up through the B-17D, as defensive airplanes. They were to protect our shores, to defend the nation. All that changed with the new B-17E. Now, there was a weapon that was offensive all the way. We built that airplane to beat [the] hell out of the enemy. We built that airplane to fight."[33]

In August 1940 the Army ordered 277 of the improved B-17Es. The first plane was delivered in late September 1941 and arrived wearing the Army's new color scheme of olive drab top and sides over a light gray undersides. Hustled immediately to the Pacific, the new bomber literally flew into the war and soon proved to have a few deficiencies.[34]

The remote controlled Bendix belly turret turned out to be a total flop. Gunners sighting through the periscopic sight experienced vertigo and nausea. Advised of the problem, Boeing replaced the useless device with a manned Sperry ball turret on the 113th B-17E produced. Literally a steel and Plexiglas ball suspended halfway out the bottom of the airplane, the new ball turret had twin .50 caliber guns and required the gunner to curl up inside the ball and sight between his knees and feet. Because of the cramped, tight fit, the ball turret gunner was usually the smallest member of the crew. Able to rotate 360 degrees and even fire straight down, the Sperry ball turret was a welcome addition to all future B-17s.[35]

Combat also taught the bomber crews that the nose armament of the B-17 was sorely lacking. With the introduction of the tail guns, enemy fighter planes avoided the deadly "stingers" and began attacking from head-on. To increase the weak defense of the nose, field modifications were made and multiple .30 or even .50 caliber machine guns were installed.[36]

By May 1942 a total of 512 B-17Es had been produced. Originally, the Army had asked for 812 planes but the order was quickly amended when Boeing made over 400 improvements and introduced the B-17F. Although most of the changes were internal, two noticeable exterior changes were the replacement of the multi-paneled Plexiglas and steel framed nose with a one piece Plexiglas nose, and wider propeller blades.[37]

One of the major internal improvements came with the installation of fuel tanks in the very tips of the wings. Nicknamed "Tokyo Tanks," the new fuel cells gave each plane an additional 1,100 gallons of gasoline and increased the range of the B-17 by 900 miles. Because of the added weight, the engines were upgraded to Wright Cyclone R-1820-97s which actually increased the speed of the plane to 325 mph at 25,000 feet.[38]

The B-17F was the first Flying Fortress to go into "wartime mass production."[39] Unable to keep up with the demands of production, Boeing subcontracted with the Douglas Corporation and Lockheed Aircraft Corporation to help produce the B-17F. However, neither corporation produced any of the 49 B-17Fs that wound up in the Pacific. All of the B-17s that fought in the Pacific were manufactured by Boeing Airplane Corporation.[40]

While the B-17 would go on to have one more model, the B-17G, equipped with a forward firing chin turret, the new design saw no combat in the Pacific. Although a few B-17Gs reached the Pacific they were coveted as personal transports by high ranking officers or were converted and used as airborne lifeboat carriers.[41] Only the B-17C (which had been brought up to B-17D standards), the B-17D, the B-17E and the B-17F saw action against the Japanese.

The crew compartment configuration of the B-17C through the B-17F was pretty much the same. At the very front of the plane was the nose compartment, housing the bombardier and navigator. The bombardier sat just behind the Plexiglas nose and sighted his Norden bombsight through a flat panel. The navigator's area was located directly behind the bombardier. A long slender table on the left side of the compartment gave the navigator a place to work and make his calculations. Gun sockets in the Plexiglas nose and above the navigator's table allowed both men the opportunity to try and defend their position during combat.

A cramped crawlspace led from the nose compartment up to the raised flight deck. Like an American automobile, the pilot sat on the left-hand side while the copilot sat on the right. Surrounded by an array of instruments, the pilots controlled the plane with a set of rudder foot peddles and a "steering wheel" control yoke that allowed the men to fly the plane with one hand while working the speed throttle levers with the other. In the B-17E and F, the flight engineer occupied the flight deck with the two pilots, helping to read the various dials and gauges during takeoffs and landings, and manning the Sperry top turret during combat.

Immediately behind the flight deck was the bomb bay. A slim catwalk stretched between the hanging bomb racks allowed access between the flight deck and the radio compartment, located directly behind the bomb bay. Situated between the huge main wings, the location of the bomb bay gave the B-17 its stability in flight and on a bomb run.

The radio compartment was the home of the radio operator and contained an assortment of transmitters, receivers and tuning units. Above the head of the operator, and firing to the rear, was the radio compartment guns. In the B-17C and D there had been two machine guns but in the B-17E and F, there was only one.

The greatest changes inside the B-17 came when the rear fuselage was widened with the B-17E. The B-17C and D had a narrow, tapering rear gunner's compartment behind the radio compartment. Just a few feet from the radio compartment door was the bathtub gun pit. With the introduction of the B-17E, the gun pit was removed and the Bendix gun turret was installed. Then, after 112 B-17Es had left the factory, the remote controlled turret was replaced with the Sperry ball turret.

Beyond the bathtub gun pit or the gun turrets were the waist gun positions. In the B-17C and D the openings had been teardrop shaped but in the B-17E and F the openings were rectangular. Single .50 caliber guns, mounted on pedestals in front of each waist gun position, was standard equipment on all of the B-17s that saw action in the Pacific.

Finally, on the B-17E and F, at the very rear of the plane was the tail gun position. While the B-17C and D had a very narrow tail that tapered to a point, the tail of the B-17E and F was made wide enough to accommodate the tail gunner. Facing backwards, the tail gunner was always the last to see where the plane was going and the last to see where the plane had been.[42]

While a 10-man crew became standard in Europe, the crew size in the Pacific varied. On the B-17C and D an eight man crew, consisting of a pilot, copilot, bombardier, navigator, engineer and his assistant, and a radio operator and his assistant seemed sufficient. More than likely, only the two pilots and the navigator were commissioned officers. During combat the engineer and his assistant, and the radio operator and his assistant, manned the radio compartment, waist, and bathtub guns. Lacking tail guns, the pilot usually rocked the tail of the plane back and forth to give the rear gunners a shot at an enemy pursuit plane.

On the early B-17Es, the crew size remained at eight but the positions were changed. Although a new crew member was needed to man the tail guns, the two waist gun positions were sometimes manned by only one man or the radio operator ignored the radio compartment gun and helped fire one of the waist guns. The Sperry top turret made the radio room gun more or less obsolete and forced the engineer to stay on the flight deck and man the turret. The assistant engineer was given the unenviable task of trying to sight and fire the nauseating Bendix belly turret. When the Sperry ball turret appeared, in the later B-17Es and Fs, the crew size was standardized at nine.[43]

Born out of a daring plan by Boeing to outdo its competitors, the B-17 proved to be a very versatile airplane. Many changes took place since the first flight of the Model 299; changes which strengthened and refined the big bomber, and which changed her shape and appearance. Yet, the overall tenacity of the plane remained the same. The planes that went to Hawaii and the Philippines in 1941 were rugged planes capable of delivering crippling blows to a belligerent nation if used correctly. On America's first day of war the Flying Fortresses had been used incorrectly and the planes and crews had suffered.

IV

Fear and Apprehension

ALTHOUGH THE JAPANESE withdrew immediately after their attack on Pearl Harbor, the shocked American troops in Hawaii believed that the enemy was intent on invasion. As the 26th BS/11th BG historian noted, "The threat of an invasion at this time was imminent."[1] With most of their heavy bombers damaged or destroyed, the 18th Bombardment Wing could only send out a few obsolete B-18s on December 7 to help locate the enemy fleet.[2]

"We were told that there were three B-18's flyable and we would take off and find the Jap Fleet," Pvt. Schaeffer recalled. Appointed a gunner on one of the planes, the 19 year old private was not thrilled with the idea. "I was scared!" he admitted. "I thought of my slim chances of coming out of this flight alive should we run into some Jap fighters. Hell! They'd blow us right out of the sky in these very vulnerable B-18's."

When the three planes took off at approximately 2:00 P.M., Schaeffer got an unforgettable view of Pearl Harbor. "When we took off we flew over Pearl," he wrote, "not directly, but close enough to see all the unbelievable ruin and destruction. It appeared that everything in the harbor was blown-up, burning or destroyed. I had the feeling that the US had had it. My stomach was full of butterflies."[3]

Ever so slowly some semblance of order descended on Hickam Field. A temporary mess was set up under a row of trees providing most of the men with their first meal of the day. While the 42nd BS/11th BG set up an interim command post at the head of one of the base by-roads, the Hawaiian Air Force moved its headquarters to the safety of the Aliamanu Crater, far away from any possible invasion beach.[4]

Having literally flown into a war, the crews from the five B-17s of the 88th RS/7th BG which had landed at Hickam had scattered in all directions after exiting their planes. "We started a search for the missing members of the crew," reported Capt. Carmichael, "but it was not until Tuesday [December 9] that we were able to locate all." Gathering together what men he could find, Carmichael took them to a wooded area on the east end of the field. "There we spent the night, listening to the hum of the mosquitos [sic] and the irregular din of antiair-craft fire."[5]

Only later did the men learn that they had bedded down over a most precari-ous spot. "Later we [found] out that underneath where we are sleeping is the ammunition dump," wrote Lt. Ramsey, "which, if we had known it then, would have made us very uncomfortable."[6]

Still fearful of a Japanese invasion, the 5th and 11th BG airmen were sent out to guard Oahu's beaches. Lt. Latham, remembered spending "most of the night in trenches we dug in the coral dirt . . ."[7] Issued a rifle and a canteen, Pvt. Belz spent the night in a defensive line facing the ocean. "We dug foxholes, with two men to a position, about 150 feet apart," he wrote. "Every fourth position was given a .30 caliber machine gun."[8] Fueled by rumors that Japanese troops were landing at different points around the island, the nervous airmen fired at any-thing that moved, including planes taking off for reconnaissance.

The 72nd BS/5th BG historian commented on the danger of the moment:

> The Air Corps was during this time caught between two fires, on one side being the enemy and on the other our own land and sea forces who did not or would not recognize any airplane as friendly. Several times while taking off the entire fleet opened up on our air-planes, and how they escaped being knocked down in the barrage that was put up is an unexplained wonder.[9]

In the late afternoon Maj. "Blondie" Saunders returned from his search mis-sion south of Oahu. As his B-17D came in low over Pearl and Hickam, antiaircraft fire suddenly filled the air. "[T]he military forces on Oahu had seen B-17s around the island for six months," Saunders noted, "but they really let go at us, like we were public enemy number one. I thought we were going to be shot down by our own forces."[10] Fortunately, Saunders was able to land his plane safely in spite of the best efforts of the Army and Navy.

When darkness fell, a sense of the unknown was added to already frayed nerves. "The night of December 7 was a hectic one . . ." noted the 72nd BS histo-rian. "All during the night guards were firing at shadows and several times the antiaircraft guns at Pearl Harbor opened up."[11] Pvt. Jenkins, manning a .30 caliber machine gun at the end of the runway, concurred. "No-one dared move that first night. You would hear a gun go off and see tracers, and everyone would start shooting. If someone made a noise, someone else would shoot at the noise. It was scary."[12]

By the time Pvt. Schaeffer's B-18 returned to Hickam Field the sun was already down. Although the B-18 pilot asked the Hickam control tower to turn on the landing lights they would not, or could not, because of the total blackout. "We flew around in a holding circle and pretty soon people started shooting at us. I could see tracers flying about us," Schaeffer wrote. "They finally turned on what I remember as a large searchlight down the runway and we landed." Needless to say, Schaeffer was "very relieved."[13]

Near 9:00 P.M., the undisciplined firing finally led to disaster when six fighter planes from the carrier *Enterprise* attempted to land at Ford Island in the center of Pearl Harbor.[14]

"We heard planes coming in and of course, everybody assumed the Japs were back," admitted Pvt. Schaeffer. "The whole sky lit up with tracers and everybody with a weapon was firing at the noises in the sky." Pvt. Blutt and a few other men were manning a .30 caliber machine gun when they heard the incoming fighters. "Sometime that night some of our Navy planes came in," he wrote. "Not knowing they were friendly we, and every other gun, let loose at them. I didn't see any shot down."[15] Unfortunately, three planes were shot down and all three pilots died.[16]

Bedded down in the woods east of Hickam, the new arrivals from the 88th RS tried to sort out the strange events of the past 24 hours. Lt. Johnson recorded, "The navy and army didn't do much coordinated work in peace time and that showed up on Dec. 7. During the night a couple of navy ships [i.e. planes] came in for a landing and were mistaken for enemy. They were shot down by a combined effort on the part of the navy, coast guard and the army, an effort which disturbed our attempt to rest out in the trees on the edge of Hickam Field." He went on to admit, "That night under the mosquito nets, occasionally dampened by showers, put the crews a long, long way from the mainland and their loved ones."[17]

While the aircrews from the 88th RS/7th BG were spending a fearful night in Hawaii their ground crews were going through a frightening time of their own. On November 21, 1941, the ground echelon of the 7th BG had boarded the Army transport ship *Republic* at San Francisco for their trip to the Philippines. Traveling in a convoy with seven other ships, the *Republic*, dubbed the "Repulsive" by some, was still at sea when, at 10:00 A.M. on December 8, the men were told of the attack on Pearl Harbor. Sgt. John W. Green (9th BS), a technician, recalled, "I was on a 12 knot boat with the ground crew . . . One day past the international date time zone, we heard the news [about Pearl Harbor] and it was quite an experience being alone without escort in that hunk of water . . ." Fearful of being detected by Japanese submarines, the convoy turned south.[18]

In addition to the ground crews from the 7th BG, the *Republic* also carried a couple of Texas National Guard artillery units with 75 World War I artillery pieces. "Somebody decided they would be a good defense for submarines," remembered L. M. "Mike" Payne (9th BS). "They brought two of them on deck and welded them onto the deck. To help reinforce them, they chained them to the railings." The idea was, as the ship rolled, the guns would be fired at any attacking subs. However, the idea was flawed. "They fired one [gun] for practice," Payne continued, "and it jumped up in the air and rolled into the ocean. So much for our defense."[19]

For defense against enemy aircraft, the *Republic* carried a number of old WWI machine guns. Pvt. Wilbur W. Mayhew (88th RS), a qualified aerial gunner with the .30 and .50 caliber air cooled machine guns, recalled, "I had never seen a water cooled .50-caliber machine gun in my life before, but I was now assigned to one and was expected to shoot Japanese planes out of the sky with it, if the occasion arose. Most of the rest of the fellows assigned to these machine guns were as untrained on them as I."[20]

Luckily, the convoy reached Papete, Fiji Islands, on December 13 without incident. Afraid of sending the ships towards the Philippines through unfriendly waters, the decision was made to divert the convoy to Australia. After spending "a very nervous 25 hours aboard ship while the convoy refueled," the *Republic* and her sister ships headed west. The historian for the 7th BG reported, "The men were now getting accustomed to the daily drill of possible air attack, submarine menace, and night blackouts, as they traveled through enemy waters."[21]

On December 22, after 32 days aboard ship, the men finally arrived at Brisbane. Since the B-17s of the 7th BG had been held up in Hawaii, the ground crews were put to work servicing and repairing Australian and American planes which had either fled the Philippines or were arriving from the States. As the group historian wrote, "With inadequate tools, salvaged parts, and anything available, planes were kept flying in the early days of combat."[22]

At daybreak on December 8, in Hawaii an uneasy calm settled over Hickam Field. Still afraid of a Japanese invasion or a second air strike the Hawaiian Air Force sent a few of the obsolete B-18s out on patrol. Noted the historian for the 42nd BS/5th BG:

> We participated in reconnaissance; our object was to sight the Japanese fleet and to observe what further attack might be forthcoming. Boy, are we scared! We haven't adequate protection, are flying antiquated airplanes with only three each GI 30 cal. machine guns and we expect to be attacked at any moment by the Japanese Zero which is an unproven factor. At this time we expect Hickam Field to be attacked again with an even larger force than before and we are almost helpless but will do what we can . . . We are wondering if replacements will arrive from the States.[23]

Since almost all of the B-17s based at Hickam had been damaged or destroyed by the Japanese, the California Fortresses were utilized to help search the waters around Hawaii. "For several days our ships [B-17s] were about all the protection Hawaii had (since) only five or six pursuits and some B-18s were Hawaii's (other) power," Lt. Johnson lamented. "Hundreds of ships [i.e. planes] had been lost on the ground. Who had let the Japs sneak in, anyways?"[24]

At first Johnson and his comrades were amazed at how unprepared the Hawaiian based troops were. Soon however, their amazement turned to disgust. "We were to become more disgusted later on," he wrote, "with the hesitancy, the disunity, the disorganization. We expected more from an outpost."[25] For the time being, the crews and planes of the 38th and 88th RSs would remain in Hawaii. Their trip to the Philippines was delayed indefinitely.

During the day, the orphaned waifs from the 88th RS left the woods over the ammunition dump and, along with the crews from the 38th RS, moved to "Splinter City," a group of newly constructed two-story wooden barracks buildings near the Hale Makai barracks. Lt. Johnson elaborated, "We took all the cots, sheets, blankets, and our personal baggage and moved as a unit into Building T1, the overflow going to the neighbor building, TX. We shared T1 with the 38th Recon., they taking one half, we the other."[26]

Also moving into Building T1 was Skipper, Sgt. Angelini's Scotch Terrier puppy. "[T]hey put us in the barracks . . .," Angelini remembered, "and we were upstairs and the dog would wee-wee on the floor and it would leak down through the floor and you could hear these officers yelling, 'Hey Joe, shut off your dog!'"[27]

By the time Skipper flew to Hawaii he was a veteran in a B-17. "He started flying when he was six weeks old . . .," Angelini explained. "I had an oxygen mask and life vest and everything [for him]." The only thing that seemed to bother the puppy was the constant drone of the four big engines. "In fact, I had to keep cotton in his ears because he wouldn't hear anything . . . when we got on the ground," the sergeant said. "One day he shook the cotton out and he couldn't hear for two days."[28]

Over the next few days, some of Hickam's heavy bomber squadrons set up shop in out of the way places. On December 8, the 23rd BS/5th BG set up operations in an undamaged officer's quarters. On December 9, the 4th RS/5th BG established it's headquarters on the skeet shooting range and the 42nd BS/11th BG moved it's command post to an "Air Corps unoccupied building." Two days later, the 72nd BS/5th BG, equipped solely with B-18s, found Hickam getting altogether too crowded, and moved to Bellows Field.[29]

While the moves were taking place, the 23rd BS was busy patrolling the Pacific Ocean and working hard to resurrect a few of the damaged B-17s. By December 10, the squadron historian was able to report, ". . . the 23rd was operating 4 B-17s . . ." On that same day, 12 B-17 pilots and copilots from the other squadrons were reassigned to the 23rd BS to help ease the burden of flying search missions by themselves.[30]

On December 12, Maj. Walter C. Sweeney, Jr. (50th RS/11th BG), who had been on detached duty in the United States, brought a "flight of B-17s" into Hickam. The welcome arrivals were the first reinforcements and bolster the morale of the base personnel. Almost immediately, the new arrivals were sent out on search missions, flying systematic pie-shaped patterns out of Oahu.[31] Then, on December 18, six more Flying Fortresses, B-17Es of the 22nd BS/7th BG under the command of Maj. Kenneth B. Hobson, reached Hawaii.[32]

2nd Lt. John Wallace Fields was the copilot for 1st Lt. Harry W. Spieth on B-17E (41-2440) and recalled the flight to Hawaii. "[W]e were told . . . that we should arrive at Hickam Field in Hawaii within about 15 hours. We flew and flew with a heavily loaded plane, and 14 hours came and went; 14-1/2 hours, and no land in sight. Fifteen hours came with no land in sight, and finally, after 16 hours and 10 minutes, we arrived at Hickam Field." Overloaded with extra gas and spare parts, each plane landed with an average of only 100 gallons of gas remaining in its tanks.[33]

Looking over the ruins of Hickam, Lt. Fields recalled, "Well, as for Hickam itself the runways had been cleared off, but many of the buildings had been bombed and there were still burned aircraft visible along the sides of the runways." When he looked towards Pearl Harbor he saw even more devastation "There was still smoke from burning vessels in Pearl Harbor and an oil slick all over the water. It was a mess."[34]

Coming into Hickam aboard 1st Lt. Frederick C. Eaton, Jr.'s. B-17E (41-2446) was Maj. Gen. Clarence Tinker, former commander of the 7th BG, who came to Hawaii to take over command of the Hawaiian Air Force after the debacle at Hickam and the other airfields around Oahu.[35]

The 22nd BS was originally destined for the Philippines but like the 38th and 88th BSs before them, soon found out that its travel plans were changed. Indefinitely attached to the Hawaiian Air Force, the planes and crews were parceled out to different Hawaiian bomb squadrons and were instantly sent out on search missions.[36] Lt. Fields wrote:

> [T]hey took over all the equipment that we had, our airplane, our hack watches for the navigators, all navigational equipment, a case of .45 automatic pistols, additional clothing, underwear, shoes; everything that we thought we might have a need for and that we had originally planned to take on into Australia and the Philippines . . . After having stripped all our equipment we had off our airplanes, the Hawaiian Department countermanded our orders, which had been to go to the island of Mindanao; confiscated our airplanes; impounded our equipment, and put us to work flying patrol missions out of Hawaii.[37]

Although the threat of invasion subsided as the days wore on, the various heavy bomb squadrons continued to fly search missions. The 42nd BS/11th BG historian typified the seriousness of the missions:

> From 7 December 1941 things were "different" within the squadron. The reality of being at war crystallized a great many plans and activities which heretofore had been training activities. The search missions which had been instituted as training exercises for the crews now became serious expeditions; bomb bays no longer were loaded with practice bombs but with live explosives.[38]

Although the majority of the searches were uneventful, occasionally a B-17 crew would claim that they had sighted an enemy submarine and on at least one occasion on Christmas Eve, a B-17 and three A-20 medium bombers bombed a couple of submarines off the Hawaiian islands of Niihau and Kauai. The results were "unobserved."[39]

On December 23, when word reached Hawaii that the American garrison on Wake Island had been overrun Col. "Blondie" Saunders, newly-promoted and in temporary command of the 5th BG,[40] was called to headquarters. Once there he learned that had Wake not fallen, he would have been ordered to take the 5th BG B-17s to Midway to refuel and then go after a pair of Japanese aircraft carriers known to be about 10 miles south of Wake. "[T]hat was about 1200 nautical miles [one way] . . .," Saunders recalled, "pretty touchy business at that range with a full load of bombs . . ." Realizing that none of the B-17s would have had enough gas to bomb the carriers and successfully make it back to Midway Saunders saw the strike as a suicide mission. "Oh God," he told headquarters, "you were gonna sacrifice old Saunders and his boys to fish heads and rice for the rest of the war weren't you?"[41]

As the Christmas holiday neared, the commanders feared that the Japanese might try to disrupt the occasion. On Christmas Eve the 5th and 11th BGs were put on special alert and given extra missions to fly. Adding insult to injury, the 4th RS/5th BG historian reported, "[T]urkey today, and free beer at the club, but flying personnel alerted and cannot imbibe—Dammit!"[42]

On December 26, 16 B-17s went on search missions around Hawaii.[43] Only 15 returned. Lt. Cooper and his crew, who had arrived at Hickam during the Japanese attack, were returning to Oahu late in the evening in B-17E (41-2402) when they got lost. "We flew about in blackness for hours," Cooper reported. "There was nothing on the horizon but sea and more sea." Finally running out of fuel, Cooper ditched the plane about 40 miles south of Kauai. "Suddenly the water was all around us and we were swimming away from the sinking plane," he wrote. Scrambling into the two life rafts which were carried in special compartments on every B-17, the eight man crew floated around for three days and nights before being spotted by a Navy PBY flying boat. "None of us will ever forget it as long as we live," Cooper stated. "It was like coming back from the dead."[44]

Although the B-17 had been designed as a strongly defended offensive weapon, the Fortresses in Hawaii were coming into their own as long range reconnaissance planes. After the Japanese attack of December 7, there were only 11 operational B-17s in Hawaii, including those that had arrived from California. By the end of 1941, through the rapid deployment of B-17s to Hawaii, the 18th Bombardment Wing had 28 operational B-17s with another 12 undergoing some form of maintenance.[45]

The men of the Hawaiian Air Force had lived through a strenuous three weeks. Torn from a life of luxurious splendor they had been plunged into the terror of a surprise attack and a possible enemy invasion. However, while their lives had certainly been thrown into turmoil, it could not compare to what was happening in the Philippines.

V

Striking Back

ALMOST IMMEDIATELY AFTER the attack on Clark Field the wounded were taken to the hospitals. Total casualties at Clark, including civilian personnel, were about 100 killed and 250 wounded.[1] Lt. Crimmins, badly wounded while trying to save his B-17, was taken to Fort Stotsenberg Hospital. He recalled, "Kids were dieing all night long, crieing out and calling for the nurses. Men who had gone to sleep would wake up shouting."[2]

While the wounded were being gathered, some of the men undertook the sad job of identifying the dead. Although the bodies were identified and tagged, an argument arose over who was responsible for burial. The Medical Department said the Quartermaster Department was responsible while the Quartermaster Department said the job belonged to the Medical Department. In the confusion and stubbornness, the bodies remained uncollected for days, bloating in the hot glare of the sun, ". . . grim reminders of the way in which the power of the enemy had been misjudged."[3]

Lt. Carpenter remembered, "At Clark Field the dead were still all over the place. . . . They lay there over a week." Although Carpenter and others volunteered to bury the dead they were told that they would be court-martialed if they touched the bodies. Finally, after a week, Carpenter could take it no more and swore that if the dead were not buried, he would bury them himself in spite of a court-martial. When push came to shove, the men were finally buried, although Carpenter never knew which department did the work.[4]

Expecting the B-17s from Del Monte to come up during the early morning hours of December 9, a flight of P-40s flew into Clark Field late on the afternoon of December 8 to cover their arrival. Near 5:00 A.M. on December 9, the fighters began taking off. Bothered by dust and darkness, one of the pilots hit a bomb crater and lost control, leaving the runway and slamming into a parked B-17D.

An eyewitness remembered, "there was a sudden flash of light, a violent explosion, and a hail of bullets all over the area as flaming gasoline from the B-17s ruptured tanks set off the loaded .50 caliber guns." The P-40 pilot was killed and both planes were destroyed. The Fortress, B-17D (40-3100), belonging to Col. Eubank, had been only slightly damaged in the Japanese attack. In the following minutes, three more P-40s crashed because of the dust. Unfortunately, the loss of the four fighters and one precious B-17 had been in vain, for the heavy bombers from Del Monte did not arrive until late in the afternoon.[5]

Unbeknownst to the men at Clark Field, the crews at Del Monte had no intention of arriving at Clark so early. It was not until 7:30 A.M., and only after Capt. Parsel went out in B-17D (40-3074) on a reconnaissance of Mindanao, that the 93rd BS left Del Monte. Leaving Lt. Tash behind with his damaged bomber, Maj. Combs led the remaining six B-17s out to attack an enemy aircraft carrier reported to be off the southeast coast of Luzon. With each plane carrying 20 small 100-lb. demolition bombs, Lt. Jacquet thought, "What could 100-lb. bombs do to a carrier? Like sticking an elephant with pins."[6]

At Clark Field, the two servicable B-17s went out at around 8:00 A.M. on separate missions. Lt. Carpenter, in B-17D (40-3063), set out to fly a photo mission over Formosa but was forced to abort because of his nagging generator trouble while Lieutenant Wheless, in B-17D (40-3096), took off to bomb Japanese ships reportedly off the northwest coast of Luzon. Although Wheless found the ships and started his bomb run, he had to abort when the bomber suddenly developed a complete electrical failure. When both pilots returned to Clark, the airbase commanders were afraid of another Japanese air raid and instructed both men not to land until after dark. In the meantime they were to stay in the clouds and circle the field.[7]

One other B-17 left Clark Field that morning. By using parts and pieces from the destroyed bombers, and working all night long, mechanics had been able to piece together B-17D (40-3098). Shortly after the other two planes left, 1st Lt. Jack Adams (30th BS) took the reworked bomber down to Del Monte for further repairs.[8]

Near 2:30 P.M., after failing to find the reported enemy carrier, and now low on gas, Maj. Combs led the 93rd BS B-17s from Del Monte towards Clark Field. In spite of the threat of another enemy air raid the planes were permitted to land and refuel. Lt. Jacquet, flying as copilot with 1st Lt. William J. Bohnaker in B-17D (40-3073) looked down at Clark Field from the air. "In each B-17 position there was just a charred mass of black earth with four projections showing the former motors sticking out . . . As we leveled for the landing [we] could see the bomb holes [we] had to dodge."[9]

Despite the cratered runway all six planes landed safely and were quickly refueled. Col. Eubank was still fearful of another air raid and personally ordered the men to "keep the ship[s] in the air to avoid getting strafed on the ground." Although tired and hungry, the aircrews took off and began circling in the clouds above Clark Field.[10] In reality, Eubank had nothing to fear from the Japanese. Thick fog over Formosa was keeping the enemy on the ground on this second day of war.[11]

Over on Mindanao, Maj. O'Donnell took seven B-17s of the 14th BS towards Clark Field at 2:30 P.M. Left behind was 1st Lt. Weldon H. Smith and B-17D (40-3079) which had developed a hydraulic leak and was undergoing repair. By the time the seven planes reached Clark Field it was already after sunset and the planes from the 93rd BS were returning. Afraid of having too many B-17s on the ground at any one airfield, the 14th BS was sent to a new airfield 30 miles to the west near the little village of San Marcelino. As the seven planes flew off, they were joined by Capt. Parsel, who had finished his reconnaissance flight around Mindanao, and by Maj. Combs. Having seen his five 93rd BS planes land safely at Clark, Combs turned and followed the 14th BS towards San Marcelino, curious to have a look at the new airfield.[12]

The new runway near San Marcelino was 200 feet wide but only 4,000 feet long and consisted of dry, sandy soil. "Walking on it was like walking on so much talcum powder," Lt. Teats recalled. Still under construction, the field lacked everything from a control tower to landing lights and everything in between.[13]

In spite of the short field, the soft soil, and the lack of landing lights, the B-17s landed at San Marcelino. "We circled the field once, then spaced out at intervals," wrote Lt. Teats. "It was so dark that at 1,000 feet you could just make out the field, but by the time the fourth or fifth man was ready to land, all he could see was the dust the man landing was kicking up. His only method of orientation for landing was the beam of the landing lights of the planes ahead."

As the planes touched down, they were fired on by jittery Filipino soldiers. Although no one was hurt, a bullet cut an oil line on one of Capt. Parsel's engines. "We found out a lot about those big fortresses that we hadn't known," penned Lt. Teats. "We discovered that we could take off from any field we could land in. We took off and landed, no matter what the wind direction was . . . We threw the book away . . ."[14]

After watching the other planes land at San Marcelino, and having seen what to expect of the new field, Maj. Combs returned to Clark Field to be with his squadron. Although the control tower refused to turn on the landing lights he landed without incident. As he climbed from his plane he could see the hooded flashlights of ground crew men who were bustling about in the dark servicing the bombers that had landed before him.[15]

Since Clark Field lacked adequate antiaircraft batteries and since there were not enough fighter planes left in the Philippines for adequate coverage, the decision was made on December 9 to evacuate the base and use it only as a forward staging field. Starting that night, and continuing each night thereafter, the obsolete B-18 bombers flew supplies and spare parts that could be salvaged from the wrecked B-17s down to Del Monte.[16]

When the 93rd BS arrived from Del Monte, they were surprised to discover that Clark Field was being abandoned. Wrote Lt. Jacquet, *Then* I found out *why* I had been carrying a sleeping bag around the world." Loaded into trucks, the airmen were taken to a temporary camp about three miles from the airfield. Throughout the night their sleep was interrupted by a blaring air raid alarm.

"This happened about five times," Jacquet recalled. "Everyone's morale had ebbed very low, and we were actually scared to death."[17]

The morning of December 10 found the Philippine B-17s widely dispersed. Seven planes, including the six from the 93rd BS and Lt. Carpenter's plane with the bad generator were at Clark Field. In addition, the ground crews were working overtime to rebuild three planes that had been damaged in the Japanese attack. Eight Fortresses were at San Marcelino, and four were at Del Monte, including Lt. Wheless' bomber. (Experiencing electrical trouble and told not to land at Clark Field until after dark, Wheless had flown down to Del Monte for repairs.) Though widely scattered, the 19th BG was finally ready to take action.

During the night of December 9–10 a P-40 pilot spotted a Japanese convoy headed towards the northwest corner of Luzon.[18] Starting their conquest of the Philippines, the Japanese planned a dual invasion at Aparri and Vigan, on the north and west coast of Luzon respectively. Although Col. Eubank had intended to send the 19th BG against Formosa, he changed his plans but did not abandon Formosa all together. At 5:30 A.M., he sent 1st Lt. James T. Connally (93rd BS) out on a photo mission of Formosa in B-17C (40-2062) and then sent his other bombers against the enemy convoy.[19]

Near 6:00 A.M. the five remaining planes from the 93rd BS, still carrying their 20 100-lb. demolition bombs, took off from Clark Field. Led by Maj. Combs, B-17D (40-3062), the planes flew north up the center of Luzon and then turned west towards Vigan. Joined by a flight of P-40s and P-35s, the B-17s came over Lingayen Gulf and immediately spotted a large concentration of enemy ships already disgorging troops onto the beach. Ignoring a wall of antiaircraft fire, the Fortresses began bombing the transports from 12,000 feet while the fighters went down to strafe the Japanese infantry.[20]

Lt. Vandevanter, B-17D (40-3066), reported, "My bomb racks didn't work at that altitude [12,000 feet] so we went down to 7,000 feet where they operated properly." In fact, all of the planes circled around for another bomb run over the transports. "There was very heavy antiaircraft fire [but] it was mostly behind us," Vandevanter wrote. "Their antiaircraft shells seemed designed more for concussion than for fragmentation. We would get bursts that would shake the whole ship, yet we wouldn't find any shrapnel." America's first B-17 bombing raid of World War II was anything but a success. The planes hit only one or two vessels, perhaps sinking one. After dropping all of their bombs, Maj. Combs led his flight back to Clark Field to rearm.[21]

Returning to Clark at about 9:30 A.M. Maj. Combs immediately called for more bombs. Incredibly, he was told to get back into the air. The airbase commanders were still afraid of a Japanese air raid and did not want the B-17s to get caught on the ground. However, since 1st Lt. Morris C. Shedd, B-17D (40-3070), and Lt. Young, B-17D (40-3073), were experiencing some form of trouble with their planes they were allowed to remain.

Maj. Combs, Lt. Vandevanter and 1st Lt. Walter R. Ford, B-17D (40-3087), were about to take off to circle the airbase when Col. Eubank asked Combs if his planes had encountered any Zeros. When he replied that they had not, Eubank said, "Thank God. I've been sending off O'Donnell's ships one at a time."[22]

Maj. O'Donnell, B-17D (40-3061), and Capt. Parsel, B-17D (40-3074), had left San Marcelino before dawn and arrived at Clark Field shortly after the planes from the 93rd BS had departed. While Parsel saw to the replacement of his severed oil line, O'Donnell was informed of the Japanese invasion force off Vigan. After quickly contacting San Marcelino by radio and telling the rest of his 14th BS to come over to Clark Field for bombs and fuel, Maj. O'Donnell loaded his plane with eight 600-lb. bombs and set out to bomb Vigan himself.[23]

Arriving over Vigan at 25,000 feet, O'Donnell started a bomb run on a cruiser and a destroyer escort but, like Vandevanter, he experienced trouble with his bomb racks and had to circle around for another run. In all, he made five passes and spent 45 minutes over the enemy ships. Although rocked by antiaircraft fire he was able to drop all eight bombs but observed no hits. With his bomb bay empty, O'Donnell headed back to Clark Field.[24]

The six remaining 14th BS B-17s reached Clark Field at 7:30 A.M. only to find that just three of their planes would be allowed to land. While Capt. Colin P. Kelly Jr., B-17C (40-2045), and 1st Lts. Guilford R. Montgomery, B-17D (40-3086), and George E. Schaetzel, B-17D (40-3091), landed, the B-17Ds of Lts. Godman, (40-3097, *Ole Betsy*), Teats (40-3078), and Donald M. Keiser (40-3079) remained airborne. "So there we were," Teats remembered, "almost 24 hours [after the attack on Clark Field], circling the valley east of our main air base on Luzon because we didn't dare take the chance that we might be caught on the ground by enemy bombers and strafers."[25]

Although the caution seemed excessive, it may have paid dividends. Close to 9:30 A.M., Clark Field received information of an incoming air raid and the three B-17s from the 14th BS scrambled off the field. However, only Lt. Schaetzel's plane was fully loaded with eight 600-lb. bombs while the other two left with partial loads. Capt. Kelly took off with only three 600-lb. bombs while Lt. Montgomery left with only one.

Also taking off was Capt. Parsel, who had finally managed to get his oil line repaired and had been able to load seven 300-lb. bombs before the alarm came. Flying individually, Schaetzel and Kelly headed towards Aparri while Montgomery and Parsel headed towards Vigan.[26]

Lt. Schaetzel arrived over Aparri first and dropped a few bombs from 25,000 feet on a number of troop transports lined up on the beach, possibly sinking one ship and hitting another. As Schaetzel turned for another pass, he was jumped by four Zeros who riddled both wings and an engine, and ruptured an oil tank. Caught unaware, Schaetzel instantly put B-17D (40-3091) into a dive and headed for a thick bank of clouds at 7,000 feet.

"The last time I looked at the air speed indicator," he said, "it read 350 and was still going up. I knew there were mountains at 6000 or 7000 feet, just under the overcast, but I didn't even think of that." Just as Schaetzel reached the clouds, his gunners ran out of ammunition. Streaming oil and nursing his damaged engine,

Schaetzel headed for San Marcelino and landed there at 2:30 P.M. In addition to the damage inflicted by the fighters, antiaircraft fire had made a sieve of the bomber's tail. Said an eyewitness, "The plane was a mess."[27]

Arriving above Aparri shortly after Lt. Schaetzel, Capt. Kelly, B-17C (40-2045), ignored the transports along the beach, and went after a concentration of warships off the coast that were firing salvoes in support of the invasion force. Spotting a large heavy cruiser, which Kelly and his crew mistook for a battleship, Kelly started his bomb run.

"Then antiaircraft fire from all the naval vessels started, but they were way off, under us," remembered Cadet Joe M. Bean, Kelly's navigator. Carrying only three bombs, Kelly's bombardier, Cpl. Meyer S. Levin, dropped all three at once. "One bomb fell short in the water," Bean reported, "the second hit amidships, setting off a fire, and the third bomb hit just beyond the ship at the waterline."

Circling back towards Clark Field, Kelly's crew had a good view of the damage they had inflicted. "A large oil streak trailed the ship, and we saw what looked like 2,500 to 3,000 men jumping off the ship and into the water," recalled Cadet Bean. PFC Robert E. Altman, the radio operator and bathtub gunner, was kneeling in the tub and got a good view of the ship. "The fire seemed to be spreading all the way to the water," he remembered, "and the ship had stopped moving altogether."

Returning to Clark Field, B-17C (40-2045) was all set to land when it suddenly came under attack. "We had just gotten down to about 11,000 feet at this point, just above some broke clouds," Cpl. Altman reported, "and these fighters jumped us from behind the tail. [I] began firing my twin .50s blindly, hoping some of my bullets would hit someone. The captain kept kicking the tail from side to side to give the gunners a wider field of fire, and all of us were firing away to the rear."

Unknown to anyone, Zero fighters had been trailing the Fortress all of the way from Aparri. Reported Saburo Sakai, "My fellow pilots and I were upset by the fact that the enemy had attacked despite our screening Zero fighters." Certain that more than one bomber had attacked the warship, Sakai was amazed when he found only a single B-17. "We had never heard of unescorted bombers in battle," he wrote, "especially a single bomber in an area known to be patrolled by dozens of enemy fighters. Unbelievable as it seemed, the B-17 had made a lone attack in the very teeth of all our planes. The pilot certainly did not lack courage."

Sakai and six other Zeros followed Kelly back to Clark Field but before they could strike, three more Zeros suddenly appeared and fired at the big bomber. Sakai and his flight soon joined the battle. "It was impossible for the ten Zeros to make a concerted attack against the bomber," Sakai reported, ". . . [so] we swung out in a long file, and made our firing passes one after the other, each plane making its run alone." All 10 planes made attacking runs from behind the bomber but when the B-17 did not go down, Sakai moved directly above and behind the plane and opened up with a stream of machine gun and cannon fire.

"Pieces of metal flew off in chunks from the bomber's right wing, and then a thin white film sprayed back," he wrote. Not sure whether the spray was gasoline or smoke, Sakai continued his attack. "I kept up my fire against the damaged area, hoping to hit either the fuel tanks or oxygen system with my cannon shells. Abruptly the film turned into a geyser." As Sakai reported, "The bomber's gun[s] ceased firing; the plane seemed to be afire within the fuselage."[28]

Cpl. Altman remembered being on the receiving end of the Japanese fire. "The first heavy burst from the fighters went right through the middle of our ship and burst the pilot's instrument panel and absolutely sliced off the top of [Staff] Sgt. [William J.] Delehanty's head," he reported. "They also set us on fire in the middle of the ship. We had all those gasoline lines and oxygen lines right in there. We were on fire like an acetylene torch." With the rear of the plane ablaze, Capt. Kelly ordered everyone to bail out. Without hesitation, Altman and the other surviving gunners quickly jumped into space.[29]

Bombardier Levin and Navigator Bean, in the nose, had a hard time getting out of the small escape hatch in the tight crawlspace behind the nose compartment but did so after a short time. With the rear of the plane fully engulfed in flames, only two men were still alive on board, Capt. Kelly and his copilot 2nd Lt. Donald D. Robins. As Kelly worked to keep the plane steady, Robins moved to open the commander's observation dome in the roof of the flight deck. As Robins fought to open the dome the B-17 suddenly exploded and he was blown out of the plane. Thinking quickly Robins deployed his parachute and began a slow descent to the ground.[30]

B-17C (40-2045) was plummeting downward, still wrapped in flames and with its two right engines out, when it suddenly exploded again. The second blast tore the plane apart. Three main sections—the forward fuselage, the rear fuselage, and one intact wing—slammed to the ground less than six miles from Clark Field. Apparently thrown from the plane, Capt. Kelly's body was found only a few yards from the wreckage. The body of Sgt. Delehanty was found inside the burned tail section.[31]

After bailing out, Kelly's crewmen were strafed by the swarming Japanese fighters. "They followed us right down to the ground," waist gunner S/Sgt. James E. Halkyard reported. "When we got to the ground, the five of us who came down close to each other counted over one hundred bullet holes in our canopies." Fortunately, only Cadet Bean was wounded, being grazed on one ankle. Coming down close to the airbase, all six survivors were quickly rescued and taken back to Clark Field.[32]

Over the years the legend of Colin Kelly, America's first hero of World War II, has grown all out of proportions. For years it was reported that Kelly had bombed the Japanese battleship *Haruna*. In reality, no Japanese battleship took part in the invasion of the Philippines. Cadet Bean believed the enemy ship was actually a heavy cruiser, judging from the size of its gun turrets. Indeed, the Japanese later reported that the heavy cruiser *Ashigara* had been bombed on December 10, 1941. Still, the report stated, "No appreciable damage was suffered by the *Ashigara* on that date."[33]

It is also claimed that the target ship was the Japanese minesweeper *W-19*, reportedly hit and subsequently beached on December 10. However, a careful study shows that *W-19* was too small and too lightly armed (only 237 feet long with three 4.7 inch guns and two 25mm antiaircraft guns) to have been mistaken for a battleship. On the other hand, the *Ashigara* measured 668 feet long and was equipped with 10 turret mounted 8-inch guns and a number of smaller guns.

Additionally, Kelly's crew remembered seeing a seaplane take off from the deck of the ship they bombed. While *W-19* carried no seaplane, the *Ashigara* did.[34] Clearly, the ship that Kelly bombed was the heavy cruiser *Ashigara*, although it suffered far less damage than Kelly's crew reported. The *W-19*, in all probability, was the vessel bombed by Lt. Schaetzel.

The legend of Colin Kelly contends that after seeing his crew safely bail out, Kelly dove his burning B-17 into the Japanese ship. This of course is false. It was also reported that Kelly was awarded the Congressional Medal of Honor. This again is false. Kelly received the Distinguished Service Cross, second only to the Medal of Honor.[35] In spite of the inaccuracies in the legend, America had its first real hero of World War II and the name Colin Kelly would be remembered by a generation of Americans.

While Schaetzel and Kelly were bombing the vessels off Aparri, Lt. Montgomery and Capt. Parsel were attacking the enemy ships off Vigan. Carrying only one 600-lb. bomb, Montgomery made a quick bomb run and then turned back towards Clark Field. Following close behind, Parsel came through a hail of antiaircraft fire and dropped four bombs on a heavy cruiser from 12,500 feet. All four fell far short. Circling back, he dropped his last three bombs on a troopship nestled close to shore. As the B-17 headed towards San Marcelino, his crew observed flames belching from the ship.[36]

Near 11:00 A.M., the three 14th BS planes which had been circling above Clark Field were running low on gas so they returned to San Marcelino. As soon as the planes landed they were covered with camouflaging palm fronds and immediately refueled. In only a matter of minutes the extra efforts to cover the planes paid off when a flight of enemy fighters followed by two Vs of bombers suddenly appeared. With the B-17s partially camouflaged, the enemy planes missed the unknown field and passed quietly on towards Clark Field.[37]

It was shortly after noon when word of the approaching planes reached Clark. Two P-40s quickly took off to get away and kicked up a great cloud of dust on the runway. As a third fighter started to take-off, it ran into the dust and plowed into Lt. Carpenter's B-17D (40-3063), slicing through the left wing and cutting the fuselage in two. As Carpenter recalled, "[The P-40] went right through my B-17." Luckily, no fire started and everyone was able to walk away unscathed.[38]

Forewarned by the alarm, Clark Field was deserted by the time the Japanese arrived. Saburo Sakai had returned with the bombers and recalled, "Over Clark Field, we found not a single target. For 30 minutes we circled the burned-out American base, but failed to sight a plane either on the ground or in the air." Down on the ground, Lt. Jacquet remembered the numerous air alarms of December 10. "That was a hectic and exhausting day. Every 20 minutes would bring a warning and away we'd run for a foxhole—run as fast as we could, too. By nightfall I was really tired . . ."[39]

Sometime after noon, Lt. Montgomery returned to Clark Field after dropping his single bomb on the ships off Vigan. Arriving in between air raids, he was allowed to land and refuel and take on 20 100-lb. bombs. At 2:00 P.M. he was back in the air. This time heading towards Aparri, Montgomery bombed one transport, reportedly setting it on fire and sinking it, before turning back towards Clark.[40]

Maj. O'Donnell, after bombing Vigan, returned to Clark Field. Allowed to land, he only had time to refuel his B-17D before he was ordered off the field and sent to Del Monte. As O'Donnell was passing south of Manila, he was unexpectedly jumped by a flight of Japanese fighters. In a running gun battle, O'Donnell's crew shot down two of the attacking Zeros while sustaining no damage to themselves or their plane. Sometime after dark, O'Donnell successfully landed at Del Monte.[41]

Only one other bombing mission was flown on December 10. At 2:00 P.M., 2nd Lt. Harl Pease Jr. (93rd BS), left Clark Field in Lt. Bohnaker's B-17D (40-3073). Carrying 19 100-lb. bombs, Pease flew to Aparri and attacked a Japanese cruiser. Facing no antiaircraft fire or enemy fighters he made two bomb runs and dropped half of his bombs from 24,000 feet. Although his bombs fell close, he claimed no hits. Still carrying a few bombs, Pease made two runs over a Japanese transport but missed again. With his bomb bay finally empty, Pease headed back to Clark for more bombs and fuel.[42]

After Pease left Clark Field, the planes still circling overhead were ordered to fly to Del Monte. Lt. Connally, who had been in the air for over eight hours, knew that he did not have enough gas for the long four-hour flight so he landed at Clark in spite of the orders. Maj. Combs, and Lts. Ford and Vandevanter however-er started out immediately. Combs and Ford were flying together when they hit bad weather. Low on fuel, they knew that they would never be able to reach Del Monte and landed at a small field on the island of Mindoro.[43]

Flying alone, Lt. Vandevanter pressed on through the storm but soon found that he too was running low on fuel. Passing near the island of Leyte, he decided to land at a short, 2,000 foot emergency runway at Tacloban. "We got in all right and confiscated some gas from Pan-American which they had cached there," Vandevanter wrote. Although fully refueled, he did not want to attempt a night take-off from the short runway so he elected to spend the night.[44]

While the B-17s over Clark Field were being sent to Del Monte, the crews at San Marcelino were still in a fighting mood. Shortly after the Japanese bombers had passed overhead, Capt. Parsel arrived to boost the number of planes at San Marcelino to five. Although Lt. Godman's plane was undergoing immediate engine repair and Lt. Schaetzel's bomber was full of holes and undergoing repairs to the battle damage, the other three planes were ready to go. With each plane carrying six 500-lb. bombs, they were about to take off at about 3:30 P.M. when they received word to cancel the attack and return immediately to Del Monte. Although frustrated, Capt. Parsel and Lts. Teats and Keiser followed orders and, even though they ran into the storm front, landed at Del Monte a little after dark.[45]

After his mission to Vigan, Lt. Montgomery tried to land at Clark Field but was told to proceed to Del Monte. Hampered by the storm and the darkness, Montgomery decided to head for an emergency airstrip at Zamboanga. However, about 10:00 P.M., Montgomery's B-17D (40-3086) ran out of gas and he was forced to ditch in the Sulu Sea. "Due to heavy rain and poor visibility the plane was landed at fairly high speed and sank almost immediately, approximately 4 miles off shore," the 19th BG historian reported. "Only minor injuries were sustained by the crew, which reached shore safely about 0200 [2:00 A.M.] that night."[46]

Surprisingly, although Lt. Pease returned to Clark Field after Montgomery, he was allowed to land and refuel while Montgomery had been sent away. At 6:30 P.M., Pease took off for Del Monte but soon ran into the same storm front that had plagued the others. Having enough gas, Pease simply turned around and returned to Clark. As he touched down in the darkness, his B-17 joined the planes of Lts. Connally and Shedd as the only B-17s spending the night at Clark Field.[47]

Late in the evening, Lts. Godman and Schaetzel, whose planes were still being worked on at San Marcelino, decided to take their planes down to the meager, but better, facilities at Del Monte. At 11:00 P.M., the two pilots finally took off. More than half way to Mindanao, Schaetzel heard a false message that Del Monte was in enemy hands and not having enough fuel to return to Clark or San Marcelino, landed on the island of Cebu. Godman, unaware of the false report, continued on but became disoriented in the heavy rain and darkness and did not reach Del Monte until 9:00 A.M., December 11.[48]

With Godman's arrival at Del Monte, the activities of the 19th BG were over for the day. December 10 had been a costly day for the group. Besides losing Capt. Kelly and Sgt. Delehanty, the 19th BG had lost three more B-17s. In the early morning hours of December 11, only 19 B-17s (17 B-17Ds and 2 B-17Cs), in various shape, remained to help defend the Philippines.

December 10 had been a learning experience for the 19th BG as well. The aircrews had seen that bombing from high altitude against a moving ship was more difficult than dropping a bomb on a motionless target. Their most successful bomb runs had been against the stationary troop transports. Although the aircrews claimed a number of hits, in reality only one ship was so badly damaged that it had to be beached.

However, the B-17s, attacking singly or in pairs, had managed to disrupt the Japanese landings whenever they appeared. Had the 19th BG been able to put all 35 bombers over the landing beaches they may have been able to cause considerable damage and throw off Japan's timetable for the conquest of the Philippines. The loss of half of the B-17s on the first day of the war prevented this. By nightfall on December 10, the Japanese were firmly established on Luzon.

The B-17 crews had gained a healthy respect for the Japanese airmen. "This business about them being a funny-looking, squint-eyed bunch of little men who have to wear glasses and who can't fly is hooey," Lt. Teats stated. The 19th BG had painfully learned that the Japanese could indeed fly and that the Zero was a top-notch fighter plane. And, unfortunately, they had also found out that the Japanese were well aware of the blind spot behind the tail of the B-17.[49]

At the same time, the Japanese had gained a lasting respect for the B-17. "This was our first experience with the B-17," Saburo Sakai wrote after shooting down Capt. Kelly's plane, "and the airplane's unusual size caused us to misjudge our firing distance. In addition, the bomber's extraordinary speed, for which we had made no allowance, threw our range finders off."[50]

Both sides had learned a lot about each other during the first few days of war. Each side would have many more opportunities.

VI

To Australia and Back Again

ON DECEMBER 11, the 19th BG continued to regroup at Del Monte. During the morning, Maj. Combs, B-17D (40-3062), and Lt. Ford, B-17D (40-3087), flew in from Mindoro, and Lt. Vandevanter, B-17D (40-3066), came in from Tacloban. "On take off the next morning," Vandevanter wrote, "we just didn't have enough room to clear the fence at the end of the [short] runway and damaged the horizontal stabilizer very badly." An inspection proved that the plane would be sidelined for about a week.[1]

When Lt. Schaetzel tried to leave Cebu, he discovered that the aileron control cable on B-17D (40-3091) was holding by only one strand. Apparently cut by the fire from the Zeros, Schaetzel would have to replace the cable before he could go anywhere.[2]

In the afternoon, 1st Lt. John W. Chiles (93rd BS), B-17D (40-3070), and Lt. Bohnaker, B-17D (40-3073), flew down to Del Monte from Clark Field.[3] When they arrived they found the air and ground crews hurriedly applying a camouflaging coat of paint to the planes already there. Maj. Elsmore had been worried that the shiny aluminum bombers would be spotted from the air, thus giving away the secret location of the airfield, and had started the men applying the camouflaging paint with whatever colors they could find. "It was a sorry camouflage job," Lt. Teats conceded. When the men were finished Teats found that some of the planes were "a splotchy green, some a dirty brown and some an indescribable color which could only be called dull."[4]

The 19th BG spent the day of December 11 painting and repairing their planes but on December 12, they went on the offense again. At 7:30 A.M., six B-17s started out from Del Monte to bomb the Japanese ships off Vigan but as Lt. Adams started his take off run he ran into trouble. His plane, B-17D (40-3098), had been damaged during the attack on Clark Field but had been hastily repaired and flown down to Del Monte on December 9. Now, as he started off, two engines suddenly quit and the plane skidded off the grass runway. When the brakes failed because of a faulty hydraulic system, Adams ground looped the plane.

Completely out of control, Adams collided with Lt. Tash's parked B-17D (40-3087), which was still undergoing repairs to the battle damage sustained on December 8. Adams' bomber tore the nose off Tash's plane before breaking in two itself. Luckily, none of the bombs detonated and no one was seriously hurt but both planes were considered a total loss.[5]

The remaining five B-17s, led by Maj. O'Donnell, took off without further incident and headed towards Vigan. Moments later, Maj. Combs took off in B-17D (40-3062) to replace Adams' plane in the flight and raced to catch up with the others. Far out in the lead however, O'Donnell's planes reached Vigan first and bombed the enemy transports from high level. Observing no hits, the flight headed back to Del Monte.[6]

Unable to catch up with O'Donnell, Combs came over Vigan all by himself at 25,000 feet. Spotting a couple of destroyers beyond the transports, Combs was already in his bomb run when his radio operator unexpectedly passed out after pinching his oxygen line. Although faced with the possibility of losing his radio operator to anoxia, Combs continued the run. When the bombardier toggled the bomb release however, only half of the bombs dropped and the bomb bay motor caught fire. Quickly the crew extinguished the fire and jettisoned the remaining bombs harmlessly into the sea. Having completed his run, Combs immediately dove his plane down to 12,000 feet, where oxygen masks were no longer needed, to help revive his radio operator and then headed towards Clark Field.[7]

Once at Clark, Maj. Combs was surprised to find that Maj. O'Donnell and the others had gone back to Del Monte. While his plane was being refueled, Combs was informed by Col. Eubank that the Japanese had landed near Legaspi, on the southeast tip of Luzon, and were reportedly being supported by an aircraft carrier. Since radio communications with Del Monte were sporadic, Eubank wanted Combs to fly down to Del Monte and tell Maj. O'Donnell to hit the carrier with everything he had. When Combs lifted off from Clark he had on board 10 evacuees from Clark Field.[8]

Running into a heavy thunderstorm south of Luzon, Maj. Combs was delayed in arriving at Del Monte. By the time he landed and passed his information on to Maj. O'Donnell it was too late to send out a strike that day. Furthermore, Maj. O'Donnell decided to wait for the arrival of Maj. Gibbs, who was still in charge of the 19th BG since Col. Eubank was busy with 5th Bomber Command, and had decided to move his headquarters down to Del Monte.[9]

At 6:00 P.M., in spite of the heavy storm between Luzon and Mindanao, and the protests of the other officers, Maj. Gibbs left Clark Field in a B-18. He was never heard from again. Presumably, the plane hit an unseen mountain in the rain and darkness. With the disappearance of Maj. Gibbs, the 19th BG lost a promising young commander.[10]

At 5:45 A.M. on December 13, Maj. O'Donnell sent two planes out to locate the enemy carrier. Although they ran into the persistent storm which was still sitting between Luzon and Mindanao, they were back by 10:30, reporting that the target was still just east of Legaspi.[11]

About that same time, word reached Maj. O'Donnell that the plane with Maj. Gibbs was missing and that he was now in command of the 19th BG. Col. Eubank wanted the new commander at his side and ordered O'Donnell to return to Clark Field and sent Maj. Birrell "Mike" Walsh down to Del Monte to take care of things there. While he waited for Walsh to arrive, O'Donnell drew up plans for the attack on the Japanese carrier.[12]

Perhaps because of the terrible storm, which was pounding Mindanao and hampering the servicing of the planes, or because of the shake-up in command, the B-17s were not ready to go until 10:00 A.M. the next day. The 19th BG now had 16 B-17s at Del Monte after Lt. Connally somehow managed to bring the last Fortress down from Clark Field on December 13, and Lt. Schaetzel finally brought his plane in from Cebu. Still, on the morning of December 14 only six planes were deemed combat worthy enough to attack the carrier.[13]

When Lt. Connally's lead plane, B-17C (40-2062) blew a tire prior to take-off, the size of the force was cut to five. With Lt. "Shorty" Wheless, B-17D (40-3096), now in the lead, the five planes lifted off and headed towards Legaspi. When the planes had gone only about 100 miles however they suddenly ran into the storm front. Hit hard by the heavy rain, Wheless lost one engine. Dropping down to a lower altitude, he was able to restart the engine and even though he had lost contact with the others, he continued on.[14]

Unknown to Wheless, Lts. Coats and Ford had also developed engine trouble but they had turned back for Del Monte. The other pilots, Lts. Adams, B-17D (40-3073), and Vandevanter, B-17D (40-3093), continued on. Flying at 21,000 feet, the two reached Legaspi with Adams in the lead by 90 seconds. Through a break in the clouds, Adams spotted a row of transports and warships and started his bomb run. Conspicuously missing was the enemy aircraft carrier, which had already left the area. Lining up on the transports, Adams dropped all of his bombs on one pass and then turned back towards Del Monte. As he did so, he spotted five enemy planes rising up to intercept him.

Sighting thick clouds far below him, Lt. Adams put his B-17 into a steep dive just as the Zeros opened fire on his tail. The first shots seriously wounded Adams' radio operator in the leg and creased navigator Harry Schrieber in the arm. "I don't think I'll ever forget the sound of those Jap slugs bouncing around in there," Schrieber said. "They'd come through the aluminum skin as easy as if it was human skin, and they'd ricochet—they sounded like somebody had slung a handful of BB shot every time a burst went through us."[15]

Adams' gunners shot down two of the Zeros but the others pressed the attack. At one point, Adams throttled back and one of the Zeros shot past, easy pickings for one of the waist gunners. The remaining two fighters continued to fire into the B-17, knocking out the two left engines before Adams' gunners shot down a fourth Zero.

Finally reaching the clouds, Adams found that he could not maintain altitude and began to look for someplace to land. Eventually, he glimpsed a tree-ringed rice paddy in the center of Masbate Island, south of Legaspi. "[Adams] pulled her nose up as high as he dared and just cleared those trees," wrote Schrieber, "and then, cutting the remaining two motors so we wouldn't have to climb out of her in flames, he made as nice a belly landing in a rice patch as you could hope for."

Still followed by the remaining Zero, the men ran for cover while the fighter repeatedly strafed B-17D (40-3073). For some unknown reason, the plane did not catch fire and the Zero eventually flew off. Rescued by armed Filipinos, Adams and his crew eventually returned to the 19th BG in mid-March 1942. Although Adams' plane was riddled, it was still in one piece and he was hoping that it could be salvaged. Unfortunately, it never flew again. The 19th BG had lost another B-17 and Lt. Adams was left with the unwanted distinction of losing two bombers in two days![16]

While the Zeros were concentrating on Adams, Lt. Vandevanter came in and made three unmolested passes over the enemy ships. Bombing from 21,000 feet, he dropped eight 600-lb. bombs on the transports, perhaps sinking one and damaging others. As he headed back to Del Monte he spotted a handful of Zeros but successfully avoided them when he reentered the clouds.[17]

Although Lt. Wheless had hoped to lead the B-17s over the invasion fleet, he arrived well after Lts. Adams and Vandevanter. "By this time, the other planes had passed over the target, dropped their bombs and pretty well stirred up the Japanese there," Wheless wrote. Unable to find an enemy carrier, Wheless started a bomb run against the transports from 9,500 feet when 18 Zeros suddenly attacked. Since he was already on his bomb run, Wheless continued on, allowing his gunners to protect the plane.

As two fighters approached, one on either side, the two waist guns fired almost simultaneously, shooting them down. However, while the radio operator, PFC W.G. Killin, was manning the bathtub guns, a burst of incoming fire from straight behind tore the top of his head off, killing him instantly. Seconds later, the rest of the crew heard the bombardier shout through the interphone, "Bombs away! Bomb-bay door closed! Kick her in the behind!" Immediately, Wheless rocked the tail of B-17D (40-3096) back and forth and his gunners managed to shoot down the trailing Zero.

Machine-gun bullets and 20-mm cannon shells ripped through the aluminum bomber and knocked out the left outboard engine. Assistant radio operator Cpl. W.W. Williams, was firing the radio compartment guns when an explosive shell ripped into his leg, tearing him open from the knee to hip. Knocked to the floor, Williams tried again and again to reach his guns but could not because of his wound.

"I was diving for cloud cover," Wheless recalled, "and all I could find were scattered cumulus clouds . . . But those scattered clouds were some good. They gave the gunners a chance to change ammunition." Unknown to Wheless, all four gunners in the rear fuselage had been hit during the first 10 minutes. In addition to the death of Pvt. Killin and the wounding of Cpl. Williams, Sgt. Russell Brown had been hit in the right wrist and Sgt. John Gootee had his right hand almost shot off. Ignoring the pain, Brown continued to fire the two waist guns with his left hand, working first one and then the other, while Gootee tried to steady the guns with his one good hand. Working together, they managed to shoot down at least three more Zeros.[18]

Wheless's B-17 was taking a beating but it was still flying. Later, Wheless summed up the damage:

> Sometime during the fight, my Number 4 gas tank was hit by an explosive bullet, knocking a hole in it about six inches in diameter and allowing all the gas . . . to leak out. The radio was shot off in the cockpit [and] . . . The oxygen system was entirely shot out. Out of the 11 control cables, there were only 4 remaining . . . which made it very difficult to maneuver the ship; and almost impossible to turn it. The tail wheel was entirely shot loose from the mount. The two front wheels were both flat. Each gas tank had approximately 15 bullet holes in it.[19]

The Zeros followed Wheless' B-17 for 30 minutes and 75 miles before finally giving up. With his plane severely damaged, Wheless fought to keep it in the air as darkness began to fall. "My control cables were shot in two and that gave me very little diving ability. All I could do was go straight ahead." Reaching Mindanao, Wheless realized that he would never be able to get the plane over the mountains surrounding Del Monte on only two engines. Instead, he headed for a small airfield near Cagayan, on the northern end of Mindanao.

Coming in too low, Wheless hit the top of some palm trees but in spite of the two flat tires and no tail wheel, he made a safe landing. Recalled Wheless, "The plane, on hitting the ground, rolled fairly straight for two hundred yards then the brakes locked, causing the plane to stand straight up on its nose. However, it settled back on the tail and all aboard managed to get out unhurt."

Miraculously, only Pvt. Killin had been killed and only two men had been seriously wounded. B-17D (40-3096) however, was a total loss. M/Sgt. Benjamin F. Kimmerle (30th BS) reported, "The insides was covered with blood, the propellers had bullet holes in them, the tail was almost completely shot away and one could hardly put his hand on the wings and fuselage without touching a bullet hole." Later, when someone attempted to count the bullet holes in the plane, he stopped at 1,200! Everyone gained a new respect for the Flying Fortress that day. "[T]he B-17-D is an excellent airplane in my opinion," Wheless said, "and unless the control cables are shot out, I don't believe the Japanese can shoot it down." When he recalled the punishment his plane had absorbed, Wheless added, "And don't let anyone tell you that the B-17 can't take it."[20]

The mission to bomb the Japanese aircraft carrier was a failure. By the time the B-17s arrived, the carrier was long gone. Maj. O'Donnell's decision to wait 24 hours to attack had perhaps cost the 19th BG a golden opportunity. Instead, the group had to settle for the possible sinking of three transports and the damage of two others.[21]

For their part in the mission Lt. Vandevanter was awarded a Distinguished Flying Cross while Lts. Adams and Wheless each received the Distinguished Service Cross. Perhaps 11 Zeros had been destroyed but two airmen had been killed and two more B-17s had been destroyed. Only 15 of the original 35 Philippine based B-17s were still around after only one week of war.[22]

When Maj. Walsh arrived at Del Monte on December 14 and saw the battered and beaten airplanes and personnel, he immediately requested that he be allowed to pull the bombers back to Australia.[23] Lt. Teats reported: "The primary fact in the whole situation was just this: We had to go some place where we could get decent maintenance on the planes, and where the crews could get some rest."[24]

Anticipating the move, the 19th BG began evacuating Clark Field in earnest. By December 14, the Japanese had captured enough airfields on northern Luzon to establish air superiority. They were now staging daily raids on Clark Field, sometimes hitting it two or three times each day. With the Japanese infantry coming closer to Clark, the 19th BG ground crews were issued rifles and ammunition while the stranded pilots, men like Lt. Kurtz who had lost his B-17 on December 8, began flying the obsolete B-18s down to Mindanao with a load of supplies and evacuees.[25]

With the Japanese firmly established on Luzon, Air Headquarters finally realized that it was only a matter of time before Japan invaded Mindanao and discovered Del Monte Airfield. On December 15, Gen. Brereton forwarded Maj. Walsh's request to move the B-17s to Australia. Hoping to avoid the total destruction of his B-17s, MacArthur gave his permission, "not as a withdrawal of forces but to facilitate maintenance in order that the remaining planes might be used to best advantage."[26]

Since the trip from Del Monte to Australia was about 1,700 miles, each B-17 would have to carry two bomb bay gas tanks. The only available bomb bay tanks were at Clark Field which meant that the B-17s had to risk one more trip to Clark before they could take off for Australia. And, since Clark could only service three planes at a time, the process was slow and tedious. "The procedure was for not more than three planes to fly in at night, pick up all the spare parts and personnel that could be taken aboard, and two bomb bay tanks each," wrote Lt. Teats. "Every tank not riddled by enemy air attack was taken out. We also took up empty oxygen bottles and flew out full ones." Most often, the spare B-17 parts came from the destroyed Fortresses.[27]

On December 17, the 19th BG began moving to Australia. At 2:00 A.M., six B-17Ds, under the leadership of Maj. Combs, took off from Del Monte and headed towards Batchelor Field, Australia, about 45 miles south of Darwin. Each plane was loaded to the maximum with parts and personnel. Priority for evacuees was

AUSTRALIA AND NEW GUINEA AREA

given to all first pilots.[28] The Army could build a new airplane but it took too long to train a new first pilot.

On December 18, three B-17Ds and one B-17C left Del Monte at 2:00 A.M. Once again, the planes were fully loaded with extra parts. "We ignored the rated maximum load. There wasn't such a thing," recalled Lt. Teats, who was piloting one of the planes. "The only criterion was how much we could carry and still get out to Australia.[29]

When the men arrived at Batchelor Field they were none too impressed with their new base. A new airstrip, Batchelor was an active Royal Australian Air Force (RAAF) training base and the 19th BG had to share the field with the Australians. Cut out of the red soil and light timber of northern Australia, the field lacked even a control tower. "When we saw our Australian base for the first time, nine hours out of Del Monte," Teats reported, "it was two roughly right-angled runways in the middle of a clear space in the brush." Each runway measured about 3,600 feet long and bisected each other near the center. "We dispersed our planes off the runways and established quarters in the tents in the light timber, from which the field had been carved."

Although Batchelor was primitive, it did have a shower fashioned from an old railroad water tank. "[B]ut we had to do all our showering before 10 A.M., or after nightfall, when the tank had cooled off," Teats recalled. "Between 10 A.M. and sunset the water was so damned hot you couldn't stand it."[30]

Cut out of the barren wasteland, Batchelor Field was home to more than just the Americans and the Australians. "First there were the ants," Teats said. "You never saw such creatures. They were green, half an inch long, and as poisonous as the devil." Called "green devils" by the Australians, the ants stung like a bee and swarmed on anything that came near. "Then there were little red-brown ants . . . that got into everything," Teats continued, "They swarmed on the tent ropes and into and over anything you owned."

Perhaps more irritating were the flies. "They swarmed around your eyes, your nose, your mouth, by the thousands," Teats went on. "They'd sit on your eyeballs if they could." Although the 19th BG airmen were bothered by the pesky insects, Batchelor Field gave them a safe haven to rest and repair their battered planes. "We became accustomed to [the insects]," Lt. Teats recalled. "We were too busy to bother about mere physical discomforts."[31]

That same day, December 18, a Japanese reconnaissance plane finally located Del Monte. Realizing that the enemy would likely be back in force the next day, the personnel at Del Monte spent the day camouflaging their planes with palm fronds.[32] Shorty after 4:00 P.M., on December 19, the Japanese returned.[33]

Hidden about the field were six B-17s, including the carcass of Lt. Tash's bomber which had been damaged beyond repair by Lt. Adams' runaway bomber. Also on the field, having just arrived from Clark Field, were three B-18s. The Japanese planes arrived so suddenly that no one had time to get the B-18s covered or into the air.[34]

For the next few minutes the Zeros continually strafed Del Monte. The

Japanese claimed that they destroyed two B-17s and three B-18s, and that they badly damaged two more B-17s and four more B-18s.[35] The first claim is true, the second is not. There were only three B-18s present on the field and all three were destroyed. Of the six B-17s present, two were destroyed, as the Japanese claimed, if Lt. Tash's plane is included. The other plane was B-17D (40-3093).[36]

At 10:00 P.M., Lt. Smith flew out B-17D (40-3079) and at 1:00 A.M. on December 20, the last two B-17Ds and the single B-17C followed.[37] In all, the 19th BG had been able to evacuate 145 men and fly 12 B-17Ds and two B-17Cs out of Del Monte. When Maj. Walsh assessed the situation with his airplanes he reported, "10 in commission, 2 out [of] commission, 2 need depot overhaul."[38]

With the Japanese in control of the land, sea and air around the Philippines, they were able to strike when and where they pleased. On December 20, they landed at Davao, on the southeast edge of Mindanao. While the troops were coming ashore, 54 Japanese bombers pounded Del Monte.[39]

Luckily for the Americans, the last of the B-17s had already left, but they were far from gone.

With its move to Australia, the 19th BG did not abandon its plans to harass the Japanese wherever and whenever possible. Almost immediately, the planes were readied for future missions in the Philippines, leaving from Batchelor and staging through Del Monte. Plans were laid for the planes to bomb a target and then land at Del Monte after dusk. During the night the planes would be rearmed and refueled, and then at dawn they would take off, hit the Japanese and be back at Batchelor before the Japanese knew what had hit them.[40]

Informed of the Japanese landing at Davao, Maj. Walsh decided to strike as soon as possible, thereby showing that the 19th BG had not abandoned the Philippines. The men used December 21 to make as many planes operational as possible and make a few necessary improvements. Realizing that the Japanese were attacking the unarmed tail of the B-17s, three sergeants from the 93rd BS rigged up a "stinger" in the tail of B-17D (40-3097, *Ole Betsy*). After cutting off the tail, they installed a .30 caliber machine gun which could be fired by pulling a cable that reached to the waist positions.[41]

Nine planes, flying in three equal flights led by Maj. Combs, took off from Batchelor Field at 10:43 A.M. on December 22. The nine planes, each carrying one bomb bay tank and four 500-lb. bombs, were the largest formation of B-17s that the 19th BG had put up. Reaching Davao just at dusk, the Fortresses dropped their loads from 20,000 feet and caught the Japanese completely by surprise, encountering no antiaircraft fire or fighter opposition.

"They didn't expect us," Lt. Teats wrote, "and we got some hits in on transports and shore installations and then put in at Del Monte on the north side of the island." Later, the Japanese admitted that the dock area was heavily damaged, that a 10,000-ton tanker had been sunk, and that one bomb struck the bow of a heavy cruiser, forcing the ship to return to Japan for repairs.[42]

The planes found Del Monte being drenched with rain but landed without trouble. As Lt. Ford stepped from his plane he nearly collapsed. Unknown to anyone he had been "suffering from a severe attack of malarial fever . . ." He was later awarded a Distinguished Flying Cross which read, in part, "The seriousness of his condition was withheld because of the shortage of pilots and the importance of the mission. . ."[43]

Working in the darkness and the driving rain, the men began servicing their planes. "We had only one refueling truck," remembered Lt. Vandevanter. Each time the truck ran dry, it was refilled from 50-gallon drums and electric pumps salvaged from some of the destroyed planes. When finished, the men were told that a large Japanese task force consisting of an estimated 80 transports and warships lay at anchor in Lingayen Gulf.[44] The 19th BG had been handed a golden opportunity and elected to act accordingly.

"We could only service six ships at a time," Teats stated, "so it was agreed that everyone who couldn't hit Lingayen would gang up on Davao. Both raids were to be made at the crack of dawn." At 3:00 A.M. December 23, with the rain still falling, the B-17s started for Lingayan Gulf. Unfortunately, Maj. Combs, commanding two three-plane elements, could not start his engines and had to abort. Capt. Parsel then took the lead and led the others into the air.[45]

The five planes were flying in one two-plane element and one three-plane element when Lt. Coats, B-17D (40-3067), leading the second element, developed engine trouble and turned back to Australia. Then, when Lt. Teats, in the second element, spotted a Japanese reconnaissance plane and went to investigate, the formation was fragmented further still.

Surprisingly, Teats arrived over Lingayen Gulf first. He later described what he found. "It was a monster aggregation—heavy cruisers, destroyers, cargo auxiliaries and transports." While a heavy, but harmless, wall of antiaircraft fire erupted below and behind him, Teats spent 15 minutes over the fleet looking for the biggest ship. Finally, he dropped his small 100-lb. bombs on two 25,000-ton transports anchored close together. When his bombs straddled the bows of the two ships Teats was sure they "must have done plenty of damage . . ." As he turned away and headed for San Marcelino, as planned, 14 Zeros came after him but they only fired one burst and then turned away. They had other targets to attack. The other three B-17s had arrived.[46]

Arriving in a loose formation at 21,000 feet, Capt. Parsel was in the lead with Lts. Tash and Keiser on his wings. Amidst a rain of antiaircraft fire, the two wingmen dropped their bomb load when they saw the first bombs start to fall from Parsel's plane. Generally, in the Pacific, only the lead bombardier used his bombsight. The other bombardiers, sometimes called "togglers" would drop, or toggle, their bombs when they saw the bombs fall from the lead plane. "[I]t is believed that the wing ships had very little effect because they didn't drop at the same time as the leader," Lt. Vandevanter had to admit.[47]

Spotting the incoming Zeros, the three pilots pushed their tired engines to the limit and reached the safety of the storm clouds. Like Teats, they started towards San Marcelino but after deciding that it would be too risky to land there in broad daylight, they turned south and headed for an alternate field on the island of

Ambon, in the Netherlands East Indies. By 4:00 P.M., all three B-17s were safely on the ground at the small Dutch airstrip.[48]

An hour later Lt. Teats also landed at Ambon. After heading towards San Marcelino, he too had decided that it would be too risky to stay there during the daylight hours so he headed south. Low on fuel, but feeling that Del Monte would also be too risky during the daylight, he landed on Mindoro at 9:00 A.M. Two hours later, after taking on fuel, he took off and six hours later landed at Ambon.[49]

Had the 19th BG been able to send a large number of B-17s against the tightly packed shipping in Lingayen Gulf on December 23, they may have been able to do considerable damage to the Japanese. Unfortunately, the numbers were not available. Their few bombs hurt the Japanese but could not stop them. That morning, the first of 80,000 Imperial troops came ashore.[50]

Shortly after the five planes had left Del Monte, Maj. Combs finally got his engines started. Instead of heading towards Lingayen Gulf, after the others had already stirred up the enemy fighters, he turned towards Cotabato in western Mindanao where another invasion force was reportedly landing. When Combs arrived however, he found nothing. Undaunted, he flew over to Davao, dropped his bombs on a Japanese destroyer and then headed back to Australia.[51]

Only three B-17s remained at Del Monte after Combs departed. Lt. Connally took off at 4:30 A.M. but because of the lack of servicing facilities, Lts. Bohnaker and Godman were forced to wait and take off at 30 minute intervals. They all tried to rendezvous above the field but because of the weather and the threat of an enemy air raid they could not. Ordered not to attack individually, Connally turned south and soon joined the other B-17s at Ambon while Bohnaker flew all the way back to Australia.

Lt. Godman, piloting the last B-17, also headed back to Australia but on his way over Davao, he bombed the docks. His crew reported seeing a "large fire" in Davao harbor before their attack, supposedly the result of the previous nights attack.[52]

The next day, Christmas Eve, the five "lost" pilots on Ambon returned to Batchelor, arriving after noon. When they landed, they learned that Maj. Walsh had sent another three planes up to Del Monte. Although he had planned a "maximum effort raid," Walsh had found that only three of the nine planes then in Australia were combat worthy. At 10:45 A.M., Lts. Smith and Alvin V.H. Mueller had taken off for Del Monte, followed by Lt. Schaetzel at 11:27. When the crews reached Del Monte, they were treated to a special Christmas dinner. The remaining ground personnel had slaughtered a cow and made beef stew, a welcome relief from the curried beans served by the Australians at Batchelor.[53]

All nine of the planes that had been sent on the first bombing mission from Australia came back without major damage. Each plane had flown approximately 4,600 miles round trip—an unprecedented mission. The four pilots that had bomb Lingayen Gulf each earned the Distinguished Flying Cross.[54] Meanwhile, the three pilots on the second mission sat at Del Monte and waited for orders from Manila and Air Force Headquarters on where to strike next. The orders never came.

On Christmas Eve, the Japanese executed a major landing at Lamon Bay less than 100 miles south of Manila. Almost immediately, Gen. MacArthur ordered all Allied troops on Luzon to concentrate on the Bataan Peninsula and the island of Corregidor. On that same date, Clark Field was finally abandoned.[55]

Around noon, Maj. O'Donnell, who was still in overall command of the 19th BG and was now at Clark Field, received an order from Manila: "The Headquarters is closing. Go to Bataan."[56]

Maj. O'Donnell wanted the installations at Clark Field systematically destroyed so that the approaching Japanese could not use them however, in the confusion of the rapid evacuation, nothing was systematic. "They blew up all the bombs and gas," O'Donnell reported. "They closed the gate and threw away the key." Lt. Jacquet recalled, "All personnel at Clark Field had been ordered to evacuate to Bataan and the protective guns of Corregidor. Everything at Clark was being destroyed and blown up." A thick, black cloud of smoke rose high over Clark Field when the men bashed in the heads of 55-gallon drums of gasoline and set them on fire.[57]

"There was no talk of Christmas and there was no talk of home," wrote Lt. Whitcomb, "for neither could have any meaning for us. Our new oriental home, which only three weeks before had been a tropical paradise where we lived in luxury such as we had never known before, had been bombed and blasted out of existence." With the destruction of Clark Field, the ground echelon of the 19th BG was redesignated ground forces and became infantry. Morale was at an all time low as the remnants of the 19th BG on Luzon boarded trucks and joined the long column of American and Filipino troops heading southwest towards Bataan.[58]

On Christmas Day, the three B-17s at Del Monte, still without specific orders, decided to hit a captured airfield at Davao. With each plane carrying seven 300-lb. bombs Lt. Smith, B17D (40-3079), began his takeoff run but suddenly blew a main tire. As Smith's crew sought a way to repair the tire, Lts. Mueller, B-17C (40-2072), and Schaetzel, B-17D (40-3062), took off for Davao at 4:30 A.M.[59]

It was dawn and Schaetzel was in the lead when the two reached Davao. Heavy antiaircraft fire filled the sky as they dropped their bombs on the captured airfield, destroying at least one of the parked Japanese planes. Schaetzel's plane was hit once while Mueller's plane was hit twice. As the two turned to leave, 10 Japanese fighters raced up to attack.[60]

Wanting to get up into the thin air of high altitude, Lts. Schaetzel and Mueller climbed to 28,000 feet where it was generally believed that the B-17, with its supercharged engines, could outperform the Zero. "The best defense was to try and fly at 30,000 feet, as the Zero got real sloppy on the controls at that height and couldn't stay with you," reported Sgt. Fesmire. Lt. Kurtz agreed, "[I]f we're up to 30,000 the Fortress is performing beautifully while the Zeros, if they can make it, are skidding all over the sky in that thin air."[61]

In spite of their sloppy handling, the Zeros came after the two B-17s. On the first pass, the Zeros went after Lt. Schaetzel, knocking out one of his engines. Moments later, his bathtub gunner was killed and both his right waist gunner and radio room gunner were wounded. Although the damaged engine forced Schaetzel to slow down, Mueller stayed with him, trying to use the interlocking fire from each Fortress to fight off the Zeros.[62]

After hitting Schaetzel, the Zeros concentrated on Lt. Mueller. For the next 20 minutes they raked his B-17C with machine-gun and cannon fire. When the Zeros finally broke away, the plane was a sieve. Miraculously, all four engines were still running and only two men, the radio room gunner and the right waist gunner, had been wounded. Staying at their guns, each man had helped shoot down one of the attackers.[63]

Although Schaetzel's plane had barely been touched he had one man killed and two wounded, and had one engine out. Dropping down to wave top height, the two planes flew back to Batchelor Field and landed at 3:30 P.M. The official report stated that Schaetzel's B-17D had "barely more than a dozen enemy hits on it" while Mueller's plane had "more than 100." However, Lt. Teats wrote, "Mueller's plane looked like the one Wheless brought back about a week before from Legaspi. It was riddled. 'More than 100 hits' is putting it conservatively. It looked as though the holes had been put together rather than the plane."[64]

Back at Del Monte, Lt. Smith's crew was working hard to repair the blown tire on B-17D (40-3079). Fearing an early morning air raid, Smith stationed one of his men at the end of the field with orders to fire three shots if he heard enemy planes approaching. Then, after finding only one wing jack, and needing two, the crew improvised. By jacking up the wing with the blown tire and digging a hole under the flat, the men were able to replace the punctured tire. However, now Smith had to get his bomber out of the hole.

At the far end of the field, the sentry crewman suddenly heard incoming fighters and fired his pistol but after only one shot the gun jammed. One shot was warning enough however and Smith's crew scrambled for cover. A lone Zero roared in and made one strafing run before flying away. Although a bullet punctured the bomb bay tank, the tank did not explode and the hole was hastily patched. Then, working quickly, the crew filled in the hole and knocked the jack out from under the wing. With Lt. Smith giving full power to both engines on that side of the plane, and with the crew pushing against the tail of the bomber, the B-17 was "horsed" out of the hole.

Still carrying his bombs, Smith took off at 10:30 A.M. and flew to Davao. After dropping his bombs on four ships in the harbor, he sighted a flight of enemy fighters coming up to get him but was able to outrun the Zeros and land back at Australia at 6:00 P.M.[65]

The Christmas raids on Davao had cost the 19th BG two more B-17s. Lt. Mueller's B-17C (40-2072) was so badly damaged that it could only be used as a transport while Schaetzel's B-17D (40-3062) was never used on a combat mission again. The 19th BG now had only 11 combat worthy B-17s to work with.[66]

While the three crews were bombing Davao, the men at Batchelor Field spent Christmas Day servicing and overhauling their planes. "We thought about Christmas and home," Lt. Teats wrote, "and that's all, and I think most of us deliberately tried not to think." In the evening, the Australian airmen who shared Batchelor Field came over to share some Christmas cheer. "That day will be forever memorable to us for an item so negligible in a normal, peace-time existence as to pass unnoticed," Teats recalled, "a bottle of beer." The Australians had brought with them a few bottles of beer and although it was served warm, Teats recalled that "no nectar of the Gods ever tasted so sweet to us."[67]

At noon on December 25, Gen. Brereton and his staff, including Col. Eubank, flew to the island of Java in the Netherlands East Indies. Ordered to "go on south" by Gen. MacArthur, Brereton was planning on moving his air force, including the 19th BG, to Java to fight the Japanese from there.[68] Already the Japanese were advancing towards the rich Dutch oil fields of the Netherlands East Indies. Unable to produce her own oil, Japan had to capture the oil fields in order to keep her military machine rolling. Using Davao Harbor as a base of operations, the Japanese began building up their strength for the eventual push into the Indies. Since the Dutch had sent all of their bombers to Malaya to help the British they desperately needed the American B-17s and Gen. Brereton was not about to let them down.[69]

On December 29, Gen. Brereton arrived at Batchelor Field and immediately called for an operations meeting. Lt. Kurtz remembered:

> He told us the United States Army Air Force of the Far East . . . was moving all its bombers to Java, and at once. Its main base would be on a field near the city of Malang. From there we would operate out of advance bases already prepared by the Dutch on the outlying islands of Borneo and the Celebes. From these our first missions would all be concentrated on breaking up an immense concentration of Jap transports which was gathering at Davao Bay, on the southern tip of the Philippines.

Naturally, the men were excited, until it was discovered that the "United States Army Air Force of the Far East" consisted of the 11 worn-out B-17s of the 19th BG. "[W]e didn't know whether to be sorry for ourselves or for Maj. Gen. Brereton for having such a pitifully small command," wrote Kurtz.[70] However, Gen. Brereton had a surprise for the men—the new improved B-17Es were on their way. As Kurtz recalled, "[S]oon Fortresses were to be flying out to reinforce us . . . with the newest planes with fresh crews and plenty of ground personnel coming by boats."[71]

The move to Java was twofold. The two long missions flown out of Australia had been hard on the men and the planes, and had used up an enormous amount of high octane aviation fuel, which was hard to obtain in Australia. By moving to Java, the 19th BG would be closer to the Japanese and at the same time they would be closer to Palembang in Sumatra, where the Dutch produced their high octane fuel.[72] Moving the 19th BG to Java would be symbiotic for both the Dutch and the Americans.

At 8:00 A.M., on December 30, Maj. Walsh led six B-17Ds and B-17C (40-2062), the one remaining combat worthy B-17C, towards Singosari airfield near Malang,

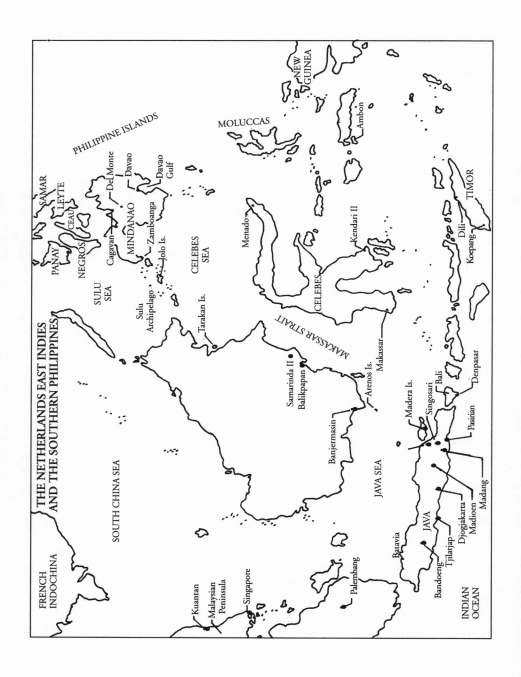

THE NETHERLANDS EAST INDIES
AND THE SOUTHERN PHILIPPINES

Java.[73] Wrote Lt. Kurtz, "From Australia to Java is a full day's work even for a Fortress." Eight hours and 1,300 miles later, the planes finally arrived at their new base.[74]

"To get [to Singosari] you have to climb a little and then enter a narrow mountain pass which usually is filled with clouds in the afternoon," Kurtz wrote. The two sod runways were 4,000-feet long and expertly camouflaged. "Looking down on it from altitude, you took it to be just an ordinary tilled field," Kurtz said. Two enormous hangars stood side by side, their roofs painted to blend into the tropical vegetation. The 19th BG men were housed in brick barracks buildings but because of a lack of bunks some of the men had to throw their mattresses on the floor. And, since Singosari had not been built for the large B-17s, the protective revetments were too small and the big bombers had to park out in the open.[75]

At 5:30 P.M. on December 31, three more B-17Ds arrived.[76] Since Maj. O'Donnell was still in the Philippines, Maj. Combs was given command of the bombers in Java.[77] His command consisted of 10 war-weary B-17s, since four planes had been left in Australia. B-17D (40-3072) had developed electrical trouble on the No. 2 engine while B-17C (40-2072) and B-17Ds (40-3062) and (40-3091) had been sent down to Laverton Repair Depot near Melbourne. Eventually, B-17D (40-3091) would be scrapped and cannibalized for parts, but B-17C (40-2072) and B-17D (40-3062) would see life as transport and supply planes.[78]

The year 1941 had come to a close. After suffering the devastating loss of almost half of their bombers on December 8, the 19th BG had waged "an epic but futile attempt to halt the Japanese invasion of the Philippines."[79] Courageously, the 19th BG had showed unsurpassed devotion to duty in attacking the enemy invasion fleets, wherever and whenever possible, with tired men and machines. Unfortunately, the number of B-17s available to the 19th BG was too little to have any overall effect.

After three weeks of war the 19th had lost over two thirds of its bombers. Yet, only two, Capt. Kelly's and Lt. Adams', had been shot down. The others had been damaged on the ground or lost to crash landings or ditchings. The men had developed a great fondness for the B-17 and knew first hand that it was a plane that could take a lot of punishment and still bring the crew home. With new men and the new improved B-17Es arriving soon, the men of the 19th BG arrived at Singosari with renewed hopes and high spirits.[80]

"No wonder our morale rose, and we took off for Java with our dander back up," wrote Lt. Kurtz. "Suppose we were only a baker's dozen [sic] against the entire Japanese Empire! That was only the tip of the spear point. The others would surely follow soon . . . All the mistakes, we were sure, had been made in 1941; 1942 would be different."[81]

VII

A New Axiom

BY JANUARY 1, 1942, the American garrison at Wake Island had been overrun, the Japanese had captured Hong Kong, pushed down the Malay Peninsula to threaten Singapore and had successfully invaded three-quarters of the Philippines. The Japanese had a toehold on Borneo and were preparing to invade the Netherlands East Indies. The New Year did not look bright for the Allies. As the historian for the 5th BG in Hawaii stated, "Offensive action against the enemy was impossible and all that could be done was to 'sweat' out the enemy who had the initiative and who was swallowing up territory at a most alarming rate."[1]

Still fearful of an attack against Oahu, and afraid that the Japanese might use Wake Island as a springboard for an invasion, Lt. Cecil Faulkner (31st BS/5th BG), flew his B-17D down to Midway for a reconnaissance of Wake. At 3:00 A.M., on January 2, he took off on the 2,000 mile round-trip. Running into strong head winds, he did not reach Wake until two hours after his scheduled time. Then, after snapping the necessary pictures, and fearful that he had wasted most of his gas in reaching Wake, Faulkner turned back towards Midway. However, the head winds that had plagued him going out were now behind him, pushing him to speeds above 250 mph. Even with the wind the plane reached Midway with only 15 minutes of gas remaining in the tanks. For their daring flight, the entire crew was awarded DFCs.[2]

In early January, the 50th BS/11th BG moved from Hickam to a newly constructed airfield near Kahuku, on the north coast of Oahu. Being a new field, some of the concrete revetments for the B-17s were still under construction when the squadron arrived. "On one occasion, while working on our B-17 in our bunker, we heard a lot of yelling and commotion in a nearby bunker," wrote Pvt. Belz. A contractor, spraying the bunker with a layer of liquid concrete, had allowed the wind to carry the spray over to a parked B-17. "It took the ground

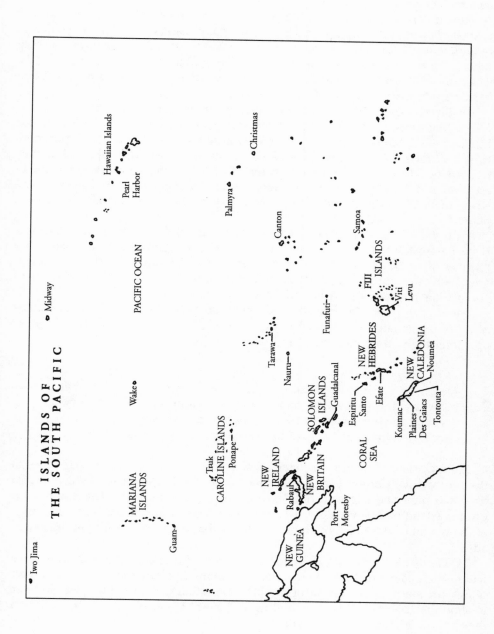

and flight crew fellows several days of delicately chipping away at that layer of concrete 'blanket' on that B-17," Belz mused.[3]

During January, the 4th RS/5th BG became a school squadron checking out first pilots in the B-18s and then qualifying them as copilots in the B-17s. Once qualified as a copilot, the men were transferred to the other squadrons to help relieve the exhausted crews that had been flying almost continuous search missions since December 8. In addition, the 4th RS also trained navigators and bombardiers who were likewise much in demand.[4]

On January 6, the first flight of B-17Es, three planes from the 22nd BS/7th BG led by Maj. Hobson, B-17E (41-2406), left Hawaii to reinforce the 19th BG.[5] Noted Lt. Fields, ". . . Maj. Hobson had repeatedly asked that the Hawaiian Department turn his crews loose so that they could go ahead to [Mindanao] . . . but they refused to let us go." Through Hobson's insistence, the bombers were finally released and left Hawaii on the inaugural flight, "hopping southwestward via a string of Pacific Islands and atolls most of which had never before seen a land plane."

With the loss of Wake Island, a new ferry route had to be found to Australia. Even before the fall of Wake the Americans had begun building airstrips on a number of far-flung islands across the Pacific. On December 28, the bare essentials had been completed and the new southern ferry route from Hawaii to Townsville, on Australia's east coast, was reported open.

The first stop for Maj. Hobson and the others was Christmas Island, 50 miles north of the equator and 1,400 miles from Hawaii. Lt. Fields, who would follow on a later flight, described the island:

> Christmas Island was a very tropical island and the strips that we landed on were just cut out of the coconut trees. It was here that I saw my first green coconut and learned that in place of a laxative it would do very nicely. Drinking the coconut milk was a new experience for a lot of us and we all experienced the same fate, too.[6]

From Christmas Island the planes flew to Canton Island, about 1,050 miles to the southwest. "Canton Island is a small coral atoll in the Pacific, which at that time had only one tree, and one landing strip," Fields noted. "The one tree on Canton Island had a look-out tower built around it so they could take advantage of the height of the tree looking for anybody that might be coming in unexpectedly."[7]

Lt. Fields also recalled one other peculiarity of Canton. "[The] landing strip had numerous goony birds on it . . . that could not fly; they ran and flapped their wings but could not become airborne. [The men stationed on Canton] would have to shoo the goony birds off the landing strip until the airplanes got in, and then they would let them back on again."[8]

The next stop on the flight was at Nandi Field, on the island of Viti Levu in the Fiji Islands. Here native laborers had constructed a fine 5,000 feet long runway.

Although it was considered "good in all weather," the runway proved to be a bit too narrow for night takeoffs.[9]

From Nandi the three 22nd BS B-17s flew to Tontouta Field on New Caledonia. A very primitive field, Tontouta consisted of a rolling, rough surfaced 5,000 feet long runway and little else. Lacking a fuel pumping facility, the planes had to be refueled by hand, using 55-gallon drums and a hand pump.[10]

From Tontouta the bombers flew to Townsville and from there took a short hop across northern Australia to Darwin. Arriving in Darwin, 1st Lt. Clarence E. "Sandy" McPherson, B-17E (41-2417, *Monkey Bizz-Ness*), experienced engine trouble and was left behind. On January 14, in spite of the long distances and the primitive conditions, Maj. Hobson and 1st Lt. Jack W. Hughes, B-17E (41-2419), landed at Singosari, Malang.[11] A back door ferry route had been opened to Java.

On January 16, the constant search missions off the Hawaiian Islands finally paid off. West of Oahu, Lt. Edmundson, now with the 26th BS/11th BG, bombed a Japanese submarine. Later, the United States Navy intercepted Japanese radio messages trying unsuccessfully to contact a submarine in the area. Acting on these unsuccessful contacts, the Navy confirmed Edmundson's sinking of the sub.[12]

On that same date, after a small detachment of Japanese warships shelled Samoa, three B-17Es from the 23rd BS/5th BG, and three B-17Es from the 50th RS/11th BG, under the overall command of the recently promoted Lt. Col. Sweeney, set out for Canton Island. Assigned to Naval Task Group 8.9 the six bombers ran into a tropical storm and were forced to stop at Palmyra Island, halfway to Canton. With visibility down to almost zero, the planes had difficulty landing on the short, narrow runway. On coming in, Lt. Robert Sullivan (50th RS) landed short of the runway and tore the tail off his plane.

On January 17, with the rain still falling, Col. Sweeney requested the Pan American station on Canton to send out homing signals. Late in the day, the five remaining planes took off. By the time they neared Canton the sun had set and the rain had increased. Although the crews listened, no one heard a homing signal. By dead reckoning, Sweeney and one other pilot managed to find Canton but two of the other planes passed the island and the fifth plane was totally lost. Furious that there had been no homing signal, Sweeney raced towards the Pan American station and chewed out the operator. Wrote Sweeney, "The radio operator on duty was shortly and properly instructed, and the fifth airplane soon picked up the signals and effected a safe landing."[13]

Over the next few days, flying search missions from Canton, a number of submarines were sighted and bombed but results were "doubtful." The aircrews soon found that the newly constructed facilities at Canton left much to be desired. Although fuel was plentiful, the gas was found to be of inferior quality, being dirty, watered, and full of metal corrosives. Additionally, the planes had to be gassed by hand from 55-gallon drums.

On January 19, Capt. George Blakey (23rd BS) made a cross-wind landing and wrecked two propellers and his landing gear. With no spare parts on Canton, Sweeney sent Lt. Francis Seeburger (23rd BS) back to Palmyra to cannibalize parts from Lt. Sullivan's wrecked B-17. After stripping the necessary parts, Seeburger was about to return to Canton when he blew a cylinder head on one engine. Once again Sullivan's plane became a donor and after a few hours, Seeburger was on his way with the replacement parts for Capt. Blakey's Fortress.[14]

For the next two weeks the five planes flew back and forth between Canton and Nandi Field on Viti Levu, every so often dropping bombs on a suspected enemy submarine. By January 30, the five B-17Es were back at Hickam.[15] Although no enemy ships had been sighted and the attacks against the submarines had been inconclusive, the crews had gained a new respect for their bombers. The B-17s, ranging far from their home fields and staging through distant airdromes, could hit the enemy anywhere and at any time. The Japanese Navy would have to be on guard.

More importantly, the crews had gained much needed experience. In his follow-up report Col. Sweeney emphasized the need for perfect dead reckoning navigation. The slightest error in a battle area surrounded by nothing but water would mean almost certain death. Dead reckoning training was not to be taken lightly.[16]

On January 23, under an overall shake-up in the command structure of the AAF, the 5th and 11th BGs were placed under the newly constituted 7th Bomber Command. On February 2, Maj. Gen. Willis H. Hale was placed in command.[17] Continuing the shake-up, the AAF established combat air forces in the different areas of operation. On February 5, the Hawaiian Air Force was redesignated the 7th Air Force (7th AF). Gen. Tinker, who had controlled the Hawaiian Air Force since December 18, was put in charge. Under his command were 7th Bomber Command and 7th Fighter Command.[18]

At its inception, 7th Bomber Command consisted of only 43 heavy bombers, the majority B-17s.[19] Throughout January and February, 7th Bomber Command continued to participate in search and training missions around Hawaii. New B-17Es continued to arrive from the United States and were still being assigned to the different squadrons to help ease the burden of activity.[20] For the time being, the 7th AF was not ready to strike out on its own.

On New Years Day, the Dutch on Java, grateful that the Americans had come to help save their possessions, treated the 19th BG air echelon to a sumptuous New Years Day dinner at the Palace Hotel in Malang. "The Dutch practically turned over the town to us," Lt. Teats wrote.[21]

Absent from the celebration was Capt. Edwin B. Broadhurst (30th BS). Assigned to inspect the forward Dutch airfields for the 19th BG, Broadhurst took off in B-17D (40-3061), flew up to Samarinda II, on the east coast of Borneo and about 120 miles north of Balikpapan, and then to Kendari II, on the southeast corner of Celebes. After discovering that both airfields had runways long enough for a B-17, contained enough high-octane gasoline, and had a sufficient number of Dutch bombs, which had been made in America and could be used by the American bombers, Broadhurst returned to Singosari, filed his report and on January 2, the 19th BG went back into operation.[22]

At 9:00 A.M., seven B-17Ds and the lone B-17C, led by Maj. Combs, left Singosari for Samarinda II but ran into such a heavy downpour that they were forced to turn back. As they sat and waited, the ground crews got another plane ready so at 8:30 A.M. on January 3, nine planes set out for Borneo.[23]

Samarinda II lay hidden in the thick jungle along a tropical river. Since Davao was only 800 miles away, the Dutch were afraid that the Japanese would locate the field and had told the Americans not to approach it directly. "We were to take an irregular course to the coast of Borneo," Lt. Kurtz wrote, "then fly so many minutes up the river, then drop down to low altitude, and at this point we should be right over the field . . ."[24] Although the planes hit a weak cold front, they pushed through and found Samarinda II without trouble.[25]

"[T]he Dutch had hewed this field out of the teeming jungle," noted Kurtz, "uprooted the stumps, leveled it off, planted it with grass and then covered it with wooden sawhorses that would knock the be-Jesus out of any plane that tried to land through them." As the B-17s appeared, native laborers moved the sawhorses. The moment the last plane was on the ground, the natives replaced the barricades. "They didn't intend that the Japs should sneak in and take that field by surprise," added Kurtz. Upon landing, it was found that Lt. Schaetzel's B-17D (40-3070) had a broken oil line and the aircrew immediately went to work repairing it.[26]

Although Maj. Combs had been ordered to launch an air strike at the "earliest possible hour," he ran into unseen problems. "The natives who helped service the planes were so slow they almost drove us frantic," remembered Lt. Teats. Each plane was to be loaded with 2,100 gallons of gas and four 600-lb. bombs. Lacking trucks and fuel pumps, 50-gallon drums of gasoline were rolled out to the planes and loaded by hand. Adding to the delay, through an error in translation, the Dutch had readied 600-kilogram bombs, about 1,100 lbs. each, which had to be rolled back to the magazine for the correct size bombs.[27]

Once the correct bombs were in place, the Americans had trouble getting the fuses lined up correctly. Additionally, the Americans discovered that the Dutch fuses were a bit touchy. "We used Dutch detonators and [they] had to be fused in the air," recalled mechanic Mike Payne. "A 5 degree temp[erature] change in 5 minutes could set them off." By the time the nine B-17s were ready, it was after dark and too late for an attack.[28]

At 5:15 A.M. on January 4, all nine B-17s began taking off but when Lt. Schaetzel's repaired oil line ruptured he was forced to abort. Flying in two three-plane elements, followed by one two-plane element, the B-17s climbed to 25,000 feet and came over Davao Gulf from the northwest. Through broken clouds they could see the water below them. "It was Lingayen all over again," noted Teats. "There was all kinds of stuff up there." Particularly congested was Malalag Bay, a small cove on the southwest side of the gulf. "It seemed to me that half the Jap navy was tied up there," Teats said. "There was a big battleship, heavy and light cruisers and destroyers, and the whole works tied up, deck to deck."

Caught completely unaware, the Japanese ships were at anchor and could only throw up a wall of antiaircraft fire and hope for the best.[29] Lt. Teats was elated as the three flights attacked at one minute intervals:

> The bombs of the first flight hit the cruisers and destroyers. Elmer Parcell [sic] was leading the second flight. His first bomb hit smack in the superstructure of the battleship [actually the heavy cruiser *Myoko*]. The first bombs of the other wingman hit around the forward turret and my bombardier planted his first one right at the water line, the other falling across destroyers nearby.[30]

A Japanese officer aboard the heavy cruiser recorded, "*Myoko* took a direct hit on No 2 turret and there were many casualties. I saw the commander was hit in the shoulder. The signal searchlight was damaged and the gunnery officer was wounded in the eye by fragments of a bomb."[31]

Besides hitting the *Myoko*, the B-17s hit a number of other ships. "One destroyer was blown practically out of the water," Lt. Teats reported, "and the entire forward end of another was lifted clear of the water . . ." Although the bay was packed with ships, and the antiaircraft fire was ineffective, Maj. Combs elected not to make a second bomb run. Experience had taught him to, "Hit 'em high, hit 'em fast, hit 'em once!"[32]

At 2:30 P.M., the planes were back at Samarinda II. Since the forward airbase could only supply 1,700 gallons of gasoline per plane, it was decided to return the bombers to Singosari before the next mission. By noon of January 5, all nine B-17s, including Schaetzel's bomber, were back on Java.[33]

The unexpected and sudden attack on the concentration of Japanese warships in Malalag Bay was the most successful mission flown by the 19th BG to date. By going over the bay at a fast rate of speed, at high altitude, and only once, the B-17s had been able to drop their bombs, avoid the Japanese antiaircraft fire and get away before any fighters could intercept them.[34]

On the negative side, while bombing from 30,000 feet was the safest altitude for the B-17, it tended to decrease the accuracy of the bomb run against a moving vessel. By the time the bombs reached the earth, the targeted ship was no longer there. With the concentration of ships found in Malalag Bay however, all standing at anchor, dropping from high altitude was not only safe, but very effective.

Also, by attacking in three flights the B-17s had managed to drop a concentration of bombs against a few ships. Likewise, by staying in a group, the bombers tended to discourage the enemy fighters. The airmen had learned in the Philippines that the Zeros loved to go after a lone bomber. Although only two B-17s had been shot down by Japanese fighters, a number of other bombers had been badly damaged because they had been caught all alone. By staying together, several B-17s could concentrate their fire against one attacker. "If we were a huge formation," Kurtz explained, "the lack of tail guns wouldn't matter, for if a Zero started climbing in on your tail and coming in on your blind spot, he'd be in easy range for the waist gunners of the planes on either side of you—and cross fire from a dozen of them converging on him would surely blow him into confetti."[35] Unfortunately, the massed flights were at a minimum.

For a few days the 19th BG sat idle while Maj. Walsh, as operations officer under Maj. Combs, tried to find a forward airbase that had gasoline. "Cannot plan mission until information is received regarding availability of 100 octane fuel at Kendari. None available at Samarinda for seven days," Walsh cabled Col. Eubank at FEAF Headquarters at Darwin.[36] In addition to the problem of obtaining gasoline, the Americans had also discovered that the highly aromatic Dutch gasoline caused troubles for the Flying Fortresses.

As early as late-December the 19th BG had reported that the Dutch aromatic additive in their gasoline was dissolving the rubber linings of the self-sealing bullet-proof fuel tanks and gumming up the engines and carburetors. Immediately warnings had gone out to dilute the Dutch gas with American gas. American gasoline was non-aromatic while that produced by the Dutch contained between 20 and 30 percent aromatics.

By January 6, the Americans were aware that the foreign aromatic fuel not only damaged the leak-proof tanks but also the fuel pump and high pressure carburetor diaphragms. Replacement fuel cells and diaphragms were ordered but until they arrived, the 19th BG had to use either foreign fuel entirely, and continue to damage their planes, or mix it half and half with American made gas whenever any was available.[37]

While the men waited for a solution to the problem, they overhauled their beaten airplanes and got acquainted with the Dutch customs. Two airmen from the 9th BS/7th BG, which would reach Java later, recalled the food at Malang. "The mess was in charge of the Dutch," recalled T/Sgt. Rowland A. Boone. "They served only one hot meal a day, and this was always at noon—usually hot soup with boiled beef and potatoes." Out in the field, the men ate canned food. 1st Lt. Cecil C. Knudson wrote, "If it is canned American it is o.k., but some of this canned cabbage and meat the Dutch make. Also we can't read the Dutch labels, and as there are no pictures, it's a gamble what turns up."[38]

On many of the missions, the Dutch provided the Americans with a basket of food, "pineapples, tropical fruit, and . . . sandwiches which were either a slab of cheese, or else raw bacon, in between two thick hunks of bread." Sgt. Boone wrote, "We found this heavy stuff made gas in your intestines and just as you got to high altitude going over the target, this gas swelled up, giving you the gripes. So we'd eat the fruit and throw the sandwiches away."[39]

Another custom that the Americans could never understand was the European tradition of rinsing one's rear end after a bowel movement. Mechanic Payne remembered, "One problem we had when we arrived in Java was, no toilet paper. They used water to wash their rear ends then washed their hands. We solved that problem by importing toilet paper."[40]

Payne, as a member of the 7th BG ground crews, had been aboard the troop ship *Republic*, bound for the Philippines, when the war started and the ship was diverted to Australia. After spending Christmas at Brisbane, complete with a Christmas dinner of cold bologna sandwiches and sweet milk, some of the 9th BS mechanics had been sent to Djogjakarta, about 160 miles west of Malang, on the south coast of Java. "We arrived there on Jan. 4th, 1942," Payne wrote. "[W]e were split up into 2 groups, part to India and part to Java to a town called Jock Tacarta [sic]."[41]

Since the air echelon of the 7th BG was slated to reinforce the 19th BG in Java, part of the 9th BS ground crews had been sent to Djogjakarta to help the Dutch and the native Javanese prepare another bomber airfield. "They started building a coral runway for us," Payne wrote, "and ran a small gauge railway down to the runway to haul the rocks down to it." Unfortunately, the railroad had a sharp bend in the tracks. "They would get these little cars rolling as fast as they could and it would jump the tracks spilling its load," Payne continued. "[Then] they would load it back up and push it to the runway in a normal manner." As Payne recalled, the Javanese would "jump with joy" every time the cars overturned. "The runway never got finished," he added.[42] The other half of the 9th BS was sent to Karachi, India, to help establish an airbase for reinforcements flying to Java via a new air route across Africa.[43]

On January 8, Maj. Combs, B-17D (40-3097, *Ole Betsy*), led the nine combat ready B-17s into Kendari II. Left behind was Lt. Schaetzel, who was still waiting for a replacement oil line.[44] Instead of staging through Samarinda II, the planes were using Kendari II. Besides the lack of gasoline at Samarinda II, the pilots had complained that the new sod runway was not firm enough to withstand the weight of the B-17 and would be a major problem in the rainy season.[45] On the other hand, Kendari II was considered an "excellent heavy bomber field . . . [with] sufficient dispersal for 35 heavy bombers . . ."[46]

After receiving bombs and gas, the planes took off after midnight for another strike against the congestion of ships at Davao Gulf. Assembling on Maj. Combs, the nine B-17s started towards Mindanao but suddenly ran into a violent tropical storm. "We expected heavy weather, but I think this is the worst night I've ever flown," Lt. Kurtz, B-17D (40-3067), recalled. Eventually Lts. Teats, B-17D (40-3078), and Smith, B-17D (40-3079), both turned back with engine trouble.[47]

Just south of Mindanao the seven remaining B-17s broke out of the overcast and Combs realized that they were ahead of schedule. Wanting to arrive over the target at dawn, when the sun would illuminate the enemy ships, he began to circle. Unexpectedly, the planes ran into a second storm even more violent then the first and Capt. Broadhurst, B-17D (40-3061), and Lt. Kurtz, were finally forced to abort.[48]

The five planes that continued on were broken even further when Capt. Parsel, B-17D (40-3074), and Lt. Connally, B-17C (40-2062), became separated from the others. Arriving over Davao Gulf first, they managed to spot at least eight transports and a few warships through the overcast. At 6:45 A.M., Parsel bombed a 25,000-ton transport and a cruiser, and five minutes later, Connally went after a single large transport. All of the bombs missed and the B-17s quickly turned back for Kendari II.[49]

Somehow, the last three planes had managed to stay together in spite of the violent storm and arrived over Davao Gulf shortly after Parsel and Connally left.

Combs and his two wingmen, Lts. Keiser, B-17D (40-3066), and Patrick W. McIntyre, B-17D (40-3064), headed immediately for Malalag Bay and found it still packed with enemy ships, although far less than on January 4. Besides a few cruisers and destroyers, and a number of lesser craft, the crews spotted the mis-identified heavy cruiser *Myoko* off to the side and under repair. Coming through a smattering of ineffective antiaircraft fire, the B-17s zeroed in on the damaged *Myoko*. They reportedly scored one waterline hit and one direct hit which started a fire. As an added bonus, one of the bombs that missed the ship entirely landed squarely on a antiaircraft shore battery.[50]

By noon on January 9, all nine planes were safely back at Kendari II. That night, Dutch flying boats attacked the *Myoko*, further damaging the ship.[51] For their part in the mission, Maj. Combs was issued a Silver Star and a DFC, Lt. McIntyre was given a DFC, and Lt. Keiser was presented with a Silver Star and Oak Leaf Cluster in lieu of a 2nd DFC. In part, their joint citation for the DFC read, "During the flight the weather conditions were extremely dangerous. Extreme carburetor icing and the turbulence of an equatorial front made forma-tion flying almost impossible and threatened the success of the mission. It was only by exceptional skill and determination to reach the objective, inspired by the urgency of the mission, that Maj. Combs led his flight to the objective, and that his two wing men were able to follow him through."[52]

Although the 19th BG did not know it at the time, their second raid on Davao Gulf would be their last offensive strike in support of the Philippines. In late December, the Americans, British, Dutch and Australians (ABDA) had gotten together to form a joint command to combine their meager forces to combat the Japanese. Headed by British Gen. Archibald Wavell, who was supported by a mixed staff from all four nations, ABDA Command was given the unenviable task of holding a 2,000 mile front with the battered remnants from four nations.[53]

Almost immediately friction developed between the various staff members as each sought to defend their own interests. All along it had been the predominant interest of the Americans to protect the Philippines. However, the British felt that the Malaysian Peninsula had to be held in order to protect Burma and India. Likewise, the Dutch wanted to protect their oil fields in the Netherlands East Indies while the Australians felt that holding the East Indies would keep Australia safe.

By January 4, the American government had come to the conclusion that the relief of the Philippines was "entirely unjustifiable." Although President Franklin Delano Roosevelt would continue to tell MacArthur that help was on the way, he had already made the strategic decision of "Europe First." While fighting a delay-ing action in the Pacific, the United States would concentrate most of its resources towards the defeat of Nazi Germany.

With America's decision of "Europe First," ABDA Command decided to pro-tect the Malaysian Peninsula, which included the important British stronghold of Singapore, and the Netherlands East Indies. The defense of the Philippines was secondary.[54]

The soldiers on the Bataan Peninsula were more like a disorganized mob than a military unit. The 19th BG evacuees, along with two squadrons from a light bomber unit, were sent to Cabcaben, on the far southeastern tip of the peninsula. From Cabcaben the battered airmen, now fighting as infantry, could look out over Manila Bay and see both Manila and the island fortress of Corregidor. Over the next few days, camped beside the beach, the airmen had a ringside seat as Japanese planes repeatedly bombed both Manila and Corregidor.[55]

Among the men that were evacuated to Bataan was Lt. Carpenter. Being a West Point graduate, Carpenter was placed in command of a group of ground crew mechanics and assigned to hold a beachhead sector. Later he was interviewed about his activities. "[H]e never saw much action there except chasing off Japs a couple of nights," the interviewer wrote. "He had a hard time training his outfit. Their minds ran to wrenches, not tactics.[56]

Carpenter also told the interviewer that there was little food at Cabcaben. "There was no need or excuse for this," Carpenter told the interviewer. "They were told to clear out of Clark Field in such a hurry that they had time to take only one truck [of food]." Although a couple of mess sergeants were able to perform minor miracles with the food on hand, even supplying a Christmas dinner of roast turkey and all the trimmings, Carpenter was disgusted with the rush and confusion of the evacuation. Starting December 25, and continuing for the next four nights, he sent trucks to Clark Field to bring back more provisions.[57]

On December 29, a select group of stranded pilots and mechanics were evacuated to Mindanao. The 19th BG personnel, comprising the only heavy bomber group in the Philippines, were deemed too important to lose. At the same time, the rest of the men were told to move across the peninsula to Mariveles, approximately eight miles west of Cabcaben. The 30th BS historian described the move, "Trucks, abandoned buses and derelicts of private automobiles composed the makeshift convoy to the new base, during which it was constantly pounded by enemy aircraft."[58]

Shortly after midnight, 109 officers and 650 enlisted men boarded the small inter-island steamer *Mayon*. Under the cover of darkness, the steamer, described as a "lovely little ship, about 4000 tons, beautifully built, and painted white," slipped through the mine fields of Manila Harbor and headed south. In order to avoid the Zeros, the *Mayon*, completely unarmed, moved at night and hid out in small coves during the day. In spite of these precautions however, the steamer was spotted by a Japanese flying boat while it was in hiding near Mindoro Island.[59]

The flying boat came in at only 2,000 feet and repeatedly criss-crossed above the *Mayon*, dropping a total of a half dozen bombs. Although a couple bombs straddled the ship there were no direct hits. The only damage was the loss of the *Mayon's* water supply.

When the enemy plane flew off, the captain of the *Mayon* feared that the Japanese would return with a squadron of dive bombers and finish off the ship. In order to save the men he ordered everyone to abandon ship. Lt. Crimmins was among the men being evacuated on the *Mayon* and recalled what happened: "The life boats were put over and everybody scrambled to get into them. People in some of the boats rowed against each other so that their boat just went in circles." Somehow, the airmen reached shore and for the next few hours sat and waited. Finally, near 5:00 P.M., when the bombers failed to materialize, the men rowed back to the *Mayon* and the ship continued on towards Mindanao.[60]

On the evening of January 1, after three days at sea the ship finally reached Mindanao. That night, as the evacuees slept among some trees on the shore, several Japanese planes suddenly appeared and repeatedly strafed the ship. The *Mayon* had reached Mindanao just in time.[61]

When the men from Bataan reached Del Monte they were informed that all of the B-17s had left for Australia. Instead of being given bombers to fix and fly, the evacuees were given rifles to shoot. Recalled the 30th BS historian, "[T]here were no airplanes to fly at the nearby field of Del Monte, so [the 30th BS] was given the assignment of defending the harbor with four water-cooled 30 caliber Browning machine guns and several Springfield rifles."[62]

The other Bataan evacuees remained at Del Monte with the 19th BG personnel that had not been removed to Australia. Hastily trained as infantry, the men "made machine-gun nests and dug tank traps and made hand grenades out of bamboo and dynamite." Being an officer, Lt. Crimmins was placed in charge of a "machine-gun platoon of 15 or 20 men (they called it a company) with 2 officers assisting him."[63]

The Allied forces in the Philippines were battered but not beaten. Whether on Bataan, Corregidor or Mindanao, they awaited reinforcements and equipment from the United States, not knowing that it would never come.

All nine B-17s at Kendari II returned to Singosari on January 10. Since January 1, the men had flown, on average, over 6,000 miles each, usually through inclement weather. Staging through forward airfields the crews had been forced to do their own servicing and repair while allowing little time for eating or sleeping. "By this time," Lt. Teats noted, ". . . we were pretty well whipped down physically." Although everyone was suffering from "overfatigue," the 19th BG was not allowed to rest. The Japanese ships that had evacuated Davao Gulf had finally been sighted.[64]

On January 10, the Japanese invaded the island of Tarakan off the northeast coast of Borneo. Tarakan contained an important oil refinery. That same day, another enemy force landed on northern Celebes. Although Col. Eubank realized that the 19th BG was "overfatigued" and he wanted to rest his men, he decided it would be impractical to wait while the Dutch sent every plane that they had against the Tarakan invasion fleet. At 5:55 A.M., January 11, seven airworthy B-17s, once again led by Maj. Combs, B-17D (40-3097, *Ole Betsy*), took off from Malang.[65]

Flying at 9,500 feet, the Fortresses ran into a tropical storm over the Java Sea. "It was like trying to fly inside a giant bale of cotton," Lt. Kurtz, B-17D (40-3067), wrote, "so dense that when you looked out at the side you could barely see your own wing tips." Somehow Kurtz and Lt. Connally, B-17C (40-2062), and Lt. Bohnaker, B-17D (40-3064), stayed together and continued on. Rising to 27,000 feet, the three finally broke out of the storm only to discover that Lt. Bohnaker was having supercharger trouble and had to turn around. As Kurtz and Connally continued on, they suddenly saw a big black funnel-shaped cloud rising up before them.

"The gallant Dutch [were] scorching the earth," Kurtz stated, ". . . burning up their Borneo oil fields right in the face of the advancing Japs . . ." At that moment, Kurtz felt a vibration in his No. 1 engine and noticed his oil pressure dropping. Slowly falling behind Connally, Kurtz adjusted the RPMs on his engines and continued on.[66]

The B-17 formation had been badly broken by the weather. Along with Lt. Bohnaker, Lts. Keiser, B-17D (40-3066), Broadhurst, B-17D (40-3061), and Teats, B-17D (40-3078), had all turned back. Separated from the others, Combs reached Tarakan first. At 11:30 A.M., Combs dropped four 600-lb. Dutch bombs from 21,000 feet, but missed everything. Turning away, Combs was suddenly jumped by three Zeros. For 35 minutes the B-17 was subjected to repeated attacks and received minor damage. Only after two fighters were shot down did the third Zero turn away.[67]

At 11:45 A.M., Lts. Connally and Kurtz reached Tarakan and dropped their bombs from 29,000 feet. Results of the bombing were reported as "uncertain." Turning back towards Singosari, Kurtz's B-17D, flying with the troublesome engine, began to fall behind Connolly's B-17C. Instead of immediately descending to 12,000 feet, where the men could come off oxygen, Kurtz decided to stay as high as possible since his plane was losing 100 feet of altitude every minute. Recalled Kurtz, ". . . I had to hang onto my precious altitude, and it would be another two hours before we fluttered down to 12,000."

Nursing his plane along, Kurtz headed towards the small auxiliary field at Soerabaja, on the north coast of Java. "When I finally saw Surabaya [sic] Field we had less than 1,000 feet of altitude left and I didn't dare think how little gas." Without circling, Kurtz made a perfect landing on the short runway. "[W]e were tired beyond any words I have to tell, from those eleven and a half hours in the air," wrote Kurtz. "The longest mission I'd ever flown." The next day, Kurtz hopped the B-17 into Singosari.[68]

Lt. Connally, out ahead of Kurtz, was low on fuel and landed at Samarinda II. Like Kurtz, he too returned to Singosari on January 12. With the return of Kurtz and Connally, all seven bombers that had flown the mission to Tarakan were back home. However, Comb's and Kurtz's planes were immediately sidelined for repairs. By the end of the second week in January, the 19th BG had only five B-17s in commission.[69]

In spite of the resistance by the Americans and the Dutch, by January 12, the Japanese were securely ashore on Borneo and Celebes.[70] With the Japanese in possession of the airfields on northeast Borneo and northern Celebes, their land based bombers were now within range of all of the Allied bases on Borneo and the surrounding islands. As the Japanese juggernaut continued to advance, the Americans awaited their first trickle of reinforcements.

B-17E (41-2428, *Ole Sh'asta*)This photo shows the modification done on the nose of the B-17 to add a forward firing heavy machine gun (above shoulder of airman.) Lost January 1943. (USAF)

B-17E (41-2523, *Goonie*) Shot down off Russell Island, 20 March 1943. (USAF)

B-17E (41-2525, *Madame-X*). Mechanics begin repairs on collision damage. (USAF)

B-17E (41-2632, *Crock O' Crap*) of the 394th BS/5th BG in Fiji. Mrs. Eleanor Roosevelt was coming to visit Fiji so the crew of *Crock O' Crap* was told to cover up the nose art. (Phil Klingensmith collection).

B-17E (41-9124, *Buzz King*). Destroyed by "Washing-machine Charlie" on Henderson Field, Guadalcanal, 23 March 1943. (USAF)

B-17E (41-9211, *Typhoon McGoone II*) of the 98th BS/11th BG. Returned to the United States, 14 December 1945. (USMC)

B-17F (41-24353, *Cap'n & the Kids*) of the 63rd BS/43rd BG. The mission and kill markings indicate that *Cap'n & the Kids* flew 79 missions, while destroying 10 Japanese aircraft (five in aerial combat and five on the ground), and eight Japanese vessels. Scrapped, 31 April 1945. (Boeing/90317)

B-17F (41-24554, *Mustang*). Prior to its return to the United States *Mustang* was painted with its mission and kill markings. It flew 109 missions, shot down 17 Japanese planes, and reportedly sank nine Japanese vessels. (USAF)

Bullet hole in the Plexiglas nose of B-17F (41-24403, *Blitz Buggy*) received on a mission to Rabaul on 5 October 1942. (USAF)

B-17F (41-24384, *Pluto*) of the 63rd BS/43rd BG. The plane is fitted with a shorter B-17E Plexiglas nose cone. Disappeared on mission while carrying Brig. Gen. Howard Ramey, 26 March 1943. (O.K. Coulter—from *Pride of Seattle* by Steve Birdsall.)

B-17E flies over Pearl Harbor on 7 December 1941 during Japanese attack. (National Archives)

Broken B-17C (40-2074) flown into Hickam Field, Oahu, on 7 December 1941 by Capt. Raymond T. Swenson (38th RS). Japanese fire ignited the flare box which in turn burned the B-17 in two. (*Arizona* Memorial Collection)

Front half of B-17C (40-2074) parked on apron at Hickam Field, 7 December 1941. (National Archives)

B-17C (40-2049, *Skipper*), piloted by 1/Lt. Robert Richards on 7 December 1941, after crash landing at Bellows Field, Oahu. (National Archives)

Clark Field, Luzon, Philippines, c. 1938. (USAF)

Remains of a B-17E burning on Java, c. February 1942. (Royal Netherlands Air Force)

B-17E (41-2483) of the 9th BS/7th BG, somewhere in Africa on the way to Java. The plane reached Java on 31 January 1942. (Ritchie B. Gooch Collection.)

A B-17E, perhaps (41-2471), wearing Japanese markings. Two B-17Es were rebuilt by the Japanese after their capture of Java and flown to Japan for further study. (USAF)

VIII

Too Little, Too Late

On January 11, while the 19th BG B-17s were attacking Tarakan, three LB-30s (export versions of the four-engine Consolidated B-24 "Liberator" bomber) arrived at Malang via a new eastern air route across Africa. The LB-30s belonged to the 7th BG, and were being rushed to the Pacific with orders to "proceed to wherever the Commanding General of the Far East might be."[1]

After the heavy loss of B-17s in the Philippines, President Roosevelt had ordered the remaining bombers to be reinforced as soon as possible. Many of the reinforcements that went to the Pacific had already been earmarked for movement to the Philippines but the outbreak of war greatly accelerated the schedule. The new schedule, termed "Project X," called for 15 LB-30s and 65 B-17Es to hurry to the Pacific as soon as possible. The planes would come from the 7th BG and the 32nd BS/19th BG, which had been left in the States when the rest of the group went overseas. "Project X" was the first major foreign ferrying project of World War II and the first overseas movement of combat units by Ferrying Command.[2]

Although planes ferried to the Middle East had already established an eastern air route as far as Cairo, the three LB-30s pioneered the rest of the route that would be used by the reinforcing planes to reach the Pacific. Taking off from Tampa, Florida, the planes flew to South America, staging through Trinidad and Brazil and then headed east across the Atlantic Ocean, landing at Sierra Leone on the west coast of Africa. After reaching the Dark Continent, the bombers staged along the west coast before crossing the desert to Khartoum, Sudan and then on to Cairo, Egypt.[3]

Bombardier T/Sgt. Charles T. Reeves (9th BS/7th BG) flew the African route in a B-17. He recalled the approach to Cairo, ". . . we sighted the Pyramids and dropped down to fly between them, only a British ack-ack gun opened up as a warning, because it seems that isn't allowed." Lt. Knudson also remembered when he and his crew stopped at Cairo. "We walked around the largest

Pyramid," he wrote. "We went into this to the very center thru a dirty narrow passageway that slanted upward to the King's chamber." Commenting on Egypt, Knudson wrote, "Beggars are everywhere, yet they only bother Americans. We are the monied easy marks."[4]

From Cairo the planes flew to Iraq and then to India where most of the aircrews received their orders to fly to Java instead of the Philippines. Heading south out of India, the planes flew down to Sumatra and then to Soerabaja on Java. Having reached Java, it was only a short hop to Singosari Airdrome at Malang. The entire trip, from Florida to Java was just over 21,000 miles.[5]

One day after the LB-30s arrived, Lt. Tash flew B-17D (40-3072) to Singosari from the repair depot at Laverton and two days later, on January 14, Maj. Hobson and Lt. Hughes from the 22nd BS/7th BG arrived at Malang after reestablishing the new Pacific air route to Australia. Lt. Kurtz was there when they arrived. "[W]e soon got our first reinforcements," he wrote. "They were Fortresses of the brand-new E model. . . . There were many improvements, but the most vital of all were the new tail guns."[6]

Only two and one half hours later, two 9th BS/7th BG pilots, Maj. Conrad F. Necrason, B-17E (41-2461, *El Toro*), and Capt. John L. "Duke" Dufrane, Jr., B-17E (41-2459), arrived in Java, along with another LB-30, by way of Africa. Noted the 7th BG historian, "The 9th Bomb and 22nd Bomb Squadrons each departing in different directions and each traveling half way around the world landed within one hour [sic] of each other at Malang, Java."[7]

The next day, Capt. Fred M. Key (30th BS/19th BG), B-17E (41-2472, *Guinea Pig*) and 1st Lt. Charles H. Hillhouse (32nd BS/19th BG), B-17E (41-2460), also came in via Africa.[8] The promised reinforcements were beginning to arrive.

The wide-eyed newcomers were somewhat surprised by the look of the ragged veterans of the 19th BG. "[W]e went down to . . . meet the 19th," Sgt. Boone recalled. "Well, there'd been quite a change. As a bunch they looked nervous and hollow-eyed . . . You had to stop and remember that those poor guys had been fighting a defensive war . . ." Sgt. Reeves agreed, "They looked dog-tired, their eyes were sunk in, and they had beards . . . I suppose it had been so futile in the Philippines, and they'd been caught so unprepared that they'd never quite got their dander back . . ."[9]

While the first planes from the 7th BG were coming in, the 19th BG went out on another raid. At the insistence of ABDA Command, seven B-17s led by Maj. Combs departed Singosari at 10:00 A.M. on January 14, heading for the Dutch forward staging airfield at Palembang, on the southeast curve of Sumatra. Losing a day at Palembang because of inadequate servicing facilities and another mix-up with Dutch bombs, the planes did not take off until 8:00 A.M. on January 15 to bomb the Japanese airfield at Sungei Patani, on the west coast of Malaysia.[10]

While heading north over the Indian Ocean the planes ran into a severe front with temperatures of -20 degrees C, causing the windows to frost. Lt. Teats, B-17D (40-3078), lost the formation and returned to Palembang. Lt. Vandevanter in the newly-repaired B-17D (40-3072) experienced faulty supercharger regulators on the two right engines, making it impossible to stay in formation, also returned to Palembang.[11]

The remaining five bombers swept in over the Japanese airfield at 27,000 feet, leaving thick vapor trails in the cold, thin air. Bombing in two elements, Maj. Combs, B-17D (40-3061), Lt. Bohnaker, B-17D (40-3064), and Capt. Parsel, B-17D (40-3074), dropped only 31 of their 42 available bombs, with only 15 hitting the airstrip. Ten bombs hung up in Maj. Combs' plane so he took the flight around for a second run. Again, however, when his bombardier attempted to drop the bombs individually, the racks failed and he was forced to drop the bombs in salvo—all at one time.

One minute later, Lts. Schaetzel, B-17D (40-3067), and Smith, B-17D (40-3066), dropped all of their bombs on one pass hitting the airfield buildings and a hangar. As the B-17s headed towards Palembang three Japanese fighters attempted to intercept them but were unable to reach the altitude of the bombers.[12]

Still hampered by the cold weather and running low on fuel, the B-17s landed at Lhoknga, a poor emergency Dutch field on the extreme northwest tip of Sumatra. Upon landing, Maj. Combs blew the tail wheel on B-17D (40-3061) and with no spare, his crew was forced to improvise. Taking a heavy duty inner tube from a Dutch truck, the crew wrestled the plane's tail over a barrel and twice wrapped the inner tube over the smaller tail wheel hub. After inflating the tube the crew left it over night. To their great relief, the tire was still inflated the next morning and Combs was able to take off with the others.[13]

By 2:00 P.M., January 16, all seven bombers were back at Malang. However, upon landing in a moderate rain, Lt. Bohnaker's B-17D (40-3064) overshot the field and slid into a ditch when the brakes failed. Although no one was injured the plane was a total wreck, the first B-17 to be lost in Java.[14]

Bohnaker's accident was the result of the deteriorating field conditions at Malang. January brought the rainy season and the men and machines suffered. Gen. Brereton recalled, "This was the worst season of the year for flying, and our pilots often had to fly through typhoons and atrocious weather." 2nd Lt. Ritchie B. Gooch (30th BS/19th BG), agreed. "Every afternoon it rained," Gooch wrote. "Our weather man said we really didn't need him. He said all he needed to do was post a notice on the bulletin board that forecast, 'rain in the afternoon'."[15]

The constant rains played havoc with the grass runways. "[Malang] had a 4000-foot turf runway which was fine when we first got in," described Teats, "but about the middle of January the heavy rains came. There was a dip in the middle of it and by the end of January that section was a sea of mud and water." Capt. Felix M. Hardison (9th BS/7th BG) remembered, "The daily tropical rains, plus the constant churning of planes taking off and landing, had turned the unsurfaced runways into a sea of mud. If you came along too slow, you'd bog down entirely; too fast, you'd skid or even go over on the nose."[16]

Sgt. Boone was on a fully loaded plane that had aborted a mission and ran into trouble upon landing. "We were worried," he wrote, "because we knew that a single pound weight on the brakes would start our twenty-five tons sliding over that slippery field like it was the frozen surface of a pond." As expected, when the big bomber touched down it started sliding. In an attempt to save the plane, the pilot ground-looped the B-17. "Of course she would then have crashed tail-first into the end of the field and blown up all of us," Boone noted, "but [the pilot] was able to stop her by gunning the motors. Even if the wheels couldn't bite into the slippery ground, the propellers could bite the air."[17]

The thick mud at Malang also caused problems for the parked B-17s. 1st Lt. John A. Rouse (30th BS/19th BG) wrote in his diary, "Was scheduled to go on a mission this morning but the plane was stuck in mud and couldn't get it out in time." Mike Payne remembered how the airmen got the planes unstuck from Djogjakarta. "We would get the natives we called Gooks to help pull them out. They tied a large rope to each wheel and had 50 or more on each wheel to pull. If that didn't work we started up the engines. You would be surprised how fast them Gooks could scatter when the plane came out of the ruts it was in."[18]

Not only did the rain and mud hamper the airmen but also the extreme temperature differences between the airfield and high altitude. Most of the airfields in the Pacific were close to the equator, forcing the men to work long, tiring hours in the energy-sapping tropical heat and humidity. "I remember doing pre-flight of my equipment in the nose of our B-17 with the sun beating down on that plastic greenhouse," recalled bombardier Gooch. "My clothes were soaked with sweat when I finished, shortly before takeoff. As we climbed to altitude, usually above twenty thousand feet, the temperature would drop two degrees Centigrade per thousand feet. By the time we were at twenty thousand feet it was about forty degrees Centigrade colder in the aircraft than when we took off, so we went rapidly from one discomfort to another."[19]

Unfortunately, because of the extremes in temperature, the aircrews were forced to dress for every occasion. While on the ground personal preference prevailed. Most men usually wore khaki summer uniforms of either long or short sleeve shirts and long or short pants. Likewise headgear ranged from the informal summer baseball-style flying caps or floppy utility caps, to the more formal khaki visored service cap. However, once in the air, personal preference took a back seat to necessity.

"Mostly, we flew in our khaki uniforms or in lightweight [one-piece] summer flying suits," recalled Lt. Edmundson. Lt. Fields agreed, "Pilots usually flew in khaki shirt and trousers." However, he also recalled flying in the one-piece summer suit. "I cut the sleeves off mine and sewed zippers to the map pocket and chest pocket." Crewman Earl Schaeffer recalled a close call while wearing the A-4 one-piece flight suit. "On one mission . . . our plane was hit by small arms fire from a Zero. One of the slugs tore out the crotch of my flying suit causing a gaping hole in my suit."[20]

Over the top of the khaki uniform or flight suit, most men wore an A-2 leather jacket. "We all had lightweight flying jackets," Edmundson wrote. Additionally, the B-17 waist gunners, who stood at the open side windows and took a constant pounding from the cold slipstream, usually wore the fleece-lined B-3 jacket, along with the A-3 winter flying trousers, and heavy fleece-lined A-6 winter flying shoes. "[These were] seldom worn in the S[outh] Pacific except for side gunners," wrote Fields. "This was a tough position."[21]

Although the nose compartment was supposed to be heated, the bombardier and navigator might disagree. "The B-17 heating system was capable of heating the cockpit to a point where eggs could be fried on the throttle quadrant," stated Edmundson, "but the heat to the nose compartment was always insufficient. The pilot and copilot would be sweltering in their shirt sleeves while the navigator and bombardier were freezing in their fleece-lined winter flying suits." As Edmundson recalled, "We used to say the B-17 was like a healthy puppy—it had the coldest nose in town."[22]

Footwear, with the exception of the side gunners, tended to be "high-top GI shoes." While in flight, the officers usually wore their visored service cap while the enlisted men wore the soft baseball-style cap. Still, this was not always the case. Pilot Edmundson noted, "Most of us wore khaki flight caps and head-phones. The waist gunners wore leather soft helmets because they had to stand in the open hatches."[23]

Atop all of the flight clothing, each crewman wore either a back type, or seat type parachute. Recalled Fields, "B-17 pilots used seat type chutes [but] chest and back types were available early on."[24] A life preserver and oxygen mask complet-ed the ensemble. "We were at these higher altitudes even before the oxygen mask was developed," wrote Lt. Godman. "The way we got our life-sustaining oxygen was to get a rubber hose and put a pipe stem in our mouth and just suck oxygen at these extremely high altitudes. It could have been fatal."[25]

Lt. John C. Minahan (28th BS/19th BG) also remembered the oxygen hoses. "Prior to the oxygen masks we simply had oxygen bottles fastened in the rack close to us with a rubber tube coming from it. As the tubes were not palatable we fitted a pipe stem—usually purchased at Woolworths—into the end. I remember some friendly bickering as to which was best a straight pipe stem or a curved one; personally I liked the curved one better."[26]

Lt. Godman added, "Later, they developed the rubber oxygen masks that were strapped onto our helmets and kept all outside air out . . ." Although an improve-ment over the oxygen tubes, the new masks were not perfect. "Those old masks on our D-model B-17 were connected with rubber tubes which plugged into oxy-gen outlets in various parts of the ship," stated Lt. Kurtz. "We learned right away that these tubes weren't long enough to use in combat." Since the machine guns on the B-17Ds and early B-17Es were fed by ammunition boxes, rather than by continuous links, the gunners had to take off their oxygen masks to retrieve new ammunition canisters. After only a few minutes without the life sustaining oxy-gen, the gunner would pass out. "A friend would see him," Kurtz recalled, "and clap his own mask on the passed-out man to bring him to. Then in about a minute this second man would keel over . . ."[27]

Also, the early masks had a rubber balloon-like bladder attached to them which filled and deflated as the crewman breathed. "After a while moisture would condense inside the balloon and had to be drained out through a bung hole in the bottom," remembered Lt. Minahan. "This was fine on normal operations but at these extreme altitudes the balloon tended to freeze up." The frozen bladder would restrict the oxygen flow and endanger the crewman's life. "This O2 mask caused problems caused by freezing up with a big lump of ice in [the] bladder," Lt. Fields wrote. "[But this] was the only one in use early on."[28]

Fighting not only the Japanese, but also the elements and, at times, their own equipment, the Pacific B-17 crewmen sometimes felt that they were fighting a losing battle. Yet, the vast majority fought on.

On January 16, while the 19th BG planes were returning to Malang, the 7th BG staged its first raid. Three LB-30s and two B-17s took off from Malang at 11:40 A.M., flying to Kendari II to refuel. At 2:15 A.M. January 17, the planes took off. The three LB-30s bombed the Japanese airfield at Menado, on northern Celebes, and ran into heavy fighter opposition. Two planes were subsequently lost and only one returned to Java.[29]

At the same time Maj. Necrason, B-17E (41-2461, *El Toro*), and Lt. Dufrane, B-17E (41-2459), bombed some Japanese transports off Menado. When one plane had six bombs hang up the B-17s were forced to make another bomb run. As the bombers left the area, leaving one transport capsized and another damaged, they were attacked by 14 Zeros.

Coming up from behind and beneath, the Zeros attacked for the next 40 minutes. Necrason's tail gunner shot down two of the fighters before being seriously wounded by an explosive bullet. Forty-three years old, M/Sgt. Louis T. "Soup" Silva, a 9th BS/7th BG mechanic, who had insisted on accompanying Necrason, because of a lack of experienced gunners, pulled the wounded airman out of the tail position and shot down two more Zeros with the deadly tail guns thereby earning himself a Distinguished Service Cross. A fifth fighter was shot down by the bombardier, who came back to man one of the side guns.[30]

Lt. Dufrane was having a tougher time. On the second bomb run, antiaircraft fire knocked out one of his engines. Falling slightly behind Necrason, Dufrane was subjected to repeated attacks by the Zeros who shot his Fortress full of holes and knocked out a second engine. In return, however, one of Dufrane's gunners shot down two of the attacking fighters before the B-17 flew into welcome cloud cover. In spite of the damaged engines, Dufrane, still accompanied by Necrason, kept B-17E (41-2459) airborne and both pilots returned safely to Kendari II.[31]

While the wounded were being helped and the planes were being refueled, five Japanese fighters appeared. Somehow, Necrason managed to take off and fly safely back to Malang but Dufrane's B-17E was grounded by the two damaged engines and suffered from repeated strafing runs. Although two more men were wounded, flight engineer S/Sgt. Jack W. Coleman stayed at his top turret guns and kept the Zeros at bay. For the next two days, the Zeros returned repeatedly to try and set the bomber on fire but each time Sgt. Coleman drove them off. The crew made three attempts to get the bomber airborne but were unsuccessful. Finally, when informed that Japanese soldiers were close by, they blew the plane up to keep it from falling into Japanese hands.[32] B-17E (41-2459) was the first B-17E to be lost in the Pacific.

Sgt. Silva, the hero of the mission, became a celebrity among the 7th BG. "Silva was known to everyone as 'Soup'," wrote Lt. Minahan, "and to me he is one of the great unsung heroes of the war." After the mission to Menado, Silva insisted on flying every mission as a tail gunner. "He loaded the guns without tracers so the Japs wouldn't see where the fire was coming from," added Minahan. "In all 'Soup' shot down some 18 or 20 Japs and these were confirmed . . ."[33]

The first mission for the fledgling 7th BG had been a disaster. Two LB-30s and one B-17E, all of which had arrived only days before, had been lost. However, two important lessons had been learned. First, it was found that the LB-30 was not nearly as rugged as the B-17. The LB-30 had only one revolving turret, lacked armor plating and had no superchargers, so it could not operate above 20,000 feet, leaving it well within range of the Zero. Second, it was found that the new tail guns of the B-17E were truly deadly. Four Zeros had been shot down by the tail guns. One of the most glaring inadequacies of the Flying Fortress had finally been corrected.

The perfected tactic used by the Japanese fighter pilot, that of approaching the B-17 from behind, knowing that the bomber lacked tail guns, soon proved deadly. Sgt. Boone recalled the first time a few Zeros came after his B-17E. "[They] came in from behind . . . [and] throttle[d] down to our speed and, in a leisurely way, [tried] to shoot the tail off." The only defense for the old C and D models was to have the pilot rock the tail from side to side and let the waist gunners try to hit the trailing Zero. Sgt. Boone went on, "[T]hey first opened up with their four little .25-caliber wing guns, getting everything nicely lined up with their tracers before cutting loose with their cannon." The tail gunner in Boone's plane waited until the Zeros came in close. "Then just as they were about to uncork their cannon, he let them have it—knocked hell out of them. If they hadn't been dead they'd have been terribly surprised."[34]

Miraculously, perhaps because of their rigid training and lack of improvisation, the Japanese took almost two months to develop new tactics to attack the B-17. It did not take the Americans that long to realize that the Japanese were beginning to fear the new tail stingers. In fact, crews still flying the C and D model Fortresses began cutting the tail cone off of their plane and sticking a pair of black painted broom handles out the back to try and bluff the Zero pilots.[35]

However, Zero pilot Sakai disagreed with the American belief that the heavy tail guns forced the Zero pilots to seek a new method of approach. "We soon discovered [tail-end attacks] had little effect on the well-constructed and heavily-armored B-17. It was this knowledge—and not primarily the addition of tail armament to the Fortresses—which brought about a sudden change of tactics." Going after another weak spot on a B-17, the Zeros started attacking the lightly protected nose. "We adopted head-on passes," Sakai wrote, "flying directly against the oncoming B-17s, pouring bullets and cannon shells into the forward areas of the enemy bombers."[36]

Sgt. Fesmire, a bombardier, reported, "From my point of view the biggest weakness on the early B-17s was the old .30 caliber gun in the nose. [The Zeros] usually attacked singly and in the early days attacks were all from the tail. When we got the E model they started coming in at the front." Additionally, the light gun was not in a fixed position. "There were a lot of [ball and socket] ports and you had to keep pulling the gun out and pushing it into a new port to follow attacks," Fesmire wrote, "and it needed a great deal of effort to do this at altitude." Lt. Edmundson noted another problem with the nose gun. "We didn't ever really fire the .30 cal. nose guns very much. You couldn't really aim them properly or hit anything with them, anyway, but when they were fired they filled the nose with junk [i.e. cartridges and links.]"[37]

Lt. Reeves, also a bombardier, noticed, "Now [the Japanese] were coming in at all directions . . . but mostly they were hitting us head-on, because they discovered that in the nose we had only a single little .30 caliber." To combat the new tactic, the aircrews improvised. "So we got bus . . .," wrote Reeves. "We mounted a big .50-caliber down in the [nose] compartment, rigging it so it would fire out of the ventilator. And for good measure we stuck in another .30-caliber."[38]

Many of the B-17 crews went so far as to mount two and sometimes three .50 caliber guns in the nose. The ball and socket mounts were rebored to take the larger barrel of the .50 caliber and, because the heavier recoil of the bigger guns actually fractured the Plexiglas nose cone, support struts were welded in place for added strength.[39]

Bombardier Minahan recalled,

> Originally, the bombardier had a .30 rifle caliber gun in the Plexiglas nose of the B-17E but when the Japs turned to frontal attacks an improvised mount was rigged up at air depots in Australia to take a pair of .50's in this position. The guns were mounted high and to the right of the bombsight, firing through an aperture cut in the top of the nosepiece. When not in use, a rubber cord kept them stowed out of the way of the bombardier's head. As soon as the bombs had been dropped and the [bomb] bay closed, the Norden [bombsight] was quickly and easily removed from its base and put on the floor behind the bombardier's position: then the two fifty calibers could be brought into play.[40]

Eventually, planes equipped with these extra guns, eliminated the bombsight altogether and flew as wing aircraft, toggling their bombs on the lead aircraft.[41]

Many of the later modifications were produced at the repair depot at Laverton but the earlier modifications, however, were all performed in the field. Sometimes, the modifications caused unexpected results. Lt. Gooch, a bombardier, recalled what happened during an attack by Japanese fighters. "I was busy firing a newly installed fifty caliber machine gun our maintenance men had improvised for the nose of our B-17E," he wrote. "The standard gun for that position was a thirty caliber (pea shooter, we called it)." The Zeros were coming in at the nose, one after the other. "My gun was hot from much firing," he went on. "Suddenly, an explosion occurred directly in front of me. The [nose] filled with smoke and the acrid smell of burning powder. I turned to see our navigator, [2nd Lt. Walter E.] Seamon, [Jr.] (30th BS/19th BG), staggering backward, with blood running from his mouth. I thought he was dying."

Ignoring the Zeros, Gooch turned to Seamon. "As the smoke cleared and the situation stabilized," Gooch stated, "I could see our navigator was not badly hurt after all. His lip had been cut by the flying shell case from a fifty caliber cartridge that had exploded in the cartridge belt of my nose gun." The gun had become too hot and had "cooked off" a round before reaching the firing chamber. Fortunately, the fighters ceased their attacks shortly after the incident. Years later Gooch wrote, "I can thankfully smile about this incident now, because what appeared to be a serious injury or death, turned out to be nothing more than a cut lip."[42]

While the added nose guns were an improvement, they were far from perfect. Lt. Minahan remembered, "They had limited travel and you could not fire far below the horizontal. As a result the Jap fighters came to make climbing attacks from 12 o'clock low and only the ball turret could reach them before they rolled away down." On the early B-17Es, the vulnerable belly was covered by the remote controlled Bendix "belly" turret.[43]

Although designed as an improvement over the bathtub gun position, the Bendix belly turret proved to be a disappointing failure. It is generally believed that no enemy aircraft was ever shot down by the Bendix belly turret. As Lt. Edmundson recalled, "The gunner laid [on his stomach and] fired the turret which was removed from him. He aimed through a mirror in which his target appeared upside down and backwards." The awkward sighting arrangement gave the gunner nausea and a feeling of vertigo.[44]

Lt. Knudson clearly described the working of the Bendix belly turret:

> This lower turret is a jinx. It is a remote control affair in which one performs tricks by the use of mirrors. The gunner supposedly picks up an attacking plane in a mirror that the gunner operates by lying on his stomach in the bottom of the plane. There are cross hairs on the mirror, and the target must be in the center of these. The guns operate by turning of handles on the mirror. Wonderful set-up if it works—which it doesn't—on our plane or any other.[45]

Perhaps no more than 100 hostile rounds were ever fired from the belly guns of all of the B-17Es equipped with the Bendix turret. Realizing that the turret was useless, some of the crews loaded the guns with tracers and rigged cords to the triggers. During combat, the waist gunners would kick the cords and send a few tracer rounds towards the enemy. More often however, to cut down on weight, the twin .50s were removed and replaced with black painted broomsticks. Sgt.

Fesmire's crew was even more practical. "We took the early under-turrets out because they were useless," he wrote.[46]

Eventually, the remote controlled Bendix turret was replaced with the Sperry ball turret. Although a vast improvement, the manned Sperry ball turret still had its deficiencies. Combat crews immediately experienced trouble with the empty ammunition links jamming in the ejection chutes, which sometimes caused the guns to jam. This was easily remedied by making wider and larger chutes.

A much scarier problem arose when it was found that the turret door hinges were much too weak. The door of the ball turret was the backrest for the gunner when the door was closed. Constant opening and closing of the door, and the vibrations from firing the twin .50 caliber guns, sometimes loosened the hinges. On a few occasions, the door came open during flight leaving the gunner crouched in a steel and Plexiglas ball beneath the belly of the plane at 20,000 feet with no parachute, and held in place by two safety straps! Heavier steel hinges, bolted and welded in place, were soon replacing the factory issued ones.[47]

For the most part, the Sperry top turret, above the flight deck, worked well but it too had some problems. In a telegram to Washington it was reported, "Gunner unable to wear oxygen mask and parachute in turret on account of room shortage." Additionally, it was noted that the gunners were having a hard time sighting enemy fighters because of steel panels in the dome. Soon, new clear bulletproof panels and a higher dome were replacing the existing ones.[48]

The top turret also had other troubles. The guns could not be depressed low enough to hit enemy fighters coming in below the horizon and, at times, the turret rotated too slowly against swift moving Zeros.' While these problems were too complex to fix in the field, a couple of other problems were more easily overcome. It was found that when the guns were fired at a high angle, the ammunition belts sometimes failed to feed into the guns. To fix this problem, the men added a coiled spring and a roller extension to the ammunition boxes to help maintain a constant upward pressure on the belts as they were raised. Another problem arose when the thin cables that charged the guns constantly broke. This was easily remedied by replacing the original cables with a very flexible ⅛ inch cable.[49]

The Pacific B-17 machine-gunners in general encountered another problem. It was soon found that the 50-round factory-issued ammunition cans contained an inadequate amount of rounds. Sgt. Reeves remembered that the men began, "[t]hrowing away those small inadequate ammunition cans, and rigging the guns so you could set a whole box of ammunition in there." The ground crews came up with a can that held 300 rounds and was equipped with a spring-loaded false bottom. As the rounds were fired, the false bottom raised the ammunition, reducing the weight and drag on the firing mechanism.[50]

Although the B-17E was not a perfect plane, it was a vast improvement over the C and D models and through trial and error, the air and ground crews were able to correct most of the problems that cropped up.

By the third week of January 1942, the Japanese had pushed the British down the Malaysian Peninsula into Singapore. Expecting Singapore to fall quickly, the Japanese renewed their move into the Netherlands East Indies, building up a strike force of airplanes on Jolo Island, southwest of Mindanao. On January 19, 5th Bomber Command decided to pay them an unexpected visit.[51]

At 9:20 A.M., five B-17s from the 19th BG and four from the 7th, under the overall command of Lt. Connally, B-17C (40-2062), with Maj. Combs as his copilot, took off from Malang in the face of a terrible storm. The operation was the first joint mission of the 19th and 7th BGs.[52]

The nine planes were to hit Jolo, fly on to Del Monte, and return to Malang with a planeload of stranded Del Monte airmen. Wrote Lt. Teats, "On the 19th we took off in absolutely stinking weather on a mission to bomb Jolo in the Sulu archipelago . . ." Every hour, the personnel at Del Monte radioed the flight, telling them to turn back because of rapidly deteriorating weather conditions. "The weather was 'zero-zero' from the water to 20,000 feet," Teats reported, indicating that visibility was practically nil. Yet, realizing the importance of the dual bombing/rescue mission, the planes continued on.[53]

Flying through ". . . very heavy rains, low visibility, and severe equatorial thunderstorms," the flight lost three planes from the 7th BG when Maj. Hobson, B-17E (41-2406), and Lt. Hughes, B-17E (41-2419), experienced engine trouble, and Lt. Hillhouse, B-17E (41-2460), had unspecified problems, and landed at Samarinda II.[54] When the others found Jolo completely "socked in" they made a direct beeline for Del Monte. On the way, the bombers suddenly entered "a kind of trough in the weather" and to their great surprise spotted enemy ships directly below them.[55]

Sgt. Fesmire, the bombardier on Lt. Connally's B-17, wrote, "When we got over Jolo it was socked in . . . [so] I took the head of the bombsight and laid it down because it was in my way. I was sitting there reading a book when the weather began to clear." Glancing down, Fesmire suddenly spotted "a tanker of around 15,000 tons, with an escort of destroyers." Fesmire instantly reported the sighting and was immediately given the green light to bomb the tanker. "I said the bombsight wanted warming up so would they give me a long turn [towards the target]," Fesmire remembered. "I didn't tell them it was off and completely out of the way. I've never hooked up a bombsight faster than I did that day!"[56]

Lt. Teats, in the second of two three-plane elements, called Lt. Connally over the radio but was not sure whether his transmission had been picked up. "Then I saw his bomb-bay doors open, he turned and, the rest of the formation following, we came back over the target course." Naturally, Teats had no idea of the frantic actions of Sgt. Fesmire. Each plane was carrying seven 100-kg. bombs and a bomb bay tank. Fesmire's frantic actions paid off however. "Of the 21 bombs dropped by the first flight," Fesmire recalled, "one went into the water one side of the tanker and two the other side and 18 hit it." Only Lts. Teats and Schaetzel, B-17D (40-3070), dropped from the second flight, hitting the stern of the tanker. Lt.

Keiser, B-17D (40-3066), had his bomb bay door motor burn out and was unable to get his bomb bay doors open.[57]

"[The tanker] must have been loaded with high test gas," recalled Fesmire, "because it really did blow all to hell." Wrote Teats, "As we turned away toward Del Monte, the tanker was burning and smoking, turning on a circular starboard course as though [its] steering mechanism had jammed, and was sinking by the stern."[58]

Leaving the sinking tanker, the flight continued on towards Del Monte. Although the B-17s ran into another fierce storm, with "big, black thunderheads" that separated the planes and forced them to fly on instrument, each plane reached Del Monte safely.[59]

There waiting for the Fortresses were the stranded personnel from the 19th BG. Overjoyed by the sight of the six B-17s, which they mistakenly believed were the first of the long-expected reinforcements, the stranded airmen began to celebrate. Only later did they learn that the planes were there to help evacuate them.[60] The United States had no intention of reinforcing the Philippines.

Shortly after midnight, January 20, the evacuation began with priority going to stranded B-17 pilots. Lt. Schaetzel, who was experiencing engine trouble, took off without a load of bombs and carried eight evacuated officers to Malang. The remaining five planes each took off with three evacuated officers, and carried a half-load of bombs and their bomb bay fuel tank, intending to hit the Jolo airstrip on their way home.[61]

Once again the bombers ran into nasty weather. "We couldn't get on top of it because we didn't have oxygen for the personnel we were evacuating," recalled Lt. Teats. The pilots started for Jolo but when they picked up engine and carburetor ice, they went directly to Malang. Shortly after noon, all six bombers were back in Java having evacuated a total of 23 officers from Del Monte. For his part in leading the evacuation flight, Lt. Connally was issued the DFC.[62]

From January 18 to January 21, seven more B-17Es of the 7th BG arrived at Malang, all via the African air route. On January 18, 1st Lt. Robert E. Northcutt (9th BS) (41-2468) arrived, followed one day later by Maj. Stanley K. Robinson (41-2456), CO of the 7th BG, and 1st Lts. Duane H. Skiles (41-2454, *Craps for the Japs*) and Donald R. Strother (41-2471), (both 9th BS). Then, on January 21, 1st Lts. Theodore B. Swanson (41-2469), Joseph J. Preston (41-2466) and Jack W. Bleasdale (41-2464, *Queenie*), all 9th BS flew in.[63] Java now contained a total of 22 Flying Fortresses, although not all of them were operational.

Initially, due to the overall shortage of B-17s, many of the first missions undertaken by the 7th and 19th BGs were flown as joint missions. Soon, a slight friction developed between the two groups over differing philosophies.

Through experience, all 19th BG pilots were fully briefed before going out on a mission and the pilots were expected to follow orders, varying only slightly under unusual circumstances. Should the bombers encounter enemy fighters, they were to close formation, fly level and go on to the target, never climbing or varying their course. On the other hand, Maj. Robinson believed that all critical decisions should be made by the flight leader while in the air. The 7th BG personnel were given their target and a few necessary facts at a briefing and then sent on their way. The flight leader was free to make as many decisions as he felt necessary to get his bombers safely to the target and back again.[64]

Furthermore, for training purposes, veterans from the 19th BG began flying with the inexperienced crews of the 7th BG. However, since promotions had lagged for the 19th BG, many of the most experienced personnel were junior in rank to the men of the 7th BG. Then, when 5th Bomber Command began sending only second lieutenants from the 19th BG to fly with the 7th BG, the men from the 7th resented taking orders from a junior officer. The veteran's advice was often ignored. 19th BG navigators and bombardiers, instead of flying in the nose compartment, were often sent to the waist area as excess baggage.[65]

When the complaints against the 19th BG became extreme, Maj. Robinson assembled the 7th BG and ordered the complaints to stop immediately. However, after the meeting, when the 7th BG planes went out on a mission, except in rare cases, they carried purely 7th BG personnel.[66] Like the 19th BG, the 7th BG would have to learn from trial and error.

On January 20, because of the sudden influx of planes at Malang, the 7th BG began moving to Djogjakarta, called invariably Jockstrap or Lockjaw by the Americans. Over the next few days, so many heavy bombers, both B-17Es and LB-30s, arrived for the 7th BG that they spilled over onto another field at Madioen, about halfway between Djogjakarta and Malang. The 7th BG Headquarters was kept at Djogjakarta, along with the LB-30s of their 11th BS. The B-17s of the 22nd BS and part of the 9th BS operated out of Madioen while the remainder of the 9th BS, plus a few crews from the 22nd BS, remained at Malang.[67] Still, the clean break between the 7th and 19th BGs never materialized. Throughout their stay in Java, planes from both groups continued to use all three airfields.

IX

Ups and Downs

With their backs to the wall in Singapore, ABDA Command pushed for another raid to relieve the pressure on the British troops. On January 21, Maj. Robinson led nine B-17s from the 7th and 19th BGs up to Palembang but deteriorating weather conditions forced him to scrub the mission. Upon landing on the rain slicked field Lt. Hughes, B-17E (41-2419), overshot the runway and completely wrecked his plane. However, when Lt. Skiles, B-17E (41-2454, *Craps for the Japs*), tried to return to Malang and blew a cylinder on one of his engines he was able to cannibalize Hughes wrecked bomber for the needed part.[1]

Japanese advances southward, and now eastward towards the important Australian harbor of Rabaul on New Britain were causing ABDA Command to worry. Reconnaissance flights were constantly trying to locate Japanese convoys to ascertain their next objective.[2] On January 22, Lt. Teats, B-17D (40-3070), was flying along the east coast of Borneo when he spotted a huge, black spiral cloud rising above Balikpapan. "[W]hen we got into it," he wrote, "we knew what it was—it was oil smoke. The Dutch had dynamited the refineries at Balikpapan. Under the monster cloud, huge flames were roaring, lapping up the oil which the Dutch were determined should not be turned against them."[3]

On January 23, the Japanese captured the deep-water harbor of Rabaul and the port of Kavieng on New Ireland. That same day, Japan grabbed the important airfield at Kendari and sent a convoy towards Balikpapan. In what would later be called the Battle of Makassar Straits, obsolete Dutch bombers attacked the invasion fleet, sinking one transport and damaging three others. Informed of the convoy, ABDA Command responded.

The next day, January 24, the Dutch bombers returned, again sinking one ship and damaging two more. A short while later, Maj. Robinson, B-17E (41-2456), leading three planes from the 7th BG and four from the 19th, attacked.[4] Having left Malang at 6:15 A.M., the eight planes bombed from 20,000 feet through a hail

114

of antiaircraft fire that was listed as "Hot, Heavy and Close." After sinking one transport and setting a tanker on fire the B-17s were turning away when they were jumped by a flight of Zeros who gave chase for 20 minutes and succeeded in damaging three of the heavy bombers.[5]

Japanese fighter pilot Kuniyoshi Tanaka was among the attackers. "We caught the Fortresses just right," he said, ". . . I could see the bullets hitting and the cannon shells exploding in the airplanes. But they wouldn't go down. These damned bombers are impossible when they work into their defensive formations."[6] By staying together and using their interlocking fields of fire the B-17 gunners were able to claim five enemy kills. By 1:35 P.M., all eight Fortresses were safely back at Singosari.[7]

During the evening, four American destroyers surprised the Japanese ships and sank three transports and one patrol boat while suffering damage to only one destroyer. Before the Japanese could react, the Americans quickly fled into the night.[8]

In spite of the repeated attacks, the Japanese convoy reached Balikpapan on January 25 and began putting men ashore. At 7:00 A.M., six planes from the 19th BG and two from the 7th, commanded by Maj. Hobson, B-17E (41-2406), left Singosari and fought their way through a tropical storm to drop their bombs on the landing force.[9] "After dropping our bombs, we were low on gas," recalled Lt. Gooch, "so our pilot [Lt. Hillhouse] broke away from the formation and headed for our home base. Our being alone out there was the signal for Japanese fighters to come in for an easy kill." Not realizing that the lone Fortress, B-17E (41-2460) was equipped with tail guns, the Japanese attacked from behind.

"Bullets ripped through our airplane as the Japanese fighters were intent on making quick work of us," Gooch wrote. In the air battle that followed the tail gunner shot down two Zeros but the Japanese were able to shoot the B-17 "full of cannon and small arms holes." Gooch continued, "While no one on our crew was killed or wounded, our aircraft was in deep trouble. Our battery power was shot out, our trim tab control cables were severed, many of our instruments were inoperative and our wings and fuselage were full of holes . . ." Slowly, the Fortress began to lose altitude.

Finding the first available airfield, Lt. Hillhouse set B-17E (41-2460) down at the Dutch airstrip at Banjermasin, on southern Borneo. "With the help of the Dutch military," Gooch continued, "we made emergency repairs on our crippled airplane and the next morning took off and limped back to home base at Malang in an aircraft that normally would be considered un-flyable."[10]

Unknown to Lt. Gooch and his crewmen, the remaining seven bombers also ran into trouble. Only three planes, all B-17Ds, returned to Malang, while the others, all B-17Es, ran out of gas and made forced landings. Lt. Bohnaker, B-17E (41-2472, *Guinea Pig*), landed safely at Soerabaja, but Maj. Hobson, B-17E (41-2406), and Lt. Northcutt, B-17E (41-2468), made wheels-up belly-landings on the open beaches of Madera Island, east of Java. Unable to take off again, both crews burned their planes to prevent them from falling into Japanese hands.[11] Due to the bad weather, which had caused the heavier B-17Es to consume large amounts of gas very rapidly, two more planes were lost.

Lt. Crimmins, B-17E (41-2469), also set down on Madera Island but was able to make a perfect wheels down landing. Sent additional fuel from Java, and aided by Dutch engineers and native laborers, the crew set about to rescue their plane. "They worked a full day," wrote Lt. Kurtz, "shoring up the plane, building a base of logs and sand under it, clearing a runway strip." Three days later, Crimmins lifted off from the makeshift runway and returned to Malang.[12]

Later that same day, January 25, Allied submarines attacked the Japanese fleet and sank perhaps one or two transports but by then Balikpapan was securely in Japanese hands.[13] Still, the Battle of Makassar Strait continued.

On January 26, 1st Lt. Philip L. Mathewson (32nd BS/19th BG), B-17E (41-2455), and Capt. Walter W. Sparks, Jr. (9th BS/7th BG), B-17E (41-2476), arrived via Africa to replace the two bombers lost the day before. A little later, two planes from the 7th BG set out again to attack the transports but the rapidly deteriorating weather forced the mission to be scrubbed.[14]

The battle continued on January 27 when three B-17s from the 7th BG and three from the 19th, led by Maj. Robinson, left Singosari at 7:50 A.M.[15] Although Lt. Preston, B-17E (41-2466), turned back after hitting nasty weather, the others pushed on and dropped their bombs in spite of heavy antiaircraft fire. The airmen claimed the sinking of one transport and waterline hits on a cruiser. In reality, the waterline hits were scored on the floatplane tender *Sanuki Maru*. In addition to the hits on the warship, two floatplanes were damaged.[16]

After dropping their bombs the B-17s were jumped by four Zeros. Perhaps aware of the tail guns in the B-17Es, the Zeros concentrated on Lt. Cox's lone B-17D (40-3074). Fortunately, Maj. Robinson kept the six Fortresses together, using the defensive firepower from all the planes to protect one another, and the B-17s were able to shoot down two of the Zeros.[17] Due to his outstanding leadership, Maj. Robinson, who had flown his fourth mission in seven days, was issued the DFC.[18]

Thus ended the Battle of Makassar Strait. The Japanese had learned an important lesson at the cost of 13 ships sunk and another 16 damaged. In her haste to gobble up territory, Japan had sent out a column of ships without a protective umbrella of fighter aircraft. In order to advance further, Japan had to establish air superiority in the Netherlands East Indies and in order to achieve this, she needed to either capture or at least gain control over the East Indies airfields. Before pushing further south, Japan elected to wait and build up her forces at Balikpapan. For the time being at least, the Allies had managed to slow the Japanese advance.[19]

While the Japanese rested, four of the old B-17Ds were flown out of Java between January 23 and 27 and taken down to Laverton Repair Depot for complete overhauls. Lt. Teats' description of B-17D (40-3067), which he flew down, was typical of the older bombers. "It had no hydraulic system. Three of the engines seemed to be running okay aside from a slight roughness, but the fourth had been hit, and a 37-millimeter antiaircraft shell had hit and weakened one of the wings. It had to be flown with one wing about 10 degrees below the other, so that it just crabbed and sobbed along at low altitude and low speed."[20]

Unfortunately, when Teats tried to take off from Darwin a few days later, B-17D (40-3067) crashed. The plane was demolished and the navigator was killed.[21] When the four B-17Ds moved down to Australia, only five B-17Ds and one B-17C of the original 35 Philippine Fortresses were still in a combat zone.

One of the planes flown to Laverton was B-17D (40-3097, *Ole Betsy*). On its last mission, on January 11, the engines had been overtaxed and needed immediate repair. Once at Laverton, besides changing all four engines, the entire tail assembly was replaced with that of B-17D (40-3091) which was being used for parts. Assembling one B-17 out of two, the plane was renamed *The Swoose*—half swan and half goose. Although B-17D (40-3097, *The Swoose*) would never fly another combat mission, it remained in the Pacific for a short time as the personal plane of Lt. Gen. George H. Brett, Deputy Commander of ABDA Command.[22]

On January 28, more relief arrived for the two heavy bomb groups when additional ground crews from the 7th BG reached Java. On January 19, the men, who had been sidetracked to Australia on December 8, had been loaded aboard the transport *President Polk*, and in convoy with three American warships and two other vessels, including the tanker *Hawaiian Planter* carrying 22,000 fifty-gallon drums of precious 100 octane American aviation fuel, left Australia for Java. With the arrival of the high octane gas, the problems with the highly aromatic Dutch fuel would be eliminated.[23]

"We were heavily laden with bombs, high explosives, [and] ammunition besides carrying two squadrons of maintenance personnel," remembered 1st Lt. Joseph W. Dalley (22nd BS/7th BG). Traveling along the east and north coast of Australia, the ships were subjected to three submarine scares and one legitimate attack but arrived safely at Soerabaya on January 28. Taken to Singosari, the men were surprised at the shape of the war-weary bombers. "We divided our men into 12 hour shifts and immediately started to work, although we were handicapped by the lack of proper equipment," Dalley wrote.[24]

Forced to do everything by hand, the Americans looked for additional help from the native Javanese. "They had a few trained as mechanics, and they could put a nut on by hand," Mechanic Payne remembered. "We had to take a wrench to loosen it."[25]

The same date that the new ground crews arrived, Maj. Combs, B-17E (41-2472, *Guinea Pig*), led two planes each from the 7th and 19th BGs on another strike to help Singapore. While ABDA Command felt that it was imperative to continue to aid Singapore, the Americans felt otherwise. The airmen believed that Singapore was already lost and that they were wasting their time. Instead, they felt that they should be going after the Japanese fleet that was assembling at Balikpapan. Additionally, a raid on Malaysia took an average of three days to complete and was hard on both men and planes while a raid on Balikpapan could be accomplished in only one day. However, Gen. Wavell wanted to "put heart in Singapore" so on January 28 the five bombers took off.[26]

After refueling at Palembang, the planes took off to hit Kuantan Airfield on the east coast of Malaya, and although Lt. Bohnaker, B-17D (40-3074), turned back with engine trouble, the bombing by the other four was deemed "highly successful." On January 29, the four operational planes hit Kuala Lumpur Airfield, on Malaysia's west coast. This time the results were listed as "doubtful." By noon on January 30, all five planes were back at Malang.[27]

While the Singapore mission was being flown, two more 7th BG B-17s arrived via Africa. After 1st Lts. Ignatius Sargent (HqS), B-17E (41-2478), and Edward C. Habberstad (9th BS), B-17E (41-2427), flew in, the decision was made to retire two more B-17Ds from combat. Dispersed to Pasirian Airfield, southeast of Malang, B-17Ds (40-3072) and (40-3078) were redesignated as transports.[28]

On January 29, three planes from the 7th BG and two from the 19th set off from Malang at 7:23 A.M. to strike Balikpapan.[29] Of the five crews, Capt. Sparks' and Lt. Mathewson's had been in Java for only three days while Lt. Habberstad's had only just arrived. Although Maj. Robinson had been grounded by Gen. Eubank and told to take a rest, he felt uneasy about sending rookie crews into combat without a seasoned leader. Pleading his case, Eubank reluctantly agreed and allowed the indefatigable Robinson to fly as an observer with Capt. Sparks.[30]

Shortly after takeoff, Lt. Habberstad, B-17E (41-2427), developed engine trouble and turned back. The others continued on and found more than 50 ships, including a number of transports and one heavy cruiser, off Balikpapan. For some unknown reason, the lead plane did not drop its bombs on the first bomb run so the planes circled for a second run. As they were approaching the target again, they were hit by 14 Zeros.

Lt. "Duke" Dufrane was flying as copilot/observer with Lt. Skiles, B-17E (41-2454, *Craps for the Japs*). "When we returned we were met by Jap Zeros," he stated. "Robby's [Robinson's] ship was hit and damaged." Hit hard in the tail, Capt. Sparks' plane, B-17E (41-2476), with Maj. Robinson as copilot/observer, began to lose speed and altitude. Protectively, the other planes circled their leader and attempted to fight off the swarming Zeros.[31]

"We've already lost altitude waiting for the Maj. (we've boxed him in so he could stay with us and the Zeros wouldn't tear him to pieces)," remembered Sgt. Reeves, the bombardier with Lt. Skiles, "and he seems to have developed engine trouble." Having come full circle, the bombers came over Balikpapan again and dropped their bombs on the heavy cruiser, scoring a few hits and setting the ship on fire.[32]

"We dropped our bombs and headed back to the base," wrote Lt. Dufrane. "Robby's ship kept falling back. I tried to stay to protect him." The Zeros attacked for the next 40 minutes. Besides the damage inflicted to the Sparks/Robinson plane, the other three B-17s were slightly damaged. In return, the Americans reportedly shot down six of their attackers.[33]

Once the Zeros gave up, the Fortresses continued to fly in formation, hoping that Capt. Sparks' badly damaged plane could keep up. B-17E (41-2476) continued to lose altitude and speed, making it difficult for the other planes to stay with it. "I pulled the throttle back as far as I could without stalling," recalled Dufrane. Soon, perhaps realizing that he would never make Malang, Maj. Robinson told Lt. Dufrane to take command of the flight and reported that he would try a crash landing somewhere.[34]

"We've drifted down to 4,000 feet altitude, protecting Robinson," Sgt. Reeves recalled. "Then, all of a sudden, Robinson's plane swoops down beneath us about 1,000 feet, and the incline sends it scooting on out in front of us . . ." As the others watched, the Sparks/Robinson plane continued to descend and then suddenly fell off to the left and hit the water.

"Just before he goes in," remembered Reeves, "his tail elevator blows off. The poor guy [Robinson] must have had the stick clutched back into his stomach trying to pull out of that dive, and the terrible air pressure on those elevators ripped them off." The Sparks/Robinson Fortress hit the water nose first at a high rate of speed. Dufrane, now in command, circled the flight and came back over the spot where B-17E (41-2476) had crashed. "By the time we had circled and returned," Dufrane said, "everything was quiet where Robby's plane had fallen."[35]

There were no survivors from B-17E (41-2476). Nine men had perished, including the CO of the 7th BG. Because of his unselfish act of wanting to fly as an experienced guide with one of his unseasoned crews, Maj. Robinson was posthumously awarded a Distinguished Service Cross. Maj. Austin A. Straubel, commander of the LB-30s of the 11th BS, assumed command of the 7th BG.[36]

Between January 30 and February 2, the 7th and 19th BGs flew four more missions against the enemy ships at Balikpapan. The heavy weather forced the planes to abort two of the missions and concealed the results of a third but on February 2, seven Fortresses managed to reach the target and sink one transport and damage another.[37]

During the same four days, four more B-17s and one LB-30 arrived in Java. On January 30, the LB-30 arrived via the Pacific air route, while the brother of Capt. Fred Key, Capt. Algene E. Key (30th BS/19th BS), B-17E (41-2458, *Yankee Diddl'er—Wouldn't It Root Ya*) and 1st Lt. Kenneth D. Casper (9th BS/7th BG), B-17E (41-2470), arrived via Africa. The next day, Lt. Rouse, B-17E (41-2453) and 2nd Lt. Paul M. Lindsey (9th BS), B-17E (41-2483), came in from Africa.[38]

Despite the best efforts by the Americans and Dutch, the Japanese continued to build up their forces at Balikpapan. Still the attacks continued. At 9:30 A.M., February 3, the 7th BG flew its first mission from Djogjakarta when Maj. Hobson, B-17E (41-2472, *Guinea Pig*), led eight other bombers against the enemy ships off Balikpapan.[39] Although all nine planes, flying in three three-plane elements at 30,000 feet, reached the target, bad weather once again interfered with their drop and the results were undetermined. Unknown to anybody at the time, February 3 was about to become one of the costliest days for the B-17 in the Pacific.

Zero fighters jumped the first element shortly after leaving Balikpapan. The Japanese concentrated their fire on Maj. Hobson's lead plane, *Guinea Pig*, wounding two men. As a Zero banked away, its wild fire sliced into the left outboard engine of Lt. Swanson's B-17E (41-2469) causing it to burst into flame. Unable to extinguish the fire, Swanson ordered his crew to bail out. Five of the eight men jumped before Swanson belly landed his stricken bomber on a beach on Arends Island, north of Java. All eight men survived but the bomber was a total loss.[40]

On Lt. Bleasdale's bomber B-17E (41-2464, *Queenie*), PFC Arthur T. Lowry (22nd BS) had trouble with his oxygen and passed out. When a fellow crewman attempted to resuscitate him, he too was partly overcome. Since Bleasdale was unable to leave the protection of the formation and drop to a lower altitude, Pvt. Lowry died from "oxygen want."[41]

While the 7th BG was hitting Balikpapan, the Japanese staged their first air raid on Java. In three separate attacks, the Japanese struck Soerabaja, Madioen and Malang. At Singosari Airdrome, the 19th BG was taken completely by surprise since the Dutch air warning system in Java was almost non-existent. Mike Payne described the setup at Djogjakarta:

> Their air raid alert was a papier-mâché ball they used hanging from the control tower. You were suppose to watch for it. The only thing was, was that they were slow in changing it. Green was always clear, Yellow for warning, and of course Red meant a raid. They never did get it changed in time. By the time they got the Red up, the raid was over.[42]

With the 7th BG putting up a maximum effort against Balikpapan, the 19th BG had been given the day off. At 10:40 A.M., nine unidentified fighter planes suddenly came up from the south at about 5,000 feet. When someone contacted the control tower he was told that they were "American planes of an unidentified type." Knowing that new types of American fighters were supposedly on the way to Java, the men relaxed. Standing outside of their quarters, the airmen calmly watched the approaching planes until all hell suddenly broke loose.[43]

"While six of the planes stayed upstairs," recalled Lt. Teats, "the other three turned, swooped and went right down the hangar line, strafing with all guns." Five B-17s were on the field, while a few more were inside the hangars, or hidden in revetments. The swooping Zeros pumped machine-gun and cannon fire into the exposed bombers for 15 minutes setting fire to B-17Ds (40-3074) and (40-3078), both veterans of the Philippines, and B-17Es (41-2427) and (41-2470). Fully loaded with bombs, B-17E (41-2427) exploded into shrapnel. Lt. Dalley wrote, "[One B-17] which was loaded with some 4800 pounds of demolition bombs blew up all over the field."[44]

Twenty enemy bombers followed the strafing fighters, dropping their bombs from 15,000 feet, but most of the bombs missed, hitting near the east end of the field. After nearly an hour of strafing the nine fighters finally flew off, leaving Singosari Airdrome a shattered, burning mess. "That was the first time our air raid warning system had failed us," wrote Lt. Teats.[45]

The two B-17Ds and B-17E (41-2427) were completely destroyed but fast work extinguished a fire on B-17E (41-2470). However, less than 24 hours later, the plane suddenly burst into flames again and burned beyond repair.[46] Four precious bombers had been lost to the surprise Japanese raid but February 3 was not yet over.

Lt. Cox, who had saved one of the B-17s from a bomb damaged hangar during the December 8 raid on Clark Field, was out test flying B-17C (40-2062) at the time of the Japanese attack. When he returned to Singosari Airdrome he was unexpectedly jumped by a pack of Zeros. Turning his bomber out to sea he tried to outrun the fighters but never made it. "Next day the plane was found shot down and burned about twenty miles from Malang Field," remembered Lt. Kurtz.[47]

Within a span of less than six hours the AAF in Java had lost six B-17 Flying Fortresses. With the destruction of Cox's B-17C and the two B-17Ds, only three veteran planes from the bloody, hectic Philippine campaign, B-17Ds (40-3061), (40-3066) and (40-3070), were still being used as combat aircraft, although five others were based at Pasirian and still in use as transport and supply planes.[48] Furthermore, the combined groups had lost eight new B-17Es out of the 21 new Fortresses that had arrived in Java. After February 3, only 16 combat ready B-17s were available to the men of the two bomb groups, including three of the old D models.[49] The attrition record in Java was almost as bad as that in the Philippines.

On February 3, the 7th BG also lost another commanding officer. Maj. Straubel was returning from a conference at Bandoeng, on the western end of Java, flying a B-18, when he ran into a pack of Zeros. Straubel tried to outrun the fighters but was shot down in a fiery wreck near Soerabaja. Although Maj. Straubel and his copilot survived the crash, they both suffered severe burns while trying unsuccessfully to save others and died before sunup.[50] Maj. Straubel had been in command of the 7th BG for only six days.

Starting on February 4, the Japanese began staging almost daily raids on Singosari. Usually, the early warning system worked and the bombers took off before the attack or the bombers were already in the air. Commented Lt. Knudson, "After the bombing raid here some of the damnest [sic] things happen—such orders as flying the planes up and down the coast in order to keep them off the field in case of another bombing raid is one example. These orders come from Col. Eubanks, six hours and a half of flying up and down the south coast . . . A machine won't last indefinitely."[51] Neither would the men.

To say that some of the men had frayed nerves would be a gross understatement. Lt. Dalley remembered what happened when he and some of his fellow airmen were eating lunch and an antiaircraft unit decided to test fire their machine guns. "They cleared their guns and our messhall [sic] at the same time," recalled Dalley. "Men dove out of doors and windows forgetting to open them first. From then on, the sound of machine gun fire brought more prompt attention than a four star general could have commanded."[52]

The Japanese raided Singosari on February 5 and when the attack was over, a new LB-30 and B-17E (41-2492) flown by 1st Lt. William J. Pritchard (9th BS/7th BG) arrived—the LB-30 by the Pacific route and the B-17 via Africa. That same afternoon, seeking a safer haven, the 19th BG Operations staff moved from Singosari Airdrome into the town of Malang.[53]

Before the Japanese raid hit on February 5, six Fortresses left Malang for Balikpapan.[54] Lt. Rouse was flying as copilot with 1st Lt. M. A. McKenzie in B-17E (41-2453) to get combat experience. "I got it," he admitted. "We were jumped about 40 miles East of Soerabaya at about 7,000' by 8 Zero fighters." Staying in formation, the B-17s shot down one Zero and damaged another as the enemy fighters came in from the front. "A formation of 17s is a pretty hard nut to crack," wrote Rouse. Unfortunately, the top turrets on two of the bombers malfunctioned during the attack and 1st Lt. Edwin S. Green, B-17E (41-2483), had his oxygen system ruptured. When the three planes turned back, the mission was scrubbed. Lt. Rouse wrote, "[We then flew] around the South coast until 15:00 [3:00 P.M.] to make sure they [i.e. the enemy] wouldn't be waiting for us when we went in to land at Malang."[55]

On February 6, after another Japanese air raid, 1st Lt. John D. Bridges (30th BS/19th BG) brought B-17E (41-2488) into Singosari from Africa.[56] By February 7, the daily raids were becoming a nuisance. "Had an air-raid alarm again this morning," Lt. Rouse wrote. "It sure disrupts all work on the field. Gooks, Dutch and Americans all take off for the woods." Gen. Brereton noted, "The Japs now have the entire eastern half of Java and adjacent islands under continual fighter and bomber attacks, menacing our air reinforcements from Australia."

On the 7th, three more B-17s arrived via Africa. The first was B-17E (41-2494) flown by 2nd Lt. William A. Lorence, Jr. (32nd BS/19th BG). Upon landing however, Lorence overshot the runway and cracked up, damaging the brand new plane beyond repair. Without ever having flown a combat mission, B-17E (41-2494) had become a war casualty. The other two planes, B-17Es (41-2486, *Lady Lou*) and (41-2489, *Suzy-Q*), flown by 1st Lt. Richard H. Beck (9th BS/7th BG) and Capt. Hardison, respectively, landed without incident.[57]

Except for the aborted raid on February 5 and a fruitless armed reconnaissance mission in search of a Japanese aircraft carrier supposed to be off the eastern end of Java, the 7th and 19th BGs had been relatively quiet. That all changed on February 8 when nine 7th BG B-17s, led by Capt. "Duke" Dufrane, B-17E (41-2456), lifted off from Singosari Airdrome at 7:35 A.M. to bomb the newly captured airfield at Kendari II.[58] Carrying seven 100-kilogram bombs and a bomb bay gas tank, the planes flew in three three-plane elements. Shortly after takeoff they spotted 12 pursuit planes slowly approaching from behind. "They should be friendly, being so close to our own base," M/Sgt. James E. Worley, bombardier on Lt. Strother's B-17E (41-2471) wrote, "but we prepare to fight." While the B-17 crewmen watched, the fighters pulled even with the Fortresses. "There's only a white splash of markings on the fuselage," Worley continued. "We can't see the tops or bottoms of the wings. Probably our own P-40s—they're long overdue."[59]

Sgt. Boone, flying as top turret gunner with Lt. Strother recalled watching the fighters. "They were flying along with us, about three thousand yards away, apparently paying no attention," he stated. Looking closely, Boone noticed the

United States AAF insignia painted on the sides of the unidentified fighters. "Only when we saw the white points of our Army Air Force star with the red disk in the middle were we relieved. It hadn't occurred to us that you can take the red sun of Japan and with a few strokes of [a] paintbrush make five white points around it."[60]

Lt. Worley wrote, "They fly ahead for about a minute, then suddenly the two lead fighters turn back directly towards us." Sgt. Boone agreed, "There was nothing about this maneuver which surprised us, for the Japs so far had always attacked us from the rear. Then they wheeled in for their nose-on attack, and too late we saw those Army Air Force stars on their fuselages had been crudely forged."[61]

Having flown alongside the big bombers, the Japanese pilots were undoubtedly aware that the American formation was made up entirely of B-17Es with tail guns. The 19th BG historian reported, "The enemy made co-ordinated attacks from the front, front quarter and front underneath simultaneously." Lt. Knudson was flying copilot with Lt. Preston, B-17E (41-2455), in the first element. He recalled, "The first head-on attack was made at our ship. It was a Zero with a belly tank, and the Lord only knows why he missed us, for he pulled up just 25 feet over our left wing tip."[62]

Flying in the rear element was Lt. Pritchard, B-17E (41-2492), who had arrived in Java only three days before. As the Zero passed through the formation it fired incendiary bullets into the extra bomb bay gas tank in Pritchard's plane. Sgt. Boone recalled, "[T]he whole Fortress flared in front of our eyes in a puff of flames and smoke." Although Boone saw two or three men parachute from the exploded plane, he felt that they were already dead. "More probably," he reasoned, "they had never pulled the rip cords themselves, but the explosion opened the chutes."[63]

The second Zero, concentrating on the lead plane of Capt. Dufrane, also scored hits on the extra bomb bay tank. "As I looked [at Dufrane]," Lt. Knudson wrote, "fire was coming from his bomb bay." Perhaps as surprised as everyone else by the Japanese ruse of changing their insignia Capt. Dufrane had taken no evasive action with the formation. Added Lt. Knudson, "Du Frave's [sic] mistake was in not heading for clouds immediately."[64]

Sgt. Boone watched the attack on B-17E (41-2456). "First we saw Duphrane's [sic] plane shudder as the Jap tracers crashed into its cockpit and into its bomb bay," Boone stated. "But she didn't go down . . . And she didn't waver or flinch, even when we could see dull-red flames . . . sprouting out of her, from the cockpit back to the tail." Remembered Lt. Knudson, "Someone yelled for him to jump, over the command radio." Unfortunately, Capt. Dufrane would never hear the call. "We surged just a little ahead of her nose," wrote Boone, "and from here we could see Duke Duphrane and his copilot both slumped over dead, their heads leaning against the shattered pane of the cockpit window."[65]

Slowly, Dufrane's pilotless bomber slipped out of the formation. "She was enveloped in red flames now from her nose to her tail," Boone noted, "and through her windows we could see flames shimmering inside her cabin, and as her plates melted she began to sink in a steepening curve . . ." Six crewmen bailed out of the dying bomber but the flight engineer did not have time to buckle on his parachute and was thrown from the harness when the chute jerked open. Then, as the other men floated down, they were strafed by the circling Zeros.[66]

Assuming the lead, a recently promoted Capt. Strother, ordered the surviving seven B-17s to close upon each other and headed for the nearest clouds. As the big planes moved closer to one another, the Zeros continued to attack. Incendiary bullets hit the extra bomb bay tank in Lt. Preston's B-17E (41-2455) but he quickly jettisoned the tank before it exploded. Knudson, copilot of the plane, wrote, "We dropped our bombs and bombay [sic]. The tank left the ship burning."[67]

Fighting desperately to protect themselves, the B-17 gunners shot down two Zeros with their small .30 caliber nose guns and downed three more with the combined fire from the tail, top turret and waist guns. As the 19th BG historian noted, "The bottom turrets [Bendix belly turret] were ineffective."[68]

Instinctively, the six pilots still carrying bomb bay tanks attempted to jettison them. Five were successful but when Capt. Strother tried to release his, he found that the release mechanism had been hit and would not function. Quickly, the crew moved to release the dangerous tank by hand. "Then all of a sudden— Bang!" wrote Sgt. Boone, "there's a hell of an explosion inside our plane, and dust, and the stink of gasoline." Fortunately, it was not the bomb bay tank that exploded. Boone explained, "[A] bullet had smashed into our compressed-oxygen tank, and also cut a gasoline feed line, so that gas was spurting all over the cabin, but we didn't know it then." The exploding oxygen tank blew a huge hole in the rear wall of the flight deck and forced open one of the bomb bay doors, which was now "swinging wildly in the slip stream."[69]

As the leaking gas streamed down the belly of the bomber and sprayed off the tail, the tail gunner warned the other crewmen not to light any cigarettes. When the plane finally reached friendly cloud cover, Sgt. Boone managed to salvo both the ruptured tank and the load of bombs.[70]

Although the Zeros had disappeared, the action was not yet over. Lt. Lindsey's B-17E (41-2483) had been riddled with bullets. "Our tail section was shot up so bad both the co-pilot and I had to hang on to the controls," Lindsey stated. "We hit turbulent air—and went into a spin." Dropping like a rock, the spinning plane fell from 17,000 to 7,000 feet in a matter of minutes, causing the copilot, navigator and tail gunner to bail out. Having a badly wounded man aboard who could not bail out Lt. Lindsey fought hard to save the plane. Aided by his bombardier, the two men braced their backs against the armor plated seats and pushed forward on the control wheels with their feet, forcing the nose of the bomber down and stopping the spin.[71]

Somehow, despite having lost his navigator and with a badly damaged tail, Lt. Lindsey managed to return B-17E (41-2483) to Malang. The plane was so badly damaged however that it would never fly again. For his act of returning the crippled bomber to Malang on his first combat mission, Lt. Lindsey was awarded the DFC.[72]

Although the Americans had lost a greater number of planes on February 3, the fiery death of the two aircrews had a more demoralizing effect on the entire group. Wrote Lt. Knudson, "This has been the most disastrous day of the war for us—two 17s shot down in flames . . . It was a most helpless feeling to watch those 12 Zero fighters of the Japs coming in for attack after attack and our guns unable to knock them off."[73]

After the February 8 fracas, 5th Bomber Command evaluated the mission to see if they could prevent such an incident from happening again. It was quickly noted that the small .30 caliber machine gun in the nose compartment was the sole defense against frontal attacks since the top turrets could not traverse fast enough.[74] It was shortly thereafter, that the men began installing multiple, and/or heavier caliber, machine guns in the noses of their planes.

Another change that came about because of the February 8 mission was a change in the AAF insignia. At the start of the war, the insignia consisted of a dark blue circle with a large white star in the center. Inside the star was a red disc. To identify an approaching plane, the aircrews looked for the white points of the star and the red central disc. Realizing this, the Japanese deliberately altered the rising sun emblem on their planes. Wrote Mike Payne, "The Japs surprised us by painting a white star around their red ball. That was when we changed our insignia." Simply whitewashing over the red center of the American insignia alleviated the problem.[75]

The most glaring area that needed improvement however, was with the bomb bay tanks. The tanks were non-self-sealing and had caused apprehension from the beginning. Since there were only a limited number of tanks in the Pacific, it was strongly suggested that the men not drop their bomb bay tanks when attacked. However, the men thought otherwise, especially if they were attacked at the end of a long mission.

"That's all the more reason for dumping them," recalled Lt. Kurtz, "because an empty tank is full of a highly explosive mixture of air and gasoline vapor. A Japanese tracer bullet often goes clear through a full gas tank without setting fire to it, but an empty tank pierced by a tracer goes off like a bomb . . ." After a time, the aircrews became reluctant to carry the dangerous tanks altogether.[76]

Unwilling at this time to tell the bomber crews to jettison their bomb bay tanks when attacked, 5th Bomber Command simply noted, "Bombbay [sic] tanks are risky." Lt. Kurtz admitted however, "We'd had to dump so many bomb-bay tanks that they were now worth their weight in gold to us."[77]

If there was one glimmer of sunlight in the dark Japanese cloud that continued to work its way southward, it was the fact that as the enemy ships drew closer to Java there was less of a need for the attacking B-17s to carry the auxiliary gas tanks. The war was getting closer to Java. Too close.

X

Hard Times

WHILE THE 7TH BG airmen were grieving over the fiery deaths of two aircrews, the 19th BG went back into action. On February 9, five B-17s set out to bomb enemy ships near Makassar.[1] Running into bad weather, all five returned to Malang but not before the navigator on Capt. Algene Key's B-17E (41-2472, *Guinea Pig*) passed out and died from lack of oxygen. Warned the 19th BG historian, "We must use more care in the use of Oxygen!"[2]

While the B-17s were in the air, the Japanese once again raided Singosari Airdrome, causing moderate damage to the runway and a few buildings. Five and a half hours later, two more B-17s arrived from Africa. 1st Lts. Harold C. Smelser and Robert W. Evans (both 9th BS/7th BG) touched down with B-17Es (41-2449) and (41-2484), respectively, and a short time later 1st Lt. Pierre D. Jacques (14th BS/19th BG) arrived in B-17E (41-2498).[3]

Over the next couple of days the 19th BG flew futile searches to find a Japanese carrier reported to be southeast of Java.[4] On February 10, 2nd Lt. Richard B. Taylor (9th BS/7 BG) flew into Singosari in B-17E (41-2505). The next day, Capt. Clayton A. Beran (9th BS/7th BG), B-17E (41-2452), and 1st Lt. Clarence V. McCauley (HqS/7th BG), B-17E (41-2462, *Tojo's Jinx*) arrived at Djogjakarta. All three planes had come via Africa.[5]

Lt. Taylor's B-17E (41-2505) was the first B-17 to be fitted with the brand new manned Sperry ball turret. Because of the constant complaints regarding the ineffectiveness of the Bendix belly turret, Boeing had finally replaced the useless contraption with the new manned ball turret. Suddenly, the weak underbelly of the Flying Fortress was not so weak.[6]

On February 11, the 7th and 19th BG, set out on a secret night mission against Makassar but aborted due to bad weather. The canceled mission was the last scheduled offensive mission for a Pacific B-17D. Lt. Montgomery, a veteran of the Philippines, became the last AAF pilot to head a B-17D into combat. Deemed too war weary, B-17D (40-3066) was placed on non-combat status a few days later.[7]

The secret night raid finally took place on February 13 when three planes from the 19th BG and eight from the 7th struck Japanese shipping in the vicinity of Makassar. The 11 B-17Es comprised the largest raid sent out by 5th Bomber Command while in Java. Before reaching the target, however, Lt. Habberstad, B-17E (41-2466), developed engine trouble and turned back but the others successfully reached the target and dropped their bombs through the clouds and darkness. The Americans reported, "Bombs were dropped on lights off shore—Results undetermined." It was believed that at least one ship was hit.[8]

Shortly after midnight on February 14, an even larger force of 14 B-17s, eight from the 7th BG and six from the 19th, set out to bomb a Japanese convoy that was reportedly heading for Sumatra and the rich oil fields of Palembang. Unable to find the ships, the B-17s returned to base.[9] However, only a short time later, Japanese paratroopers dropped near Palembang and quickly moved to capture the vital oil refineries and a nearby airfield.[10]

When a reinforcing convoy was spotted in the Strait of Bangka, ABDA Command quickly responded. At 2:00 A.M., February 15, three LB-30s took off to attack the convoy. At 6:10 A.M., five 19th BG B-17s roared into the air for a follow-up strike. Carrying eight 300-kg bombs each, the B-17s flew through a barrage of "moderate to heavy" antiaircraft fire to deliver their payload. The 19th BG historian reported, "Bombs hit to the left of several transports. One near hit was seen on auxiliary vessel. Due to broken clouds all bombs were not seen to hit. Later smoke was seen to be emerging from the stern of a cruiser."[11]

Although the 7th BG was scheduled to follow close on the heels of the 19th BG major mistakes caused an unnecessary delay. Bombardier Lt. Raymond O. Carr wrote, ". . . four B-17s which were supposed to get off at dawn got off at 11:00 A.M. The crews weren't awakened and bombs weren't loaded. It was the worst inefficiency I have ever witnessed." Only three planes finally got airborne but they quickly ran into terrible weather and returned to Djogjakarta.[12]

The 7th BG, a fledgling unit which had lost two commanding officers in a matter of days, was still experiencing growing pains. Also, the daily arrival of new crews did not help the matter. Two new LB-30s had come in on February 12 and 15, the first by way of Africa, the second across the Pacific, and 1st Lt. James O. Cobb, B-17E (41-2481, *Topper*), had arrived on February 14, via the African route.[13]

In spite of the best efforts by the Allies the Japanese seized Palembang on February 15. Unfortunately, the Dutch and Australian defenders had been driven out of the city before they could destroy all of the oil installations. The capture of Palembang now gave Japan control of half the oil reserves of the Netherlands East Indies and they were bound and determined to capture the other half before they were done.[14]

That same date, February 15, the British fortress of Singapore finally capitulated. ABDA Command had built its entire strategy around the belief that Singapore could hold on in spite of everything that the Japanese could throw against it. With the rich Malay peninsula in their hands, the Japanese juggernaut rolled onward—west towards Burma and south towards Java.[15]

Still hoping to slow down the invasion of Sumatra and give the Dutch and Australian troops time to regroup and reorganize, 5th Bomber Command again sent the B-17s of the 7th and 19th BGs against the Japanese warships. On February 16, six planes from the 19th BG set out for Palembang but were turned back by weather.[16] Originally scheduled as a follow-up attack, six planes from the 7th BG took off from Djogjakarta and Madioen shortly after the 19th BG Fortresses. Although Lt. Lindsey, B-17E (41-2452), turned back due to engine failure, the others went on in spite of a heavy cloud cover. Carrying eight 300-kg bombs apiece, the six Fortresses came in at less than 2,000 feet and found two transports and two barges loaded with Japanese troops crossing the Banjoeasin River.[17]

Author Priscilla Hardison, wife of Capt. Hardison who was flying B-17E (41-2489, *Suzy-Q*), wrote of the attack: "They went into the bomb-run at one thousand feet . . . [a]nd hit the transport. With an explosion so powerful it actually tossed the *Suzy-Q* into the air, tearing the fabric off her ailerons and elevators, and splattering her belly with bomb fragments." After dropping their bombs the Fortresses returned, flashing over the sinking ships and strafing the startled invaders with machine-gun fire. All four Japanese vessels were reportedly sunk. Still hampered by bad weather, the B-17s landed at Batavia, the capital of the Netherlands East Indies, on the west end of Java.[18]

Following the successful February 16 raid, five planes from the 19th BG set out to repeat the attack on February 17 but were forced back by the impenetrable storm front. Later that afternoon, another new bomber, B-17E (41-2497) flown by Lt. Coleman Stripling (HqS/7th BG), arrived via Africa, but the plane overshot the landing in the rain and darkness and collided with B-17E (41-2472, *Guinea Pig*). Although neither plane was seriously damaged, both were grounded for repairs.[19]

Again, on the 18th, both the 7th and the 19th BGs attempted to return to Sumatra but the weather turned them back.[20] During the five day period between February 14 and 18, 5th Bomber Command had sent nine heavy bomber missions, involving fifty-three planes, against the Japanese on Sumatra. Only two of the missions had reached the target, one by the 7th BG and one by the 19th. Only 12 planes had been able to reach the target and only 11 had been able to drop their bombs. Seven missions, 41 planes, had either failed to find the target or had been turned back by the deteriorating weather conditions.

At the same time, the Japanese considered the bad weather to be a godsend. Not only did the front stop the Allied attackers, but it screened Japan's subsequent moves toward Bali, Timor and eventually Java.[21]

With the fall of Singapore, Gen. Archibald Wavell, the ABDA commander, felt that the fall of Java was imminent. It was estimated that Japan had almost the entire strength of their navy and between 400 to 500 fighter planes, and 300 to 400 bombers in the Southwest Pacific. In turn, the Allies had a combined strength of less than 15 warships, and less than 150 fighters and bombers. Realizing the inevitable, Wavell decided to abandon Java.

On February 16, Gen. Wavell wrote, ". . . Burma and Australia are absolutely vital for war against Japan. Loss of Java, though a severe blow from every point of view, would not be fatal. Efforts should not, therefore, be made to reinforce Java which might compromise defense of Burma and Australia."[22] The very next day, Gen. Brett diverted a convoy with almost 3,000 American airmen bound for Java to India. Earlier, Generals Brett and Brereton had decided to move all of the American airmen and airplanes already in Java back to Australia for rest and recuperation, and to help defend Australia. Meanwhile, Brereton would fly to India with Gen. Wavell and help build up an Allied force there that would strike back at Japan through China.[23]

To the men of the 7th and 19th BGs, the fall of Singapore meant the fall of Java. "[Singapore] was the key to the defense of the Netherlands Indies, and the doom of Java was sealed," wrote Lt. Teats. "As far as we were concerned, Java rapidly was becoming untenable." Java had become the Philippines all over again. Once again, morale suffered. "All we grasped was that for the second time in less than three months, a delaying action would have to be broken off by withdrawal in the face of overwhelming enemy offensive superiority."[24]

Lt. Godman wrote, "Our morale was terrible because our planes were being shot up on the ground and in the air . . . Soon we felt like we were being fed into [a] meat grinder and the only thing coming out the other end was dead people. We were losing one island, one city, one base, one air strip, one after another." Godman summed it up precisely when he wrote, "I was getting a sense of defeat."[25]

Adding to the low morale was the battered and beaten condition of the planes. Mechanical failure was grounding more Fortresses than enemy action. Replacements were nonexistent. Priscilla Hardison wrote of the aircrews in Java, "These men were strictly on their own, as cut off from sources of supply as if they'd been on another planet. They received from the United States no replacement parts, no supplies, no equipment, no clothing, no medical materials, no money."[26]

As early as January 26, Brereton, in Melbourne, had telegraphed ABDA Command, "There are no parts available here for B-17s." Unfortunately, by the time even the newest plane reached Java, it was already showing signs of wear and tear. The AAF Historical Division commented, "While medium bombers and fighters could be dismantled and shipped by water, the only practicable way of delivering heavy bombers was to fly them to their destination." Since many of the ferrying stops had inadequate servicing facilities, many of the B-17s that reached Java were in need of a major overhaul.[27]

Although speaking about the earlier activities in the Philippines, Lt. Crimmins had correctly identified the problems of the B-17s in the Southwest Pacific. "Speaking of the planes in the Philippine Islands it was a saying that when a ship [i.e. B-17] was worn out [in the States] it was sent to Hawaii; and when they thought in Hawaii that it was worn out, they passed it on to the Philippine Islands. And it was not far from the truth."[28] The same could be said about Java.

Unable to get new replacement parts, the ground crews became scavengers. Lt.

Dalley commented, "There were no spare parts available so when an airplane came in badly damaged, or 'washed out' in landing, often we would be there stripping it of spare parts and replacing parts before the crew had a chance to get out." Even later on, mechanics had to be on constant guard against other ground crews. Remembered Sgt. Green, "You had to keep an eye out for any crew chief/mechanic walking close to a damaged B-17 with tools in his pockets."[29]

In trying to keep their planes airborne and out of reach of the Japanese fighters, the ground crews often tried to boost the performance of the B-17s. "We tried everything to try to outrun their Zero," wrote Mike Payne, ". . . We even took the stops off of the superchargers, [but] that didn't work. It blew the plugs out of the cylinders." The blown plugs only added to the frustration of the ground crews since spare spark plugs were a rare commodity in Java.[30]

Understandably, the aircrews appreciated the efforts put forth by the ground crews. "I know that we would have been unable to do the work [i.e. bombing] we accomplished," Lt. Vandevanter wrote, "if we had not had wonderfully trained mechanics and crew chiefs on our airplanes." Sgt. Fesmire echoed those words, "We had some of the best mechanics you could want; they were all regular Air Corps old timers and they knew how to make an airplane fly."[31]

Capt. Hardison was glowing in his praise for the heavy bomb group mechanics:

> [T]hey never get near enough credit . . . It's easy enough for a flier to be a glamour boy. But where would the fliers be if the ground crews weren't on the job? My ground echelon was wonderful—you couldn't ask too much of them. Changing an engine . . . Changing tires, patching bullet holes, repairing oxygen lines, taking care of the guns, loading gas and ammunition, checking the hydraulic systems—everything. Sometimes planes would come in all shot up until you couldn't see how they'd ever get off the ground again, let alone fight. And the ground crews would fix them up—working all day long . . .[32]

The combination of combat fatigue, beaten and battered planes, and the lack of supplies all contributed to the low morale. Sgt. Green summed it up best when he wrote, "The USA forgot that there was a war going on in that area . . ."[33]

In an attempt to raise the morale, Gen. Brereton flew to Malang on February 17 and assembled the "whole 5th Bomber Command" for the "first Air Force decoration ceremony since the war." Seventy-four awards were handed out. Although Brereton claimed to have assembled both the 7th and 19th BGs, not a single award went to a member of the 7th BG. The 7th BG historian did not even mention the event in the official group history. Another historian of the 7th BG wrote, "It appears that the Gen. recognized the 19th because of his earlier and longer association with them . . ."[34]

At 2:30 A.M., on February 19, 5th Bomber Command suddenly ordered three

19th BG planes into the air as soon as possible—a Japanese convoy was landing troops on the south coast of Bali, the small island off the east coast of Java. Having captured Sumatra to the west, thereby cutting off reinforcements from Africa, Japan was now trying to take Bali on the east and stop the flow of reinforcements from Australia. Working frantically to hit an enemy that was too close for comfort, Lts. Godman, Vandevanter and Mathewson were airborne by 5:00 A.M. with orders to bomb individually in the darkness.[35]

Lt. Mathewson, B-17E (41-2484), was the first to reach the target. At 7:05 A.M., he made his bomb run from only 4,000 feet under a heavy cloud cover. Carrying eight 300-kg bombs, Mathewson went after an enemy cruiser and dropped six bombs on the first pass—missing with all six. On the second run, he dropped his last two bombs and had better luck with one of them, hitting "center-right of ship." Encountering "heavy and close" antiaircraft fire, Mathewson flew back to Singosari.[36]

The next to reach the target, Lt. Godman, in B-17E (41-2478), began his attack on the enemy convoy at 7:45 A.M. from 7,000 feet. "I didn't realize it at the time," he wrote, "but that altitude was just a perfect range for their three-inch antiaircraft guns. They were going off like crazy under my wing when it dawned on me that I had better get out of there and climb to a higher altitude—and fast."

Going up to 23,000 feet, Godman made another run over the convoy but found the targets obscured by the heavy cloud cover. Dropping a bit lower, Godman made two more bomb runs, both at 16,000 feet, but found that the target was still hidden by the clouds. "To make matters worse," Godman continued, "There were those ever-present Japanese Zero fighters, and this day I found four of them headed straight for me." Although Godman's gunners managed to shoot down two of the Zeros, when he found out that his top turret was not functioning properly, he salvoed his bombs into the sea and fled back to Malang.[37]

Lt. Vandevanter, B-17E (41-2498), came in 10 minutes behind Godman and caught the full effect of the antiaircraft barrage. Flying at 4,000 feet, under the cloud base, Vandevanter was forced to make a second bomb run when his bombs hung up on the first. Sgt. Fesmire, Vandevanter's bombardier recalled, "Our target was a destroyer and all I could see through the bombsight were flashes from his guns as he fired broadsides at us." On the second run, all eight bombs fell short. ". . . [T]he destroyer maneuvered out from under our bombs," wrote Vandevanter. "None were close enough to damage the vessel." By 10:30 A.M. he was back at Malang.[38]

An hour behind the first three B-17s was one bomber from the 7th BG and three from the 19th, led by Capt. Schwanbeck, B-17E (41-2458, *Yankee Diddl'er*). Intending to strike the landing forces coming ashore opposite Denpasar Airfield, the four planes reached the target area at 8:35 A.M., at 11,000 feet. Although the landing beach was obscured by the thick clouds and the antiaircraft fire was heavy, the bombers dropped their Dutch bombs and then fled when enemy fighters were sighted.

The copilot, Lt. Knudson, flying in the lone 7th BG plane, B-17E (41-2452) piloted by Lt. Lindsay, recalled, "There were six and they made passes for the next one-half hour as we headed along the south coast of Java." Two Zeros flew out in front of the B-17s and made a simultaneous head-on attack. "Practically all [the] guns in our planes fired on the plane on the left," wrote the 19th BG historian. "It started smoking and passed out of sight underneath. It was believed shot down." The other Zero, concentrated on Capt. Schwanbeck's lead plane but quick evasive maneuvering saved the B-17 from serious damage.

Two more Zeros attempted an attack from the left front but heavy concentrated fire and quick evasive action from the B-17s caused one of the fighters to pull away before getting in range and the other to pass beneath the B-17s without firing. Having survived both the antiaircraft fire and the fighter attacks, Capt. Schwanbeck decided not to press his luck and headed back to Java. After landing Schwanbeck reported, ". . . evasive action taken just as the fighter puts his sights on is the most effective solution to their head on attacks."[39]

Hoping to keep the pressure on the Japanese at Bali, three 7th BG LB-30s went out to bomb the beachhead but were turned back by enemy fighters. Shortly thereafter, two 7th BG B-17s from Madioen caught the Japanese almost completely unaware. Facing no antiaircraft fire, the two planes dropped their bombs on a cruiser from the height of 14,000 feet, and scored one hit. The ship was ". . . smoking badly when last seen." Attacked head-on by two Zeros, the B-17s managed to make their escape unscathed and returned to Madioen by 2:20 P.M.[40]

At 12:30 P.M., the air raid alarm sounded at Madioen and Lt. Casper took his fully loaded bomber into the air. Casper had been scheduled to fly the Bali mission with the other two bombers but engine trouble had forced him to abort. Taking off with only three engines, he resolved that his plane was stable enough for operations and decided to go after the Bali convoy by himself.

Running into a storm, Casper continued on and dropped his eight 300-kg bombs from 28,000 feet alongside a Japanese destroyer, hitting just below the waterline. The B-17 airmen claimed that they thought they saw the ship turn over and sink but Japanese sources said otherwise. Whatever the final outcome, Casper's one plane raid had been the most successful of the day to date but the B-17 crews were not yet finished.[41]

Having bombed early in the morning, Lts. Godman, Vandevanter and Mathewson were eager to go out again as soon as their planes could be serviced. At 12:45 P.M., when the air raid alarm sounded at Singosari, the three planes were ready and headed back towards Bali but Lt. Mathewson, B-17E (40-2484), soon developed a cracked cylinder head on one of his engines and aborted. Continuing on, Lts. Godman and Vandevanter once again went over the enemy ships on individual runs.

Remembering the heavy antiaircraft fire that had greeted him in the morning, Vandevanter took his plane over the area at 35,000 feet. Bombardier Fesmire wrote, "That was the highest I ever flew in any plane during the war and we got hits on a couple of ships." Pilot Vandevanter recalled, "We noted near misses on a destroyer and transport. There was no enemy pursuit and we encountered no antiaircraft."[42] Lt. Godman, attacking from 27,000 feet, tried to hit a cruiser but the ship, ". . . turned as the bomb release line was reached and the bombs fell 200 feet [to the] right."[43]

While the 7th and 19th BGs were trying to impede the invasion of Bali, the Japanese on Sumatra staged their first massive air raid on western Java. Flying out of the newly captured airfield at Palembang, the Japanese arrived over Bandoeng in time to find two brand new B-17Es, which had just arrived from Africa, sitting on the ground. B-17E (41-2493), brought in by Maj. Francis R. Feeney (7th BG), was demolished by strafing and B-17E (41-2503), flown in by Lt. Charles F. Franklin (7th BG), caught fire and burned. Also destroyed by strafing was B-17E (41-2466) and one LB-30.[44]

Two more brand-new planes, B-17E (41-2500) piloted by 1st Lt. Robert C. Lewis (9th BS/7th BG), and B-17E (41-2507) with 1st Lt. Robert L. Williams (30th BS/19th BG), had just reached Java and were headed towards Bandoeng when they ran into the retiring Japanese bombers. In a short but spirited fight, the startled American crews managed to shoot down one Japanese plane but B-17E (41-2500) was so badly damaged that it would never fly again. Although Lt. Lewis successfully landed at Bandoeng, the new bomber could only be used for parts. Eventually, it would be burned just prior to the final evacuation of Java.

Lt. Williams was able to outdistance his attackers and land at Bandoeng in one piece. On February 20, he brought his plane into Singosari and added it to the depleted ranks of the 19th BG.[45] With the fall of Sumatra, the African air route was no longer safe. B-17E (41-2507) was the last Flying Fortress to successfully reach the Southwest Pacific via the eastern air route across Africa.[46]

The very last B-17 to arrive in Java before the Japanese closed off the two reinforcement routes was B-17E (41-2417, *Monkey Bizz-Ness*) piloted by Lt. "Sandy" McPherson, who had started out from Hawaii on the pioneer flight with Maj. Hobson and Lt. Hughes on January 6. Sidelined in Darwin with engine trouble and while waiting for a tail-wheel assembly, McPherson had finally gotten his plane repaired and set out on February 19 to join his mates. Leaving Darwin in the face of a typhoon, McPherson started out leading a flight of P-40s towards Java but when the weather worsened, the P-40s turned back and McPherson went on alone.

Battling the elements all the way, Lt. McPherson managed to reach Bali and decided to land at the Denpasar airstrip for fuel and information. Lowering his landing gear, he had only touched down when a fusillade of machine-gun fire peppered the side of *Monkey Bizz-Ness*. Hearing the slap of the bullets and the cry from his tail gunner that he had been wounded in the foot, McPherson quickly pushed the throttles forward and made his getaway. Unknowingly, McPherson had set down on a newly captured airfield. If the Japanese had shown a bit more patience, they may have been able to finally capture and closely study one of the new B-17Es. As it was, their impatience had gotten the better of them.[47]

Among those watching in amazement as McPherson made his mistaken landing was Saburo Sakai. He and his fellow pilots were relaxing inside one of the base buildings when they suddenly heard the unmistakable sound of a B-17. "We ran to the window . . ." he wrote. "There it was, the impossible! A giant Flying Fortress, its landing gear and flaps extended, engines throttled back, easing out of it's approach for a landing." As they watched, they tried to figure out how a Japanese pilot had managed to capture a B-17. "In a moment we were rushing through the door, excited with the prospect of being able to study the defenses of the powerful American bomber."

However, the pilots pulled up short when they heard a burst of machine-gun fire. "The B-17 wasn't captured!" Sakai wrote. "Its pilot had landed in error at our field, and some idiotic soldier was firing at him even before the plane stopped rolling!" Warned by the gunfire, the American plane picked up speed and flew off. "We were stunned," Sakai admitted. "A B-17, intact, right in our hands, and the priceless opportunity had been thrown away by some trigger-happy baboon of a machine gunner! . . . For the next several days we cursed the Army and bemoaned the loss of the enemy bomber."[48]

Although low on fuel and still bothered by the weather, Lt. McPherson managed to reach Singosari Airdrome and get his wounded gunner to the hospital without any further trouble. As B-17E (41-2417, *Monkey Bizz-Ness*) was taxied off the field, all four engines suddenly quit for lack of fuel. McPherson had literally landed on fumes.[49]

With the invasion of Bali, the Japanese were closing the noose around Java. Having already captured the surrounding islands and airfields, Japan had finally established air superiority over the region. Japanese airplanes were free to roam at will over the Indian Ocean and northern Australia and their transports were free to move on Java. On February 19, the Japanese staged a massive air raid on Darwin. Over 100 planes struck without warning, demolishing the harbor and setting the town on fire. Two hours later, when the attackers finally flew away, 243 people were dead and more than 300 were wounded.[50]

The attack on Darwin and the capture of the islands surrounding Java spelled the end of "Project X." No more heavy bombers could be sent to relieve the battling remnants of the 7th and 19th BGs. Of the 65 B-17s earmarked for the Pacific, only 39 ever reached Java. Of the intended 15 LB-30s, only 12 reached the island. Three B-17s and five LB-30s were flown to Java utilizing the Pacific air route—all the rest came in via Africa.[51]

On February 20, three B-17Es from the 7th BG at Madioen and seven B-17Es from the 19th BG at Singosari followed close on the heels of an attack by American dive-bombers and LB-30s on the Japanese warships near Bali. Led by Capt. Hardison, the 7th BG planes reached Bali first, at 11:30 A.M., and bombed a large transport from 22,000 feet, setting the ship on fire and causing it to list.

As the Fortresses flew away, they spotted nine Zeros in the distance but the fighters did not attack. At this point in the war, the enemy pilots had found that it was a lot safer to attack the B-17s on the ground than to try and shoot them out of the air. Sgt. Reeves recalled, "We'd be flying along pretty as you please when a flock of Zeros would come into view, but staying well out of range—just looking us over . . . Towards the last they only tried to get us on the ground. They knew we had no protection there to speak of—no fighters and no pom-poms [i.e. anti-aircraft]. They'd come in insolent as could be."[52]

The 19th BG B-17s, led by Capt. Parsel, B-17E (41-2458, *Yankee Diddl'er*), arrived 25 minutes later. Parsel lined the flight up on a Japanese destroyer towing a second destroyer but when two of the B-17s experienced bomb rack trouble he took the planes around for a second run. Coming over at 26,200 feet, the second run wasn't any better. Although all the bombs were dropped, they fell between the two ships. Wrote Rouse, "Arrived over the target O.K. but lead ship [i.e. B-17] gave us a poor run so everybody's bombs missed . . ." Attacked by one Zero fighter, the combined fire of the B-17s managed to chase it away and the big bombers returned safely to Singosari.[53]

Once on the ground, two planes were put into a hangar and revetment for minor repair while the other five were dispersed about the field. Near 3:45 P.M., nine fighter planes suddenly appeared overhead. "We all thought they were our ships," admitted Lt. Rouse, "as they were in plain sight below the clouds and there was no alarm." Unconcerned with the fighters, Rouse turned away. "All of a sudden I heard the familiar pop, pop, pop sound of exploding cannon shells. Those ships were Japs."[54]

S/Sgt. Oscar D. Hansen was on the field when the planes struck. "There had been no air raid alarm and everybody was caught in a very embarrassing position," Hansen wrote. He and another man hid behind the tire of a B-17 as the Zeros swept over the airstrip. "On the first pass the tires were shot out and the nose [was] set on fire," he recalled. Fearing an explosion of the Fortress, the two men eventually found protection in an "overcrowded sand-bagged gun pit."[55]

By the time the Japanese planes withdrew, nine men had been wounded, two seriously. All five B-17s left in the open had been set on fire. B-17Es (41-2455), (41-2484) and (41-2488), burned completely but quick action extinguished the fire on B-17E (41-2478) and B-17E (41-2498). However, both planes had been burned beyond repair. Wrote Lt. Rouse, "They burned up five ships and wounded about 9 crew members. We were sure lucky." The historian for the 19th BG wrote, "Quick work by many officers and EM [enlisted men] saved considerable equipment out of these airplanes, i.e. guns, ammunition, tail sections, wing tips, engines, etc." Still, five more B-17s had been lost. The historian added, "Men worked all night preparing every available plane for a mission the following day."[56]

During the early morning hours of February 21, two LB-30s attacked Denpasar airport. Intending to carry out a follow-up raid, six B-17Es of the 19th BG left Malang and headed towards the airfield. Unfortunately, along the way, the flight lost four planes to mechanical failure and other reasons and although two Fortresses managed to reach the target, they were unable to drop their bombs due to a heavy haze and the "inability to spot [a] target."[57]

That same day, three B-17Es from the 9th BS/7th BG took off from Madioen to bomb the enemy shipping south of Bali. Finding no ships, Lt. Swanson, leading the flight, took the planes over Denpasar Airdrome at 26,000 feet at 12:15 P.M. Although each plane dropped eight 300-kg bombs apiece, the airmen reported, "Results unknown due to clouds over target at time of impact."[58]

Still trying to damage the Denpasar airfield, three B-17s of the 19th BG tried to take off at 4:15 A.M. on February 22, but ground fog delayed their take off 45 minutes. Then, as a newly-promoted Capt. Godman, B-17E (41-2507), started down the runway, his speed was retarded by the slick surface and he was forced to come back around for another try. As he was taxiing back, he rolled into an unseen bomb crater and became hopelessly stuck.[59]

Taking off without trouble, Lt. Vandevanter, B-17E (41-2486, *Lady Lou*), bombed the enemy runway while Lt. Mathewson, B-17E (41-2472, *Guinea Pig*), bombed the hangar. Vandevanter wrote, "We laid our train of bombs from 25,000 feet, directly down the cross runway along which the Japanese ships [i.e. planes] were parked. Several fires were started—we believe we destroyed at least 16 enemy bombers on the ground. The second ship bombed and destroyed the hangar. We returned to Malang." Although a flight of Zeros chased the two pilots, they were unable to catch up with the B-17s. As the Zeros turned back towards Denpasar however, one of the Japanese pilots made a startling discovery.[60]

Toyo-o Sakai was flying low over the east end of Java when he spotted a collection of planes sitting camouflaged on the ground. Without hesitation, he attacked. In actuality, Sakai had finally discovered Pasirian airfield. Among the planes sitting on the ground were the four transport and supply B-17Ds, (40-3062), (40-3066), (40-3070), and (40-3072). After one strafing run, Sakai returned to Bali to inform his superiors.

Armed with the important information, Sakai and five other pilots returned in the afternoon, bombing and strafing the undefended Allied planes at will. By the time the attack was over, all four B-17Ds, and one P-40 and two or three Dutch bombers, had been destroyed or damaged beyond repair. Four more veterans of the Philippines were gone.[61]

That same date, February 22, Lt. Rouse wrote in his diary, "1st notice that we are going to evacuate pretty soon." In reality, two days earlier, Gen. Brereton had asked Gen. Marshall for permission to pull out of Java. On February 22, with the fall of Java imminent, not wanting one of his top air generals to be taken captive, Marshall told Brereton to move his headquarters. Later the same day, Brereton received word to begin the evacuation of his airmen and ground crews as soon as possible.[62]

On February 23, ABDA Command was dissolved and the defense of the Netherlands East Indies was left solely in the hands of the Dutch. Unfortunately, ABDA Command had been given too little to work with to try and stop the onrushing Japanese tide. Internal squabbles had only added to the problem. On February 24, Brereton left Java for India and command of the newly-formed 10th Air Force. With him he took a number of experienced officers from the 7th and 19th BGs, thus further weakening two battered bomb groups. As he left, Brereton confided to his diary, "I was glad to leave. Everyone realized that it was a completely hopeless task to defend Java."[63]

XI

Evacuation and Reinforcement

WHILE ABDA COMMAND was shutting down, the 7th BG staged another raid on Denpasar airfield. Three B-17s left Madioen at 5:30 A.M. on February 23 but after only a short time, one of the planes aborted with engine trouble. Continuing on, Lts. Preston, B-17E (41-2462, *Tojo's Jinx*), and Lewis, B-17E (41-2461, *El Toro*), dropped their bombs from 27,000 feet through a thick layer of clouds. Lt. Knudson reported, "Doubt if we came any place close to the target tho [sic] may have caused some worry to the Japs."[1]

A little after midnight, a newly promoted Capt. Hoevet, B-17E (41-2497), flew the first planeload of airmen from Java to Broome, on the northwest coast of Western Australia. Lt. Rouse described Broome as ". . . a pretty desolate, deserted town." However, he noted, "This is evidently going to be the evacuation center from Java."[2]

That same date, six B-17s of the 7th BG, led by Lt. Habberstad, B-17E (41-2452), attacked a concentration of enemy ships in the port of Makassar. "We encountered no fighter opposition, which we feared most, but the antiaircraft fire was intense," Habberstad wrote. Dropping their bombs from 20,000 feet, Habberstad reported, "One large transport seemed to disintegrate under the impact of the bombs, and another was burning intensely as we left the target . . . I always felt it was the most successful mission I flew during my year of combat."[3]

Things continued to disintegrate in the Pacific. Back on February 20, the Japanese had invaded the island of Timor, only about 500 miles northwest of Darwin, and by February 24, most of the island was under Japanese control. Gen. Wavell left Java on February 25, and at 4:30 A.M., that same day, the ground crews from the 7th and 19th BGs began evacuating the airfields. Lt. Dalley wrote, ". . .

[W]e received secret orders to proceed to Djogja-karta, the residence of the Sultan of Java. From there . . . we traveled overland by truck convoy to Tjilatjap, the last port not occupied by the advancing Japanese forces."[4]

Fortunately, Col. Eubank had anticipated the evacuation and had the 12,000-ton Dutch freighter *Abbekerk* waiting at Tjilatjap for the men.[5] Still, with only limited room on board, some men were asked to stay behind. Recalled Mike Payne, "Late in February, 1942 a radio message was sent to our company asking us to stay and fight a delaying action. The CO asked the radio man if he had acknowledged it. He said no. The CO broke the radio and told us to get out the best way we could. We went [to] a harbor at Tillivap [sic] to get out."[6]

When the convoy finally reached Tjilatjap, the ground crews found the waterfront crowded with servicemen from several different units all trying to get on board the *Abbekerk*. Since the ship had no side hatches, the men found that they could not get their vehicles aboard. Aside from a few personal belongings, the only thing the airmen could take aboard were some machine guns salvaged from some of the destroyed planes. Then, to make matters worse, in the middle of the loading, an air raid alarm sounded. Although it proved false, for a few tense moments, the men crouched in darkness until the "All Clear" was sounded.[7]

Throughout the night of February 26 and well into the next day, the long line of evacuees continued to crowd aboard the ship, amidst the constant wail of false air raid alarms. Along with the ground echelon of the 5th Bomber Command, the *Abbekerk* took hundreds of other Army and Navy personnel. Finally, a little after 5:00 P.M., February 27, the *Abbekerk* steamed into the Indian Ocean carrying an estimated 1,700 people.[8]

Lt. Dalley wrote, "There were Americans, Dutch, Javanese, English and Australians on board, making living conditions rather jammed. We had to sleep on deck[s] that were rain [and] windswept . . ." On February 28, the crowded ship was spotted by a Japanese bomber. "[W]e were shadowed by a lone Japanese bomber, which bombed and straffed [sic] us unsuccessfully," Lt. Dalley continued. "There was fear that he would report our position back to his base and although he got away, he carried quite a few souvenirs from machine guns which were hastily strapped to the rails and fired." The bomber made four passes at the ship, each time receiving fire from numerous small arms, .50 caliber machine guns, and the lone aft deck gun. As the plane flew away, a few men thought they saw it wobbling in the darkening sky.[9]

"After the raid we held services in the hold of the ship," remembered Mike Payne. "There were no Atheists in a tight situation." Deep inside the freighter, the men discovered an American locomotive and tender surrounded by tons of bombs. Amazed, Payne wrote, "We could have been back to the [S]tates in pieces had we been hit hard enough." Although fearful of further air or sea attacks, the *Abbekerk*, successfully reached Freemantle, on the far southwest coast of Australia on March 5.[10] The ground echelon of the 7th and 19th BGs had successfully evacuated Java.

While the ground crews were leaving Java, the 7th and 19th BGs aircrews attempted another raid against Bali. Although eight Fortresses from the 7th BG were scheduled for a raid on Denpasar airport on February 25, only two were able to get into the air but did no damage. Meanwhile, Capts. Keiser, B-17E (41-2453), Algene Key, B-17E (41-2486, *Lady Lou*), and Godman, B-17E (41-2507), from the 19th BG, took off from Malang for Denpasar but all three developed some form of trouble and were back on the ground within a couple of hours. Lt. Knudson, in one of the 7th BG planes that got airborne, commented, "The planes are reaching the limit of their endurance. All of them need repairs of some nature."[11]

On February 26, three more B-17s, loaded down with evacuees, departed Malang for Broome. As the evacuation sped up, Japanese airplanes continued to raid Java at will. That same day Lt. Knudson wrote in his diary, "Had three air raid alarms today . . ." The historian for the 19th BG, writing from Malang on February 26 noted, "Some bases around here must be catching hell, brings home value of rapid and careful camouflage when an airplane is not flying."[12]

Having achieved air superiority, the Japanese began moving towards the invasion of Java. Two separate fleets converged on the island from the east and west. The Western Invasion Force traveled south from Indochina, while the Eastern Invasion Force left the Philippines and moved south through the Celebes Sea and the Strait of Makassar. To cover the approach of the Eastern Force, the Japanese stationed a cruiser/destroyer flotilla at the south end of the Strait of Makassar. And finally, to block any escape from Java, a heavy battle group moved into the Indian Ocean.[13] The trap was set and waiting to spring.

On February 26, Capt. Hardison, B-17E (41-2452), and 2nd Lt. Bernice S. Barr (9th BS/7th BG), B-17E (41-2417, *Monkey Bizz-Ness*), made the first attack on the converging convoys. Lifting off from Madioen the two headed towards the south end of the Strait of Makassar. Spotting 18 enemy ships, which threw up a light and inaccurate screen of antiaircraft fire, the two pilots dropped their bombs from 21,000 feet but missed by at least 100 feet. Again it was proven that hitting a moving vessel in the open sea from high altitude was almost impossible.[14]

The attacks continued the next day. Lt. Teats wrote, "Four of us [from the 19th BG] took off [but] . . . Only one ship got over the target. The other three had to turn back because of engine trouble." Once again, worn-out equipment had cost the Americans a chance to injure the Japanese. Although all alone, Lt. Mathewson, B-17E (41-2507), attacked a small convoy of ships north of Java. Afraid of fighters, Mathewson quickly fled for the safety of the clouds and was unable to observe the results of his attack. "A lone ship [i.e. B-17] couldn't fool around with the stuff they had up there," Teats added. "Once again, it was 'hit 'em high, hit 'em fast, hit 'em once'—and then scram as though the Devil were after you."[15]

An hour later, two B-17s of the 7th BG, flown by Lts. McPherson and Casper attacked the same small convoy, reported to be one large ship accompanied by four smaller ones. Very heavy antiaircraft fire filled the sky as the two dropped eight 300-kg bombs from 26,500 feet. Although clouds obscured the strike, a second pass showed that the bombs had landed close to the large ship, which was now stopped dead in the water.[16]

Although the B-17s had tried to sink the ships, it was probably best that they had missed. In all probability, the targeted ships were what was left of the Allied navy in Java, out looking for the Eastern Invasion Force. The 7th BG historian noted, "It is not known whether or not the ships bombed . . . were ours."[17]

All four 19th BG planes that had bombed the unidentified ships were ordered to land at Djogjakarta instead of Singosari, which was under constant air attacks. 5th Bomber Command had finally decided to abandon Singosari in favor of Djogjakarta. "It was out of the frying pan into the fire," wrote Lt. Teats, "for the field at Djogjakarta was expecting a raid any time." Within a short time the air raid alarm sounded and Teats and the others took to the sky. Although the raid turned out to be a false alarm, the airborne crews happened to spot a large formation of Japanese planes off to the west. Upon their return to Djogjakarta they were informed that the USS *Langley*, America's first aircraft carrier, had been sunk in the Indian Ocean. "We had no doubt whatever that this big formation which we had seen and evaded was that which bombed the Langley . . ." Teats wrote.[18]

By the end of the day, only two officers and 10 enlisted men were still at Singosari destroying everything that had to be abandoned. "When we were forced to leave . . ." Teats recorded, "a clean-up crew of our men demolished all of our property which could not be taken out or repaired." Hoping to prevent the Japanese from learning anything about any of the big American bombers, one damaged LB-30 and four crippled B-17s were set on fire and destroyed. Among those burned were B-17Es (41-2478) and (41-2498) which had been set on fire by the Japanese on February 20. On February 27, the American clean-up crew completed the job.[19]

That night, the small convoy of Allied naval vessels met the Japanese in the Battle of the Java Sea, one of the few ship-versus-ship battles in World War II. By the time the sun rose on February 28, half of the Allied ships had been sunk and the others had been scattered. Japan had only one destroyer damaged. Later, the American cruiser *Houston* and the Australian cruiser *Perth* were sent to the bottom when they ran into the Western Invasion Force. Although both ships managed to sink or damage about a dozen transports, the Japanese juggernaut rolled on.[20]

Utilizing the cover of darkness, three B-17s from the 7th BG left Madioen for one more strike against the Eastern Invasion Force. Before reaching the area however, Capt. Preston, B-17E (41-2449), turned back with faulty guns but Lts. Skiles, B-17E (41-2417, *Monkey Bizz-Ness*), and Evans, B-17E (41-2464, *Queenie*), went on.[21] Sgt. Reeves, Lt. Evans' bombardier, wrote, "We came in at 28,000 watching this first ship [Skiles] plunking direct hits on two parallel strings of transports—seventeen in each string . . . with fifteen or twenty naval craft circling them."[22]

Dropping his own bombs, Reeves recalled, "From that altitude there isn't much to see when they first crack the deck. There's a little pause, then there's the sweetest geyser of deck splinters, and foam, and machinery, and Japanese infantry corporals you'd ever hope to gaze down at." The two B-17s sank one transport and damaged another. Returning to Madioen, they reported the number of ships they had sighted.[23] It was no mystery what the Allies were up against.

That night, one LB-30 and three B-17s, loaded to the rafters with personnel, evacuated more men to Broome.[24]

At 12:20 A.M., on March 1, 1942, Japanese troops finally set foot on Java. The Eastern Invasion Force landed on the north shore, about 100 miles west of Soerabaja, while the Western Invasion Force landed on the northwest coast near Batavia. Almost immediately, one B-17E from the 19th BG and one LB-30 from the 7th BG left Djogjakarta, and five B-17Es from the 7th BG started out from Madioen to hit the Eastern Invasion convoy. At the last minute, just as Capt. Hardison was about to take off from Madioen, his bombardier became violently ill. Quickly scrounging up another, Hardison took off an hour after the others.[25]

Lt. Beran, B-17E (41-2489, *Suzy-Q*), arrived first, at 2:30 A.M., and aided by a full moon, dropped a train of bombs from 7,000 feet atop two transports, scoring a direct hit on one and possibly the other. Fifteen minutes later, Lt. Barr, B-17E (41-2461, *El Toro*) arrived. Meeting a heavy barrage of antiaircraft fire, Barr dropped his bombs on the transports from 10,000 feet. As he circled around, his tail gunner noticed two ships on fire.

At 3:00 A.M., a newly promoted Capt. Smelser, B-17E (41-2449), arrived. Meeting "intense" antiaircraft fire, Smelser went up to a higher altitude and attacked from 15,000 feet. Results of his high altitude bomb run were listed as "uncertain." After a 35-minute respite, Lt. Beck, B-17E (41-2417, *Monkey Bizz-Ness*), came in. Running into the same heavy antiaircraft fire, Beck went over the convoy three times from varying heights. He too had to report, "Results unknown." When he arrived back at Madioen, Beck discovered that he had a "busted tailwheel" but landed without incident.[26]

Lt. Vandevanter, B-17E (41-2507), piloting the only B-17 from Djogjakarta, reached the target while Beck was making his second run. He recalled, "As my plane was the last tactical airplane in commission [in the 19th BG], I ran a night mission against this convoy. We could not see the convoy at first until we were fired on by antiaircraft guns. Then we picked them up clear enough for the bombardier to see them through the bomb sight because of a brilliant moon." Hoping to get under the umbrella of heavy antiaircraft fire, he came in at only 4,000 feet. "However," he remembered, "as we approached the target they were obscured by clouds so we lined up on the flashes of antiaircraft fire and dropped our bombs. The results are unknown."[27]

After the lone LB-30 failed to locate the convoy, Capt. Hardison arrived at 5:00 A.M. At least an hour behind the others, Hardison discovered that the Japanese had already quit firing their antiaircraft guns and that the clouds had obscured the moon. Having trouble pinpointing the enemy ships, Hardison flew back and forth over the area in an attempt to goad the Japanese into turning on one of their spotlights and revealing their position. Unfortunately, the Japanese would not cooperate. Forced to wait until sunrise, Hardison and his crew spent a nervous hour flying up and down the northern coast of Java.

Finally, around 6:00 A.M., Hardison spotted the enemy vessels and dropped a few bombs on a 10,000-ton transport, scoring a direct hit. As the transport began to sink, Hardison returned to let his replacement bombardier drop his remaining bombs. Remembering the Japanese attacks on the crews of Capts. Kelly and Dufrane as they hung helpless in their parachutes, Hardison's aerial gunners strafed the surviving Japanese as the B-17 passed overhead. Already, the war in the Pacific had turned vicious. Despite antiaircraft holes in the floor, side, and one wing, Hardison's B-17 returned safely to Madioen without any casualties.[28]

At 9:00 A.M., still hoping to damage the Japanese Eastern Invasion Force, Lts. McPherson and Casper took off from Madioen but Casper soon developed engine trouble and turned back. Lt. McPherson, B-17E (41-2417, *Monkey Bizz-Ness*), carried on and went over the convoy at 30,000 feet, dropping eight 300-kg bombs in the midst of the transports. His crew reported a direct hit on one ship and waterline hits on another.[29]

Near 2:00 P.M., Zero fighters struck Djogjakarta and caught two LB-30s on the ground, damaging both beyond repair. Fifty minutes later, when another air raid alarm sounded, Lt. Mathewson took off in B-17E (41-2507) to get his bomber off the field. Finding himself with a fully loaded bomb bay, Mathewson elected to try one more strike against Bali. Unknowingly, he was about to fly the last B-17 bombing mission from Java.

Reaching Bali at 5:50 P.M., Mathewson sighted two destroyers and four transports off the south coast and roared over at 25,000 feet, dropping four bombs on one destroyer and four bombs on a transport. The bombs missed the destroyer but bracketed the transport, which began to smoke. As he started for home, two enemy fighters raced up to give battle. The combined defensive fire from the Fortress guns chased one fighter away almost immediately but the other kept up a running battle for fifty miles before breaking away. With nobody injured, Mathewson was back at Djogjakarta by 8:00 P.M. The last B-17 mission from Java was over.[30]

By the time Mathewson returned to Djogjakarta, the field had a different look to it. Near 2:00 P.M., Col. Eubank had received orders to destroy Madioen and Djogjakarta and move back to Singosari. Knowing that Singosari was still receiving daily air raids, Eubank refused. It was time to pull out of Java, not move to another airfield.

Still hoping to prevent the Japanese from capturing a heavy bomber to study, Eubank issued orders to destroy any plane that could not make it to Australia. Three LB-30s and three B-17s were summarily destroyed. At Singosari, B-17D (40-3061) was put to the torch, while at Djogjakarta, B-17E (41-2471) was destroyed, and at Madioen, B-17E (41-2483) was burned.[31]

Things were happening rapidly all over Java. At 6:00 P.M., Col. Eubank left and flew to Australia on B-17E (41-2507) piloted by Lt. Vandevanter. With the removal of Eubank, the Dutch decided to blow up the airfields to keep them from falling into Japanese hands. "We had to use all of our persuasion that night on the Dutch," recalled Lt. Teats. "They wanted to blow one of the runways, leaving only the other one. We were afraid that the debris tossed up by the demolition would riddle our planes, which were scheduled to leave just before midnight with the last of our remaining personnel."[32]

Only two Flying Fortresses were still at Madioen when the Dutch began to destroy the field. Sgt. Reeves and his fellow crewmen were refueling their bomber by hand when the destruction began. ". . . [A]ll of a sudden came a terrific Bang! it shook the ship so badly it knocked one guy off the wing, and he fell face-down on the field," Reeves wrote. Unable to see in the darkness, the airmen thought it was another air raid. "But no. Oh, no!" Reeves continued. "It was just the methodical Dutch, carefully scorching the earth by blowing up our ammunition dump . . . It seemed the order had just come through to evacuate, because the Japs were coming . . ."[33]

It wasn't until 2:00 A.M. March 2, that the two B-17s finally took off for Australia. "As we climbed for altitude," Reeves reminisced, "we could see refineries flaming all over the island—fires and explosions— and as we circled the field in the dark for the last time, the Dutch down below us threw a switch and blew up [the] beautiful new concrete hangar." Despite having no brakes on the right main wheel, Sgt. Reeves' bomber successfully carried 24 men out of Java.[34]

The other bomber that took off from Madioen was flown by Lt. McPherson and was in worse shape. B-17E (41-2417, *Monkey Bizz-Ness*) had been brought back from bombing the Eastern Invasion Force with a "busted tail wheel." With no spare parts or planes to cannibalize, the crew improvised. After fashioning a wooden tail skid braced with cable, the crew loaded everybody aboard and successfully took off. After landing at Darwin and finding that the skid was still in good condition, McPherson took off again and managed another good landing at Melbourne.[35]

At Djogjakarta, quick talking by the Americans had also bought them some time. "We managed to persuade the Dutch to hold up their demolition until we got off . . .," Lt. Teats remembered. "At that time, our planes were in such bad condition that a maximum safe load of 20 personnel to each plane was established." However, unwilling to leave anyone behind, the pilots jammed as many people as they could into each bomber. Late on the night of March 1, Lts. Teats and Green each carried 25 people to Broome while Capt. Godman took 32.[36] When two LB-30s left Djogjakarta a few hours later, the military evacuation of Java was complete.[37]

A total of 16 B-17Es had been evacuated from Java.[38] Added to the remaining B-17C (40-2072) and the two B-17Ds, (40-3079, now nicknamed *The Gazelle*) and (40-3097), from the Philippines, and 10 newly arrived B-17s from the 14th RS, which were at Townsville, on the east coast of Australia, a grand total of 30 Flying Fortresses were on Australian soil after March 1. However, perhaps only one half of that number were in combat flying condition.

A total of 32 B-17s had been lost in Java. Twenty-two planes were either strafed or bombed during Japanese air raids and/or destroyed during the evacuation, six were destroyed during landing accidents, and four were shot down by the Japanese. Although the Flying Fortress was considered the best heavy bomber in the world, it continued to take a beating as the Japanese moved almost unabated across the Southwest Pacific.

For their undaunted courage in the face of overwhelming odds, both the 7th and 19th BGs received the Distinguished Unit Citation for actions against ". . . enemy aircraft, ground installations, warships and transports during the Japanese drive through the Philippines and Netherlands [East] Indies."[39]

When the Americans left Java the Japanese rushed onto the different airfields intent on capturing a B-17E. After the evacuation of Clark Field in the Philippines, the Japanese had managed to piece together a B-17D, using spare parts and the body of (40-3095), which had been destroyed on December 8. In late 1942, B-17D (40-3095), marked with the Rising Sun of Japan, flew to Japan for further study.

Rushing onto the Java airfields, the Japanese found mostly battered, burned and twisted wreckage. However, at Djogjakarta, B-17E (41-2471) was found to be missing only its nose and all four engines. The Japanese quickly went to work, salvaging parts from a dozen other damaged planes. At the same time, the Japanese attempted to put together three more B-17Es. Almost a year later, two B-17Es were flown to Japan. "We got a tremendous kick out of flying the bomber," remembered Saburo Sakai, who flew the plane in January 1943, "which impressed us with its excellent controllability and, above all, the precision workmanship of its equipment. No large Japanese airplane I had ever seen was in its class."

For the next two and a half years the planes were studied as the Japanese attempted to learn the secrets and characteristics of the B-17. However, when Japan was occupied by American forces in August 1945, the three captured planes, B-17D (40-3095), B-17E (41-2471) and one unidentified B-17E, were nowhere to be found. Their final fate remains a mystery.[40]

When the battered veterans of the 7th and 19th BGs arrived in Australia, they were surprised to find that a squadron of B-17s was working out of Townsville. After the Japanese capture of Rabaul on New Britain, Adm. Chester W. Nimitz, commander-in-chief of the Pacific Ocean Area, reacted quickly. On February 9, Nimitz assigned 12 B-17s from the 7th Air Force in Hawaii to Naval Task Force 11. The next day, six planes from the 88th RS and one from the 38th RS, all of which had flown into Hickam on December 7, and five from the 22nd BS, which had been the first reinforcement squadron to arrive in Hawaii, left Hickam under the overall command of Maj. Carmichael. Designated the 14th RS, their instructions were to move south and protect the vital supply line to Australia.[41]

Island hopping to the Fiji Islands, the 12 planes flew 16 missions over 5 days from Fiji and then moved on, landing at Townsville, Queensland, on February 18 and 20. One of the copilots was Lt. Fields. "We were very well received by the Australians," wrote Fields, "because they thought that their great saviors had arrived when we tooled in there in these first B-17Es that they had ever seen." The airmen were based at Garbutt Field, an Australian airbase outside Townsville, and housed in comfortable barracks.[42]

Unfortunately, Garbrutt lacked friendly fighter cover and antiaircraft guns which forced the Americans to disperse their planes into the interior to protect them from unexpected enemy raids. The two dispersal fields were at Charter's Towers, about 50 miles southwest of Townsville, and at Cloncurry, about 300 miles west. "The Japs couldn't find Cloncurry," Fields noted, "we could barely find it, and we were friendly." Unfortunately, the two dispersal fields were rather primitive and the men were constantly harassed by hoards of flies. "Flies were much more than plentiful and we were constantly fighting them," noted Fields. The only recreation the Americans had at Cloncurry, beside the local movie theater, was hunting kangaroos. "I'll say this," wrote Fields, "we hunted them; we saw them, but I never had the good fortune to kill one. I couldn't hit them, they bounced up and down so."[43]

On February 20, the 14th RS was to fly its first mission, a joint venture with the US Navy, against the captured harbor of Rabaul but the raid was called off when the naval convoy was discovered and attacked by Japanese aircraft. On February 22, however, the orders to hit Rabaul came through again.[44]

Headquarters planned for the B-17s to attack the ships in Rabaul's Simpson Harbor, (1,200 miles away), refuel at Port Moresby, New Guinea (only 525 miles from Rabaul) and then return to Townsville (750 miles from Port Moresby). It was supposed to be a maximum effort but due to the lack of maintenance personnel, only nine planes were deemed capable of making the long raid. Then, as Lt. Rawls, B-17E (41-2434), was taxiing into position, his left wing tip cracked into the No. 4 engine and right wing of Lt. Bostrom's B-17E (41-2416, *San Antonio Rose*). Both planes were scratched from the raid. *San Antonio Rose* was damaged beyond repair and immediately became a donor plane so that B-17E (41-2434) could fly again.[45]

Then, when 1st Lt. James R. DuBose, Jr., developed engine trouble and had to drop out, only six B-17s headed towards Rabaul in two three-plane elements.[46] Led by Maj. Carmichael, the planes took off at midnight, hoping to attack at dawn and catch the Japanese by surprise. About 90 miles out from Townsville the flight ran into a severe tropical storm which forced 1st Lt. Harry E. Spieth, in the second element, to turn back. Only five Flying Fortresses flew on to stage the first Allied bombing raid on Rabaul.[47]

Somehow, the second element, consisting of Capt. William Lewis, Jr., and Lt. Eaton reached the target first. Flying over at 20,000 feet at 6:47 A.M., the two pilots found Simpson Harbor closed in by heavy clouds and steam from a nearby volcano. "After circling the target for 25 minutes," Capt. Lewis reported, "we found an opening at [the] north end of [the] harbor and dropped our bombs toward a 10,000-ton cargo vessel . . ." While Lewis managed to drop his bombs, Lt. Eaton, B-17E (41-2446), had trouble releasing his bombs and was forced to make a second pass, thereby losing contact with Lewis. On his second bomb run, Eaton's plane was hit by an antiaircraft shell which passed completely through the right wing without detonating. Though unsure of the results of their strike because of the clouds and volcanic steam, the two planes had managed to sink one cargo ship and damaged one other. As the two B-17s turned to leave a dozen Zeros raced up to intercept them.[48]

Now far behind Capt. Lewis, Lt. Eaton was caught by the Zeros over Gasmata, on the southern coast of New Britain. While Lt. Eaton took evasive maneuvers, his crew shot down two Zeros and crippled another. Cannon fire however pierced the rudder of the B-17 and somehow inflated the left life raft, stored in a compartment outside of the bomb bay. The left waist gunner had to shoot it full of holes to deflate it.[49]

By the time the Zeros flew away, Eaton was nearing New Guinea. Realizing that he could never get enough altitude with his damaged plane to get over the dangerous Owen Stanley Mountain Range that ran across the center of New Guinea, he began looking for a safe spot to land. Low on fuel, he set B-17E (41-2446) down in Agaiambo Swamp, 220 miles short of Port Moresby. Even though the plane was not badly damaged, it would never fly again. Five weeks later, the malaria-thinned crew returned to Australia.[50]

After Lewis and Eaton went over Rabaul, the first element finally showed up. After each plane dropped their four 600-lb. demolition bombs through the clouds and steam, the planes were headed towards Port Moresby when they too were jumped by enemy fighters. 1st Lt. Raymond T. Swenson's bombardier was slightly wounded, and even though only two bullets entered Carmichael's plane, the radio operator and tail gunner were both slightly wounded. 1st Lt. Harry N. Brandon, B-17E (41-2408), however, ran into the most trouble. One of his engines was set on fire and the other one on the same side suddenly stopped. After extinguishing the fire, Brandon managed to get his third engine working again and reached Port Moresby. All four remaining B-17s, including Capt. Lewis' plane, were quickly refueled and back at Townsville by 2:30 P.M.[51]

The first mission against Rabaul was only a minor success but it afforded combat experience to five crews and was a "shot in the arm" for both the fledgling American aircrews and to the Australians themselves. Since the beginning of the war the Australians had been pulling back from one forward base to another until they had been pushed almost all the way back to Australia. Without adequate long range bombers, the Australians had been forced to wait for the United States to try and stem the rush of the Japanese. Although small in scale, this first offensive strike against Rabaul did much to bolster the morale of Americans and Australians alike.

The February 23 attack by the 14th RS on Rabaul can be considered the first 5th Air Force (5th AF) bombing mission of World War II. When ABDA Command was dissolved and Gen. Brett assumed command of 5th AF on February 23, the 7th and 19th BGs were still in Java, flying missions with any available plane, and with aircrews made up of personnel from each group. On the other hand, the 14th RS was flying as an integral new squadron. This integrity earned them the right to claim that they formed the backbone of Gen. Brett's 5th AF and to argue that they were the first of the 5th AF units to reach Australia and fly the first 5th AF bombing mission of World War II.[52]

The next mission for the 14th RS was scheduled for February 28 but had to be canceled when six crews were weakened by dengue fever. Dispersing the planes to Cloncurry, the ailing individuals were sent to a hospital in town. Soon, parts of 10 crews were sidelined and by March 5, one-sixth of the personnel were laid up.[53]

What Japanese planes and bullets could not do, an infectious disease could—laying waste an entire squadron.

By March 8, a sufficient number of men felt well enough to begin operations again. The day before, the Japanese had landed unopposed at Lae and Salamaua, on the coast of British New Guinea. Wanting to disrupt the embarkation of troops, the 14th RS struck the shipping off Salamaua on March 8 and 9, and both communities on March 11. The March 11 mission was flown in connection with the U.S. Navy. After carrier-based planes bombed the shipping at Lae and Salamaua, eight 14th RS B-17s arrived. "The chief purpose of the mission," Walter Johnson, now a first lieutenant, wrote, "was to cover up for the navy while their planes returned to the carrier." The combined attack sank two enemy ships and left another four burning. The 14th RS damaged one transport and scored a near miss on a destroyer. Two Zeros were damaged and two more were shot down, one by a tail gunner on Capt. Thacker's B-17E (41-2432, *The Last Straw*), and one shared by two side gunners on Capt. Maurice C. Horgan's B-17E (41-2435).[54]

Planning to deal Rabaul another blow, five planes from the 14th RS moved up to Seven Mile Airdrome, located seven miles from Port Moresby, New Guinea, on March 12 to be 2½ hours closer to the target. "[W]e lived in grass huts that the natives had built," Lt. Fields wrote, "and flew off of a field that was metal stripping placed on swampy ground." Aviation fuel was stored in 55-gallon drums that had to be brought to Port Moresby by ships and floated to shore. A hand pump was used to pump the fuel into each plane. "We could use the fuel transfer pump from the aircraft itself," Fields remarked, "but we didn't like to do this because we might need that fuel transfer pump in flight and we didn't want to wear it out . . ."[55]

Another problem with Seven Mile Strip was its proximity to the Equator. "The moment we let down to land we felt the humidity," stated 2nd Lt. James T. Murphy (63rd BS, 43rd BG) who flew into Port Moresby at a later date. "When we arrived and got out of the airplane, each of us immediately soaked our clothes with perspiration." The high humidity quickly rotted fabric and wood. "When we set up our tents for a temporary stay, we thought we were fortunate to have wood floors," Murphy went on. ". . . But we found that the wood would mildew and rot almost overnight . . . Dry washcloths and towels were unheard of."[56]

Being a tropical island, New Guinea was drenched by daily rains during the rainy season. Sgt. Green remembered, "[I]t rained a lot which became a big problem keeping clothing dry . . . [and] with the very high humidity you were wet most of the time." Likewise, metal parts were subject to the rain and high humidity. Lt. Murphy noted, "Metal rusted so rapidly you could almost see it become useless in a day. Our only salvation was to keep it greased and covered."[57]

Leeches and insects were also a big problem in New Guinea. Whenever the men bathed in the nearby streams they came out covered with leeches. "They were extremely hard to dislodge from the skin," wrote Murphy. "We later found only one means to have them quickly separate and that was put a rag with

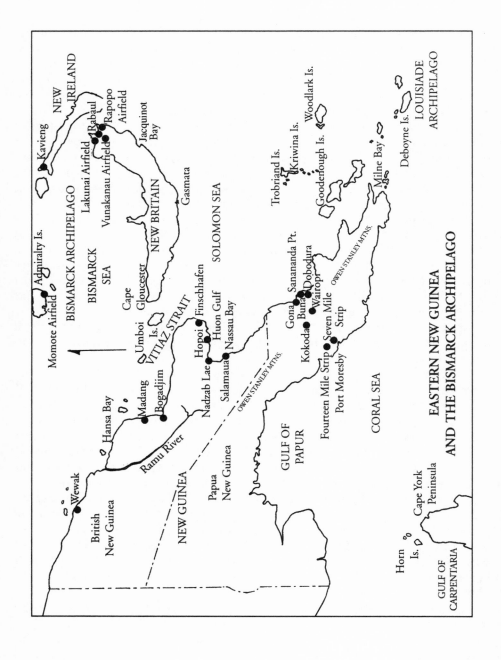

EASTERN NEW GUINEA AND THE BISMARCK ARCHIPELAGO

kerosene on them. That was effective, but it was hard to remove both the odor and the skin blemish."[58]

Sgt. Green remembered the insects. "Many of the insects in the jungle was [sic] the type that they wanted to suck blood," he wrote, "and the only way you could get any relief was to put finger nail polish on them, but it caused sores." Along with the ever-present mosquitoes, ticks were a big concern at Port Moresby. "Those ticks were very thirsty," Green said, "and the only way to get them off was to place a cigarette to them and they would back off. A lot of man hours were lost by sickness . . . I was a victim of malaria, dengue fever and amebic dysentery all at one time and lost 54 lbs. in 5 weeks . . . Somehow I always ended up in some godforsaken place . . ."[59]

On Friday the 13th, Capt. Lewis, B-17E (41-2435), led five B-17s of the 14th RS out of Port Moresby at 2:30 A.M. Although the planes attempted to assemble over the airfield, bad weather interfered and four planes turned back. Believing that the others were headed towards Rabaul, Capt. Lewis climbed to 21,000 feet and followed. Flying through "very rough weather" that caused one of his engines to throw oil, Lewis pushed on. Reaching Rabaul and nearby Vunakanau Airfield at 6:55 A.M., he circled and waited for the others. Finally, nobody having shown up, he started his bomb run.

Forced to make two runs after his bombs failed to release on the first pass, Capt. Lewis dropped seven 300-lb. bombs on 16 enemy bombers parked wing tip to wing tip along the runway. Two bombs landed directly on the parked planes, while the others hit nearby, damaging the Vunakanau runway and other parked planes. In all, 12 Japanese bombers were destroyed.

Low on fuel after buffeting the bad weather, Capt. Lewis landed at Port Moresby but discovered that an enemy air raid was expected. His crew loaded just enough fuel by hand to get them to an emergency airfield on Horn Island, off the northern tip of Australia's Cape York Peninsula. Taking off again, Lewis had a hard time locating Horn Island. He began circling, finally finding it on the third try. After landing and refueling a second time, the B-17 left Horn Island and arrived at Townsville at 8:30 P.M., 18 hours after starting out. For his Friday the 13th solo mission, Capt. Lewis was awarded a DFC.[60]

On March 14, the 14th RS, still at Townsville, were made a part of the 19th BG, which was now stationed at Melbourne.[61] Three days later, four crews from the 14th RS were called on for a very important mission. The 19th BG was going back to the Philippines.

During the evacuation of Java, the surviving airmen and airplanes of the 7th and 19th BGs flew to Broome. As quickly as they came in however, they went out. Commented Lt. Teats, "My plane, loaded to the guards, hit Broome just at sunrise, refueled immediately, and went on through to Perth on the southwest coast of Australia, 7½ hours and 900 miles in a direct airline farther south." On March 2, realizing that Broome was within easy reach of the Japanese and was untenable as a forward airbase, 5th Bomber Command directed all of the evacuated airmen to report to Perth and then to Melbourne, as soon as possible.[62]

Hundreds of men, women and children, all being evacuated from Java, almost doubled the population of Broome. "This place looks like La Guardia Field at its busiest," Lt. Rouse commented. "The entire small airdrome is covered with [planes]." As Teats explained, "The Dutch were flying civilian evacuees, principally women and children, out of Java, and the Aussies were picking them up at Broome and flying them on south . . ."[63] Such a tempting target was not about to be overlooked by the ever vigilant Japanese.

Near 10:00 A.M., on March 3, the Japanese struck. In a devastating attack, nine Zero fighters suddenly appeared out of nowhere and tore into the crowded airfield and harbor. One B-24 was shot down while taking off with 34 people aboard. Only one man survived. For a full 15 minutes the Zeros continued to deal death and destruction. When it was finally over, 33 airmen and 45 civilians were dead, and 22 planes had been destroyed, including B-17E (41-2449) and B-17E (41-2454, *Craps for the Japs*). The Japanese lost one plane.[64]

Fearful of another raid, 5th Bomber Command ordered all of the B-17s that had already gone on to Perth to go back to Broome to rescue the remaining airmen. Five or six pilots set out immediately. After picking up everyone that they could find, the planes flew south to Perth and then, on March 4, flew on to Melbourne, the new home of 5th Bomber Command.[65]

Located on the extreme southeast corner of Australia, Melbourne was far removed from any Japanese air raid or impending invasion. At Melbourne, the battered Flying Fortresses of the 7th and 19th BGs could be repaired at Laverton Repair Depot, while the men recuperated. For the next few weeks, the men of the two groups were given a chance to rest and rebuild their morale. After three months of constant warfare, the men of the 19th BG were finally being given some time off.

Fortunately, the tired aircrews found welcome relief at Melbourne. Working at Laverton Repair Depot were the squadron personnel from a brand-new heavy bomb group, the 13th RS of the 43rd BG (Heavy). Originally trained with B-17Ds at Bangor, Maine, the men of the 13th RS had left from Boston by ship on January 18 and had reached Melbourne on February 26. Arriving without planes, the men were put to work at Laverton Depot trying to repair the battle damaged and war-weary planes of the 7th and 19th BGs. "Working under the more experienced men," the 13th RS historian wrote, "the new men whose total schooling in aircraft engineering had been theoretical lectures on the boat coming over, came across like champions and performed wonderfully. Everyone—engineers, armorers, radio maintenance men—worked night and day to put the ships [i.e. planes] in operating condition."[66]

After Java, the 7th and 19th BG aircrews found life in Melbourne more to their liking. Far removed from the horrors of war, military discipline became lax. Low on morale, feeling as though they had been forgotten by the people of the United States, and with many of their key officers siphoned off to India, most of the men took residence in Melbourne hotels and loafed around, ignoring all things military. "Slept for 12 hrs. last night," Lt. Rouse wrote in his diary on March 6. "Feel better now. First real city I have seen since leaving the States. Nothing to do except loaf around." On March 9 he wrote, "Still loafing." On March 10, "Loafing." On March 11 he visited an amusement park.[67] Rouse's inactive lifestyle was typical of most of the men of the 7th and 19th BGs during the first two weeks of March 1942.

After arriving at Freemantle aboard the *Abbekerk*, the ground crew personnel of the 7th and 19th BGs were taken by train to Melbourne, "a tiresome three-day trip . . ." At Melbourne, the men were sent to a tent city set up in the middle of Royal Park, an Australian horse race track. "We arrived in Freemantle, Australia on March 4, 1942," recalled Mike Payne. "We were sent to a race track in Melbourne where we signed our name, rank and serial number. They had no correct record of us."[68]

On the night of March 2, a handful of American servicemen waited at Andir Airfield near Bandoeng, Java, for a B-17 to pick them up. Although almost everyone from the 7th and 19th BGs had been evacuated from Java, a few men had stayed behind to destroy Army files. Assembling at Andir Field, the men waited in vain for a plane that never arrived. In actuality, Capt. Schaetzel and Lt. Green, flying out of India, reached Java as scheduled but when the agreed-upon flares were not lighted, they turned back. Perhaps, however, in the darkness, they had failed to find the small airfield and were actually circling the wrong area.[69]

While most of the men gave up hope, T/Sgt. Harry Hayes decided that he was not going to spend the rest of the war as a Japanese prisoner. Looking over three shot-up and damaged B-17s at Andir, Hayes found that B-17E (41-2460), which had been mauled on January 25 on a mission against Balikpapan, was salvageable. With the help of native laborers he managed to repair most of the damage and completely rebuild two engines. Although he had doubts about one engine, he declared the plane ready for flight and went in search of a pilot.

Even though American civilian pilot Gerald L. Cherymisin, and Dutch air officer Lt. Sibolt J. Kok had never flown a B-17 before, Sgt. Hayes managed to talk them into flying as pilot and copilot, respectively, on his rebuilt Fortress. On the night of March 4, Cherymisin and Kok took the controls, and with the help of Hayes as flight engineer, lifted off from Andir Field. Flying on only three good engines, and carrying a total of 18 refugees, including Cherymisin's Dutch wife, B-17E (41-2460) flew for eight hours and made a safe landing at Port Hedland, Australia.[70] B-17E (41-2460), flown by a makeshift crew, was the last B-17 to evacuate Java.

XII

To The Rescue

ON MARCH 11, after weeks of ignoring direct orders to leave the Philippines, Gen. MacArthur finally relented. Wanting to wait until it was psychologically beneficial to his beleaguered troops on the Bataan Peninsula, MacArthur waited for the situation to stabilize before pulling out. By March 11, the Japanese had settled into defensive positions opposite the Allied lines. Along with his wife and young son, the son's nurse, and a few staff members, MacArthur climbed into one of four waiting PT boats and left Corregidor, heading south towards Mindanao and Del Monte Airfield.[1]

On Bataan, the airmen from the 19th BG who had not been evacuated to Mindanao or Australia had been put to work as infantry soldiers fighting side by side with the American and Filipino troops.[2]

Capt. Ralph L. Fry, the executive officer of the 5th Air Base Group in the Philippines, reported on the activities of the 19th BG personnel on Bataan: "Some continued to service the few remaining pursuits, [i.e. fighter planes] which were based on Bataan Airfield . . . The remainder of the Air Service personnel was used as infantry on Bataan, along with the ground echelon of tactical squadrons." He admitted, "Few were evacuated."[3]

Lt. Carpenter, in charge of a group of airmen and infantry, recalled that they were bombed repeatedly while on Bataan, and were all "pretty well fed up with it." On one occasion, Carpenter witnessed a Japanese Banzai charge. "The Japs came out of the woods across a clearing squeaking and yelling and were mowed down." From the very start the men were put on half rations and as time went on the rations were cut to one-fifth. Lacking fresh beef, the airmen slaughtered the Philippine carabao. In less than four weeks time, Carpenter lost 20 pounds. Fortunately for him, at the end of January he and 23 fellow Army and Navy airmen were evacuated to Java by submarine.[4]

Very few members from the 14th BS ever got out of Bataan, prompting the 19th

BG historian to admit, "The records of the War Department have officially declared that the 14th BS was not evacuated from the Philippine Islands." Almost equally as unfortunate were the men from the 28th BS. Although a few men were evacuated to Mindanao, most of them were stranded at Del Monte. The 28th BS historian declared, "Of the men left in the Philippines [on both Bataan and Mindanao] belonging to the 28th Squadron only 25 officers and 12 enlisted men reached Australia alive."[5]

A large number of airmen from the 30th BS had been left on Bataan and suffered from disease and malnutrition along with everyone else. Wrote Sgt. Kimmerle, "The general health of everyone was getting worse and worse. Malaria and malnutrition was taking its toll. The food by March was issued in quantities that was far from being enough to keep anyone fit . . ." In spite of being sick and hungry, the personnel from the 30th BS assisted in successfully repelling a Japanese amphibious landing that tried to circumvent the Allied lines on January 23.[6]

Likewise, the men from the 93rd BS also saw heavy action on Bataan. Fighting under the command of Maj. "Moe" Daley, the ground crews from the 93rd were "attempting to hold a bridge against armored Japanese forces," when the enemy started their final push. Reported the 19th BG historian, ". . . Maj. Daley was able to withdraw with the bulk of the Squadron to Signal Hill, Bataan for a final stand."[7] Nothing further is written about the men of the 93rd BS on Bataan.

By the end of December 1941, after the 19th BG took their planes down to Australia, Del Monte was a ghost town. Sgt. Kimmerle noted, "Only a small number of men were required to carry on the work of the Air Corps at this time as there were so few planes left and all the rest [of the men] were assigned to infantry units." Issued rifles, the men were moved to strategic locations around Mindanao to help combat the Japanese invaders.[8]

In spite of Japan's success in the Philippines, Del Monte stayed open. Well equipped with American 100-octane gasoline, which had been delivered before the start of the war, Del Monte was able to fully refuel every heavy bomber, small evacuation plane, and occasional fighter plane that made its way to Mindanao.[9]

The first major effort to evacuate the stranded airmen came on January 20. [See Chapter Seven] Twenty-three officers were taken out by five B-17Es. A week later, an LB-30 and a B-24 flew into Del Monte with critically needed medical supplies and ammunition and carried out 40 enlisted men and two officers. On February 4, another LB-30 and B-24 flew into Del Monte and picked up a group of Air Force personnel, including 10 officers and 11 enlisted men from the 19th BG. For the next few weeks, an LB-30 or B-24 would show up unexpectedly with a cargo of much needed supplies and take off with a handful of evacuees.[10] However, the most important evacuation flights were yet to come.

On March 11, three B-17Es from the battered 19th BG and one from the 7th BG moved from Melbourne to Daly Waters for "a special mission to the north." Wrote Capt. Godman, B-17E (41-2507), "That was all the instructions that I was given . . . The planes were really in terrible shape." Moved to Batchelor Field at

Darwin, the four crews were finally told about their mission—they were to fly much needed arms and ammunition into Del Monte and bring out Gen. MacArthur and his family and staff.[11]

Intending to reach Del Monte after dark, the planes started taking off near noon on March 12. Right from the beginning the flight ran into trouble. Lt. Casper, B-17E (41-2452), in the lone 7th BG B-17, developed engine trouble and did not even attempt a takeoff, while Capt. Adams, B-17E (41-2486, *Lady Lou*), experienced difficulties with his engines and turned back after going only fifty miles. The other two planes, flown by Godman and Lt. Pease, B-17E (41-2453), continued on even though Pease lost the use of his hydraulic system which in turn rendered his superchargers and brakes inoperative. With the loss of his superchargers, Pease was forced to fly at low altitude through airspace literally crawling with Japanese.[12]

Flying individually, Capt. Godman had been flying for four hours when his crew chief began transferring the gas in the bomb bay fuel tank to the half-empty wing tanks. By mistake, the chief did just the opposite, suctioning the gas from the wing tanks into the already full bomb bay tank. Looking into the bomb bay Godman saw, ". . . gasoline cascading in niagara proportions out of the overflow, down the sides of the tanks, and into the bomb bay and out into the atmosphere." By the time the mistake was corrected, the damage had been done. Having already passed the half-way point, Godman had no choice but to continue on and hope he had enough gas to reach Mindanao.[13]

Reducing power on his engines to get maximum range, Capt. Godman coaxed B-17E (41-2507) along as best he could. As night descended, Godman took the plane lower. "There was no moon, just the ugly overcast of clouds," he recalled. "The night was just black, black, black." Spotting the irregular coastline of Mindanao, Godman flew around the island to approach Del Monte from the north. He wrote, "Just as I leveled the airplane out and started a descent, we hit the water at 170 miles an hour with the altimeter reading 1,200 feet!" Without warning, the B-17E hit the still waters of Iligan Bay, bounced into the air and then slammed back down nose first, killing two of the gunners in the rear.[14]

Godman's navigator, 2nd Lt. Carl E. Epperson, recalled, "I was thrown on impact into the nose of the airplane and knocked unconscious for a moment. My back was severely strained and ribs were broken." Feeling warm water dripping in on him and realizing that the plane had crashed, Epperson, although partly paralyzed, swam up to the flight deck.[15]

Capt. Godman wrote, "We hit so hard that the parachute on [my co-pilot] Lt. Carlisle broke open." Although Carlisle's feet were tangled in the shroud lines of his parachute, and the flight deck was quickly filling with water, he remained calm, dove under water, and untangled his feet. Once untangled, Carlisle slipped easily through the right-hand side window.

In the meantime, Capt. Godman had crawled through the left-hand cockpit window and inflated his "Mae West" life vest. Looking back into the flight deck, he spotted Lt. Epperson and helped pull the half-paralyzed man from the sinking plane. "We turned around," Godman recalled, "and saw the airplane slowly getting perpendicular, and then slowly the tail disappeared."

B-17E (41-2507) sank about one mile off shore. Slowly Godman and the other surviving crewmen began swimming through the shark-infested waters towards shore. "All of us were scared to death," confided Godman, who was helping his injured navigator. "We realized that at any moment the sharks could hit and that our stroking, kicking, and bleeding certainly were not helping." Four exhausting hours later, all five survivors finally reached shore.[16]

Lt. Pease, B-17E (41-2453), was not faring much better. Forced to fly at an extremely low altitude past enemy infested islands, Pease finally reached Del Monte well after dark, setting down near 11:00 P.M. Upon landing, Pease had to ground loop his plane because of the failed brakes. When Maj. Gen. William F. Sharp, Senior Commander on Mindanao, saw the youthful appearance of Pease and the battered look of the B-17E, he had second thoughts about sending Gen. MacArthur to Australia with Pease and B-17E (41-2453).

When Pease discovered that MacArthur was not yet present, and was not expected for at least another 12 hours, he spoke to Gen. Sharp and expressed concerns about exposing his bomber to daylight air raids. When he suggested that he be allowed to leave with a planeload of evacuees and send another plane back for MacArthur, a relieved Gen. Sharp quickly agreed. Unloading the much needed ammunition and arms, Pease took aboard 16 AAF passengers and returned safely to Australia, again having to ground loop B-17E (41-2453) to bring it to a stop.[17]

On March 13, upon reaching Del Monte, MacArthur went into one of his highly publicized tirades when told that there was no Flying Fortress ready to take him to Australia. Immediately MacArthur sent a dispatch to Washington requesting that the best plane and crew in the whole Pacific, or in the United States for that matter, be sent to Del Monte with all haste.[18] It was now time for the 14th RS, the newest member of the 19th BG, to go to work.

Between March 4 and March 14, plans were laid for the reorganization of the 19th BG. On March 14, the 7th and 19th BG evacuees were officially combined and reorganized into the 19th BG, with a newly-promoted Lt. Col. Hobson, the surviving senior officer of the 7th BG, placed in command. At this same time, the independent 14th RS, still at Townsville, was officially assigned to the 19th BG. Personnel and equipment from the 22nd BS were "relieved from assignment" with the 7th BG and transferred to the 14th RS while crews from the 9th and 11th BSs/7th BG, along with the surviving members of the 28th BS/19th BG, were banded together to form a reorganized 28th BS. When it was all said and done, the newly reorganized 19th BG consisted of the HqS, the 28th, 30th and 93rd BSs, and the 14th RS.[19]

In the process of reorganization, the highly decorated 14th BS, which had been among the first units to move to the Philippines, almost ceased to exist. Members of the squadron were parceled out to the other units of the 19th BG, and the 14th BS was assigned to the 7th BG, which was reorganizing in India. With no planes or personnel, the 14th BS existed only on paper while in India and was never manned. Years later, James Edmundson wrote, "So one of the most illustrious and decorated squadrons of WW II got dropped between the stools and no longer exists today. The 14th Sqdn. is the lost squadron of the Pacific War."[20]

Also on March 14, a newly-promoted Capt. Skiles was landing at Daly Waters in B-17D (40-3079) when his No. 1 and No. 2 engines suddenly quit. Hitting hard, two men were killed and four others, including Capt. Skiles, were badly injured. B-17D (40-3079), a veteran of the Philippines, was completely destroyed.[21]

Two days later, four B-17Es from the 14th RS left Townsville for Batchelor Field. There, the crews were augmented by four experienced airmen from the 19th BG who climbed aboard as copilots. "We were to fly up to Del Monte," Lt. Teats recounted, ". . . and bring out MacArthur." The 5th Bomber Command had decided to send the fresher crews and newer planes of the 14th RS to retrieve Gen. MacArthur and wanted someone to go along who knew the area. "The four of us making the trip as copilots had operated from the field at Del Monte on many occasions," Teats went on, "the crews and pilots [from the 14th RS] had never been there. It was a tricky place to find and safely approach, even in good weather, without knowledge of the surrounding terrain." Taking off at 2:00 P.M. on March 17, the men hoped to reach Del Monte by midnight.

Like the first rescue flight, things went wrong from the beginning. Again, two planes developed engine trouble and could not even get off the ground but Capt. Lewis, B-17E (41-2429, *Why Don't We Do This More Often*), and Lt. Bostrom, B-17E (41-2447, *San Antonio Rose II*), took off without difficulty. Although the pilots knew the intent of the mission, the crew members did not until the planes were airborne. Commented Bostrom's tail gunner, PFC Herbert Wheatley, "It is always nice to know when one is designated as a volunteer. We were well aware of how the war was going [in the Philippines]. To me it looked like a one way trip . . ."[22]

Without incident Lt. Bostrom, with Lt. Teats as his copilot, reached Del Monte first and a short time later, near midnight of March 17, Capt. Lewis landed safely.[23] Surprisingly, there to meet the airmen was Capt. Godman. After swimming ashore, Godman had found his way to Del Monte. After seeing that his crewmen were taken care of, Godman had gone for a personal interview with Gen. MacArthur. Afraid of being left behind, Godman told MacArthur his story and requested permission to be evacuated from Mindanao.

Wrote Capt. Godman, "He looked at me and paused for a moment with his long corncob pipe held securely in his hand, and he said, 'Godman, anybody as lucky as you who can crash at night into the sea at 170 miles an hour and live to tell about it can work for me'." It was the start of a long friendship. Godman would indeed be evacuated, and before long would become MacArthur's private pilot.[24]

Knowing that the Japanese were swarming about Mindanao, the B-17 crewmen were anxious to be on their way. "We wanted to leave the minute we could refuel and get the personnel and cargo aboard," wrote Teats. Quickly Gen. MacArthur and his wife and son, the son's nurse, and a few of his staff members boarded Lt. Bostrom's plane. Recalled Pvt. Wheatley, "In almost total darkness it was hurry, hurry."[25]

While Bostrom's plane was being loaded, the rest of the staff was trying to fit into Capt. Lewis' bomber. Having expected four planes, the evacuees suddenly realized that someone would have to stay behind. Assured that a third B-17 would be up in a few days, a few of the men agreed to wait and stepped back from the two planes.[26]

Still, a few of the stranded airmen from the 19th BG tried to talk their fellow airmen into smuggling them aboard. At least one airman managed to sneak aboard Capt. Lewis' plane. Capt. Godman's copilot, Lt. Carlisle, had made his way to Del Monte and was looking for a quick ride back to Australia. With the help of Godman, Carlisle sneaked into the tail gunner's position of the B-17. "Now this position in the airplane was not supposed to have anyone in it during take off or landing," Godman wrote, "because it was at the extreme end of the airplane and would be a very dangerous place to be in case of any accident." Realizing that the added weight in the tail would throw off the delicate balance of the plane on takeoff, Godman whispered to Lewis that Carlisle was in the tail and Lewis quietly adjusted the trim tabs.[27]

With the planes fully loaded, the two pilots were all set to take off when Lt. Bostrom suddenly experienced trouble. "[O]ur number three engine wouldn't catch," recalled Pvt. Wheatley. Afraid of running down the batteries, Bostrom sent Wheatley and another crewman out to use the long handled inertia crank. On the second try, the engine caught and B-17E (41-2447, *San Antonio Rose II*) started down the runway. "[W]e dropped the crank and ran for the door," Wheatley said. "If there had been three of us somebody would not have made it."[28]

Although Capt. Lewis, B-17E (41-2429, *Why Don't We Do This More Often*), also experienced engine trouble both planes were airborne by 2:30 A.M. For the next eight hours, the tired pilots and copilots, who were flying from Australia to Mindanao and back without sleep, took turns flying the big planes. Near 10:30 A.M., March 18, the two B-17s finally reached the Australian coast and a few minutes later set down at Batchelor Field.[29]

Grateful to be back on the ground, Gen. MacArthur, who did not like airplanes, decided to go to Army Headquarters at Melbourne by train. However, when he discovered that the closest rail depot was at Alice Springs, in the very center of Australia, he and his family and staff were forced to take one more flight. Climbing aboard a couple of transport planes, the general and his entourage were soon on their way to Alice Springs and Melbourne.[30]

On March 18, while Gen. MacArthur was being flown out of the Philippines, Lt. Chaffin, B-17E (41-2408), finally managed to take off from Australia and reach Del Monte. At 10:30 P.M., he left Del Monte with 21 evacuees. "From the tiny cubby of the tail gunner to the glass-cased nose, the big bomber is an unbroken mass of men and baggage," recalled Col. Allison Ind, one of MacArthur's stranded staff members.[31]

Eight hours later, Lt. Chaffin, assisted by Capt. Adams as his copilot, landed at a secret airfield in northern Australia for more gas. Once refueled, the plane started on the 1,900 mile flight over the center of Australia to Melbourne. Less than halfway there, however, Chaffin ran into strong headwinds. Slowed by the strong winds, Chaffin began to watch his gas gauges while his passengers began to watch for any sign of civilization. "This is the great interior," Ind wrote, "a vast and terrifying desert where a forced landing would have meant almost certain disaster through inexorable thirst and starvation."

Almost everything that could go wrong did go wrong with Chaffin's flight across central Australia. First he hit the heavy headwinds, then his navigator found that he had faulty equipment that put him 40 miles off course, then, when the heading was corrected, the B-17 ran into a heavy rain storm that interfered with the radio signal when Chaffin tried to contact Melbourne. Low on fuel, and now flying through the dark of night in a pounding rain, Chaffin eventually found Melbourne but had to circle the field twice when he had trouble finding the runway and almost ran into some buildings and trees. On his third try Chaffin finally set B-17E (41-2408) down, only to find that he had once again missed the runway.

Col. Ind recalled, "The big 17 heels, rights, and seems for all the world to be trying to pitch herself over her own nose." When the plane finally stopped and the engines were cut, the grateful passengers and crew gave a collective sigh of relief. Wrote Col. Ind, "We simply tumble out onto the mud beneath the bomber, safe, safe—safe!"

Miraculously, Chaffin had landed down the center of a wide, deep ditch. "It is a problem to get out, even for a man," wrote Ind, "not to speak of a huge twenty-ton airplane with a wing span of one hundred and twenty feet!" The next morning, the local Australians built a special ramp and towed B-17E (41-2408) out of the ditch.[32]

Gen. MacArthur, his family, and staff had been successfully evacuated from the Philippines, due in large part to the skill and devotion of the men of the 14th RS of the newly reorganized 19th BG. They had managed, with the help of the veteran 19th BG copilots, to make a 1,500 mile flight ". . . almost entirely over open seas, through enemy controlled air, and through an area beset by tropical storms." In spite of a lack of sleep for at least two days, the crews had managed to carry MacArthur out of harm's way.[33]

On April 5, every single member of the five aircrews, including the crews of Capt. Godman and Lt. Pease, was awarded a DFC. Thirty-eight DFCs, (two posthumously), were passed out to the men who ". . . had completed a mission of tremendous service to the Allied Cause." Wrote 1st Lt. Bob Roy Carruthers, Lt. Bostrom's navigator, "We had delivered our precious cargo safe and sound and we all felt pretty swell about it."[34]

On March 30, the Pacific Ocean was divided into two Allied commands. Gen. MacArthur was placed in command of the Southwest Pacific Area which included the Philippines, the Netherlands East Indies, the Bismarck Archipelago, New Guinea and Australia. Admiral Nimitz was made commander of the larger Pacific Ocean Areas, which included the mostly water-filled Pacific area west to the 160th meridian. Subsequently, Nimitz's domain was sectioned into the North Pacific, the Central Pacific, which included the Hawaiian Islands, and the South Pacific. Although he had been forced to flee the Philippines, the Allied commanders had shown their faith in MacArthur's ability and tenacity by keeping him in Australia and putting him in charge of the volatile Southwest Pacific Area.[35]

After the successful rescue of Gen. MacArthur, three aircrews from the 14th RS assembled at Townsville on March 26 for another special mission. Moving up to Batchelor Field to refuel, Lts. Spieth, DuBose and Ted S. Faulkner took off in the middle of the afternoon and headed for Del Monte Field to rescue Philippines President Manuel Quezon.[36]

Instead of sending the same crews and bombers that had just recently rescued Gen. MacArthur, headquarters elected to send three new crews but had sense enough to send along the experienced navigators from the MacArthur mission. "The crews were changed," navigator Lt. Carruthers noted, "with the exception of the navigators who were chosen a second time for it was figured that they would have less trouble finding the place, having once been there."[37]

Running into a tropical storm, the three planes were forced to alter course a bit but managed to reach Mindanao without incident. "We were scheduled to land during the hours of darkness, which we did," recalled Lt. Fields, copilot for Lt. Spieth. "They had no lights on the runway, with the exception of smudge pots which they lit for us to line up on . . . These were old highway markers that looked like a bomb, a black smudge pot that burned diesel fuel." Once the planes were on the ground, the smudge pots were quickly extinguished.

In total darkness, the planes were serviced and the crews ate. After President Quezon, his wife, two daughters and family nurse were taken aboard Lt. Faulkner's B-17, priority was given to any remaining members of Gen. MacArthur's staff. Like before however, some of the stranded airmen from the 19th BG tried to get aboard the planes. "People were crying, wanting to be smuggled aboard," Fields remembered, "and we told them we couldn't take them; that we didn't have parachutes for them. They would say, 'Well, don't worry about a parachute; I don't need one; I won't use one.' Anything to get on that plane and off that island." In all, Lt. Spieth took aboard 17 passengers, including a couple of Filipino generals.[38]

When the planes were full, the Fortresses took off immediately for Darwin. "We flew 32 hours out of 36," Lt. Fields recalled. Reaching Batchelor Field on March 27, the planes were quickly refueled and took off for Alice Springs, where President Quezon and the others would catch a train to unite them with Gen. MacArthur.[39]

On the way to Alice Springs however, Lt. Dubose's B-17, carrying President Quezon's nurse, suddenly ran out of gas and made a forced landing in the desert. Search planes set out immediately but the downed bomber was soon spotted by Lt. Faulkner, who was still carrying President Quezon and his family. Landing beside the stricken bomber, Faulkner transferred some fuel to DuBose's plane and both pilots were soon on their way to Alice Springs. "You can imagine the concern of Gen. MacArthur," Capt. Godman wrote, "especially because of his own dislike for flying, listening to the stories the president of the Philippines was telling about his forced landing in the Australian desert."[40]

Once again each member of the three crews was given a DFC or Oak Leaf cluster in lieu of a second DFC. Still, in place of medals, the aircrews wished for another chance to go back and rescue more of their stranded airmen. "The crews would have jumped at the chance to fly back there again," wrote Lt. Carruthers. "There was something about these flights that made them quite different from the routine bombing missions that we were engaged in at our base."[41]

The 19th BG would fly many more routine bombing missions before ever going back to the Philippines. But they would go back.

On March 28, the rest of the 43rd BG, the other heavy bomb group in Australia, finally reached the continent. On February 18, the air and ground personnel from the 63rd, 64th and 65th BSs, along with other troops, had set out from Boston Harbor for an undisclosed destination aboard the converted luxury liner H.M.S. *Queen Mary*. Noted the historian for the 64th BS, "Finally, after thirty-nine days of English food, storms, views of Rio and Capetown, calisthenics, boat drills and sub scares, the ship arrived in Sydney, Australia . . ." Having traveled completely around the tip of Africa, the trip covered 19,000 miles.[42]

Arriving at Sydney, the 43rd BG, minus the 13th RS which was still working on the planes of the 19th BG at Laverton Repair Depot, set up camp on the grounds of Randwick Race Course. "As no cots were available, the men slept on straw and blankets on the floor." Arriving without any B-17s, the historian wrote, "Calisthenics, a few hours of military drill each day, an occasional lecture, and the job of keeping the area clean, constituted our daily tasks as the group had no airplanes at that time."[43]

Although Sydney turned out to be a relative haven for the men of the 43rd BG they soon learned that the town literally shut down on Sundays. "Here Sunday was truly a day of rest," admitted the 63rd BS historian. "After a while the American officials did succeed in having a law passed to allow one theater to be open each Sunday evening for men in uniform." Of course, the most interesting thing in Sydney was the Australian girls. "The men found the Sydney girls very friendly and some of them were married while there," commented one squadron chronicler. Perhaps noting the high rate of unwed mothers in town after the airmen left, the historian added, "Others should have married."[44]

It was not only the 43rd BG personnel that had fun with the girls of Sydney but also the airmen from the 19th BG, who were sent to Sydney for rest and recuperation. Mechanic Mike Payne recalled, "Along about this time some of the crew took R & R in Sydney. That's when Felix Hardison decided to fly under Sydney harbor bridge with an Aussie girl as co-pilot." Hardison had been drinking and fortunately, the attempt was never made. "He had to turn around because a boat got in the way . . . he probably couldn't have made it."[45]

While at Randwick Race Course the 43rd BG was plagued by fleas. "There was an epidemic of fleas while we were in Sydney and many of the men were a mass of red welts from these vicious specks," wrote a squadron historian. Around the end of April the bomb group received cots to sleep on and happily burned the straw and blankets that they had been sleeping on. Unfortunately, the fleas remained. As the 63rd BS historian wrote, "They went merrily on."

Food was another problem at Randwick. The food, mostly mutton and bread, was considered "poor" by some individuals and the long mess lines were almost unendurable. After standing in line to retrieve their meal, and then eating the unfamiliar food, the men were forced to wash their mess kits in dirty, usually cold water. Luckily, most of the men managed to supplement their Army diet by purchasing a steak or a milkshake in town. In time however, the rarity of Australia wore off. "By the middle of April," noted a squadron historian, "the men were pretty well used to the new customs. . . . Traffic keeping to the left, open trams, intermissions at the movies, and mutton were now commonplace things."[46] Still, the 43rd BG had no planes and the men of the newly reorganized 19th BG continued the war without them.

XIII

Victory at Last

WHILE MOST OF the men of the 19th BG were granted a period of rest and relaxation, the 14th RS, at Townsville, continued to work, becoming the only heavy bombardment unit in operation in Australia until April.[1]

On March 18, three B-17s from the 14th RS attacked the ships in Rabaul's Simpson Harbor again. Coming in at 31,000 feet, the planes met a blanket of heavy but inaccurate antiaircraft fire. "[Y]ou thought they were accurate," admitted Lt. Fields, copilot with Capt. Spieth, "because you didn't know where the antiaircraft was until it exploded and you saw the smoke, and when you saw that smoke, the fire, the danger was over. They made it look like it was pretty close always." Lining up on a 6,000-ton cruiser, Spieth's bombardier laid his bombs squarely across the stern. "[It] was the first time we had been over Rabaul . . .," said Fields. "We didn't learn until the next day how much damage we had inflicted on this cruiser, but we found out on March 19th that we had hit it pretty severely. It was a high altitude attack, about as high as a B-17 would go."[2]

Keeping the pressure on, the 14th RS returned to Rabaul on March 19 and 20, and then changed targets, attacking enemy aircraft installations at Lae, New Guinea, on March 21. Coming in without warning, the Fortresses destroyed 17 Japanese planes on the ground and returned to Australia without any damage to themselves. Four days later, while three crews were on their way to Mindanao to rescue President Quezon, a flight of B-17s bombed Koepang on Timor. On March 27, the 14th RS aircrews, who had been repairing and servicing their own planes, received some much needed help from the ground crews from the 22nd BS/7th BG. Having been evacuated from Java, the mechanics had been absorbed by the 19th BG during the reorganization. Almost as important, the men brought with them some much needed supplies and parts for the rapidly aging B-17s. Closing out the month of March, the 14th RS staged another successful strike against Simpson Harbor.[3]

162

While the 14th RS was keeping busy, the rest of the 19th BG was getting ready to move out of Camp Royal Park in Melbourne. On March 23, advance elements of the group moved to Cloncurry, one of the dispersal bases previously used by the 14th RS. Although the men were led to believe that Cloncurry would be "completely equipped and ready for immediate occupancy" they found it sorely lacking in everything. "They found only a few half-finished buildings," wrote the historian, "no facilities for housing men or equipment, a temperature of 103 degrees in the shade, endless clouds of red dust, and hordes of flies."[4]

Over the next two weeks the rest of the group moved up to Cloncurry. Like the men from the 14th RS before them, the men from the other squadrons of the 19th BG found Cloncurry to be "pretty desolate." Although the town reminded some men of a sleepy little town in the western United States, Lt. Rouse summed it up by writing, "All it is is a railway junction." In time, Cloncurry was dubbed, "The Bush Base."[5]

Instead of the Japanese fighter planes that had plagued the men in Java, mosquitoes seemed to be the big problem at Cloncurry. "The mosquitoes were a constant bother," recalled Sgt. Green. "At night if you wanted a good nights sleep, a mosquito bar [holding aloft a mosquito net] was necessary and if your bare body came in contact with the netting, you had a big red spot on you with an infection coming if you did not medicate it." Likewise, Sgt. Green remembered the desert snakes. "[I]t was always a good habit to wear boots all the time," he wrote. "I almost got nailed by a 6 foot cobra."[6]

However, it was the ever present hoards of flies that plagued everyone the most. "[T]he flies were terrible," wrote Capt. Boris M. Zubko (28th BS). "They covered your back so heavily you thought you were wearing a black shirt." Lt. Gooch recalled that at Cloncurry, ". . . we contended not only with the Japanese but also with dust and flies." Although he admitted that the flies looked like ordinary house flies, they were not. "They didn't concentrate on garbage and food, but on people and animals. All day long swarms of them would alight on us and stick there. They wouldn't fly away with a swat, they had to be wiped off."[7]

In early 1942, Gen. Hap Arnold had issued a directive stating that the two heavy bomb groups presently in Australia, the 19th and 43rd, should maintain a minimum of 40 planes per group. In order to achieve this number, plans were made to send two bombers to Australia each day, beginning about March 20. However, a breakdown occurred almost immediately when the Hawaiian Department refused to release any Fortresses until they had built up their own allotment. When the War Department in Washington decided to temporarily suspend all movement of heavy bombers to Hawaii and Australia "pending reconsideration of allocations of this type of aircraft to all theaters," the trickle of B-17s from the States halted. By the end of March, the Southwest Pacific had received only nine bombers from Hawaii.[8]

Forced to wait for new planes, the 19th BG began a period of reorganization and retraining. Wrote the historian for the 28th BS, ". . .a rigorous training schedule was initiated which included navigator, bombardier and pilot training, gunnery and turret practice, radio operation training, physical training and other courses designed to bring the [group] to a high peak of fighting efficiency."[9] Slowly but surely the fighting edge was being honed back onto the 19th BG.

When not training, many of the men took up kangaroo hunting. On April 3, Lt. Rouse wrote in his diary, "Went kangaroo hunting tonight in a jeep. Never laughed so hard in my life. 5 of us in [a] jeep. 2 with rifles all with 45's . . . Went tearing along with everybody firing . . ." Unfamiliar with the jumping movement of the kangaroos, the airmen found them very difficult to hit. Lt. Knudson wrote, "They are very wild, and it is almost impossible to hit one on the run, jump I mean . . ." Still, the men continued trying.[10]

On April 7, Brig. Gen. Ralph Royce, Gen. MacArthur's staff operations officer, inspected the bombers of the 28th BS. Although unknown at the time, Royce was undoubtedly inspecting the planes to see if they were capable of flying back to the Philippines. On Good Friday, April 3, the Japanese troops on Bataan had launched a major offensive which easily broke through the thinly held Allied lines. By April 9 in order to stave off further bloodshed, 76,000 troops were surrendered into Japanese hands.[11]

Although Bataan had fallen, the Allies still held Corregidor and small sections of Mindanao, including Del Monte Field. In an attempt to bolster the sagging morale of the remaining defenders, and show them that they were not forgotten, Gen. MacArthur had decided to send a strike force back to the Philippines. Gen. Royce's inspection tour of April 7 was undoubtedly undertaken with this mission in mind. However, perhaps after seeing the condition of the 19th BG B-17s at Cloncurry, Royce decided to send only three Fortresses to Mindanao and supplement them with B-25 Mitchell medium bombers.

At 11:00 A.M., April 11, Lts. Bostrom and Rawls from the 14th RS, and Lt. Teats from the 30th BS lifted off individually from Batchelor Field. Flying with Lt. Bostrom, B-17E (41-2447, *San Antonio Rose II*), was Gen. Royce, who would personally command the vital mission.[12]

Late in the afternoon the three B-17s landed at Del Monte while 10 B-25s, utilizing long-range bomb bay tanks, flew into a fighter base about 60 miles away. When Bostrom touched down on Mindanao, he reported that one of his engines was inoperative and needed replacement. As the ground crews at Del Monte scrambled to find a new engine, Gen. Royce adjusted his plans accordingly.[13]

On the morning of April 12, the American bombers took to the air. The B-25s headed for a fleet of Japanese transports docked off the coast of Cebu Island. At the same time, Lt. Bostrom, flying Lt. Rawls' B-17, headed out to bomb Nichols Field, the former American fighter base near Manila, and Lt. Teats headed towards a Japanese convoy reported to be midway between Luzon and Mindanao. Arriving over Nichols Field, Bostrom caught the Japanese completely by surprise, scoring direct hits on the runway and a big, newly constructed hangar.[14]

Meanwhile, Lt. Teats found no sign of the convoy so he turned to hit Nichols Field, too. However, when he developed engine trouble that consumed gas at an alarming rate, he switched targets again and went after Batangas Airfield on the southwest tip of Luzon. Although he found the airfield deserted, he spotted a large cargo ship tied up to a nearby dock. Targeting the enemy freighter, one bomb hit the ship's superstructure and another hit almost dead center on the rear cargo hold. As Teats turned away, the entire stern of the vessel was engulfed in flames. "Three minutes later," Teats added, "as we were speeding towards Del Monte, the bombardier exulted: 'The whole damned ship blew up!' There was deep satisfaction in his fatigue-cracked voice."[15]

Arriving back at Del Monte, Teats found that Lt. Bostrom was already back and getting ready to go out on a second mission. Although Gen. Royce had hoped to send Teats out again also, the bad engine changed all that. Then, as the ground crews went to work to replace the defective engine, the air raid signal sounded. While everyone rushed for the safety of the slit trenches, two Japanese floatplanes flew over and dropped a string of bombs on the B-17s.

One bomb hit close behind Lt. Teats' bomber, cutting the elevator cables and riddling the fabric on the elevators and control surfaces, and another landed close to the Bostrom/Rawls plane, badly damaging the tail. Although both planes were repairable, the second mission had to be canceled.[16]

Then, while the planes were being repaired, the Japanese returned. Although a flight of American fighters tried to intercept, the Japanese managed to unload a few well placed bombs. Lt. Bostrom's original B-17E (41-2447, *San Antonio Rose II*) disintegrated in a flash of flame and smoke and the Bostrom/Rawls plane was further peppered with shrapnel. Only quick action by his crew saved the plane from being consumed by a grass fire.[17]

When Lt. Teats inspected his plane, he found that it too had been seriously damaged. "The shrapnel tore up the wings badly," Teats recalled, "the rear spar of the left wing was practically knocked out and there was a lot of damage to the sides all of the way back." The side cockpit windows on both sides of the plane had been shattered and the No. 4 engine oil tank had a hole in it the size of a man's fist. Foregoing sleep, Teats and his crew joined the small group of ground mechanics in attempting to get their plane airworthy again.

"With nothing but a pair of pliers, a screwdriver and their bare hands, that gang spliced the heavy control cables," Teats wrote glowingly of the mechanics. Scavenging a bullet riddled oil tank from an abandoned B-17, the men plugged the holes and used it to replace the damaged tank on Teats' plane. "They cut sections of metal from the skin of the old B-17 and covered up the worst rips in the wings and the tail section." By 3:00 A.M., April 13, the tired men had done everything they could. After running up all four engines, including the one that had been consuming gas, Teats decided to try to fly the plane back to Australia.[18]

While Teats' bomber was being repaired, the other crews tried to repair the Bostrom/Rawls plane. Although they managed to repair the damaged tail section, they discovered that the plane had faulty superchargers and a leaky hydraulic system. Without the hydraulics, there were no brakes. Unwilling to subject anyone to a questionable flight, the two pilots took off for Australia around 5:30 A.M., with only about half of their original crews. Although the battered plane managed to reach Batchelor Field without further trouble, the bomber had to be ground looped to get it to stop.[19]

A little after 6:00 A.M., Lt. Teats was ready to take off. "Dawn was our deadline," he wrote. "We had a badly damaged plane on our hands, and we were dog-tired." On board were 16 people, including his own flight crew and the leftover crewmen from Bostrom and Rawls. Just as Teats was about to take off, a Japanese floatplane flew over the far end of the field but missed sighting the battered B-17. When the enemy plane disappeared from view, Teats took off, skimming the tops of the trees to hide his silhouette from the searching enemy. Wrote Teats, "Gen. Royce later told [me] in Australia that the Japs came over and bombed the hell out of the field, just at dawn." The B-17 had gotten away none to soon.

Thirty minutes out of Del Monte, Lt. Teats lost the use of his finicky engine and was forced to feather the propeller. In addition to the dead engine, two other engines began running rough. "It was practically a miracle how that plane flew, considering its structural and engine weakness and the fantastic overload," Teats said. In addition to the mechanical problems with the plane, Teats' copilot, 2nd Lt. Theodore "Ted" Greene, had been hit in the back with a piece of shrapnel and was suffering from intense pain, forcing Teats to do most of the flying. In spite of all the handicaps however, Teats made it safely back to Batchelor Field.[20]

The B-17s returned to Australia on April 13 but the B-25s of the Royce Mission remained on Mindanao for another day, striking at the Japanese ships and installations at Cebu Island. In all, the B-17s and B-25s of the Royce Mission managed to sink four Japanese ships, damage almost a dozen more, bomb the airfield and installations at Nichols Field, and disrupt the conquest of Cebu. While the official cost to the United States was only one B-17, the Fortress flown by Lt. Teats was only good for spare parts.

Although the Royce Mission actually inflicted minimal damage on the Japanese it was a boost to the morale of the beleaguered defenders on Corregidor and Mindanao. It came at a time when they needed to know that Gen. MacArthur, and all of America, had not forgotten them. Regrettably, the Royce Mission was the last offensive action in the Philippines for the 19th BG. In less than a month, the Allied defenders would be forced to surrender to superior numbers.[21]

With the fall of Bataan on April 9 the only organized areas of Allied resistance in the Philippines were on Mindanao and in the central islands known as the Visayan island group. The Japanese immediately set out to finish their conquest of the Philippines. On April 10, starting with the island of Cebu, the Japanese invaded one small island after another until by the end of the third week in April the central Philippines was securely in Japanese hands. All that remained was the conquest of Mindanao.[22]

On April 29, a large invasion force landed on the west coast and drove inland in an attempt to link up with the forces already holding the southeast corner of Mindanao. Near the center of the island they ran into Allied resistance, including air and ground crew personnel from the 28th BS. More familiar with fighting a war from the air or with wrenches and pliers, the airmen gave ground and retired towards Del Monte.[23]

Already the final evacuation of Del Monte was under way. On the night of April 23, Lt. Mueller flew a B-17 filled with supplies into Del Monte and took out another planeload of passengers. As the Japanese drew ever closer, one last plane flew into Del Monte to evacuate the officers in charge. "On the 29th April 1942, I left Del Monte on the last airplane to leave the field," wrote Capt. Fry. Included on the last plane was Maj. Elsmore, who had managed to keep Del Monte open for so long in spite of the lack of fighter protection and antiaircraft batteries.[24]

On May 3, the Japanese landed on the north coast of Mindanao. Although the Allied troops, including elements of the 30th BS armed with rifles and fighting as infantry, put up stiff resistance, they could not stem the Japanese tide. By May 4, the defenders had been squeezed into three small areas, including the Cagayan River valley which was being defended by groups of stranded airmen from the 19th BG. On May 5, Capt. Mueller ran another evacuation flight up to Del Monte in a B-24A. Upon reaching the airfield, he circled a few times but did not receive the proper recognition signals. Trying two alternate fields Mueller ran into the same problem—no recognition signals. Finally, low on fuel, he headed back to Australia but never made it. Almost completely out of gas, he crash landed on an inhabited atoll, from which he and the crew were eventually rescued.[25]

On May 6, Corregidor surrendered. Although the surrender included the men on Mindanao, fighting continued on the island for four more days until it was finally realized that further resistance was futile. The Japanese were too numerous and there was no place to run. All of the surrounding islands had been either occupied by the enemy or were already under Japanese control. On May 10, Mindanao surrendered. After five months of hard fighting, the Japanese had finally conquered the Philippines.[26]

With the fall of Mindanao, the defenders were gathered together at Camp Casisang near Malaybalay in the center of the island. The men were told to bring all of their belongings, but the orphaned airmen and ground crews from the 19th BG who had evacuated Clark Field, then Bataan, and then Del Monte, had only the clothes on their backs. Eventually, the 19th BG survivors would suffer the same harsh treatment as all of the other Allied personnel taken prisoner in the Philippines.[27]

The heroic stand in the Philippines was an inspiration to Americans throughout the world. While the Allied forces were retreating all across the Pacific, the stubborn defenders in the Philippines had held on throughout the spring of 1942. By holding on for five months, the American and Filipino defenders had shown the world that the Japanese soldier was human and that he could bleed and die like everybody else.

On April 18, Gen. MacArthur was made overall commander of all Allied forces in Australia and quickly made the decision to go on the offensive. Intent on keeping the Japanese from reaching Australia, MacArthur intended to use his air force to harass the Japanese build-ups at Rabaul and along the northern coast of Papua

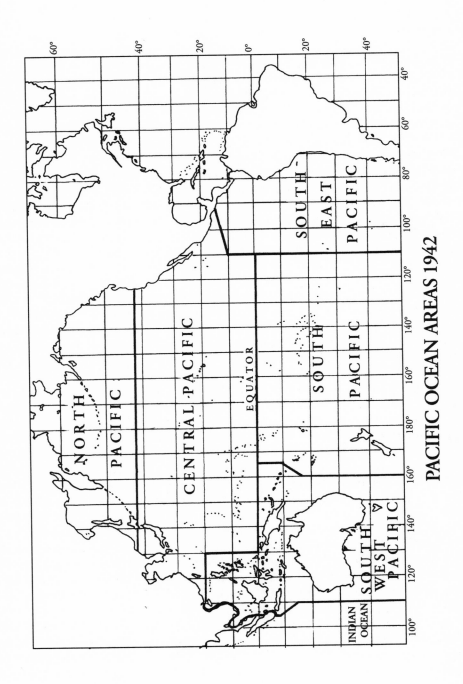

PACIFIC OCEAN AREAS 1942

New Guinea, and use his ground troops to stop the Japanese drive across the Owen Stanley Mountains. Two days later, the job of commanding all Allied air forces in the Southwest Pacific Area was given to Gen. Brett.[28]

Almost immediately Gen. Brett found that he was facing an almost impossible task of trying to defend Australia with the meager forces at hand. He had too few fighter planes to protect the entire coast of Australia so he concentrated most of his fighters around Darwin and along the northern coast, and used his reconnaissance planes to keep an eye on the eastern and western coastal waters.

Since his bombers were built as offensive weapons, Gen. Brett continued to base his B-17s in the interior of Australia, far away from the raiding enemy planes, and use Seven Mile Airstrip outside of Port Moresby as a forward staging field. Having only a few antiaircraft guns and a rudimentary air warning system, Seven Mile Strip could not be utilized as a forward airbase until the Allies won air superiority over New Guinea. The same enemy planes that could reach northern Australia, could easily reach Port Moresby. Crews caught on Seven Mile Strip during the day had to be ready to get their planes off the ground at a moments notice or risk losing them to a surprise Japanese air raid.[29]

On April 21, one day after Gen. Brett took command of the Allied air forces in the Southwest Pacific Area, the 14th RS was redesignated the 40th RS. Still the only active heavy bombardment squadron in Australia, planes from the newly named squadron continued to strike at the Japanese. Along with a few missions to Rabaul, the 40th RS flew a couple of missions over the Solomon Islands, and against Kavieng, on the northwest tip of New Ireland Island. Although a few reconnaissance missions were flown to close out April, the next bombing raid did not occur until May 2, when the 40th RS returned to Rabaul and sank a 10,000-ton freighter and damaged the main dock installation. Then, on May 5, the 40th RS was put on alert. Something big was brewing and excitement was in the air.[30]

The rest of the 19th BG was slowly coming back to life. On April 14, four brand new B-17Es (41-2636), (41-2641), (41-2653, *Craps for the Japs*), and (41-2655) arrived from the States followed three days later by two more (41-2621, *The Daylight Ltd.*) and (41-2657, *Old Faithful*). On April 15, the 93rd BS flew its first mission since its reorganization when a B-17 flew a photo-reconnaissance mission over New Ireland. "Observations were made but no enemy planes were encountered," reported the 93rd BS historian.[31]

On April 15, a newly promoted Lt. Col. Connally succeeded Lt. Col. Hobson as commanding officer of the 19th BG and immediately began sending his planes back out on strike missions. Even though planes from the 28th, 30th and 93rd BSs attempted a number of missions throughout the middle of April, consistently bad weather hampered their success. A lack of reliable data about weather conditions was one of the main factors in the failure of many missions. "[The] chief difficulty encountered in missions flown thus far has been weather . . . ," wrote Capt. John E. Dougherty (28th BS). "Difficulty is encountered in keeping formation on the way to [the] target because of weather." On April 24, the problem with data and communications was greatly improved when teletype equipment was installed at Cloncurry.[32]

One day later, weather played a fatal role in the loss of B-17E (41-2505), the first B-17 to be equipped with the manned Sperry ball turret. Flying at only 9,000 feet, 2nd Lt. Daniel W. Fagan slammed into the north side of Mt. Obree in the Owen Stanley Mountains, killing the entire eight-man crew. That same day, the Japanese caught Lt. Montgomery, B-17E (41-2461, *El Toro*), on the ground at Port Moresby. By the time the Zeros flew away, *El Toro* had to be relegated to the scrap heap as a donor for spare parts. On April 28, B-17s from the 93rd BS flew to Lae to repay the Japanese but found the area socked in by bad weather. A return to Lae the next day found the weather clear and the Flying Fortresses were able to drop their bombs, completely demolishing five Zeros and damaging four more.[33]

The build up of B-17s in Australia continued throughout the last week of April with four or five airplanes arriving at one time. By the end of the month there was a total of 40 B-17s in Australia, including two old B-17Ds. However, only about 20 were operational.[34]

On May 4, Gen. Brett divided his air forces into two commands. Command No. 1 was headquartered in Darwin and was responsible for the northwest area of Australia while Command No. 2, working out of Townsville, protected the northeast area. That same day, Brig. Gen. Martin F. Scanlon, the newly appointed commanding officer of Command No. 2, and Col. Connally went out as observers with Weldon Smith, now a captain, on a 19th BG raid on Rabaul.

Finding Rabaul closed in by weather, the B-17s detoured to their alternate target, the airdrome at Lae on northern New Guinea. While Gen. Scanlon and Col. Connally watched, the B-17s dropped their bombs on three Japanese planes. Returning to Cloncurry, the tired aircrews suddenly found themselves on immediate alert. On May 6, three aircrews were moved to Townsville to supplement the nine B-17s of the 40th RS that had been alerted the day before. The Japanese were making a major thrust towards Port Moresby and the 19th BG had been called upon to lend a hand to stop them.[35]

It was the intention of the Japanese to take Port Moresby with a bold amphibious strike from Rabaul. Massive air raids were staged against Port Moresby for eight of the 12 days prior to May 7. Meanwhile, on May 3, in an attempt to secure their left flank, Japanese troops moved down through the Solomon Islands and captured Florida and Tulagi Islands, near Guadalcanal. Tulagi was perhaps the more important of the two acquisitions, containing one of the best ship anchorages in the Solomons. Although the Americans attacked and managed to sink a few enemy vessels off Tulagi, the Japanese went ashore and within a few days had occupied both islands.[36]

The main Japanese invasion fleet, consisting of 11 troop transports and a number of lesser warships, and all covered by the light carrier *Shoho*, left Rabaul on May 4 and steamed towards the Coral Sea. At the same time, a strong naval force built around the carriers *Shokaku* and *Zuikaku*, which had sailed from Truk in the

Caroline Islands, circled around the Solomon Islands and approached New Guinea from the east. Thanks to the 40th RS reconnaissance flights, the Americans were well aware of the enemy build-up at Rabaul and, having broken the Japanese codes, knew exactly when the Japanese began their move, although they did not know their final destination. Hoping to turn back the Japanese, three American task forces, accompanied by the carriers *Lexington* and *Yorktown* quickly moved into the Coral Sea. Each side was hoping to spot the enemy first and sent out reconnaissance planes. For the Americans, that included the B-17s of the reinforced 40th RS.[37]

At 10:30 A.M., on May 6, Capt. Henry M. "Hotfoot" Harlow, and Lts. Wilber Beasley and Harry Spieth, scouting in three B-17s near the Solomon Islands, spotted the *Shoho* and her escorts and made a high altitude attack. "We sighted an aircraft carrier of the Japanese fleet and made a run on it," reported Lt. Fields, copilot with Spieth. In his diary Fields added, "Bombed on carrier, pursuit attacked us, A.A. fire, but no injuries on board." Although the B-17s inflicted no damage, one Japanese task force had been sighted. Immediately the B-17s crews reported their sighting and the American carrier force adjusted course. After the war, Rear Adm. Aritomo Goto, in command of the transports and the *Shoho* task force, admitted that this discovery by the B-17s eliminated all secrecy and meant that a battle in the Coral Sea was imminent.[38]

At 7:05 A.M., on May 7, a flight of B-17s took off from Townsville to bomb the small Japanese carrier. Lt. Rouse was flying one of the planes and noted, "Found plenty of Japs but no aircraft carrier." Having happened upon the transport fleet, the B-17s spent the next half hour flying over the vessels, avoiding their antiaircraft fire, and fruitlessly searching for the enemy carrier. When the ship could not be found the B-17s decided to attack the transports. "[The] leader, a 40th Sqd. man, finally gave signal to break formation and bomb ships singally [sic]," recorded Rouse. "Bomb sight went out so couldn't bomb. No one else hit anything. Should have bombed in formation. Impossible to hit maneuvering ship with one aircraft." The B-17s returned to Townsville, landing a little after 3:00 P.M.[39]

In spite of the B-17 attack, the Japanese appeared to have gained the upper hand on May 7 when a searching scout plane reported that it had found the American carriers. At almost the same time however, the American carriers received word that the Japanese flattops had finally been located. Each side quickly scrambled their planes only to find that both reports were false. With no enemy carriers in sight, both groups headed back to their respective ships.[40]

Then, by chance, a Japanese floatplane finally sighted the American task force and quickly sent back a message. For some unknown reason the main Japanese battle fleet did not receive the message but Admiral Goto did. While his transport group lagged behind, Goto moved into the Coral Sea with the *Shoho* and her escorts. As his airplanes began returning to refuel, a scouting 40th RS B-17 finally sighted the *Shoho* through a break in the clouds. Luck had run in favor of the Americans this time as the radioman flashed out the location of the Japanese carrier.

Already in the air, the planes from the American carriers struck with vengeance. At 11:00 A.M., the Americans attacked with torpedoes and bombs, and by 11:35, the *Shoho* keeled over and slipped beneath the waves of the Coral Sea. The *Shoho* was the first Japanese aircraft carrier of any kind to be lost in World War II.[41]

While the Navy planes were attacking the *Shoho*, the B-17s from Townsville went after the heavily laden transports. Having returned from their earlier attack, eight B-17s were quickly refueled and rearmed and took to the air again. Flying in two three-plane, and one two-plane element, the flight was cut to three equal flights of two planes each when two pilots turned back with engine trouble.[42]

Flying at 25,000 feet, the B-17s found the transport fleet near the Louisiade Archipelago and immediately came under antiaircraft fire. "We could see the convoy clearly," reported Lt. Teats, whose crew was one of the three 19th BG aircrews that had been rushed to Townsville to augment the 40th RS. "All [the] ships were maneuvering wildly in all directions, like an aggregation of excited water-bugs." As the air erupted around the B-17s, the pilots took evasive action. "Neither before nor after have I seen such heavy and well placed antiaircraft fire as those cruisers and destroyers threw at us. We could see the orange flashes as the ships' batteries fired. Things grew hotter and hotter." Due to the high altitude bombing, the heavy antiaircraft fire, and the wild evasive maneuvers of the ships, only one 8,000-ton transport was damaged by the B-17s.[43]

While the Fortresses were returning to Townsville, three of the aircrews suddenly spotted a large task force below. As the men watched, they could see bombers attacking the ships. "We were coming in at about 18,000 feet and could see some planes flying below and diving at low level," Lt. Fields wrote. Knowing that there were medium bombers in the area, the B-17 crews thought that the planes below them were American planes attacking Japanese ships. "The Navy had told us that everything north of a certain parallel would be enemy, and everything south of a certain parallel would be friendly," Fields remembered. "We were north of this certain parallel . . . so we lined up on the battleship that they were bombing and dropped our bombs on it. It turned out that it was the Australian flagship *Australia*, and the planes that we saw diving were Jap bombers."[44]

Although the Allied ships sent up a wall of antiaircraft fire, neither side scored any hits. "We didn't hit the *Australia*, luckily, and they didn't hit us . . ." Fields reported. When the Australian commander complained about the B-17 attack, he said, "Fortunately their bombing, in comparison with that of the Japanese formation minutes earlier, was disgraceful."[45]

Another one of the three aircrews that was attached to the 40th RS was Lt. Habberstad's. Returning on his own, Habberstad, B-17E (41-2652), became lost in the growing darkness and ran out of fuel. When he ordered his crew to bail out, he did not know whether they were jumping out over water or land. Luckily, they all landed safely on land, only 25 miles from Townsville, but B-17E (41-2652) crashed near Ewan, Queensland, Australia, and was completely destroyed.[46]

As May 7 drew to a close, the Japanese, who had finally located the main

American carrier group, attacked through a series of rain squalls and storm clouds but did no damage. Unwilling to commit their ships to further night attacks, both the American and Japanese commanders refueled and rearmed their airplanes and waited for daybreak.[47]

Even before dawn on May 8, the B-17s from Townsville were in the air, searching for the evasive main Japanese task force while keeping an eye open for the transport fleet. At almost the same time, the commanders of the opposing carrier groups sent out their own search planes. At 8:15 A.M., an American Navy pilot finally spotted the main Japanese carrier force. Almost immediately all of the American carrier-based planes were in the air. In spite of heavy cloud banks, which effectively hid the *Zuikaku*, the American planes located the *Shokaku*. Although 66 American planes were shot down, the attackers caused enough damage to *Shokaku* to send her limping back to Truk for immediate repair. At almost that same instant however, less than 200 miles away, the two American carriers came under attack by the Japanese.

Having located the American carriers, the Japanese struck both ships at once, inflicting major damage to the *Lexington*, but only slight damage to the *Yorktown*. Having lost 70 planes, the Japanese broke off the attack believing that both ships would eventually sink. Accepting the claims as fact, and happy to still have both the *Shokaku* and *Zuikaku* afloat, the Japanese headed back towards Truk, at the same time notifying the transport fleet and the covering fleet of their intention.[48]

Although badly damaged and listing to port, the crew of the *Lexington* eventually managed to bring the ship back to an even keel. Then, a tremendous explosion tore through the center of the ship and started an uncontrollable fire. As the carrier burned, the order was given to abandon ship. Near 10:00 P.M., an American destroyer fired a number of torpedoes into the *Lexington* and sent her quickly to the bottom.[49]

While the planes from the two opposing carrier groups were going at each other, the transport covering fleet, minus the sunken *Shoho*, came under attack from the B-17s again. Located far north of the Louisiade Archipelago, the 13 enemy ships were attacked by the Flying Fortresses from high altitude through a fusillade of antiaircraft fire. "No damage by our bombs," recorded Lt. Fields. Unable to score any hits, the planes returned to Townsville as the Japanese fled back to Rabaul.[50]

Although the Battle of the Coral Sea was effectively over, the Americans did not realize it. Still believing that the Japanese ships were in the area, hidden by the heavy weather, and still not knowing the intended destination of the invasion, the B-17s of the 19th BG continued their search patrols. On May 9, a few planes from Cloncurry were rushed over to Townsville to relieve the tired airmen of the reinforced 40th RS. "We are running 6-12 ships [i.e. planes] a day from our Sqdn," recorded Lt. Fields. That morning, a Navy scout plane thought he saw a Japanese carrier through the rain and notified the American fleet. As the Navy scrambled their planes a call went out for the 19th BG to assist. Augmented by the planes from the rest of the group, 14 B-17s set out from Townsville. In one of the best coordinated attacks of the battle, the Fortresses arrived almost simultaneously with the Navy only to learn that the reported enemy carrier was nothing more than a coral reef.[51]

On May 10, the airmen at Townsville, still believing that the Japanese were in the area, were put on alert for an enemy air raid. "Went on alert early this morning to take planes off field in case of air raid alarm or an Air Raid," wrote Lt. Rouse. "Never so scared in my life as two Jap aircraft carriers reported about 300 miles off shore. Could hardly light cigarette." When word finally reached Townsville that the enemy carriers were retiring, six B-17s were sent out at 1:30 P.M. to ". . . find and bomb [a] crippled Jap carrier." Unable to locate the Japanese fleet anywhere, the planes landed at Port Moresby near 9:00 P.M., joining three Fortresses which had been flown up to New Guinea earlier in the day.[52]

At 5:40 A.M. on May 11, all nine B-17s, flying in three three-plane elements, left Port Moresby with orders to ". . . bomb crippled aircraft carrier." Two hours into the flight, the plane carrying bombardier Lt. Gooch developed engine trouble. "We were flying on the wing of our flight leader in formation," recalled Gooch. "Our pilot decided we must leave the formation. As our airplane pulled ahead to signal the flight leader we were leaving the formation (radio silence was mandatory), the tail of our airplane came in contact with the propellers of the lead plane." The midair collision resulted in the loss of about two thirds of the tail of Gooch's B-17E. "What was left of our rudder no longer functioned, and instead of a tail section, we had a large pile of chopped up aluminum sheet metal clinging to the back of our airplane. It's a wonder it flew at all, but the B-17 is a remarkable airplane." Fortunately, the plane continued to fly and an emergency landing was made at a coastal airport near Cooktown, in northeastern Australia.[53]

A half hour after the collision, Lt. Teats, flying as flight leader, was forced to shut down one of his engines and abort. Taking over as leader, Lt. Rouse continued to head the group in a northeasterly direction towards Rabaul expecting to see the Japanese fleet at any minute. Before long however, Rouse too developed engine trouble. Maintaining radio silence, he signaled the next plane to take the lead and turned back to Port Moresby only to find out a few minutes later that the entire formation had followed him. Although Rouse quickly turned back around, hoping for the others to turn with him again, the other B-17s continued back towards Port Moresby. Surprisingly, in a short time, Rouse heard that the others had started their bomb runs.[54]

"[I] thought we might have overshot [the target]," Lt. Rouse confided in his diary for May 11, "so turned back also. Made run where they did but only little islands there." Perhaps hampered by the weather, the other bombers had mistakenly identified some scattered islands as enemy warships. Returning to Port Moresby, Rouse was waved off because of an impending air raid and flew on to Horn Island. After refueling his plane, Rouse flew on to Townsville, arriving there at 8:10 P.M. Upon landing he was given some glorious news. "Hear our navy defeated the Japs in Coral Sea. Great news," he wrote.[55]

The Battle of the Coral Sea was over. Going down in history as the first battle ever fought between opposing warships in which neither fleet saw each other, the battle was fought entirely with aircraft. Although unknown at the time, this engagement set the pattern for all of the other carrier actions of 1942. Generally considered a tactical victory for the Japanese and a strategic victory for the Americans, the Battle of the Coral Sea meant much more to the Allies since it was the first time in World War II, with the exception of the first assault on Wake Island, that a Japanese invasion force had been turned back. Coming shortly after the fall of the Philippines and the retreat from Java, the strategic victory at the Coral Sea was a great boost to Allied morale.[56]

The Battle of the Coral Sea cost the Japanese 77 airplanes and the light carrier *Shoho* while the Americans lost 66 aircraft, the fleet carrier *Lexington*, and two lesser vessels. Additionally, and often forgotten, the 19th BG lost one more plane, B-17E (41-2652). Although a tactical victory, Japan had lost a larger number of experienced airmen, which it could ill afford to lose as it spread its invasive tentacles in all directions at once.[57]

XIV

Japanese Luck

BY THE MIDDLE of February 1942, while the Allied forces, including the 19th BG, were fighting a delaying action in the Netherlands East Indies and busy defending Australia, life in Hawaii had fallen into a quiet routine. Sgt. Horst Walter Handrow (50th RS/11th BG) wrote, "[W]e took life easy for February, March, April and most of May. It looked like we were going to spend the duration right in Hawaii. We flew 900-mile searches every other day and spent our days off in Honolulu fooling around the beaches and having all kinds of fun."[1] In reality however, the men were fully aware that the Japanese juggernaut was still steamrollering across the Pacific. Although the enemy seemed to be concentrating on pushing southward into the Solomon Islands, the Americans in Hawaii feared a push to the east, towards Hawaii itself. B-17s from the 5th and 11th BGs, aided by Navy PBY flying boats, continued to fly wedge-shaped search missions to the west and north of Hawaii, keeping a wary eye open for any Japanese activity.

Wanting to find out what the Japanese were doing on Wake Island, 7th Bomber Command sent a lone B-17 on a photo reconnaissance mission toward Wake on February 14. Staging through Midway, the crew was back in Hawaii within a couple of days, reporting nothing out of the ordinary. Unfortunately for the Americans they had been looking too far to the west.

During the early morning hours of March 4, two Japanese flying boats from the Marshall Islands flew over Oahu and dropped their bombs. By sheer luck and because of bad weather both planes missed the ships at anchor in Pearl Harbor.[2] Wrote the historian for the 50th RS, "Lone [sic] enemy four-engined flying boat dropped four heavy bombs in the mountains north of the city of Honolulu at 0215 (no damage)." The presence of the two Japanese bombers however had brought the war back to Hawaii and had shown the airmen of 7th Bomber Command that there was no such place as a safe haven.[3]

In spite of the need for training, especially on the part of new pilots, bombardiers and navigators fresh from the States, Admiral Nimitz, as Commander in Chief Pacific Ocean Areas, had placed the 7th Bomber Command under the control of the Navy searching PBYs. Instead of being given time to develop their skills correctly, the new B-17 crews were given a pie-shaped wedge of the Pacific Ocean to patrol. Those crews not flying patrol were held on alert, thus leaving little time for the necessary training. It was not until April 1 that orders were amended, allowing approximately 25 percent of the crews time to train.[4]

In late March, Col. "Blondie" Saunders, in command of the 5th BG since January 12, was transferred to command of the 11th BG while Col. Arthur W. Meehan was placed in command of the 5th.[5] As new B-17Es continued to arrive from the States, each commander argued for time to train the crews properly, and Saunders attempted to build up the recently activated 98th BS. Wrote the 11th BG historian, "Every possible training concept was put to use to insure that bomber crews could traverse the long distances of the Hawaii-South Pacific area."[6]

Near the end of March, the 4th RS/5th BG, which had been designated a school squadron, received four B-17Ds and Es and set up a pilot's training course. Noted the 4th RS historian, "[The squadron] checked out first pilots in the B-18s and then qualified them as B-17 co-pilots. They were [then] transferred to other squadrons." Later, when some training time was finally made available, the 4th RS also began training navigators and bombardiers.[7]

The month of April opened ominously for the 7th Bomber Command when it lost another B-17 and crew. On April 5, Lt. Charles O. Allen (42nd BS/11th BG) was out on a routine search patrol when he got lost in extremely foul weather and crashed into Keaheakahoe Peak on Oahu. The entire crew was killed and B-17E (41-2443) was left a mass of scattered, burning wreckage.[8]

In late April and early May a few changes took place within 7th Bomber Command. On April 29 the 50th RS was redesignated the 431st BS/11th BG and a few days later, the 4th RS was changed to the 394th BS/5th BG. Noted the historian for the 394th BS, "The Squadron's primary function as a bombardment outfit was recognized in May when it was given its present designation. It must be noted that this change did not mark a sudden change in work but simply capped a long period of development. The metamorphosis of the Squadron [from reconnaissance to bombardment] was now complete in name as well as in fact."[9]

Even in the spring of 1942, new crews arriving from the States were surprised at the devastation they found at Pearl Harbor and Hickam Field. New arrival Roy Davenport (394th BS/5th BG) wrote, "Getting to Hawaii in April 1942, we [had] heard many different versions of what had happened on [December] 7th. After seeing the condition the Japanese left Hickam Field in . . . [it] didn't make me feel that great. This increased the bitterness and made me more determined to get even. It surely changed one's attitude toward the enemy."[10]

With more crews and planes arriving every day, the 72nd BS/5th BG finally received it's first B-17s on May 1, and one day later, the airmen of the fledgling 98th BS/11th BG finally acquired their very first planes, one B-18 and one B-17D. Over the next two weeks, the 98th BS was given 10 more B-17s and began operating alongside the other heavy bomber squadrons on Oahu. However, as the squadron historian reported, "As far as the enlisted men were concerned, the 98th did not become a complete entity until May 19. It was upon that date that the Squadron's own mess was set up. Even an air echelon travels—as did Napoleon's infantry—upon its stomach."[11]

The reorganization and replenishing of the bomb squadrons came just in time. From May 18 to May 28 the B-17s were put on special alert. While the obsolete B-18 bombers suddenly replaced the B-17s on the constant search missions, the Flying Fortresses were loaded with bombs and kept on the ground in anticipation of action. Something big was brewing in the Central Pacific and the B-17s of 7th Bomber Command were going to be a part of it.[12]

Back on April 18, 16 twin-engine B-25 bombers from the American aircraft carrier *Hornet*, under the overall command of Lt. Col. James H. Doolittle, unexpectedly bombed Tokyo and several other Japanese cities, before continuing on towards China. Although the Doolittle raid did little damage to Japan, it was a gigantic boost to American morale and a necessary payback for Pearl Harbor. More importantly however, the unexpected raid helped push the Japanese towards a critical decision in the Pacific war.[13]

Prior to the Doolittle raid the Imperial General Staff had been divided over whether Japan needed to push her defensive perimeter further east. Arguing against the plan, some admirals and generals felt that Japan's eastern perimeter had been extended far enough and that Japan should concentrate on an invasion of Australia. Among the men arguing for expansion was Adm. Isoroku Yamamoto, the architect of the Pearl Harbor attack, who argued that an attack on Midway Island, which lay 2,250 miles from Japan and only 1,100 miles from Oahu, would push the Americans into making a decision with dire consequences. If the Americans made a strong effort with their carrier forces to keep Midway, Yamamoto, who had supreme confidence in the ability of the Imperial Navy, felt that he could defeat the Americans in the "decisive naval engagement" of the war. But, if the Americans decided to avoid a fight, Japan would conquer Midway and advance her defensive perimeter further east.[14]

Two days after the Doolittle raid, the Imperial General Staff, greatly embarrassed by the raid, finally came together and agreed to extend Japan's defensive perimeter. Yamamoto was given the green light for the invasion of Midway. Already in the planning stage, along with the planned invasion of Port Moresby and a follow up move into the Solomons, all three assaults were now squeezed into a narrow timetable which allowed little room for unexpected setbacks. Conceived and planned by Yamamoto, the strike against Midway was to be the biggest operation ever attempted by the Imperial Navy.[15]

In early May, Yamamoto's planned strike against Port Moresby unexpectedly met defeat at the Battle of the Coral Sea. Intent on keeping to their tight timetable in spite of the loss of two carriers (one sunk, one badly damaged), Yamamoto put the conquest of Midway into full swing. Assembling a vast array of warships, Yamamoto planned to split his force and send a diversionary strike against

Alaska's Aleutian Islands. When the Americans went after the diversionary force, Yamamoto's main force would strike at Midway.[16]

An extremely complex plan, the success lay in the need for the Americans to react accordingly. Hoping to draw the American ships toward Alaska through a screen of attacking Japanese submarines, and then back through the same screen, Yamamoto expected the American warships to be greatly reduced in numbers by the time they reached Midway. Then he would attack with his carrier planes and achieve his "decisive battle." Unfortunately, Yamamoto did not know that America had broken Japan's secret codes and by the end of May knew that the Japanese were planning an invasion of Midway.[17]

The United States Navy moved quickly and built a task force around the carriers *Enterprise*, *Hornet* and *Yorktown* (still being repaired from her damage at the Coral Sea as she rushed to help). PBY flying boats were sent to Midway to begin searching for the enemy convoy while 7th Bomber Command readied their planes for the upcoming fight.[18] In order to flesh out the other 5th BG squadrons, the B-17s were taken away from the 394th BS, which was still acting as a training unit, and given to the other squadrons of the group.[19]

On May 18, when Gen. Tinker put his 7th Air Force on "special alert," 7th Bomber Command had only 27 B-17Es and seven old B-17Cs and Ds divided between the 5th and 11th BGs. Realizing the importance of stopping the Japanese at Midway, a steady stream of bombers was rushed to Hawaii from the United States. With the new planes flying into Hickam, the airfield became a bit too crowded so on May 23, the 31st BS/5th BG moved to Kipapa Field, and a week later, the 394th BS/5th BG personnel, now without any B-17s, moved to Bellows Field.[20]

Roy Davenport remembered the move to Bellows. "We carried full field pack with the belt filled with ammunition plus bayonet, two bandoleers of ammunition, a 1903 Springfield rifle, canvas army cot, [and] two barracks bags (the blue ones) filled with our belongings . . ." The most constant complaint about Bellows Field concerned the mosquitoes. "Our worst enemy was those pesky mosquitoes that filled the night sky," Davenport commented. "After we moved to Bellows Field, they were the worst because of the [surrounding] sugar cane fields . . . [At night,] we had to cover up to keep away from the mosquito netting because the mosquitoes would find you with their long siphons and the part exposed would be like hamburger the next morning."[21]

By May 31 there were 56 B-17s in Hawaii but only 44 were in commission with trained crews. Although the newly arriving B-17s, all model-Es, needed little modification to get them combat ready, it took weeks to adequately train a new crew. In all, a total of 60 new Fortresses arrived from the United States between May 18 and June 10.[22]

On May 25, the 26th BS/11th BG traded three old B-17Es equipped with the remote control Bendix belly turret, and one old B-17D to the other squadrons for four new B-17Es with the more effective Sperry manned ball turret. The 26th BS had been selected as the first B-17 squadron to reinforce Midway and was being given the best planes.[23] Five days later, six planes, designated Striking Force V92, left Hawaii, accompanied by Gen. Hale, the CO of 7th Bomber Command.

When the 26th BS reached Midway they were put on full alert. Noted the squadron historian, "The crews were on a constant alert, requiring that they sleep alongside their planes in the revetments. Often during the next few days they 'scrambled' in search of the huge Japanese naval force reported in those waters." Unfortunately, the aircrews had brought along only a handful of ground crew personnel and were forced to service their own planes and refuel the thirsty bombers by hand from 55-gallon drums. On May 22, Midway had experienced an accidental explosion of its fuel dump and refueling facilities.[24]

Realizing that moving a large portion of the PBYs and B-17s from Oahu to Midway left Hawaii blind to the movements of the Japanese, 16 B-17s from the 303rd BG, 2nd Air Force (2nd AF), assigned to the protection of the west coast of the United States flew to Hawaii near the end of May. Almost as soon as the new planes arrived, newly-promoted Lt. Col. Sweeney, led a conglomerate group of 10 B-17s, carrying a few mechanics, to reinforce Striking Force V92 at Midway. The flight consisted of seven crews from the 431st BS/11th BG, two from the 31st BS/5th BG, and one from the 72nd BS/5th BG.[25]

Earl Schaeffer, now a corporal, was the radio operator and waist gunner on 1st Lt. Edward A. Steedman's B-17E (41-2523, *Goonie*), the lone representative from the 72nd BS. "It wasn't until we were well on our way that we knew our destination. Midway Island . . . ," Schaeffer wrote. Arriving late in the afternoon of May 31, the airmen were informed by the Marine garrison that rumors were afloat that between 30 and 40 Japanese ships had been spotted by an American submarine and were only 700 miles away. For the B-17 crews, the expected fight would be their first taste of combat. "Now we had something to think about and it gave us all a spine tingling sensation to know that [we] were finally getting into action," wrote Schaeffer. "We were scared too."[26]

With the arrival of Sweeney's 10 B-17s, tiny Midway, consisting of two small islands surrounded by a coral atoll, became extremely crowded. Only one island, Eastern Island, had landing strips and air facilities and became the sole home for dozens of Marine, Navy and now AAF planes.[27]

For most of the B-17 airmen, the move to Midway provided them with their first look at the tiny outpost. Most were amazed by what they saw. "[It was] just like any other island in the Pacific only it was armed to the teeth with guns," recalled Sgt. Handrow, who was flying as the tail gunner with Capt. Clarence P. Tokarz (431st BS/11th BG) in B-17E (41-2404, *The Spider*). "I never saw so many guns in one place; they weren't going to pull another Wake here, I thought."[28]

As Midway built up its defenses, Adm. Jack Fletcher moved his carrier task force to a spot northeast of Midway. Figuring that the Japanese would approach from the west, Fletcher wanted to hide his ships from the enemy yet be in position to react when the Japanese attacked Midway. Knowing that the Japanese were intent on capturing the island, Fletcher decided to give the enemy the initiative and let them strike first. In the meantime, the PBYs and B-17s continued to search.[29]

As early as May 31, when Sweeney's B-17s arrived at Midway, six B-17s from the 26th BS/11th BG and six from the 431st BS/11th BG went on search missions 800 miles out from Midway. Sent out late in the day, mainly on orders from Admiral Nimitz to scout the expected rendezvous spot of the Japanese fleet, the B-17 crews, unfamiliar with the area, promptly got lost. By homing in on a "combination of radar and radio direction finder bearings," all 12 planes made it safely back to Midway, but the last one did not return until 3:50 A.M., June 1, more than four and a half hours late.[30]

Despite sending only the best planes to Midway, Lt. John Van Haur (431st BS/11th BG) returned from an early morning search on June 2 in need of a complete engine change. Thomas Bradshaw, Van Haur's crew chief, recalled, "About the second day my aircraft lost #2 engine and I requested a new engine be sent from Hawaii. I started working to remove the old engine . . . I had diarrhea caused by eating in the over-crowded mess facility with only salt water to wash your gear in, so it was tough trying to work with your pants at half mast." At 9:00 A.M. on June 3, Capt. Faulkner flew his B-17 in from Hickam, replacing Van Haur's bomber in the strike force.[31]

Late in the afternoon of June 2, the six 26th BS B-17's, once again carrying Gen. Hale, headed back to Oahu. Knowing that the endless searches were hard on both men and machines, the 7th AF had decided to shuffle planes in and out of Midway. While the planes of the 26th BS were on their way home, six planes from the 42nd BS/11th BG, at Barking Sands on Kauai, were preparing to replace them. Their arrival at Midway was scheduled for the early afternoon of June 3.[32]

At 4:30 A.M. on June 3, Col. Sweeney's nine operational planes took to the air as a precaution against a surprise air raid. By now the many hours of flying and constant alert were beginning to wreak havoc on the men's nerves.[33] At 8:25 A.M., the B-17s returned from the false air raid and the men began refueling their planes. Then, suddenly, at 9:25 A.M., Midway received word that the Japanese ships had been spotted 700 miles to the west. Sweeney wanted to take off immediately but was told to wait. As Sweeney reported, "The Commanding Officer of the Midway Defense Forces . . . refused rightly to commit this striking force, consisting of nine (9) B-17E type Airplanes, until positive information was received as to the exact location and composition of the main body." For three hours the anxious airmen waited as more sightings were reported. Finally, around 12:30 P.M., when it was determined that three smaller groups of ships were maneuvering to rendezvous with a larger group, Sweeney's Flying Fortresses began taking off.[34]

Preceding Sweeney's strike force was a lone Fortress flown by Lt. W. A. Smith (394th BS/5th BG). Having just arrived at Midway that morning, Smith's plane was quickly refueled and lifted off at 11:58 A.M., heading west, towards the first reported sighting. Carrying no bombs, Smith had been told to find the enemy fleet, shadow it and pinpoint its exact location for Col. Sweeney. It had been decided that a big, rugged B-17 would stand a better chance than a PBY of tracking the enemy vessels in case Smith located the carriers and was attacked by pesky Zeros.

At 4:11 P.M. and about 700 miles west of Midway, Lt. Smith spotted two enemy transports escorted by two destroyers. Circling at 8,000 feet, Smith kept an eye on the ships and reported their location while the destroyers threw antiaircraft fire in his direction. For almost two hours he shadowed the four vessels but the B-17 strike force never showed up. Finally, low on fuel, Smith turned back towards Midway. Unknown to everyone, Lt. Smith had located another small task force of enemy ships. While he was tracking their movement however, Col. Sweeney's Fortresses had come across the main body of the invasion fleet.[35]

Sweeney's nine B-17s headed west in three three-plane elements, with each plane carrying four 600-lb. bombs and a bomb bay fuel tank. At exactly 4:23 P.M., the B-17s spotted the enemy invasion fleet 570 miles west of Midway. Recalled Cpl. Schaeffer, "The flight was uneventful until we were about 650 [sic] miles out. There they were!" Undoubtedly excited, the airmen counted varying numbers of enemy ships. Capt. Gregory reported an "enemy force of approximately forty (40) ships of all classes except carriers"; while Cpl. Schaeffer recalled, "We counted 35 transports escorted by several Destroyers and Cruisers." In actuality, the convoy consisted of a total of 27 transports and escort vessels. Lt. Steedman was the closest when he reported a total of 26 ships.[36]

Sgt. Handrow, in B-17E (41-2404, The Spider) with Capt. Tokarz, was amazed by the size of the task force:

> [T]his day hunting was good and there below was a task force that spread all over the Pacific. What a sight, everything from cans [destroyers] to battleships but no carriers in this force. Strange, there was suppose to be five of them around somewhere. We didn't have enough gas to look any farther so we picked out the biggest battlewagon we could find and started to make a run on it . . .[37]

Col. Sweeney, B-17E (41-2409, *Old Maid*), brought his flight in from the east, with the sun at their backs. Capt. Paul Payne (431st BS/11th BG), B-17E (41-2463, *Yankee Doodle*), wrote "We came in out of the sun—there were clouds but not many—perfect bombing weather." While Sweeney and his two wing men, Capt. Gregory and Lt. Willard G. Woodbury (431st BS), went in at an altitude of 8,000 feet, the second element went in at 10,000, and the third at 12,000. As the B-17s drew near, the Japanese sailors finally noticed them. "Our flight immediately went into the bombing run," Schaeffer wrote, "but they spotted us and went into evasive maneuvers . . . ." Col. Sweeney, leading the first element, reported, "At the bomb release line very heavy antiaircraft fire was encountered and continued throughout the attack."[38]

Sweeney's element dropped their bombs against a heavy cruiser and then headed for safety. "The antiaircraft fire was so intense," admitted Sweeney, "that it was not deemed wise to remain in the target area for close observation of bombing results . . ." As the first element flew off, the second element, led by Capt. Tokarz and flanked by Capt. Payne and a newly promoted Capt. Sullivan, flew in.

"The antiaircraft was coming up now and the sky was black with it," recalled Sgt. Handrow, "bang, we had a hit in No 4 engine, on we went on our run, bombs away!"[39]

While Capts. Tokarz and Sullivan dropped their bombs, Capt. Payne had two bombs hang up and circled around for a second run. Coming in over the Japanese transport *Argentina Maru*, he was met by a hail of antiaircraft fire. "They were good gunners," he admitted. "They got the altitude and range. A-A fire was bursting all around in precise bursts of four. We weren't hit; we let the bombs go and headed for home." Fearful of the antiaircraft fire and one wrong spark near the half empty bomb bay tank, Payne ordered his radio operator to get rid of all of the flares. When the radioman opened the side fuselage door and began discarding the flares, the wind unexpectedly slammed the door shut on his finger, causing the only injury of the entire formation of B-17s.[40]

The third element, consisted of Capt. Faulkner, leading Lt. Steedman and 1st Lt. Robert B. Andrews (31st BS/5th BG) came in at a higher altitude and dropped their bombs on the maneuvering ships. Looking back, Cpl. Schaeffer acknowledged that the vessels managed to ". . . dodge most of our bombs." Out of the four bombs dropped by Faulkner, only one exploded, while Steedman was able to drop only one bomb because of trouble with his release mechanism. Although the B-17 crews claimed numerous hits, Col. Sweeney felt that his B-17s had scored only five hits but had several near misses. He felt that his own first element had hit the stern of one heavy cruiser, that the second element had left one heavy cruiser or battleship on fire, and that Capt. Payne had hit one transport on his solo bomb run.[41]

Unfortunately, Sweeney's claim of five hits and several near misses was optimistic. Dropping from high altitude, the B-17s had completely missed the wildly maneuvering ships. When the nine B-17s flew away, the only damage suffered by the Japanese was a few bomb splinters from a near-miss to one transport.[42]

Heading back towards Midway, Sweeney's B-17 strike force suddenly ran into a bad storm. "About 400 miles from Midway we ran into a storm and had to break formation and it was every aircraft for itself," recalled Cpl. Schaeffer. An hour later, when Schaeffer's pilot, Capt. Steedman, finally broke out of the storm clouds, he found that he was lost. "Being the radio operator," continued Schaeffer, "the pilot ordered me to contact Midway, but I was unable to because I hadn't [been given] the frequency of the Midway station. (This info was only given to the lead aircraft.)" Although Schaeffer was able to contact Pearl Harbor, 1,400 miles away, they were unable to give him the correct frequency. Almost frantically, Schaeffer searched all over the dial until he picked up a strong signal. "Knowing we were somewhere in the vicinity of Midway," he said, "we figured this signal must be Midway station. I challenged them with our code and they answered correctly." Picked up by the Midway radar, the lost crew was safely guided back to the island. "This was the first time I had seen what radar could do," commented Schaeffer.[43]

Caught in the storm and the darkness, it wasn't until 9:45 P.M. that Lt.

Woodbury set the last bomber down on Eastern Island, more than eight hours after taking off. Relieved to be back at Midway, Woodbury felt that his plane did not have enough gas left in the tanks "to fill a cigarette lighter."[44]

As Sweeney's aircrews dropped exhausted from their planes, they were met by the six crews from the 42nd BS/11th BG which had been brought in by Brooke Allen, now a lieutenant colonel. Having left Barking Sands at 2:05 P.M. the planes had reached Midway only a few hours before the return of Sweeney's strike force. Although 1st Lt. Carl E. Wuertele, B-17E (41-9157, *Hel-En-Wings*), had developed a problem with the automatic pilot shortly after takeoff, he was aware of the importance of the mission and had refused to turn back, manually flying the big bomber all the way to Midway.[45]

With the arrival of Allen's planes, and including Lt. Smith's bomber, 16 combat ready B-17s were now at Midway. Although the Japanese aircraft carriers had yet to be sighted, the Army airmen believed that they had already hurt the Japanese Navy and were ready to go out early the next morning. Wrote Sgt. Handrow, "We had really done some good that day and we all remembered December 7th. We worked all that night loading bombs, gassing the ships and trying to get No. 4 engine in shape because we knew we would really need it next day."[46]

The first attack by either side in the battle of Midway had come from the American B-17s of Striking Force V92 and while no damage had been done, the psychological effect weighed heavily upon the minds of the Japanese admirals intent on capturing Midway without much of a fight. Wrote one of the pilots of the 11th BG, ". . . I'm sure the biggest surprise for the Nipponese Navy was finding itself under attack by B-17s out in the middle of the Pacific Ocean." Although Navy PBYs carried out a torpedo attack during the night, scoring one minor hit on a transport, June 3, 1941, ended with the Japanese Navy still fully intact.[47] However, the next day would be quite a different story.

At 4:05 A.M., on June 4, 15 B-17s took off from Midway and headed west towards the enemy transport fleet. Left behind was one of the planes from the 42nd BS/11th BG, grounded with mechanical trouble.[48] Realizing that the Japanese would attack Midway on this date, Lt. Van Haur's stricken bomber was sent back to Hawaii. By this time, Pvt. Bradshaw had been able to replace the damaged engine. "I told [my sergeant] that my plane was ready but hadn't had a test flight," Bradshaw wrote. "He got hold of a lieutenant and the two of them cranked up that B-17 and took off and, of all things, they flew it back to Hawaii, leaving me there on Midway Island!!" Having gone without sleep for the past three days and nights, Bradshaw retired to his tent and fell asleep.[49]

With Col. Sweeney leading the first of five three-plane elements, the 15 B-17s pressed on. Before leaving Midway, Sweeney had been warned that his target could be changed at any moment if the Japanese carriers were spotted. So, near 6:00 A.M., when Sweeney was less than 200 miles from the transport group and received word that "another enemy task force complete with many carriers" had been sighted only 145 miles northwest of Midway, he was not surprised by the order to turn around and go after the carriers. Turning to intercept, the massed flight ran into thick clouds that extended from 1,000 up to 18,000 feet. Believing that it would be suicide to attack from below the clouds, Sweeney took his bombers up to 18,000 feet and headed for the enemy carriers.[50]

While the B-17s were turning to attack, the Japanese struck at Midway. Near 6:30 A.M. Japanese bombers began hitting the twin islands of Midway. Moments later, Zero fighters raced in to strafe the defenders through a fusillade of American antiaircraft and small arms fire. Only a few AAF ground personnel were present on Eastern Island when the raid came. Pvt. Bradshaw, who was sound asleep, was glad to find a slit trench directly behind his tent. "As I rolled out of my army cot into that slit trench an anti-personnel shrapnel bomb exploded several feet from me and I received a few slugs from it," he wrote. "One nearly tore my nose off, [and] another lodged in my right hip."[51]

During a lull in the attack, Bradshaw tried to find an aid station, but was caught out in the open when the Japanese staged another attack. "I jumped into this pit along side the runway and got chewed out by a Marine already in there," Bradshaw recalled. "He informed me that that was HIS command post." Moving on, the plucky private managed to find a command bunker and get his wounds treated.[52]

S/Sgt. Joseph Soler (42nd BS/11th BG) was also having trouble finding an empty slit trench. During the first attack, Soler jumped into a slit trench only to find it already occupied by a large gooney bird. "The Japs were lacing the field with machine guns," he remembered, "so I picked up that gooney and tossed him the hell out of there." Figuring that he was done with the bird, Soler dropped to the bottom of the trench to await the end of the attack. "Whereupon," he continued, "that damned gooney bird jumps in on top of me and beats the bejesus out of me with his wings."[53]

By 7:01 A.M. the attack was over. The enemy inflicted considerable damage to Midway. On Eastern Island alone, besides wrecking a number of buildings, the runways were cratered with shellholes and littered with tiny pieces of shrapnel. Fortunately, because of the advance warning afforded by breaking the Japanese code, countless slit trenches had been dug and numerous sandbag bunkers had been build by the defenders. In all, only 11 men were killed and 18 were wounded. Among the dead however, were three Army airmen.[54]

While the Japanese were hitting Midway, the Americans were attacking the enemy carriers. At 5:45 A.M. a Navy PBY had spotted the Japanese Carrier Force of four large carriers, the *Akagi*, *Kaga*, *Hiryu* and *Soryu*, and reported the sighting to Midway. Col. Sweeney's airborne B-17s were immediately notified. At the same time the Midway-based planes took off.[55]

Near 7:00 A.M. six torpedo planes from Midway, followed by four torpedo-carrying Army B-26 bombers attacked the Japanese Carrier Force. Although a total of seven planes were shot down, and no torpedo hits were scored, the attack by land-based bombers convinced Adm. Osami Nagumo, the Japanese commander, that the American carriers were hundreds of miles away, rushing to defend

Alaska. Deciding on another attack on Midway, Nagumo ordered his second wave of planes armed with general-purpose demolition bombs, generally used against land-based targets, instead of torpedoes.[56]

At 7:30 A.M., almost 15 minutes after making his fateful decision, Nagumo finally received word that an American convoy had been sighted. Not knowing if any carriers were in the convoy, Nagumo waited an additional 15 minutes before ordering his crews to reverse the armament and change from general-purpose bombs to torpedoes. To help speed up the process, the armament crews removed the bombs, and instead of returning them to the magazines, stacked them in piles on the hangar or second deck while the torpedoes were being installed.[57]

Unknown to the Japanese, at that very moment his fleet was under the watchful eyes of Sweeney's B-17 crews. Somewhere along the flight path Col. Sweeney had lost one of his bombers, which apparently flew back to Midway, so that his strike force now numbered only 14 bombers, flying in four three-plane elements followed by one two-plane element.[58] Arriving unseen over the Japanese Carrier Force at 7:32 A.M., the B-17 crews failed to see any carriers through the thick cloud layers. "The carriers were circling under the clouds," Sweeney believed, "and we had to search for them." Knowing that the carriers were somewhere below, Sweeney began to circle.[59]

In between breaks in the clouds the aircrews could see the enemy ships suddenly going into wild evasive maneuvers. "There isn't much doubt that they had spotted us and were trying to avoid our planes," Sweeney felt, "and this served to break up their formation." In reality, the B-17s had not been spotted. The Japanese ships were taking evasive action because of a flight of 16 dive-bombers from Midway. When the attack was over, eight bombers had been shot down and again, not a single bomb had hit home.[60]

For nearly 40 minutes the B-17s circled the enemy fleet in search of the enemy carriers. Finally, near 8:10 A.M., Lt. Wuertele, B-17E (41-9157, *Hel-En-Wings*), leading the two-plane element at the rear of the formation, spotted a carrier through the clouds. Although he tried to contact Col. Sweeney on the radio, he was unsuccessful. Grasping the initiative, Wuertele signaled his wingman, 1st Lt. Hugh S. Grundman (42nd BS/11th BG), to follow him and then went after the carrier before it disappeared from sight again.[61]

Lt. Wuertele released three 500-lb. bombs on the carrier and then lined up on a second carrier that suddenly loomed into view. Following close behind, Lt. Grundman dropped a couple of his eight bombs on the first carrier and then followed Wuertele against the second ship. Before Wuertele could drop his remaining five bombs however, he spotted a third carrier and decided to go after that vessel. Grundman nevertheless emptied his bomb bay on the second carrier but admitted that his bombs went wide. Braving heavy antiaircraft fire, Wuertele made a long, level run on the third flattop and dropped his remaining five bombs in train. As he flew away Wuertele believed that he had scored one direct hit, one possible hit, and one near miss.[62]

Flying just in front of the two-plane element, Col. Allen and his two wingmen,

Lts. Richard Eberenz and Paul Williams, (both 42nd BS/11th BG) sighted the *Soryu* and immediately went after it. As the carrier went into wild evasive action and sent up a string of antiaircraft fire, the three planes dropped a total of 24 bombs from 20,000 feet. As Allen and his wingmen headed back to Midway, they believed that they had scored at least one direct hit and two near misses.[63]

Col. Sweeney, B-17E (41-2409, *Old Maid*), was still leading nine planes on his search for the carriers. He recalled, "All elements of the main body of the fleet could be observed except the carriers." Then, Capt. Payne, B-17E (41-2463, *Yankee Doodle*), in the third element, spotted a carrier. After notifying his element leader, Capt. Tokarz, he called Col. Sweeney. "Our three-plane element was dropping, but our commander [Sweeney] apparently hadn't seen those babies yet," recalled Payne. "We were alone, off to one side. We informed him and he ordered us to attack." Having by now sighted "three or four" carriers, Capt. Tokarz, with Capts. Payne and Sullivan on his wings, picked the closest flattop and started his bomb run.[64]

Sgt. Handrow, in the tail of Tokarz's lead plane, remembered, "We found the carriers and started our run but couldn't get in—the clouds covered up the target and the antiaircraft was thick." Still, Capt. Payne dropped half of his bombs. He later reported, "Four bombs were dropped—near-misses. Four were left." In the lead plane, Capt. Tokarz suddenly lost his No. 4 engine again and was forced to circle his element around for another bomb run while he tried to restart his engine. "Then we saw a big *Kaga* [class] carrier come out from under the clouds," wrote Handrow. Forgetting the troublesome engine, Tokarz led his element over the enemy flattop. "Down went the bombs from three ships," wrote Handrow. With a bit of exaggeration he added, "the flight deck got three hits, the water line four; she was sinking and burning at the same time."[65]

As the three B-17s turned from their run, they were jumped by a handful of Zeros. Sgt. Handrow reported, "Zero fighters attacked us on the way home but wouldn't come in close enough [to our plane] so we could get a good shot at them." Although the fighters avoided B-17E (41-2404, *The Spider*), three of them went after Capt. Payne, B-17E (41-2463, *Yankee Doodle*). As one fighter flew to within 50 feet of the left side of the bomber, Corp. Donald C. Bargdill (431st BS/11th BG), the waist gunner, suddenly opened fire. "I later counted 72 heavy machine-gun shells fired," Bargdill said, "and tracers were going into his engine and belly." As Bargdill watched, the enemy pilot gyrated wildly in the cockpit before his plane spun into the ocean. "Those other two fighters never did follow up the attack," he added.[66]

Capt. Faulkner, Lt. Steedman and Lt. Andrews in the second element, believed that Col. Sweeney had yet to see the carriers. Acting on his own, Capt. Faulkner led his wingmen against "the largest of the 4 carriers," undoubtedly the *Akagi*, Admiral Nagumo's flagship. Flying with Lt. Steedman, B-17E (41-2523, *Goonie*), Cpl. Schaeffer was awestruck by the size of the Japanese convoy. "It was an awesome sight to behold," he recalled, "square miles of enemy ships, among them four big aircraft carriers, several battleships, cruisers and destroyers."[67]

Spotted by the enemy ships, the second element ran into a gauntlet of antiair-craft fire. Braving the fire, Capt. Faulkner dropped all eight of his bombs and got away safely but Lt. Steedman was not so lucky. Wrote Cpl. Schaeffer, "In the first thirty seconds we were hit by antiaircraft fire knocking out [our] number one engine, the electrical wiring to the bomb bay and the wiring to the ball-turret." Although Steedman's bombardier was able to manually release his bombs, Schaeffer felt that only two hit the carrier. "The other six bombs," he added, "straddled all around it." As the element flew away, Capt. Faulkner believed that the three planes had scored one direct hit on the port bow, one possible hit on the starboard side, and five near misses.[68]

Unknown to Faulkner, Lt. Andrews had dropped only four bombs and felt that he had missed completely so he decided to make a solo run on a "large carrier." Encountering no antiaircraft fire, he released his last four bombs and was than chased by two Zeros. "[B]y diving and pouring the coal to it," Andrews succeed-ed in outrunning his pursuers and making it safely back to Midway.[69]

Down to a two-plane element now, Capt. Faulkner and Lt. Steedman were also hit by Zeros which shot up Faulkner's fuselage, knocked out his No. 4 engine and caused the only injury of the entire formation, hitting his tail gunner in the left index finger.[70] Zeros also struck at Steedman's Goonie. Wrote Cpl. Schaeffer, "We were flying at 25,000 feet and were using oxygen, but the aircraft, being a training ship, was not fully equipped for combat and there were no oxygen outlets at the waist guns." Without the proper hook-ups, Schaeffer and the waist gunner, Sgt. Albert St. Jean, had improvised a tag-team method of defense while the plane approached the target. "[We] took turns at manning the guns, staying there until we became dizzy from the lack of oxygen," Schaeffer noted. "Then we would return to the radio compartment. One of us would remain at the guns at all times."

When the Zeros attacked, both gunners left the safety of the radio room. "Now both St. Jean and myself were manning the waist guns," Schaeffer said, "com-pletely forgetting that we needed oxygen." Together, the crew of the Goonie suc-cessfully defended their aircraft, and shot down two of the attackers. Recalled Schaeffer, "By this time both St. Jean and myself were overcome from the lack of oxygen, but were revived by [ball turret gunner] Cpl. [Frank] Frucci using a walk-around-bottle of the life saving oxygen." Having beaten off the Zeros, Faulkner and Steedman flew back to Midway.[71]

Finally informed of the location of the Japanese carriers by Capt. Payne, Col. Sweeney had swung the first element around for an attack. "The enemy started firing as soon as we opened our bomb bays," Sweeney wrote. "The fire wasn't effective but it was disturbing." Lt. Wessman, flying as copilot, however felt that the antiaircraft fire was a little more than "disturbing." One of the first rounds exploded the cockpit window to his right. "From then on," Wessman wrote, "all of us were sorry we stopped at 20,000 feet."[72]

Although a flight of Zeros was spotted, Col. Sweeney felt that "their heart was not in their work, and in no case was their attack pressed home." Capt. Gregory, flying on one wing, believed that the enemy pilots had a cautious respect for the new B-17E with tail guns. He reported, "enemy pursuit appeared to have no desire to close on the B-17E modified." Ignoring the Zeros, Sweeney, in *Old Maid*, led Gregory and Lt. Woodbury over *Kaga*. All three planes dropped their full bomb loads around the stern of the carrier causing Sweeney to feel that they had scored at least "one bomb hit . . . causing heavy smoke."[73]

By 8:20 A.M., after only 10 minutes, the attack was over. By 9:30 the 14 B-17s were back on the ground at Midway. Upon landing, Lts. Wuertele, B-17E (41-9157, *Hel-En-Wings*), and Grundman rolled over pieces of shrapnel scattered about the field from the Japanese air raid and suffered blown tires. As the few ground crewmen scrounged for replacement tires and began rearming the planes, the air crews formed a bucket brigade to help refuel their thirsty bombers. As they worked, they talked excitedly of their success. They were certain that they had critically damaged two or three of the enemy carriers and wanted to get back into the air and finish them off. In reality however, the B-17s had once again proven the fact that it was almost impossible for a high altitude bomber to hit a wildly maneuvering ship on the open sea.

On June 7, three days after the attack, Col. Sweeney admitted that the 14 bombers had scored only one direct hit. Reportedly, Capt. Faulkner's flight had landed one bomb on the port bow of one carrier. For his own part, Sweeney felt that his own flight may have scored a few hits or near misses on the stern of another carrier. Later however, Japanese records showed that out of the 112 bombs dropped by the B-17s, not a single one hit.[74]

As the B-17s flew away, 11 Midway-based torpedo planes showed up. Attacking the battleship *Haruna*, two of the planes were shot down before they flew away. The *Haruna*, already reported sunk by Capt. Kelly on December 10, 1941, continued to lead a charmed life. Every one of the torpedoes missed.

Although five waves of American planes, including the B-17s, had missed with every single bomb or torpedo, the attackers had unknowingly accomplished two important things. First, they had managed to throw the fleet into confusion, scattering the ships and breaking their defensive screen around the aircraft carriers. Second, and more importantly, the almost continuous air strikes had wasted precious time. Knowing that his Midway attack planes were about to return, Admiral Nagumo made the fatal decision to halt the rearming of his second wave of planes so that he could reclaim his first wave. The second wave planes, already rearmed and refueled and being brought up from the hangar decks, were sent back down to leave the flight deck open for the first wave.

Shortly after, the American Navy carried out perhaps the most devastating attack of World War II. Starting at 8:37 A.M., three successive waves of carrier-based torpedo planes attacked the Japanese carriers. Although 35 planes were lost in less than one half hour, and not one torpedo found its mark, the attacks were critical. The repeated attacks by the low-flying torpedo planes, skimming just above the surface of the ocean, had pulled the Zero fighter cover down to water-top level. The skies above the carriers were left wide open.

Less than five minutes later, the high-flying American dive-bombers showed up. In just six minutes, the dive-bombers shattered the decks of the *Akagi*, *Kaga*, and *Soryu*, starting uncontrollable fires on each ship when the American bombs crashed into the piles of carelessly discarded general-purpose bombs.[75] The six-minute attack is perhaps the most devastating six minutes in naval history. Although the Japanese managed to shoot down 47 of the dive-bombers, three major fleet carriers, with almost 200 aircraft, were left burning uncontrollably. Japanese luck had finally run out.

XV

The Turning Point

THE COMMANDERS IN Hawaii, knowing of the action around Midway from the constant radio transmissions between the two points, decided to send all available B-17s to Midway. At 12:30 P.M., six B-17Es from the 23rd BS/5th BG carrying a half load of bombs and a bomb bay gas tank left Hickam. A few hours later, the 72nd BS/5th BG, at Bellows Field, received orders to stand by for a mission to Midway.[1]

Having escaped the American attacks unscathed, the *Hiryu* sent its planes out in search of the American carriers. Finding the *Yorktown*, the Japanese planes managed to drop three bombs on her decks and set her on fire. Returning to the *Hiryu*, the pilots reported that they had sunk the American carrier. At almost the same time, the Japanese learned that there were two more American carriers in the area and quickly dispatched another strike force.

Although the *Yorktown* was seriously wounded the crew managed to put out the fires. Just then, the second Japanese wave appeared and, believing that they were attacking a second American carrier, slammed two torpedoes into her side. Again, the Japanese pilots returned to the *Hiryu* to report the sinking of a carrier. Again, however, their reports were premature and the *Yorktown* stayed afloat.

Believing that two American carriers had already been sunk and knowing that there was a third in the area, the Japanese decided to send out another strike force as soon as possible. While the planes were being re-armed and refueled, the Americans struck first. At 5:00 P.M., a flight of dive-bombers found the *Hiryu* and attacked. Hit by four bombs, the Japanese carrier burst into flames and was rocked by a number of internal explosions. At 5:12, when another flight of dive-bombers arrived and found the *Hiryu* wrapped in flames, they went after two cruisers. While the Navy bombers were attacking, two flights of B-17s, one from Midway and one from Hawaii, suddenly appeared.[2]

Near 11:00 A.M., the B-17s on Midway were still being refueled by the bucket brigades and Lts. Wuertele and Grundman were still fixing their punctured tires.

191

"Wheels and tires were taken as replacements from planes damaged by antiaircraft and fighter fire and placed on otherwise effective airplanes," Col. Sweeney wrote, "all of which was completed in a remarkably short time."[3]

Near 11:15 A.M., the Midway air-raid alarm suddenly sounded. "All of the airplanes, seven in number, that were fueled and ready for flight cleared the airdrome and proceeded back to Hickam Field," continued Sweeney. "This left eight B-17E airplanes at Midway, of which four were, at that time, effective." In addition to the sidelined bombers of Lts. Wuertele and Grundman, two bombers were still out with engine trouble, including Col. Sweeney's own B-17E (41-2609, *Old Maid*). As it was, the air raid turned out to be a false alarm so at 3:00 P.M., when Sweeney received orders to take his planes out for another strike on the Japanese transport, he had only four operational planes at his disposal.[4]

Flying as an observer with Capt. Payne, B-17E (41-2463, *Yankee Doodle*), Col. Sweeney led Capt. Woodbury from his own 431st BS/11th BG, and Col. Allen and Lt. Williams from the 42nd BS/11th BG, towards the convoy reported to be southwest of Midway. About an hour later, having finally replaced their blown tires, Lts. Wuertele and Grundman followed Sweeney's four-plane flight into the air. The tire on Wuertele's *Hel-En-Wings*, had been replaced with the last tire available, a defective one with a large blister. Changed with improvised tools, Wuertele was told that he could make only one more landing on the tire.[5]

About halfway to the target, the two separate flights suddenly received a message from Midway. "En route we got orders to attack a carrier . . . about 180 miles from Midway," recalled Sweeney. Although still separated, all six planes turned north and raced for the Japanese carrier force. Near 5:30 P.M., Sweeney's four-plane element arrived on the scene and spotted the burning *Hiryu*. Believing that an undamaged carrier was still in the area, Sweeney led his flight on a search to find it.[6]

Forty minutes later, Lts. Wuertele and Grundman reached the area and immediately made their bomb runs on the *Hiryu* and the battleship *Haruna*. Although the two crews claimed to have landed two direct hits and three near misses on the burning carrier, and one direct hit and two near misses on the battleship, the actual tally totaled only one near miss on the stern of the *Haruna* which bent a few plates and jammed the main battery range finder.[7]

As Lt. Wuertele turned from the area, his left outboard engine on his battered airplane, which was already being flown with no autopilot and a defective tire, unexpectedly caught fire. Successfully extinguishing the blaze, Wuertele cut power to the engine and, accompanied by Grundman, headed back to Midway.[8] Seconds later, a flight of six B-17s from the 23rd BS/5th BG, fresh from Hawaii, suddenly arrived.

The six B-17s had been approaching Midway when the flight leader, Maj. George Blakey, suddenly received alternate orders. "We were flying in formation off Midway," Blakey recalled, "when we got word that the enemy warships were about 170 miles away, and we were ordered to proceed there. We'd been waiting for action ever since December 7, and here it was." Although low on fuel, Blakey immediately turned his two three-plane elements towards the enemy.[9]

Near 6:15 P.M., Maj. Blakey spotted the Japanese carrier force. "After a while we saw two Jap carriers down ahead of us," wrote Blakey. Sgt. George Scherba, Blakey's ball turret gunner, recalled, "The sun was on the horizon when we turned in toward the carrier, we got the sun on our backs and came in low, so damn low they could see our teeth." Hampered by low clouds, Blakey brought the first element, consisting of himself, Capt. Ernest R. Manierre and Lt. Francis Seeburger, in at only 3,600 feet and concentrated on the damaged *Hiryu*.[10]

Spotting the incoming B-17s, the Japanese warships began firing their antiaircraft guns. "One thing I'll remember forever, was the Jap battleship [*Haruna*] firing broadsides at us from his big guns," Blakey recalled. "[O]ur whole squadron of B-17s went through a wall of antiaircraft fire, right on through the whole Jap force, took everything they could fire at us and we didn't lose a plane or have a casualty." Added Sgt. Scherba, "[T]he Japs couldn't get it into their heads to shorten the range, thank God. Their shots seemed to be breaking above and behind us." At one point however, a shell burst close to the wing of one plane, and another exploded near the nose of a second, momentarily knocking the bombardier out of his seat.[11]

As the bombers started their bomb run, a squadron of Zeros showed up. "People think we just make a straight run, but we don't," stated Lt. Herbert Henckell, Blakey's copilot. "We had to keep our formation with Zero fighters coming from all directions, and the ships zigzagging below us." As the planes passed over the Japanese ships, Sgt. Scherba opened fire on a large cruiser with his twin .50 caliber ball turret guns. "My guns started at the stern and went over the whole length of it. I don't think anybody ever figured on a B-17 strafing, it is a little big for that kind of horsing around, but I was doing it." While Scherba strafed the enemy ship, the Japanese crewmen fired back. Recalled Scherba, "My only thought was, 'I hope I don't get it between the eyes.'"[12]

Coming in quick and low, Blakey's lead element dropped seven bombs on the *Hiryu*. Only one bomb hit. "When we saw that bomb hit the carrier you could have heard us yell clear back to Hickam," recalled Lt. Henckell. Once past the carrier, however, the first element was once again attacked by the Zeros. "It is a funny feeling when that first fighter makes his pass and you know he is not kidding," Henckell wrote. "Your stomach lets go."[13] When one fighter making a head-on attacked rolled up and away, exposing his belly, Blakey's top turret gunner shot it down. "[W]hen you see the Jap blow up—that is something else," Henckell remembered. One more Zero was shot down by Blakey's crew and two more were shot down by the other two Fortresses. Although this was their first time in combat, the Fortress crews were learning fast.[14]

Capt. Narce Whitaker, and Lts. Jack Whidden and Otto Haney, composing the second element, also came in at 3,600 feet. Perhaps because of their inexperience, Whitaker's and Whidden's bombardiers completely missed the *Hiryu* while Haney's bombardier failed to drop his bombs. Adjusting quickly, the bombardier dropped his bombs on a destroyer and reported scoring one direct hit. As the planes raced away, the Zero fighters attacked. Although the second element was able to shoot down two Zeros, a cannon shell hit Whidden's left wing and knocked out his No. 1 engine.[15]

As Maj. Blakey led his six B-17s towards Midway, he looked back at the scattered Japanese fleet which was still sending up a wall of antiaircraft fire. Suddenly he spotted a few geysers of water shoot into the air. "My Lord," Blakey thought, "those are really big shells." Unknown to him, Col. Sweeney's B-17s from Midway had finally arrived and were at that moment dropping their own bombs.[16]

Flying at a height of 25,000 feet, high above Blakey's bombers, Col. Sweeney, in Capt. Payne's bomber, had finally concluded that there was no undamaged carrier in the area. He wrote, "We searched the vicinity, but although a burning carrier and a burning capital ship were sighted, no commissioned carrier was located." Near 6:30 P.M., Sweeney decided to attack a heavy cruiser. "Visibility was perfect and the bombing run excellent," he wrote. Once again under attack, the Japanese sent up a fusillade of antiaircraft fire. "At the bomb-release line an antiaircraft shell burst at our altitude off the wing of the number three plane, followed by fairly heavy fire," Sweeney reported. Although rocked by the fire, Sweeney and his wingman Lt. Williams were able to drop their 500-lb. demolition bombs. Concluded Sweeney, "We scored hits on the cruiser and left it burning, a heavy cloud of smoke issuing amidships." Close behind, Col. Allen and Capt. Woodbury attacked another ship but were unable to determine the results.[17]

It was after dark when Col. Sweeney's flight landed at Midway. Only a few minutes ahead of him, Maj. Blakey's six planes had landed literally on fumes. After flying all the way from Hawaii to Midway, and then being diverted to attack the enemy warships, Blakey's planes reached Midway with not a second to spare. Having never been to Midway before, Blakey found the small atoll only after spotting a huge oil fire which had been ignited by the Japanese attack. As Blakey taxied to the end of the runway, his two starboard engines suddenly quit—he was completely out of gas. "Five minutes more and we would have been in the drink," Blakey admitted.[18]

With 14 B-17s now at Midway, the commanders looked at their meager supplies and found that there "were only sufficient bombs left to load eight airplanes for the dawn mission." Deciding to send six planes back to Hawaii, Sweeney selected his own bomber and the other 431st BS/11th BG B-17 that was sidelined with engine trouble. Additionally, he chose two more planes from the 431st BS that were deemed unfit for combat "due to damaged wings, bombbay [sic] doors and engines . . . ," and Lt. Whidden's plane from the 23rd BS/5th BG, because of the hole in the left wing and the damaged No. 1 engine, and Lt. Wuertele's *Hel-En-Wings* of the 42nd BS/11th BG, which was in overall bad shape. Before leaving, however, the men caught what little sleep they could or ate what little food they could find. As Capt. Payne recalled, his crew "lived on a gallon of fruit salad and a gallon of tomato juice and some chocolate bars" while on Midway.[19]

Near 2:00 A.M. on June 5, the Army aircrews were suddenly awakened when a Japanese submarine began shelling Midway. Wrote Pvt. Bradshaw, "Soon Maj. Sweeny [sic] and crew showed up and, as fast as it could be accomplished, we got airborne and headed back to Hawaii." Piloting his own plane, in spite of the damaged engine, Sweeney managed to take off on all four engines. "I took over as flight engineer," Bradshaw recalled, "and shut down the bad engine, flying to Hawaii on three good engines, then starting the 4th engine for the landing process." When Col. Sweeney left Midway, the five remaining B-17s from the 23rd BS/5th BG and the three planes from the 42nd BS/11th BG were placed under the overall command of Col. Allen.[20]

A little after 4:00 A.M. an American submarine reported "many unidentified ships" close to Midway. Believing that the Japanese were still intent on invading the islands, Col. Allen led the eight remaining B-17s into the air at 4:30 A.M. Hampered by heavy weather, the Fortress crews were unable to locate the enemy ships and turned back towards Midway. By 6:00 A.M. the eight planes were casually circling Kure Island to the west of Midway.[21]

Throughout the night, the four Japanese fleet carriers continued to burn. By sunup however, the *Soryu* and *Kaga* had gone to the bottom and shortly thereafter, the Japanese scuttled both the *Akagi* and *Hiryu*. On the American side, the fires on *Yorktown* had been put out again and it was soon being towed back towards Hawaii. Unfortunately, on June 6, the *Yorktown* was spotted by a Japanese submarine which quickly put two torpedoes into its side. Unable to control the flooding, *Yorktown* sank at 4:58 A.M. on June 7.[22]

At 8:30 A.M., June 5, Col. Allen's eight bombers were still circling Kure Island when they received new orders. Maj. Blakey was leading the second four-plane element and recalled, "We weren't out very long on this second day when we got word two Jap battleships were out there, trying to get away." In reality, the two "battleships" were the heavy cruisers *Mogami* and *Mikuma* which had accidentally collided during the night leaving the *Mogami* with a crushed bow. As *Mogami* turned back to the west, the *Mikuma* went along as an escort.[23]

Arriving at 20,000 feet, the two B-17 elements spotted the heavy cruisers, which the airmen still believed to be battleships. "We found the battleships and my flight dropped on one, Blakey's on the other," recorded Col. Allen. The first element, consisting of Allen, and Lts. Williams, Grundman and Haney, dropped a total of 19 500-lb. bombs on the *Mogami*. "We put a pattern over the battleships and think we got two hits," wrote Allen. Following close behind, Maj. Blakey, accompanied by Capts. Manierre and Whitaker, and Lt. Seeburger, dropped 20 500-lb. bombs on the *Mikuma*. "We were at high altitude, but we scored direct hits on ours, and the other flight got theirs, too," believed Blakey. Japanese reports later confirmed that the eight Fortresses scored only one near miss on the *Mogami*, which killed two men.[24]

Throughout the rest of the day the Japanese continued to withdraw from Midway. The B-17 crews were still hoping to deal the enemy another blow and quickly reloaded their planes with bombs and fuel. "We were helped by

Marines," remembered Col. Allen. "We were delayed in getting oxygen which had to be brought by barge from the other island to Eastern. We went back out in the afternoon." Told that the Japanese Carrier Force had been relocated, at 1:20 P.M. seven of Allen's B-17s departed Midway. Left behind was Capt. Manierre, whose Fortress had developed engine trouble.[25]

"There was no sign of carriers when we got to the point of interception," Col. Allen reported, "but we found a heavy cruiser steaming back toward Midway." The enemy ship was the *Tanikaze*. Acting upon a false report that the *Hiryu* was still afloat, the *Tanikaze* had gone back to rescue any remaining crewmen. Believing that the cruiser was a decoy to divert the Americans away from the retiring carrier force, Col. Allen ignored the ship and led his seven planes westward for another 140 miles. When nothing else was sighted, Allen went back to attack the *Tanikaze*. At 4:35 P.M., the lead element, consisting of Col. Allen and Lts. Williams, Grundman and Haney, dropped a total of 32 500-lb. bombs from 16,000 feet, while the second element, led by Maj. Blakey, accompanied by Capt. Whitaker and Lt. Seeburger, dropped 24 bombs from 14,000 feet. "We dropped a salvo right on the Jap ship with probably one or two hits," concluded Allen. Actually, none of the 56 bombs hit their target.[26]

Close on the heels of Allen's bombers was a flight of Flying Fortresses under the command of Capt. Donald E. Ridings (72nd BS/5th BG). At 8:15 A.M., five B-17s from the 72nd BS, and one from the 394th BS/5th BG, had taken off from Bellows Field to replace the six bombers brought back to Hawaii by Col. Sweeney. Arriving at Midway in the early afternoon, the planes were sent out at 3:45 P.M., when word arrived that an enemy carrier had been spotted to the west of Midway. Left behind when the others took off was Capt. Orin H. Rigley Jr. (72nd BS), whose B-17 had been throwing oil on the trip from Oahu.[27]

Unable to locate the reported carrier, Capt. Ridings' five planes found the *Tanikaze* near 6:45 P.M., but only after Navy dive-bombers had unsuccessfully tried to sink the ship. "My bombs would not go," Ridings found, "so I circled the cruiser at 10,000 feet waiting for the other planes to drop theirs." As antiaircraft fire filled the air, Capts. Glenn Kramer and Richard Stepp (both 72nd BS), and 1st Lt. Ira M. Bird (394th BS) attacked, "scoring no hits but several near misses. . . ." Then, as 1st Lt. Robert Porter (72nd BS) attempted to drop his bombs, he seemed to run into trouble.

While the other crews watched, Lt. Porter, B-17E (41-2415, *City of San Francisco*), which had been paid for by the citizens of San Francisco and donated to the AAF, suddenly dropped both his bombs and his bomb bay tank. Then, *City of San Francisco* swerved out of formation but otherwise appeared to be all right. Figuring that Porter was okay, Ridings led his planes back towards Midway as the sun began to set. Unfortunately, Porter never made it. Apparently hit by antiaircraft fire during the bomb run, B-17E (41-2415, *City of San Francisco*) went down somewhere in the Pacific with its entire crew.[28]

Returning to Midway in the darkness, Ridings' B-17s suddenly found themselves lost. Guided by radar, Capts. Ridings and Stepp, and Lt. Bird finally reached the atoll but Capt. Kramer, B-17E (41-2529), received conflicting directions and before long he was out of gas. Forced to make a water landing, the plane hit the water hard, shattering the Plexiglas nose piece and tearing loose a number of bulkheads. Although the crew had taken up emergency positions in the radio compartment, the radio operator was killed and the others received minor injuries. With the fuselage buckled at the waist gunner positions the plane sank in only 30 seconds, but all eight of the survivors were able to get into the two B-17 life rafts. The next day they were rescued by a Navy PBY.[29]

On Oahu, 7th Bomber Command remained busy throughout June 5. Tasting victory, and wanting to seal the fate of the Japanese fleet, six B-17s from the 31st BS/5th BG, carrying four 600-lb. bombs and a bomb bay tank left Hawaii at 12:05 P.M. A few hours later, six planes from the 26th BS/11th BG, carrying four 1,000-lb. bombs, also set out. After all of the planes had landed, a total of 24 Fortresses were at Midway, although two were still sidelined with mechanical problems.[30]

Around 9:30 A.M., on June 6, American carrier planes attacked the *Mikuma* and the damaged *Mogami*. By the time it was all over, the *Mikuma* was on fire and the *Mogami* had taken further punishment. Eventually the *Mogami* made it back to the protection of Wake Island but the *Mikuma* was too far gone. After sunset, the *Mikuma* capsized and sank.[31]

At 10:45 A.M., reacting to a false report that a Japanese task force was north of Midway, all available combat-worthy B-17s went out on a search. Breaking into small formations, the B-17s searched the area in vain. However, at 11:40 A.M., the six planes from the 26th BS suddenly spotted what appeared to be an enemy cruiser and dropped twenty 1,000-lb. bombs. The airmen reported two definite hits and swore that the cruiser "sank in 15 seconds." In reality, the B-17s had bombed the American submarine USS *Grayling*, which had made a crash dive. Understandably, the infuriated skipper sent a blistering report back to headquarters.[32]

The Battle of Midway was over. Although the Japanese diversionary force was able to occupy the Aleutian islands of Kiska and Attu, the loss to the Imperial Navy at Midway was devastating. Four fleet carriers and one heavy cruiser had been lost, along with 332 planes, and 2,500 men, including many highly-skilled pilots. For the Americans, the battle had cost them one aircraft carrier and one destroyer, and 137 carrier- and land-based planes, including two B-17s. In addition, 307 American servicemen lost their lives.[33] The rolling Japanese war machine had finally been stopped. The Battle of Midway was the first clear-cut victory for the Americans in the Pacific and sent the morale of the troops soaring. Noted the 431st BS/11th BG historian, "The result of this battle was total victory for the U.S." Not beyond celebrating, Sgt. Handrow recalled, "The Japs had been turned around and were taking their beat up fleet with them. Victory was ours and we took it by all getting tight in Honolulu . . ."[34]

Having the advantage of flight, the B-17 crews made it back to Hawaii before any of the Navy personnel and on June 12 they gave their stories to the Honolulu *Advertiser*. Greatly exaggerating their success, the B-17 crews claimed that they had bombed an accumulation of seven battleships or cruisers, seven aircraft carriers, one destroyer, and two transports. The airmen believed that they had scored 22 direct hits, 6 probable hits and 46 near misses. In addition, they claimed that they had shot down eight Japanese fighters and had damaged two more. Days later, when the Navy finally arrived back at Oahu they sent up a wail of protest, rightly claiming that it had been Navy and Marine Corps planes that had sunk the Japanese ships.[35]

In reality, the B-17s had dropped a total of 314 bombs during the Battle of Midway, from heights ranging from 3,600 up to 25,000 feet. In spite of the number of bombs dropped, the hits were minimal. On June 3, Capt. Payne, on his solo run, had scored a near miss on the Japanese transport *Argentina Maru*. On June 4, Lts. Wuertele and Grundman combined to drop one near miss off the stern of the battleship *Haruna*, causing damage to some of her plates. Later that same afternoon, Lt. Haney, attacking from 3,600 feet, probably scored a direct hit on a destroyer. Beyond this, the other hits and near misses were pure optimism. The bomber crews were inexperienced and insufficiently trained. They had made their bomb runs in small numbers and against quickly moving targets. They were lucky to have scored one direct hit and two near misses.[36]

Additionally, the B-17 crews had been greatly overworked. Lt. Col. Sweeney, who had led three of the B-17 bombing runs said, "Our morale was high throughout, but after it was over we were as tired a bunch of flyers as you ever wish[ed] to see."[37] Even after the battle, the Flying Fortresses and the Navy PBYs were kept on patrol, flying pie-shaped search patterns from Midway out towards Wake Island looking for any signs of a retaliatory strike by the Japanese.

Officially, the AAF recognized the dedication of the overworked airmen. Lt. Col. Sweeney was awarded the Distinguished Service Cross for his leadership, and Lt. Col. Allen and Lts. Grundman and Williams were each commended for flying four missions in less than 48 hours.[38] Given more rest prior to the arrival of the Japanese warships, the contribution of the B-17s in the Battle of Midway might have been more substantial. Thrown in piecemeal, even before some of the bomber crews had reached Midway, the poor results of their bombing runs should have been expected.

Never did more than 14 B-17s come over a portion of the Japanese fleet at one time, and even then the planes went after different targets. For the most part, the Flying Fortress crews attacked in flights of four or less, and from varying heights, allowing the enemy ships room to maneuver out from under the falling bombs. "We were green," admitted Lt. Edmundson, "and had much to learn about bombing maneuvering targets." The results of the B-17 strikes in the Battle of Midway might have been more successful if the bomber crews had been given more time to train in formation flying and bombing instead of devoting numerous hours to exhaustive search flights.[39]

In spite of the lack of experience and the poor bomb runs, Japanese survivors admitted that the attacks by the big Flying Fortresses had caused the neatly arranged attacking warships to break formation and go into wild, erratic maneuvers to avoid the falling bombs. Although the B-17s had scored only a couple of hits, they had managed to scatter the Japanese vessels and drive the aircraft carriers away from the protecting antiaircraft fire of the escort ships. Once the fleet was scattered, the flattops had become vulnerable to the Navy dive-bombers.

Additionally, the B-17 reasserted itself as the top reconnaissance plane in the Pacific. While the Navy PBY had about the same range as the Army B-17, the PBY was about 100 mph slower and was less heavily armed so that once the enemy was found the B-17 was far superior. Able to withstand the punishment of attacking Zeros better than a PBY, the B-17 could more easily shadow enemy ships and report their location to headquarters. Impressed by the search and tracking capability of the B-17, Adm. Earnest J. King, Chief of Naval Operations, placed a bid to have a sufficient number of B-17s and B-24s on hand for long-range reconnaissance use by the Navy. However, with the AAF in both Europe and the Pacific fighting for more heavy bombers, Admiral King's bid was quietly ignored.[40]

Although the contribution played by the B-17 in the Battle of Midway is often overlooked, it can be said that the Flying Fortress played an important role in the defense of the atoll. It was a flight of B-17s that dropped the first bombs on the Imperial Invasion Fleet, surprising the Japanese and informing them that their expected conquest of Midway was not going to be easy. Likewise, it was repeated flights of B-17 bombers, interspersed with Navy and Marine Corps torpedo-bombers, that had scattered the tight formation of Japanese ships, thereby leaving the enemy carriers open for the Navy dive-bombers. As the historian for the 23rd BS/5th BG wrote, "We have had a large part in what is apparently a great victory for the US."[41]

On the night of June 6, after the Battle of Midway had ground to a close, four LB-30s lifted off from Midway for a surprise attack on Japanese held Wake Island. Capable of flying a greater distance than a B-17, the LB-30s were recent arrivals from the United States and had flown to Midway from Hickam Field on the night of June 5. With Gen. Tinker along as an enthusiastic observer, the four LB-30s left Midway and headed southwest towards Wake. They never made it. Lost almost from the start, the four planes droned on until Gen. Tinker's plane disappeared into a thick bank of clouds and was never seen again. Although the other three planes continued on, they never found Wake Island and were forced to return to Midway before running out of gas. On June 7, with the disappearance of Gen. Tinker, Brig. Gen. Howard C. Davidson assumed command of the 7th Air Force. Then, 13 days later, the more experienced Maj. Gen. Hale succeeded Gen. Davidson as commander.[42]

XVI

Rabaul and Lae

ALTHOUGH THE AMERICAN airmen in the Southwest Pacific Area felt that the Battle of the Coral Sea had been a strategic victory, they knew that they could not sit back and relax. There was still a war to be won. The American airmen in Australia knew that there was still a lot of hard fighting ahead of them.

There were two hot spots in the Southwest Pacific—Rabaul and Lae. Even though the immediate threat against Port Moresby was gone, Japanese transports could still move under a protective umbrella of land-based aircraft flying out of Rabaul or Lae. In an attempt to cut off the vital supply line to Australia, the Japanese had already captured Tulagi and Florida Island in the Solomons. At the same time, they had been building up their forces at Lae and Salamaua on the north coast of British New Guinea, and it was only a matter of time before Japan started pushing her troops over the Owen Stanley Mountains towards Port Moresby. Something had to be done to harass the Japanese and keep them back on their heels, and the Allied air force was called on to handle the job.[1]

With only a limited amount of resources, the Allied strategic planners had to make a decision as to the importance of each target. Realizing that Rabaul was the major staging area for transports ferrying troops to both New Guinea and the Solomons, the commanders selected Rabaul as the primary target.[2] However, Lae and Salamaua would not be overlooked.

Although there were two heavy bombardment groups in Australia, the 43rd BG at Sydney, minus the 13th RS, which had been redesignated the 403rd BS (Heavy) on April 22, and which was still helping out at Laverton Repair Depot, did not have any B-17s. The harassment and isolation of Rabaul and Lae would be left up to the tired veterans of the 19th BG.[3] In preparation for the upcoming campaign, around the middle of May, the 28th and the 93rd BSs moved out of Cloncurry and into an airbase at Longreach, about 400 miles to the southeast.[4]

The airbase at Longreach was a vast improvement over the base at

Cloncurry. "Looks like a swell place," a newly promoted Capt. Rouse wrote. "Much cleaner and larger than Cloncurrie [sic] . . . Flies aren't any where near as bad. Mosquitoes not so bad but plenty of them."[5] With a population of roughly 1,200 people, Longreach was somewhat overwhelmed by the sudden influx of over 500 American airmen. With most of the men under the age of 20, they naturally became a little mischievous at times. "The streets in Longreach were exceptionally wide," recalled mechanic Mike Payne. "They parked on the sides and in the middle as well . . . We flew [our Fortresses] down the main street looking in the second story of the buildings . . . It was interesting to look in 2nd story windows of hotels, looking out gunports in a B-17." The men also discovered that the strong B-17 prop wash could be used in a playful manner. "You can also upset a outdoor toilet by banking close to it close to the ground," added Payne.[6]

In spite of Longreach's improvement over Cloncurry, all of the movement and readjustment for the war-weary veterans had its effect. The 19th BG continued to be based at small, out of the way places, far from any large Australian city and its diversions. The constantly changing facilities, the lack of recreation, and even the unfamiliarity with the Australian food and drink, played havoc with the fragile morale of the 19th BG. Additionally, it was hard to maintain their battered B-17s on a supply line that stretched 7,500 miles back to the United States. A shortage of spare parts and trained mechanics, along with bad landing fields, ever-changing weather, long missions, and unending combat left only 50 percent of the airplanes ready at any given time.[7] Yet, in spite of these hardships, the 19th BG continued to function.

Over the next few days, while the 28th and 93rd BSs were moving to Longreach, the B-17s from the 40th RS struck Rabaul, and also the seaplane base at Deboyne Island in the Louisiade Archipelago. On May 13, nine Zeros came after three Fortresses that struck at Rabaul, and for the first time, the Japanese from Rabaul used the more successful head-on attacks. In spite of these new tactics however, only one Fortress was damaged while one Zero was shot down by Capt. Bostrom's gunners in B-17E (41-2434).[8]

On May 16, the 40th RS was renamed the 435th BS but as the squadron historian noted, "The changes in the squadron were in name only, all personnel remained practically the same throughout."[9] In mid-May the squadron received a few Australian pilots who were brought in to fly as copilots with the American crews. Since so many of the 19th BGs original pilots had been transferred to India or been given staff positions in the newly reorganized group, and since so many copilots had become first pilots, there was, in the words of Gen. Brett, "a crying need" for copilots. To try and relieve the shortage, the decision was made to use Australians as copilots on the B-17s. "The caliber of these men in every way met the highest standards of pilot performance," wrote 1st Lt. Horace Perry. Although trained on twin-engined British aircraft, the Australians "assiduously set themselves to master the technique of four engined B-17 flying. . . ."[10]

At almost the same time, the 435th BS was improving their planes. Faced with the new head-on attacks, the ground crews began installing twin .50 caliber machine guns in the nose compartment. Lt. Perry reported on the improvisation: "At the time we had a wrecked B-17 that had been stripped for parts. A trial installation was made in this ship to determine if the plastic cell material [of the nose] would withstand the shock of twin 50 caliber machine-guns firing together." When the guns were test fired against the side of a hill, Lt. Perry wrote, "They worked—and how! Tracers set the grass afire and the squadron spent the afternoon fighting a grass fire."[11]

On May 18 and 20, the idle planes from the 93rd BS got back into the shooting war. In an attempt to help the struggling Dutch on Timor Island, five Fortresses staged through Batchelor Field and hit the shipping off Koepang.[12] On May 21, the 93rd BS went to Rabaul. Recorded the squadron historian, ". . . despite a great deal of ice on the planes, bombs were dropped on the target." Two days later, the squadron repeated the flight but could not drop their bombs because of thick clouds over the target.[13]

The B-17s from the 28th BS got back into the war on May 24 when two separate flights from the squadron hit both Rabaul and Lae. Japanese ace Sakai was stationed at Lae and recalled, "For the first time . . . four B-17s attacked with an escort of twenty fighters. Over the towering Owen Stanley Mountains, all hell broke loose when 16 Zeros plummeted into their ranks. Five enemy [i.e. American] fighters went down, but the Fortresses escaped." Because of bad weather, the Lae mission was unsuccessful.[14]

Six B-17s from the 19th BG, led by Maj. Elbert Helton, the CO of the 28th BS, hit the Rabaul area again on May 25. Bombing from 27,000 feet, the planes attacked Rabaul's Vunakanau airfield in two three-plane elements but when Maj. Helton's bombsight went out, only the second element released their bombs, setting fire to several parked aircraft.[15]

While the planes were returning to Port Moresby, they were jumped by 12 Zeros. Concentrating on the first element, the Japanese attacked for 45 minutes and lost two planes. Reporting the damage to the B-17s, Capt. Rouse wrote, "Maj. Hilton's [sic] ship had two shell holes, [and] several machine gun [holes]. Top gunner badly wounded. [Lt.] Evans, 3rd ship, one shell hole in tail—tail gunner slightly hurt in head. Our ship one machine gun bullet in vertical stabilizer . . . We were lucky."[16]

The next afternoon, the three planes from the second element led by Capt. Hardison in B-17E (41-2489, *Suzy-Q*) took off to bomb Rabaul's Simpson Harbor. Running into a storm front, Hardison continued on while his two wingmen turned back.[17] Reaching the target area, Hardison found an opening in the clouds and aided by a full moon dropped a string of 500-lb. demolition bombs and incendiaries on the docks and warehouses from 5,000 feet. Circling back, he dropped down to 1,000 feet and let his gunners strafe a military camp at the edge of town.[18]

Without the threat of an effective Japanese night fighter, the 19th BG employed a unique bit of warfare over Rabaul. By attacking at night, the Americans chased the Japanese into the malaria-carrying, mosquito-infested slit trenches. Noted the 435th BS historian, "Disease is a weapon in warfare."[19]

Turning back towards Port Moresby, Capt. Hardison dropped down further still, to 150 feet, and let his gunners strafe the parked airplanes at Lakunai Airfield, a few miles northwest of Rabaul, and at Gasmata Airfield along the south coast of New Britain.[20] Having wasted precious gas during his strafing runs, Capt. Hardison ran into trouble when he finally reached Port Moresby and found it socked in by fog. Turning towards Horn Island, and fighting a 60-mph headwind, he shut down two engines and throttled back on the other two to conserve gas. This, however, only caused the *Suzy-Q* to lose altitude at the rate of 50 feet per minute.

With only 15 minutes of fuel remaining, the airmen finally spotted land and although Hardison suggested that the crew bale out, everyone elected to stay. Finding a flat piece of ground, Hardison set the *Suzy-Q* down with the airspeed indicator showing only 70 miles per hour, 20 miles less than the usual controlled landing. When the sun came up on May 27, the airmen were surprised to find that they had miraculously landed in a field pockmarked with waist-deep melon holes.[21]

Unbeknownst to the crew, the plane had come down on the northern tip of the York Peninsula. Radioing Townsville, the crew called for "200 gallons fuel, shovels and water . . ." but it wasn't until the night of May 31 that an Australian rescue team reached them. After filling in the melon holes, stripping the plane of all unnecessary weight, and clearing a 900-foot long runway, the *Suzy-Q* was backed up with her tail between two scrub trees. Reported Sgt. Fesmire: "[Capt. Hardison] held her on the brakes and gave her full power until the tail pulled up then let her roll. About a third of the way down he gave her one-third flaps and when they reached the end of the strip and pulled her off she was only doing 80, but they made it."

Twenty-five minutes later Capt. Hardison landed at Coen, Queensland.[22] This was the last combat mission for B-17E (41-2489, *Suzy-Q*). Like some of the older planes with the remote-control Bendix belly turret, the *Suzy-Q* was pulled from combat and replaced with the newer model B-17Es. In May alone the 19th BG received nine of the newer models, thus allowing the older models to be relegated to transport and supply duties. However, on May 26, the group lost one of the new planes when Lt. Jacques was taking off in B-17E (41-2631) from Charters Towers and the controls locked up unexpectedly. Although the crew was uninjured, the plane was wrecked beyond repair.[23]

Rabaul continued to be the primary target of the 19th BG throughout the rest of May and during the first week of June. Small numbers of B-17s hit Rabaul on May 28 and 29, and went back again on June 1, and for three consecutive nights beginning June 3.[24] At the same time, the Fortresses did not forget the Japanese installations on northern New Guinea. On May 30, planes hit Lae and Salamaua and, on June 1 one plane hit Lae again. This time, however, in addition to dropping bombs, the aircrews showered the areas with empty beer bottles. As Lt. Sargent, the pilot, wrote, "Beer bottles were thrown out on the second pass which drew antiaircraft fire." Perhaps discarded purely for fun, the falling bottles made an eerie whistling sound as they twirled downward. The antiaircraft gunners, perhaps fearing that the noise was from some new type of bomb, concentrated on the whistling bottles and left the B-17 alone. Flying unmolested, Lt. Sargent dropped his bombs and made a quick getaway before the "new bombs" could be investigated.[25]

Although the rest of the 19th BG was inactive from June 6–8, the 435th BS continued to fly reconnaissance missions of Rabaul and northern New Guinea. Although officially designated a bomb squadron, the 435th continued to act as the fact finding squadron for the 19th BG, designated by their unique squadron patch depicting an airborne kangaroo holding a bomb in its tail and a spyglass to its eye. Usually, single planes from the "Kangaroo Squadron," as they became known, were sent over a target before and after a raid to photograph and obtain pertinent information. When chased by enemy fighters, the B-17 usually headed for the clouds—but not always. During a flight on June 8, Capt. Eaton, B-17E (41-2666, *Lucy*), was jumped by a few Zeros at 18,000 feet and managed to positively shoot down one plane and possibly a second.[26]

On June 9, two B-17s aided in a massive American air raid on Lae and Salamaua. Originally, three Fortresses set out but Lt. Fields' plane was badly damaged when his own top-turret guns malfunctioned and shot his tall tail to pieces. "[T]he rudder was shot in two," Fields recalled. Without a rudder, Fields dumped his bombs and returned to Port Moresby. "Gen. Scanlon and Gen. Royce were there on an inspection tour, and they saw us come in," Fields wrote. Believing that the crew had run into enemy opposition, the two generals raced over to hear what had happened. "[W]e told them that our guns had run away; that we shot our own tail off," Fields admitted. "Well, they were pretty much disgusted; they turned around and got in their jeep and drove away. They weren't very happy."[27]

Both Horn Island and Port Moresby were being relied upon more and more as forward staging areas. Problems arose however, as neither field was ever intended to take the amount of traffic that was now coming into them. Seven Mile Airstrip at Port Moresby, the busier of the two, had only one landing strip and no dispersal area. Cut into a circle of low hills, the runway ran up hill so that there was only one direction of takeoff, regardless of the wind. When first put into use, there were no fighter planes or antiaircraft guns at Seven Mile Strip, but as these units arrived in Australia they were sent over to help defend the B-17s while they were on the ground. Likewise, the airfield itself was eventually improved. "By May. . . ," Col. Kurtz recalled, "we began to get the situation in hand at Moresby. We got some dispersal fields back in the hills for our planes and an operational alarm net[work] . . ." Unfortunately, the improvements attracted the attention of Japanese bombers—which caused more problems. "For a while we had a labor problem," Kurtz continued. "The tame village natives we'd hired to work on the field didn't like the bombs, and when the alarm sounded, instead of jumping into the foxholes they'd beat it into the jungle, and maybe not come back for a couple of days. However, this soon stopped, because the cannibal head-hunters who lived in the jungle used to stalk them and chase them back, and as between the bombs and the head-hunters, the natives chose the bombs, so we got plenty of work done."[28]

The constant Japanese air raids on Seven Mile Strip, forced the B-17 crews to avoid keeping their planes on the ground for any length of time. "It was bombed and strafed almost daily by the enemy and we couldn't afford to expose our Flying Fortresses to destruction on the ground," recalled Capt. William Crawford, Jr. (65th BS/43rd BG), who flew into Port Moresby at a later time. The typical mission called for the B-17s to take off from Australia late in the evening followed by a risky night landing at Seven Mile Strip. The planes would then be refueled and take off before sunup since the Japanese were always expected to bomb the airfield before noon. The planes stayed in formation going to the target but once the bombs were dropped, the planes returned individually, stopping at Port Moresby to refuel before flying back to Australia, where once again they were forced to make a night landing.[29]

If the men could avoid the Japanese bombers, fighters and antiaircraft fire, and land safely in the darkness, they still had to contend with the constant, and violent, tropical storms. Fighting so close to the equator, the airmen often flew through thick, almost impenetrable weather on their way to and from the target. The pilots were often forced to use maximum power on all four engines to keep the plane under control. Engine life was subsequently diminished and the stress and strain on the pilots was unbelievable. Since the AAF had yet to decide on the requirements of how many combat missions or combat hours a crew had to fly before being sent home, there seemed no end in sight for the veterans of the 19th BG.[30]

As bad as Port Moresby was, however, the airstrip at Horn Island was worse. The disadvantages at Horn Island were listed as "the ocean, the hills, and the heavy jungle forest." The island sported two runways which crossed each other in the center. The first terminated at the ocean edge and the other came to an end at the foot of the heavily forested hills. When using the ocean strip, the pilots had to hope that they had enough wind blowing off the water to give them lift or they would end up in the drink. When using the other runway, the pilots had to hope that they had enough power and enough height to clear the forest.[31] In spite of these disadvantages, the two forward bases were all that the 19th BG had and they continued to use them until they could find something better or improve what they already had.

During the second week of June the 19th BG sent small flights of bombers, usually three B-17Es, against the airfields on Rabaul on four separate occasions. Each time 5th Bomber Command hit Rabaul, the Japanese went through the process of rebuilding and resupplying. The *United States Strategic Bombing Survey* reported, "Stubborn adherence to a preconceived plan [by the Japanese] was clearly evident in many instances but nowhere was this operational inflexibility more apparent than in the enemy's continuing to reinforce Rabaul . . . After a large portion of the air garrison had been destroyed or rendered nonoperational by damage, a delay of a few days to a week would insure the presence of new air units and/or airplanes in strength." The enemy kept resupplying Rabaul, and the 19th BG kept tearing it apart.[32]

Curious for a look at how the war in the Southwest Pacific was progressing, President Roosevelt sent Senator and Lt. Comdr. Lyndon B. Johnson, future president of the United States, on a tour to report on the morale of the men. On June 11, Johnson, Gen. Royce and 11 other VIPs, were flying from Darwin to Melbourne with Capt. Kurtz in B-17D (40-3097, *The Swoose*). Trouble with a navigator's octant and sloppy flying when each of the VIPs was given a chance to fly the plane put *The Swoose* terribly off course. Low on fuel, Kurtz was forced to land his planeload of VIPs in the Australian outback. Using a farmer's telephone, Johnson called for help and the next morning, after receiving some gas, Kurtz eventually flew his important cargo on to Melbourne.[33]

On June 15, Gen. Brett held an awards ceremony at Longreach. Wrote Lt. Knudson in his diary, "Both squadrons[,] the 28th and 93rd[,] were in their shining best and in formation. The awards were for the Java Campaign mostly."[34] That same date a reconnaissance plane from the 435th BS flew the first mission over the island of Guadalcanal in the Solomon Islands. With the Japanese having already invaded Buka, and Bougainville, and a number of smaller islands in the northern Solomons, and Tulagi and Florida Island in the southern Solomons, the Americans were keeping a sharp eye on developments in the area.[35]

Three B-17s from the 435th BS hit Lae on June 16 and drew the Zero fighters after them, allowing B-25s and B-26s to go in low and bomb and strafe everything in sight. "This was a disastrous day for the Japs," reported the historian of the 435th BS.[36] On June 18, B-17s from the 30th and 93rd BSs attacked Vunakanau airdrome and Rabaul's Simpson Harbor, scoring direct hits on a 10,000-ton transport. In the middle of the bomb run, bombardier Lt. Gooch felt a tap on his shoulder. "I turned and looked around the armor plate behind me to see our navigator surrounded by silk," he wrote. "The [nose] was full of his released parachute. Somehow he had opened it by mistake and the silk blossomed all over the place. I completed the bombing run, and when I was not firing the nose gun to fight off Japanese fighters, I helped him stuff his parachute back into its packet." Writing years later, Gooch added, "This episode seems humorous to me but I suspect it wasn't at all funny for him at the time."[37]

On June 19, the 19th BG set out from Port Moresby to attack Rabaul with a maximum effort. Seven planes from the 30th BS and six from the 93rd took off around 6:00 A.M., followed two hours later by three Fortresses from the 28th BS. Later, around 2:30 P.M., three B-17s from the 435th BS headed towards Rabaul. The first flights ran into a storm south of New Britain and became widely separated. "[R]an into light clouds which changed to a very bad snow storm," Capt. Rouse wrote. "Formation broke up. Ship iced up. Engines completely covered with ice." After 45 minutes, Rouse broke out of the storm and found that he was all alone: "Couldn't see any other planes so went on towards Rabaul. Decided to go in alone at 30,000 feet indicated." However, when the ball turret gunner passed out two times due to a faulty oxygen feed, Rouse decided to forego the mission and headed towards Horn Island.[38]

Although Rouse was unable to reach the target, some of the other planes did. Five B-17s went over Rabaul at 29,000 feet and were attacked by 17 Zeros. In the ensuing air battle, one Zero was shot down and three more were listed as "probably lost." Later, three more Flying Fortresses, perhaps from the 28th BS, attacked Rabaul and in turn were jumped by two Zeros which inflicted slight damage to one of the Forts.[39] Meanwhile, the planes from the 435th BS never got off the ground. Before they could take off, the mission was canceled.

On June 20, the three 435rd BS planes finally took off, heading towards Lae. Led by Lt. Fields, the flight was crossing over the Owen Stanley Mountains when they were suddenly attacked. "We had two Jap pursuit planes attack us," Fields recalled, "but they didn't persist, and they didn't do any damage to us. We dropped our bombs on the airstrip at Lae, but the visibility was not such that we could tell what kind of damage we did."[40]

For the last week in June, the 435th BS reverted back to a reconnaissance unit flying daily missions all over the Southwest Pacific. Although most of the missions were "milk runs," a few were memorable. On a flight over Kendari on June 24, flown at 14,000 feet, 1st Lt. James A. Gibb was attacked by three Zeros who promptly knocked out his ball turret. When Gibb attempted to jettison his two bomb bay gas tanks only one fell while the other remained "frozen" in place, causing the bomb bay doors to remain stuck open. For 55 minutes the crew fought off the attackers as Gibb put the plane into wild evasive maneuvers and dropped down to only 2,500 feet. When the Zeros finally gave up, the bomb bay doors were cranked closed by hand and the plane returned safely to Australia.[41]

"Probably the roughest reconnaissance mission," flown by bombardier 1st Lt. Theodore I. Pascoe (435th BS) took place on June 25. The B-17 crew had flown a photo mission to Kavieng and was only 100 miles from Port Moresby when 15 Zeros attacked. "We were under attack for 45 minutes," Pascoe recalled. "Two motors were shot out and we were trapped. We couldn't get altitude to get over the mountains while under attack. But we made it home through a pass." Three Zeros were destroyed and two more were badly damaged. When the B-17 finally landed at Port Moresby, Pascoe found that three crewmen had been wounded and that the plane, "was battered with many cannon gaps and numerous machine gun holes."[42]

While the 435th BS was keeping an eye on the Japanese, the other three squadrons, the 28th, 30th and 93rd, continued to attack Rabaul and Northern New Guinea. Attacking at night and dropping incendiary bombs, the B-17s were sometimes able to start "large fires . . . which were visible 60 miles away."[43]

On June 30, two Fortresses from the 28th BS and three from the 93rd BS flew "the longest combat mission ever flown by the group with return to the same base."[44] Taking off from Batchelor Field near Darwin at 1:45 P.M., the B-17s bombed Kendari airfield on Celebes just before sunset from 8,000 feet through a heavy cloud layer. "Hit the field good," Capt. Rouse put in his diary. "Looked like about 150-200 Zeros and bombers on the ground. Figure we damaged or destroyed about 40 of them . . ." Turning from the attack, the three 93rd BS planes were suddenly jumped by one lone Zero. "He made six separate passes," wrote Lt. Teats. The crews from the three Fortresses concentrated their firepower and eventually shot the persistent fighter down but not before he had caused some damage himself. "Evidently," Teats reasoned, "the pilot was killed or badly hit and 'froze' to the gun triggers; but his last pass got one of Smitty's [Capt. Weldon Smith] engines." Throughout the flight, Smith had been losing oil on his No. 3 engine and had planned to feather the propeller after the bomb run. Now, hit in the No. 4 engine, Smith checked his gauges, found that No. 4 was still operating properly and shut down his No. 3 engine.[45]

Unaware of Smith's troubles because of the surrounding darkness, the other four planes turned south to hit Dili, on Timor. "Here a night bombing attack was made from a low level," noted the 93rd BS historian, "and despite more heavy AA fire the planes continued on towards Darwin." Near 1:25 A.M. on July 1, almost 11 hours after taking off, the four B-17s returned to Batchelor and found a dense cloud of thick smoke hanging over the landing strip. "Smoke so thick I couldn't see the field from ¼ mile away," Rouse noted.[46] Unknown to them, the smoke was caused by the crash of Capt. Smith's bomber B-17E (41-9014).

Having already feathered his No. 3 engine, Smith was coming in for a landing when the damaged No. 4 engine suddenly quit. At the same time, the control cables on the right side of the plane, failed him, causing him to dive nose first into the ground. Three crewmen were killed in the fiery crash and the other six were badly shaken and injured. Ignoring his own injuries bombardier Lt. Everett "Stinky" Davis went back into the burning plane to save his fellow crewmen. Wrote a war correspondent, "While the ship blazed furiously, he fought his way through the confusion of twisted white-hot girders and roaring flames to pull out the tail gunner. He went back for a side gunner, returned for the other side gunner. Finally, he even thrust himself into the center of the conflagration and struggled out with the radio operator." A week later Lt. Davis was recommended for the Distinguished Service Cross.[47]

The June 30 mission had covered 3,560 air miles, of which 1,506 had been flown over enemy controlled territory.[48] Perhaps 40 enemy airplanes had been destroyed at the cost of three American lives and one more B-17. Although Flying Fortresses continued to arrive in Australia via the Pacific air route, the planes continued to disappear. In addition to the loss of B-17E (41-9014), the 19th BG lost B-17E (41-2667) when it exploded from an unknown reason at Whenuapi, near Auckland, New Zealand on June 9, leaving a small crater in its place.[49]

July began with a raid by the 28th BS on the newly constructed airfield on Buka Island in the northern Solomons. Unfortunately, the mission was aborted when the flight ran into bad weather.[50] On July 3, the 435th BS hit Lae while the 93rd BS attacked Koepang on Timor. Both flights managed to drop their bombs and both flights were attacked by Zeros as they flew back to Port Moresby.

Although no B-17s were knocked down, the plane flown by Lt. Clyde B. Kelsey (93rd BS) was badly damaged. Lt. Rouse summarized the damage in his diary, "[Kelsey] had 6-8 shell holes plus machine gun holes in his plane, #3 engine hit, right wing two holes, right horizontal stabilizer 2 holes, vertical fin pulverized, left horizontal stabilizer one hole, left wing one hole, one hole thru #3 prop, one hit just forward of lower turret, one piece of shell through gas line." Although battered, the plane brought its crew safely back to New Guinea.[51]

Independence Day found the 19th BG sending six B-17s from the 93rd BS, led by Capt. Hardison, B-17E (41-2640, *Tojo's Physic*), to start a fireworks display at Lae. Coming along for the ride was war correspondent Howell Walker, of *National Geographic Magazine*. "As we drew nearer the target area," Walker reported, "I felt remarkably confident from the knowledge that six Fortresses in tight formation made up the attacking force. Contemplation of even one of these ships with its bomb bay wide open, all guns ready, and the four engines droning on a steady course through the frigid substratosphere is mighty comforting over enemy territory." Dropping their bombs on the Lae airfield, the six B-17s hit the dispersal area and set fire to an oil dump. "A tremendous fire blazed on the edge of the airdrome," Walker noted, "and huge masses of black smoke billowed up from two other fires in the same area."

The B-17s were 10 minutes away from the target when they were suddenly jumped by six Zeros. "Their tracer shots poured past our windows like a horizontal hail of red-hot rivets," admitted Walker. "Never before had I been in actual combat. Now that I was, it did not seem real." As Walker watched, he was impressed by the maneuverability of the Japanese Zero. "Swerving, darting, and diving," he wrote, "they streaked the atmosphere around our big bomber like chimney swifts exercising for fun near their nesting place."

In spite of their maneuverability, however, one of the Zeros was damaged by the converging fire from the six Fortresses. "Our side gunner [then] poured round after round from a .50-caliber machine gun into the faltering plane," Walker wrote. "His face lit up as the Zero exploded, and trailing thick, black smoke, started its 28,000-foot swan flight from stingy substratosphere to steaming jungle below."[52]

Having lost one, and possibly two planes, the fighters broke off the attack. Remarkably, B-17E (41-2640, *Tojo's Physic*) had only one bullet hole in it, and this in spite of the fact that the ball turret had gone unmanned. Thirty minutes before reaching Lae, the gunner had turned "white as dough . . ." from a faulty oxygen feed which was becoming a recurring problem with the ball turret. Returning in the darkness to Horn Island, five planes landed without incident but Lt. Richard Smith hit a runway light with B-17E (41-2633, *Sally*) and blew out the left tire. The plane dropped with such force that the "landing gear plowed up through the No. 2 engine." Although repairable, the plane would be sidelined for some time.[53]

On July 5, the 19th BG returned to Lae airfield with two independent flights.[54] More importantly, while the planes were engaged at New Guinea, a reconnaissance plane flew a mission over Guadalcanal. Passing along the middle of the north coast, near Lunga Point, the crew noticed and photographed a new Japanese airfield. Tipped off by an Australian "coastwatcher" that a Japanese work party had crossed over from Tulagi and was working on a new airfield, the B-17 came back with the first concrete evidence of the fact. The Japanese were preparing to move their planes onto Guadalcanal, 560 miles to the southeast of Rabaul. When the field was finished, planes stationed on Guadalcanal could fly cover for ships anchored at Tulagi. Then, utilizing the anchorage at Tulagi, and the airfield at Guadalcanal, the Japanese could move south and attack Samoa or the Fiji Islands, thereby threatening or breaking the Allied lifeline between the United States and Australia. Something had to be done to prevent the Japanese from occupying the Guadalcanal airfield and something had to be done fast.[55]

The very next day, seven 435th BS B-17s flew up to Guadalcanal and bombed a motor boat.[56] When reconnaissance indicated that the Japanese were building up a concentration of ships in Kavieng and Rabaul harbors, the American commanders figured that the Japanese were going to send reinforcements to Guadalcanal. On July 11, six planes from the 28th BS set out to bomb Rabaul. Attacked by five Zeros while still close to New Guinea, the B-17s jettisoned their bomb bay gas tanks and bombs and concentrated on fighting off the attackers. "The tactics employed by the enemy in making their attacks upon our formation consisted mainly of attempting head on attacks," reported Lt. Knudson. Although the Zeros attacked for 45 minutes, none of the bombers or crewmen were seriously wounded. However, having dropped their bombs and bomb bay tanks, the B-17s were forced to return to Port Moresby.[57]

On the morning of July 13, 1st Lt. Donald O. Tower (435th BS) flew a reconnaissance mission over Kavieng and then headed for a look at Rabaul. Unfortunately, the enemy at Kavieng were able to notify Rabaul that Tower was on his way. Once over Rabaul, Tower managed to get his photographs but as he was leaving the area he was jumped by enemy fighters. "One by one three Jap Zeros zoomed over and under us, giving us all they had of machine gun fire and cannon shots," he said. Cannon shells tore into each wing of B-17E (41-9206) and shot open the bomb bay doors. The manual winding mechanism was also hit, making it impossible to close the doors. A bullet passed through the cockpit front window and shattered the copilot's side window, and the No. 4 engine was "shot away," making it impossible to feather the windmilling propeller. Chased for 40 minutes, Tower's nose gunner managed to shoot down one Zero before the B-17 reached the safety of some clouds.

"But now we had serious trouble on our hands," Tower remarked, "with one engine gone and the bomb bay doors making a drag." Although Tower had hoped to find a pass through the Owen Stanley Mountains, when he reached the area the mountains were shrouded with clouds. Giving full throttle to the three good engines, Tower managed to get B-17E (41-9206) above the overcast and find a pass. When Tower landed at Port Moresby he estimated that he only had "approximately twenty minutes gas left."[58]

On that same date, July 13, the 30th BS lost two planes. Lt. Lindsey crashed into a mud flat while taking off from Horn Island in B-17E (41-2655), killing three of the crew and wrecking the plane beyond repair. Later, Lt. Curtis J. Holdridge was forced to ditch B-17E (41-2636) more than 500 yards off shore at Horn Island. Both planes had been in the combat zone for less than three months, both having arrived in Australia on April 14. Still, they had beaten the odds. Statistics compiled by Gen. Brett in May had shown that the average life of a B-17 in a combat area was 66 days.[59]

On July 15, the announcement was made for the planned occupation of Buna, on the north coast of Papua New Guinea. Early in July, the Joint Chiefs of Staff had developed a three-task plan to defeat the Japanese in the South and Southwest Pacific. Task I, was the occupation of the Santa Cruz Islands and Tulagi in the southern Solomons; Task II, was the parallel move to reoccupy the northern coast of New Guinea; and Task III, was the conquest and reoccupation of New Britain and Rabaul. Although Task I was to start first, MacArthur had already developed his plans for the re-conquest of New Guinea. By July 17 Australian troops were advancing through the Kokoda Pass in the Owen Stanley Mountains towards Buna.[60]

The 19th BG lost B-17E (41-2421) from the 435th BS on July 16 when "Sandy" McPherson, now a major, and Lt. Lucius Penick, with 17 other people on board, crashed at Horn Island. Not a soul survived. "When I heard of that accident, I had a pretty good idea of what had happened," commented Lt. Fields, "because McPherson was a person that just took everything out of an airplane that it had in it." Eyewitnesses stated that the plane was coming in for a landing but overshot the runway and made a "very steep turn" to come around again. As it did so, one of the wing tips dug into the ground and the plane crashed and exploded. Rumor stated that the less experienced Lt. Penick had been in control.

Lt. Fields, however, disagreed. "Penick was a classmate of mine and I know that McPherson did not let him fly very much," he stated. "[The crash] sounded to me like something that McPherson would pull because he was pretty caustic; he probably just took the airplane over and made a sharp turn and dug a wing in the ground on his go-around. Anyway, nobody will ever know, because they were all killed."[61] Among those killed in the fiery crash was 43-year-old Sgt. "Soup" Silva, the living legend of the 19th BG.[62]

The dawning of July 17 found B-17s from the 28th and 93rd BSs hitting Rabaul's Simpson Harbor.[63] On that same date, Lt. Ramsey from the 435th BS, flying in B-17E (41-2639), took two officers from the 1st Marine Division on a personal reconnaissance of Guadalcanal. Attacked by two Japanese floatplanes, the top turret gunner downed one, while the side gunner got the second.[64] Although only a few people may have realized it at the time, the two Marine Corps observers were scouting Tulagi and Guadalcanal in an attempt to find the best place for a simultaneous amphibious invasion. Fearful of the Japanese airfield at Lunga Point, the Joint Chiefs of Staff had decided to launch an American invasion of the two islands. Although the operation was to be handled by the U.S. Navy and the 1st Marine Division, plans called for the AAF to play an important role in the upcoming offensive.[65]

By the third week in July, changes were taking place for the 19th BG again. On July 10, Lt. Col. Connally, the CO of the 19th BG, had been replaced by Lt. Col. Carmichael, late CO of the 435th BS. On July 18, Carmichael began moving the battered veterans from the 19th BG to a new airbase at Mareeba, at the base of the York Peninsula, leaving the Kangaroo Squadron at Townsville. Mareeba was only 525 miles from Port Moresby, which meant less flight time on planes going out on combat missions and less fatigue on the men. The consolidation of the 28th, 30th and 93rd BSs at Mareeba brought these squadrons together for the first time since the evacuation of Java in late February and was made to improve the morale and performance of the men.[66]

Almost everybody agreed that the new airbase at Mareeba was a vast improvement over Longreach and Cloncurry. "This place is pretty nice," a newly-promoted Maj. Rouse concluded. "1500 ft. high in a big wood with a deep river in back of the camp, mountains all around it, and two good long runways. I am going to like it here very much." Sitting on a plateau between high mountains, the airfield consisted of two dry, 7,000 feet flat and wide runways running at right angles from each other. "Besides the runways," recorded historian Priscilla Hardison, "there were curving strips, just the width of a Fortress. These were used for paths along which to taxi the planes to the woods themselves . . . Except for these strips, the forest was left intact; the trees were tall, their high overhanging branches practically concealed the dispersal paths."[67]

Although living quarters at Mareeba consisted of high-peaked tents placed among the shade of the tall trees, the men were generally happy and found few things to complain about. "Mareeba, in Australia, was a big improvement over Cloncurry in almost every way," Lt. Gooch reported. "While we did live in tents away from any towns, unlike Cloncurry, there were trees around us, and nowhere near as many flies, and fewer mosquitoes. Rain and mud were not problems at Mareeba." Echoing Gooch, Mike Payne recalled, "There we lived in pyramid tents. Things were good though. They had open range land there and when we got tired of mutton we could kill a cow or hog and cook that."[68]

The airbase at Mareeba also included post exchanges and a base hospital "made of slabs of wood, hastily nailed up and roofed with tin sheets," all of which were administered by American personnel. While the exchanges gave the men access to American goods when they were available, the on base hospital meant that wounded or sick airmen would not have to be transported over miles of bumpy, dusty roads to the nearest hospital and be treated by Australian doctors and nurses.[69]

As usual, the American airmen quickly found ways to entertain themselves. "We used to have a stripped down B-17 used to haul cargo," Payne remembered. "When watermelons were in season we used to load it up with melons and take them up to altitude to cool them . . . A good use of taxpayers gas." While visiting the small, nearby town of Mareeba, the airmen taught the native Australians a few things about American life. "[W]e had to teach them to cool their beer," Payne wrote. "They drank it room temp. We also taught them to make hamburgers. We showed them how to make milkshakes the American way."[70]

While the 19th BG was moving, the war continued. Unknown to the Americans, the Japanese had also come to the conclusion that Buna would make a splendid base for operations against Port Moresby. In spite of the vigilance of the 435th BS, a Japanese task force arrived safely off the shore of Buna on the afternoon of July 21. During the night, troops were put ashore at both Buna, and Gona, a few miles to the north.[71]

Apprised of the situation, the Allies mounted a "maximum effort" on July 22, sending American and Australian bombers and fighters, and 12 B-17s against the landing force. Two lone B-17s attacked Buna at two different times, but the 19th BGs best chance came when a group of 10 Fortresses from the 28th and 30th BSs came overhead. Targeting two destroyers and a transport, the planes dropped 72 500-lb. bombs. Unfortunately, they all missed. "Found a perfect target and weather and no opposition but missed," wrote a dejected Maj. Rouse. "The largest formation we have had and we missed." Though unsubstantiated, Rouse felt that the bombardier in the lead plane had gone "haywire," causing the other bombardiers, who toggled on the lead plane, to drop their bombs harmlessly into the sea.[72]

By midday of July 23 the Japanese were strongly entrenched at both Buna and Gona. Still, the Allies continued to attack. On July 23, the fighters and bombers were back, and so were the B-17s. Apparently disappointed with the results of the July 22 mission, Col. Carmichael personally led five B-17s over the enemy ships this time. Although the B-17s dropped 28 more 500-lb. bombs on the enemy ships they scored only one direct hit.[73]

It was too little, too late. In spite of knowing the Japanese codes, the Allies had been taken completely by surprise. Within a matter of days, 13,000 Japanese troops came ashore at Buna and Gona. MacArthur's capture of Buna had to be postponed as the Australian infantry on the Kokoda trail, who had gotten as far as the village of Kokoda, 50 miles inland from Gona, suddenly went on the defensive. Almost immediately, although the Allied fighters and bombers continued to harass the Japanese, Imperial troops started pushing inland over the Kokoda Trail towards Port Moresby. "Situation looks bad with Japs just across the Island from Moresby," admitted Maj. Rouse.[74]

Threatened with the loss of Port Moresby and New Guinea, Gen. MacArthur wrote, "I led one lost cause [i.e. the defense of the Philippines] and am trying not to have it two." Facing an Australian High Command that was already making preparations to resist a Japanese invasion of Australia, MacArthur said, "We'll defend Australia in New Guinea." Tired of the defeatist attitude of those around him, MacArthur declared, "We must attack! Attack! Attack!" As men, machines and supplies slowly trickled into Australia, MacArthur was bolstered by the appointment to the Southwest Pacific Area of another individual with a strong character and the will to win—Gen. George C. Kenney.[75]

XVII

Target: Guadalcanal

When Gen. Hale took charge of the 7th AF on June 20, there were 63 B-17s in the Central Pacific, 47 at Oahu and 16 at Midway.[1] The planes at Midway continued to fly search missions in the general direction of Wake Island. Wondering what was taking place on Wake, four B-24s flew to the island on June 26, dropping a handful of bombs and taking the first pictures of Wake since February. Unbeknownst to anyone, this first successful long-range mission by B-24s spelled the eventual doom for the B-17 in the Pacific. With a larger bomb load and greater range, the B-24 would eventually replace the B-17 as the premier heavy bomber in the Pacific.[2]

By early July, the Joint Chiefs of Staff had decided that it was only a matter of time before the Japanese tried to expand down through the Solomon Islands and threaten the sea and air routes to Australia. Before that could happen, the American war machine wanted to set Task I of their three-task plan into motion, the occupation of the Santa Cruz Islands and Tulagi. On July 4, Lt. Gen. Delos C. Emmons, in command of the Hawaiian Department, received orders from the Joint Chiefs to designate either the 5th or 11th BG as the Hawaiian Mobile Air Force, ready to strike at the enemy within a moment's notice. Although Emmons strongly objected, stating that he needed both groups to protect the Hawaiian area, he obeyed orders and selected Col. Saunders' 11th BG as the designated unit.[3]

When reconnaissance reports from Australia (carried out by the 435th BS/19th BG) indicated that the Japanese were building an airstrip on Guadalcanal, a "carefully selected group of 107 men [of the 11th BG]", boarded the Navy supply ship USS *Argonne* on July 10 and steamed towards New Caledonia. Their destination was known to only a few.[4] Also on July 10, the fledgling 98th BS/11th BG, which had only been activated on December 2, 1941, and had only gotten its mess facil-

214

ities set up in May, was deemed too inexperienced to accompany the rest of the bomb group to the South Pacific and was summarily transferred to the 5th BG. Later however, on July 13, there was a change of heart and the 98th BS was transferred back to the 11th BG. Noted the squadron historian, "Three days later it was decided that Junior could go with Daddy after all."[5]

With the Japanese move onto Guadalcanal, 7th Bomber Command began preparing the 11th BG planes for the move to the South Pacific. "The aircraft [all B-17Es] were all cycled through the Hawaiian Air Depot where an additional .50 caliber manual gun was mounted on a ring sight to be fired from the upper hatch of the radio compartment," recalled the newly promoted Maj. Edmundson. Three planes in each squadron were fitted with a "very rudimentary radar system" and space was made in the radio room for a tenth crew member, "a radar operator . . ."[6] Additionally, the Hawaiian Air Depot installed extra gasoline tanks in the nose section of planes equipped with radar, and in the radio rooms on many of the other planes. By doing this, the need for the extra bomb bay gas tanks was eliminated and the entire bomb bay could be filled with bombs.[7]

"We packed the airplanes and got ready to get on our way," recalled Sgt. Handrow of the 431st BS. "Where we were going or what we were going to do nobody knew." On July 17, nine B-17s, led by black-haired Col. "Blondie" Saunders, took off from Hickam on an "unknown mission." Surprisingly, the first squadron to leave was the 98th BS, which had almost been left behind. Heading southwest, the planes crossed the Equator and passed from the Central Pacific Area to the South Pacific Area, reaching their new home at Plaines des Gaiacs, New Caledonia four days later. Newly constructed, the Plaines des Gaiacs airfield consisted of a dusty, red dirt runway that had been hacked out of a swamp. It took less than two weeks to find out that the red dust sifted through the engine filters and damaged the cylinders, causing tremendous oil leaks and dropping the life expectancy of a B-17 engine down to only six hours with a full load of oil.[8]

Life at Plaines des Gaiacs was anything but the idyllic life of Hawaii. Lacking any shelter whatsoever, even tents, all the airmen, including group commander Col. Saunders, slept on cots set up under the wings of their bombers. The food was prepared and served by native New Caledonians but as the squadron historian noted, ". . . [it] was better left untouched in the opinion of the fliers." Added the historian, "On one occasion they fared exceptionally well when one gunner shot a deer on the runway."[9]

Next to leave Hawaii were the nine Fortresses of the 26th BS, led by the squadron CO, Maj. Allen J. Sewart, which took off from Wheeler Field around 8:00 A.M. on July 19.[10] Almost immediately the long range reconnaissance flights and lack of maintenance on all of the bombers began to take their toll. Before the planes reached Efate Island in the New Hebrides they had lost Lt. William Kinney, B-17E (41-9060, *Zero-Six-Zero*), when a push rod went out on one engine, and Maj. Edmundson, B-17E (41-2611), when he found a hole in one piston. Additionally, B-17E (41-9220) was delayed when the spark plugs suddenly needed changing.

"Ours were the first bombers to land on the newly-constructed field at Efate," noted the squadron historian. A Naval Construction Battalion (Seabees) had been working night and day on Efate and had been able to hack a landing strip slightly over 4,000 feet long and 350 feet wide out of the jungle, and had managed to construct bunkers for nine Fortresses. "We are the only B-17s here and share the field with a Marine fighter squadron," an unnamed squadron member wrote in his diary.[11]

"Conditions at Efate were fairly primitive," recalled Maj. Edmundson. "Col. Saunders had his office in a Quonset hut and we all slept in tents or in huts, when we slept at all." Since only nine maintenance men had accompanied the 26th BS from Oahu, the aircrews assisted in "repairing battle damage, manually loading bombs and in refueling." Lacking proper refueling equipment, the airmen refueled their B-17s from 55-gallon drums. Since the new arrivals lacked their own mess facility the airmen relied on the generosity of others. "The crews will never forget the aid given by a few artillery officers and men," wrote the squadron historian, "who provided hot food for the air corps in those early trying days." In time, the airmen began sharing the Marine Corps mess hall. "Each man was permitted one meal a day at the Marine mess hall," recalled Edmundson, "and he took this, day or night, whenever the flying and work schedule permitted. . . . Our mess kits, like our canteen and cup, were vital pieces of equipment which we were never without."[12]

On July 22, nine B-17s from the 42nd BS, led by Ernest Manierre, now a major, and the HqS joined the 98th BS at Plaines des Gaiacs. Two days later, eight B-17s from the 431st BS, carrying both combat crews and a handful of maintenance men, reached Nandi Field on Viti Levu Island.[13]

A total of 35 11th BG B-17s (including the two 26th BS planes in need of repair) had been transferred to the South Pacific. Left behind in Hawaii with the 5th BG were an additional 35 B-17s but they were far from top-of-the-line aircraft. The number included three B-17Cs, seven B-17Ds and 25 B-17Es. Additionally, 13 of the B-17Es were equipped with the old Bendix remote control belly turret. Left with rejects and outdated models, Col. Meehan, CO of the 5th BG, recommended that all the B-17Cs and Ds be sent back to the United States and be replaced with "properly armed B-17Es and B-17Fs."[14]

While the scattered aircrews from the 11th BG were flying to their new homes, the USS *Argonne*, carrying the forward echelon of the 11th BG ground personnel finally arrived at Noumea, New Caledonia. Although the forward echelon was suppose to arrive before the aircrews and have the scattered airbases up and operational when the planes arrived, the plan had quickly gone awry. "It is believed that there was a sudden change in the tactical situation—possibly unexpected speed in the construction of [the Guadalcanal] airfield—which forced the departure of the air echelon from Oahu before the scheduled time," noted the 11th BG historian.[15]

Backed now by a handful of ground crew personnel, the 11th BG immediately took to the air, taking over the job of photo reconnaissance of the Solomon Islands from the hard-fought 19th BG in Australia. On July 23, three planes from the 98th BS left Plaines des Gaiacs and flew a photographic mission over the Tulagi-Guadalcanal area. Lacking the proper equipment and trained personnel, the Navy provided the cameras and the Marines furnished the photographers.[16]

On July 29, Maj. Sewart, B-17E (41-9076), took off from Efate and landed the first heavy bomber on the island of Espiritu Santo. Located northwest of Efate, planes attacking from Espiritu Santo were 125 miles closer to Guadalcanal than any of the other airfields. Although the 11th BG would still base their planes out of the distant fields of Efate, Plaines des Gaiacs, and Viti Levu, they would use Espiritu Santo as a forward staging field.[17]

"Espiritu's airdrome was no Randolph Field [Texas]" wrote the 11th BG historian. "A narrow strip cut partly from a coconut grove, partly from the encroaching jungle; revetments barely deep enough to keep a B-17s nose off the runway and so narrow a man had to stand at each wing tip to guide the pilots out to the short taxiway . . ." The airfield at Espiritu Santo, code-named "Buttons," lacked any electric lights whatsoever. During night takeoffs or landings, jeep headlights illuminated the ends of the runway and bottles of oil with paper wicks marked the sides of the strip. However, every time a plane went by, the flames were extinguished and had to be re-lit, necessitating a long delay between each takeoff or landing.[18]

Also, Espiritu Santo lacked proper fueling facilities. The Navy had moved 300,000 gallons of gasoline to Espiritu Santo in preparation for the arrival of the 11th BG, estimating that the fuel would last at least two weeks. Unfortunately, the supply was exhausted in only 10 days. Only the timely arrival of a ship with another 150,000 gallons of gas in 50-gallon drums kept the B-17s airborne. However, this brought other problems. "For refueling we used a hand operated wobble pump from 50 gallon barrels that they had dumped off of a ship, floated them ashore and rolled them up to the airstrip," recalled Pvt. Bradshaw. "Boy, you soon realized how much 1700 gallons is when you pump it by hand."[19]

A few days after the 42nd BS and the HqS joined the 98th BS at Plaines des Gaiacs, the airfield became too crowded and the 98th moved to a new airfield at Koumac, near the northwest end of New Caledonia. On July 31, the 11th BG launched its first raid against Guadalcanal, sending two planes from the 98th BS, and six from the 26th BS (the only planes equipped with radio room gas tanks) against the island.[20]

"[W]e ran into a murderous overcast that kept us within five hundred feet of the water," wrote Col. Saunders. "Flying at that altitude for that distance is a fluttering horror. A sudden down-draft can flip a plane into the sea before you can say Guadalcanal." As the formation neared the island, the Fortresses climbed through the clouds. "We finally broke out of the soup at 18,000 feet and circled Lunga Point," Saunders said. "Ack-ack was heavy but we got our bombs away on the target and returned to base undamaged."[21]

Ironically, the 98th BS, which had almost been left behind on Oahu, not only flew the first 11th BG reconnaissance mission over the Solomons, but also dropped the first bombs for the group. Lt. John H. Buie, B-17E (41-2523, *Goonie*), with Col. Saunders riding as an observer, and his wingman, Lt. Frank T. "Fritz" Waskowitz, B-17E (41-2616, *The Blue Goose*), both from the 98th BS, led the formation and dropped eight 500-lb. demolition bombs on the Japanese airfield.[22] Interestingly, Waskowitz' plane, *The Blue Goose*, was actually painted a bright, light blue. Perhaps as a test for a new camouflage scheme, B-17E (41-2616) had been given a coat, top to bottom, of Light Glossy Blue Duco paint at the Hawaiian Air Depot. With its highly unusual color, the B-17 and its crew were soon known to everybody.[23] After bombing the enemy airfield on Guadalcanal, the light blue colored B-17 was now known to the Japanese as well.

Following immediately behind the first two planes, the six Flying Fortresses from the 26th BS, flying in two three-plane elements, came in low and dropped 20 100-lb. bombs apiece on the airfield supply dump. "Antiaircraft fire was ineffective," noted the 26th BS diarist, "and no enemy fighters were encountered." The first heavy strike against Guadalcanal by the 11th BG had been a complete success.[24]

At 12:45 P.M., on July 21, the rest of the 11th BG ground crews finally left Hawaii on the transport USS *President Tyler*. For the next 10 days the ship zigzagged to the southwest, crossing the Equator on July 26, and the International Date Line on July 30. On the afternoon of August 1, after traveling 3,200 miles, the ship arrived at Suva on Viti Levu where the 431st BS ground personnel disembarked and boarded trucks for the long overland drive to Nandi Airfield.[25]

Recalled a member of the 431st BS, ". . . after sailing through what seemed to be an endless chain of coral reefs and small islands the entire day [August 1], we reached Veti Levu [sic], the second largest island in the Fiji group. Upon entering the harbor all members of the 431st breathed a sigh of relief as their part of the voyage was over." While the men were disembarking, the Fiji native residents came down to greet the ship. "[T]he troops were quite awed by their large mops of black bushy hair and wrap-dress that made both women and men look alike," continued the unnamed squadron member. Noted the 42nd BS historian, "For a quarter, placed in a paint bucket and lowered over the side, the natives would fill the container with Fiji oranges, which were about six inches in diameter and made excellent eating. Coconuts were likewise on sale."[26]

On August 3, the *President Tyler*, accompanied by a destroyer escort, set off for Efate, reaching that island on August 5. After a submarine scare outside of the harbor, in which the escorting destroyer dropped five depth charges while the anxious mechanics looked on, the troop ship entered the harbor. The 98th BS mechanics stayed on board the *President Tyler* while the 26th BS and HqS personnel disembarked. The 42nd BS people were transshipped onto the SS *Cape Flattery* and taken to Noumea on New Caledonia, arriving there on August 10.[27]

After reaching Noumea, the 42nd BS mechanics were taken by truck on an all-night 150 mile ride through driving rain to Plaines des Gaiacs. Far removed from Hawaii, the men began their stay at Plaines with a meal of Army rations. Soon however, the men found that they could supplement their diet with venison. "The

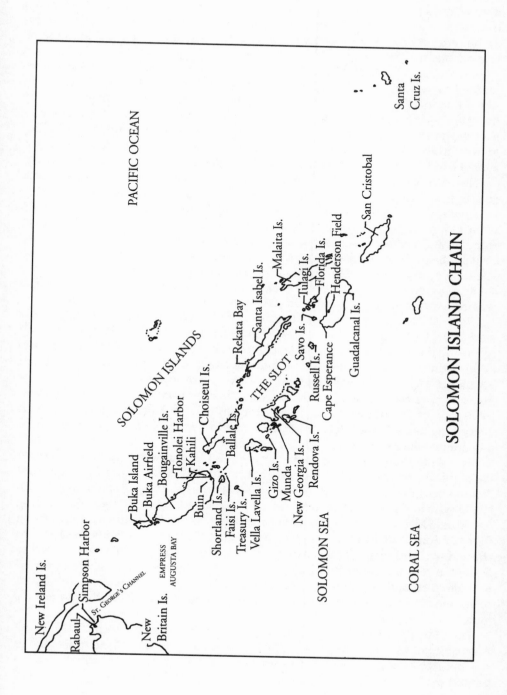

SOLOMON ISLAND CHAIN

deer were so plentiful," noted the 42nd BS historian, "that open season extended throughout the year . . . For the first few weeks the venison was a distinct delicacy, but after it appeared in the menu daily, it soon became relegated to the same unenviable category as Spam."[28]

On August 11, the *President Tyler*, still carrying the 98th BS ground crews, reached Espiritu Santo where the men were put ashore. As the mechanics began unloading their equipment they found that most of it had been "appropriated" by the other squadrons. "Next time," wrote the squadron historian, "the men promised themselves, if they aren't to be the first outfit to leave the ship they will post guards on the kitchen equipment and other supplies." The 98th BS ground personnel had been left with only one complete field stove and no tents whatsoever.

The 98th BSs home base at Camp Santo, about a half mile from a newly constructed airfield dubbed "Bomber Number 1," was primitive to say the least. Borrowing tents from a local Marine Corps unit, the men slept eight men to a tent, or in two-man pup tents, until better accommodations could be brought over from New Caledonia. Lacking a mess facility, the airmen received food from a detachment of Black soldiers from a nearby camp, eating the food in the open air, standing up and resting their mess kits on boards nailed between trees. Wrote the squadron historian, "To the process of eating was added the necessary ritual of waving away swarms of flies before each bite was conveyed to the mouth."[29]

The first bombing raid on Guadalcanal by the 11th BG on July 31 marked the start of the first major land offensive by the Americans in World War II. Intent on capturing the enemy airfield at Lunga Point before the Japanese could get it operational, the Americans scheduled a simultaneous invasion of Guadalcanal and Tulagi for August 1. However, because of a number of unforeseen problems, the invasion date was pushed back to August 7. In the meantime, Col. Saunders was told to strike Guadalcanal and Tulagi from July 31 to August 6, inclusive, with everything he had. The Allied High Command intended to damage the Japanese defenders before putting a single man ashore.[30]

Following the eight plane strike on July 31, Col. Saunders gathered together the eight planes with radio room gas tanks, and added two more from the 431st BS, and sent them against "the town and seaplanes at Tulagi" on August 1.[31] Lt. Waskowitz in *The Blue Goose* dropped 14 300-lb. bombs on a storage area, scoring four direct hits and leaving the area ablaze. As the ten B-17s turned for home, a flight of Zero floatplanes attempted to intercept them but the B-17s were able to shoot down two planes and chase the others away. When the planes returned to Efate, the 26th BS crews found Lt. Kinney waiting for them. He had been forced to make a complete engine change on B-17E (41-9060, *Zero-Six-Zero*) to make it operational. Now, the 26th BS was operating at maximum strength, but not for long.[32]

The 26th BS set out to hit Guadalcanal and Tulagi again near 1:00 A.M. on August 2 but as Maj. Edmundson, B-17E (41-2520, *Jap Happy*), began his takeoff run his right wing clipped an unseen tree and he accidentally turned into the parked B-17E (41-9155) of Capt. Rolle W. Stone (42nd BS). All four propellers of

Edmundson's plane tore into the nose of Stone's bomber and left the plane a complete wreck. Although Edmundson's *Jap Happy* could be repaired, the plane was out of action indefinitely. In spite of the accident, Lt. Kinney, B-17E (41-9218), and 1st Lt. Robert D. Guenther (26th BS), B-17E (41-2610), took to the air for a dawn attack. Unfortunately, the two ran into bad weather and returned to Efate after a 12 hour flight.[33]

Lt. Kinney reported on the terrible weather often encountered by the crews of the 11th BG:

> To the boys flying the Solomons circuit, weather was the worst foe of all. Massive fronts, turbulent and unpredictable, would roll across the Coral Sea without warning, blotting out the sky and water . . . You were crazy if you tried to fly into them and you couldn't always fly around or over them. We tried every dodge possible, but sometimes it was no go . . . The Japs never stopped us from making a mission, but the weather often did.[34]

While Lts. Kinney and Guenther were still airborne, Capt. Jack Thornhill, B-17E (41-2527), and 1st Lts. Hugh W. Owens, B-17E (41-9145), and John W. Lancaster, B-17E (41-2524), (all 26th BS) started off from Efate at 5:00 A.M. to hit Guadalcanal. In the dark, Capt. Thornhill's plane brushed wing tips with Lt. Owens, causing only minor damage to both planes but sidelining two more aircraft from the attack. Instead of going off on his own, Lt. Lancaster attached himself to the next element, consisting of Maj. Sewart, B-17E (41-9076), and 1st Lts. Edwin A. Loberg, B-17E (41-2611), and John W. Livingston, B-17E (41-9060), (all 26th BS). Taking off at 5:45 A.M., the four planes missed the storm and carpeted the Lunga airfield with 21 500-lb., and 14 300-lb. bombs. Noted the 26th BS diarist, "Hits were scored with 75% of the bombs—runways were smashed and two hangars left burning."

On the return flight to Efate, the B-17s were hit by Japanese Zeros which caused serious damage to Lt. Lancaster's right outboard engine. As the plane began trailing smoke, the other Fortresses circled around him and shot down one of the Zeros and chased the others away. As the four Fortresses headed for home, two pilots from the 98th BS, 1st Lts. Robert B. Loder and Vincent M. Crane, bombed Lunga Field again.[35]

Col. Saunders continued his attacks against Guadalcanal and Tulagi on August 3 when Capt. Thornhill, B-17E (41-2527), and Lt. Owens, B-17E (41-9145), bombed Tulagi with 28 300-lb. bombs from only 6,000 feet. Noted the 26th BS diarist, "The rest of the squadron took a well needed rest . . . The squadron personnel is being administered 2 tablets of attabrine (substitute for quinine) twice a week. Malaria is prevalent in the New Hebrides and Solomen [sic] Islands."[36]

Col. Saunders also recalled the fight against malaria. "[M]alaria was the biggest threat," he wrote. "It was difficult to prevent under such conditions. Quinine lowered flying qualities and we used it only after malaria had been contracted instead of as a preventative . . ." Only the 42nd BS and the HqS, on Plaines des Gaiacs did not suffer from malaria. For some unknown reason, the island was devoid of mosquitoes. Native legend suggested that the mosquitoes did not like the white-barked gaiacs trees that were peculiar to the island. Whether true or not, the Americans did not care. There were no mosquitoes on Plaines des Gaiacs and the airmen that were stationed there did not complain.[37]

Continuing with his attacks against Guadalcanal, Col. Saunders sent three planes from the 431st BS to bomb the airfield on August 3, and sent the same three planes back again on August 4.[38] On that same date, he sent the 26th and 98th BSs out to hit Tulagi. Maj. Edmundson, B-17E (41-2527), was leading Lt. Guenther, and 1st Lt. Rush E. McDonald, B-17E (41-9218), from the 26th BS towards the Japanese base when they were suddenly jumped by seven Zero floatplanes. One enemy plane was shot down almost immediately and another was set aflame by the fire from Lt. Guenther's plane. As the flaming floatplane veered out of control it crashed into the left wing of Lt. McDonald's B-17. Wrote the 26th BS diarist, "The plane [i.e. B-17] was set afire and was last seen diving off to the right with the ship's #1 engine in flames." Nine crewmen and B-17E (41-9218) were gone.[39]

Seeing the flaming loss of McDonald's B-17, Maj. Edmundson turned the tables on the Japanese and gave chase to one of the floatplanes. Caught completely by surprise, the fighter was quickly shot down which earned Maj. Edmundson a DFC for his daring. For 30 minutes the remaining four fighters kept attacking but the Americans were able to knock down one more plane and drop their bombs along the southeast coast of Tulagi.[40]

As the two surviving 26th BS planes flew away, three planes from the 98th BS showed up. The lack of radio silence among the 98th BS pilots while they were approaching Tulagi became a bone of contention between the 26th and 98th BSs. "In regards to the loss of McDonald & crew," wrote the 26th BS diarist, "severe criticism and a good deal of resentment was directed against the 98th BS flight ... for failing to preserve radio silence. The command frequency was filled with their idle small talk during the trip up to the Japanese base—as a result, our first flight was confronted by 5 or 7 Zeros at their altitude."[41] Later that day, three more 26th BS planes hit Tulagi and despite the earlier attacks, caught the Japanese completely by surprise.[42]

While the Navy was carrying the 1st Marine Division towards Guadalcanal and Tulagi, the 11th BG continued its nuisance raids on the Japanese. On August 5, the 26th BS returned to Tulagi with a three-plane strike followed closely by seven planes from the 431st BS. Originally, eight planes from the 431st BS were scheduled to attack but the aircrews had run into trouble with the lone fuel pump at Espiritu Santo and 1st Lt. Warren S. Wilkinson could not get his B-17 refueled in time. "[W]e had to refuel my ship by means of a 5 gallon can, by hand," wrote Wilkinson. "This process was slow, we didn't get away in time to make the raid."[43]

The planes that did get away dropped their 500-lb. bombs on the buildings alongside Tulagi's docks. Although one building was marked as a hospital, the airmen believed that it actually contained Japanese munitions. "Last one [i.e. bomb] went right into a hospital," noted Sgt. Handrow. "It flew even higher than the rest. They must have been treating T.N.T. for a cold." No enemy fighters appeared and in spite of the fact that the bombers flew through a heavy barrage of antiaircraft fire, Handrow was able to state, "No ships [planes] were lost that day."[44]

The last mission of the day was flown by Col. Saunders, B-17E (41-9145), at 8:30 A.M. Undoubtedly intent on seeing first hand what effect his maximum effort was having, and knowing full well that the Marines were scheduled to land on August 7, he flew over the island to inspect the positions and take mental notes. Satisfied with what he saw, he dropped a load of bombs on the western edge of Lunga Point and returned safely to Espiritu Santo.[45]

With only one day left before the invasion, Col. Saunders scheduled more air strikes against Guadalcanal for August 6 but unseen circumstances delayed the usual early morning takeoffs. A driving rainstorm and the loss of the lone fuel pump at Espiritu Santo kept the planes grounded until well into the afternoon. The 11th BG historian noted, "On 6 August, all available hands—and available hands included Col. Saunders and Brig. Gen. William C. Rose, who commanded ground forces on Espiritu and Efate—worked a bucket line for 20 hours in a driving storm to put 25,000 gallons of gasoline aboard the bombers. But such labors were not enough, and the strike missions were delayed for lack of service facilities."[46]

Perhaps no more than five bombers struck Guadalcanal on August 6 and an unknown number of planes flew search missions north of the island. Noted Sgt. Handrow, "August 6, 1942 we went out on search for the Jap navy. We got word that the Marines were going to take Tulagi and Guadalcanal the next morning and that they didn't want any Jap fleet hanging around while they were landing." After the mission he added, "Didn't see a thing."[47]

One of the planes that attacked Guadalcanal on August 6 was flown by Lt. Buie, B-17E (41-2523, *Goonie*). His ball turret gunner, Sgt. Harold C. Miller (98th BS), wrote:

We took off quite late and arrived at Guadalcanal just as the rest of the group was leaving. The Zeros picked us up and we wound up making 2 dry runs on the airstrip, plus 2 more to drop all of our bombs. What we figured out later is that the Japs had run out of ammunition on the group and only fired a few shots at us, hoping to drive us away. One [bullet] did hit [our] tail strut and kept stunting around while we were making our runs.[48]

Although Capt. Stone, B-17E (41-9221), also managed to bomb Guadalcanal he ran into a bit of bad luck on his way home. Lt. Wilkinson recorded the next day, "Rolle Stone got lost the night before, and unable to find the field in the darkness made a water landing just off shore [of Espiritu Santo]." Fortunately, all nine crewmen were not seriously injured but the 11th BG had lost another B-17 in the campaign to win Guadalcanal.[49]

D-day in the Solomons arrived on August 7, 1942, when the Marines went ashore at both Guadalcanal and Tulagi. Virtually unopposed on both islands, the Marines quickly pushed inland.[50] Prepared to assist the Marines and Navy in any way possible, most of the 11th BG B-17s were kept on full alert. "The 26th Squadron had six planes on 1 hour alert," noted the 26th BS diarist, while Lt. Wilkinson of the 431st BS wrote, "As this was 'D' Day—the invasion of Guadalcanal—we all remained on 15 minute alert, except for the search planes." Keeping a wary eye open for the enemy, a few B-17s from the 98th and 431st BSs covered the area north of the islands. "We were out on search again way to the north of the Solomons and didn't spot a thing," recalled Sgt. Handrow. "Maj. Pharr also went out and that was the last we ever heard of him or his crew."[51]

Maj. Marion Pharr, the CO of the 431st BS, and Capt. Sullivan took two planes out from Espiritu Santo in the early morning hours. "Someone cooked up the bright idea of three A.M. take-offs for search missions," complained Lt. Wilkinson. "Pharr and Sully drew the first one on 7 Aug 42. Sully came back, but nothing was ever heard from Pharr." Patroling far to the north, it was assumed that Maj. Pharr, in B-17E (41-2426), had run into enemy fighters and was shot down. Later, captured Japanese documents indicated that a B-17 had been downed by Zero fighters on the morning of August 7.[52]

In addition to the loss of Maj. Pharr's plane, the 11th BG also lost another plane on August 7 when Lt. Loder, B-17E (41-9224, *Kai-O-Keleiwa*), took off on a search mission from the 98th BS airfield at Koumac and failed to return. The Squadron Operational Diary stated, "Weather was extremely poor and it is believed that Lt. Loder may have crashed in mountains on New Caledonia." Although a plane circled over Koumac late that night and the headlights from 20 jeeps were played across the runway in an attempt to illuminate the airstrip, the plane never landed. "Thus," noted the squadron historian, "the 98th Bombardment Squadron (H) lost its first crew and plane."[53]

By the end of the day, the Marines had a substantial toehold on both Tulagi and Guadalcanal. The only air opposition the Marines faced was a weak attempt late in the day by forces from the Northern Solomons. Although everyone had expected the Japanese at Rabaul to retaliate with a strong counterstrike, the attack never materialized. Perhaps unknown to most of the Americans in the South Pacific Area, the Japanese at Rabaul had been too busy to stage a counterattack. The 19th BG, under their new commander, Gen. George C. Kenney, was giving them hell.

On July 25, Gen. Kenney was still a week from arriving in Australia and the 19th BG was still carrying on operations as normal, and still taking it on the chin. That morning, Capt. Horgan, B-17E (41-9193), was flying a 435th BS reconnaissance mission of Rabaul and Kavieng when he was jumped by 15 Zeros. In the 45 minute air battle, the B-17E had two engines knocked out, a big cannon hole in the elevator that caused a few control cables to snap, and the ball turret knocked out. Additionally, three crew members were wounded. However, the gunners were able to shoot down six of the Zeros, including one by the bombardier when

Capt. Horgan dove his Fortress straight at a Zero. Although B-17E (41-9193) made it safely back to Port Moresby, it would be some time before it was ready to fly again.[54]

Two days later, on July 27, nine Fortresses, led by "Pinky" Hoevet, now a major and in command of the 30th BS, set out to bomb Buna. "Overcast all the way to ground so couldn't bomb," noted Maj. Rouse. As the planes were landing at Horn Island, Lt. Edward J. Bechtold (93rd BS), B-17E (41-2460), came in a bit too fast and slammed into the waiting bomber of Capt. Carey O'Bryan (30th BS), B-17E (41-2640, *Tojo's Physic*). O'Bryan's bomber had been flown up to Horn Island with an extra crew to retrieve B-17E (41-2633, *Sally*) which had been badly damaged while landing on July 4. Maj. Rouse commented on the whole affair, "Becktold [sic] ground looped on landing and tore the nose completely off one of our ships and smashed up his pretty badly. Purely pilot error due to inexperience, I believe. Two more ships gone that we need badly." No one was hurt but both B-17E (41-2460) and B-17E (41-2640, *Tojo's Physic*) were written off as complete losses.[55]

When Gen. Kenney arrived in Australia on July 29 he immediately went to see Gen. MacArthur. When he exited the meeting both men had a new found respect for one another. Although neither man had ever met before, MacArthur knew of Kenney's reputation for running an efficient air force, and Kenney knew that MacArthur would expect nothing less. MacArthur informed Kenney of the upcoming invasion of Guadalcanal and Tulagi, and told his new air chief that 5th Bomber Command had been called upon to give whatever assistance they could to the operation. Having just arrived in the Southwest Pacific Area, Kenney immediately set out to see what he had on hand to work with.[56]

After borrowing Gen. Brett's personal plane, B-17D (40-3097, *The Swoose*), one of only two B-17s remaining from MacArthur's stand in the Philippines [The other surviving B-17 was B-17C (40-2072) which was still in use as a transport.] Kenney flew up to Port Moresby to look over operations at the forward air base. Finding the base in need of a full overhaul, Kenney flew down to Mareeba to check on the 19th BG. "The crews were thinking only of going home," Kenney commented. "Their morale was at a low ebb and they didn't care who knew it." Kenney found only 14 planes ready for combat and 18 planes out of commission awaiting engine repairs or new tailwheel assemblies. Half of the 32 B-17s sported the worthless Bendix belly turret, and all of them were pretty much worn out. "Anywhere else but this theater," Kenney reasoned, "they would probably have been withdrawn from combat, but they were all we had so I'd have to use them if we wanted to keep the war going."

When Gen. Kenney looked into the supply system for the 19th BG he found it "appalling." Planes were being robbed to get parts to keep other planes in the air because the supply depot at Charters Towers was taking too long to fill requisition forms or was returning the forms because they were improperly filled out. Needing every available plane to assist in the invasion of Guadalcanal and Tulagi, Kenney swore to speed up the delivery of parts, and instructed Col.

Carmichael to rest his men and repair his planes. Returning to Gen. MacArthur, Kenney stated that with enough rest and repair, he would have at least 16 Fortresses and their crews ready to hit Rabaul in conjunction with the Marine landings on August 7.[57]

While most of the B-17s were getting a general overhaul, Col. Carmichael sent four planes against Buna on July 31, and six against Salamaua on August 1. The flight to Buna dropped 14 300-lb. bombs but ran into nine Zeros on the way home and lost B-17E (41-2641). Nothing is known about the demise of this plane except for a handwritten notation on a 19th BG A-3 Airplane Status Section Folder. The notation simply reads, "Lost in Combat."[58]

On August 2, five planes set out to locate and bomb two enemy ships reported to be near Buna. When the ships were not sighted, and nine enemy fighters showed up, the bombers jettisoned their bombs and headed back to Port Moresby. Unfortunately, a Lt. Watson, piloting B-17E (41-2435), was shot down and another Fortress was damaged before the fighters gave up and went home. One more plane and nine more lives had been lost to the 19th BG.[59]

Two days later, Gen. Brett left for the United States in B-17D (40-3097, *The Swoose*) and Gen. Kenney was officially named the Southwest Pacific Forces Air Commander. *The Swoose* became the first B-17 to return from combat in World War II and was quickly sent on a bond raising drive across America.[60]

True to his word, by August 6 Gen. Kenney had 16 B-17s ready to bomb the Japanese stronghold of Rabaul in conjunction with the Marine landings on Guadalcanal and Tulagi.[61] Moving in small flights up to Port Moresby, six planes from the 93rd BS set out from Horn Island on the evening of August 6 after flying an aborted mission to Lae during the day. Fifty miles out, however, Capt. Pease, B-17E (41-2668), blew a valve on an engine and hurried over to Mareeba for a new plane. Every serviceable plane, five each from the 28th and 30th BSs, and the remaining five from the 93rd BS, had already moved up to Port Moresby. Determined to be a part of the big raid on Rabaul, Pease looked around and found B-17E (41-2429, *Why Don't We Do This More Often*). The plane was one of the older model Es, sporting the useless remote-controlled belly turret, and had been plagued with electrical problems and "weak" engines. Although it had aborted several missions, it could still fly so Pease and his crew quickly took it up to Port Moresby.[62]

When Capt. Pease reached Seven Mile Strip at 1:00 A.M. on August 7, the engineering officer of the 93rd BS, Lt. Snyder, "raised hell in no uncertain terms" about the safety of Pease's replacement bomber. Undaunted, Pease spoke to Maj. Hardison, his CO, and convinced him to allow B-17E (41-2429) to fly the mission. Unwilling to give up, Snyder implored Hardison to at least put Pease in the middle of the formation where it would be safer but the major had already assigned the positions of the planes and the B-17s were parked along the runway according to take-off positions. Pease would fly the right-wing position on the second three-plane element, led by Capt. Jacquet. Ironically, Lt. Snyder had little right to complain. Snyder's own plane, B-17E (41-2464, *Queenie*), was one of the older E-models whose remote-controlled belly turret had been ripped out and replaced by a board with a fake gun barrel sticking out of it.[63]

At 7:30 A.M. on August 7, the 16 planes began taking off. Right from the start the flight was plagued by trouble. A runaway supercharger on Lt. Hillhouse's B-17E (41-2617) caused the plane to bolt forward during his takeoff run. Lt. Gooch was Hillhouse's bombardier and recalled, "Our B-17E, carrying a full load, veered off the runway and crashed into a rock pile. The plane was a total wreck but all the crew escaped with only a minor injury to our navigator's leg. The bombs were torn from their shackles, but fortunately none detonated."

Seeing the crash, Capt. Pease's bombardier, 1st Lt. Bruce Burleson, rushed over to see if Lt. Gooch was okay. "After seeing I was all right," Gooch wrote, "he said as only Bruce Burleson could say it, 'Gooch, you have used up all your luck.' He said this because he knew I had been shot down over Borneo, was involved in a mid-air collision, and then the crash that day on takeoff." Satisfied that Gooch was uninjured, Burleson went back to Pease's bomber and took off for Rabaul.[64] Once in the air the formation lost two more bombers when Lt. Fred F. Wesche, B-17E (41-2657), suffered an engine failure, and Lt. Sargent, B-17E (41-9015), experienced electrical failure.[65]

Climbing to 22,000 feet, the 13 remaining planes, under the overall leadership of Col. Carmichael, flying as flight commander and copilot with Capt. Dougherty, B-17E (41-2536), headed towards Vunakanau airfield. Recent reconnaissance pictures indicated that at least 150 enemy bombers and fighters were at Vunakanau, perhaps waiting to be moved to the new airfield on Guadalcanal. Flying in a large V-formation made up of flights of squadrons, the planes reached New Britain just after 11:30 A.M. and were 25 miles short of the target when they were intercepted by 20 enemy fighters.

As the Japanese swarmed all over the American formation, bullets tore into the B-17s. Lt. Snyder's No. 3 engine was already running rough when a cannon shell knocked out the *Queenie's* oxygen system. "We continued in formation," Snyder wrote, "though the lack of oxygen became noticeable to all the crew . . ." Cannon and machine-gun fire ripped through the other Fortresses but miraculously no one was injured and the planes pressed on. At the same time, the B-17s gave as much as they got. Lt. Claude N. Burcky's gunners in B-17E (41-2452) shot down two Zeros, while those on Lt. Snyder's plane downed one more.[66]

In one of the lead bombers, bombardier Lt. Emanuel Snitkin, manned the nose guns and fired back at his attackers. As the B-17s neared the target, Snitkin put down his gun, leaned over his bombsight and dropped his string of bombs, "causing considerable damage to [the target]." With his bombs gone, Snitkin returned to his machine gun and continued his fight with the Zeros, thereby earning himself a Silver Star, America's third highest award for valor.[67]

Gen. Kenney, duly proud of his airmen, later wrote, ". . . the kids closed up their formation and fought their way to Vunakanau where they dropped their bombs in a group pattern that was a bull's-eye." The 150 Japanese planes were still beside the runway as 96 500-lb. bombs fell on the airfield. Wrote Kenney, "The [strike] pictures looked as though we got at least 75 of them, besides setting fire to a lot of gasoline and blowing up a big bomb dump on the edge of the field."[68]

As the B-17s turned from the bomb run, the Zeros renewed their attack. Enemy fire rocked B-17E (41-2536) with Capts. Dougherty and Col. Carmichael, killing one of the gunners, injuring another, and rupturing the oxygen system. Carmichael immediately called Maj. Hardison, B-17E (41-2643), on the command radio to inform him that they would have to go down to a lower altitude and then put the B-17 into a dive. Following his leader, Maj. Hardison, who was leading the 93rd BS planes, dove also. Lt. Snyder, flying off Hardison's left wing, and already groggy from a lack of oxygen, saw the two planes start to descend and put his own plane into a crash-dive, almost colliding with Maj. Hardison. This unexpected action by the lead planes caused the tight formation to breakup and the Zeros immediately went after the stragglers.[69]

Although the Zeros killed one man and wounded another on Capt. Jacquet's plane, B-17E (41-2462, *Tojo's Jinx*), they seemed to concentrate on Capt. Pease's bomber. Already suffering from "weak" engines, the plane fell behind when the formation broke apart. The first to notice that Pease was in trouble was Capt. Bridges, flying off Pease's left wing. He reported seeing Pease's bomber descend about 1,000 feet with the left inboard engine out and Japanese planes buzzing all around it. As Bridges watched, a blazing bomb bay tank fell from Pease's B-17 but it was too late, B-17E (41-2429, *Why Don't We Do This More Often*) was already wrapped in flames.[70]

While nobody saw Capt. Pease crash, most everyone believed that the flaming bomber made a crash landing in the water and that the whole crew was killed, including Lt. Burleson, who had chided Lt. Gooch about using up all his luck. "It's ironic that, after his comment about my bad luck, gutsy Bruce did not return from that mission," Gooch lamented. It wasn't until 1946 that the wreckage of B-17E (41-2429, *Why Don't We Do This More Often*) was found along the Powell River on New Britain. Two bodies were found inside the wreck and identified as Pease's Australian copilot, and his radio operator. Natives also reported that three other bodies had been seen around the wreckage shortly after the crash but had been washed away by the river.[71]

Later, evidence taken from captured Japanese records indicated that Capt. Pease and one of his gunners, Sgt. Chester Czechowski, had successfully parachuted from the burning airplane and had been taken prisoner. Brought to Rabaul, the two were held captive until October 8, 1942, when they were marched out and executed. Their remains were never found.[72]

Reaching the safety of clouds, nine of the remaining 12 Fortresses reformed and returned safely to Port Moresby. Within the next hour, the last three came in.[73] Ten men had been killed, including all eight on Capt. Pease's plane. One plane was lost and several more were badly shot up. Still, the mission was a success. The Fortress crews were credited with shooting down seven Zeros and destroying at least 75 airplanes on the ground, thereby preventing the Japanese from assaulting the Marines on Guadalcanal and Tulagi.

Gen. Kenney and others believed that the maximum effort by the 19th BG played a significant role in the success of the Marine landings. He wrote, "[Vice] Admiral [Robert L.] Ghormley [Commander of the South Pacific Area] wired Gen. MacArthur a congratulatory message on the success of our attack on Vunakanau and the fact that it had broken up the possibility of Jap air interference with his landings in the Solomons." The successful raid, plus congratulatory notes from Ghormley, MacArthur and Kenney, did wonders to help boost the morale of the 19th BG. And later, Capt. Pease was posthumously awarded the Medal of Honor and each member of his crew was posthumously awarded the Distinguished Service Cross. After eight months of almost continuous combat, the 19th BG had its first, and subsequently only, Medal of Honor recipient.[74]

The invasion of Guadalcanal and Tulagi had been a success. It is hard to evaluate the success of the AAF in conjunction with the landings. Surely Gen. Kenney's attack by his 19th BG destroyed and distracted a number of enemy planes at Rabaul that would have been used to attack the American transports. Likewise, Col. Saunders' week long bombing by his 11th BG destroyed a number of Japanese floatplanes stationed around Tulagi, and perhaps even harassed the Japanese enough to prevent their completion of the airstrip on Guadalcanal.

The Guadalcanal Campaign had finally spotlighted the perfect use of the B-17 in the Pacific. The Flying Fortress had moved to the forefront as the prime airplane for long-range armed reconnaissance, and had proven its worth for damaging stationary targets from high altitude. The constant bombing of the Rabaul, Buna and Lae airdromes had kept the enemy on the defensive, checking his reinforcement of both the Guadalcanal and Buna area. More importantly, however, the endless surveillance of the Solomon Islands, and even the Rabaul area had kept the Americans well aware of any changes in enemy disposition.[75]

XVIII

Hanging On

ALTHOUGH THE JAPANESE had managed to put up only token air resistance against the American invaders of Guadalcanal and Tulagi on August 7, they came back the next morning with a fury, sinking one ship and damaging two others. At the same time, a Japanese naval strike force set out from Kavieng. Although the ships were sighted early in the morning by B-17s from Gen. MacArthur's command and the Japanese expected an air strike, it never materialized. By a quirk of fate and bad planning by the Americans, the Japanese ships were allowed to steam unmolested through the center of the Solomon Islands, through an area soon to be called "The Slot."

Since the boundary between MacArthur's Southwest Pacific Area and Admiral Ghormley's South Pacific Area bisected the Solomon Islands, it was the responsibility of each section commander to search and patrol his portion of the Islands. Unfortunately, two B-17s from the 11th BG missed sighting the strike force by only 60 miles. On the night of August 8–9, the Japanese ships moved up next to Guadalcanal and in the ensuing battle of Savo Island sank four Allied heavy cruisers, earning the area southeast of Savo Island the nickname "Ironbottom Sound." Having handed the U.S. Navy its worst defeat in history, the Japanese ships turned around and retired back up The Slot.[1]

Near 8:00 A.M., eight B-17s of the 11th BG set out to bomb the retreating enemy task force which was said to be north of Guadalcanal. Although visibility was good, the enemy ships could not be found and the crews settled for dropping their bombs on a Japanese installation on the southern end of Santa Isabel Island.[2]

Prior to the battle of Savo Island the American aircraft carriers, which had aided in the invasion, had been pulled back out of range of the enemy aircraft from Rabaul and the northern Solomon airfields, leaving reconnaissance to the Navy PBYs and the 11th BG B-17s. On August 10, Col. Saunders moved his HqS from Plaines des Gaiacs to the forward airfield on Espiritu Santo. Each day he sent out a handful of bombers on search missions while maintaining an alert strike force of nine aircraft on 30 minutes notice. Additionally, a reserve force of about five planes was held on four hours notice. The strain of keeping all of the planes airborne was eased somewhat on August 11 when the transport *President Tyler* arrived at Espiritu Santo with the ground crews of the 98th BS. When the air echelon of the 98th BS moved from Koumac to Espiritu Santo, Col. Saunders had 14 Flying Fortresses at the forward airbase at all times.[3]

Although Col. Saunders tried to maintain his daily search quota, by August 18 the supply situation for the group was critical. Six ball turret doors had broken off, sidelining six planes for lack of spare parts. Additionally, the crews were having trouble with turbo-supercharger regulators, and flight and engine instruments. The dusty new airstrips were necessitating constant engine changes which quickly exhausted 12 spare engines. And, in addition to losing almost a dozen planes to mechanical failure, Saunders found that because of the wide dispersal of the 11th BG, and unreliable radio communications, he could only exercise direct control over the 14 B-17s at Espiritu Santo. Wanting to consolidate his group at Espiritu Santo, Saunders requested that additional airfields be built on the island as soon as possible.[4]

On August 17, the airstrip at Lunga Point, which had been captured from the Japanese, was finished by Navy Seabees and named Henderson Field in honor of a Marine flier that had been killed at Midway. That night, the Japanese made the first of their almost nightly naval runs to bring reinforcements in from Rabaul, landing 900 men to the west of the Marine position. The following night, the Japanese landed another 1,500 troops to the east. At the same time, in order to cover the withdrawal of the transports, six escorting destroyers moved opposite the Marine position and opened fire. Almost immediately the Marines put out a call to Espiritu Santo and Maj. Edmundson, now the CO of the 431st BS, immediately took off in (41-9217, *Fiji Foo*). "At that time," he recalled, "my aircraft was the only one that was bombed up, fueled and ready to go . . ." His tail gunner Sgt. Handrow remembered, "Our crew jumped into the plane and in fifteen minutes we were on our way to Guadalcanal . . . 'Get a cruiser,' those were our orders and we were out there to fill them. And alone too."[5]

As the sun began to rise, Edmundson arrived and spotted a large ship off Guadalcanal. "We started to circle it," wrote Handrow. "It slowly circled with us so we couldn't make a good run on it." Antiaircraft fire filled the air as Edmundson took his B-17 around again and came out of the sun, trying to blind the Japanese gunners. "[W]ith the sun at our backs, down we came with bomb bay doors open," recalled Handrow, "down until we were at 5,000 feet. Mighty low to be fooling with anything [that] big." Added Maj. Edmundson, "We made our bomb run from 5,000 feet, an altitude when the flak was rough but from which my bombardier Lt. Al Thom . . . could not miss." Thom dropped four 500-lb. high explosive bombs on the ship. Noted the 431st BS historian, "Nos. 2 and 4 bracketed the vessel and No. 3 hit back of the after turret . . ."[6]

The vessel hit by Edmundson was actually the destroyer *Hagikaze*. Struck on the after gun mount, it caught fire and began burning fiercely. "The ship started burning like a Roman candle and evidently her steering mechanism was damaged because she started steaming in circles," Edmundson wrote. Taking his plane lower, he stayed around for about 30 minutes, letting his gunners strafe the burning warship. "While waiting," said Edmundson, "we buzzed low over the Marines on the beach who waved and jumped up and down."[7]

One of the men standing on the shore was journalist Richard Tregaskis, who would eventually write the best-selling *Guadalcanal Diary*. "We knew the aircraft had dropped bombs," Tregaskis wrote in his book, "for we saw a mushroom of dark-brown smoke rising from a point aft of the rear mast, and a steady torrent of smoke followed." Although Edmundson believed that the enemy ship would eventually sink, Tregaskis wrote otherwise. "The Jap [ship] was crippled, but not stopped," he noted. "He made full steam for the passage that leads to the sea, between Florida and Savo Islands. Clouds of brown smoke were still rising from the fantail." Nonetheless, Maj. Edmundson was awarded an Oak Leaf Cluster in lieu of a second DFC for his daring.[8]

Single bombers continued to patrol the sea-lanes around Guadalcanal and occasionally spotted an enemy submarine or reconnaissance plane. On August 20, Capt. Walter Y. Lucas (98th BS), B-17E (41-9211, *Typhoon McGoon II*), received the DFC for his battle with a Japanese flying boat. For 25 minutes the crews from both planes slugged it out in the air over Santa Isabel Island, with both sides scoring hits. Finally gunfire from the B-17 set the enemy plane on fire and forced it down for a water landing. As the flying boat taxied, Lucas passed overhead in a strafing run which finally exploded the plane. The *Typhoon McGoon II* returned to base with a 20-mm hole in the right wing, two bullet holes in the rudder, one in the nacelle of the No. 4 engine, and six in the fuselage. Fortunately, no one was injured.[9]

The hard flying and bad weather was sidelining the B-17s faster than the ground crews could repair them. In mid-August Maj. Gen. Millard Harmon, in charge of all Army troops, both ground and air, under Admiral Ghormley, was given the authority to requisition any of the 29 brand-new improved B-17Fs passing through on their way to Australia. On August 15, Capt. Edward Steedman, B-17F (41-24446, *Jezabel*), was on his way to the 19th BG, when his orders were changed and he wound up with the 42nd BS/11th BG. The first B-17F in the South Pacific Area, the *Jezabel* soon ran into trouble when a propeller governor failed on one of the engines and there was no replacement parts for a B-17F in the area. Ultimately, the crew stripped the plane of all unnecessary equipment and made a three-engined takeoff and flight to Efate, where the Navy manufactured a new gear. However, when Steedman attempted to return to Espiritu, the propeller proved to be out of balance and the engine ran away. Ignoring the problem, Steedman flew to Espiritu where B-17F (41-24446) was sidelined until the proper replacement parts could be flown in from the States.[10]

Japanese ships, nicknamed "Tokyo Express," continued to enter Ironbottom Sound by night, usually dropping off reinforcements and shelling the Marine perimeter. Each time, the planes of the 11th BG responded and each time the enemy ships steamed north before the sun came up and the B-17s arrived.[11] Before dawn on August 21, the Japanese soldiers that had landed on Guadalcanal on the night of August 18/19, struck the eastern flank of the Marine position. In a vicious battle fought along the Ilu River, the Marines killed nearly 800 Japanese, winning America's first victory over Japan's jungle-trained, battle-hardened troops and inflicting a severe blow to the ego of the Imperial Army.[12]

Having deciphered a number of Japanese coded messages, American Intelligence notified Admiral Nimitz that the Japanese were sending a strong strike force containing the light carrier *Ryujo* and the heavy carriers *Zuikaku* and *Shokaku*, along with the battleships *Hiei* and *Kirishima*, toward Guadalcanal to cover another reinforcement run. Duly notified, Nimitz stationed his Navy to intercept the Japanese and called on the Allied long-range planes to keep him apprised of the approach of the enemy.[13]

Immediately 11th BG B-17s, Navy PBYs and Australian Hudsons began searching. Near 12:15 P.M. on August 24, Col. Saunders was told that an enemy carrier force had been sighted northeast of Guadalcanal, and 720 miles from Espiritu Santo. Knowing that an immediate air strike would result in a hazardous night landing back at Espiritu, Saunders quickly decided that the opportunity was worth the risk. By 1:30 P.M., three planes, led by Maj. Manierre, and four more, commanded by Maj. Sewart, were in the air.[14] While the B-17s winged northward, Navy planes located portions of the Japanese fleet and started the Battle of the Eastern Solomons.

Spotting the light carrier *Ryujo* and her escorts, the navy planes dropped a number of bombs on her deck and slammed one torpedo into her hull. Engulfed in flames and without power, the *Ryujo* was under tow when the first flight of Flying Fortresses arrived near 6:00 P.M. Coming in almost unopposed, since most of the *Ryujo's* planes had abandoned the burning carrier, Maj. Manierre and his two wingmen made one bomb run but overshot with their bombs. On a second pass the bombardiers were more accurate and four 500-lb. bombs struck the *Ryujo*, administering the coup de grace. At 8:00 P.M. the carrier sank to the bottom of the South Pacific.[15]

Sixty miles to the east, Maj. Sewart's flight of four bombers found another segment of the Japanese fleet. Shortly after 6:00 P.M., in gathering darkness, the B-17s came across a support section containing a battleship and what appeared to be a seaplane carrier. Targeting the carrier, the B-17s flew through a storm of very accurate antiaircraft fire and fought their way through a swarm of enemy fighters to drop at least three and perhaps five bombs amidships on the vessel. Chased by the Zeros, the B-17s managed to shoot down five fighters with no damage to themselves. As the planes flew away, Maj. Sewart was sure that they had badly damaged a Japanese carrier. Instead however, confused in the darkness, they may have bombed a heavy cruiser since one of the ball turret gunners noticed that their bombs had "knocked her turrets off."[16]

Returning to Espiritu Santo, Maj. Sewart's flight found the island engulfed in a torrential downpour. Although low on gas, Sewart elected to fly the extra hundred miles to Efate rather than try a night landing on a rain slicked field. Upon touching down at Efate, the airmen found that all four planes had been damaged by antiaircraft fire, with B-17E (41-9060) requiring a new horizontal stabilizer, and B-17E (41-2527) requiring patching of "numerous holes."[17]

Maj. Manierre's element reached Espiritu Santo during the same torrential storm. Dangerously low on fuel, Manierre decided to try the hazardous night landing. Two planes landed safely before the No. 4 engine on Lt. Guenther's B-17E (41-2610) failed as he was making his approach. Going into a steep bank, the plane crashed into a small hill at the edge of the jungle airfield. Guenther and four others were killed while the rest of the crew were all injured. As the plane began to burn, the assistant engineer S/Sgt. Franklin E. Beattie, although semi-conscious himself, pried open the bomb-bay doors and helped his fellow crewmen to safety. For his heroic actions, Sgt. Beattie received the DFC.[18]

During the day, Japanese planes had attacked Henderson Field on Guadalcanal, causing little damage. At the same time, the Battle of the Eastern Solomons continued when a flight of Japanese carrier planes found the American carrier *Enterprise*. Although hit by three bombs, her crew was able to quickly repair her deck and reclaim all of her airborne planes.[19] The first day of the battle had gone to the Americans.

Near 3:00 A.M. on August 25, Col. Saunders was informed that yet another enemy carrier had been spotted near the Solomons and the 11th BG crews worked throughout the rainy night on Espiritu Santo to get their planes ready for an early morning strike. Around 5:30 A.M., with the rain finally at an end, eight B-17s headed north in search of the Japanese warship. Unfortunately, the enemy carriers had already left the area but there was still more than enough targets lingering around Guadalcanal.[20]

Near 8:35 A.M., Navy dive-bombers found the Japanese transports and scored a few hits on the *Kinryu Maru*. At 10:15 A.M., as the destroyer *Mutsuki* lay alongside the sinking transport taking off passengers, and the destroyer *Uzuki* stood guard, the eight B-17s suddenly appeared. Showing total disregard for the ability of the Flying Fortresses to hit an enemy ship, the commander of the *Mutsuki* decided to remain alongside the *Kinryu Maru* instead of taking evasive action. Flying a perfect bomb run, the B-17s hit the *Mutsuki* with three 500-lb. bombs, breaking the ship in two. At the same time near-misses blew a hole in the side of the *Uzuki*. Later, the disrespectful commander of the *Mutsuki* remarked, "Even the B-17s could make a hit once in a while!"[21]

With the sinking of the *Mutsuki* the Battle of the Eastern Solomons ended. The Americans had won a strategic and tactical victory. The Japanese had lost the light carrier *Ryujo*, the destroyer *Mutsuki*, and the transport *Kinryu Maru*. Additionally, Japan lost almost 90 planes, including at least five which were shot down by the B-17s. On the other side, the Americans had lost less than 20 planes, including B-17E (41-2610), and although the *Enterprise* had been hit it would only be out of action for a little more than a month.[22] Once again the Imperial Navy had come away with a bloodied nose and Guadalcanal was still in United States hands.

Although Japan had felt the Marine invasion of Guadalcanal was nothing more than a distraction to keep them from capturing Port Moresby, the subsequent naval actions and the failure to reinforce the island suddenly forced a change in strategy. By the end of August, the recapture of Guadalcanal was given top priority. Troops, aircraft, and ships originally destined for New Guinea were now divided between the two points of interest.[23]

Following the successful maximum effort raid by the 19th BG planes against Rabaul on August 7, Gen. Kenney continued his regular bombing of northeastern New Guinea, and Rabaul. Six B-17s hit the Lae airdrome on August 8, and the next day, seven planes led by Maj. "Pinky" Hoevet, took off to punish Rabaul again.[24] Running into heavy weather one plane became separated from the others and hit the airdrome at Gasmata, starting fires across the runway. The others however, continued on and dropped a string of bombs on Lakunai airdrome, a small fighter field north of Rabaul, wrecking another 15 parked enemy planes. Attacked by at least 15 Zeros, the B-17s fought a 20-minute air battle and although they managed to shoot down five fighters, Lt. Grundman, B-17E (41-2643), was shot down and crashed into the ground at Rondahl's Plantation on New Britain, killing everyone on board.[25]

As the six remaining Forts withdrew, the weather closed down again, making it difficult to maintain formation. Capt. Harry J. Hawthorne, B-17E (41-2452), became separated from the rest and, low on fuel, made a crash landing on a coral reef near Malapla Island off the east coast of New Guinea. Commented the 93rd BS historian, "Due to Capt. Hawthorne's skillful piloting no injuries were sustained by the crew." Able to radio their location to headquarters, the crew was soon rescued.[26]

On August 9, after attaining permission to organize his 5th Bomber Command and 5th Fighter Command into an American air force, separate from the Australians, Gen. Kenney designated his new outfit the 5th Air Force (5th AF). Kenney then placed Brig. Gen. Kenneth N. Walker in charge of 5th Bomber Command in Australia and sent Brig. Gen. Ennis Whitehead to command Seven Mile Strip at Port Moresby.[27]

Trying to determine the exact numbers of his new air force, Gen. Kenney asked for a tally of all of the planes and men under his command and found out that among other aircraft, he had a total of 62 Flying Fortresses in the 19th BG. However, two planes had been lost on August 7, and another two on August 9, and 19 were listed as being "overhauled and rebuilt." Still, new planes were trickling into Australia. On August 2, B-17E (41-2656, *"Chief Seattle" from the Pacific Northwest*), paid for through the sale of Defense Bonds by the people of Seattle and the Pacific Northwest, had arrived at Charters Towers. Intended for the fledgling 43rd BG, the plane was eventually flown to Townsville and flew reconnaissance missions with the 435th BS/19th BG.[28]

Four new planes, all improved B-17Fs, had arrived in Australia on August 6 and five days later, six more were landed at Brisbane. Another plane, B-17F (41-24383), flown by Lt. Lewis A. Anderson, developed engine trouble on the way and was delayed at Christmas Island, arriving at Charleville shortly after the others. The crews were originally destined for the 43rd BG but were quickly assigned to the war-weary 19th BG for training purposes and to gain combat experience, and to relieve the pressure on the overworked veterans.[29]

Many of the new crews however, were irritated at having to fly combat missions with the 19th BG. Many of the men had hundreds of hours of flight time in the B-17 and were combat veterans themselves, having participated in the battle of Midway. In fact, some of the men had been among the flight of B-17s that had stumbled into Hickam Field on December 7, 1941.[30] And, the training that they received, in some cases, was negligible. "I assumed I would receive some kind of training from experienced combat pilots," wrote Lt. Murphy who was shipped to the 435th BS. "But that was not the way it happened." After arriving at Townsville, the operations officer gave Murphy a map of Northern Australia, New Guinea, New Britain, and the Solomon Islands. "He then said that was our area of reconnaissance," Murphy continued. "After that lengthy indoctrination, he left." Selected to fly a photographic mission over Rabaul only one day after arriving, Murphy flew up to Port Moresby for further instructions. "My orders were to fly to Rabaul, New Britain, take pictures, fly south to Bougainville, take more pictures, and then return to Port Moresby," said Murphy. "We were then instructed to go back to our plane and wait for word to take off. That was the only training and indoctrination that I received before going into combat. We had no experienced pilot, navigator, or crew member to fly our crew."[31]

On August 10, after Gen. Kenney was informed of the number of planes that he had at his disposal, he was finally informed that there was a second heavy bombardment group in Australia—the 43rd BG. Incredibly, Gen. Kenney had been in Australia for two weeks without the knowledge of the existence of the 43rd BG. Shortly, he took steps to gather together the scattered squadrons of the 43rd BG and mold it into a cohesive fighting unit. Kenney recalled, "I ordered the pieces picked up and assembled in the Townsville area, where I decided to equip them with B-17s as fast as I could get them out of overhaul and repair, or from the United States as replacements."[32]

Although every air commander in the Pacific complained about the lack of Flying Fortresses being sent to the theater, the truth is that at the very beginning of the war, two out of every three B-17s produced were sent to the Pacific. Eleven B-17Cs saw combat in the Pacific Theater and 41 out of 42 B-17Ds wound up in Hawaii or the Philippines. Then, with war looming, and after the attack on Pearl Harbor, the Pacific Theater continued to get Flying Fortresses. Sixty-six of the first 100 B-17Es were sent to the Pacific. Unfortunately, every single one sported the highly ineffective Bendix remote-controlled belly turret.

However, when the United States decided on the policy of "Germany First," the flow of B-17s to the Pacific turned into a trickle. Out of the next 412 B-17Es produced, only 108, including six more with the Bendix belly turret, went to the Pacific, roughly one out of every four. And, with the Central, South, and Southwest Pacific Areas all clamoring for heavy bombers, the flow to any one area sometimes appeared as though it had dried up completely. When the B-17F came along, only 49 ever reached the Pacific. By that time however, the decision had already been made to replace the B-17 Flying Fortress with the B-24 Liberator. The air commanders in the Pacific would have to make due with what they had.[33]

By the time Gen. Kenney found out about the 43rd BG, the 63rd BS was at Torrens Creek, Northern Territory, about 550 miles north of their old base at Charleville and the 64th BS was at Fenton Field, about 80 miles inland from Darwin. The 403rd BS was still at the Laverton Repair Depot at Melbourne, but in an attempt to consolidate the group, the 65th BS and HqS left Williamtown, near Sydney, during the second week in August and joined the 63rd BS at Torrens Creek on August 15. One day earlier, four B-17s had been assigned to the 63rd BS, thus making it the first squadron of the 43rd BG to be activated. However, as already stated, the planes and crews were quickly hustled off to the 19th BG. Noted the 63rd BS historian, "Within a week, most of the 63rd personnel had been flown either to Townsville, Queensland, or to Mareeba, Queensland, to train with the 19th BG for actual combat operations."[34]

Those that stayed behind at Torrens Creek found the place less than admirable. "This was not Mareeba," noted Lt. Murphy when he came back to the squadron, "just dust, flies, and food as bad as that in New Guinea." Flies seemed to be a common complaint at all of the American airfields in Australia, but the combination of flies and bad food at Torrens Creek made it particularly bad. "None of us had a great love for Torrence [sic] Creek, principally because of the food," remembered Murphy.[35]

While Gen. Kenney was trying to consolidate the 43rd BG, the 19th BG continued to fight. On August 12, a conglomerate flight of eight B-17s from the 28th, 30th and 93rd BSs went after merchant shipping in Rabaul's Simpson Harbor. Attacked by Zeros before reaching the target, the formation, led by Capt. Hillhouse of the 30th BS, kept a tight grouping and managed to drop 48 500-lb. bombs from 26,000 feet and either sank or badly damaged at least three transports. In a 45-minute running fight, the B-17 gunners shot down two or three Zeros while the Flying Forts received only slight damage. For his coolness in leading the flight through both antiaircraft fire and persistent fighter attack, Capt. Hillhouse was awarded a Silver Star.[36]

In New Guinea, the Japanese infantry were steadily forcing the Australians back along the Kokoda Trail through the Owen Stanley Mountains. On August 11, the Japanese took the settlement of Kokoda, almost midway along the trail. By August 13, the Imperial troops were a few miles beyond the settlement when they decided to stop and consolidate their holdings and wait for reinforcements.[37]

At Rabaul, the Japanese commanders had decided to send a convoy of four transports and their escorting warships to reinforce Buna. At 6:25 A.M., on August 13, while the convoy was still 76 miles northeast of Gona, it was spotted by 1st Lt. Andrew H. Price (435th BS). Immediately the warships opened up on the lone reconnaissance B-17 while Price's radio operator sent a message of the sighting to Port Moresby. "We kept just out of firing range and near to good cloud cover,"

Price reported. After almost four hours of shadowing the ships, five Zeros appeared. "We immediately dove into cloud coverage just as [the] fighters started to come in on us," wrote Price. "We flew thru [sic] heavy rain for about 20 minutes, occasionally breaking out only to see the Zeros off to the left and above. At 1040 o'clock we broke out into the clear and saw seven B-17s coming from the direction of Port Moresby."[38]

Alerted by Price's discovery, 10 B-17s left Seven Mile Airstrip at 8:40 A.M. Running into terrible weather, only seven planes rendezvoused with Price, who by now had lost sight of the convoy while eluding the fighters and had to double back to find it. As the B-17s followed, the strike force broke down again. "We saw only three B-17s reach the target and drop bombs," Price admitted, "but could not observe [the] results because of [the] clouds." Only 24 500-lb. bombs were dropped by the three B-17s from an altitude of 16,000 feet but the moving ships easily avoided them.[39]

Still intent on damaging the transports, a flight of B-26s went after the enemy ships while the B-17s returned to Port Moresby to refuel. Like the B-17s, the B-26s missed their targets and returned to base just as a few of the Fortresses were going out for a second run. At 4:15 P.M., Maj. Hoevet and two other planes lifted off from Seven Mile Strip but ran into thick weather again and were forced to abandon the mission. Thirty minutes later, Maj. Rouse and two other planes tried to find the convoy but instead found a lone Japanese cruiser. "I got through O.K. with my flight and bombed a cruiser," Rouse wrote. "He maneuvered and we missed." Taking his flight back over Buna, he was surprised to discover the enemy transports laying at anchor. "Found three transports (what we wanted to bomb) in Buna Bay on way back," he wrote. "Intelligence had told us they wouldn't be there yet. Was disgusted that we missed them especially as this may have been a decisive factor in the New Guinea Battle."[40]

Determined to strike at the enemy ships at first light, Lt. Wilson L. Cook (435th BS) left Port Moresby in B-17E (41-2656, *"Chief Seattle" from the Pacific Northwest*), to scout Buna, Gasmata, and the sea-lanes towards Rabaul. Cook's B-17 lifted off at 6:02 A.M. on August 14 and was never seen again. The *"Chief Seattle"* and 10 men simply disappeared. Whether the plane was shot down or crashed due to mechanical failure is unknown but the *"Chief Seattle"* disappeared on only its third mission.[41]

At 6:30 A.M., seven B-17s followed the *"Chief Seattle"* off the runway and headed towards Buna. By then, however, 3,000 Japanese troops had been landed and the ships were gone. "Convoy not at Buna so searching for it," Maj. Rouse wrote in his diary. A few hours later, the B-17s located the convoy. "Found it 100 miles NE of Buna," Rouse added. "[S]tarted bombing run at 3,800 ft. (weather very poor) but fighters jumped us and in first pass injured two men in Pincky's [Hoevet] ship. Chased us a long way." About 10 Zeros tried to defend the convoy and inflicted slight damage to the B-17s. Concluded Maj. Rouse, "Put 3 shells in Pinck's ship, one in engine of another ship, shot top window out above co-pilot's head on another ship, [and] hit rocker box rod in our ship. One ship had one gun in top turret blown up." Miraculously, only one crewman was wounded. In return, the Americans shot down two Zeros and damaged three others but the tenacious attack by the enemy fighters had given the convoy time to slip away and the bombers had to settle with dropping their bombs on the Buna Bay landing area.[42]

Reinforced with fresh troops, the Japanese renewed their drive over the Kokoda Trail. As their infantry pushed steadily forward, the Japanese fighters and bombers continued to disrupt the Allied resistance. By the middle of August, Port Moresby had suffered 78 air raids, while Darwin had been bombed 27 times. On August 17, over 100 enemy planes appeared over Port Moresby and Seven Mile Strip and destroyed the operations building, several trucks, 200 drums of precious gasoline, and 11 American planes, none of which were B-17s.[43]

Unfortunately, the 19th BG did lose another B-17 that day while Lt. Lindsey was out testing flares in B-17E (41-2434) with 11 other men, including Maj. "Pinky" Hoevet, CO of the 30th BS. For some unknown reason the plane caught fire and crashed near the shore of Yorkey Knob, near Cairns. For several days the authorities searched the shark-infested waters for the bodies of the 12 men. Only six were ever found. Noted Maj. Rouse on the loss of Maj. Hoevet, "[He was] one of the best men in the 19th Group." The next day, Maj. Rouse was given command of the 30th BS.[44]

Over the next few days the B-17s of the 19th BG attacked the Japanese at Kavieng on New Ireland, a convoy off Faisi on Shortland Island off the southern tip of Bougainville in the Solomons, and the airstrip at Lae. While the bombings of Kavieng and Lae were successful, the attack on the convoy was less than impressive.[45] Once again, the B-17s were showing that their worth was in hitting stationary targets.

Gen. Kenney's attempt to activate the 43rd BG took a giant leap forward on August 24 when he placed Maj. William Benn, his aide, in charge of the 63rd BS. Eleven B-17s and 12 crews from the 43rd BG, which had been flying reconnaissance missions with the 435th BS/19th BG, were deemed nearly ready for aerial combat and were returned to the 63rd BS at Torrens Creek, where they began training as a unit. Two weeks later, the 403rd BS, which had been working in the repair depot at Laverton since mid-March, was brought up to Torrens Creek to train in the airplanes from the 63rd BS.[46] Slowly but surely, the 43rd BG was coming together.

About the third week in August, the Japanese decided to open up a second arm of a pincer move to capture Port Moresby. Already pressing southward along the Kokoda Trail, the Japanese loaded a few transports at Kavieng and headed towards the deep-water anchorage at Milne Bay, on the far southeastern tip of New Guinea. For some time, the Australians had been utilizing two small airfields a few miles west of Milne Bay, and more recently, the Americans had begun building a bomber strip with the intention of having a forward staging area a few hundred miles closer to Rabaul and the Solomons. The Japanese planned on capturing the three airfields and using them as forward staging areas for their drive on Port Moresby and the eventual invasion of Australia.[47]

Allied intelligence had already decoded the fact that the Japanese were intent on capturing the Milne Bay airfields so when a strong force of enemy planes raided Milne Bay on August 24, Gen. Kenney was convinced that the Japanese were about to move. Calling Gen. Walker at Townsville, he ordered two bomb squadrons from the 19th BG moved to Port Moresby immediately, and wanted the other two there by the afternoon of August 25. Then, to keep the enemy off balance, he ordered a night strike against Rabaul.[48]

Near 10:00 P.M., August 24, eight B-17s began taking off from Seven Mile Strip. From the very start things went wrong for Maj. Rouse. The last plane in the flight, Rouse was about to take off when he received word of an incoming air raid. Unknown to Rouse, four of his crew abandoned the plane. "Didn't discover this until after take off," he wrote. "Only 5 men left on ship. Bombardier, navigator, pilot, co-pilot, and eng[ineer]. Decided to go on to Rabaul as we were." Flying in formation with the other bombers, Rouse pushed his plane through a violent tropical storm and made a respectable bomb run on Vunakanau Airdrome. As the planes turned for home, Rouse felt fortunate that only one lone Zero made a desultory pass at his undermanned B-17. Running into the same storm that had plagued the bombers on the way to the target, Rouse's plane iced up over the Owen Stanley Mountains but he made it safely over the top. Upon approaching Port Moresby, he found the area socked in by clouds. "Clouds down to 400' over Moresby," he wrote. "Bad time finding it. Navigator really on the ball." At 5:00 A.M. on August 25, the B-17s set down at Seven Mile Strip, their night raid on Rabaul at an end.[49]

Around noon on the 25th, a reconnaissance plane sighted the convoy from Kavieng about 120 miles north of Milne Bay. By 2:00 P.M., nine Fortresses from the 93rd BS lifted off from Mareeba, but bad weather shielded the convoy from sight and the B-17s returned empty-handed. Later that afternoon, the convoy was eventually found by a flight of Australian planes who managed to sink a minesweeper and damage one of the transports. Still, in spite of the best efforts of the Allies, under the cover of the rain and the darkness on the night of August 25, about 1,200 Japanese marines landed on the north shore of Milne Bay, about eight miles east of the unfinished American airstrip.[50]

At 4:00 A.M. on August 26, eight B-17s from the 93rd BS flew to Milne Bay to attack the Japanese ships. "Weather was horrible, ceiling approximately 2,000 feet, sometimes less," reported Lt. Lewis Sutton, navigator on Lt. Bruce Gibson's B-17E (41-2663). Led by Maj. Hardison in B-17F (41-24391, *Hoomalimali*), the formation disintegrated into flights of two or three planes as the aircraft hit heavy rain clouds. "We were supposed to assemble in an eight ship formation," wrote Lt. Jim Dieffenderfer, copilot on Capt. Chiles' B-17E (41-9234), which sported a light blue top and white bottom, "but due to darkness and weather never made it. When we got an airplane on each wing we headed for Milne Bay and got there in daylight." As the planes arrived at Milne Bay the Japanese ships responded. "Antiaircraft very accurate," noted Lt. Sutton.[51]

The planes were hit hard as they leveled out at about 1,500 feet for their bomb runs. Capt. Kenneth Casper, B-17E (41-2621, *The Daylight Ltd.*), had one tire flattened, two engines and his hydraulic system shot out, the flaps shot away, and the wings and fuselage peppered with small shell fragments. A shell exploded just above the nose section of Capt. Chiles' light blue Fortress, hitting bombardier Sgt. Earl Snyder in the back of the head and almost severing the left leg of the navigator, Lt. David Hirsch. Though mortally wounded, Snyder released four 500-lb. bombs before passing out. Flight engineer Sgt. Wathen Cody left his top turret position to check on the men in the nose. He wrote, ". . . Hirsch was bleeding badly all over, his face speckled with Plexiglas from the nose, big hole. His leg looked like it was blown off. Snyder was lying over the bomb sight with his hand on the bomb release handle, and when I got over him I could see a piece of jagged metal in his head, size about three inches around and about two inches deep in his head." Realizing that the bombardier was dead, Cody tied a tourniquet on Hirsch's leg and pulled him onto the flight deck.[52]

A large naval shell passed completely through the wing of Lt. Gibson's plane and barely missed the wing fuel tank. "The hole was flowered up in a mushroom pattern on top of the wing," wrote navigator Sutton. Not so fortunate was Capt. Clyde Webb, B-17F (41-24354). An antiaircraft burst hit his plane in the left inboard engine and fuel tank, setting it on fire. Wrote Lt. Dieffenderfer, "Just before the bomb drop we saw Webb get a direct hit in No. 2 engine—he went over on his back and into the water, no sign of parachutes." Before sinking, the plane skidded along the surface of the water, leaving behind a burning gasoline slick. Capt. Webb and his crew were all killed and B-17F (41-24354) became the first F-model Fortress to be lost in the Pacific war.[53]

In spite of the heavy ack-ack fire and the loss of Capt. Webb, the remaining seven Fortresses made their bombing runs from between 1,500 and 2,000 feet. Lt. Percy Hinton, B-17E (41-2668), thought that he hit a transport which was "observed sinking," and the unknown pilot of B-17E (41-2599, *Tugboat Annie*) reportedly laid five 500-lb. bombs alongside a cruiser, damaging the ship enough to cause it to list. Capt. Hardison had trouble with his bomb racks and spent one and a half hours over the enemy ships, making perhaps 12 passes, before his bombardier was able to salvo half of the bombs close enough to the stern of one of the cruisers to do some damage. Accompanied all the time by his wingman, Lt. Bruce Gibson, B-17E (41-2663), Hardison made one more pass over the ships and dropped four more bombs before heading for home.[54]

Several crewmen were injured on the various planes and although all seven B-17s made it safely back to Seven Mile Strip, Capt. Caspar ran into trouble while trying to land *The Daylight Ltd.* Since his plane was badly shot up and hard to handle he was forced to circled the field several times before coming in. Touching down at 130 mph he tried to slow the plane but could not because of the damaged hydraulic lines. When one wheel suddenly shot off, the plane spun to the right in an uncontrolled ground loop and cracked into a tree. Although smoke billowed from the wreck, the plane did not catch fire and everyone walked away. However, B-17E (41-2621, *The Daylight Ltd.*) was a total loss.[55]

Though the 28th BS sent nine planes out after the 93rd BS, they were unable to find the convoy through the continuing rain and instead dropped their bombs on the Milne Bay beachhead.[56] The overall raid on the Milne Bay convoy had cost the 5th AF two more B-17s and 10 men while the Japanese may have lost one transport. Able to put their troops ashore, the Imperial marines quickly began moving inland towards the Allied airfields. Only the coming of day stopped the advance, as the badly outnumbered, but not outfought, Imperial marines faded back into the safety of the jungle to await the coming of night and reinforcements.[57]

Despite the best reconnaissance efforts of the 435th "Kangaroo Squadron," the Japanese took advantage of the terrible weather and slipped another convoy of troops into Milne Bay on the night of August 26–27. Reinforced, the Japanese marines fought westward toward the unfinished American bomber strip, fighting their way to the very edge of the runway. At that point the Australian defense stiffened and held firm.[58]

On the evening of August 29, another Japanese convoy entered Milne Bay and landed a small contingent of 750 men. Although the 28th and 30th BSs attempted to intercept the fleeing warships they were unsuccessful because of the continuing bad weather. On August 31, the 30th BS fought their way through the terrible weather and bombed Rabaul. Noted Maj. Rouse, "Four ships [i.e. B-17s] finally made it to Rabaul and dropped their bombs on a moving cruiser and missed."[59]

The month of August was finally at an end. The Allies were still holding on in New Guinea, though just barely, while the Americans were strengthening their toehold on Guadalcanal. Although nobody realized it, August 1942 had been the third costliest month for the B-17 in the Pacific. A total of 17 B-17s had been lost to either accident, weather, or enemy action. Only December 1941, and February 1942, were costlier months for the B-17 in the Pacific. In December 1941, 31 B-17s had been lost in Hawaii and the Philippines, and in February 1942, another 25 B-17s had been lost in the Netherlands East Indies. The new model B-17Fs continued to arrive but not nearly fast enough to offset a loss rate of one B-17 every two days. Something had to be done to counter the attrition rate of the B-17 in the South and the Southwest Pacific Areas. Unfortunately, it would take quite some time.

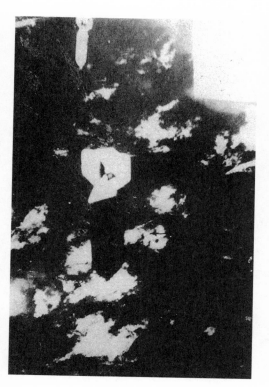

On 7 May 1942, three B-17s of the 19th BG, while returning from the battle of the Corel Sea, accidentally bombed the *Australia* and her Allied escorts. The B-17 bombs missed the *Australia* and its escorts as the ships went into wild evasive maneuvers. Fortunately, all bombs missed. Needless to say, the Australian commander was none too happy about the bombing while Col. Eugene L. Eubank, commanding officer of the 19th BG, was none too happy with the results. (John Wallace Fields Collection)

B-17D (40-3097), *The Swoose*) in Australia. Third from right is Senator and Lt. Comdr. Lyndon B. Johnson, future president of the United States. (USAF)

Twin .50 caliber machine guns protruding through the radio compartment roof on B-17E (41-9121, *Buzz King*). Such modifications were often done in the field.

B-17E in a camouflaged hangar at Mareeba, Australia. (USAF)

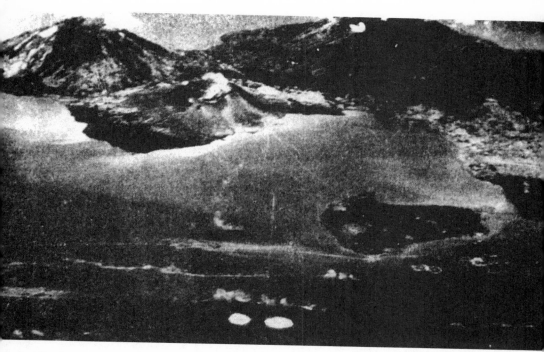

The harbor of Rabaul, New Britain Island, 1942.

B-17E (41-2432, *The Last Straw*) receives a load of bombs at Port Moresby in August 1942. The useless remote-controlled Bendix ball turret has been removed and replaced with a pair of .50 caliber machine guns. (USAF)

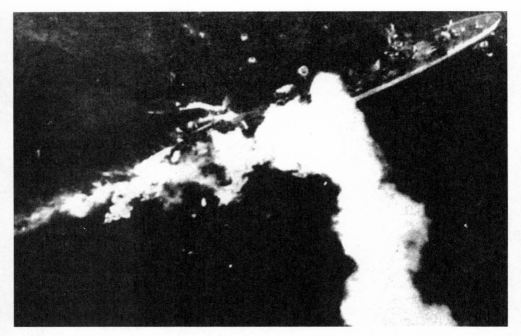

Japanese destroyer *Yayoi* hit by bombs from B-17E (41-2645, *Miss Carriage*) near the Trobriand Islands, off the northeast coast of New Guinea on 11 September 1942. Though badly damaged, the destroyer stayed afloat and was later beached until it could be repaired and refloated.

Flight Officer A. J. Davenport, one of the many Australian airmen that flew with the 19th BG. Davenport was mortally wounded on 5 October 1942 on a raid against Vunakanau Airdrome, Rabaul, New Britain Island. (Ritchie B. Gooch Collection.)

1/Lt. John Wallace Fields (435th BS/19th BG) receiving the Distinguished Flying Cross from Gen. George C. Kenney on 16 October 1942. (John Wallace Fields Collection)

B-17s sitting in revetments at Seven Mile Airstrip, Port Moresby, New Guinea. (Signal Corps)

On 15 November 1942 a B-17 airlifted a 105-mm. howitzer, a tractor to pull it with, the gun crew of eight men, fifty rounds of ammunition, a tool kit, and a camouflage net from Australia to Port Moresby to help the American infantry fighting on New Guinea. (USAF)

B-17F (41-24550) lies partly submerged after ditching in Bootless Inlet, near Port Moresby, on 14 December 1942. (Signal Corps)

Loading 250-lb. bombs at Guadalcanal. (USAF)

B-17F (41-24457, *The Aztec's Curse*) flying over the coast of Gaudalcanal, c. late 1942. A beached Japanese ship burns in the background. (USAF)

A stretcher-carrying jeep awaits wounded from B-17F (41-24403, *Blitz Buggy* aka *The Old Man*) after a fight with Japanese Zeros on a mission over Gasmata, 8 March 1943. (Signal Corps)

Shell casings litter the waist compartment of B-17F (41-24403, *Blitz Buggy* aka *The Old Man*) after a fight with Japanese Zeros on a mission over Gasmata, 8 March 1943. (Signal Corps)

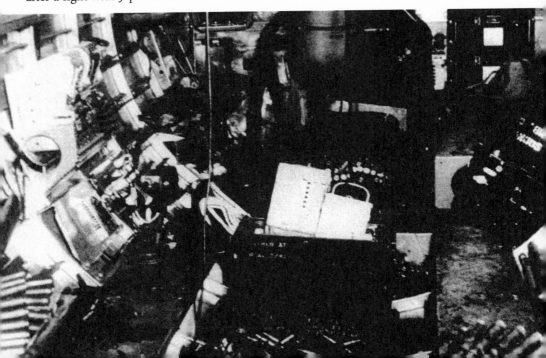

A B-17E of the 11th BG taking off from Guadalcanal, December 1942. (USMC)

B-17F (41-24537, *Talisman*) takes off from Seven Mile Airstrip, Port Moresby, New Guinea on 5 September 1943 with Gen. Douglas MacArthur to view the parachute drop at Nadzab. (USAF)

Crash landing of B17F (41-24548) at Tadji, New Guinea, 4 May 1944. The plane was damaged beyond repair. (Signal Corps)

A SB-17G on Okinawa in early 1945. Six B-17Gs were fitted with a lifeboat and special radar used to search and rescue downed B-29 crews returning from bombing Japan. (USMC)

Capt. Colin P. Kelly Jr., (14th BS/19th BG) killed 10 December 1941 after bombing the Japanese heavy cruiser *Ashigara*. (USAF)

Col. Laverne G. "Blondie" Saunders, commanding officer of the 11th BG during the Guadalcanal Campaign. (USAF)

Capt. Harl Pease Jr. (93rd BS/19th BG). The only Medal of Honor recipient from the 19th BG. (USAF)

Captain Jay Zeamer (65th BS/43rd BG), Medal of Honor recipient for a photographic mission off Buka Island, 16 June 1943. (USAF)

Lt. Joseph R. Sarnoski (65th BS/43rd BG), Medal of Honor recipient (posthumously), bombardier with Captain Zeamer on the photographic mission of Buka Island, 16 June 1943. (USAF)

M/Sgt. Louis "Soup" Silva (9th BS/7th BG) became a living legend among the 7th and 19th BGs. Although 43 years old he insisted on flying every mission as a tail gunner and is credited with shooting down between 18 and 20 Zeros. He died 16 July 1942 when B-17E (41-2421) crashed while trying to land at Horn Island. (USAF)

XIX

Reversing Positions

IN EARLY SEPTEMBER, Gen. Kenney decided to move the supply depot at Tocumwal, on the far southeast tip of Australia, to Brisbane and eventually Townsville. Unable to get the flow of new bombers that he needed, he was hoping to keep those already in Australia in the best shape possible. By moving the supply depot closer to the front, he was hoping to get his planes back into the air much quicker.[1]

In the meantime, the ground crews had to make do with what they had. Sgt. Green recalled, "Requisitions for spare parts were back ordered by the depot. I even had to use empty 50 cal. ammo cans to store critical parts from damaged acft [aircraft] in a hole covered with boards under my bunk." Summing up his experience, Sgt. Green stated, "Our existence was due to our ability to get the job done without help and salvage what we could from damaged acft [aircraft]."[2] By moving the supply depot closer to the front, Gen. Kenney was hoping to alleviate the existing situation.

Terrible weather continued to be a factor in the Southwest Pacific Area through the first week of September. "Failed to locate target due to weather," and "Returned—bad weather," were only a couple of entries in the Daily Summary for the 5th Bomber Command for the first week of September. On September 5, eight planes left Port Moresby for Rabaul but ran into ". . . snow, rain, and icing," and returned to New Guinea. At 4:00 P.M., however, four of the crews were sent back out after a few Japanese warships that had entered Milne Bay to evacuated the exhausted Imperial Marines. Hitting foul weather, the planes flew low over the waves to get under the storm. "Found them [i.e. enemy ships] at [the] mouth of Milne Bay just at dusk at 700 feet. Almost ran over them," Maj. Rouse wrote. "Opened up on us with everything they had including a broadside. Came pretty close. Tried to bomb them at 3,300 ft. but couldn't find them because of the darkness and clouds."[3]

Tired from two exhausting flights, all of the bombers turned aside and headed towards Mareeba. Noted Maj. Rouse, "Returned to Maruba [sic]. Very tired. Almost cracked up on landing." Unfortunately, Lt. William R. Humrichouse (30th BS) in B-17F (41-24428) crashed into the jungle trees when the landing gear collapsed as he touched down. Wrote Maj. Rouse, "No one hurt but a near thing, plane washed out (a new F)."[4]

The Australians had taken the initiative at Milne Bay on the last day of August and pushed the Japanese marines away from the unfinished airstrip. With her troops exhausted, and their supplies gone, Japan elected to evacuate the remaining troops. The westward drive on Port Moresby had been shattered by the hard fighting Australian infantry, the Allied airplanes, and by the strangling jungle. On the night of September 5–6, the Japanese evacuated approximately 1,300 broken down and diseased survivors.[5]

Notified of the presence of the evacuating warships, three 28th BS B-17s went after the vessels but were unable to make a bomb run because of the weather. "No bombs were dropped, no attack made, no enemy aircraft were sighted," wrote the squadron historian. Over the next two days the planes from the 28th BS tried to punish the retreating convoy but the results were always the same. Noted the historian, "A third mission was flown on September 7th . . . Nothing was sighted and no bombs were dropped. Three planes flew the same mission on September 8th with the same negative results."[6]

The Battle for Milne Bay was over and the Allies claimed their first land victory in New Guinea. Coming ahead of the total conquest of Guadalcanal, the victory was the first large-scale land victory over the Japanese since the beginning of the war. A morale defeat for the Japanese, it was a necessary boost for the Australian infantry who were becoming more and more acclimated to the rigors of jungle fighting, and were now confident that they could defeat the Japanese on their own terms. The defeat of the Imperial marines at Milne Bay was exactly the morale boost the Australians needed to help them stop the Japanese drive over the Kokoda Trail.[7]

On September 5, the day the Japanese pulled out of Milne Bay, the Imperial troops on the Kokoda Trail reached the summit of the mountain trail and began attacking downhill towards Port Moresby.[8] Something had to be done to slow the Japanese push until Australian reinforcements could be brought over from Milne Bay so on September 6, the 5th AF went to work, bombing and strafing several points along the Kokoda Trail that were in Japanese hands.[9]

Five days later, on September 11, two enemy destroyers were spotted near the Trobriand Islands, off the northeast coast of New Guinea. Nine B-17s, led by Maj. Helton, CO of the 28th BS, in the light blue B-17E (41-9234), took off from Port Moresby and broke into three three-plane elements. Spotting two enemy destroyers on the open sea in broad daylight, the B-17s went in for the kill. "The Japs in both warships began blazing away with everything they had," stated Capt. Crawford, copilot with Capt. Jack P. Thompson, B-17E (41-2645, *Miss Carriage*). "It was like all hell let loose. They knew they were caught with their pants down."[10]

Although Maj. Helton's first element, flying at 1,500 feet, missed with their bombs, Lt. James Ellis, B-17E (41-2660), flying with the second element at 1,600 feet, scored a direct hit on one of the ships and buckled her plates. "[T]iny specks of men could be seen swarming over the [destroyer's] decks, over the sides in lifeboats, sliding down ropes into the churning water . . . rats deserting the sinking ship," wrote Crawford. But even Crawford admitted that the ship did not sink. Though badly damaged, the destroyer stayed afloat and was later beached until she could be repaired and refloated.[11]

The third element went after the second ship, the destroyer *Yayoi*, and flew through a barrage of antiaircraft fire. On the *Miss Carriage*, a shard of shrapnel sliced through the copilot window to the right of Crawford, went on through the cockpit, narrowly missing the pilot, and continued out through the left-hand window. "[I]t was all over so quickly we didn't have time to be scared," recalled Crawford. Only 1,400 feet above the destroyer, the gunners of the three Fortresses strafed the warship as the bombardiers unleashed their 500-lb. bombs. As two direct hits from Capt. Thompson's plane hit the stern of the *Yayoi*, bullets from his ball turret gunner mistakenly exploded the last bomb from the B-17 while it was only a few hundred feet below the plane.

"Suddenly, without warning," wrote Capt. Crawford, "came a petrifying explosion, more terrific than anything I had ever heard." The plane shuddered violently and was knocked upward, throwing the two pilots against the cockpit ceiling. "The huge 28-ton plane was tossed like a feather and hurtled straight upwards for 500 feet," explained Crawford. "Clouds of smoke and flame surrounded us. Acrid fumes burned our nostrils. Smoke stung our eyes. Flying fragments whistled and zinged in all directions . . . we could hear them tearing into the fuselage."

As the two pilots fought to get the *Miss Carriage* under control, the waist gunner, who had been watching to make sure the bombs fell from their shackles, and who had been knocked forward and almost thrown out of the open bomb bay doors, finally informed the rest of the crew what had happened. Miraculously, no one had been injured and the plane, although battered and beaten, took the crew home. Below them, the *Yayoi* was wrapped in flames and beginning to sink.[12] The B-17 crews were learning that the way to hit and sink an enemy ship was from low altitude.

On September 11, the Japanese continued to strengthen their drive across the Owen Stanley Mountains and moved 22 planes to the Buna airstrip. At first light American light and medium bombers, followed by the B-17s of the 19th BG, attacked the airfield. Coming in low again, at between 1,000 and 3,000 feet altitude, the B-17s flew through a storm of antiaircraft fire dropping a total of 84 300-lb. bombs. The airfield received only medium damage, but one of the Fortresses was seriously damaged.[13]

Lt. Gilbert E. Erb (28th BS), B-17E (41-2663), was just finishing his bomb run when his plane was hit by antiaircraft fire. "The huge machine," Capt. Crawford, B-17E (41-2645, *Miss Carriage*), wrote, ". . . was hit on the nose by a shell, right before my eyes. I saw the flames spurt out, the Fortress reel like a drunken man and then plunge down on a crazy path towards the water." The official report stated that B-17E (41-2663) was "hit in the fuselage, causing fire and explosion of a gasoline tank." As the other aircrews watched, four men parachuted from the stricken bomber, leaving five men still inside. "Just as the plane was about to strike the water, it leveled out and made a neat water landing," stated Crawford. Somehow, Lt. Erb had gained enough control of the plane to make a controlled belly landing 20 miles south of Buna and about 50 yards off shore.

While two of the men that had parachuted from the burning B-17 were captured, the other two got away and fled into the jungle. Of the five men inside the plane when it ditched, three were drowned but Lt. Erb and his bombardier got out and made it safely ashore. Although the bombardier was injured, the two men began moving through the jungle towards Milne Bay. Miraculously, they ran into the other two crewmen and all four eventually made their way to an Australian encampment. For his actions in leading his fellow crewmen to safety through hostile territory, Lt. Erb was issued a DFC.[14]

Very early on the morning of September 13, a lone reconnaissance plane located and strafed a Japanese convoy south of Kavieng in the Bismarck Sea. Informed of the convoy, nine B-17s from the 30th BS quickly set off from Mareeba to stage through Port Moresby. Unfortunately, by the time the flight left Seven Mile Strip, they had lost three planes due to mechanical failure. Then, instead of finding the reported convoy, the six remaining B-17s found a cruiser towing a destroyer near Jacquinot Bay, midway along the southeast shore of New Britain. Dropping 48 500-lb. bombs from 14,000 feet, the aircrews believed that they damaged the cruiser but admitted that they did not sink it. By 3:00 P.M., the planes were back at Port Moresby and six hours later they were back in Australia.[15]

Convinced that the two vessels bombed by the 30th BS were not from the same convoy spotted on September 13, a search plane went out and found the large convoy south of Rabaul. Near 3:30 A.M. on September 14, seven B-17s from the 63rd BS/43rd BG started out from Mareeba on the first independent mission for the 43rd BG.[16] The fledgling 43rd BG was finally ready to spread its wings and take flight on its own.

Slowly but surely the 63rd BS had grown to maturity. Since coming together at Torrens Creek after being parceled out to the 19th BG for training, the 63rd BS aircrews had been engaged in further training, learning to fly as a squadron, and gaining the cohesiveness they needed to survive in combat. At the same time they had been working with the aircrews from the 403rd BS, the next 43rd BG unit scheduled to become operational. When the 403rd BS first moved to Torrens Creek, they had no airplanes but by the beginning of September four new B-17Fs and their crews, fresh from the States, had been assigned to the squadron. The area commanders were eager to get the 43rd BG into the air, and send the tired veterans of the 19th BG back home, so the 403rd BS was steadily beefed up until by the end of September there were a total of 12 new planes in their arsenal.[17]

One of the new planes that was assigned to the 403rd BS was taken away from them twice. Before leaving the United States, B-17F (41-24534, *Omar Khayyam, The Plastered Bastard*), piloted by Lt. Edward C. McAnelly, was originally assigned to the 403rd BS. Halfway to Australia the plane was diverted to New Caledonia and reassigned to the 11th BG. Having classmates among the 43rd BG, McAnelly was irritated at his sudden change of orders and the next day, on the pretext of testing some troublesome engines, took off and never came back. Reaching Australia, McAnelly was reassigned to the 403rd BS and flew up to Torrens Creek to join his friends. Soon however, the B-17 and its crew was reported missing from the South Pacific and Gen. Harmon asked Gen. Kenney to send his plane back. "[McAnelly] had three combat missions to date and I hated to let him go," Kenney wrote, "but after all he had broken too many orders, so I had to let him go back . . ." Reluctantly, Kenney sent McAnelly and B-17E (41-24534, *Omar Khayyam*) back to Gen. Harmon.[18]

On September 12, headquarters had decided that the aircrews of the 63rd BS were finally ready to go into combat as a unit and moved seven planes to Mareeba. Two days later, on September 14, the decision was made to send the 63rd BS into action. Noted the 43rd BG historian, "Everyone was eager to get started because now the Squadron was operating on its own, and it was time to start making a reputation."[19]

Unfortunately, the 63rd BS got off to a disastrous start. As the B-17s took off, Capt. Hershell R. Henson, B-17F (41-24391, *Hoomalimali*), suffered an engine failure when he was only about one half mile off the end of the runway. With the engine on fire, the big bomber went into a nose dive and crashed into a small valley. Fully loaded with bombs and fuel, the plane exploded with a terrific noise and concussion. Chaplain Lt. William C. Taggart (19th BG) was sound asleep in his tent when the plane crashed. He wrote, "During the night I was thrown from my cot by an explosion . . ."

Rushing to the crash site, Taggart found that there was little that he could do. "We stood at a distance watching the flames and waiting for all the bombs to explode." With the coming of dawn, the chaplain and others began recovering the bodies. "Dismembered bodies and the wreckage of the Flying Fortress were strewn all over the field," Taggart wrote. "It was a gruesome, sickening task," admitted the chaplain. "Some of the men [helping out] became ill and had to leave."[20]

The other 63rd BS Fortresses took off without incident and headed towards Milne Bay, believing that the convoy might be headed in that direction. Hampered by bad weather, the six planes found nothing and eventually returned to Mareeba. One B-17 had been lost and nine men had been killed on the first independent raid by the 63rd BS. Wrote the historian for the 43rd BG, "It was obvious that glory was coming to the 63rd—the hard way if at all."[21]

Despite the hardships faced by Gen. MacArthur in New Guinea, with the Japanese on the Kokoda Trail having pushed their way to within only 30 miles of Port Moresby, Admiral Ghormley in the South Pacific Area contacted MacArthur on September 14 and again asked for help. The admiral was going to reinforce

Guadalcanal and wanted MacArthur's bombers to attack and harass Rabaul, much as they had done prior to the Marine invasion. Although facing a critical situation in New Guinea, MacArthur relayed the request to Gen. Kenney, who in turn promised to put one squadron of B-17s over Rabaul each day, and have the RAAF bombers harass the Japanese by night, until reinforcements were put ashore.[22]

Accordingly, the B-17s of the 5th AF went back to Rabaul. Late on the night of September 14, four B-17s left New Guinea for an early morning bombing. Flying over the harbor at roughly 25,000 feet, the crews were hindered by the absence of any moon and had a hard time identifying their targets. Releasing only 16 bombs, the men claimed that they set fire to one ship and shot down one Zero from a flight of fighters that came up to intercept them.[23]

On the night of September 15, seven Fortresses from the 28th and 30th BS, led by Capt. Carpenter, flew through "extremely heavy weather" which included "rain, lightning and thunder storms," to reach Vunakanau Airdrome. Two of the planes turned back, and Capt. Knudson in B-17F (41-24403, *Blitz Buggy*) became separated from the others. After reaching the southwestern tip of New Britain, Knudson decided to approach the target by traversing the center of the island. "Our approach was entirely over land," he reported, "which may have been one reason we caught the Japs unaware, for as we came to the target area we could see lights both on [at] Vunakanau aerodrome and in the town."

Coming in under a 10,000 feet overcast, the *Blitz Buggy* unloaded eight 500-lb. bombs on Vunakanau. "The lights began to be extinguished about the time the bombs were released," Knudson wrote. Still, the bombs were all on target, starting on one side of the runway and crossing the strip diagonally. By 7:20 A.M., September 16, Knudson was back at Port Moresby, leaving behind him a shattered runway and two crippled Japanese planes.[24]

Due to the lack of a moon, the four other planes came over the enemy field at 6,500 feet and unleashed a total of 32 500-lb. bombs on the aerodrome. At such a low altitude, the antiaircraft fire was fairly accurate, knocking out two engines on Lt. Ray Holsey's B-17E (41-2659, *Tojo's Jinx* aka *Frank Buck*). Newly-promoted Capt. Robert Williams in B-17F (41-24427) fared even worse. After the others returned to Port Moresby, they discovered that Capt. Williams was nowhere to be found. Maj. Rouse wrote, "Sure hope he shows up for he is one of the best. It will be a big loss to the Squadron and bad blow to me if he is lost." Unfortunately, B-17F (41-24427), with its entire crew, was never found.[25]

Lt. Holsey, nursing his plane back to Port Moresby with two dead engines, and with another giving him trouble, was forced to land on a sandy beach near Hood Point along the south coast of New Guinea, about 65 miles short of Port Moresby. Unwilling to abandon his plane, Holsey radioed Seven Mile Strip for help. Forty-five tons of steel matting and a handful of mechanics were shipped over to Lt. Holsey and while the crew and mechanics worked on the engines, 400 native laborers laid a 3,000-foot-long runway along the beach. Sixteen days later, on October 2, the *Frank Buck* was ready to go. Climbing into the plane, Holsey started all four engines and rumbled down the make-shift runway. Just as the wheels lifted off of the steel matting, one of the engines cut out and the left wing tip dipped into the water but Holsey had enough power to stay airborne and 20 minutes later B-17E (41-2659, *Tojo's Jinx* aka *Frank Buck*) landed safely at Seven Mile Strip.[26]

On September 18, the 93rd BS bombed Rabaul and the antiaircraft gunners claimed another victim. While passing over the target, Lt. Burcky, B-17E (41-2650) was hit. Nursing his plane back to New Guinea, Burcky and his crew bailed out over the Carpenteria Peninsula. Rescued and brought back to Port Moresby, Burcky and his crew continued to fight the Japanese but B-17E (41-2650) was lost forever.[27]

By September 18, the Japanese on the Kokoda Trail began to run out of steam. Gen. Kenney's aggressive air war against the supply depots at Buna and Gona, and the reinforcing supply vessels, was having its effect on the Imperial soldiers at the far end of the trail. During the same period, Japan had switched her emphasis to the Solomon Islands, sending most of her supplies and reinforcements towards Guadalcanal. Setbacks there affected the amount of supplies and men sent to New Guinea. The longer it took Japan to retake Guadalcanal, the less material and men would be sent to New Guinea. With the supply situation on the Kokoda Trail critical, and with most of her men suffering from malaria and dysentery, Japan suspended operations to capture Port Moresby and recalled her troops.[28]

Of course, the Japanese decision was unknown to the Americans. On September 18, Admiral Ghormley's Marine reinforcements landed on Guadalcanal and Gen. Kenney shifted his bomber campaign back, attacking the Japanese forces on the Kokoda Trail and along the north coast of New Guinea.[29] On September 19, the 63rd BS/43rd BS went out again when a flight of B-17s led by Capt. Carl Hustad attacked enemy supply ships in the Dampier Strait, between New Britain and New Guinea. Finally drawing blood, Lt. William M. Thompson managed to sink a 5,000-ton cargo ship.[30]

Although Gen. Kenney's high-altitude bombers had been able to claim a few enemy ships, he was convinced that it was too hard to hit a moving vessel from high altitude. It was estimated that only one percent of the bombs dropped from high altitude on moving ships actually hit their mark. Back in July, Gen. Kenney and Maj. Benn had discussed the possibility of a low level skip bombing attack from about 50 feet altitude. When the bomber was about 100 feet away from the ship, it would release a bomb which would skip across the surface of the water until it bumped into the side of the vessel. Then, with a five-second delay fuse, the bomb would sink beneath the ship and blow a hole in the hull when it detonated.[31]

The idea of skip bombing had originated with the British but they had been unsuccessful in perfecting the technique and had abandoned its use as being too dangerous. Reviving the idea, Gen. Kenney gave it to Maj. Benn's 63rd BS to perfect. Experimenting with different size bombs and different length fuses, and practicing against the hulk of the SS *Perth*, an old freighter that had been hung up on a reef just inside the harbor of Port Moresby, the 63rd BS finally came up with the right combination and technique. Although each pilot preferred his own speed and altitude, the general practice was to fly at approximately 2,000 feet altitude and search for an enemy ship. Once one was spotted, the B-17 dropped down to about 250 feet and approached the ship from the side, in level flight and at a speed of about 220 mph. "We had no positive means to ensure that we were at an exact altitude," remembered Lt. Murphy, "so we always tried to take care of a potential error by coming in a bit high. My sight was an X on my [front] window, and I used the nose of the B-17 as my forward point of reference . . ."[32]

Usually, the bombardier dropped the bomb 60 to 100 feet away from the side of the ship. If done correctly, the bomb would hit the surface of the water, skip into the air, strike the side of the vessel, and sink beside it. "From that low altitude," reported the 43rd BG historian, "the bombs did not have time to point down. Instead they struck the water, still with more forward than downward momentum, skittered across the waves and struck the side of the freighter." Lt. Murphy added, "At that time I would fly directly over the ship, retaining my same airspeed and altitude. With the 4- to 5-second delay fuse in the bomb, I had time to get away while the bomb sank by the side of the ship. The explosion underwater often broke the ship in half, and it created almost immediate fire and explosions."[33]

Maj. Benn expected to use skip bombing only at early dawn or on moonlit nights when the B-17s were aided by the backlighting glare of the rising moon off the surface of the water. Noted Lt. Murphy, "I made my approach into the rising moon or toward the east at daybreak to catch the first light of day. My bombardier and I could then see the ship before its crew saw us."[34]

On the morning of September 20, Gen. Kenney watched a skip bombing practice. Capt. Ken McCullar, proved to be "especially good," skipping six out of ten bombs against the side of the *Perth*. To get the bombs to detonate at the precise moment, Kenney learned that the airmen had been able to modify Australian 10- to 12-second delay fuses to 5-second fuses. Noted Gen. Kenney, "So far they worked pretty well. Sometimes they went off in three seconds, sometimes in seven, but that was good enough." Until American 5-second fuses could be supplied, the men would have to rely on the modified Australian fuses. Overall, Kenney liked what he saw but he knew that it was still too early to risk the skip bombing technique in combat. The 63rd BS was told to keep practicing.[35]

Back on September 15, Gen. Kenney's transport planes had successfully airlifted a regiment of American infantry to Port Moresby to help the Australians regain the Kokoda Trail. The operation was so successful that Gen. MacArthur subsequently asked Gen. Kenney if he could move the rest of the division by air as soon as possible. Pressing every available plane into service, Kenney wrote, "[T]wo B-17s, replacements from the United States flown by civilian crews . . . landed at Amberley Field, [Brisbane, on September 21]." Although the men wanted to go into town, Gen. Kenney had other plans. "I told them the next town they saw would be Port Moresby, New Guinea," wrote Kenney, "as I was loading thirty doughboys in each of those B-17s and they were to fly them to the war at the rate of one load every twenty-four hours" Although the crews were excited with the idea of helping out, Kenney was taking a risk. "If anything happened to these civilian ferry crews," stated Kenney, "I'd catch hell, but if we didn't get troops into New Guinea I'd catch hell, too." Noted Lt. Fields, "[W]e were pretty desperate to use B-17s to fly troops with."[36]

With the Japanese retreating along the Kokoda Trail, Port Moresby was no longer in immediate danger, so seven B-17s from the 30th BS, constituting an "alert striking force," were relocated from Mareeba to a new bomber strip outside of Port Moresby called Fourteen Mile Strip. No improvement over Seven Mile Strip, Maj. Rouse reported, "Bad field here with hills on both ends and a perpetual cross-wind. Built on a swamp through a thick tall forest. . . . Pretty dusty and dirty here. Quite a few mosquitoes and food very bad."[37]

On September 23, the "alert striking force" went out carrying one 2,000-lb. bomb apiece in search of a Japanese battleship supposed to be near Faisi in the Solomons. When the ship was not found, the three planes, led by Maj. Rouse, B-17E (41-9196), bombed Buna. "2000-lb'ers sure make a big explosion," admitted Rouse. The following day, the B-17s went out again, this time to bomb a few Japanese transports reported north of Buna. When bad weather prevented the planes from finding the ships, or even bombing Buna, they returned to Fourteen Mile Strip.[38]

Perhaps the same weather that plagued the 30th BS on their mission also caused the loss of another 19th BG B-17. On September 24, B-17E (41-9206) made a crash landing in Orangerie Bay, New Guinea, close to Milne Bay.[39] The next day, however, the weather cleared and at 9:20 A.M. the 30th BS went out for the third time in three days. This time, six B-17s went after two ships that were supposed to be anchored off Buna. "Searched entire area," wrote Maj. Rouse. "No trace. Another false report."[40]

In spite of Gen. Kenney's intent to relieve the 19th BG and send it back to the United States, the 19th continued to be his only fully operational group. Planes from the 435th BS continued to fly reconnaissance missions out of Townsville, while the 28th, 30th, and 93rd BSs, continued to attack the Japanese ships and airfields around New Britain and on the north coast of New Guinea. On September 25, Gen. "Hap" Arnold, Chief of the AAF, visited Australia during a tour of the Pacific Theater and Gen. Kenney immediately asked him for a new bomb group to replace the 19th. "He said he could not give me any more groups but would do the best he could on giving me replacement aircraft," Kenney recalled, "although he warned me that every time an airplane came out of the factory about ten people yelled for it, with the European Theater getting the first call."

Both Arnold and Kenney agreed to send the veterans from the 19th BG back to the States as soon as possible, and send the newer arrivals in the 19th to Hawaii in exchange for the 90th BG which was then flying B-24s out of Hawaii. Remembered Gen. Kenney, "Gen. Emmons, in command there [i.e. Hawaii], needed an experienced group and I needed a fresh one." When Gen. Arnold asked Kenney if he would have a problem using B-24s instead of B-17s, Kenney said that it really did not matter. He needed replacements and he needed them now. "The B-17 was preferred in Europe," he wrote, "but I was not particular. I'd take anything."[41]

The 30th BS Alert Strike Force was relieved at Fourteen Mile Strip by the 63rd BS/43rd BG on September 26. "63rd arrived and we took off . . ." commented Maj. Rouse. Fresh to New Guinea, the 63rd BS began sending out two planes a day to raid and harass the Japanese at Buna. "We began to fly in pairs made up of two planes and two crews," wrote Lt. Murphy. "That was our basic combat unit. Each was responsible for the other. Under all conditions, these two had to stick together. It was an unpardonable sin to return without your buddy."[42] Unlike the 19th BG, which tended to fly in three plane elements, the 63rd BS preferred the two plane system which allowed more flexibility in flying. Continued Murphy, "We gained additional maneuverability, and that permitted the commander to fly his plane smoothly without worrying about which of his wingmen were going to cut off his tail. It allowed the other pilot to fly on either side, above, or below the flight commander as he saw fit or as the combat demanded."[43]

In spite of continuing storms, by September 29 the 63rd BS/43rd BG was hitting northern New Guinea on a regular basis. On that date, Lt. Murphy, B-17F (41-24543, *Pluto*) and his partner, Lt. Folmer J. Sogaard, B-17F (41-24520, *Fightin' Swede*), took off during a driving storm to bomb a light cruiser reported to be near Buna. After searching for two hours through the battering storm, the pilots were notified that the report had been in error. "Those dumb son-of-a-bitches should have been with us," Lt. Murphy wrote in anger, "we would have put them back in the waist gun section without belts or tie-down equipment." Turning towards their alternate target, Murphy and Sogaard dropped 20 500-lb. bombs on the Japanese airfield at Buna. Attracting enemy antiaircraft fire, the *Fightin' Swede* took one hole in the right wing and two more in the left but made it safely back to Port Moresby.[44]

Out on the Kokoda Trail, the Australians had finally taken the initiative. On September 27, reinforced by their victorious brethren from Milne Bay, the Australians began pursuing the quickly retreating Imperial soldiers back towards Buna. Due to Gen. Kenney's aggressive campaign against the New Guinea airfields, the Japanese had no fighter planes to cover their withdrawal. The Japanese were at the mercy of the pursuing Australians and the fighters and bombers of the 5th AF and the RAAF.[45]

September had been a time of reversal in the Southwest Pacific. The Allies had gained air superiority over New Guinea, while the Japanese had been repulsed at Milne Bay and were retreating on the Kokoda Trail. Gen. MacArthur and the Allies had gained the upper hand and were looking for ways to exploit it. In the South Pacific, however, the American toehold on Guadalcanal was still in jeopardy. While the Japanese had all but abandoned New Guinea, they were putting renewed emphasis on Guadalcanal.

XX

Stopping the Tokyo Express

AFTER THE BATTLE of the Eastern Solomons the 11th BG resumed its patrols around Guadalcanal. The Marines saw the first B-17 make an emergency landing on Guadalcanal on September 2. While flying a search mission around Guadalcanal, Lt. Owens, B-17E (41-9145), spotted the Japanese trying to bring in reinforcements on a number of open barges. Coming down low, Owens made a couple of long sweeping passes as his gunners fired into the barges and set a few on fire. Low on fuel, Owens made a forced landing at Henderson Field, making B-17E (41-9145) the first Flying Fortress to land on Guadalcanal.[1]

In spite of the best efforts of the 11th BG, and the Navy and Marine planes at Guadalcanal, the Japanese continued to use the Tokyo Express almost nightly. By the end of the second week in September, it was estimated that at least 6,000 Japanese troops were on Guadalcanal. Although the Americans controlled the air and the sea-lanes around Guadalcanal during the day, the Japanese decisively controlled the waters at night.[2]

On September 8, the 11th BG lost another plane when B-17E (41-9071) mysteriously disappeared near Rendova Island. Piloting the plane was Capt. Richards, who had flown into the surprise Japanese attack on Pearl Harbor and had made a forced landing at Bellows Field. Noted the 42nd BS historian, "Capt. Richards' plane and crew were never heard from, and it was presumed that they were lost at sea."[3]

By September 11, with the Japanese building up their forces in the northern Solomons, Gen. Harmon was beginning to wonder if the Marines could hold Guadalcanal. Targets for the B-17s were plentiful but because of the distance that the planes had to fly from Espiritu Santo, and because of a lack of aviation fuel in the area, massive air raids were impossible. Although Guadalcanal could be used as a forward staging area, the critical lack of fuel at Henderson Field meant that the island should only be used in an emergency. Although careful not to criticize the Navy, Gen. Harmon felt that Admiral Ghormley was too cautious in bringing in supplies and reinforcements to Guadalcanal. If Henderson Field could be extended, if revetments could be made, and if gasoline could be brought in, the B-17s could use Guadalcanal as a forward staging base to reach further into the northern Solomons. Until these changes took place however, the 11th BG would have to operate as best they could.[4]

On the afternoon of September 11, a couple of B-17s were flying through terrible weather over New Georgia Island, about 100 miles northwest of Guadalcanal, when Lt. Woodbury, B-17E (41-9226), was suddenly hit by antiaircraft fire. Sgt. Roy Storey, Woodbury's bombardier, wrote, "One engine was knocked out and our left wing was torn up. All we could do was turn back and head for our base at [Espiritu Santo]." Although buffeted by the weather, Woodbury tried to follow the other plane which was equipped with the rudimentary form of radar. Storey went on, "We were depending on another plane which was better equipped for 'blind flying,' but she fell back with engine trouble and we were left on our own."

After six hours, Woodbury was totally lost. "Just after midnight [September 12] we hit the water," recalled Sgt. Storey. "I was in the radio compartment helping one of the younger crewmen get into proper position for a crash landing. We touched down with such impact that he rolled on top of me and drove me through the bottom of the plane and into the sea." Storey's right leg was badly mangled and he was in terrible pain when he was pulled from the rapidly sinking plane and pushed into one of the two rubber life rafts. Luckily the crew managed to reach a small island and were eventually rescued by a Navy PBY.[5]

On September 12, the South Pacific Area lost another plane by ditching when four B-17s from the 431st BS took off from Nandi Field to hit a Japanese aircraft carrier supposedly only 350 miles away. Unable to find the warship, the planes started back when Lt. Van Haur, B-17E (41-2402, *The Spider*), lost one engine. Near 11:00 P.M., having fallen far behind the others, and with *The Spider* almost out of fuel, Van Haur attempted a dangerous night ditching.

After ordering the crew into their emergency landing positions in the radio compartment, Van Haur dropped down on an angry sea. As he attempted to drag the tail and slow the plane down, the nose suddenly dipped and *The Spider* stopped "as though it had hit a brick wall." Two of the crewmen were catapulted through the radio compartment door and into the bomb bay but were uninjured. In a matter of minutes all nine crewmen scrambled out of the sinking plane. Only one of the two B-17 life rafts had deployed but someone had managed to grab a two-man raft and a few provisions from inside the plane before it went under. Exposed to the elements and lacking adequate food and water, two men died from exposure before the seven survivors were rescued seven days later.[6]

That same day, September 12, six B-17s set out to attack a large enemy task force reported to be northwest of the Santa Cruz Islands. Poor weather interfered with their mission and by the time the leader decided to call off the search it was dark and the planes were running low on gas. Just after midnight, Maj. Philip M. Rasmussen, B-17E (41-9219, *Hellzapoppin'*), ditched his plane. The *Hellzapoppin'* hit the water and came to an abrupt stop, knocking Maj. Rasmussen temporarily unconscious and badly shaking up the radio operator. Also injured was Sgt. Angelini, who was still flying with his puppy Skipper. Reportedly, Angelini suffered a broken ankle because he ". . . was more concerned with wrapping a Mae West [life vest] around Skipper, the ship's mascot, than in guarding his own safety. The dog . . . was unhurt and paddled around in the water in the Mae West." All nine men and the little puppy reached the two life rafts and made their way to shore near Plaines de Gaiacs where they were rescued the next day.[7]

In a span of a little more than 24 hours, the 11th BG had lost three more B-17s, the largest single-day loss for the group since Pearl Harbor. At a time when Gen. Harmon was worried about the lack of new B-17s arriving from the States, he could ill-afford to lose three heavy bombers to nothing more than faulty engines or exhausted gas tanks.

The enemy aircraft carriers and warships that the B-17s had been hunting were actually a part of a large scale plan by the Japanese to retake Guadalcanal. On September 12, while Japan's navy went hunting for any American vessels around the Solomons, 2,000 Imperial soldiers struck the Marine defensive perimeter around Henderson Field. For two days the fighting raged back and forth along "Bloody Ridge" but when it was all over the U.S. Marines had held firm and 600 Japanese were dead. Once again, the Marines had proven to themselves, and to the world at large, that they were more than a match for the Imperial soldier.[8]

At 12:30 P.M. on September 14, a mixture of seven B-17s from three different squadrons set out from Espiritu Santo to hit a part of the enemy fleet that had been sighted east of the Solomon Islands.[9] Although hampered by bad weather, the B-17s, flying in one three-plane element and one four-plane element, attacked from only 10,000 feet and dropped 25 500-lb. bombs through intense antiaircraft fire. The aircrews reported probable hits on two battleships, but actually caused only slight damage to the heavy cruiser *Myoko*.[10]

During the low-level attack, Lt. Owens, B-17E (41-2527), with the second element, was hit in the No. 4 engine by antiaircraft fire. As his element headed back to Espiritu Santo, Lt. Owens lagged behind. When the element hit bad weather, Owens apparently got lost and went down. B-17E (41-2527) and its crew of nine men were never seen again.[11]

On September 14, Admiral Ghormley contacted Gen. MacArthur and asked for assistance in protecting a reinforcing convoy that he was sending towards Guadalcanal. While the planes from the 5th AF hit Rabaul [see Chapter Nineteen], two protecting carrier groups, and six transports carrying the Marine reinforcements set out from Espiritu Santo. On September 15, a Japanese submarine spotted the American aircraft carrier *Wasp* and slammed three torpedoes into it. Enveloped in flames, the *Wasp* was finally sunk by a Navy destroyer at 9:00 P.M.[12]

While the reinforcing American convoy was moving forward, Col. Saunders' B-17s remained active. For three consecutive days beginning September 16, a single B-17 from the 26th BS dropped bombs on Gizo Harbor on Gizo Island, northwest of Guadalcanal, while other planes flew daily reconnaissance flights. On September 18, the reinforcing convoy finally reached Guadalcanal and 4,000 Marines and much needed equipment, including 400 drums of aviation fuel, went ashore. Thanks to the fine work being done by the Guadalcanal fighter planes of the "Cactus Air Force," so named because of the American code name for the island, and the bombers of the 11th BG in the Solomons, and the 19th BG against Rabaul, the unloading of the men and supplies was carried out without the appearance of a single Japanese airplane.[13]

On September 23, the 11th BG, which had been operating as the only heavy bombardment group in the South Pacific since late July, finally received their first large group of reinforcements. The 72nd BS/5th BG, fresh from the quiet war in Hawaii, arrived at Espiritu Santo after having been assigned to the Mobile Force, Pacific. Attached to the 11th BG, it was hoped that the 72nd BS would help ease the workload of the constant combat and reconnaissance flights.[14]

Like the 19th BG in Australia, it was more than apparent that the constant use of the 11th BG Flying Fortresses was beginning to take its toll. Although a few planes had been lost to enemy action since the 11th BG moved to the South Pacific, mechanical failure was still the number one source for sidelining a plane. Additionally, the rudimentary airfields and the strong tropical storm fronts did not help. Notations in the 26th BS diary told the story: "#[41-24]531 'out' with defective bomb racks," "#[41-2]524 is 'out' with bad right brake." Unfortunately, the notations could have come from any 11th BG squadron. All four squadrons were suffering a war of attrition and operating with only about half of their planes "in commission." New planes and new crews were slowly arriving from the United States but not in numbers enough to be effective. And each new crew needed time to train before going into combat. Therefore, in mid-September, the decision was made to send a veteran unit from the 5th BG in Hawaii to bolster the 11th BG in the South Pacific.[15]

On September 15, Gen. Emmons in Hawaii received orders to "move one heavy bombardment squadron of B-17s to the South Pacific at once." Furthermore, the order stipulated, "The squadron dispatched should be the best trained and fitted for immediate combat of all those under your command." Selecting Maj. Don Ridings' veterans of the Battle of Midway, the air echelon of the 72nd BS started out from Bellows Field at 9:00 A.M. on September 18. Along the way, the flight lost Lt. Wayne W. Thompson when B-17E (41-2612) showed metal filings on the spark plugs of two engines and had to be left at Christmas Island until the two engines could be changed completely. The rest of the planes continued on however, arriving at Espiritu Santo on September 25.

Having traveled light, the 72nd BS aircrews had to borrow cots, tents and almost everything else to get operational. Fortunately, or unfortunately, the 98th BS provided the hungry new arrivals with C-ration hash and dehydrated potatoes. On September 21, three LB-30s left Oahu with the maintenance men of the squadron but it would be almost a week before they arrived at Espiritu Santo. In the meantime, the aircrews had to arm, fuel and service their Fortresses by themselves. Still, by the afternoon of September 25, Col. Saunders had 11 fresh B-17s and their crews at his disposal.[16]

In Hawaii, Gen. Emmons quickly contacted Washington. Deprived of the 72nd BS, and aware of the rumor that the other 5th BG squadrons would soon follow, Emmons argued that with the loss of both the 5th and the 11th BGs, it would be impossible for him to maintain the minimum force of 35 heavy bombers that he deemed necessary to defend Hawaii. Appealing directly to Gen. Marshall, Emmons managed to stop the 90th BG, a B-24 unit, from being sent to Europe and got it assigned to Hawaii.[17]

True to Gen. Emmons' worst fears, at the end of September, the 5th BG began to leave Hawaii a few bombers at a time. Trickling into Espiritu Santo they were quickly parceled out to the 11th BG squadrons most in need. Pressed for planes and personnel, Gen. Harmon had sent repeated pleas to the War Department for more heavy bombers until finally the planes from the 23rd and 31st BSs/5th BG, were sent to the South Pacific. By October 28, 24 planes and crews, 12 from each squadron, had been taken from Gen. Emmons and sent to Espiritu Santo where they were quickly placed on detached service with the 11th BG, filling the holes in the group's depleted ranks.[18]

On September 24, while the planes of the 72nd BS were en route to the South Pacific, three B-17s from the 98th BS/11th BG and one from the 42nd BS/11th BG penetrated "bad weather" and dropped 24 500-lb. bombs on a large concentration of enemy ships near Tonolei Harbor, southeast of Bougainville.[19] The four planes scored a direct hit on one enemy cargo ship and near misses on another, while the escorting warships sent up heavy but inaccurate antiaircraft fire. As the B-17s fled the area, 20 Japanese floatplanes came up to intercept them. In a furious air battle, two of the floatplanes were shot down and several more were damaged but Capt. Charles E. Norton's (42nd BS) B-17E (41-2420, *Bessie the Jap Basher*) was hit repeatedly and began trailing smoke. Peeling away from the others, the bomber was last seen "descending to the water, smoking and disabled, with enemy fighters pursuing it to the surface."[20]

Although Lt. Cecil Durbin's (98th BS) B-17E (41-2523, *Goonie*) and Lt. Waskowitz's B-17E (41-2616, *The Blue Goose*) were both slightly damaged they reached Henderson Field without trouble while Capt. Lucas, B-17E (41-9215, *Gallopin' Gus*) continued on to Espiritu Santo. For his "extraordinary heroism" in the face of the enemy, Capt. Norton was posthumously issued the Distinguished Service Cross and each of his eight crewmen received the DFC.[21]

Having witnessed the large concentration of ships near Tonolei Harbor the day before, Lts. Durbin, now flying B-17E (41-9124, *Buzz King*), and Waskowitz, B-17E (41-2616, *The Blue Goose*), returned on September 25 and made individual attacks on the ships. After scoring a direct hit on an enemy cruiser from 14,000 feet, Lt. Durbin was attacked by 15 enemy floatplanes. After shooting down three of the attackers, Lt. Durbin somehow got away without damage. Noted the 98th BS historian, "The Japs never laid a glove on the *King* in the entire bout."

A little later, Lt. Waskowitz showed up and also bombed a cruiser, perhaps even the same one. As he retired from the area, the crew could see "smoke and flame" pouring from the stricken vessel. In all reality, the Japanese ship was probably laying down a smoke screen. However, enemy records indicated that the light cruiser *Yura* was attacked by B-17s on September 25, and received a direct hit on an after turret.[22]

With a large grouping of enemy ships outside Tonolei Harbor, Col. Saunders sent out nine Fortresses on September 26. Led by Maj. Ridings, and including four other planes from the 72nd BS/5th BG, the B-17s took off from Espiritu Santo at 6:00 A.M. and flew in three three-plane elements. Flying at only 7,500 feet to get under a thick overcast, the bombers were attacked intermittently by about 10 Zero fighters but were able to shoot down two or three of them. Facing "heavy and fairly accurate" antiaircraft fire, Maj. Ridings' first element had two near misses and two direct hits on a cruiser and set the ship on fire. The other two elements dropped their bombs on a transport, scoring three hits "between bow and stern," and left that ship in flames also. Although a number of the Fortresses were hit by antiaircraft fire, none were seriously damaged and all nine landed at Guadalcanal, constituting the largest force of B-17s to use Henderson Field to date.[23] The 72nd BS had passed through its baptism of fire in the South Pacific Area with flying colors.

The next day the B-17s went back to Tonolei Harbor. The four Fortresses from the 72nd BS/5th BG and one from the 26th BS/11th BG, took off from Guadalcanal to repeat the attack on the Japanese warships. An element of three planes, led by Maj. Ridings, made it safely through a rain of antiaircraft fire but counted no hits. As the first element turned back towards Espiritu Santo the last two planes, piloted by Capt. Kramer, B-17E (41-9122, *Eager Beavers*), and Lt. Raphael Bloch (72nd BS), B-17E (41-9059, *Boomerang*), were still several miles behind. As they approached the target, they were jumped by 15 Zeros. In the ensuing air battle, a 20-mm shell exploded inside the ball turret of the *Eager Beaver*, seriously wounding the gunner in the eye, arm and chest, and another exploded in the nose compartment, injuring the navigator and bombardier. On the *Boomerang*, Lt. Bloch's engineer was hit in the thigh but he continued to man the top turret guns and was credited with shooting down one Zero. In all, at least two fighters were shot down and three more were listed as "probably damaged or destroyed."[24]

Turning back towards Guadalcanal, the two pilots made an emergency landing at Henderson Field. Robert H. Graham, an infantryman with the 1st Marine Division on Guadalcanal, spoke to a friend who was present when Capt. Kramer landed. Years later, Graham recalled:

> He stated that he was down at the airfield when he saw this B-17 landing. Not too many B-17s were seen around Guadalcanal so it attracted his attention. He got as close as he could when it pulled off

the runway. It was then that he noticed that they were taking a crewmember from the ball turret and he remarked that the ball turret looked like "a goldfish bowl filled with blood." I seem to recall that the gunner was still alive.[25]

More and more the forward airfield on Guadalcanal was being used for the relief of wounded airmen and as a haven for stricken bombers.

On the morning of September 29, a composite force of 11 B-17s from the 26th, 98th and 431st BSs/11th BG, and the 72nd BS/5th BG, returned to Tonolei Harbor. Led by Maj. Sewart, B-17E (41-2611), the planes were nearing their objective when they were suddenly attacked by at least 15 Zeros. "I had a funny feeling already when we got into the plane," wrote Sgt. Handrow, tail gunner with Capt. White, B-17E (41-9156, *Uncle Biff*). "Today we are coming back with holes and lots of them I said to the mechanics." As the bombers dove through a thick cloud cover, the Zeros attacked and Handrow's premonition became reality.

"The sky was full of the little sons of guns and they started hitting us," Handrow recalled. "One went past the tail and I gave him both barrels and down he went in flames." A 20-mm shell slammed into Handrow's tail position and send hot shards of steel through the seat he was sitting on, over his shoulder, and past his leg. Bullets ripped through the thin aluminum wall not more than two inches from his heel and cut his oxygen line, and later, a hail of hot lead tore through the tail section door, about three feet behind him. Having suffered enough, Handrow waited for another fighter to come into range and then blew him to pieces. At almost the same time, two other gunners on *Uncle Biff* each shot down a Zero. Wrote Handrow, "Four in one day; not bad shooting."[26] A total of eight Zeros were shot down by the B-17 crews, and perhaps three more were damaged. Only one American crewman was wounded.[27]

Upon reaching Tonolei Harbor, the 11 B-17s found the target completely covered by fog. Having chased away the enemy fighters, the flight searched along the west coast of Bougainville for a target of opportunity until they found a lone Japanese cruiser. "The target was bombed . . . from 5,500'—all missed," admitted the 26th BS diarist. Both Lts. Kinney, B-17F (41-24457, *The Aztec's Curse*) and Waskowitz, B-17E (41-2616, *The Blue Goose*), made another pass over the cruiser when their bomb release mechanisms failed. By this time the cruiser was throwing up a wall of antiaircraft fire and as Lt. Waskowitz in his bright blue Fortress flew past, an antiaircraft shell scored a direct hit.

"[It was] a sight I'll never forget," wrote Sgt. Handrow. Riding as the tail gunner in the *Uncle Biff*, he had a panoramic view of the tragedy. "There was a little trail of smoke right back of the radio compartment," Handrow recalled. "The plane went into a spin, then exploded, fire shot out all over, the wings tore off and she hit the sea. Nobody got out." The glossy blue B-17E (41-2616, *Blue Goose*) was gone, along with nine crewmen. Continued Sgt. Handrow, "It left me with a cold sweat and I have feared antiaircraft fire since."[28]

Very low on gas, the rest of the flight returned to Guadalcanal and landed at

3:30 P.M. Almost every plane had been damaged by the enemy fighters but none as much as B-17E (41-9156, *Uncle Biff*). When Sgt. Handrow and his fellow crewmen counted the holes in their plane they found 450 in all, including 17 in the tail compartment, two in the No. 3 engine, and one big hole in the nose compartment. In addition, the tall rudder was shredded and one tire was flattened. "We had had a close call and we really were lucky that nobody got hit," Handrow concluded. "The raid was a flop, but he who runs away today comes to fight again another day."[29]

October brought a spell of warm weather to the South Pacific and the Seabees on Guadalcanal took the opportunity to patch up the holes in Henderson Field created by the almost nightly shelling from the Japanese navy or from *Washing-Machine Charlie*. Named for the erratic sound of its engines, *Washing-Machine Charlie* was a multi-engine plane that bombed the Marine position each night, causing weary men to abandon their sleep and jump into muddy, rain-filled foxholes.[30] Cpl. Schaeffer remembered:

> Guadalcanal was a very active island. Every night we were there, weather permitting, we were visited by a lone Japanese bomber we called "Washmachine Charlie" (because he sounded like a washmachine). He never did much damage to the installations, but he sure had an effect on our morale, keeping us awake much of the time, dropping a bomb every five or ten minutes. Then we had another visitor called "Bathtub Pete," a Jap submarine who would surface early in the morning and throw some shells in on our airstrip. Also "Millimeter Mike," a Jap gun located up in the hills somewhere who made it uncomfortable for us until one of our P-39s silenced it. There were also many day raids by the Japanese Air Force who did considerable amount of damage to our runway and gasoline dump. On top of all this we were visited by Jap cruisers at night who bombarded us with "pretty" star shells. Aside from all this it was a nice tropical island.[31]

With Henderson Field repaired, four B-17s from the 26th BS/11th BG, and Lt. David C. Everitt, Jr., from the 72nd BS/5th BG, moved up to Guadalcanal on October 3 for a planned strike against the Buka airstrip. Flying out of Henderson Field, the B-17s could dispense with carrying a bomb bay gas tank so at 3:00 A.M. on October 4, the five planes set out carrying a full load of 20 100-lb. bombs. Although the planes ran into a heavy storm and could not bomb the airfield because of a heavy cloud cover, they unexpectedly came across six Japanese warships off the coast of New Georgia Island while they were returning to Guadalcanal.[32]

Almost instantly, six enemy floatplanes and six Zero fighters suddenly appeared. In the ensuing air battle, two floatplanes and two Zeros were shot down, but Lt. Livingston, B-17F (41-24351), had his No. 3 engine shot out, and Lt.

Everitt, B-17E (41-9118), was lost. One of the Zeros, shot down and perhaps out of control, flew into the formation of B-17s and collided with Everitt. After knocking off the Fortress wing tip, the fighter continued on, slamming into and tearing off a part of the vertical stabilizer. Everitt lost control of the B-17 and went into a spin. The Fortress was last seen in a spiral entering an overcast at 11,000 feet altitude. Although two crewmen were believed to have bailed out, no one was ever found alive and all eight crewmen were posthumously awarded the DFC.[33]

A maximum strike by the 11th BG B-17s in conjunction with the Navy and the Cactus Air Force was scheduled for October 5 but the weather did not cooperate. Although the Navy and Marine planes took off, they had a hard time finding their appointed targets and did little damage. At the same time, acting on the belief that the other forces were meeting with success, seven Fortresses from the 72nd BS/5th BG, three from the 26th BS/11th BG, and three from the 98th BS/11th BG, 13 planes in all, started off from Guadalcanal to hit Buka. Unfortunately, two planes from the 72nd BS taxied into bomb craters and became stuck in the mud but the other 11 managed to get airborne. Almost immediately however, the flight ran into a fierce electrical storm and weather front. Capt. Lucas of the 98th BS, leading the strike, finally emerged on the other side of the front only to find that he was all alone. Deciding to carry on with his mission, he headed for Buka Airfield.[34]

Arriving at 5,000 feet, through heavy rain and scud clouds, Capt. Lucas succeeded in dropping his 20 100-lb. bombs along the entire length of the runway, "undoubtedly destroying and damaging many aircraft parked along both sides and dispersed in revetments." While returning to Espiritu Santo, Lucas somehow managed to link up with a Naval task force, as originally planned, and flew air cover for them for two hours. Because of his "tenacity, aggressiveness, skill and courage," Capt. Lucas was awarded an Oak Leaf Cluster in lieu of a second DFC.[35]

Although the electrical storm had prevented the other planes from reaching Buka, it did not prevent some of them from hitting alternate targets. The bombers from the 26th BS, along with one plane from the 72nd BS, bombed Gizo Harbor, while Lt. Robert M. Creech (72nd BS), B-17E (41-2396), went after Rekata Bay. Although all alone, Creech dropped down to 2,000 feet after releasing his bombs and let his gunners strafe the area. However, the Japanese gunners proved equal to the task and shot out Creech's No. 1 engine. With no further damage or casualties, Creech headed for Guadalcanal and landed at Henderson Field without any trouble.[36]

For the next week or so the B-17s continued to scout the area north and west of Guadalcanal, searching and gathering intelligence on Japanese naval movements. At the same time, both the Americans and the Japanese were planning to reinforce Guadalcanal. Hoping to land 3,000 American soldiers from the Americal Division on Guadalcanal on October 13, Admiral Nimitz sent an advance task force towards the Solomon Islands around October 9. At almost the same time, the Japanese were making their move to reinforce the 'Canal. Planning to land their men on the night of October 14, the Japanese planned to send an advance cruiser force into Ironbottom Sound on the eve before the move. Without even knowing it, both sides were maneuvering for an unexpected clash.[37]

By October 11, the American advance force was in the vicinity of Ironbottom Sound, on the lookout for Japanese ships. That same afternoon, a searching B-17 spotted the Japanese screening squadron only 210 miles away from Guadalcanal. Almost immediately four B-17s from the 26th BS and two planes from the 431st BS left Espiritu Santo for Henderson Field. While the B-17s were en route, two more air contacts were made and at 6:10 P.M., it was reported that the Japanese cruiser group was near Cape Esperance on the northwest tip of Guadalcanal.[38] Although it was too dark for the B-17s to attack, the American Navy moved forward to do battle. Hoping to avenge their defeat at the Battle of Savo Island, the American ships used their radar and at 11:46 P.M., in total darkness, opened the Battle of Cape Esperance with a massive and well-placed salvo. For the next 20 minutes the two sides were locked in battle. Eventually, the Japanese gave up and turned about, having lost a heavy cruiser and a destroyer. On the American side, three ships had been badly damaged but were still afloat. However, although the Americans had avenged their defeat at Savo Island, they had not prevented the enemy from reinforcing Guadalcanal. While the night battle was taking place, 800 more Japanese troops had landed on Guadalcanal.[39]

With the Japanese ships gone, and still acting to protect the expected American transports, the six plane strike force on Guadalcanal took off at 6:00 A.M. on October 12 to bomb Buka airport. Unfortunately, the flight ran into bad weather and returned to Cactus empty-handed. Still, a flight of Fortresses from the 72nd BS/5th BG was more successful. Noted the 26th BS diarist, "The 72nd went in and managed to bomb Buka by entering from the west side."[40]

On October 13, the strike force from the 26th and 431st BSs set out again to bomb Buka airfield. Flying in two three-plane elements, Col. Saunders commanded the mission and flew with Maj. Sewart, B-17E (41-2611), leading the first element, while Maj. Edmundson, B-17E (41-9217, *Fiji Foo*), led the second. Each plane carried two 1,000-lb. and four 500-lb. bombs as they headed northwest. "The weather was bad and we got on the bomb run just as a storm was closing in on the place," remembered Sgt. Handrow, Maj. Edmundson's tail gunner. The first element dropped their bombs among the parked enemy planes while the second element bombed the runway itself. "We could see fighters taking off as we were on our bombing run," wrote Maj. Edmundson, "and Zeros were soon at our altitude and continued to work us over as we proceeded south to our second target, a collection of ships at anchor in Buin Harbor at the south end of Bougainville Island."[41]

Bothered by a shortage of gas, Capt. Payne, B-17F (41-24528), in the second element, dropped all of his bombs on Buka and headed for Guadalcanal as the others headed towards Bougainville. "Three Zeros started in attacking," stated Sgt. Handrow, "and [since we had] only two ships in our formation they went after us." As one Zero came in on the tail of the *Fiji Foo*, Handrow opened fire. "He went down like a spin wheel in the Fourth of July," Handrow recalled. "The other ship's side gunner got one, he just blew up above us and the pieces went right past the tail. It looked pretty good."[42]

Although both planes in the second element had received a few bullet holes, no one was hurt and the B-17s carried on until they were over Buin Harbor. Surprisingly, the B-17s found at least 34 enemy ships at anchor, including "battleships, cruisers, and destroyers, not to mention troop and cargo transports." Immediately the B-17s went into a bomb run from 11,000 feet, as a hail of antiaircraft fire filled the air. Scoring direct hits on a cruiser and a transport, the Fortresses were returning to Guadalcanal when 10 Zeros intercepted them.

In a running air battle back towards Guadalcanal, six of the fighters were shot down but one B-17 crewman was killed and two more were wounded. "[A]ll our ships were hit with varying degrees of severity by antiaircraft and machine-gun fire," noted the 26th BS diarist. Losing the Zeros in thick clouds, the flight reached Guadalcanal only to find that Henderson Field was under attack from Japanese bombers. "It was easy to see that the B-17s couldn't land on the pock-marked strip," noted the 431st BS historian, "so they began circling high above the area to await developments. From their grandstand seat the B-17 boys saw quite a show."[43]

As the airmen watched, Marine fighters engaged the Japanese attackers amid antiaircraft fire from U.S. warships offshore. At the same time, American landing craft landed the first troops from the Americal Division. Immediately after the Japanese bombers were driven off, the Navy Seabees rushed out to repair Henderson field. "We were low on fuel and out of ammunition," recalled Maj. Edmundson, "and by the time the field was clear for us to come in and land we were mighty glad to get on the ground." However, no sooner had the five B-17s been dispersed around the runway when 20 Japanese bombers returned. Fortunately, only three bombs hit the runway and although one B-17 was hit by shrapnel the damage was minimal.[44]

Glad to be on the ground after a harrowing day, the crews were in for a worse night. "A miserable night was spent by all personnel on Cactus," concluded the 26th BS diarist, "because of intermittent air raids and a terrific artillery barrage laid down by a few Jap shore guns and huge Jap naval guns on the warships off Guadalcanal." Starting at 6:30 P.M., Japanese artillery began shelling Henderson Field, forcing everyone into bomb shelters. Then, near 1:30 A.M. on October 14, the Japanese Navy opened fire. For over two hours enemy battleships, cruisers, and destroyers lobbed their shells into the Marine position. At one time, a shell exploded near a dugout holding six Army airmen. The side walls collapsed and buried all six men but S/Sgt. Sebastian Maraschiello was able to extricate himself and dig the others out.[45]

"That night . . . ," Maj. Edmundson remembered, "will forever be known as 'The Night of the Big Shelling' to all of us who were there . . . Several [Marine and Navy] aircraft were hit and fires were started in the ammunition and fuel dumps." Two of the B-17s were caught in the heavy barrage and received considerable damage. "[T]wo of the Forts were so sieved that night by shrapnel that they had to be abandoned," noted the 431st BS historian. Among the bombers lost was Capt. Payne's B-17F (41-24528) and an unnamed Fortress which had probably been stuck on Guadalcanal awaiting repairs. With the approach of dawn the enemy ships retreated up "The Slot."[46]

With a temporary cessation of shelling Col. Saunders decided to pull his remaining B-17s out. Although only 2,000 feet of runway was intact, he wanted to get his bombers off the island before any further damage could befall them. At 7:00 A.M., just as the enemy artillery began shelling the airfield again, the four planes from the 26th BS, and Maj. Edmundson's B-17E (41-9217, *Fiji Foo*), took off. Left behind were the two destroyed B-17s and two that were awaiting parts. "On instructions from Marine headquarters," the 11th BG historian reported, "officers of the 67th [Fighter Squadron] went through the two derelict B-17s, destroying radios, maps, charts, and confidential papers, and hiding the Norden [bomb] sights." Additionally, since the Henderson Field fuel dump had been hit by the naval gunfire, the Marine fighter pilots drained the gas tanks of the two dead B-17s and transferred the fuel to their few remaining fighters. Noted the 11th BG historian, "For the time [being] Henderson was useless as a heavy bombardment base."[47]

Under the cover of the heavy bombardment, the Japanese had landed another 4,000 men on Guadalcanal and perhaps believing that they had neutralized Henderson Field, attempted to land more troops during the daylight hours of October 15. While the few planes on Cactus attempted to interfere with the landing, nine B-17s left Espiritu Santo to attack the enemy transports. Flying in three three-plane elements, the formation arrived off Guadalcanal and found five transports and a collection of enemy warships sitting offshore. Marine fighters had already set one transport on fire so, following orders, the B-17s went after the other transports. "We'd rather have gone after some bigger bait," Sgt. Handrow admitted, "but orders are orders." The antiaircraft fire filled the air as the B-17s made their bomb runs from 11,000 feet. "I have never seen ack-ack so thick," wrote Handrow.

The first element, led by Maj. Manierre, missed with their bombs but the second element, led by Maj. Edmundson, B-17E (41-9217, *Fiji Foo*), scored a direct hit. "Down went our bombs and four 500 pounders hit [and] blew [the transport] all to heck," Sgt. Handrow reported. "What a sight, the water was full of swimming Japs." Close behind, the third element, led by Capt. Chambers in B-17F (41-24457, *The Aztec's Curse*), reportedly scored three direct hits on another transport, setting the ship on fire. As the bombers finished their runs, perhaps 20 Zeros attacked from out of the sun.

Unusually aggressive, the Zeros made numerous runs at the B-17s, shooting up the noses of three of the bombers and injuring three different bombardiers. At the same time, a lone Zero came straight in on the tail of the *Fiji Foo*. "Was this guy nuts?" tail gunner Handrow wondered. "They never do it because it's sure death, yet here he was coming and getting closer. I started firing with all I had. He kept coming. He was going to ram us!" Sgt. Handrow fired 200 rounds before the enemy plane finally went down. "Boy, was I sweating blood," he wrote. "He was only 25 yards away when he went down. Ten more yards and I would have got out of the tail." Each B-17 was slightly damaged but all nine planes returned safely to Espiritu Santo while at least 10 Zeros had been shot down. Three Japanese transports had been sunk or stranded by the combined efforts of the Cactus Air Force and the 11th BG B-17s, yet, once again the enemy had managed to successfully land another batch of troops on Guadalcanal.[48]

During the nights of October 14–15 and October 15–16 Japanese cruisers fired more than 2,000 rounds into the Marine position, and during the day the long range artillery pieces worked over the airfield. Knowing full well that it was only a matter of time before the Japanese made another attempt to break through the Marine defenses, six B-17s left Espiritu Santo on the afternoon of October 17 to bomb an enemy concentration near the Kokumbona River on Guadalcanal. Bombing in two elements from 10,000 feet, the planes hit an ammunition dump, which exploded with enough force to rock the departing B-17s.[49]

On October 18, the delicate morale on Guadalcanal took an immediate upward turn when it was learned that hard-nosed Vice-Adm. William F. "Bull" Halsey had replaced Admiral Ghormley. The South Pacific was lacking in men, ships, planes, and supplies, and Halsey knew that his job was not going to be an easy one. "Europe was Washington's darling," he would write, "the South Pacific was only a stepchild." Among other things, almost immediately Halsey instituted construction of a bomber airstrip at Koli Point, approximately 12 miles southeast of Henderson Field. The men on the island knew that they had a fighting admiral at the helm now and if anybody could rescue them from annihilation, Admiral Halsey could.[50]

On that same date, Col. Saunders made further moves to consolidate the 11th BG. The 42nd BS, which had been working out of Plaines des Gaiacs since July 22, was moved forward to Espiritu Santo. Lt. Paul Williams, B-17E (41-2445, *So Solly Please*), flew the first plane in, loaded from nose to tail with "a conglomerate assortment of stoves, rations, garbage cans, cutlery and other mess components, including three cooks, and four K.P.'s." Having gotten used to Plaines des Gaiacs, the men were less than enthusiastic with Espiritu Santo. "The weather here was miserable," noted the 42nd BS historian, "with rain falling daily, resulting in ankle-deep sticky gooey mud . . ." Disease was also a factor at the new camp. At least 80 percent of the men eventually came down with dengue fever, while nearly 100 percent contracted malaria.[51]

While the 42nd BS was getting settled in, the Japanese paid a surprise visit to Espiritu Santo. At 2:35 A.M. on October 23, a Japanese submarine lobbed a few shells into the base area of the 26th BS. Although Lt. Loberg, B-17E (41-9076), with journalist Ira Wolfert aboard, went out looking, the sub was nowhere to be found. Returning to Espiritu Santo, Loberg suddenly ran into trouble. Wrote Wolfert, ". . . Lt. Loberg put on the brakes. Then we found out there were no brakes . . ." Reacting quickly, Loberg tried to lock the brakes on one side and ground-loop the bomber. Recalled Wolfert, "But there not only wasn't enough brake for that, there wasn't any brake at all, and what finally stopped us was the wing of another plane, a parked one." The plane Loberg hit was a fighter plane, carrying a 100-lb. bomb. Jarred loose in the collision, the bomb rolled under Loberg's B-17E (41-9076). "When we saw that," wrote Wolfert, "we didn't think of anything at all, just held our ears and waited for the explosion." Luckily, the bomb failed to detonate. Wolfert later wrote, "The ordnance man from whom I tried to find out why the bomb didn't go off just said we were damn fools to hold our ears. 'If that bomb had gone off,' he said, 'you never would have heard anything.'"[52]

By October 23, Henderson Field was back in operation and after another unsuccessful attempt by enemy bombers to knock it out again, the Japanese finally made their push against the Marine perimeter. Shortly after sundown, the enemy attacked with armor and infantry. Although their armor was quickly knocked out, the infantry kept coming. Still, the Marine position held and at sunup, the Japanese retreated into the jungle.[53]

October 24 saw the arrival of the entire ground echelon of the 72nd BS/5th BG on the troopship *William Ward Burrows* at Espiritu Santo. After operating for more than a month with only the handful of mechanics brought in by the three LB-30s, the aircrews were glad to receive their grounds crews. At the same time, the mechanics were glad to be on dry land. Placed on board the *Burrows* on October 4, the men had been at sea for nearly three weeks.[54]

That night, October 24–25, the Japanese infantry renewed their attack on the Marine perimeter. Pressed to the breaking point, the Marines brought forward the Americal Division and managed to hold the line. Once again, at daybreak, the Japanese faded back into the jungle. Meanwhile, the Japanese sent a powerful naval task force out from their strong naval base at Truk Island. With five aircraft carriers and four battleships, this was the greatest task force yet assembled against the American forces in the Solomons, and was intended to attack any American naval vessels in the area and threaten the vital supply route to Guadalcanal.[55]

Out on a routine search mission, 1st Lt. Mario Sesso (26th BS), B-17E (41-2409, *Old Maid*), happened across a portion of the task force off the northeast coast of Sewart Island on the morning of October 25. As he shadowed the group and radioed its position to Espiritu Santo, six Zeros attacked. Flying in and out of cloud cover, Sesso tried to evade the fighters while still keeping an eye on the enemy ships. Unfortunately, on one occasion when he was out of cover, a fighter fired a long burst into the nose of the *Old Maid*. At that same instant, bombardier T/Sgt. Eldon M. Elliott, flying on his first mission, fired his nose gun. The bullets from each plane passed each other in flight. The Zero exploded at the same time Sgt. Elliott keeled over with a bullet in his heart. For more than an hour Lt. Sesso remained over the enemy ships, darting in and out of the clouds, and radioing their position to base. Two more Zeros were damaged before Sesso finally broke away and headed for home. For some unknown reason, perhaps because of bad weather over Espiritu Santo, the other B-17s never arrived.[56]

Near 11:00 A.M., a squadron of Japanese destroyers, led by the light cruiser *Yura*, moved into Ironbottom Sound and began shelling Henderson Field.

Attacked by the Cactus Air Force, the *Yura* was left badly damaged. Then, near 5:00 P.M., as the Cactus Air Force retired, the 11th BG arrived.[57]

Although the weather over Espiritu Santo was extremely bad, six B-17s responded to the later call for help. Although flying on instruments, the flight somehow stayed together and arrived in formation. In spite of heavy and accurate antiaircraft fire, which put a hole through the horizontal stabilizer of Lt. Loberg's B-17E (41-2433), the Fortresses dropped 23 500-lb. bombs from 12,500 feet and got two direct hits on the crippled *Yura*. Although the ship was already badly damaged, the 11th BG B-17s had administered the coupe de grace. Burning throughout its entire length, it was abandoned by its crew and was finally sunk by torpedoes from two of its escorts. For their part in the Battle of Lunga Point, the B-17 pilots, who had managed to hold formation in spite of the weather and the heavy antiaircraft fire, were awarded the Silver Star medal.[58]

On October 26, two separate missions were flown against the main Japanese task force coming down from Truk but on both occasions the B-17s dropped their bombs from high altitude and completely missed their targets.[59] Unable to be stopped by the B-17s, the Imperial Navy ships continued on and eventually ran into the United States Navy near the Santa Cruz Islands, over 200 miles east of the Solomons. In the ensuing Battle of Santa Cruz, the Americans lost the aircraft carrier *Hornet*, and the carrier *Enterprise* was badly damaged. For the Japanese, two light carriers were mauled but still very much afloat. For the Americans, the battle was a tactical defeat but a strategic victory. Failing to follow up on their success, the Japanese returned to Truk. The sea-lanes around Guadalcanal remained open to the Americans.[60]

XXI

New Blood, New Techniques

THE JAPANESE WERE still pulling back along the Kokoda Trail on October 1 when Folmer Sogaard, now a captain, and Lt. Murphy from the 63rd BS/43rd BG attacked the Wairopi Bridge on the trail and knocked out a 30-foot section.[1] Early the next morning, six B-17s from the 63rd BS took off from Port Moresby to hit Rabaul. "This was going to be our first bomb run using the extremely low- altitude bombing tactics we had developed and practiced," wrote Lt. Murphy. Although the 63rd BS felt that they were ready to try skip bombing, persistent trouble with the five-second delay fuses caused Maj. Benn to delay using the technique. Instead, his planes would use a new low-altitude attack. Flying in two three-plane elements, the B-17s reached Rabaul before sunup and broke formation to reduce the noise and for individual runs against different targets.

Carrying four 1,000-lb. bombs apiece, the pilots selected their targets and attacked. Flying at just 2,500 feet altitude, Lt. Murphy lined up on a huge transport ship as the Japanese antiaircraft batteries opened fire. "Everything around the harbor seemed to be firing at us," Murphy recalled. "I had a good 20-second run, straight and level. The bombs went exactly as we hoped—one hit the ship directly, with the other three very close to it. Major fires broke out all over the ship." The 63rd BS planes scored big. Lt. Murphy, B-17F (41-24543, *Pluto*), hit a 15,000-ton transport while Capt. McCullar, B-17F (41-24521, *Black Jack*), set a 7,000-ton cargo ship on fire. Capt. Sogaard, B-17F (41-24520, *Fightin' Swede*), hit a destroyer, and Capt. Byron Heichel had a number of near misses on a 7,000-ton cargo ship. The other two planes, flown by Capt. Hustad and Lt. Bill O'Brien, hit an ammunition dump and a seaplane area, respectively. All six Fortresses were damaged by antiaircraft fire but no one was hurt. "Extremely low-altitude bombing was dangerous," Murphy concluded, "but it worked."[2]

The October 2 mission was a success but it could have been better. In actuality, every available plane from the 19th BG, along with the planes from the 63rd BS/43rd BG, had been scheduled to bomb Rabaul but at the last minute the maximum effort had to be scrubbed when somebody "talked too much."[3] Instead, the 63rd BS had been sent out alone, the only squadron trained in low-altitude bombing.

On October 5, Gen. Kenney began an airlift of Australian troops to the north coast of New Guinea. Gen. MacArthur was determined to open a second front against the Japanese, and intended to strike along the coast while pushing hard along the Kokoda Trail. While the Australians were being airlifted, the 28th and 30th BSs/19th BG went after the airfields near Rabaul.[4]

Taking off at 2:30 P.M., six planes from the 30th BS set out to bomb Vunakanau. Flying at 24,000 feet, and led by Maj. Rouse, the B-17s reached the airfield only to find it covered by clouds. As they circled to make another approach, 25 Zeros swarmed all around them. Lt. Gooch, Rouse's bombardier, recalled, "Being in the lead of the formation, we were their prime target. They made many frontal attacks on us with their small caliber machine guns and explosive cannon shells. We were badly shot up." On the first pass, while the B-17s were still in their bomb run, a Zero flicked through the formation, firing machine-gun bullets into the nose of Rouse's bomber. "A front window was shot through inches from my head," Gooch wrote, "injuring my forehead around my right eye with glass fragments. Fortunately for me, my eye was pressed against the bombsight, thus protecting my eyeball from the splintered glass."

Finished with the bomb run, the Fortresses turned away from the airfield as the Zeros continued to attack. "On the second attack they knocked out our #2 engine and [1st Lt. Earl L.] Hageman's #3 engine," reported Rouse. "On third attack they hit [Flight Officer A. J.] Davenport my navigator in the leg almost blowing his leg off." An Australian navigator, Davenport, though mortally wounded, began cussing because his gun had jammed just as he was hit and he could not fire back anymore. Lt. Gooch, immediately put a tourniquet on the wounded leg.

Down to only three engines, Maj. Rouse was beginning to slow down so Lt. McKenzie, one of his wingmen, shot past and took the lead. At about the same time, Rouse lost sight of his other wingman, Lt. Hageman. "Lost sight of Hageman but last I saw of him his #2 engine was smoking," said Rouse. "Gunners say he dove out of formation with 11 Zeros chasing him." Lt. Hageman and his crew in B-17E (41-9196) were never seen again.[5]

On B-17F (41-24403, *Blitz Buggy*), flown by Lt. Wesche, bombardier Lt. Bernard Anderson was creased in the back by a machine-gun bullet but stayed at his position. With Zeros buzzing all around, Wesche's navigator, Lt. Francis Sickinger, was trying to man both side guns while Anderson fired the nose guns. "I was trying to man both side guns and my oxygen hose wouldn't stretch to the right.

Consequently I was on oxygen only about half the time." At one point in the air battle, machine-gun bullets shattered the radio compass beside Sickinger. "I was sweating," he recalled, "and because the glass caused me to close my eyes I thought, 'I'm hit! I'm bleeding!' and it was just the sweat running down my face."[6]

Almost every plane in the formation took a beating. Capt. Charles H. Giddings had a shell explode in the cockpit, hitting the top turret gunner in both legs, and starting a fire. Ignoring his wound, the gunner extinguished the fire and then went back to his turret until another shell knocked out the electrical system. Lt. McKenzie eventually lost one engine and his ball turret gunner was burned in the arm by an incendiary bullet. And Maj. Rouse, in addition to losing his No. 2 engine, had three bullets pass through the ball turret, narrowly missing the gunner but shooting shards of glass into his eyes. Additionally, Rouse's radio operator had a close call when a bullet cut his parachute harness but left him unharmed.[7]

Battered and short on fuel after a fifty minute running fight, the five Fortresses headed for Port Moresby but ran into lousy weather. "Got lost and flew for 9.25 [hours]," Rouse put in his diary, "finally landing with the aid of a radio beam at 1155. Almost out of gas." His bombardier, Lt. Gooch concurred, "It was an anxious journey back to our staging base, Port Moresby, in our damaged aircraft, short on fuel." During the time that they were lost, Rouse's mortally wounded navigator, Flight Officer Davenport, tried to get up and identify some islands. "Never a word of complaint or pain," Rouse wrote admiringly. "Bravest kid I ever saw." Lt. Gooch agreed wholeheartedly. Gooch wrote, "After he was blasted off his feet by the impact of the bullet, [Davenport] looked at his shattered leg and said to me, 'I wonder how I'll look with a wooden leg.' He was indeed a brave, courageous young man."[8]

At the same time that the 30th BS was hitting Vunakanau, eight B-17s from the 28th BS set out to hit Lakunai airfield. Running into terrible weather, only three planes reached the target. Unfortunately, the bad weather restricted visibility and the results of the strike were unobserved.[9]

Gen. Kenney was informed on October 6 that Admiral Ghormley was planning to bring reinforcements (the Americal Division) into Guadalcanal again and had asked for the Southwest Pacific to support the move with repeated attacks on Rabaul again. Deciding to ". . . burn out the town of Rabaul," Gen. Kenney staged the largest raid by B-17s in the Pacific to date. On the afternoon of October 8, 36 Flying Fortresses, belonging to the 28th and 93rd BSs/19th BG, and the 63rd BS/43rd BG, all under the overall command of Maj. Helton, set out from Mareeba and flew into Port Moresby. Just before midnight, the first of the bombers began taking off, bound for a rallying point 100 miles south of Rabaul. "It was a beautiful sight as our little air fleet maneuvered in the faint moonlight and got into formation at 7,000 feet," remembered Capt. Crawford, B-17E (41-2645, *Miss Carriage*). Although the planes flew the entire route through perfect weather, six planes turned back for one reason or another. Still, 30 B-17s were now poised to bomb the unsuspecting town of Rabaul.[10]

Prior to the arrival of the Fortresses, four Australian Catalina flying boats had dropped incendiary bombs on the city. Now, as the Fortresses bore down on Rabaul, they found the target nicely lit up. Each B-17 was carrying 10 500-lb. bombs and flew over the city at varying heights to confuse the antiaircraft gunners and searchlight crews. "It was a colossal fireworks display," Capt. Crawford remembered. "Against a sky reddened by the glow of the burning town, antiaircraft fire and shafts of light pointed upward. Tracer bullets from the ground interlaced with tracer bullets from the thirty-six [sic] Fortresses. Shells exploded so close that they almost blinded me."[11]

Lt. Murphy, B-17F (41-24543, *Pluto*), was caught by the probing search lights, becoming an instant target for the antiaircraft guns. "[A]t 6,000 feet, every search light in the place picked us up, and I believe every antiaircraft battery also fired at us," he wrote. "With the search lights totally blinding us except for the lights in the cockpit, there was nothing else I could do except stay fixed on instruments to fly the B-17." Suddenly, his copilot panicked, grabbed the controls and tried to put the plane into evasive action. "I said, 'You-son-of-a-bitch, get off'," Murphy wrote. "He came around almost immediately and stopped trying to take over control, and we were able to finish our bomb run and then get out of the search lights and the antiaircraft fire."[12]

Although the antiaircraft fire damaged almost every single Fortress, all 30 planes made it safely back to Port Moresby. Behind them they left a devastated city. Fifty-four tons of bombs had been dropped on Rabaul. "An hour after we left the target the fires could still be seen as far as 80 miles away," noted Capt. Crawford. "Rabaul burned fiercely through the night and was almost completely destroyed as flames from the ammunition dumps and gas tanks spread to the flimsy structures of the town."[13]

Radio Tokyo chastised the American bomber crews for violating the sanctity of Rabaul by bombing the city itself, even though the Japanese were already in violation for storing war materiel in the town. The radio went on to state that the raid had killed 50 Geisha girls at the Rabaul hotel, guests of Japanese officers. Wanting to document the success, on October 9 the 435th BS sent 1st Lt. Arnold R. Johnson, B-17E (41-9207, *Texas #6*), to photograph the damage. Flying over at 27,000 feet, Johnson managed to avoid the antiaircraft fire and get his pictures but could not avoid four Zeros. "About 15 minutes after we left Rabaul the first Zero made his first attack," reported Johnson. During the attack, a bullet penetrated the control column of the Australian copilot, Sgt. David Sinclair, and struck him in the chest. The impact knocked Sinclair from his seat and left him motionless on the cockpit floor.

During the ensuing air battle, the Zeros made approximately 10 passes at the bomber. On the third pass, Johnson's tail gunner, Cpl. Ralph C. Fritz, shot down one of the Zeros but was in turn struck in the back and killed. After the third attack, Sgt. Sinclair revived and climbed back into his seat. "There he remained until the ship landed," Johnson recalled. When the fighters finally left, Lt. Johnson found that one bullet had hit a cylinder in his No. 4 engine, and that he was leaking gas from his left wing. Feathering the damaged engine, Johnson radioed his course, distance and estimated time of arrival, and asked for fighter protection the rest of the way to Townsville. "Fighters escorted us in the last 50 miles," he reported. "On the final approach No. 3 engine went dead." B-17E (41-9207, *Texas # 6*) was pretty badly shot up but would fly again. Sgt. Sinclair was seriously wounded but would survive. Miraculously, Cpl. Fritz became the only man from the 435th BS to be killed in combat operations.[14]

Lt. Johnson's photographs showed that Rabaul was still on fire four hours after the initial raid but Gen. Kenney wanted a follow-up strike. On the night of October 9–10 another 21 Fortresses, from the same three squadrons from the previous night, set off to punish Rabaul again. Like before, Navy Catalinas preceded the B-17s to drop incendiary bombs but found that it was unnecessary since portions of Rabaul were still on fire.[15]

Three B-17s turned back for unknown reasons but 18 planes dropped their bombs through the rising smoke. After dropping his bombs, Lt. Murphy, B-17F (41-24543, *Pluto*), once again had trouble with his copilot. "That night we had completed our bomb run and dropped our bombs when, suddenly, the enemy search lights exposed us," he wrote. "Antiaircraft fire intercepted us. We were again blinded and had to resort completely to the use of instruments. Simultaneously, we were hit twice by flak." Momentarily panicking, the copilot once again grabbed the column and tried to wrest control of the plane from Murphy. "I yelled at him, 'You bastard, you'll kill all of us, let go.'" Unable to get control back, Murphy instructed his flight engineer to knock the copilot out. "The only thing available was the fire extinguisher," Murphy recalled. "He struck a resounding blow to the side of the co-pilot's head . . . I was then able to keep the plane in a safe flying position and escape quickly from the Rabaul area."[16]

Once again, the raid was a success. Rabaul was left aglow. All 18 bombers returned safely to Port Moresby where, upon landing, Lt. Murphy immediately requested a new copilot. "The bizarre behavior of my co-pilot was not precipitated by fear of flying," Murphy understandably wrote, "nor by a case of trying to avoid having to serve in an extremely risky environment where his very life was in jeopardy. His momentary mental deterioration was a result of the blinding search lights and direct hits to the aircraft by antiaircraft ammunition." Still, Murphy was wise enough to know that he needed a new copilot. "While I could empathize with the poor guy, I could not jeopardize future missions."[17]

Again, after the mission, a 435th BS reconnaissance plane went out to photograph the damage. This time, however, he returned without incident. The 435th BS, the premiere reconnaissance squadron in the entire Pacific, was ranging far and wide from its home field at Townsville so, during the first part of October, half of the unit was moved to the new bomber field at Milne Bay, closer to the action in both the Southwest and South Pacific.

For the men who made the move, their new camp was more primitive than their base at Townsville, which they had been using since February. "A camp which can not be seen from the air was set up in impressive jungle," wrote the

435th BS historian. "A lot of improvisations were necessary in tent city." Perhaps accustomed to the easy life, the men brought a washing machine to the Milne Bay base to help them with their laundry. "Everyone in the area was jealous of the 435th washing machine," stated the 435th BS historian. "It's real—a real factory-made washing machine."[18]

Another luxury was the "putt-putt" or 435th scooter which consisted of a pair of P-40 fighter tires, a gasoline motor, and scraps of iron. Lt. Fields recalled, "[I had a] motorscooter, which I'd pieced together using the tailwheel of a P-40, a gasoline engine, and some sprockets. I hunted up a guy that could weld, and he welded part of a maintenance frame together, and I had a motorscooter, which I pushed to get started."[19]

In October, most of the 43rd BG was brought together when the 65th and 403rd BSs joined the 64th BS at a simple base at Iron Range on the Cape York Peninsula. The 65th BS arrived on October 13, while the 403rd BS arrived four days later. Iron Range had been the location of a gold mine, prompting the group historian to write, "It is interesting to note that when planes flew into Iron Range they landed on what was called 'Golden Runway'; the dirt around here was very rich in gold content."[20]

Very early on the morning of October 13, Gen. Kenney again sent his B-17s out to bomb the two major airfields around Rabaul. Five planes each from the 30th and 93rd BSs went after Vunakanau while eight planes from the 28th BS struck at Lakunai. Due to problems with dropping the guiding flares, the strike on Vunakanau was mediocre at best while the results at Lakunai were listed as "unascertainable."[21]

All set to send the 19th BG home as soon as the 90th BG replacements arrived, Gen. Kenney flew to Townsville and Mareeba on October 15 to award the veteran airmen with over 250 decorations. The ceremony at Townsville, involving the 435th BS, took almost one hour while the one at Mareeba, involving the rest of the group, took over two hours. Gen. Kenney personally pinned each decoration on each proud chest. "By the time I got through," Kenney wrote, "I had worn most of the skin off the thumb and forefinger of my right hand. It was a great show."[22]

While the 19th BG was being decorated, four B-17s from the 63rd BS/43rd BG went out on an armed reconnaissance mission over the Faisi area in conjunction with the South Pacific Area. After the heavy shelling of Guadalcanal by the Japanese Navy on the night of October 13/14, the South Pacific once again asked the Southwest Pacific for assistance. Spotting an enemy cruiser near Treasury Island, off the southern tip of Bougainville, Capt. McCullar, B-17F (41-24521, *Black Jack*), went into his bomb run and scored a direct hit. Although the ship did not sink, the 63rd BS had served notice that their planes were capable of reaching the Northern Solomons and of inflicting damage on enemy ships.[23]

On October 16, the 63rd BS served notice again. After seven B-17s hit shipping in Rabaul Harbor, they flew to the Buin-Faisi area. Utilizing their low-altitude bombing, they struck the airfield at Buin, and then bombed shipping off the Shortland Islands. Then, on the night of October 17, with Henderson Field still out of commission, all available planes of the 19th BG and the 63rd BS/43rd BG, went out again. As six B-17s of the 63rd BS hit the Buin-Tonolei area, a combined seven Fortresses from the 30th and 93rd BSs bombed ships in Faisi Harbor, and seven planes from the 28th BS hit the Vunakanau aerodrome.[24]

In the Buin attack, Capt. Hustad hit a 8,000-ton cargo ship, while William Thompson, now a captain, and Capt. Edward W. Scott, Jr., destroyed five Japanese flying boats and eight floatplanes on the water. At Tonolei, Capt. McCullar, B-17F (41-24521, *Black Jack*), hit another 8,000-ton cargo ship before being intercepted by three Zeros. Dropping down to the top of the water, McCullar kept the enemy away from his vulnerable underbelly. Making only one pass, the Zeros started to leave when McCullar turned the tables and went after them. More maneuverable and quicker than the B-17, the fighters soon got away.[25]

After the South Pacific flights, Gen. Kenney informed Gen. MacArthur that his bomber crews were worn out. "[R]egardless of anyone's needs," he said, "they needed a rest and the airplanes needed maintenance." Fortunately, Gen. MacArthur had just been informed that 12 B-24s from the 90th BG were on their way. Overjoyed, Kenney recalled, "I recommended that we send home 12 crews of the 19th Group most in need of rest, in 12 of the old-model B-17s immediately and follow with the rest of the 19th Group as fast as the crews and planes of the 90th Group arrived from Hawaii." Understandably, MacArthur readily agreed.[26]

Although the rumor about an eventual return to the States had been circulating within the 19th BG for weeks, when the 12 B-24s arrived on October 22, the rumor became reality. "[H]ere at last was the order to return," Chaplain Taggart wrote. "The 93rd Squadron was to leave first under the leadership of Col. Carmichael. Soon the others would follow." On October 23, Maj. Rouse wrote in his diary, "93rd is leaving tomorrow. They are sure happy."[27] Twelve 93rd BS combat crews and their planes were ready to leave Australia and begin the long but happy journey back to the United States when word reached Australia that an American hero was missing.

On October 21, Capt. Eddie Rickenbacker, the World War I ace, was lost on a B-17 flight from Hawaii to Canton Island. "I had hoped for a converted B-24 bomber," Rickenbacker wrote, "because it is roomier, but the only long-range four-engine plane available was a tactically obsolete Boeing Flying Fortress which had been earmarked for return to the US . . ." Climbing into a B-17D piloted by Capt. William Cherry of Army Air Transport Command, Capt. Rickenbacker, with two other passengers and four crewmen, took off at 1:30 A.M. bound for Canton Island. They never made it. Overshooting Canton, Capt. Cherry tried to double back but became further disoriented and, running low on fuel, eventually made a hard water landing. "The crash was a violent jumble of sounds and motions," recalled Rickenbacker. "A moment later, while we were still stunned from the first crash, a second one came and with that the plane lost motion." Rickenbacker estimated that the Fortress skidded only fifty feet before coming to a complete stop. "As I struggled to unfasten myself," he went on, "green water was pouring over my legs and down my back. The window beside me had been broken and the topside [radio compartment] hatch had [been] carried away. The whole Pacific Ocean seemed to be rushing in."

Climbing into two four-man rafts and a smaller two-man raft, all eight men made it safely out of the plane and watched as the B-17D sank. "The tail swung upright," Capt. Rickenbacker wrote, "in true ship's fashion, hesitated, then slid quickly out of sight." Adrift on the ocean with only four oranges and no water, one man eventually died from exposure. Rickenbacker and the others survived for 21 days before being picked up by a Navy PBY on November 12.[28]

Almost immediately after Capt. Rickenbacker was reported lost, everyone was out looking. Notified in Hawaii, Gen. Emmons immediately dispatched 11 B-17s of the 23rd BS/5th BG, to Canton to aid in the search. For the next four days the Fortresses flew fruitless search missions out from Canton until finally, on October 26, having failed to locate "Capt. Eddie" and the others, the B-17s returned to Hawaii.[29]

The first skip bombing raid in American history took place on the night of October 22–23 when the 63rd BS/43rd BG attacked a build-up of Japanese shipping at Rabaul. At midnight October 22, six Fortresses from the 63rd BS took off from Port Moresby behind six planes from the 64th BS/43rd BG. While the 64th BS bombed the town of Rabaul from 10,000 feet, attracting the searchlights and the antiaircraft fire, the 63rd BS engaged the enemy ships in skip bombing. Before even entering Simpson Harbor, Capt. Franklyn T. Green successfully skip bombed a light cruiser and a 5,000-ton cargo ship, then climbed in altitude and entered the harbor to score two direct hits on a 15,000-ton cargo ship. As he turned away, Green noted that both cargo ships were sinking and that the light cruiser was on fire with her stern already under water.[30]

Inside the harbor, Capt. Hustad skip bombed a 10,000-ton cargo vessel, setting it on fire, while Capt. McCullar, B-17F (41-24521, *Black Jack*), skipped two bombs into the side of a Japanese destroyer, sinking or damaging his fifth vessel since arriving in Australia less than three months before.[31]

In only a matter of minutes the 63rd BS had managed to sink or damage at least five Japanese ships. "This was jackpot night," noted the 63rd BS historian, "and the first use of skip-bombing. It paid dividends." Informed of the success of the mission, Gen. MacArthur immediately congratulated Maj. Benn for his persistence in the development of skip bombing and presented him with a Distinguished Service Cross.[32]

The date of October 23, 1942, will always be remembered by the 93rd BS as the day they went home. In addition to each bomber crew, headquarters allowed each plane to carry as many passengers as was deemed safe. Overjoyed at the prospect of finally going home, the airmen joked and carried on like children. Chaplain Taggart drove one load of men down to the waiting B-17s and recalled, "My little Chevrolet car was overflowing with 15 men who behaved like kids on their way to the circus. They were going home."[33]

The first plane to leave Mareeba was B-17E (41-2489, *Suzy-Q*) piloted by Maj. Hardison, with a newly promoted Col. Carmichael in the copilot seat beside him.

Flying in a loose formation, the 12 battered B-17Es headed towards Noumea, New Caledonia. From there, the planes flew to Nandi field on Viti Levu, Fiji, where they got the shock of their lives when they were suddenly informed that they would be delayed for a few days in case they were needed to relieve the tired B-17 crews in the Solomons. While the Battle of Santa Cruz was being fought, the airmen waited. Finally, near the end of October, the men received word to continue their homeward journey. From Fiji the men flew to Samoa, then to Christmas Island, and then finally to Hawaii. About November 1, the first planes landed at Hickam Field. For the 93rd BS/19th BG, the fighting war was over.[34]

The men of the 93rd BS remained in Hawaii for almost three weeks, as they readied their planes for the long over-water flight back to California. Three of the better 19th BG B-17Es were traded to the 394th BS/5th BG and replaced with B-17C (40-2059), and B-17Ds (40-3085) and (40-3092). Tired relics of the Hawaiian Air Force, the three obsolete B-17s would be returning with the 93rd BS. Finally, around November 19, the men took off from Hickam and flew to Hamilton Field, San Francisco. For many of the crews, the trip to war had come full circle. The first of the 19th BG was home by Thanksgiving.[35]

Unfortunately for Gen. Kenney, he began to miss the 12 B-17s almost as soon as they were gone. Shortly after the 90th BG B-24s arrived, each plane was inspected and found to have a cracked nose-wheel gear. Unable to safely land the plane with the bad gears, Kenney had to sideline the B-24s until the damaged gears could be repaired or replaced. In the meantime, he would have to continue to rely on his B-17s.[36]

On the night of October 25, the 63rd BS/43rd BG which, according to Kenney, "now constituted about all the heavy-bomber strength I had," set out to skip bomb the ships in Rabaul's Simpson Harbor again. The 43rd BG historian dramatically wrote, "[E]ight planes nosed towards Rabaul like winged tigers who had the taste of blood still in their mouths." Once again the 63rd BS scored big. Lt. Jack Wilson, B-17F (41-24551, *Fire Ball Mail*), sank a 5,000-ton cargo ship and Capt. Hustad badly damaged another. In addition, Capt. Green bombed and set fire to a coaling jetty next to the harbor. As the planes fled the scene, the fire from the jetty was still visible 80 miles away.[37]

On the 28th, the South Pacific again asked Gen. MacArthur for assistance. A request was made for his bombers to hit the Japanese ships in the Buin-Faisi area. Having hit Buin two weeks ago, Gen. Kenney informed MacArthur that the shipping in the Buin-Faisi area was too transitory, and suggested that his bombers continue to attack Rabaul. However, perhaps believing that the Japanese ships retreating from the Battle of Santa Cruz could be found around the Buin-Faisi area, Gen. MacArthur directed Kenney to send his B-17s back again.[38]

Utilizing the 63rd BS, 10 planes bombed the Buin-Faisi anchorage at Tonolei on the night of October 28–29. Bombing from low-altitude, the planes set fire to a 8,000-ton cargo ship, and damaged a cruiser and a destroyer. On the night of October 29–30, the B-17s of the 63rd BS, along with a few from the 30th BS/19th BG, went over the anchorage again. This time, as Gen. Kenney recalled, the 14

Fortresses "got direct hits on a battleship and two other unidentified vessels and damaged a light cruiser and an aircraft carrier."[39]

Unfortunately, the 30th BS lost another bomber when Maj. Allen Lindberg, B-17E (41-9235, *Clown House*), for some unknown reason, made a nighttime water landing about 20 miles off the Cape York Peninsula. "We crashed early in the morning," Lindberg recalled. "We just had time to shove off on two rubber rafts without a crumb of food or a drop of water." Lindberg continued, "You've no idea what hell is like until you're crowded in a rubber bubble without food or water and left to drift beneath the broiling sun." Adrift for two days, the men were eventually found by a group of Australian aborigines and returned to the mainland.[40]

Unwilling to ease the pressure on Rabaul, Gen. Kenney sent a total of 10 planes from the 403rd BS/43rd BG and the 28th BS/19th BG, against Simpson Harbor on October 30. Having trained with the crews of the 63rd BS, the 403rd BS went in low, utilizing skip bombing and claimed hits on a large cargo ship and two destroyers. Noted Gen. Kenney, "Photos taken the next day showed all three vessels half under water and aground."[41]

That same day, the 435th BS/19th BG sent at least two individual planes out on daylight reconnaissance missions. Lt. Fields flew nine hours through "rotten weather" and ice to count 23 enemy vessels at Faisi and Tonolei Harbor, while Capt. Eaton, B-17F (41-24554, *The Mustang*), counted 33 ships at Rabaul. Additionally, Eaton also spotted "1-3,000 ton cargo ship half sunk off Lesson Point," and "[m]uch oil on the water and a lot of debris," in Rabaul Harbor, the results of the recent visits by Gen. Kenney's B-17s. As Eaton turned back towards Port Moresby, 11 Zeros jumped him. In a running fight, Capt. Eaton's gunners shot down two Zeros and damaged another, and kept the others at bay long enough for Eaton to reach protective cloud cover. "There were about 12 separate attacks in all," recalled Eaton, "and our airplane did not receive any damage whatsoever."[42]

Acting on the information gathered by Lt. Fields, nine B-17s from the 30th BS/19th BG, staging through Milne Bay, went back to the Faisi area for a Halloween night attack on Tonolei Harbor. Reportedly, the B-17s sank "two destroyers and a large cargo vessel." At the same time the Fortresses from the 63rd BS/43rd BG acted upon the intelligence brought back by Capt. Eaton and struck at Rabaul but the results went unrecorded.[43]

On November 1, 12 B-17s from the 28th and 30th BSs/19th BG left Port Moresby and once again staged through Milne Bay on their way to strike the Buin-Faisi area. On one of the last missions for the 19th BG, the planes managed to damage a Japanese destroyer and a couple of cargo vessels. Then, the inevitable happened. Gen. Kenney had hoped to avoid sending out the planes of the 19th BG since most of the men were going home soon and he wanted to avoid the chance of anybody getting killed or wounded. However, being so short of planes and crews, he had been forced to use the 19th BG on the last few raids against Buin and Rabaul. "We were keeping our fingers crossed," Kenney wrote, but on November 1, one of his bombers failed to return.[44]

Writing about the November 1 raid in his diary, Maj. Rouse wrote, "They did pretty good but Hancock missing. Afraid he was shot down over target." Lt. John S. Hancock, B-17E (41-2635), never returned from the mission. Lt. Hancock's crew and B-17E (41-2635) have the unenviable distinction of being the last crew and bomber from the 19th BG to be lost in combat. When Chaplain Taggart heard of the loss a few days later, he wrote, "Last week we lost a plane with the entire crew. They had been only one week from home."[45]

By November 1, the Japanese had pulled back completely from the Kokoda Trail and were concentrating their remaining troops in the Buna area. On November 2, the Australian soldiers captured the village of Kokoda and the accompanying airfield. Over 2,000 dead Japanese soldiers had been counted along the trail since the Australians started their advance on September 28. With the success along the trail, Gen. MacArthur intended to assault and reduce the Buna pocket on November 15. In the two weeks prior to the attack, he intended to soften up the area with an air assault. As the 43rd BG historian wrote, "Fighters, attack planes, light and medium bombers, and the heavies were called out."

On November 1, after Japanese air activity in the Buna area increased, Gen. Kenney wrote, "This looked like the preliminary to another Jap convoy movement to re-supply or reinforce Buna, and there I was caught with my only heavy group worn out." Calling on the over-worked 43rd BG again, Kenney asked the CO of the group, Col. Roger Ramey, to send all of his combat-worthy planes up to Port Moresby in preparation for an attack on enemy shipping at daybreak on November 2. Unfortunately, Ramey did not have much to choose from. Lt. Murphy reported on the condition of the 63rd BS, "At the start of November we had only four of our twelve airplanes available." Since the planes from the 403rd BS were being used almost entirely for reconnaissance work, slowly taking over the job of the 435th BS/19th BG, Col. Ramey augmented the 63rd BS with a few planes from the 28th BS/19th BG.[46]

As Gen. Kenny had predicted, early on the morning of November 2, a reconnaissance plane spotted a convoy of two transports, escorted by two destroyers, coming down from Kavieng. Perhaps sidelined by bad weather, the B-17s were delayed and did not go out until 7:30 A.M. on November 3, when six planes from the 28th and the 63rd BSs, under the overall command of Capt. Scott, took off to damage the convoy. Although hampered by terrible weather, the B-17s spotted the ships and went into their bomb run at only 1,000 feet altitude, just below the overcast. In spite of heavy antiaircraft fire, and the interference of nine enemy fighters, each bomber was able to drop their eight 500-lb. bombs on the ships. No direct hits were observed, but the Fortresses scored five near misses on one of the transports. "Damage was positive," noted the 43rd BS historian, "for oil slicks and bilge spread in the water surrounding the ships." In the air battle that followed, six Zeros were shot down while two B-17s were damaged and two bomber crewmen were wounded.[47]

In the afternoon, having damaged only one transport, Gen. Kenney's medium and light bombers, accompanied by fighter planes, attacked the enemy vessels while they were opposite Gasmata. Then, three B-17s from the 28th BS/19th BG along with three from the 30th BS/19th BG went after the ships and sank the previously damaged transport and set fire to another. Unfortunately, Capt. Richard Hernlund's (28th BS) B-17 was hit by antiaircraft fire, mortally wounding tail gunner M/Sgt. Robert D. Chopping. "We got the ship, but an explosive shell hit our tail," recalled Hernlund. "I heard Chopping call: 'They got me!'" Quickly, somebody went back to the tail to give aid. "There was a large hole in the body of the plane," Hernlund continued. "Choppy was hanging partly out of the plane. His leg was gone. The pull of the air stream was sucking the blood out of him. We dragged Choppy to a flat place and wrapped him up. We tried to give him some dope, but he was gone." Sgt. Chopping became the last combat casualty of the 19th BG while it flew B-17s in the Pacific.[48]

Ken's Men

By NOVEMBER 1, the 403rd BS/43rd BG had eight crews ready for action. Selected as the reconnaissance unit for the group, an advance echelon of the squadron moved from Iron Range up to Milne Bay to replace the forward element of the 435th BS/19th BG. "[The advance echelon] took over the camp area which had been occupied by the 435th Bombardment Squadron," commented the 43rd BG historian.[1] Perhaps Milne Bay was an improvement over Iron Range for the men of the 403rd BS, but it was a last outpost for the men of the 435th BS. Lt. Fields had managed to avoid being stationed there and was glad when he got word that the 435th BS was being sent home. "Although we wanted to get out of Townsville, we weren't too anxious to go to Milne Bay," he admitted. ". . . Milne Bay was really kind of a last outpost for us, and we certainly weren't looking forward to going there."[2]

Although the 19th BG was still being sent home squadron by squadron, a rotation system had also been instituted whereby the older crews within each squadron were being sent home first. Recalled Lt. Fields:

> As we rotated home, we came up on a rotation list, by virtue of the number of 'points' we had, and every mission that we flew added so many points toward our rotation. The 19th BG, although they had been kicked around pretty severely in the Philippines, had reorganized in Australia, and although they ran quite a few missions, they never did catch up with the missions that the 435th had run. We in the 435th always felt like the 19th BG reaped the glory and the 435th did the work, after they came to Australia. In any event, the crews that had been shot up pretty bad and had a little tougher time seemed to be given some preference, and they came home ahead of us before they ever got on schedule on number of missions, but at

least with the 51 missions that I had, I was pretty high on the list to go home.[3]

Because of the point system, the 28th BS/19th BG suddenly found itself being detached from the parent group. Although the 28th BS had been in the Pacific since 1922, it did not become a part of the 19th BG until November of 1941. Then, since it did not get its first B-17 until well after the start of the war, the aircrews from the 28th BS still needed a few more missions to reach enough rotation points to go home. To achieve this, the 28th BS was temporarily attached to the 43rd BG.[4]

During the first week in November, 12 more B-24s of the 90th BG arrived from the South Pacific. They arrived at a good time. At the end of October, Gen. Kenney had learned that he had only a handful of heavy bombers in operational status in the Southwest Pacific. Since he was still having trouble with his B-24s, and since he was no longer getting any new B-17s, he decided to amend his earlier orders about sending the 19th BG home with their battle-worn planes. Instead, Kenney decided to transfer the B-17s to the 43rd BG and send the 19th BG home via Ferry Command.[5]

While the 19th BG prepared for their departure, the 43rd BG continued to carry on the war. On November 3, the 43rd BG bombed the airfield and wharf at Lae and then attacked a Japanese ship south of Gasmata. The next day, the planes were in the air again, attacking the town and harbor of Salamaua. Leading both flights, and gaining precious rotation points, were the crews from the 28th BS.[6]

After the November 4 mission, the B-17 units were sidelined for a week while 5th Bomber Command tried to sort out the intricacies of who was to go home, who was not, and who was to go where. As the 19th BG got ready to go home, the 43rd BG got ready to move to Mareeba and take over where the veteran group was leaving off. Somehow, during all of this activity, the 19th BG lost another bomber when B-17E (41-9012) caught fire and burned on the ground at Mareeba. Apparently, no one was hurt but the cause and circumstances behind the fire are unknown.[7]

Signifying his belief that Port Moresby was now safely in Allied hands, Gen. MacArthur established an advance headquarters at Port Moresby on November 6 and promised to stay there until the Buna campaign was over. Bringing Gen. Kenney along to personally supervise the air force in New Guinea, MacArthur began airlifting the American 32nd Infantry Division to Dobodura, about 10 miles south of Buna, as he readied his forces for a final push against the Japanese defenders. While he waited for the Australian infantry on the Kokoda Trail to move forward, MacArthur instructed Gen. Kenney to keep bombing the Buna perimeter.[8]

On November 7, the 43rd BG moved into Mareeba. "There," recalled the 43rd BG historian, "each squadron of the 43rd was assigned the area occupied by a squadron of the 19th Bombardment Group which was under orders to return to the states [sic]." For many of the members of the 43rd BG, who had been stationed at such remote fields as Daly Waters, Fenton Field, Torrens Creek, and Iron Range, the move to Mareeba was a vast improvement. "The food was something to write home about," commented the group historian, "fresh vegetables, milk, ice cream, and Beer!"[9]

That same day, the next batch of lucky airmen from the 19th BG started home. Wrote Maj. Rouse, "One [crew] from 30th and one from the 435th. They are going by air transport. Not taking any more planes back. . . . 2 more going tomorrow and then 2 every day until all are gone." Climbing aboard their battered B-17s, the crews flew the planes down to Brisbane where they traded them in for a seat aboard a Ferry Command C-47 or LB-30 bound for the United States.[10]

About this time, the 19th BG crews that had filtered in from the States one-by-one, and which did not have enough rotation points to go home, were transferred to the 43rd BG. Noted the group historian, "In addition to those [403rd BS men] who had been at Iron Range, the Squadron was now joined by nearly a hundred former members of the 435th, some of whom had been up to Milne Bay previously. These men were duly assigned to [fly search] sectors."[11]

By the middle of November, the 19th BG was disbanding at an alarming rate with crews either going home or being transferred to the 43rd BG. In addition to the men from the 435th BS, and the air crews from the 28th BS being transferred to the 43rd BG, a large number of men from the 30th BS were also transferred. In fact, the 43rd BG historian was able to write, "Quite a few combat and maintenance men of the 30th Bombardment Squadron were transferred to the 64th making the organization equipped to start flying combat missions."[12]

While all the internal movement was taking place, Gen. MacArthur was once again contacted by the commanders of the South Pacific Area and asked to maintain surveillance of the northwestern Solomons. "This agreement was limited because our 43rd BG had very few B-17s in commission because of losses in combat," noted Lt. Murphy. Still, on November 11, three planes from the 63rd BS attacked shipping in the Buin-Faisi area. Bombing from low altitude, Lt. Anderson hit a medium-sized cargo ship and Lt. O'Brien had a possible hit on a 10,000-ton cargo vessel in Tonolei Harbor. As the B-17s left, the crews spotted several enemy transports lining both the east and west side of the harbor.

With plenty of targets available, four more planes from the 63rd BS took off to strike Tonolei Harbor at 1:30 A.M. on November 12. Flying the buddy system, the flight broke into pairs, with one pair attacking the transports on the west side of the harbor while the other pair went after the ships on the east side. Approaching the harbor at 2,000 feet, Lt. Murphy, B-17F (41-24543, *Pluto*), spotted the phosphorescent wake of a 10,000-ton transport moving across the harbor and dropped down to 200 feet altitude for a skip bombing run. "When I leveled off at 200 feet, I picked up the wake of the ship," reported Murphy. "As I move closer, the 'X' marks on my window met the middle of the ship. I called, 'Bomb, bomb, bomb, bomb.'" With each command, Murphy's bombardier toggled loose a bomb. As the *Pluto* passed over the ship, the antiaircraft guns finally opened fire but it a bit too late. "Our bombs had been delivered very accurately," Murphy continued. "The transport was immediately on fire—explosions were seen on board, and [my wingman, Capt.] Heichel and his crew confirmed that it had turned on its side."

On the other side of the harbor, the other pilots were having similar luck. Also using skip bombing, Capt. Scott hit a 8,000-ton cargo ship with two bombs, causing substantial damage, while Capt. Sogaard, B-17F (41-24520, *Fightin' Swede*), sank a 10,000-ton transport with one bomb amidships and two more on the water line.[13]

On the same date, November 12, the 43rd BG lost another plane and crew when B-17E (41-2536) failed to return from an unknown mission. Information on the loss is sketchy at best. The only thing that is known for sure is that B-17E (41-2536) and her eight man crew did not come back and was eventually listed as missing in action.[14]

At 1:00 A.M. on November 13, Lt. Murphy, still flying B-17F (41-24543, *Pluto*), and his wingman Capt. Heichel, set out from Port Moresby for another raid on Tonolei Harbor. Immediately, they ran into bad weather. Murphy recalled:

> We had seen many weather fronts between New Guinea and New Britain or en route to the Solomon Islands. Most of them dissipated at night and then built during the day into severe thunderstorms with extremely turbulent winds and heavy rains. . . . The weather during that mission made me believe that the airplane just couldn't continue to fly. We were tossed all over at every altitude but especially above 500 feet. We flew through the storm, just holding our breaths that the engines would continue running and that the turbulence would stay above us.

Passing through the front, the planes reached Tonolei Harbor just as the moon was rising. Spotting a 10,000-ton cargo ship, Murphy was just starting his descent for a skip bombing run when an antiaircraft shell hit his No. 4 engine. Quickly feathering the engine, Murphy steadied the *Pluto* at 200 feet and dropped two 1,000-lb. bombs on the ship. As the vessel erupted beneath him, Murphy took the *Pluto* low over the harbor and circled for another run. "We then flew over a runway and became the target for more antiaircraft fire," he wrote. "There was another 8,000-ton cargo vessel at the harbor by the runway, so we dropped the other two 1,000-pound bombs and hit the ship; fire erupted immediately." A second later, an antiaircraft shell tore through the upper left side of the *Pluto*'s Plexiglas nose, leaving a hole about two feet in diameter.

"It felt as though we were in a hurricane," Lt. Murphy said as the air stream rushed in through the hole. "Everything was flying around in the nose and up in the cockpit. We couldn't stop the air from coming in, but did tie everything down to prevent the blowing of paper and other items." Also blown around was a small dog named "Pluto" that had become the mascot of B-17E (41-24543, *Pluto*). "We not only had Pluto on the side of the airplane," recalled Murphy, "we also had a mongrel dog we found in Charleyville, Australia, that we named Pluto. We took him on a number of missions with us and had an oxygen mask for him. He always stayed up in the nose . . . He was with us the night our nose was blown out by antiaircraft over the Solomon Islands."[15]

After a loss of power on another engine, Murphy turned back towards Port Moresby on only two and one-half engines. Unexpectedly, he suddenly flew past an enemy aircraft carrier and prayed that the Japanese would not send any fighters after his crippled bomber. While climbing for altitude to get over the Owen Stanley Mountains, Murphy reentered the violent storm and the *Pluto* was tossed around again. "The crew really took a physical pounding," Murphy wrote, "and I still have great praise for the ability of the Boeing Flying Fortress to take punishment." Finally, when Murphy was clear of the front he was able to reach 18,000 feet and a few hours later landed safely at Seven Mile Strip. "We ran out of gas in our third engine on landing," he wrote. "That was by far the longest mission we ever flew."[16]

On November 14, Capt. Knudson flying as a passenger aboard a departing LB-30, took off from Brisbane, for the long flight back to Hawaii. Delayed a short time at Canton Island, the plane landed at Hickam Field at 7:10 A.M. on November 17.[17] The delay at Canton was explained by Lt. Fields. Leaving Brisbane on a LB-30 one day later, Fields was delayed at Nandi Field. "Our first stop was in Fiji," Fields wrote, "and we had to stay in Fiji several days because they had run out of their supply of aviation fuel on Canton Island while looking for Eddie Rickenbacker's B-17." When more fuel was shipped to Canton, Fields and the others moved on, arriving at Hawaii on the same date as Capt. Knudson.[18]

For the next few days, the 19th BG personnel waited in Hawaii for available transportation to take them the rest of the way home. "Loafed around," wrote Lt. Fields on November 18, "waiting on ship [i.e. plane] to take us home . . ." The next day he added, "Same old thing. Waiting." On November 19, the available transportation finally arrived and the men were sent home. Once back in the United States Lt. Fields wrote in his diary, "This is far enough with this thing. I have too many things to do to fool with it. I've got to live like a human being again."[19]

Although rotated back to "God's Country," the tired men of the 19th BG were still members of the United States Army Air Force. After being granted leave to visit loved ones the men returned to start new army careers. Almost all of the men, including Captain Hardison, Lts. Fields, Jacquet, and Gooch, and Sgt. Fesmire were assigned to training facilities and utilized their war experience to prepare new aircrews for overseas service.[20]

On November 14, Gen. Kenney was approached by Maj. Benn and was told that the men of the 43rd BG wanted to call themselves "Ken's Men" in his honor and wanted to know if the general had any objections. "I told him I had none and to tell the gang that I felt highly honored," Kenney wrote. The next time that Kenney inspected the 43rd BG, he found that the men had replaced the scantily clad figures of girls adorning the front of their bombers with the words "Ken's Men." Remarked Kenney, "I was flattered, of course, but I sort of missed the pretty gals."[21] From then on, the 43rd BG was known as Ken's Men.

Having finally fixed the nose-wheel collars on the B-24s, the 90th BG staged its first bombing raid on November 15. However, after ignoring a lecture on tropical storms, two pilots were forced to ditch off New Guinea and three planes were badly damaged when eight planes ran into a heavy storm on their way to bomb the Buin-Faisi area. The next day, November 16, when the B-24s and four B-17s from the 63rd BS/43rd BG headed towards Rabaul, one B-24 crashed and exploded on takeoff, damaging two others. Two more failed to return. Needing further training, Gen. Kenney pulled the 90th BG from combat and went back to relying on the 43rd BG.[22]

As if to showcase the ruggedness of the B-17, the four B-17s on the November 16 mission made it through the storm to reach Rabaul and bomb a few enemy cruisers. Bombed from about 7,000 feet, the highly-maneuverable ships were able to easily circle away from the falling bombs. The B-17s returned to Port Moresby without any hits.[23]

Later, the 64th BS/43rd BG, augmented by the men from the 30th BS/19th BG that were short on rotation points, were finally put on alert and ordered up to Port Moresby. Eager to show what they were made of, the 64th BS B-17s flew up to Buna a few hours later and attacked Japanese shipping. Unfortunately, the results of the first combat mission of the 64th BS are unrecorded. Still, Gen. Kenney had another B-17 squadron ready to fight just when he needed it most.[24]

With the Japanese dug in at Buna, the American infantry commanders put in a special request for artillery to knock out the enemy bunkers. Since sending the guns by ship would take too long, Gen. Kenney asked for permission to try dismantling a field piece, placing the pieces aboard a B-17, and airlifting them to New Guinea. Recalled Kenney, "[On November 15,] a B-17 landed at Seven Mile Airdrome carrying a 105-mm. howitzer, a tractor to pull it with, the gun crew of eight men, fifty rounds of ammunition, a tool kit, and the camouflage net to shield it from the eyes of Jap aviators." That night, a DC-3 took the artillerymen and all the equipment to Dobodura. "How they ever stuffed that 10,000 pounds of gun, ammunition, crew, and miscellaneous equipment into a B-17 I don't know," admitted Kenney, "but they went back to Brisbane that night to get the other three guns of the battery."[25]

Another B-17 was lost to the 63rd BS/43rd BG on November 16 when B-17F (41-24402, *E-Z Mary 4th*) was badly damaged during a landing accident in Australia and could only be used for salvage. Two days later, the Australian infantry started their push against Gona through a driving rain. At almost the same time, a Japanese light cruiser and two destroyers, thought to be rushing reinforcements to New Guinea, were spotted north of Buna. Six 63rd BS Fortresses caught the ships when they were only 50 miles from Buna. "Orders were that it was imperative that the convoy be stopped," wrote the 43rd BG historian, "and stopped it was." Bombing from only 1,200 feet, Lt. Anderson scored a direct hit on the light cruiser, while Capt. McCullar, the bombing ace of the 63rd BS, hit one destroyer, and Capt. William Thompson broke the other one in two with three direct hits. "This again was a demonstration of low-altitude bombing versus the ineffectiveness of trying to hit maneuvering ships from a much higher altitude," concluded Lt. Murphy.[26]

After the second week in November, the rainy season set in and grounded all flights over the Owen Stanley Mountains. While the Australians slowly slogged their way towards Gona, the American 32nd Division started a slow advance against Buna. With the air war grounded for awhile, the decision was made to finally detach the 28th BS from the 43rd BG and send it home. Between November 17 and 20, the veteran air crews left Mareeba in their own B-17s and flew down to Brisbane. Wrote Capt. Paul E. Cool (28th BS) as he left on November 20, "Almost a tear as I drove away from the camp to the airplane." Almost, but not quite.

Once in Brisbane, the B-17s were taken away from the men and reassigned to the 43rd BG but because of a lack of transport planes, the men were forced to wait until enough planes could be found. "Awaiting Air Transport now to go home," Capt. Cool wrote. "It seems too good to be true. The war seems far away now. Never forget my friends who are dying today and every day." On November 27, the men were put aboard transport planes of the Southern Cross Air Lines and sent to Hickam Field. Once again however, because air transportation back to the United States was scarce, the men were forced to wait in Hawaii for more than a week before setting out for home, finally reaching Hamilton Field on the morning of December 10.[27] The last complete squadron of the 19th BG was finally home.

By November 20, in spite of the heavy rains, the remainder of the planes and personnel of the 403rd BS/43rd BG had left Mareeba to join the advance echelon of the squadron already operating out of Milne Bay.[28] The 403rd BSs replacement of the 435th BS/19th BG as the lead reconnaissance unit in Australia was now complete.

The Allied drive against Buna and Gona was slowing down as the Japanese perimeters constricted and their defense stiffened. On November 22, the weather cleared somewhat and the 5th AF went on the offensive again. B-17s and B-25s bombed the airfield at Lae, strafed a few barges found between Lae and Salamaua, and attacked Japanese warships in the Solomon Sea.[29]

Two days later, on November 24, the Flying Fortresses of the 43rd BG were flying missions in direct support of the Allied infantry. In preparation for the final push against Buna and Gona, almost all of the planes of the 5th AF went out to soften up the Japanese positions. Early in the morning, the B-17s of the 65th BS pounded the airstrips at Buna while the planes from the 63rd BS hit a small concentration of enemy troops at Sanananda Point, almost midway between Buna and Gona. Pushed into a tight perimeter and fighting for their lives, the Japanese threw everything they had at the attackers. "Zeros by the dozens swarmed all over the place," recalled Capt. Crawford. ". . . It was remarkable that they did so little damage to our forces."

Rushing back to Port Moresby, the B-17s refueled and took on a load of 20 100-lb. demolition bombs and 150 20-lb. fragmentation bombs. "We'd go down as low as 1,500 feet to drop our demolition bombs, and we'd hit their antiaircraft batteries, fuel and ammunition dumps and food stores almost every time," wrote

Crawford. "We even went below 1,000 feet to scatter our fragmentation bombs on troops, trenches and pill-boxes. When our bombs were all gone, we dived down to 300 feet to machine gun the Japs with our 3,000 rounds of ammunition." Later, a captured Japanese diary contained the following statement, "November 24— His air attacks are furious. Today's bombing was so terrific I did not feel as if I was alive." When the planes were finished, they returned to Port Moresby and were immediately refueled and reloaded with bombs for a third mission, this one against an enemy convoy.[30]

Five Japanese destroyer/transports carrying reinforcements and supplies, accompanied by a few warships, had been spotted by a reconnaissance plane. At sunset, as the enemy ships were starting their run towards Buna, the B-17s of 5th Bomber Command were called on to stop them. "With our troops already in trouble around Buna," Gen. Kenney remembered, "we didn't want the Nips to get any more men or supplies ashore, so before the B-17 crews took off . . . I told the gang there was a Silver Star for each member of a crew that sank a destroyer."[31]

Seven planes from the 63rd and 65th BSs took off before 9:00 P.M. from Seven Mile Strip and flew through bad weather over the Owen Stanley Mountains. Spreading out near the Huon Gulf, the planes searched for four hours before eventually locating the ships about 80 miles off the New Guinea coast. Aided by the light of a crescent moon high in the night sky, the attacking B-17s went in for the kill. Capt. Crawford took two bomb runs against the destroyer *Hayashio* at 2,000 feet before scoring two direct hits which set the ship afire and caused her to eventually explode and sink.[32]

At about the same time, Lt. O'Brien scored a direct hit on a destroyer which caused it "to burn fiercely, completely gutting it" and, Capt. James L. Harcrow (65th BS) reportedly "bagged a destroyer." Additionally, Capt. McCullar, B-17F (41-24521, *Black Jack*), came in at only 200 feet altitude and skipped a couple of bombs against the stern of a destroyer. "The bombs hit just off the end of the boat," McCullar reported, "and the AA [antiaircraft] hit in [our] tail gunner's ammunition can exploding about 70 shells and starting quite a fire." While McCullar circled for another bomb run, the rest of the crew frantically extinguished the fire.

Staying at 200 feet, McCullar hit the destroyer again, "starting a fire on the right front of the ship." Again antiaircraft fire hit McCullar's Fortress, wounding two of the men and damaging the No. 1 engine. Climbing to 4,000 feet, McCullar attempted to feather the propeller but found that the controls had been shot away and the engine continued to windmill. Undaunted, he took his plane over the burning ship for a third time. While his bombs dropped harmlessly into the sea, the antiaircraft fire from the stricken warship hit again. Shrapnel hit the fuel system of the No. 3 engine causing the engine to quit. With only two good engines, McCullar turned the *Black Jack* around and headed towards Port Moresby.[33]

Having already sunk the *Hayashio*, Capt. Crawford turned his attention towards a Japanese light cruiser and hit it with two bombs. "A gigantic geyser of flame shot up from her stern, a direct hit!" he exclaimed. Just before leaving the area, Crawford's plane was heavily damaged by antiaircraft fire, which made it hard to handle. Yet, Crawford managed to gain enough altitude to get over the Owen Stanley Mountains and reach Port Moresby. Once there, however, he found Seven Mile Strip under attack by the Japanese and was forced to wait one and one-half hours before landing. "When we limped in and finally hit the landing strip," he stated, "one engine was completely out of gas and red [warning] lights were showing on the other three gauges. Also there were more than two hundred flak holes in the plane."[34]

Having trouble of his own, Capt. McCullar was far behind the others as he struggled with the *Black Jack* and its two bad engines. "No. 1 engine got red hot from the windmilling of the prop and it looked like any minute the whole thing would catch fire and blow up," he reported. Fearing that the propeller might break loose and slice into the nose compartment, the bombardier and navigator vacated and moved into the radio room. "Evidently," McCullar continued, "the prop ground loose from the engine at the reduction gear, for after a while the engine cooled off. Still losing altitude we began to work on No. 3." Eventually, McCullar managed to get half-power out of engine No. 3, and by throwing out all excess weight, the plane began to climb. "Two and a half hours later we were at 10,000 feet, our ceiling, and luckily we found a pass [in the Owen Stanley Mountains] to sneak through, landed O.K., and forgot about it."[35]

Having sunk a cruiser and the destroyer *Hayashio*, Capt. Crawford and his crew received Silver Stars, as Gen. Kenney had promised. Two other destroyers had been badly damaged and the convoy had been turned back. The reinforcement of Buna had been stopped completely. "We had done a good night's work . . ." commented Capt. Crawford.[36]

Over the next two days, the Allied ground forces continued battering the Japanese defenses at Gona, Buna and Sanananda. Dug into their pillboxes and trenches, the Japanese repelled the assaults with relative ease. Once again the 5th AF was called on to soften up the area. On November 26, three 63rd BS B-17s dropped a total of 23 500-lb. bombs in the Buna area.[37]

Since the 63rd BS had shouldered the burden of picking up where the 19th BG had left off longer than any other squadron of the 43rd BG, the crews and their planes were sent back to Australia for a much needed rest and refit on November 28. As luck would have it, the men were in Australia for less than 24 hours before they were called back to New Guinea. A 403rd BS reconnaissance plane, B-17F (41-24546), flown by 2nd Lt. John E. Titus and carrying the squadron CO, Maj. Thomas N. Charles, had spotted four Japanese destroyer/transports in the Vitiaz Strait, between northern New Guinea and the southwestern tip of New Britain. Although Lt. Titus was able to shadow the destroyers for some time the plane never returned to base and B-17F (41-24546) and 11 crewmen, including Maj. Charles, were never heard from again. The 403rd BS had suffered its first loss.[38]

While waiting for the veterans from the 63rd BS to return to Port Moresby, Gen. Walker sent five B-17s of the 64th BS against the destroyers. Undoubtedly optimistic, the crews claimed 10 direct hits and one destroyer left in flames. At the same time, seven Fortresses from the 65th BS bombed the enemy infantry at Gona. The captured Japanese diary stated, "November 29—The position of the command section was completely destroyed by aerial bombing. Company Commander Yamasaki and Master Sgt. Toda are missing. They were probably killed." After the strike on Gona, the 65th BS B-17s were diverted to the Vitiaz Straits and made a few bombing runs against the fast approaching enemy ships. One aircrew claimed a direct hit on one destroyer while another claimed a near miss. Finally, near 6:00 P.M., five planes from the 63rd BS reached Seven Mile Airstrip and immediately began to refuel and arm up for their own run at the destroyers.[39]

Although having just arrived from Australia, the 63rd BS planes took off after dark and immediately ran into thick cloud cover. Unable to locate the ships, the B-17s returned to Port Moresby for more fuel and then took off again. Running into the same thick clouds, the planes once again missed the convoy and returned to Port Moresby. As the exhausted airmen climbed from their planes, Maj. Benn approached Gen. Kenney and asked that his crews be relieved. "General, this is a tired gang," Kenney recalled Maj. Benn saying. Although Kenney empathized with Benn, he knew that the reinforcing destroyers had to be stopped. Gen. Kenney told the major that he was willing to risk the lives of a few airmen to save thousands of American soldiers. Kenney wrote:

> The whole gang was standing around listening. Before I could say anything more or Bill could reply, we heard some sergeant back there in the dark say, "Come on, what the hell are we waiting for? Let's put a load of bombs aboard and get going. There's 10,000 Yanks over there we gotta look after." All five B-17s made another mission, found the Jap destroyers, and nailed two of them.[40]

Once again a Japanese attempt to reinforce and resupply Buna met defeat. Two of the ships were sunk and the other two turned back. The 63rd BS was quickly becoming Gen. Kenney's ace in the hole, and the 43rd BG was living up to the sobriquet of Ken's Men.

Although the 19th BG aircrews had gone home, the ground crews were still in Australia. On December 2, the long awaited day finally arrived and the happy men were placed aboard the Norwegian ship *SS Torrens* at Townsville. Recalled mechanic Payne, "The CO said no booze on board the ship . . . Needless to say our barracks bags clanked when we boarded the ship." En route home, the ship had a couple of submarine scares but each one was a false alarm. On December 20, the ship finally steamed into San Francisco Bay. "As we neared the Golden Gate [Bridge]," wrote Lt. Dalley, "the boat had a definite dip at the bow as everyone crowded for the first glimpse of the United States. As we passed underneath the bridge, there were tumultuous tears of happiness."[41] The entire 19th BG had made it home for Christmas.

XXIII

Protecting the 'Canal

THE MONTH OF November started out slow in the South Pacific Area. The battle of Santa Cruz had left both sides drained. Although the B-17s of the 7th AF continued their daily searches, enemy ships remained hidden within well-protected harbors. On Guadalcanal the Marines opened an offensive on November 1, driving westward towards Point Cruz, about one mile outside of their small defensive perimeter. At the same time, a detachment of Marines advanced eastward, attempting to stop the Japanese from landing fresh troops at Koli Point, about five miles away.[1]

Providing assistance for the Marines, 19 B-17s from the 11th BG left Espiritu Santo at 3:30 A.M. and bombed the Japanese position at Kokumbona, a mile west of Point Cruz. The largest attacking force ever sent out by the 11th BG up to that time, each plane carried 20 100-lb. fragmentation bombs and dropped from only 4,000 feet, causing considerable damage. After completing the bombing run, the planes, aided by three P-39 fighters from the Cactus Air Force, made repeated strafing runs over the Japanese strong point, inflicting further damage.[2]

On the same date, the ground crews of the 431st BS/11th BG moved from Viti Levu to Espiritu Santo to join their squadron combat crews. However, no sooner had the 431st BS mechanics unpacked their bags when the aircrews were suddenly granted rest leaves and were shipped south to Auckland, New Zealand. They would not return to combat until December 1.[3]

Over the next two weeks, the air war around Guadalcanal was limited to the strafing and bombing sorties of the Cactus Air Force, to the regular reconnaissance flights of the B-17s and PBYs, and to a few attacks against Tonolei Harbor by the Fortresses of the Southwest Pacific Area. At night, the Tokyo Express continued to make their nightly reinforcing runs. Around the Marine perimeter however, the fighting war was as bitter as ever. The Marine drive towards Point Cruz had successfully eliminated a pocket of Japanese resistance but the detachment driving to the east had been unable to stop the enemy from landing 1,500 new troops east of Koli Point.

Acting quickly, and controlling the sea-lanes and the air over Guadalcanal during the daylight hours, the Americans rushed reinforcements to the island to encircle Koli Point. By November 11, the position was completely surrounded. On November 12, in an all out attack by the Marines and reinforcing Army units, the Japanese positions were overrun and entirely eliminated.[4]

At Point Cruz, the Marines had gone on the offensive again. Reinforced by Army units from the Americal Division, on November 10 the Marines pushed west towards Kokumbona. Fighting a tenacious enemy, the men had gone only a short distance when they were suddenly halted and ordered to return all the way back to their original perimeter around Henderson Field. Unknown to the griping, arguing men, headquarters had received word that the Japanese Navy was going to make another attempt to reinforce Guadalcanal. And this time, the Japanese were going all out. It was all or nothing.[5]

Tipped off by cryptanalysts to the intended Japanese reinforcing move, a searching B-17 of Col. Saunders' 11th BG counted 61 enemy ships in the Buin-Tonolei area on November 11. That same day, it was found that more ships were massing at Rabaul. Knowing that the Japanese intended to land their men during the early morning hours of November 13, the American troops on Guadalcanal were pulled back into a tight defensive perimeter. At the same time the United States Navy commanders, along with the men of the Cactus Air Force, and the crews of the 37 B-17s of the 7th AF at Espiritu Santo were duly notified. Near 2:00 P.M. on November 12, a scouting B-17 spotted a strong Japanese battleship force built around two battleships moving towards Guadalcanal.[6]

As the battleship force headed down The Slot to bombard Guadalcanal, a large Japanese carrier force consisting of two aircraft carriers, two battleships, and escorting warships, steamed full speed towards the island, preceding 11 troop transports. As the Japanese battleship force drew closer to Ironbottom Sound, Lt. Sesso, B-17E (41-9227, *Yankee Doodle, Jr.*) spotted the carrier group about 350 miles north of Guadalcanal. Although subjected to intense antiaircraft fire, and attacks by an unknown number of enemy fighter planes, Sesso managed to shadow the carrier force for two hours, shooting down six Zeros in the process, before heading back to Espiritu Santo. By reporting the direction and movements of the ships, Sesso managed to alert everyone that the expected Japanese reinforcing move was under way.[7]

Just before 2:00 A.M. on the morning of November 13, the Japanese battleship force ran into a small force of American warships. In a veritable slugfest fought in the illumination of gun salvos and flickering spotlights, the two sides exchanged broadsides at point-blank range. A half hour later the Japanese force retired, but not before suffering the loss of two destroyers and heavy damage to the battleship *Hiei*. Again, the Americans had come away second best, losing one light cruiser, and four destroyers. Still, it was the Japanese that had retreated. The battle of Guadalcanal was over and both sides were content to let one another go.

However, as the American ships were about 25 miles south of the Solomons, a Japanese submarine slammed a torpedo into the light cruiser *Juneau*, carrying among others, the five Sullivan brothers who had become famous for enlisting together and insisting that they fight together aboard the same ship. Fearful of more torpedoes, the other ships fled the area while the *Juneau* sank.[8]

While the naval battle was taking place, word reached Col. Saunders at Espiritu Santo. Responding quickly, eight B-17s took off at 3:00 A.M. during a torrential downpour. Three hours later, 17 more Fortresses took to the sky in ones and twos, and a couple of hours later 14 B-17s assembled over San Cristobel Island, south of Guadalcanal. Led by Maj. Ridings, the B-17s went after the Japanese battleship *Hiei*. Already further damaged by repeated attacks from Navy torpedo-bombers and the Cactus Air Force, the B-17s came in at 14,000 feet and dropped a total of 56 500-lb. bombs on the ship. Only one hit. Their bomb run over, the planes headed back to Espiritu Santo leaving the final destruction of the *Hiei* to the Navy dive bombers and torpedo planes.[9]

1st Lt. Robert L. Gill (98th BS) was starting out on a search mission and was still south of the Solomon Islands when he spotted the retiring battered American warships and was amazed at the damaged condition. Although maintaining radio silence, Gill was able to determine through Morse code blinker light that a ship had been torpedoed. Going to investigate he flew over the spot where the *Juneau* had gone down and found about 150 survivors clinging to wreckage. Returning to the American warships, he informed the lead ship that there were survivors in the water and then flew on to personally report what he had seen to Guadalcanal. Waved off from Henderson Field because of an expected air raid, Gill continued on his search mission and then flew back to Espiritu Santo where he reported the survivors to a debriefing officer. Unbelievably, the officer was more concerned with the results of Gill's search mission and only made a brief notation about the survivors in his Daily Operations Report.[10]

On the night of November 13, a Japanese heavy cruiser force shelled Henderson Field with over 1,000 shells in an attempt to neutralize the airstrip. When the ships finally fled up The Slot, the American Seabees began immediate repairs on the field.[11]

By the time the sun came up on November 14, the airstrip was repaired and the Marine planes were ready. All they needed was a target. Within a short time, Capt. James E. Joham (98th BS/11th BG), B-17E (41-9211, *Typhoon McGoon II*), located one. Reconnoitering the area northwest of Guadalcanal, Joham spotted the Japanese carrier and transport force and quickly radioed his position to Guadalcanal. Almost immediately the air around Joham was filled with "heavy and accurate" antiaircraft fire which slightly damaged his B-17. Undaunted, he continued to shadow the task force and radio its position to headquarters.

As Capt. Joham continued to circle, more than a dozen enemy fighters came up to attack. During a 25-minute air battle, six enemy planes were shot down, and two more were damaged before Joham finally gave up the game and headed back to Espiritu Santo. When he landed, the *Typhoon McGoon II* had literally been riddled with cannon and machine-gun fire. "Projectiles had ripped through the tail of the plane with such frequency," noted the 98th BS historian, "that it was scarcely possible to place a hand on an untorn section of the fabric. Only a tiny fragment of cloth remained on the elevator." Miraculously, there were no casualties and by 5:00 A.M. the next morning B-17E (41-9211, *Typhoon McGoon II*) was patched up and ready to go out on another mission. The 98th BS mechanics had performed another miracle.[12]

With daylight, the Cactus Air Force and Navy carrier planes from the *Enterprise* attacked the heavy cruiser force and sank one heavy cruiser and damaged two heavy and one light cruiser. Then, after being advised of the transport group, the planes turned and attacked the reinforcements. Again and again, the planes returned to Henderson Field to refuel and rearm. It was no wonder that the Japanese had insisted that the Guadalcanal airfield be put out of commission. Then, as the enemy ships maneuvered wildly to avoid the Marine and Navy planes, 15 B-17s, carrying four 500-lb. bombs apiece, suddenly arrived overhead.[13]

Having left Espiritu Santo at 10:18 A.M., the Fortresses reached the battle area at 2:45 P.M. Attacking in two elements, the first element scored only one direct hit on a transport while the second scored "several near-misses" on a light carrier. When 15 Japanese planes came up to intercept the Fortresses, the crews promptly shot down six of the attackers. Fourteen years later, when the commanding Japanese officer wrote about the frenzied attacks of that morning, the one thing that stood out clearly in his mind was the wobbling fall of the bombs from the high-flying American B-17s. As the Fortresses flew away, the smaller American planes continued to attack. In all seven enemy transports were sunk while the other four, carrying 4,000 reinforcements, beached themselves near Tassafaronga, several miles west of Henderson Field.[14]

During the night of November 14–15, while the beached transports were quickly being unloaded, a Japanese Emergency Bombardment Group, built around one battleship and two heavy cruisers, moved forward to bombard Henderson Field. As they moved into The Slot they unexpectedly came under fire from an American task force consisting of the battleships *Washington* and *South Dakota*, and their accompanying escorts. In a one-hour battle, the American ships, aided by their radar, badly damaged the lone Japanese battleship and one destroyer. The Japanese Navy, still excellent at night fighting, sank two American destroyers, and damaged the *South Dakota* and a third destroyer. However, fearful of suffering the same devastating daylight air attacks which had sunk the *Hiei*, the Japanese scuttled both damaged vessels and quickly retreated. Once again, as in the battle of Cape Esperance, the American Navy had stopped the Japanese from bombarding Henderson Field, and once again, the Japanese would pay the price.[15]

When the sun came up on November 15, the Cactus Air Force immediately attacked the beached enemy transports and the supplies on the shore. Adding to the fireworks display were the B-17s of the 11th BG. Taking off from Espiritu Santo at 6:20 A.M., the planes dropped their 500-lb. bombs from 16,000 feet, scoring "an unknown number of hits." The massive Japanese attempt to reinforce Guadalcanal had ended in utter failure. Only 2,000 fresh troops had been put ashore, minus most of their equipment and supplies, and two battleships, one heavy cruiser, three destroyers, eleven transports, and an unknown number of planes had been lost. Shocked by this latest setback, Admiral Yamamoto decided that the Imperial Navy could no longer afford the losses it was taking in reinforcing an Army campaign. Although the Tokyo Express would continue to make runs to reinforce Guadalcanal, the number of men put ashore each time was minimal. The battle for Guadalcanal had finally reached a turning point.[16]

As an addendum to the small strike on the four beached transports on November 15, the B-17s turned around, broke formation and flew individually back towards Espiritu Santo. As Lt. Livingston, B-17F (41-24531), was flying home, he and his crew spotted "survivors from a sunk cruiser (American) hanging on wreckage and floating on rafts . . ." Upon arrival at Espiritu Santo, Livingston reported the position to the debriefing officer. At the time he did not know that the men were the victims from the sunken *Juneau*.[17]

That same day, Lt. Gill came across the survivors again. Shocked to see the men still floating in the ocean two days after his initial sighting, Gill eventually returned to Espiritu Santo and again repeated his sighting to the debriefing officer. However, this time he reported the number of survivors as much smaller than before. Again, the debriefing officer took his statement and did nothing more.[18]

In spite of the inactivity of the debriefing officer, the Navy finally found out about the *Juneau* survivors on November 16. Admiral Halsey immediately called for a search. In spite of the search, however, the survivors were still at sea on November 18 when Lt. Gill once again flew over the area. By now, the number of survivors had dwindled to about fifty. "My God!" Gill thought when he saw the men for the third time. "The Navy apparently doesn't give a damn about them. They are being left to die." Once again Gill reported his finding to his debriefing officer. This time the officer did not even include the sighting in his report.[19]

With the arrival of a P-38 Lightning fighter squadron at Guadalcanal on November 14, the Americans finally had a long-range fighter plane capable of escorting the 7th AF bombers all the way to the major Japanese supply bases far to the north. In the early morning darkness of November 18, 11 B-17s, escorted by 12 P-38s set off from Guadalcanal to attack Tonolei Harbor. Reconnaissance reports indicated that the harbor was filled with Japanese ships which had escaped the latest naval battles. Almost immediately the mission ran into trouble. While maneuvering his B-17F (41-24457, *The Aztec's Curse*), Capt. Chambers became stuck in the mud. In spite of his best efforts he was unable to extricate the plane until long after the others had left. Then, finally, he took off and tried to catch up with the flight. Unable to do so, he bombed Tonolei Harbor individually at 9:00 A.M., dropping four 1,000-lb. armor-piercing bombs on a cargo ship. Attacked by two Zeros, Chambers' crew shot down one of the attackers and *The Aztec's Curse* returned safely to Guadalcanal.[20]

In the meantime, the main strike force, led by Maj. Sewart, B-17F (41-24531), with Col. Saunders along as an observer, attacked and ran into plenty of trouble. While the P-38s circled overhead, the 10 B-17s split into two five-plane elements, with Maj. Sewart leading the first and Maj. Whitaker leading the second. Coming in at 12,000 feet through heavy and fairly accurate antiaircraft fire, Maj. Sewart's bombardier was unable to release his bombs and since the other four following planes intended to drop on the lead plane, the other bombardiers also failed to drop their bombs. Not wanting to go home empty handed, and still escorted by the P-38s, Col. Saunders decided to circle to the right and make another bombing run over the harbor.[21]

As the first element began their turn, Maj. Whitaker's element dropped 20 1,000-lb. bombs on a large transport, apparently scoring a few direct hits. Having dropped their bombs, the second element started for home, turning in the same direction as the first element. From 16,000 feet altitude, the watching P-38s assumed that the B-17s were all going home and broke off their escort service to chase after a few Zero fighters. As the P-38s flew away, Maj. Sewart's first element completed their turn and came back over the target.[22]

Once again running into "heavy and nearly accurate" antiaircraft fire, the five planes lined up in a huge "5 ship V" and started their bomb run. Capt. Philip Sprawls (42nd BS/11th BG), B-17E (41-9216, *Alley-Oop*), recorded, "The AA seemed to diminish some in our turn, but picked up again as we approached the target. Then, just before we dropped the bombs, the Zeros hit us!!! and I do mean hit!!! They were all over the sky!" At least 15 Zeros came at the five B-17s as they entered their bomb run and once again the bombs in Maj. Sewart's lead B-17 refused to fall. Fortunately, the bombardier in the second plane, Maj. Manierre's B-17E (41-9213), released his bombs and the others followed suit. "Hits were scored," was the comment from the 26th BS diarist.[23]

Finished with the bomb run, the B-17s started for home as the Zeros continued their attack. Wrote Capt. Sprawls, "The enemy fighters were coming from both sides, front and back, and bottom and top!!! Just like a big bee hive turned loose! . . . Once, I was so scared, I tried to duck behind the instrument panel!"[24] Seemingly concentrating on the lead plane, the Zeros pumped a murderous fire into Maj. Sewart's B-17F (41-24531). "The Zeros made head-on attacks and they were pretty good—better than any I'd seen before," recalled Col. Saunders. "They came at us in a string." Machine-gun fire tore through the forward compartments of the plane, wounding the bombardier in the knee, grazing Maj. Sewart's arm, and hitting copilot 1st Lt. Jack Lee (26th BS/11th BG) in the right ankle. As Col. Saunders turned to get a first aid kit, another Zero raked the B-17 and a bullet slapped into Lt. Lee's stomach. Quickly, Saunders dragged Lee from his seat and took his place. Then, no sooner had Col. Saunders climbed into the vacant copilot seat when another burst of machine-gun fire struck Maj. Sewart in the chest, killing him instantly.

Taking control from the copilot seat, Col. Saunders tried to keep the plane airborne as the Zeros continued to attack. "First one, then the second engine in the left wing was shot out," Saunders wrote. To make matters worse, the left wing fuel tank suddenly caught fire and flames began streaming from the left wing. "The left wing was red hot," Saunders recalled. "The bank and turn indicator showed we were in a spin. I was afraid to open the bomb bay doors and jettison the bombs that remained for fear that we would lose flying speed and stall. I leveled the plane as best I could and tried to get Sewart's body out of the pilot's seat where the trim tabs were located, but Sewart was jammed in and the shifting weight as I moved caused the plane to lurch. I jumped back in the copilot's seat and leveled the ship again."[25]

The rest of the crew aboard B-17F (41-24531) was having troubles of their own. During the running battle, one of the side guns failed and the ball turret was damaged and wouldn't traverse. Later, the ball turret guns themselves went out. Additionally, the upper turret stopped working and its two guns locked up, while the two .30 caliber nose guns quit firing, leaving the plane open to frontal attacks. "I was flying by the seat of my pants," Saunders said, "as there wasn't an instrument left working in the plane except the clock—and I surer than hell wasn't interested in what time it was." As the Zeros continued to attack, Saunders aimed the Flying Fortress for a thick cloud formation. "Fortunately, a cloud formation appeared and I headed for it," he wrote. ". . . At last we made it, shaking off the last Zero. Through the cloud formation the bomber continued to lose altitude."[26]

By the time B-17F (41-24531) exited the cloud, it was down to 500 feet altitude. Somehow, the other Fortresses had stayed with Saunders. Having fought a running battle for 70 miles and over 20 minutes, Saunders found himself near Baga Island in the New Georgia Island Group. "We were about a mile and a half out," recalled Saunders. "The navigator was up with me and the rest of the crew was in the radio compartment, all set for a water landing." Coming in at 95 mph, Saunders tried to slow the plane by dragging the tail but when the wings hit, the Fortress stopped suddenly, throwing Saunders against the windshield, and splitting open his forehead.

B-17F (41-24531) was broken in two by the impact and was settling fast. While the crew members in the radio compartment exited the plane at the break, Saunders and the navigator started to squeeze through the cockpit side windows. "We thought the co-pilot was dead," Saunders wrote, "but he said, 'Hey, get me out' and we did." Although the two men were able to get Lt. Lee out of the forward section and into one of the two lifeboats, he died before reaching shore.[27]

Having seen B-17F (41-24531) hit the water, Capt. Thornhill, B-17E (41-2524), in spite of a damaged main spar on one of his wings, circled the area and watched the progress of the men in the water. For almost an hour he continued to circle and when the two rafts finally reached Baga Island, he dropped Saunders some supplies and then returned to Guadalcanal to immediately report the location of the men.[28]

Unknown to Saunders or Thornhill, an Australian coast watcher on nearby Vella Lavella Island had seen the Flying Fortress go down and had immediately sent a radio message to Guadalcanal. At almost the same time, he sent two boatloads of natives to Baga Island to help the Americans. The next day, November

19, a PBY picked the men up and flew them to Tulagi, where the bombardier's wounds were dressed. From there they returned to Espiritu Santo, battered and bruised but still very much alive.[29]

The aerial gun battle of November 18 had shown Col. Saunders first hand the "toughness and aggressiveness" of the Zero pilots over Buin, fighting to protect their own backyard. The difficulty encountered in trying to shoot down the Zeros told Saunders that the Japanese had finally installed armor in some of their planes, and the head-on attacks showed him that the B-17 needed a powered gun turret in the nose. Additionally, Saunders believed that armor plating in the entire nose section of the B-17 would have stopped the enemy bullets from killing Maj. Sewart and mortally wounding Lt. Lee. In Saunders' estimation, the B-17 had been refined as far as possible and perhaps it was time to build a totally new heavy bomber.[30] Unfortunately, for the two dead pilots and B-17F (41-24531), the improvements would come too late.

On the same date that Col. Saunders and Maj. Sewart's crew were rescued, Lt. Keyes was flying B-17E (41-9060) on a routine search patrol south of Guadalcanal. Reported the 26th BS diarist, "1255 [P.M.,] three life rafts filled with survivors were seen SE of San Cristobel, 2 PBY were circling, trying to land and effect rescue. A shark was seen in the vicinity." After more than six days, the few remaining survivors from the *Juneau* were finally being rescued. While an estimated 140 men had survived the initial sinking, only 10 were eventually rescued. Nearly 700 men, including all five Sullivan brothers, had perished in the sinking and the time left in the water. Almost immediately the U.S. Navy opened an investigation.

When it was learned that Lt. Gill had spotted the survivors on the morning of November 13, the pilot was called in for questioning. During the inquest it was learned that Gill had not only reported the survivors on November 13, but also on the 15th and the 18th. "They must have thought I acted correctly," Gill said, "because I never heard anything more about it." Based on the information provided by Gill, the Navy found his initial reports among the records of the debriefing officer, and both the reports and the officer were never seen again. Someone was finally paying for one of the worst blunders of World War II.[31]

For the rest of November, the B-17s of the 11th BG and the attached 72nd BS/5th BG flew routine reconnaissance missions with an occasional dash of excitement. Having been in the South Pacific Area for almost four full months, the B-17s of the 11th BG were beginning to show signs of wear and tear.[32] During September and October, 24 combat crews from the 23rd and 31st BSs/5th BG had been sent piecemeal to the South Pacific and were already flying with the different squadrons of the 11th BG. Still, on October 26, Gen. Emmons had received orders to dispatch another heavy bomber squadron to the South Pacific. Since only the 394th BS/5th BG was left in Hawaii, and since Emmons did not want to send that unit to the South Pacific and lose all of his heavy bombers, he sent all the ground crews from the 23rd and 31st BSs to Gen. Harmon to bring those two squadrons up to full strength.[33]

With the transfer of three entire squadrons of the 5th BG to the South Pacific,

Gen. Emmons told headquarters, "Also since three of the four tactical squadrons will be in SOPAC, we are sending the group headquarters of the 5th Bombardment Group (H) for proper administration and supervision of the three squadrons."[34] On November 9, a total of 900 men from the HqS, 23rd and 31st BSs boarded the Liberty ship *Peter H. Burnett* under secret orders and set out from Hawaii. Escorted by a Navy destroyer, the two ships steamed southwest, where 17 days later, on December 1, they arrived at Viti Levu. Reported the historian for the 23rd BS, "the trip on the *Burnett* was very uncomfortable with poor ventilation, bad food and overcrowding . . ." With the exception of the 394th BS, which was still stationed at Bellows Field on Oahu, the entire 5th BG was now in the South Pacific.[35]

With the move of almost the entire 5th BG to the South Pacific, it was only a matter of time before the last combat squadron of the group would follow. Since mid-July the 394th BS had been flying search patrol missions out of Hawaii in old B-17Ds but in early November, the squadron received some of the 19th BG B-17Es that were being flown home from Australia. Almost immediately, the 394th BS was ordered to proceed to the South Pacific.[36] "In late '42 the 394th received orders to move to the Solomons," Phil Klingensmith wrote. "The three 17s we had were to fly down first, then the squadron personnel and equipment to move down by boat." Klingensmith took off in a B-17 piloted by the 394th BS CO, Capt. Rigley (late 72nd BS). Also on board was a flight surgeon and several boxes marked "medical supplies," —the Army euphemism for "booze."

"We had been flying through one heck of a front," Klingensmith recalled, "falling, climbing, right side, left side, over, you name it. It eased up a bit and I looked out and down and [for] a very brief instant I saw a carrier with a plane taking off and then solid cloud again. [I had] no time to identify." Not knowing if the carrier was American or Japanese, Klingensmith and the others got ready to throw out all their gear, including the crates of booze, to lighten the plane and increase their airspeed. "C.O. [Rigley] hit the I.F.F. [Identify—Friend or Foe] button . . ." Klingensmith recalled. "[A] few minutes later he informed everyone all clear—no dumping." The unidentified carrier turned out to be American and the precious "medical supplies" were saved.[37]

The rest of Klingensmith's flight to the Fiji Islands was uneventful. Upon reaching Fiji, the 394th BS was stationed at Nandi Airdrome on Viti Levu. Having arrived far ahead of the rest of the squadron, Klingensmith and the others tried to get comfortable. "During the first few days," he noted, "most of us slept in the planes or on cots under the wings of our planes lined up along the runway, using mosquito netting of course."[38]

At the time that the 394th BS moved to Viti Levu, the American aircraft carrier *Saratoga* was anchored just off shore for the repair of a bent propeller shaft. "Their planes flew cover 'round the clock," wrote Klingensmith, "to protect her . . . [They] landed and took off from our field at Nandi." Continued Klingensmith, "The U.S. Navy can claim credit for the name and nose art on [B-17E (41-2440)] '*Calamity Jane*'." At dusk one night near the end of November, Klingensmith watched as three Navy planes lined up wing tip-to-wing tip on the far end of the runway and began to take off. As the middle plane took off slightly ahead of the others, it kicked up a cloud of dust that blinded the other two pilots. "Each one ran into a B-17," said Klingensmith. "Fortunately no one had their cot set up yet under the wing of a plane but I believe one or two had already gone to bed in[side] one of the planes." One of the Navy planes tore the right wing tip off one of the B-17s and then slammed into the fuselage. The other fighter knocked the right landing gear out from under B-17E (41-2440), causing the bomber to collapse to one side, damaging the No. 3 and 4 engines and propellers. "That put us down to one plane," noted Klingensmith. "I noticed the C.O. [Rigley] used a hanky to get some 'dust' out of his eyes while looking over the mess."

When word of the accident reached the Hawaiian Air Depot, a detachment of mechanics was flown out and by using parts from each wrecked plane, managed to build one functional aircraft. "We wound up with a *Calamity Jane* from the two," recalled Klingensmith. The name stuck and B-17E (41-2440) was forever after known as *Calamity Jane*. Wrote Klingensmith, "I believe this event in naming a B-17 is not too well known."[39]

Eventually a total of seven B-17s were assigned to the 394th squadron and the airmen soon settled into a regular routine of search and training. Although life on Viti Levu was rough, Phil Klingensmith found a way to relieve the monotony. After meeting a fellow mechanic from a fighter squadron who had the uncanny ability to procure alcohol no matter where he was, Klingensmith had the man transferred to the 394th BS and the airmen never suffered for alcohol again. "The guy knew how to get it," Klingensmith praised. "[The] natives couldn't buy booze but the New Zealand and Australian and Indians from India had [liquor] ration cards. He bought the cards from many who didn't drink or had too much stock on hand. With the cards, he stocked up on booze, my kinda guy . . ."[40]

While the 7th Bomber Command was consolidating its forces, the Japanese continued to try and resupply their beleaguered troops on Guadalcanal. Although the Japanese Navy had soured on the idea of any large scale reinforcement of the island, they were still making their nightly runs with the Tokyo Express. On the night of November 30, the Japanese tried a new form of resupply. Placing food and equipment into sealed drums, the Japanese planned to jettison the drums over the sides of their ships and let the tide carry them to the beach. Unfortunately for the Japanese, before the ships could jettison the drums, they were intercepted by an American task force. In the ensuing Battle of Tassafaronga, the Americans suffered the loss of one heavy cruiser and had three more damaged while the Japanese lost one destroyer and had another one badly damaged. Although the battle was a Japanese victory, showing once again that the Japanese were more disciplined and better trained for night engagements, the Americans had once again thwarted an enemy attempt to resupply the Imperial troops on Guadalcanal.[41]

Although Japanese attempts to float supplies to their men on Guadalcanal would continue, the battle of Tassafaronga was the last major sea battle fought around the Solomons. The Americans, who already claimed air superiority around Guadalcanal, had slowly gained control of the waters. Although the Battle of Tassafaronga had been a defeat, the Americans had been numerically superior. While the Japanese were constantly losing ships, the Americans were constantly gaining ships. Although they would continue to suffer occasional losses, the American Navy was gaining precious experience and with their increasing numbers, the overall outcome was easy to foresee. It was only a matter of time before Japan lost Guadalcanal.

By the close of November, the B-17s of the 7th AF had been operating in the South Pacific for a full four months, long enough for an assessment to be made of their performance in the area. The B-17 crews had reported contacts with 610 Japanese aircraft of all types, and claimed to have destroyed 21 planes, while damaging 57 more. On the other hand, 21 Fortresses had been lost, but more than half due to operational problems, most of them ditching in the water after running out of fuel. Only six planes were recorded as combat losses, excluding the B-17s that had been destroyed by naval gunfire while parked at Henderson Field. By November 30, the 5th and 11th BGs had lost a total of 101 officers and men, mostly to operational losses rather than to combat with the enemy.

Commanders and crews of the 7th Bomber Command B-17s had learned a number of things about their planes during their four months in combat. The B-17 was a plane that could take a beating and bring its crew back home. While the crews had full confidence in the ability of the B-17, the commanders were beginning to doubt that the B-17 was the right plane to damage enemy shipping. From July 31 to November 30, the South Pacific B-17s had made contacts with 1,163 enemy ships of all types. Sixty ships had been attacked with a total of 828 bombs causing the sinking of four ships and damage to 15 others, while nine more may have been damaged by near misses.[42]

On November 20, Gen. Harmon gave Admiral Halsey a detailed analysis of the difficulties confronting his 7th Bomber Command. Although Gen. Harmon was critical of the performance of the B-17s, he also realized that there were a number of factors that weighed heavily upon the success or failure of the planes. The ever changing weather in the South Pacific was a big factor. Likewise, the long distances flown by the bomber crews had to be factored in, adding a fatigue and stress level to the bomber crews and reducing the number of bombs carried because of the long-range bomb bay gas tanks. Although Gen. Harmon had hoped to get a suitable bomber airstrip built on Guadalcanal to help alleviate the long range missions, by the end of November the strip was still not finished.

Perhaps the most serious problem was the tactical employment of the B-17. Although Col. Saunders had hoped to be able to put at least nine B-17s over a target at any given time, the lack of aviation fuel in the South Pacific Area and the primitive conditions at the island airfields made it all but impossible. If Saunders could get six B-17s into the air at one time, he was lucky. From July 31 to November 15, only five formations went over the target with more than six bombers, but never as many as nine.

Still however, in spite of these many disadvantages, the B-17 had proven its worth as a heavy bomber. When hitting a stationary target, the Flying Fortress could not be beat. For taking and absorbing punishment, one could not find a better plane than the B-17. And, in spite of its poor showing against moving ships, captured documents indicated that Japanese naval commanders had a natural fear and a high degree of respect for the Flying Fortress. To stress his point, Harmon pointed to the fact that since August 24 no enemy aircraft carrier had approached to within 500 miles of Espiritu Santo and the vital sea-lanes between Hawaii and Australia. Harmon felt that if the B-17s had been regularly operating out of Guadalcanal, they may have been able to seriously hinder enemy construction efforts at Buin and Buka, and may have been able to stop the build-up of enemy shipping in the Faisi-Tonolei area.[43]

Unfortunately, one of the problems facing Gen. Harmon lay in the fact that the B-17 had proven itself to be such an effective reconnaissance plane. In spite of his best wishes, by the end of November, with the Japanese cutting back on their daylight naval expeditions around Guadalcanal, B-17 strike missions were curtailed and the planes were relegated to more reconnaissance. To add to his problem of trying to reduce the reconnaissance work of the B-17, the Navy officially praised the bombers for their early detection of the Japanese warships prior to the Battles of Santa Cruz Islands, and Guadalcanal.

When Gen. Harmon contacted Gen. Arnold in Washington regarding his concerns, Arnold tried to persuade Admiral Halsey to use more of his PBYs for reconnaissance work. Although he admitted that the bombing record for the B-17 in the South Pacific was less than glamorous, Arnold believed that the reasons were threefold. First, the strike forces had been weakened by the use of so many B-17s for reconnaissance. If more PBYs were used, more Fortresses would be available for strike missions. Second, Arnold pointed to the poor servicing facilities at Espiritu Santo and Efate. If the facilities were improved, the results of the strike missions would improve. Finally, a lack of aviation fuel on Guadalcanal had seriously hampered the staging of planes through Henderson Field. In spite of Arnold's best efforts however, Halsey continued to employ the B-17 as the main reconnaissance plane in the South Pacific, especially if it was believed that a searching plane would face enemy fighter opposition.[44]

In the end the B-17 turned out to be too good at reconnaissance. While coast watchers could report the movement of ships past a certain point, only the B-17 had proven capable of locating an enemy convoy and clinging to it, despite heavy air opposition or antiaircraft fire. Not until late 1943, when the Navy started employing PB4Ys (Navy B-24s) for long range reconnaissance, were the search activities of the B-17 in the South Pacific curtailed, and then it was only a matter of time before the B-17 was almost completely phased out of the war in the Pacific.[45]

XXIV

Continuous Air Strikes

NEAR THE END of November Col. Saunders had reason to believe that the Japanese were building a secret airstrip at Munda Point on New Georgia Island. "We discovered that the Japs were unloading supplies and equipment at Munda," Saunders said, "so we raided it and kept photographing it. Soon what looked suspiciously like a landing field started to develop under a coconut grove and grew longer every day."[1] On December 1, Capt. Willis E. Jacobs (431st BS/11th BG) took off in B-17F (41-24534, *Omar Khayyam, The Plastered Bastard*) from Guadalcanal on a routine photographic mission. Near New Georgia the plane was suddenly attacked by seven Zeros. While six planes circled, the seventh dove down and slammed into the top of the B-17.

"There was a grinding crash and everything went black!" recalled tail gunner Cpl. Joseph E. Hartman. Hit just behind the radio compartment, the *Omar Khayyam* broke in two. While the front section burst into flames, the tail section, containing Cpl. Hartman, rolled to one side and began to slowly drift down. Although knocked unconscious, Hartman eventually regained his senses and prepared to bail out.

"I struggled with my parachute and became frantic when my heavy winter flying suit prevented fastening of the leg straps," Hartman wrote. With only his shoulder straps fastened, Hartman jumped out of the descending tail section and was again knocked momentarily unconscious by the impact of the opening parachute. "When I hit the water I was pretty badly dazed from the batterings in the plane and parachute," he recalled. Managing to struggle out of his heavy winter clothing and parachute harness, Hartman made his way to shore and was soon rescued by two friendly natives. Cpl. Hartman was the only survivor of B-17F (41-24534, *Omar Khayyam, The Plastered Bastard*).[2]

With the move of the entire 5th BG to the South Pacific, Col. Saunders was given command of both the 5th and 11th BGs and was able to release the combat crews of the 11th BG for a week at a time for rest and relaxation in Auckland, New Zealand.[3] Since there were no ground personnel stationed at Henderson Field, a small detachment of mechanics from the 31st BS/5th BG moved from Espiritu Santo to Guadalcanal on December 8 and began servicing all heavy bombers, including B-24s, that landed at Henderson.[4]

Maj. Francis Brady, in charge of the 31st BS ground crews recalled, "We started with 35 ordnance/engineering experts (hard workers) and supported as many as 24 multi-engined aircraft at one time." Being new arrivals on the 'Canal, Maj. Brady listened to an armament officer who was "new from the States" and instituted a new way to load bombs into a B-17. Later, Brady asked one of the mechanics how the new system was working.

"He looked me right in the eye," Brady wrote, "and in the usual 31st honest way said: 'The dumb S.O.B. who approved this system should have his balls shot off.'" Pretending not to know who had instituted the new system, Brady was shown how to load the bombs the old way and the new way. Finding the old way much easier, Brady ordered his armament officer to load six planes the old way and six planes the new way and then report which was easier. "Much later," Brady said, "an exhausted officer showed up soaking wet and a little apprehensive. 'You know, I'm convinced the old way is better, he said.'" Brady quickly rescinded his earlier order and the mechanics returned to the old way of loading bombs.[5]

On December 9, 18 B-17s set out to bomb the new Japanese airfield at Munda Point. Led by Maj. Whitaker of the 72nd BS, the planes took off from Guadalcanal and dropped 350 100-lb. bombs on the runway and adjacent revetments. The following day, Maj. Whitaker led 12 B-17s to bomb enemy shipping in the Shortland and Tonolei Area. Carrying 1,000-lb. bombs and escorted by eight P-38s the bombers set fire to two tankers and one cargo ship. Attacked by a flight of Zeros that flew above the bombers and dropped aerial bombs through the formation, the Fortress gunners shot down two of the attackers while the P-38s got five more.[6]

Over the next few days the B-17s returned repeatedly to Munda Point, trying to knock out the airfield before the Japanese could get it fully operational. At the same time, they hit Kahili Airfield on the southern tip of Bougainville. On December 19, Capt. Charters, B-17E (41-9214, *The Skipper*), made a very early morning harassment raid on Kahili. In addition to scattering 100-lb. and 20-lb. fragmentation bombs, Charters flew over the area for two hours tossing out beer bottles. As the bottles fell and made their eerie whistling noise, the Japanese searchlights suddenly went out, for fear that the Americans had developed a new "secret weapon." Upon impact with the ground, the bottles exploded with a sharp report and were reduced to jagged brownish crystals. Later, it was observed that the Japanese shunned the impact areas for days just in case some "insidious gas" had been spread.[7]

Later that day, for the ninth time in 10 days, B-17s hit Munda Field. Arriving at dawn, 12 Fortresses were met by heavy antiaircraft fire. Sgt.

Handrow recalled, "[As] we started on our run, the antiaircraft was so close that day that you could smell it in the airplane." As each plane dropped its 20 100-lb. bombs Sgt. Handrow watched. "Hits were scored all over [the] place," he wrote. "We left the place burning and [the] Zeros couldn't take off. It was a nice bombing mission."[8]

Almost like clockwork, the B-17s returned the next two nights, each time dropping 500-lb. bombs on the base buildings, runway, and fuel dump. On December 22, however, the 11th BG was given some time off so that Gen. Harmon and Col. Saunders could hand out 438 well-deserved decorations. That night however, it was business as usual when Sgt. Handrow's crew ran a "keep-them-awake night raid" up to Buin Airfield and Shortland Harbor, tossing out both bombs and beer bottles until early dawn.[9]

On Christmas Day, 15 11th BG B-17s took off from Guadalcanal to fly 644 miles on the first South Pacific Area raid against Rabaul. Before reaching the target, B-17E (41-2531, *G.I. Angel*), flown by Capt. Durbin, turned back due to heavy fuel consumption and B-17E (41-9059, *Boomerang*), with Sgt. Handrow as the tail gunner, and which he called "the worst ship in the 98th Bomb Sq.," was only 15 minutes from the target when engine No. 4 suddenly went out. Although close to Rabaul, the pilot decided not to take a chance and aborted. Thirty minutes later, on the flight back to Guadalcanal, the No. 2 engine went out and a short time later, the No. 1 engine began acting up. Wrote Sgt. Handrow, "[I]t really looked like we were going to sit the plane down in the Pacific . . . But luck was with us and we made it okay. We came in with ten minutes gas left . . . [T]he 31st Bomb. Sq. took the ship apart. It was # [41-90]59's last mission."[10]

For the planes that got through to Rabaul, they found the weather excellent for bombing. Maj. Lucas, B-17E (41-9211, *Typhoon McGoon II*), and Capt. Crane, B-17E (41-2523, *Goonie*), found an estimated 50 ships in the harbor. Delivering their 500-lb. Christmas presents on three transports, they scored direct hits on one and damaging hits on the other two.[11]

The rest of the 394th BS/5th BG finally joined their advance echelon at Nandi Field, Fiji on Christmas Day. Mechanic Roy Davenport wrote, "The start of working on the line 18 hours a day began; our food was mostly dehydrated with canned Spam as our meat supply. Our cooks were the best to make this palatable day after day. When I look back on those days, I really don't know how we managed to keep going."[12]

Luckily, fellows like Pvt. Klingensmith knew how to keep everyone going. "When the Sqdn. came in, I had a party for my friends . . .[that] got off to a roaring start . . ." Sometime during the party, two Navy airmen came over to join the celebration. Wrote Klingensmith, "We invited them in and then searched every bottle here and there [but] could find only empty ones." Undaunted, the Navy airmen took some empty bottles and left the party. "Well, they came right back with the bottles full of torpedo juice," remembered Klingensmith. "When the party finally broke up [it] must have been the wee hours of the morning. The New Zealanders had open slit trenches running from the huts down to the lagoon. We mostly crawled up the hill through the trenches—what a mess . . ." Years later, he recalled, "[I] heaved green a couple of days after the party."[13]

Christmas Day was somewhat better for Col. Saunders. Admiral Halsey showed up at a cocktail party thrown by Gen. Harmon, and pinned the stars of a brigadier general on Saunders. Although well deserved, Saunders was a bit dazed by the presentation. Well aware of the efforts of the 11th BG personnel for the past seven months, Saunders said, "Fifteen hundred men are pinning those stars on my shoulders." Five days later, Col. Frank F. Everest was given command of the 5th and 11th BGs while Gen. Saunders moved back to the States where he was eventually placed in command of B-29s.[14]

For the 98th BS/11th BG, Christmas almost did not come. On Christmas Eve, Capt. Joham and his B-17 flew to Efate to retrieve a few cases of alcohol but was delayed a day in returning. Noted the squadron historian, "Probably no plane ever based in that area was more eagerly awaited than that of Capt. Joham . . ." On Christmas morning, men from "all sections of the squadron gathered around the Operations Office" and waited for Joham's B-17 to appear. When a small speck suddenly appeared in the sky, an "exultant shout went up from the watchers on the ground." Within a few moments, Capt. Joham and his crew were distributing whisky, brandy, gin, beer and wine to the happy crowd. Noted the squadron historian, "To the men of the 98th . . . [Capt. Joham] is revered as the Santa who brought Christmas to [Espiritu] Santo."[15]

The day after Christmas it was business as usual when the 98th BS/11th BG went out and set fires in the Munda area. On December 28, 1st Lt. James R. Harp (42nd BS/11th BG) failed to return from a mission in B-17E (41-2428, *Ole Sh'asta*). And finally, 1942 closed for the 11th BG with the loss of one more plane and two more lives. Without permission, two drunken officers, a Capt. Levi and a Lt. Andrews from the 431st BS, decided to get more alcohol for a party they were attending on Espiritu Santo. Climbing into B-17E (41-9227, *Yankee Doodle, Jr.*), the two officers got the plane airborne but quickly lost control. Slamming into the jungle, Capt. Levi burned to death in the crash while Lt. Andrews lived until January 2. At a time when there were only 47 B-17s in the South Pacific Area, the 11th BG could ill afford to lose a bomber on a stupid joyride.[16]

For the men of the 43rd BG, the month of December started out rather badly. The Japanese dispatched four more transport/destroyers towards Buna under the cover of a major storm front. On December 2, five B-17s from the 65th BS, accompanied by six B-25s, took off from Port Moresby and caught the convoy midway between Buna and Gasmata. One destroyer received a direct hit, and the B-25s strafed the enemy warships, but while the Fortresses were returning to Port Moresby, 1st Lt. Robert K. Freeman, B-17E (41-9194), crashed into a mountain, killing the entire crew.[17]

The next day, the 63rd BS sent nine planes after the destroyers. Running into terrible weather, the flight missed the ships and bombed the Lae airfield instead. Upon their return to Port Moresby, they found that they were short one bomber. A note on the 43rd BG Casualty Reports states: "The only sighting of anything possibly connected with this missing aircraft was made by a member of another crew in the same formation. While trying to skirt a severe storm 5 miles off Finschhafen, New Guinea, a light was seen to signal 'S.O.' About 30 seconds later, directly ahead, a reddish yellow explosion was seen." B-17F (41-24429, *Dumbo*), flown by Lt. Anderson, was never seen again.[18]

On December 7, 1942, the one year anniversary of the surprise attack on Pearl Harbor, the 43rd BG staged a surprise attack of their own. Four B-17s from the 63rd BS hit a few Japanese transports off Gasmata and bombed the Gasmata airfield. Running into Zero fighters, the Fortress gunners expended 11,900 rounds of ammunition and shot down three fighters. The next day, a reconnaissance B-17 spotted six enemy destroyers south of Rabaul heading towards the Buna/Gona area and immediately notified Port Moresby.[19]

Four B-17s from the 63rd BS and six from the 65th BS set off almost immediately. Reaching the area first, the 63rd BS planes went after the enemy warships from only 2,000 feet. As the four pilots broke formation to bomb individually, about 15 Zeros suddenly attacked. Lt. Murphy, whose regular Fortress, B-17F (41-24543, *Pluto*) had been claimed by Col. Ramey, was flying a new B-17 and was able to hold steady for 20 seconds to give his bombardier a nice level bomb run. "One of the bombs hit a destroyer on the stern," he wrote, "there was a lot of smoke, but it continued to move." With Zeros coming at him from every angle, Murphy dove for the water, reaching a speed of 270 mph.

Pulling out about 30 feet from the water, Murphy leveled off as the Zeros continued to attack. While three Zeros gave chase, another one circled around for a head-on attack. "It was at that time my .50 caliber gun, which could fire out of the nose, proved to be an excellent weapon," Murphy wrote. Having lost the *Pluto*, Murphy had modified his new B-17 with a forward-firing fixed machine gun fired by a button on the pilot's control column. As the Japanese fighter drew closer, Murphy opened fire. "He was at our same altitude," Murphy recalled, "I can still see him screaming as he pulled off and crashed into the water." Although Murphy's radio operator was able to shoot down one other Zero, the others continued to pump rounds into the big bomber, eventually knocking out one engine and wounding the copilot. "[My copilot] had a number of wounds in the legs and arms, and two on the fleshy side of his rear," Murphy said of his copilot. "In addition, he was hit in the groin on his left leg. You should have heard him . . . saying, 'My God! They almost got the head of my family!'"[20]

Capt. Sogaard finished his own bomb run and came over to give Murphy a hand, linking up in the 63rd BS "buddy system." At the same time, Capts. McCullar and Scott, flying the other two B-17s, had also finished their bomb runs, and also linked together to fight off the swarming Zeros. "Between the four of us we produced a great deal of firepower," Murphy reported. "The Japanese Zeros had been hurt badly. Four of us had shot down seven Zeros and damaged at least three." By staying together the four Fortresses made it safely back to Port Moresby, although Lt. Murphy had to ground loop his bomber after finding out that his left tire had been shot out. In all, Murphy's plane had over 150 bullet holes in it and two engines had to be replaced. Although two men were wounded, the crew was credited with damaging one destroyer and shooting down three Zeros, including the one by Murphy. Hit almost as hard, B-17F (41-24574, *Tuffy*), piloted by Capt. McCullar, came back with 111 bullet holes and one wounded airman.[21]

Coming in on the enemy convoy behind the planes from the 63rd BS were the six B-17s of the 65th BS. While Capt. Jay Rousek and Lt. Melville V. Ehlers scored hits on the enemy destroyers, leaving one "burning and listing," the covering Zeros again hit the B-17s in force. Although no bomber was shot down, the light blue B-17E (41-9234) took a pounding, receiving 75 bullet holes, including hits in the main spar and hydraulic system. In turn, four more Zeros were shot down.[22]

With three more B-17s badly damaged and out of commission for awhile, Gen. Kenney wired Gen. Arnold for more planes, ". . . because those I had were getting worn out fast and, in spite of everything we did about it, we did lose airplanes once in a while and others got so badly shot up that they were only good for spare parts to repair others."[23] Unfortunately, until new planes arrived, Gen. Kenney was forced to use what he had.

Deprived of their reinforcements and supplies, the Japanese at Gona were overrun by the Australians on December 9, leaving only 3,000 Japanese defenders crammed into a small area around Buna, and another 2,000 at Sanandana Point. While the American infantry continued to collapse the Buna pocket, the 43rd BG went back to pounding the Japanese at Lae and Salamaua, hitting the two strongholds on three concessive days beginning December 11.[24]

In spite of bad weather on December 13, five Japanese supply/destroyers were sighted in the Bismarck Sea, north of Madang, British New Guinea, headed for Buna. Four B-17s from the 65th BS went out to give them a warm reception and in turn were intercepted by a flight of Zero fighters. "For the first time," the 65th BS historian reported, "the Japs dropped aerial bombs which they tried to hit our aircraft. Although some of the aerial bombs exploded very close to our planes, no damage was suffered." Unfortunately, no hits were scored on the ships. However, instead of going to Buna, the ships turned in at the mouth of the Mambare River, about 50 miles north of Buna, and began dropping their drums of food and supplies over the side.[25]

It wasn't until late in the afternoon that the warships were spotted again. While they were headed back to Rabaul, the B-17s from the 63rd BS and the B-24s from the 90th BG started out to harass them. Upon takeoff from Port Moresby, Lt. Ealon Hocutt, B-17F (41-24550), lost an engine while only 300 feet off the ground. When a second engine went dead Hocutt was unable to stay airborne and made a crash landing in shallow water in Bootless Bay. Although his ball turret gunner had his left foot nearly severed, and another crewman received head injuries, the others managed to walk away with only minor injuries but the 43rd BG had lost another plane.[26]

Unfortunately, the rest of the planes from the 63rd BS, and the B-24s, did not fare much better. Intercepted by protecting Zeros, the B-17s were badly shot up and did little damage to the destroyers while the B-24s managed to get through the screen of Zeros but likewise scored no hits. Noted the 63rd BS historian, "[The] only satisfaction to the crews was that they had downed several Jap fighters . . ." On their first mission since being sidelined for more training, the B-24s shot down eight Zeros, and every plane returned to Port Moresby. Wrote Gen. Kenney, "The morale was now so high [in the 90th BG] that I decided they were ready to work and take some of the load off the 43rd Group." That same day, American troops captured the village of Buna, leaving only a handful of Japanese defenders in the immediate vicinity.[27]

Four days after the Japanese convoy of destroyers successfully evaded the heavy bombers of the 5th AF, four more destroyers, a light cruiser, and two transports tried another reinforcing run into northern New Guinea. When the convoy was still north of Madang, it was hit by four B-17s of the 63rd BS. Capt. Harry Staley spotted the ships first but missed with his bombs when he was intercepted by Zeros. His ball turret gunner was hit in the shoulder by an explosive bullet but not before shooting down one of the Zeros.

Next to come over the target was Lt. O'Brien who had one engine knocked out by the swarming Zeros and a two-foot square hole punched through his elevator by antiaircraft fire. Following close behind, Capt. Sogaard also had one engine knocked out, which began trailing thick black smoke, that acted as a beacon to the circling Zeros. Quickly eight Japanese planes turned for the kill. Recalling how Sogaard had come to his rescue on December 8, Lt. Murphy moved in to return the favor. "I pushed all four engine throttles to the firewall and caught up in a real hurry," Murphy wrote. "[Sogaard] had feathered the engine, but black smoke from the oil was still pouring out. The fighters were really after him." By maneuvering above, below, or to either side of Sogaard, Murphy was able to add his firepower to the guns of Sogaard's crew.

Even as Murphy escorted Sogaard's crippled bomber back to base, six of the Zeros refused to give up. "I had never seen the Zeros continue an attack to such a long distance from their nearest landing sight," Murphy stated. As the B-17s began to climb to get over the Owen Stanley Mountains, the fighters persisted. Finally, only after two planes had been shot down, did the other four Zeros turn around. When Capt. Sogaard landed at Seven Mile Strip, his plane was found to be riddled with bullet holes, including over 30 in the nose. As Lt. Murphy taxied to a stop, Sogaard's bombardier rushed over to his crew and shook everyone's hand. "He kept saying, 'You saved our ass,'" recalled Murphy.[28]

During the evening, a couple of planes from the 63rd BS went after the convoy again, now located at Madang Harbor. Hoping to use skip bombing against the ships, Capt. McCullar came in low over the water while Lt. O'Brien dropped flares to create a backlight. When antiaircraft fire from the cruiser *Tenryu* set one of McCullar's engines on fire, he ignored the flames and circled the ship, letting his gunners knock out the deadly deck guns. While the fire in the engine eventually died out, the *Tenryu* gunners were able to knock out another engine before

McCullar's crew silenced the deck guns. Finally, with the *Tenryu* practically help-less, McCullar skipped a couple of bombs into the side of the ship and sank another Japanese vessel.

Flying on only two engines, Capt. McCullar ordered his crew to start throwing out all unnecessary weight to lighten the plane so that it could reach the mini-mum height of 6,500 feet to get through the Kokoda Pass in the Owen Stanley Mountains. Although McCullar ordered his crew to stand by to bail out he was eventually able to get the B-17 high enough and land safely at Seven Mile Strip. Said McCullar's navigator, "We didn't have to bail anybody out but when we came to the pass it looked so bad I closed my eyes and counted to fifty before I opened 'em. Sure was a pretty sight to see that slope falling away to the south."[29]

Over the next few days B-17s from the 65th BS attacked two enemy transports near Finschhafen, on New Guinea's Huon Peninsula, and at Arawe, on the south-ern coast of New Britain. Although the transports at Finschhaven had been cam-ouflaged, the three 65th BS pilots located them and scored hits on both vessels. At Arawe, Capt. Daniel Cromer scored three near misses on another transport but on Christmas Eve, he was able to redeem himself when he was one of 13 B-17s that went out after enemy shipping.[30]

Seven B-17s went after enemy ships off Aware, while six planes from the 65th BS went after two transports at Gasmata. At Arawe, the Fortresses sank the 623-ton transport *Koa Maru* while at Gasmata, Capt. Cromer sank the 515-ton *Tama Maru No. 2* with two direct hits, and Lt. Ray Dau and Lt. Ehlers damaged the sec-ond ship with one direct hit apiece. That night, as the crippled ship fled back towards Rabaul, it was caught by a reconnaissance B-17 carrying four 500-lb. bombs. Around midnight, Port Moresby received a radio call from the plane: "Found ship twenty miles east of Gasmata. Dropped four bombs. All missed. Peace on earth, good will toward men."[31]

By Christmas Day the 43rd BG had gotten word to pack all of their belongings for an expected move to Port Moresby. With the Japanese along the northern coast of Papua New Guinea holding on by a thread, Gen. Kenney had decided to move his B-17 group closer to the action. Since terrible weather grounded most of the planes on Christmas Day, the airmen were able to begin packing their equipment and then sit in peace and enjoy a traditional turkey dinner with all the trim-mings.[32]

The weather cleared enough the next day to allow the B-17s to hit Rabaul again. Although the 43rd BG, assisted by the 90th BG, had been able to damage all of the convoys that had tried to resupply the Japanese in northern New Guinea, the root of the problem was still Rabaul. The convoys were still using Rabaul as a staging center before making their final run to New Guinea. On December 26, Capts. McCullar and Scott from the 63rd BS, led four more B-17s from various squadrons, towards Rabaul.

Arriving well after dark, the six Fortresses searched the harbor for any likely targets. Capt. Scott spotted a transport tucked in beside the shore and dropped four bombs on it. Although the ship began to burn, Scott did not see it sink and could not claim credit for the vessel. However, a few hours later, when a reconnaissance plane took after-strike photos of the harbor, the 5,859-ton *Italy Maru* was found laying on its side at the spot where Capt. Scott had dropped his bombs.[33]

Four days later, on December 30, after it was reported that Rabaul's Simpson Harbor was full of enemy shipping, seven B-17s, including three from the hard working 63rd BS, returned to Rabaul. While the four other planes went in at 6,000 feet, attracting the attention of the antiaircraft gunners and the spotlights, the three pilots from the 63rd BS went in low to skip bomb.

Once again Capt. McCullar found an enemy ship and hit it with at least one bomb, causing the vessel to belch fire and smoke, while Lt. Barry Rucks scored a hit on another. At the same time, in a secluded part of the wide harbor, Lt. Murphy found two ships moving at a slow speed in line with one another. "Both of them were perfectly silhouetted in the light of the rising moon," Murphy recalled, deciding to drop two of his four 1,000-lb. bombs on the first ship, and then two on the other.

"I had never seen such an opportunity," Murphy wrote. "The stage was set just right." Dropping down to skip bombing height, Lt. Murphy waited until the first ship lined up with the "X" on his front window before calling to his bombardier to drop the first two bombs. As both bombs fell and Murphy flew over the top of the ship, the vessel's antiaircraft guns opened fire at him. Ignoring the incoming fire, Murphy immediately lined up on the second vessel. "When we had dropped our bombs on the second ship," he recalled, "[my crew] yelled, 'Pull up! Pull up!' I did and just cleared the mast of the second ship. Our tail gunner said we missed its tower by five or ten feet. Our bottom turret gunner said it was so close he just closed his eyes and prayed."

Dropping down close to the water to avoid the antiaircraft fire which now seemed to be concentrated at him, Lt. Murphy circled around and looked at his targets. "[B]oth ships were filled with fire, and smoke was billowing from the decks," he wrote. "It looked like an early New Year's celebration, with all of the light from the fires." Although Murphy was credited with sinking two large transports, and Capt. McCullar was credited with damaging another, the Japanese later confirmed that only one transport, the 3,821-ton *Tomiura Maru*, was sunk on December 30. However, the Japanese also reported that two transports, the *Italy Maru* and the 3,108-ton *Tsurugisan Maru*, had been sunk on December 26/27, while the 43rd BG claimed only one. Perhaps the Japanese got the dates mixed up. Still, by the end of 1942 the Japanese had lost three more transports to Ken's Men.[34]

To close out the year, three veteran crews from the 63rd BS led three green crews from the 64th BS towards Lakunai Airdrome. Fighting their way through terrible weather, the six planes caught the Japanese completely by surprise. "We had surprised them because some lights were on at one end of the runway," reported Lt. Murphy. While the three new crews dropped their bombs down the center of the field, putting the runway out of commission, the three veteran pilots salvoed their 500-lb. bombs on the lighted area. "We had hoped that the Zeros were parked on that end where we had seen the lights," Murphy said. "The bombs really did damage, as there were a number of explosions following our bomb impacts."

Taken completely by surprise, the Japanese antiaircraft fire was nonexistent. As Lt. Murphy and the others turned back towards New Guinea, he recalled, "That was a very noisy New Year's Eve for the Japanese and a very sober one for all of us . . . It was a good way to end 1942. That attack was also a good start to begin the dawning of a new year."[35]

XXV

Missing Stars

Sometime after Christmas Day 1942, 12 B-17s from the 11th BG, including six from the 26th BS, left the South Pacific Area and flew over to Port Moresby to help supplement Gen. Kenney's bomber force. Although the Buna Campaign was at an end, Gen. Kenney wanted to keep the pressure on both Rabaul and the Japanese strongpoints at Lae and Salamaua as he moved his 43rd BG up to Port Moresby. While he had 55 B-17Es and Fs in the Southwest Pacific Area, at least 20 were in the repair depot at Townsville, and only about another 14 were considered combat ready. Now, supplemented by the planes from the 11th BG, Kenney could continue his air war against the Japanese.[1]

At 2:00 A.M. on January 1, nine bombers from the 11th BG set out to hit Simpson Harbor but almost immediately, two planes aborted with mechanical problems, and three more turned back because of the weather. Although the other four were supposed to rendezvous south of Rabaul, the weather interfered with the meeting so each plane bombed on its own. Lt. Kinney went over Simpson Harbor and dropped three 500-lb. bombs on a transport, while Capt. Thornhill and another pilot, after finding the harbor socked in, dropped their bombs on the Gasmata airfield.[2]

On January 2, after weeks of heavy fighting, the combined Australian and American infantry finally captured Buna mission, leaving the Japanese troops at Sanandana Point as the only enemy troops in Papua New Guinea. With the fall of Buna, the objective of the 5th AF shifted to the reduction of Lae and Salamaua in British New Guinea and to preventing any new convoys from reaching the two Japanese strongpoints.[3] However, this would have to wait until the 43rd BG was settled into their new quarters at Port Moresby.

During the first week in January advance elements of the group reached Seven Mile Strip and began to set up camp. Established in the jungle, the new base was vastly different from the old base at Mareeba. "Food at Port Moresby wasn't as good as at [Mareeba]," noted Capt. Crawford. "Our diet was plain, staple and monotonous. We ate so much bully beef and other canned meats and stews that . . . [the men] won't ever want to see canned meats again. The bitter chickory—called coffee—and the powdered milk were horrible . . ." While setting up camp the men were visited by the native peoples. "When we first reached Port Moresby, the women used to wander aimlessly around in their skirts of shredded palm, wreathed in their beads and smiles, completely unabashed by their topside nudity," Crawford continued. "The native men in their G-strings didn't pay any attention to the roaming of the ladies, but we did and got a big laugh out of it." Felt to be too distracting to the airmen, the topless women were soon restricted from coming near the camp.[4]

While the 43rd BG was moving to New Guinea, unbeknownst to the Americans, on January 4, the Japanese sent out a directive to evacuate Guadalcanal. Having realized that they could never reconquer the island, and having lost too many men and too much equipment already, Japan decided to abandon Guadalcanal and act to secure the northern Solomons from further American advancement. At the same time, Japan decided to reinforce their bases at Lae, Salamaua, Madang, and Wewak along the north coast of New Guinea.[5] Although pulling back her tentacles, Japan was far from defeated.

Although the Americans were unaware of the Japanese directive, daily reconnaissance had discovered a large amount of shipping at Rabaul and Gen. Kenney guessed that the Japanese were planning to send another convoy towards Lae. Planning to strike the enemy before he even left the harbor, Kenney ordered Gen. Walker to schedule an early morning raid on Simpson Harbor for January 5. Perhaps because of the persistently bad weather, which had prevented a few of the 11th BG planes from reaching Rabaul on the morning of January 3, Walker decided to change tactics and try a daylight raid. Planning on using six B-17s and six B-24s, Walker felt that the 12 planes would have a hard time finding their rendezvous point if they tried a early morning strike. Additionally, he felt that a daylight raid would allow his pilots to see one another and fly a tight formation which was better for both defensive and offensive purposes.[6]

However, Gen. Kenney ordered that the bombers strike at dawn. Knowing that the Japanese still lacked a good night fighter, Kenney felt that the dawn strikes were much safer for the aircrews. He felt that a daylight strike would meet strong fighter opposition. With regards to a tight formation, Kenney was willing to forego a tight bombing pattern in return for the safety of his men and planes. In spite of Gen. Kenney's orders however, Gen. Walker changed the takeoff time and sent the bombers over the target at noon.

In further violation of Gen. Kenney's orders, Gen. Walker himself went along on the mission with Maj. Bleasdale, 43rd BG Executive Officer, and Maj. Lindberg, CO of the 64th BS, in B-17F (41-24458, San Antonio Rose). Leading four other B-17s from the 64th BS, and one from the 403rd BS, Maj. Lindberg took the Fortresses over Rabaul's Simpson Harbor at about noon. Noted the 64th BS historian, "This was the first daylight raid on this harbor in many days. It was a very successful mission in as far as shipping hits were concerned. Our planes scored four and possibly five direct hits on enemy shipping." Sunk in the attack was the 5,833-ton *Keifuku Maru*. However, as the bombers turned south for Port Moresby, they were jumped by enemy fighters "laying in wait just outside of the target area," reported Lt. Jean Jack (403rd BS), B-17F (41-24538).[7]

In the ensuing air battle, Maj. Lindberg's *San Antonio Rose* was hit repeatedly until one engine was set on fire. When only 25 miles from Rabaul, the plane fell behind the others and began to lose altitude. Japanese records indicated that one officer baled out and landed safely on New Britain, and managed to evade the enemy for three weeks before being captured. More than likely, the officer was not Gen. Walker. The capture of such an important member of Gen. Kenney's staff would certainly have been exploited by the Japanese. It is believed that Gen. Walker died either during the fighter attacks or in the crash of B-17F (41-24458, *San Antonio Rose*). Having often accompanied his planes on bombing missions, much to the chagrin of Gen. Kenney, and for developing new tactics for his bombers from "lessons personally gained under combat conditions," Gen. Walker was posthumously awarded the Medal of Honor.[8]

Also hit hard by the attacking Zeros was Lt. Jack. B-17F (41-24538) received gunfire through the radio compartment and the left wing, which knocked out the ball turret and tore a hole in the left main wing spar. Cannon fire, also severed the No. 1 engine controls, holed the fuel tank, and destroyed the oil cooler. Unable to feather the damaged engine, Lt. Jack and his copilot flew a "very rugged" trip back towards Port Moresby. Although only four of the 11 guns on the B-17 were working, the crew managed to shoot down four Zeros. Crippled beyond repair and unable to make it over the Owen Stanley Mountains, Jack set the B-17 down in the water just off Urasi Island, near Goodenough Island without injury to the crew.[9]

The expected Japanese convoy to reinforce Lae was spotted by 2nd Lt. Guyton M. Christopher, B-17F (41-24383), near 10:00 A.M. on January 6 off the southwest coast of New Britain. Reporting the location of the ships, Christopher shadowed six Japanese warships and four transports until he began to run low on fuel. As he headed back towards Port Moresby, he ran into a heavy storm, which consumed more of his gas. Reaching the Gulf of Papua on the south side of New Guinea, Christopher suddenly turned towards land. Copilot Lt. John Barbee recalled, "Then we ran into the heaviest storm, flying little more than wave height. The situation was hopeless, and suddenly all the motors stalled. The Fortress plunged into the sea . . ."

Only three men, including Lt. Barbee made it to the B-17 emergency life rafts. One of the men killed in the ditching was Meyer Levin, now a master sergeant, who had been the bombardier for Capt. Colin Kelly Jr. on December 10, when Kelly attacked the Japanese heavy cruiser *Ashigara* in the Philippines. "The last I remember of Levin," wrote Barbee, "was that he was standing grasping the safety catches on the raft. He probably released the raft which saved the three survivors before he was knocked unconscious." Including Lt. Christopher and Sgt. Levin, four other men perished in the ditching of B-17F (41-24383).[10]

Although Lt. Christopher never saw the 5th BG planes attack the convoy, eight B-17s and fifteen P-38s struck the enemy ships while they were fifty miles east of Gasmata. Running into a protective screen of Zeros, the B-17s scored no hits on the enemy ships but managed to shoot down six Zeros while the P-38s got another nine.[11]

Over the next four days, in spite of terrible weather, Gen. Kenney's 5th AF made repeated attacks on the convoy. On January 7 and 8, the B-17s of the 43rd BG scored a number of "hits and near misses [which] destroyed a destroyer and severely damaged several transports." Although the convoy was cut down in size, four warships and three transports still managed to reach Lae on January 8 and put 4,000 troops ashore.[12] While the ships were unloading, Capt. Thompson, B-17F (41-24381, *Panama Hattie*), and Lt. Dau, in the light blue B-17E (41-9234), attacked but were met by about 12 Japanese Zeros. Machine-gun fire ripped through the nose of Lt. Dau's plane and hit his bombardier, Lt. Albert Cole, in the jaw, breaking the bone and ripping off the tip of his tongue. Although Dau offered to abort, Cole refused.

As Lt. Cole was looking through the bombsight during the bomb run, an antiaircraft shell exploded outside the nose of the bomber and sent shrapnel into his knees. While the bombs fell, the B-17 was hit three more times by antiaircraft fire which badly wounded the tail gunner, and knocked out the top turret and both left engines. In a 30-minute air battle with the attacking Zeros, the gunners of B-17E (41-9234) shot down three Japanese planes.

Flying on only two engines, Lt. Dau realized that he would never be able to get over the Owen Stanley Mountains, so he decided to land near Wau, New Guinea. "We glided in on the side of a mountain at about 110 miles an hour," he reported, "and as luck would have it, there were no trees—nothing but nice soft grass—so we slid along into a crash landing." In the crash landing and ensuing fire, the wounded tail gunner was killed and the radio operator was mortally wounded, dying six days later. Although the others were injured and shaken, they were eventually rescued and taken to Port Moresby.[13]

On January 9 and 10, as the enemy ships fled back towards Rabaul, the 5th AF gave them a few parting shots. After four B-17s from the 65th BS struck on January 9, the squadron historian wrote, "Seven direct hits were scored on transport ships." In all likelihood, the report was greatly exaggerated. Although the Allies had been able to sink two transports, damage a few warships, and shoot down a total of about 80 enemy planes, the Japanese had once again been able to carry out a successful reinforcement of northern New Guinea. 5th Bomber Command had lost three more B-17s and its commanding officer.[14]

With the loss of Gen. Walker, Gen. Kenney temporarily named Gen. Whitehead as the replacement until January 18 when Brig. Gen. Howard Ramey (no relation to Col. Roger Ramey, CO of the 43rd BG) flew in from Hawaii and took over 5th Bomber Command.[15] By this time the 43rd BG was beginning to get additional crews from the United States who were quickly parceled out to beef up the 64th and 65th BSs. With the arrival of the new men, many of the 43rd BG veterans were given promotions, including Ken McCullar. Promoted to major, McCullar was given command of the 64th BS and quickly started training his men at skip bombing. Noted the squadron historian, "Capt. [sic] McCullar inspired the officers and men with his flying tactics. The Capt. was a skip bombing expert."[16]

On January 16, eight planes from the 65th BS flew a night raid on Simpson Harbor. Capt. Jay Zeamer Jr. sank an 8,000-ton transport while another pilot set fire to a second transport, and the others bombed the dock area. On the flight home however, the planes ran into a heavy storm and a Lt. Lien ran out of fuel and crash landed B-17E (41-2599, *Tugboat Annie*) north of Buna.[17]

In mid-January it was decided to move the 403rd BS out of Milne Bay because of malaria. Noted the 403rd BS historian, "It was decided at higher headquarters to return the Squadron to the main land for a period in order to recuperate from the effects of the Malaria germ." While the men were getting ready for the move, the Japanese staged a massive raid.

"Just after noon chow on Sunday, January 17th, the alarm sounded," wrote the historian. Twenty-three enemy bombers, flying in their usual V-pattern, crossed from one end of the field to the other, dropping their bombs along the way. Practically everything on the field was destroyed. In addition to several P-39s, and one B-24, the 403rd BS lost B-17E (41-2639), B-17F (41-24540) and B-17E (42-24551, *Fire Ball Mail*). Fortunately however, no one was hurt.[18]

Over the next few nights the Japanese returned, albeit in smaller numbers, and harassed the 403rd BS personnel as they continued to pull out. By the second week in February the men were safely encamped at Mareeba, away from the Japanese bombers and the malaria-ridden mosquitoes. Making it possible for the 403rd BS to move to Mareeba was the fact that by January 23, the combat squadrons of the 43rd BG had all been moved to Port Moresby, closer to New Guinea and closer to Rabaul.[19]

On January 18, Gen. Kenney received a "real shock" when he learned that his ex-aide and good friend, Maj. Benn, was reported missing in action. Going out in a B-25 in bad weather to scout for possible locations for new landing fields, it was believed that he had crashed into a mountain. Having taken charge of the 63rd BS when it was still learning to walk, Maj. Benn had been instrumental in the development of skip bombing. Gen. Kenney wrote, "Benn's loss hurt. He was the one who put across skip-bombing out here and if it hadn't been for that 63rd Squadron of his, we might have been fighting the war in Australia instead of New Guinea. No one in the theater has made a greater contribution to victory than Bill Benn." Maj. Benn's plane was never found.[20] Another star had fallen from the sky.

During the third week in January the Allies finally overran the Japanese position at Sanandana Point, completely wiping out all organized resistance in Papua New Guinea. On January 22 the Allied victory in the Papuan Campaign was declared complete. While keeping a wary eye on the northern coast of New Guinea and at a new Japanese airfield being built at Wewak, the 43rd BG returned to Rabaul.[21]

Three planes from the 63rd BS hit Blanche Bay near Rabaul in the early morning hours of January 21 and two pilots managed to score hits. Ed Scott, now a major, B-17F (41-24353, *Cap'n & The Kids*), skipped a 500-lb. bomb alongside a 8,000-ton transport causing it to lift out of the water. Later, the Japanese were seen to be trying to beach it. Lt. Murphy hit a 4,000- to 5,000 ton cargo ship with at least two 500-lb. bombs. "The ship rocked violently," Murphy wrote, "and an oil slick was seen all around the ship." Added Murphy, "During the remainder of January, we continued bombing everything we could find in Rabaul Harbor . . . We severely limited any opportunity for the ships to leave the harbor."[22]

During the first week in February the B-17s concentrated on crippling the enemy air force around Rabaul. On February 1 the 65th BS hit Rapopo airdrome and on February 2, six planes from the 63rd BS hit Vunakanau. "Our mission was to keep the runway out of action," wrote Lt. Murphy. Dropping their bombs on the airdrome, the Americans left the field pockmarked with craters. "The Japanese [airplanes] had been in revetments the night we made the run," Murphy continued, "and it took them three days to repair the runway." Almost immediately seven planes from the 63rd BS returned to drop incendiary bombs on both ends of the airfield, trying to hit the enemy planes in the revetments. "Many fires were started off the northeast end of the runway," Lt. Murphy stated. "The fire became visible for over 100 miles. It looked as if a fuel dump had exploded, or enemy bombers had been caught in a revetment."

For the first time in the Pacific war, Japanese night fighters struck with determination as the seven B-17s attacked. "The Japanese night fighters were building a capability to attack," recalled Murphy. "Two of them hit us when we flew over the runway at Vunakanau. Our aircraft received some damage."[23] Although the Japanese had used night fighters before, they had never been a nuisance. Now, however, the Japanese pilots were becoming a bit more aggressive and the nights were becoming a bit more dangerous for the Americans.

By January 2, there were only 25 B-17s in commission in the South Pacific Area, of which 12 had been sent off to Port Moresby to help Gen. Kenney. Although the 5th BG had been moved to the area, only the 394th BS, based in the Fiji Islands, had any airplanes, and all of those had been acquired from the 19th BG. In spite of the lack of planes, the 5th and 11th BGs were given no time to rest. For four consecutive days, starting January 2, the B-17s assaulted a large Japanese naval force found at Buin. On January 2, six planes from the 431st BS/11th BG scored four near misses in an attack against 14 Japanese destroyers. The next day, the 431st went back and bombed a cruiser, and on January 4, they went back again and sank an enemy transport. On January 5, B-17s from the 394th BS/5th BG joined the planes from the 431st BS for another attack on the enemy ships. Although only one ship was sunk, the combined strike force managed to shoot down several attacking Zero fighters.[24]

On January 5, the burden was lessened a bit when the 12 planes sent to Gen. Kenney returned to the South Pacific Area. Having flown only two missions while in the Southwest Pacific, the aircrews felt that their trip to Port Moresby had been a waste of time. "Our force is ready to leave New Guinea," the 26th BS/11th BG diarist had recorded on January 4, "we feel we're not needed here." Five planes from the 26th BS flew directly from Port Moresby to Guadalcanal and on January 6 were back in the fray.[25]

At 10:00 A.M. five 26th BS planes, escorted by a small group of American fighters, set off to attack shipping in Tonolei Harbor. When Capt. Thornhill, B-17E (41-9145), could not reach high altitude, he turned back and made a solo run against Rekata Bay. The other four B-17s continued on and although they met light anti-aircraft fire, they managed to damage one Japanese transport with their 1,000-lb. bombs. At the same time that the 26th BS planes were hitting Tonolei Harbor, a flight of 42nd BS B-17s struck the airport at Kahili.[26]

Having returned to Guadalcanal, three of the planes from the 26th BS were returning to Espiritu Santo on January 7 when Capt. Thornhill, B-17E (41-2396), ran into trouble. Near San Christobal, engine No. 2 went out and was successfully feathered. A few minutes later engine No. 1 began to lose oil and shortly thereafter, engine No. 3 began to miss. Deciding to return to Guadalcanal, Thornhill found that he could not maintain altitude. When the oil pressure continued to drop on engine No. 1 and the propellers could not be feathered, Capt. Thornhill decided to make a water landing. "Everything was thrown out (loose material), the whole crew, excepting pilot and copilot crowded into radio compartment, and a successful water landing was made near a reef," recorded the squadron diarist. "Crew disembarked on the reef and walked to the beach." Uninjured in the ditching, the crew was ultimately rescued and forwarded to Espiritu Santo.[27]

During the first week in January the Japanese, in response to their directive of January 4, began evacuating Guadalcanal and reinforcing the Northern Solomons. On January 13 a new American air force was created in the South Pacific to fulfill the obvious need for centralized command and improve the handling of the units in the area. Both the 5th and 11th BGs were relieved from assignment with the 7th Air Force, which was still headquartered in Hawaii, and reassigned to the brand-new 13th Air Force (13th AF), headquartered at Espiritu Santo and commanded by Brig. Gen. Nathan F. Twining.[28]

Twining's initial objectives were to maintain air superiority in the Central Solomons, and to destroy the enemy supply bases in the Northern Solomons. At the time that the 13th AF was created the 5th BG was still under the operational control of the 11th BG. With the exception of the 394th BS, the 5th BG had no planes. As a solution, crews from the 5th BG began flying 11th BG planes, while the 11th BG crews were given a period of rest, usually in New Zealand. Noted the 5th BG historian, "Combat Crews would carry out their missions from Cactus for periods ranging from 7 to 10 days, returning their plane and crew to Buttons [Espiritu Santo] for maintenance and rest for the crew. Throughout December and January combat crews . . . were visiting Auckland, New Zealand for rest leaves."[29]

Early in December a detachment of 31st BS/5th BG mechanics had been moved to Guadalcanal to service any heavy bombers that landed there. On January 14, the rest of the 31st BS ground personnel boarded the USS Crescent City and moved to the 'Canal. "The 31st established itself on the beach near Lunga Point, taking over a camp site formerly occupied by U.S. Marines," noted the 5th BG historian. Designated a "Service Squadron," the mechanics were responsible for servicing all of the heavy bombers and crews that flew into Henderson Field. "The squadron housed, fed, and generally took care of the personnel and maintained the aircraft of three heavy bombardment groups, the 5th, 11th, and 307th [a B-24 unit.]"[30]

Making themselves right at home and showing great ingenuity, the 31st BS mechanics soon built an "imposing outdoor theater boasting individual seats for unit personnel and coconut logs for guests." Shows were given whenever the personnel could obtain movies. Wrote the 5th BG historian, "Some evenings it took about half the night to see the complete picture because of interruptions by Jap bombing raids." Additionally, the men showed great ingenuity when they posted the following words above their latrine: "31st thunderpit—Capacity 6 Pfc's."[31]

On January 14, seven B-17s from the 72nd BS, accompanied by a few crews from the 394th BS, both 5th BG, flew up to Guadalcanal to form an advance strike force for a period of about one week. That night, as if by design, Japanese bombers struck Henderson Field on three different occasions. Fortunately, none of the B-17s were damaged and the very next day, six Fortresses from the 72nd BS took off to intercept six enemy destroyers that had been sighted near Vella Lavella Island. Dropping their bombs from high altitude against the wildly evading ships, none of the B-17s scored any hits but an escorting flight of P-38s and P-40s shot down 11 Zeros that tried to intercept the Flying Fortresses.[32]

That same day, January 15, B-17s from the 42nd BS/5th BG were called upon to help resupply the Marines on Guadalcanal. On January 9, the Marines had begun an offensive to eliminate all Japanese resistance on the island. Moving surprisingly fast, the Marines had soon outdistanced their native supply handlers. Then, having run into strong resistance near Mount Austen, the Marines began using up food, water, and especially ammunition at an alarming rate. On January 15, B-17s from the 42nd BS began airdropping tons of supplies to the troops, utilizing what little amount of cargo parachutes they could find. Then, when the parachutes ran out, the airmen wrapped the supplies in burlap or canvas in hopes that the items would survive the drop. In most cases, they did not. However, by January 17, the native supply lines had been reestablished and the B-17s went back to their bomb runs.[33]

During the night of January 15, some advance strike force planes bombed Kahili Airfield. "This mission was the first one in the [South Pacific] area in which 2,000-lb. bombs were used," wrote the 72nd BS historian. The next day the Fortresses hit Ballale airfield on Ballale Island, and on January 18, five planes from the 72nd BS attacked a cargo vessel in Shortland Harbor. "[O]ur flight scored three direct hits and some near misses on an enemy transport of 15,000-tons," wrote Cpl. Schaeffer, the radio operator in Capt. Robert E. Hawes' B-17E (41-2521, *G.I. Angel*). "This flight was flown at 9,000 feet and the antiaircraft fire was so accurate and heavy that the windshield of our aircraft was broken by flying fragments of the bursting antiaircraft fire. On withdrawal from the target, our formation success-fully fought off an interception and shot down two enemy fighters."[34]

The advance strike force continued to attack the enemy whenever and wher-ever possible. On January 19 the B-17s, escorted by American fighters, struck the revetments and runway at Munda. The next day they hit shipping in the Shortland Island area, and on January 21, they went back to Munda, accompanied by P-39s and B-26s and hit the bivouac area. On January 22, the planes from the 72nd BS returned to Espiritu Santo and some much-needed rest, while the com-bat crews from the 431st BS/11th BG moved up to Henderson Field to carry on the continuous air strikes.[35]

While some of the South Pacific B-17s were being used for raiding Japanese airfields and harbors, a large number were still being used for reconnaissance. Although most of the reconnaissance missions were uneventful, a few were not. On January 19, Capt. Buie was flying a 98th BS/11th BG B-17 on a photographic mission off the east coast of Bougainville when he was suddenly jumped by six Zeros. Seeking protection in the clouds, Buie lost two Zeros but the others stayed with him. Although attacked from all quarters, the undersides of the bomber suf-fered the most damage. When the rudder control cable was severed, the flight engineer managed to splice the cable in flight. Flying at 10,000 feet, the Zeros kept after the Fortress for 90 miles, turning back only after two were shot down and one was damaged. Although the B-17 had been hit repeatedly, only two men were slightly wounded and Capt. Buie was able to return safely to Henderson Field.[36]

Since the 11th BG had been engaged in almost continuous combat with the Japanese since July 31 at the beginning of the Guadalcanal Campaign, the War Department finally recognized the accomplishments of the group and issued it a Presidential Unit Citation on January 23. Additionally, the 11th BG was included in the Naval Distinguished Unit Citation which was eventually presented to the 1st Marine Division for its actions in the Solomons. As Maj. Edmundson wrote, "To my knowledge, this is the only B-17 unit to be so honored by a sister service." Along with the group citations, each individual squadron was awarded a Presidential Unit Citation.[37]

Having moved up to Henderson Field as the advance strike force, the 431st BS B-17s hit Ballale airdrome on the night of January 25. That same day, five planes from the 26th BS/11th BG joined the advance strike force. On January 26, three planes dropped fifty-six 500-lb. bombs on the Ballale airport amidst a hail of anti-aircraft fire. At 4:00 P.M. on January 28, three planes from the 26th BS and three from the 431st BS, bombed Kahili airfield starting "huge fires and explosions . . ." On return to Henderson Field at 8:00 P.M., B-17E (41-2520, *Jap Happy*), piloted by 1st Lt. F. Steinman (26th BS), was badly damaged when it was taxied into a jeep, ripping the skin on the tail of the B-17 and tearing off the rear gunner's door.[38]

On the night of January 27, Gen. Twining and a few members of his staff left Guadalcanal aboard B-17E (41-2403), piloted by a Capt. Woodruff (23rd BS/5th BG), for a shuttle flight to Espiritu Santo. For some unknown reason, Capt. Woodruff had to make a forced water landing. Crowded with 15 passengers and crew, the men scrambled out of the sinking plane and into the two rubber liferafts just before the plane nosed under water. Finding that neither of the rafts contained a radio set, Twining and his party floated around on the Pacific for five days before being spotted on February 1 by a searching B-17 from the 431st BS/11th BG. After being rescued Gen. Twining instantly set about making sure that every liferaft contained a radio set.[39]

On the last day of January 1943, the 98th BS/11th BG received its first B-24 when a new plane and crew arrived at Espiritu Santo. By February 7, a total of seven B-24s had been delivered to the 98th BS. "Little bombing was done this first part of February," declared the 98th BS historian. "New pilots and crews conducted familiarization flights in the new B-24's assigned to the Squadron."[40] The end of the B-17 era in the Pacific, and the dawning of B-24 domination was beginning.

Near the end of January the 72nd BS/5th BG went back to Guadalcanal, relieving the 431st BS/11th BG. On February 1, nine B-17s set out to bomb enemy shipping around Bougainville. Breaking into two elements, the first element, consisting of five planes from the 72nd BS, set fire to a large cargo ship with two or three direct hits and several near misses. Following close behind, the second element, made up of one plane from the 72nd BS and three from the 42nd BS/11th BG, flew through heavy antiaircraft fire to bomb another supply vessel. Midway through the bomb run B-17E (41-9122, *Eager Beavers*), piloted by Capt. Frank L. Houx (42nd BS), was hit in the bomb bay by an antiaircraft shell and disintegrated in midair.[41]

After scoring two hits on the enemy ship, the three remaining planes turned back towards Henderson Field but were intercepted by some 20 Zeros. In the ensuing air battle, B-17E (41-2442, *Yokohama Express*), flown by Capt. Harold P. Hensley, was attacked repeatedly and seriously damaged, necessitating a water landing. Capt. Hensley and his crew were never seen again. The two remaining planes, flown by Capt. Earl O. Hall, CO of the 42nd BS, and a Capt. Thomas, continued to fight off the persistent attackers, shooting down four planes before Capt. Hall's B-17E (41-9151) was shot out of the sky.

All by himself now, Capt. Thomas continued to try and fend off the attackers. The Zeros chased the Flying Fortress for almost 200 miles, seriously wounding the radio operator and bombardier, and knocking out the tail guns, and the ball turret and top turret guns. Two engines were damaged, one main tire was flattened, and all of the ammunition for the nose and radio compartment guns was expended but the B-17 would not go down. After three more Zeros were shot down, the Japanese finally gave up and Capt. Thomas was able to make a successful crash landing on Guadalcanal. Having had a total of only four planes assigned to the 42nd BS, the loss of all four planes and three entire crews effectively eliminated the 42nd BS from any further operations in the South Pacific.[42]

On February 2, the 72nd BS sent five planes escorted by friendly fighters against shipping in the Shortland Island area. The mission was called "the most perfect bombing mission we ever made," by the personnel of the squadron when a cargo ship was hit by a "perfect bomb pattern." Noted the squadron historian, "Explosions of the bombs in the concentrated area around the ship made it impossible to count the exact number of direct hits." Attacked by at least twenty Zeros, the bomber crews shot down three planes, while the American fighters accounted for another five. No American planes were shot down.[43]

With Japan's decision to evacuate her troops from Guadalcanal, the Japanese Navy once again began making nightly runs to the island, this time to take men off. During the daylight hours of February 5, four individual planes from the 72nd BS, went out in search of the Japanese Navy. While conducting his search, Capt. Hawes in B-17E (41-2521, *G.I. Angel*) sighted an enemy minelayer but passed it by to continue his search. After going 700 miles, the plane was intercepted by five Zero fighters and Hawes spent the next 45 minutes going in and out of rain squalls to get away from them. Finally turning back towards Henderson Field, Hawes happened across the enemy mine layer again and although carrying no bombs, decided to attack.

Cpl. Schaeffer, Hawes' radio operator, recalled, "We gunners were able to silence the machine guns, fore and aft, in the initial phase of the action. Repeated attacks damaged the steering device of the enemy vessel and he began to circle out of control." By directing their machine-gun fire into the stern of the ship, the B-17 crew managed to touch off a large explosion. "The superstructure and stern of the ship were completely blown away," Schaeffer continued. "Since our fuel supply was running low and the supply of ammunition was down to the emergency limit, we were unable to remain to see whether or not the damage done was enough to sink the ship." The 72nd BS historian noted that the B-17 crew had expended 3,000 rounds of ammunition against the enemy ship.[44]

Upon his return to Guadalcanal, Capt. Hawes filed his report and was promptly reprimanded for endangering his plane and crew by attacking the Japanese minelayer. Noted the 72nd BS historian, ". . . Capt. Hawes quoted to him the President's words, 'We shall hit the enemy whenever and wherever we find him.'"[45]

XXVI

Enough

By February 1943 the 11th BG was pretty well spent. Only 19 of its original 35 crews remained due to combat loss and attrition. Forced to fly long missions over great expanses of water, the men were exhausted beyond belief. Gen. Harmon had recognized the problem and had worked tirelessly to bring replacement crews and planes to the South Pacific, even stealing men headed to the Southwest Pacific. By February the pressure was relieved somewhat when the 307th BG, a B-24 unit, arrived from Hawaii. Although Gen. Emmons in Hawaii continued to protest over the lack of heavy bombers in the Hawaiian Area, Admiral Nimitz ignored him and started the first 15 B-24s south on February 4.[1]

With a new heavy bomb group in the area, and the 11th BG fatigued beyond effectiveness, official orders were signed on February 7 relieving the 11th BG from further duty. While new arrivals among the group were to be transferred to the 5th BG, the veteran crews were to be pulled back to Hawaii. Men with enough rotation points were to be sent home while those lacking enough points were to be retrained in B-24s. At almost the same time, on February 9, all organized enemy resistance on Guadalcanal officially ceased. Although small pockets of Japanese troops would continue to give the Americans trouble, the six-month struggle for Guadalcanal was finally over.[2]

By the middle of February, the Navy Seabees had two operational bomber airfields on Guadalcanal; Henderson Field, sometimes known as Bomber No. 1, at Lunga Point, and Carney Field, called Bomber No. 2, a half mile to the east on Koli Point. With two operational bomber fields, more and more heavy bombers began to stay on Guadalcanal for longer periods of time.[3]

Although the 11th BG was relieved from duty and the fight for the 'Canal was effectively over, the 5th BG continued to fly search missions over the Northern Solomons. At 3:00 A.M. on February 9, Capt. Thomas J. Classen, B-17F (41-24450, *My Ever Lovin' Dove*), took off from Guadalcanal to search an area far to the northeast. The *My Ever Lovin' Dove* was the only B-17F in the 5th BG and had once been the personal plane of Gen. Harmon but because of the shortage of bombers, he had been forced to give it up. Near 8:30 A.M., Classen saw Nauru Island, 750 miles northeast of Guadalcanal, and gave it a wide birth, knowing that the island held an enemy airstrip. As he passed the island however, two Zeros rapidly overtook him. "I was not immediately concerned with the situation," Classon reported, ". . . the crew was well trained and capable of holding their own with the best of them. The two Zeros, however, were quickly joined by six more . . ."

The eight Zeros attacked the B-17 for the next 45 minutes, knocking out two engines and lightly wounding three crewmen, in spite of the wild evasive maneuvers made by Capt. Classen. Although seven of the B-17's guns jammed during the fight, the gunners managed to shoot down two Zeros. Eventually, the Zeros broke off the attack and Capt. Classen turned his battered plane back towards Guadalcanal.

Having fallen to 4,000 feet, Capt. Classen found that he could not maintain altitude on two engines and ordered his crew to lighten the plane. "To add to our immediate trouble," Classen recalled, "one of the two bomb bay tanks refused to salvo. The tank, which was still full of gas, hung half in the bomb bay and half out. The added drag of the open bomb doors was not helping any in maintaining altitude . . ." By cutting a hose, the men were able to drain the tank and lose the added weight of the gas. Then, engineer T/Sgt. Donald Martin climbed atop the stuck tank and tried to kick it out. When the tank finally fell free, Martin almost went with it, only saving himself by catching hold of a couple of dangling fuel lines.

Down to only 50 feet above the waves when the tank fell, Classen kept the plane airborne and over the next two hours was able to get the *My Ever Lovin' Dove* up to 800 feet. Having jettisoned his extra fuel however, Classen knew that a landing at sea was inevitable. "Before the fuel supply was exhausted," Classen wrote, "another engine decided that it could carry the burden no further and this ended our worries regarding the gas supply."

Studying the rolling waves, Capt. Classen timed his landing perfectly. "Things must have been just right because we went in as graceful as could be expected," he wrote. Scrambling out of the sinking B-17F (41-24450, *My Ever Lovin' Dove*), the crew had trouble ejecting the two liferafts and when they finally got them out, found that one would not inflate properly. "The airplane was sinking rapidly," Classen continued, "and only the tail remained visible above the surface of the water. As both rafts were tied to the airplane with a piece of parachute cord, we were becoming increasingly concerned about losing the collapsed one . . ."

As half of the crew climbed into the inflated raft, the other half fought to break the line holding the uninflated one. "It was about this point that the airplane nosed down, the tail rising majestically out of the water in a final salute, and slid gently out of sight beneath the waves," recalled Capt. Classen. "The boys clinging to the deflated raft refused to let go and were pulled about twenty feet under water before the line finally broke." With the help of a hand pump, the men were able to inflate the second raft and climb inside.

For the next 16 days Classen and his crew floated about on the Pacific Ocean until finally reaching shore in the Carteret Island group. Seven weeks later, using a native outrigger canoe, Classen and three others finally reached American troops on Choisel Island, 150 miles away. "Thus ended the 66-day mission . . ." Classen concluded.[4]

The end of February and the beginning of March was a relatively quiet time in the Solomons. The Japanese were trying to strengthen some of their bases in the Northern Solomons while, on Guadalcanal, the Marines were mopping up. The timing was just right to send the 11th BG home and start the 5th BG on a training program with the B-24.

On February 12, the 431st BS/11th BG received word that its combat crews were to be transferred to Hamilton Field, California. Sgt. Handrow received his personal notification two days later. He wrote, "February 14, 1943 best news I ever got. My sailing papers for home came today . . . We're going home after three years away from it." While Handrow and his friends waited for transportation, the first batch of men from the 11th BG, 54 officers and enlisted men from the 98th BS, started back to the United States on February 14, some by ship and some by plane. On February 27, Sgt. Handrow and the other joyous members of the 431st BS finally boarded a ship and set sail the next day for home.[5]

The old B-17s of the 11th BG were passed on to the 23rd and 31st BSs of the 5th BG while new B-24s were going to the 72nd BS. Also, since no additional parts existed in the South Pacific Area for the B-24s, the mechanics began stripping the old B-17s for parts for the B-24s. "Most of our B-17s were past due for change," wrote mechanic Roy Davenport, "many hours plus the damage was the reason some were pushed over into a bone yard. We used some of the B-17 parts that would fit to keep the 24s in the air, as parts were going to England at that time."[6]

Having been in the South Pacific Area longer than any other 5th BG squadron, the 72nd BS became one of the first units to make the full change from B-17s to B-24s. Near the end of February, the original crews of the 72nd BS were grounded and their B-17s were given to the 23rd and 31st BSs. While the veterans were retrained to fly B-24s, new B-24s and their crews began arriving from the States and were assigned to the 72nd BS.[7]

Starting in March, the 5th BG, for the first time since moving to the South Pacific Area, began operating as an independent unit. After acquiring the old B-17s from the 11th BG, and from the 72nd BS, its sister outfit, the 31st BS became the first operational unit. On March 14, nine B-17s from the 31st moved up to Guadalcanal for "two or three weeks of prolonged night striking," joining their hard-working ground crews that had been on the 'Canal since December 8. Given the task of neutralizing Kahili Airfield on the southern tip of Bougainville, and the airfield on Buka Island, the squadron set out almost immediately, sending two planes over Kahili on March 16.[8]

Maj. George E. Glober, CO of the 31st BS, B-17E (41-9216, *Alley-Oop*), and Capt.

Jim Carroll, B-17E (41-9124, *Buzz King*), took off for the night mission against Kahili Field with each plane carrying eight 500-lb. bombs and three new M-26 flares. Intending to test the new 800,000-candlepower flares, the two planes made four passes over the airfield through heavy antiaircraft fire. Although each plane was hit by shrapnel, neither plane was badly damaged and nobody was hurt.[9] The first independent bombing mission of the 31st BS had been a success.

On March 19, B-17s of the 5th BG, along with B-24s of the 307th BG, bombed Kahili Airfield again, and dropped a few bombs on Ballale Airfield. On March 20, the 13th AF worked in conjunction with the Navy and Marine Corps to inaugurate aerial mine laying in the South Pacific Area. While B-17s and B-24s would hit Kahili Airfield, effectively drawing the attention of the Japanese searchlights and antiaircraft gunners, the Navy and Marine Corps planes planned to come in low and sow mines in nearby Shortland Harbor. Late on the evening of March 20, nine B-17s and nine B-24s set off from Guadalcanal. Leading the B-17s was Lt. Col. Marion Unruh, the 5th BG Executive Officer, B-17E (41-2523, *Goonie*).[10]

Capt. Carroll, leading one of three three-plane elements recalled, "The sky was clear except for a few scattered white fair-weather cumulus clouds." Worked out before hand, the B-17s were supposed to stay over the airfield for nine minutes. "Tonight the Jap gunners were confused," Carroll wrote as the planes started their runs. "The mission plan worked wondrous well, the [Navy and Marine bombers] were having a free run. The B-17s were getting all of the attention, as planned. Early on, the antiaircraft was wildly inaccurate. As the decoy run progressed, the bursts came closer and closer. Black puffs were appearing right off the wing tip."

Ignoring the incoming fire, the B-17s stayed around as planned, dropping fragmentation bombs on the enemy positions. Although the other bombers came away unscathed, Col. Unruh's B-17E *Goonie* was hit by antiaircraft fire and developed a runaway engine. Unable to remain airborne, Unruh made a safe water landing off the Russell Islands, near Guadalcanal and the crew was rescued the next day.[11]

In spite of the loss of B-17E (41-2523, *Goonie*), the mine-laying mission was successful, so the next night, March 21, 19 B-17s and B-24s returned to bomb Kahili while the Navy and Marine Corps bombers planted mines in the 20-fathom curve of the Buin-Tonolei area. This time, fortunately, all American planes and crews returned safely to Guadalcanal.[12]

Having run at least two very successful missions against Kahili airport, many of the 5th BG B-17s were crowded along Guadalcanal's two bomber airstrips on the night of March 23, loaded and ready to take off on another mission, when "Washing Machine Charlie" arrived. "Washing Machine Charlie was not to be denied," wrote Capt. Carroll. "His bomb struck [B-17E (41-9124, *Buzz King*)] amidships and triggered her bomb load, which ignited her fuel load. She disappeared in one magnificent swoosh!" A little later, B-17E (41-9060, *Zero-six-zero*) was hit by the nuisance bomber. Recalled reporter Mack Morriss, ". . . [the B-17] was blown to hell by Charlie, who dropped one alongside the plane which was loaded with eight 500-pounders . . . [The explosion left] a hole 40 feet wide & 30 feet deep—that was all." Two more B-17s had disappeared in the blink of an eye.[13]

In late March, the heavy rains came to the South Pacific Area turning the taxiways and revetments into seas of mud and cutting down on the missions flown by the 5th BG. Only the main runways, covered with steel matting, were not affected. At Espiritu Santo, the constant rains ended all work at trying to improve the squadron base camps. "Between the 5th Group Headquarters and the 23rd Squadron a river 100 feet wide and 20 feet deep with a raging current formed, and the roads became seas of mud," reported the 5th BG historian. "Clothing and equipment started to mold and mildew. The latest Spring fashion on Espiritu Santo: a form-fitting suit of khaki, bespattered with rain, caked with mud, against a mottled background of mold."[14]

Facing the rainy season, Movement Order #1, dated March 17, 1943, went into effect and the remaining veterans from the 11th BG began boarding the U.S. Army transport *President Polk* at Espiritu Santo on March 27. The next day, along with a convoy of other ships, the *President Polk* steamed off for Hawaii. Recalled Pvt. Belz, "The troop ship we had was a reconditioned German vessel that had been scuttled somewhere in South America by the Germans in the early days of the 'Hitler War,'. . . It didn't roll a bit, but it sure rocked when [the] waves became larger." For 11 days the *President Polk* steamed towards Hawaii, moving through waters infested with Japanese submarines. "The big trouble was that the engines would quit working periodically, and we would be left stranded," recalled Belz. "We watched our small convoy sail away, over the horizon, on numerous occasions. Once the crew got the engines working again, it didn't take us long to catch up with the convoy, as the [*President Polk*] sure had speed."[15]

Eleven days later, on April 8, the ship finally reached Oahu. "The 8th. The glorious 8th!" wrote a member from the 431st BS. ". . . [W]e gawked down upon clean uniforms—and WOMEN! . . . In turn they stared at our bearded faces and dirty, torn, damaged clothes—our shorts and shabby, make-shift attire. What the hell—we had been to war!" Surprisingly, one of the first orders the men received was to always carry their gas masks— "You are in a war zone now!"[16]

Upon reaching Hawaii, the different squadrons of the 11th BG were sent to separate sites around Oahu. The 26th BS was stationed at Bellows Airfield, the 42nd was assigned to Kualoa Point, the 98th joined the early arrivals from their unit at Mokuleia, and the 431st moved to Hickam Field. Planning to retrain the group on B-24s, the men were given the option of taking a 30-day furlough in the United States before returning to the 11th BG, or going to the United States to be reassigned to another B-17 unit. Commented the 42nd BS historian, "Approximately one third of the men chose the first course." The ratio was similar in the other 11th BG squadrons—two-thirds of the men went home for reassignment. The 11th BG had ceased to be a B-17 unit.[17]

The majority of the men that elected to be reassigned remained stateside. Among the number, Carlton Belz began work as a mechanic on a B-24 training base but later transferred to a B-29 base. Seymour Jenkins became an instructor at

Lowry Field in Colorado, and Seymour Blutt became an assistant crew chief at a training base in Tennessee. Only a few men ever went back into combat. Among them was Maj. James Edmundson who went on to command a B-29 unit, and Lt. Edwin Loberg who flew "about 40 missions" out of India and China in a B-29 Superfortress.[18]

With the removal of the 11th BG from the South Pacific, only two B-17 groups remained to fight the Japanese, the 5th BG in the Solomons, and the 43rd BG in New Guinea.

Bad weather grounded most of the 43rd BG B-17s in early February but did not prevent the B-24s of the 90th BG from moving up to Port Moresby on February 10. Almost immediately a friendly rivalry began between the B-17 crews and the B-24 crews. At one point, a B-24 crew, flying at high altitude, mistook a formation of rocks for a Japanese convoy. When a B-17 was sent out to confirm the sighting, the pilot radioed back, "The presence of the convoy of rocks in the Vitiaz Straits reported by a recco plane of the 90th Bombardment Group has been officially confirmed." Vowing vengeance, the 90th BG officers invited a bunch of 43rd BG officers to dinner at 90th BG base camp. When the 43rd BG officers arrived, they noticed a latrine off to one side displaying a placard proclaiming, "Headquarters, 43rd Bombardment Group." Able to hold their tongues through the evening meal, a lone 43rd BG B-17 showed up at daybreak and pumped a stream of incendiary bullets into the structure. "The little building blazed up as the B-17 kept on going until it disappeared behind the hills," Gen. Kenney wrote. "In a few minutes there was only one building in Port Moresby labeled Headquarters 43rd Bombardment Group . . ." Fortunately, no one was inside when the outhouse was strafed and although Kenney encouraged friendly competition between the two groups, he made it definitely clear that he did not want anything of that kind to take place again.[19]

By February 11 the bad weather had cleared enough for Gen. Kenney to turn his attention back to Rabaul. Utilizing both B-17s and B-24s, Kenney planned a massive raid against the Rabaul area on February 14–15. "Our 'St. Valentine's Day Massacre' raid on Rabaul was one of the biggest ever staged in that area," recalled Capt. Crawford. A total of 32 B-17s and four B-24s took off from Port Moresby to administer a thorough pounding of the Japanese stronghold. "Our attack had been carefully planned and our planes zoomed in at various heights over the town and over the docks lining Simpson Harbor," stated Crawford. While Gen. Kenney's reliable 63rd BS attacked the harbor area, the other squadrons hit the surrounding areas. "We blasted the Vunakanau, Rapapo [sic] and Lakanai [sic] airfields with their fuel and ammunition dumps, camp buildings, runways, sitting planes—anything that could be destroyed," Crawford noted. In all, the 36 American planes dropped approximately 50 tons of demolition bombs and over 4,000 incendiary bombs in the Rabaul area. "As we headed back to base," Crawford continued, "flames danced madly against a backdrop of rolling smoke that hung like a pall over the burning town."[20]

While most of the bombers returned to Port Moresby with only a few small antiaircraft holes, Capt. Staley, B-17F (41-24521, *Black Jack*), had a hard time over the target. Somehow arriving over the harbor 30 minutes early, he made a pass over the town and threw out some incendiaries. As he was pulling out of his bomb run, he was caught by a searchlight. "A few seconds after that," Staley wrote, "an ack-ack shell hit us, and went through the No. 3 engine supercharger, and up through the nacelle. It got the oil lines and all control levers to the No. 3 engine." Feathering the damaged engine, Staley eventually linked up with the other 63rd BS B-17s and dropped the rest of his bombs around Simpson Harbor. On the way home, the supercharger on his No. 2 engine went out and he was forced to fly back on two engines. "Got back this morning about 0730 after a hectic, rough mission," he wrote. Although the *Black Jack* made it safely back to Seven Mile Strip, it would take two weeks to replace the damaged engines and get the plane back into the air.[21]

Having run such a successful mission on February 14–15, Gen. Kenney sent his bombers back to Rabaul during the early morning hours of February 16. "We took off at 1 A.M. into beautiful weather and a starry sky," noted Capt. Crawford. "It was nice flying until we got about half way there, when we ran into a storm that gave us a terrific tossing around and broke up the formation." Only 17 B-17s managed to reach Rabaul and drop 35 tons of demolition bombs and 1,400 incendiaries but even these planes had a hard time finding something to hit. "Below us was a layer of clouds through which gigantic searchlight fingers kept poking up," stated Crawford. "We cruised around for nearly three-quarters of an hour, searching for a hole in the undercast to give us a view of the target . . . Then a strange thing happened . . . the undercast disappeared completely, vanished right before our eyes. It left us in a nasty fix, right over the center of Simpson Harbor."[22]

Although Crawford tried to get out of the exposed area, he was caught by the enemy searchlights and suffered severely. "The Japs were shooting hell out of us," he recalled. After jettisoning his bombs on the enemy docks, Crawford's B-17 was hit numerous times by shell fire. "While our bomb bay doors were closing, a shell hit our left wing, shot right through its gas tank and out again without exploding . . . A second later another shell exploded in our right wing, knock[ing] off a portion of the aileron and cut[ting] the aileron cable on that side." Unable to take evasive action because of the cut cables, Crawford was forced to fly a straight line until he was beyond the range of the searchlights and guns.

"The plane was so badly damaged that I was barely able to keep it under control," Crawford remembered. Turning the steering wheel around one and a half times he was able to tighten the slack on the left aileron cable, giving him some control of the plane. Running into the same terrible weather that had plagued the B-17 formation on the way to Rabaul, Crawford struggled to keep the plane airborne until he was safely on the ground at Port Moresby. "Those Boeing Fortresses can stand terrific punishment," he praised, "but to this day I can't see how that one kept in the air."[23]

When Radio Tokyo finally announced that the Japanese were giving up on

Guadalcanal, Gen. Kenney feared that the enemy would step up operations in New Guinea. Figuring that the Japanese would take advantage of the bad weather and send another large convoy towards Lae, Kenney told his reconnaissance planes to keep their eyes open. However, before anything could be sighted, he received word from Gen. MacArthur that the South Pacific needed the B-17s of the Southwest Pacific again. Admiral Halsey was planning an invasion of the Russell Islands, 55 miles northwest of Guadalcanal on February 21 and since the 11th BG was being dismantled, and Gen. Harmon had only a handful of operational heavy bombers at his disposal, Halsey was asking for Gen. MacArthur to bomb shipping in the Northern Solomons prior to the invasion. As usual, MacArthur agreed.[24]

Luckily, the bad weather cleared enough for Gen. Kenney to send 11 B-17s from the 63rd and 64th BSs, led by Capt. McCullar, against the Buin-Faisi area on the night of February 17–18. Carrying four 1,000-lb. bombs each, the planes left Port Moresby at 4:30 P.M. and flew to Milne Bay, where they topped off their gas tanks. Since the bombers had been ordered to skip bomb the enemy ships, the planes began lifting off at 11:00 P.M., hoping to arrive over the target just as the full moon was rising, thus providing back-lighting for the skip bombing.

"Each was on his own to search and destroy," wrote Lt. Murphy. Reaching the Buin-Faisi area, the 63rd BS planes swept in low, skipping bombs across the surface of the water at a number of different vessels. Lt. Dieffenderfer struck the bow of a 8,000-ton cargo ship, stopping it dead in the water, and then Lt. Murphy came along and placed two bombs alongside, sinking the vessel. In addition, Murphy skip bombed another cargo ship which was eventually beached to save it from sinking. Capt. McCullar once again badly damaged an 8,000-ton transport, while Capt. Staley caused damage to a 7,000-ton vessel, and Lt. Woodrow W. Moore caused considerable damage to a 3,000-ton cargo ship. In return, a few of the Fortresses were slightly damaged by heavy antiaircraft fire but nobody was injured and all 11 planes returned safely to Port Moresby.[25]

The following night, February 18–19, eight B-17s and six PBYs returned to the Buin-Faisi area again. After discovering that the Japanese had moved all of their shipping out of the area the planes bombed the seaplane base and the airfields at Kahili and on Ballale Island, destroying a number of aircraft and setting fire to large stores of aviation fuel. The next night, B-17s from the 65th BS hit the landing strip at Kahili and set fire to the floatplane base at Ballale.[26] On February 21, American Army troops stormed ashore in the Russell Islands, meeting no opposition whatsoever.[27]

Having completed their obligation to bomb the Buin-Faisi area for Admiral Halsey, Ken's Men turned their attention back to Rabaul. Six planes from the 65th BS attacked the enemy shipping in Rabaul's Tahili Bay during the night of February 22–23. Capt. Dollenberg dropped four bombs close beside a cargo vessel, which caused the ship to list to one side. Another bomber started fires in the dock area, and still another dropped his bombs on a heavy cruiser with unobserved results. During the bombings, one of the B-17s was caught in the enemy searchlights and the pilot put the plane into a steep dive before leveling out. Perhaps thinking that the plane was going down, the tail gunner bailed out and was lost forever.[28]

The following night the B-17s returned to Rabaul, hitting shipping in Simpson Harbor, and on the night of February 24–25, six planes from the 63rd BS went back again. In spite of heavy antiaircraft fire and the sweeping searchlights, Capt. Thompson made two successful skip bombing runs against a 7,000-ton seaplane carrier, and Lts. Dieffenderfer and O'Brien scored near misses on Japanese cargo vessels.[29]

During the day, Gen. Kenney received word that the Japanese were assembling a convoy for a run to either Lae or Madang that was expected to be at least twice the size of the January 7 convoy. With the news in hand, Kenney instructed Gen. Whitehead to have his reconnaissance planes cover the Wewak-Admiralties-Kavieng-Rabaul area to insure an early sighting of the ships. Then, Kenney told him to hit the convoy with everything he had, night and day, until every ship was sunk. Since Kenney expected the Japanese to bring a large number of airplanes to Lae and Gasmata to cover the arrival of the convoy, he instructed Whitehead to move his fighter planes up to the American airfield at Dobodura to counteract the enemy fighters. And finally, since he wanted to have all the heavy bombers in good condition and ready to fight, Kenney told Whitehead "to go easy on all bomber missions from now until March 5th, so that the maintenance crews could get the squadrons up to maximum strength."[30]

On the morning of February 26, a reconnaissance plane spotted a convoy of four large and three small cargo vessels 100 miles southwest of Rabaul, in the Bismarck Sea. Although the convoy seemed too small to be the anticipated convoy, eight planes from the 63rd BS set out immediately but were unable to find the ships because of deteriorating weather conditions. While the 63rd BS planes were out looking for the enemy ships, four planes from the 65th BS hit the Wewak area. Capt. Arthur Fletcher skip bombed an enemy transport, which sank in five minutes, while the other planes started fires on the Wewak airdrome. Additionally, a flight of B-17s and B-24s bombed the airfield at Gasmata, while single B-17s hit the airfields at Lae and Salamaua.[31]

Late in the afternoon of February 27, while Ken's Men were "working like mad getting every airplane in shape so that we could strike with everything we owned when the time came," a reconnaissance plane picked up the small convoy about 100 miles from Kavieng, headed west. Still doubtful that the convoy constituted the major reinforcing move, and with bad weather still hampering any American strikes, Gen. Kenney held his planes in check and continued his searches.[32]

The next day, the weather worsened north of the Vitiaz Strait, over the Bismarck Sea, and no sightings were reported. Early on March 1, while a flight of B-17s bombed the runway at Gasmata, a searching B-24 suddenly spotted a convoy of eight Japanese destroyers and eight cargo ships about 150 miles west of Rabaul, in the Bismarck Sea and heading towards the Vitiaz Strait. Seven B-17s from the 63rd BS, led by Capt. Tommy Thompson, took off immediately from Port Moresby. "The ceiling and visibility were so limited that they had to search at 50 to 100 feet off the water," reported Lt. Murphy. "They even turned the aircraft lights on to attract enemy fire from the warships." Unfortunately, the B-17s had been given the wrong coordinates and after four hours of fruitless searching returned to Port Moresby empty handed.[33]

Knowing that the convoy was out there, Lt. Herbert Derr (63rd BS) took off at 4:00 P.M. in B-17F (41-24384, *Pluto*), heading towards the right coordinates. Although hindered by bad weather and thick clouds, Derr somehow managed to find the convoy and began shadowing it. Antiaircraft fire and enemy Zeros rose up to greet the B-17 but Derr kept circling above the ships, all the while radioing its location and direction to headquarters. Even though the *Pluto*, carrying two bomb bay fuel tanks, was hit repeatedly by the attacking Zeros, Derr hung onto the convoy for 11 hours and 20 minutes. When he finally returned to Port Moresby everyone knew where the convoy was. The hungry hunters from the 43rd BG had been given the information they needed to attack.[34]

XXVII

The Bismarck Sea

Capt. Crawford, B-17E (41-2609, *Loose Goose*), picked up the Japanese convoy, actually consisting of eight destroyers, seven transports and one special service vessel, around 2:00 A.M. on March 2. "The weather was thick and it was raining hard," Crawford wrote. "It was a grueling job tailing those ships through the night. The difference in speed between a Flying Fortress and a slow cargo or warship is tremendous, but I was determined not to let that convoy get out of my sight." For almost four hours Crawford hung tenaciously to the convoy. "As the skies grayed into morning, the weather cleared enough for us to distinguish our quarry . . . They were rounding the northwestern tip of New Britain from the Bismarck Archipelago and heading southward towards Lae." Near 6:00 A.M., Crawford was instructed to return to base, as the 43rd BG went to work.[1]

Near 6:30 A.M., eight planes from the 63rd BS carrying 1,000-lb. bombs, took off from Seven Mile Strip. Led by Maj. Scott, the squadron CO, B-17F (41-24537, *Talisman*), and escorted by a flight of P-38s carrying long-range gas tanks, the bombers started out over the hump of the Owen Stanley Mountains. Running into terrible weather, the B-17s lost their protective escorts but went on as planned, reaching the Japanese ships about 10:00 A.M.[2]

Coming over the mountains, a supercharger went out on Capt. Staley's Fortress, and Maj. Scott and Lt. Frank Denault sidled in beside him for protection. "The other Fortresses went ahead and we stayed behind," recalled Scott, "but we hit the convoy first. Suddenly, the clouds cleared slightly and though it was still raining like hell we could see the ships below us." Coming in at 6,500 feet, the three B-17s went after a 10,000-ton transport. "Then the Zeros hit us," Scott went on. "There were eight of them. They made a double coordinated attack both high and low." As their gunners fought to keep the Zeros away, and antiaircraft fire thundered around them, the three pilots went into their bomb runs. While three of Maj. Scott's bombs hit the vessel amidships, Capt. Staley placed one on the bow

333

and Lt. Denault put one on the stern. "These were all 1,000-pound bombs and the big transport went up in one huge puff of smoke."[3]

While Scott's bombers were on their run, Lt. Murphy, B-17F (41-24381, *Panama Hattie*), with Capt. Sogaard, B-17F (41-24520, *Fightin' Swede*), on his wing, went after one of the escorting destroyers. "We were bounced violently by the heavy guns of the cruiser [sic] . . ." Murphy remembered. "We released two of our 1000-pound bombs. I had never felt such violent turbulence as that created by those cruiser guns. I had been hit in many instances by antiaircraft guns but had never been tossed through the sky like that." Unfortunately, Murphy's bombs missed so he circled through the protective clouds, dropped down to 1,000 feet and made a skip bombing attack on the 8,000-ton transport *Kyokusei Maru*.

"With the warships and Zeros firing at me, I had to drop our remaining bombs and get away quickly," Murphy said. Dropping to masthead height, Murphy came in on the ship's broadside and dropped his last two bombs. "I quickly dove for the water," he wrote, "and headed for the nearest weather to get away from all the guns." Hearing the joyful shouts of his crewmen who had witnessed the destruction of the Japanese transport, Murphy turned around to get his own look at the ship. "I turned the plane around, dropped closer to the water, and saw one end of the transport pointed toward the sky," he said. "The ship had been split apart and was sinking."[4]

Not to be outdone, Capt. Sogaard skip bombed a 5,000-ton transport and stopped the ship dead in the water.[5] The eight 63rd BS B-17s had dropped a total of 28 bombs, sinking two large transports while seriously damaging a third.[6] However, the Japanese achieved a bit of retribution.

Lt. Dieffenderfer, B-17F (41-24455, *Old Baldy*), was jumped by the swarming Zeros in the midst of his bomb run and put his plane into a steep dive. Reaching a speed of 280 mph he tore the fabric skin off both of his elevators. Using all of their strength, Dieffenderfer and his copilot somehow managed to pull out of the dive but without the elevator fabric, the plane would not fly level. The slightest turbulence caused the plane to shoot straight up or dive straight down. For nearly three hours the two pilots struggled to keep the plane level while trying to gain altitude to get over the Owen Stanley Mountains. Somehow, the *Old Baldy* stayed aloft, climbed high enough and brought Dieffenderfer and his crew safely home to Port Moresby.[7]

Sometime later, near 11:00 A.M., twenty B-17s led by Maj. McCullar, reached the convoy. Ignoring heavy antiaircraft fire and enemy fighters, 11 B-17s from the 64th BS went after the transports, scored one direct hit on a 6,000-ton transport, which exploded and sank, and had a near miss on another.[8]

Five planes from the 65th BS and four from the 403rd BS, working together, bombed from about 6,500 feet. Capts. Cromer and Fletcher each managed to hit a cargo ship and set it on fire. Lt. James L. Easter (65th BS) scored a near miss on a destroyer, while Capt. Harcrow had a direct hit and two near misses on a transport. Easter and Harcrow were attacked by a dozen Zeros but Capt. Harcrow's crew managed to shoot down two of the pesky fighters. Reported the 43rd BG historian, "The Jap fighter pilots are not the inexperienced type we have been meeting, these are good pilots." When the B-17s finally left, three enemy fighters had been shot down, two transports had been sunk and two more were left burning and dead in the water. While the other ships continued southwest, two destroyers stayed behind to pick up survivors.[9]

Still unsure of the final destination of the convoy, a reconnaissance B-17 began shadowing the ships shortly after the other B-17s left. At 3:30 P.M. it was reported that two more destroyers had joined the convoy, perhaps the same two destroyers that had stayed behind to rescue survivors. Two hours later, the two destroyers broke away and headed for Lae under forced draft. Near 6:30 P.M., with darkness closing down, five B-17s from the 64th BS and three from the 403rd, all led by Maj. McCullar, returned.[10]

Braving a fusillade of antiaircraft fire and an attack by 18 Zeros, the B-17s dropped a total of 43 bombs on the enemy ships but landed only one hit. Capt. Robert L. Schultz (64th BS) dropped one 1,000-lb. bomb directly on the bow of a 6,000-ton transport. As he climbed for altitude, the ship was quickly settling by the bow. Ken's Men had accounted for another transport, their fifth, and one more Zero.[11]

During the attack, the persistent Zeros wounded five members of Capt. Holsey's crew and cut his hydraulic fluid line, which sprayed flaming liquid all over the bomb bay. "They've got us—we're falling—so long," Holsey shouted into the command radio as his B-17 began to descend towards the sea. Capt. Giddings heard the words and called out, "Hold on Ray, I'll be right down," and quickly pushed his bomber into a steep dive.

Grabbing a fire extinguisher, Holsey's copilot, Lt. Vernon Reeves, and two of his crewmen, Sgts. Young and Rosenberg, soaked their heavy flying coats with extinguisher fluid and worked hard to smother the flames. "It's sure hot in here," Holsey told Giddings over the command radio. "Yeah, Ray," Giddings answered, "does look kind of warm. Y' look like a kettle on a stove." As Giddings circled for protection, Holsey's crewmen managed to extinguish the blaze. Both Lt. Reeves and Sgt. Rosenberg received second degree burns, and although only the naked spars of the belly fuselage remained, Holsey somehow nursed his plane home and landed safely at Seven Mile Strip.[12]

The afternoon air strike concluded the attacks for March 2. Throughout the night, a Royal Australian Air Force PBY kept contact with the convoy, watching its every twist and turn and at 5:45 A.M. on March 3, Lt. William Trigg (63rd BS) relieved the PBY just as the sun was coming up. Though hit repeatedly by about 10 Zeros, Trigg continued to stay with the convoy and report its position. Having passed through the Vitiaz Strait, the convoy had rounded the tip of the Huon Peninsula and had turned southwest for Lae.[13]

Unfortunately for the Japanese, the weather had cleared considerably. Taking advantage of the nearness of the convoy and the good weather, 106 Allied planes assembled over Cape Ward Hunt and prepared to attack the convoy in waves. Having had previous knowledge of the enemy ships, the Allies had worked out a well-coordinated plan. Seven torpedo-carrying RAAF Beauforts attacked first but had no success. Next came 13 RAAF Beaufighters, each armed with four nose cannons and six wing machine guns. Sweeping in just above the water they sprayed the enemy ships with deadly fire. At almost the same time, 15 B-17s, led by Maj. McCullar, and escorted by a squadron of P-38 fighters, came in overhead. "It was a beautiful tropical morning," recalled Maj. Harold T. Hastings (64th BS). "Just a few scattered clouds at 10,000 feet, and below us the convoy spread out over an area of 15 miles. Two cruisers [sic] led the parade, with destroyers flanking the big fat transports. As always with Jap transports, the decks were packed with troops."[14]

A band of Zeros ignored the Beaufighters and went after the Fortresses but the circling P-38s reacted quickly and went after the Zeros. As individual dogfights broke out, the B-17s attacked.

Once again the planes from the 65th BS claimed a number of hits, although no ships were sunk. Four different pilots claimed at least one hit on the transports while Capt. Fletcher claimed a hit on a large destroyer. Unfortunately, while Lt. Easter was making his bomb run he was jumped by the Zeros. His radioman, engineer and one gunner were wounded but Easter kept on the run. Then, suddenly, bullets slashed through the flight deck and hit Easter in the head and chest, mortally wounding him. Easter's copilot, Lt. Russell Emerick, took control of the plane, finished the bomb run and then quickly pulled out of formation. Despite having never landed a B-17 by himself before, and in spite of the fact that the plane was full of holes and had no brakes, Emerick made a perfect landing at an emergency field at Dobodura. Unfortunately, Lt. Easter died later in the day.[15]

Capt. Crawford and Capt. Ealon S. Halcutt (403rd BS) were flying in echelon and were beginning their bomb run at 7,000 feet when they were suddenly hit by about 15 Zeros. "Making pass after pass, they rolled under us, peppering away with their machine guns, then diving on top of us," Crawford wrote. "Antiaircraft shells were coming up on all sides right through their own Zeros . . . Suddenly I saw Halcutt's plane lurch, right itself and peel out of our two-plane formation." Unknown to Crawford, Japanese bullets had come through Halcutt's flight deck, wounding the engineer and hitting Halcutt in the head. Halcutt's copilot took control and immediately left the battle zone without dropping his bombs, racing back to base in time to save Halcutt's life.[16]

Left all alone, Crawford's B-17 suffered from repeated attacks by the sweeping Zeros. "Our bomb-sight and our hydraulic and oxygen system were knocked out," Crawford reported. "Part of our tail fabric was shot off, holes riddled the rudder, wings, and fuselage. Shattered glass littered the floor." Crawford's bombardier was hit in the knee, and two gunners were wounded by antiaircraft fire. Without his hydraulic system, the ball turret was useless. In addition, the top turret jammed because the guns overheated, one of the two tail guns jammed, and one of the waist guns suffered a broken extractor.

With most of his guns out, and three wounded men aboard, Crawford dropped to 4,000 feet and made a bomb run on a destroyer. Since his bombardier was wounded, and the bomb sight out, Crawford's navigator toggled the 1,000-lb. bombs by guesswork, scoring two near misses. Heading back to Port Moresby, Crawford ran into more trouble. "The engines started acting up and not developing anything like full power," he recalled. "Highly flammable hydraulic fluid was running all over the ship, gas was leaking out and a spark might set us on fire at any minute. I felt damned uncomfortable."

Successfully reaching Seven Mile Strip, Crawford next faced the hazard of landing his bomber without any brakes because of the loss of hydraulic fluid, and at high speed because of the damage to his elevators. Coming in fast and hard, Crawford got to the end of the runway and tried to ground loop the plane. "The Fort swung round like a top and spun round seven times," he wrote. "I tried to slow the spin by opening up the two right engines to counteract the pull. It stopped the spin but started the plane directly down the runway at a pretty good clip." Turning off the runway, Crawford finally stopped the bomber by running into some soft mud. "We'd had an awfully narrow squeak," Crawford admitted.[17]

Four planes from the 63rd BS, flying the buddy system, were intercepted by the enemy fighters before they could hit the transports. Capt. Bill Thompson, B-17F (41-24381, *Panama Hattie*), and Lt. Neil Kirby were hit by about 10 Zeros but Thompson's gunners were able to shoot down three of the attackers. At the same time, Lt. Denault, B-17F (41-24358, *Lulu Belle*), and Lt. Moore, B-17F (41-24356, *Ka-Puhio-Wela*), were hit by eight Japanese fighters. Although Denault's gunners shot down two of the planes, a third attacked from below and started a fire in Moore's wing root or radio compartment. Moore pulled away from Denault and salvoed his bombs before a small explosion rocked the B-17 and the plane began to go down. Seven men baled out but one man had apparently failed to secure his harness and plummeted to his death. As the others floated helplessly towards earth, the buzzing Zeros strafed the unarmed men and shot the parachute canopies full of holes.

Lt. Moore, still flying the plane, held the nose up a few minutes longer before suddenly going into a steep dive. Just before he hit the water, B-17F (41-24356, *Ka-Puhio-Wela*) exploded and disintegrated. It is believed that Moore and his copilot were killed in the explosion, while the seven crewmen were never seen again.[18]

Justly upset over the strafing of the men in the parachutes, Ken's Men swore vengeance against the Japanese. However, during the early morning attack only two crews scored crippling hits on the enemy vessels. Capt. Giddings dropped a bomb smack on the center of one transport, causing it to crack open and sink, and Maj. Hastings caused severe damage to another. "We dropped four 1000-pounders and they walked right up to the ship," Hastings said. "The last one missed the bow by only twenty feet and [the ship] started smoking. He was a lame duck, just sitting there waiting for the B-25s, which came in on the next wave at masthead height and blew him out of the water."[19]

By their own account, the B-17s had managed to sink one transport, their sixth in two days, and badly damage another, and had scored hits on five more ships.

As the B-17s and the low-level Beaufighters flew away, 13 B-25s made a bombing run from medium altitude but scored no hits. However, hot on the heels of the first group were 12 more B-25s, flying at 500 feet and using skip bombing. Easily the most successful attack wave of the day, the second group of B-25s hit 11 different ships, sinking one destroyer and one transport. Joining the attack were 12 A-20s, who scored 11 more hits, and six more B-25s, who reported an additional four hits. Having lost only three P-38s and one B-17, the Allies returned to base, rearmed and refueled their planes, and started back in the midafternoon to finish what they had begun.[20]

By now the weather had turned sour again and a large number of Allied planes failed to get over the Owen Stanley Mountains. When Maj. Scott's wingman, Lt. Dieffenderfer developed engine trouble and was forced to turn back, Scott, B-17F (41-24574, *Tuffy*), attached himself to five other B-17s from other squadrons. At 3:12 P.M., all six B-17s, seeking revenge for Lt. Moore's crewmen, struck at the remaining enemy ships. Spotting a destroyer making a run back towards Vitiaz Strait, Scott dropped two bombs on the ship and set it on fire, stopping it dead in the water. As the Japanese abandoned ship, Scott and the other B-17s came down to 50 feet above the water and began strafing the men. "Everyone in the Group would have given much to have been in on the strafing after what had happened to Lt. Moore and his men," reported the 43rd BG historian. "One gunner expended 1,100 rounds and burned out 2 guns."[21]

Eight B-25s followed the strafing attack by the B-17s, going after Maj. Scott's damaged destroyer. Again, the B-25s caused heavy damage, sinking the destroyer and one other, and causing severe damage to two transports. Ten minutes later, 15 more B-25s showed up and claimed 10 more direct hits on the enemy ships. Five RAAF Boston bombers arrived next and went after a destroyer, scoring two direct hits and sinking it. And, while the B-25s and Bostons were attacking, the six B-17s circled around and came over on a bomb run from medium altitude. Unfortunately, they made no hits.[22]

The afternoon strikes were the last coordinated attacks of the Battle of the Bismarck Sea. For the remainder of the day, single reconnaissance planes flew over the area and strafed anything Japanese, and during the night a few American PT boats came out and finished off a crippled destroyer. On the morning of March 4, Capt. Dollenberg spotted a lone destroyer streaking back to Rabaul. Dropping bombs alongside the ship, Dollenberg managed to stop the ship dead in the water, leaving it easy prey for three B-25s that came along later and sank it.[23]

At almost the same time, Lts. Murphy, Derr and Dieffenderfer from the 63rd BS, having failed to find any more surviving Japanese ships turned towards Lae and spotted six large landing barges about 10 miles off shore. "The flat-bottom boats were filled with soldiers and some sailors," reported Murphy. "I took my two wingmen down to twenty or thirty feet. I had my nose gun loaded and ready. I then initiated a strafing exercise that was unmerciful." Avenging Lt. Moore's crew, the three B-17s strafed the loaded barges time and again. Four Zeros eventually showed up to defend their countrymen but the B-17 gunners shot two of them to pieces. However, three people were hit on Lt. Dieffenderfer's B-17, including Dieffenderfer himself. Still, by the time the B-17s flew away the six barges were left sinking and hundreds of Japanese soldiers were dead. "We didn't miss anyone or anything," wrote Murphy. ". . . When we left the area, not one Japanese was seen alive in the water."[24]

The Battle of the Bismarck Sea was over. The battle was a complete, resounding victory for the Allies. For the loss of three fighters and one B-17, and the loss of 13 airmen, the Allies had stopped a maximum effort by the Japanese to resupply their forces in New Guinea. The Japanese lost a total of seven transports, one special service vessel, and four destroyers, along with 59 planes destroyed, another twenty-four probables, and nine damaged. Although many Imperial soldiers and sailors were rescued from the sinking ships, only about 850 made it to Lae, the others being brought back to Rabaul. Still, it was thought that the Japanese lost approximately 3,000 men. For their part in the battle, the B-17s were credited with sinking six vessels, and damaging many more, thus allowing the other Allied planes a chance to swoop in and administer the killing blows.[25]

Rightfully overjoyed with the Battle of the Bismarck Sea, Gen. MacArthur extended his thanks to the Allied airmen and Gen. Kenney sent his own message of thanks to Gen. Whitehead. "Congratulations on that stupendous success," he wrote. "Air Power has written some important history in the past three days. Tell the whole gang that I am so proud I am about to blow a fuse."[26]

Although the 43rd BG had helped achieve a major victory over the Japanese, it had not come without cost. Almost every plane in the Group had received some form of damage. Consequently, only individual planes went out over the next few days on harassment strikes against Lae and Gasmata. On March 8, Lt. Ehlers took off in B-17F (41-24403, *Blitz Buggy*, now painted with the likeness of "Uncle Sam" and rechristened *The Old Man*) for a routine reconnaissance of Gasmata. Spotting bomb craters on the enemy runway, the crew felt relatively safe until they saw enemy planes taking off over the painted artificial craters.

"We started climbing fast," recalled bombardier Lt. Lloyd Boren (65th BS), "and I salvoed the bombs and bomb bay tank. We were hopped by 13 Zeros, and had about a ten-to-fifteen minute running fight with them." Ehlers tried staying in the clouds while his gunners fought hard to defend the Fortress. Five Zeros were shot down but *The Old Man* took quite a pounding. Using head-on attacks, the Zeros wounded all four of the officers in the nose and on the flight deck, including Lt. Ehlers. With the wounded copilot and the flight engineer flying the plane, *The Old Man* was landed safely at Dobodura where Ehlers and Lt. Boren, who had been wounded in five places, were quickly evacuated to a hospital.[27]

On March 10, the 43rd BG received a new commanding officer when Col. Roger Ramey was promoted to chief of staff of 5th Bomber Command and Maj. John A. Roberts, the CO of the 65th BS, was promoted to lieutenant colonel and given command of the group.[28] That same date, a flight of B-17s hit Wewak and on March 12, twelve planes from the 65th BS struck Lakunai Airdrome at Rabaul.

Noted the squadron historian, "The bombing results were excellent as many fires and explosions were observed."[29]

The next day, a B-17 from the 403rd BS spotted another Japanese convoy in the Bismarck Sea headed towards Wewak. At 5:00 P.M. six planes from the 63rd BS set out to stop the convoy, this time consisting of three warships, four transports and a tanker. While a couple of planes dropped illuminating flares, Maj. Scott, B-17F (41-24574, *Tuffy*), made a skip bombing run. The 4,000-ton tanker and a 8,000-ton transport were in perfect alignment and Scott scored direct hits, sinking both vessels with one bomb run. "For the first time in the Pacific war as far as is known," commented the 63rd BS historian, "two boats were sunk on a single bomb run." Only slightly less successful were Lts. Murphy and Kirby. Murphy caused major damage to a transport and a destroyer, while Kirby hit another 8,000-ton transport.[30]

Five B-17s from the 64th BS tried to hit Wewak on March 15 but the weather turned to heavy rain and fog and the mission was aborted. On the way home however, Lt. Arthur McMullen, B-17F (41-24424, *Hell from Heaven Men*), ran out of fuel and made a crash landing at sea off Buna. Only the copilot, bombardier and radio operator managed to get out of the rapidly sinking bomber but as the three men were swimming to shore, the radio operator fell behind and eventually drowned. The copilot and bombardier reached shore after 14 hours of swimming but one more bomber and seven more men were gone.[31]

For the rest of the month, Ken's Men repeatedly bombed Wewak, Gasmata, Finschhaven, and Rapopo airfield south of Rabaul, and Lakunai airfield north of Rabaul. On March 22, 10 planes from the 63rd BS flew a special mission to Rabaul. While nine planes dropped incendiaries and demolition bombs on the city, Capt. Hustad dropped two 2,000-lb. bombs directly into Rabatana Crater, an active volcano near Rabaul. "Everyone hoped that the bombs could cause the lava to flow again," wrote Lt. Murphy. "That, of course, would necessitate the evacuation of the town as well as the runway and aircraft." Unfortunately, the volcano never erupted.[32]

On March 26, 5th Bomber Command lost another commander. While on a long-range reconnaissance mission to the Carolina and Mariana Islands, Gen. Howard Ramey and six other men, in B-17F (41-24384, *Pluto*) disappeared without a trace. Although flights of B-17s searched for the missing plane, nothing was ever found. Once again Gen. Whitehead took temporary charge of 5th Bomber Command.[33]

XXVIII

The Isolation of Rabaul

By THE BEGINNING of April 1943 Gen. MacArthur was staring at Rabaul. MacArthur knew that Rabaul was the key to Japanese resistance in the Southwest Pacific. If he could get the supplies and men that he needed, which seemed unlikely at this stage in the war, he wanted to start a drive up the coast of New Guinea to capture Lae and Salamaua. Then he planned to capture a number of islands around Rabaul and isolate the Japanese stronghold. In the meantime, he wanted Gen. Kenney to keep the pressure on the Japanese and prevent any further build-up of his forces in New Guinea.[1]

After Rabaul was bombed repeatedly during March, the Japanese moved most of their shipping to Kavieng harbor, so on April 4, and for the next four days, the B-17s and B-24s of the 5th AF hit Kavieng. In the four days, five pilots from the 63rd BS scored damaging hits on the Japanese vessels. Capt. Bob Keatts hit a destroyer, Lt. O'Brien hit a cargo vessel, and Lt. Dieffenderfer hit a light cruiser. Lt. Murphy continued his good luck and skip bombed a cargo vessel carrying a load of petroleum, which exploded in a roar of flames, and Capt. Bill Thompson sank the 5,854-ton *Florida Maru*.[2]

Keeping the heat on, single B-17s went out during April 5 to 9 and struck at targets of opportunity at Cape Gloucester on New Britain, and at Wewak, Finschhaven, Lae, and Salamaua on New Guinea. Not all of the strikes were milk runs. On April 7, Capt. Harcrow received 20 holes from antiaircraft fire but returned safely to Port Moresby. On April 10, a combined force of B-17s and B-24s struck at Wewak again, hitting the town and dock area, and on April 11, nine B-17s were sent out to hit Vunakanau, Lakunai, and Rapopo airfields around Rabaul. Running into bad weather, five of the planes turned back but the other four that got through started a number of fires in the area.[3]

"In April of 1943 the 64th [BS] received its most severe blow to 64th's morale," noted the squadron historian. In fact, the severe blow fell upon the entire 43rd BG. Added the group historian, "Monday, April 12, 1943. A sad day in camp for all. Maj. Kenneth D. McCullar, . . . popular C.O. of the 64th Squadron and 8 members of his crew and 2 NCO's of the 63rd Squadron were killed when their fortress crashed in taking-off for a joint 64-65th Squadron attack on Rabaul." Around midnight on April 11–12, nine B-17s began taking off from Seven Mile Strip when Maj. McCullar, B-17E (41-9209, *Blues in the Night*), ran into trouble.[4]

Capt. Crawford was directly behind McCullar "As [McCullar's plane] lifted its nose and cleared the ground, I pushed my throttles wide open and started down the long strip," Crawford wrote. "McCullar's plane had risen only about fifty feet when it burst into flames, fell off on one wing and nose-dived to earth. There was a ghastly explosion as its bomb load detonated by the impact. Then followed great stabs of flame from burning gasoline." Already halfway down the runway, Crawford pulled up hard to get his plane into the air. "As soon as we were off the ground I tilted her nose up as much as I could and passed over the burning bomber, through the dense smoke and fingers of flame that seemed to be reaching up for us," he wrote. "It was awful. But we had to keep going."[5]

Although there was not enough left of B-17E (41-9209, *Blues in the Night*) to make a positive assessment of what had happened, most people felt that as McCullar was racing down the runway, a kangaroo hopped in front of his plane. Said the 43rd BG historian, "As a dead wallobie [sic] or kangaroo was found on the runway at daybreak, it is presumed Maj. McCullar's aircraft hit it, some part of the wheel assembly breaking and rupturing the hydraulic system."[6]

Lt. Murphy offered more on the accident:

> An automatic reaction of most people would have been to avoid hitting the animal. Ken may have lightly touched his brakes, but because of his speed, he may have created just enough friction to have the expander tube explode. The ground crews reported that when he raised his wheels, the fire was brought into the engine nacelle . . .[7]

The group historian continued, "The 43rd Group has lost a great guy, the Allied cause a gallant soldier and airman." Wrote Gen. Kenney, "[McCullar's] courage, his ability, and his accomplishments had become an inspiration to the rest of us."[8]

Maj. McCullar's loss seemed even more of a waste when the remaining B-17s ran into a heavy thunderstorm on the way to Lakunai and only Capt. Crawford reached the target. However, three other planes hit the airdromes at Gasmata and Rapopo. Although Crawford had ruptured an oil line in his No. 3 engine and was flying on only three engines, he bombed the Lakunai airdrome in the morning daylight, hitting an oil and ammunition dump. Getting clean away, Crawford ran into further trouble when his wings iced up over the Owen Stanley Mountains. "Ordinarily," Crawford wrote, "the plane would have rubber de-icer boots [along the leading edges of the wings] that we could inflate and deflate so as to crack up any ice and let it blow off. But, as luck would have it, our de-icer had been rotted by the intense heat and wasn't working."

"I had a feeling that everything was going wrong that day, and I wondered what would happen next," Crawford said. Although he made it safely over the mountains, he ran into a terrible hailstorm on his way to Port Moresby. "The hail-stones that pelted our plane sounded as if they were as big as a man's fist," he recalled. "The storm buffeted us so severely that some of our machine guns were knocked loose on their moorings. The ammunition boxes [were] tossed around crazily inside the plane and the hailstones cracked the plexi-glass in the turrets. Never before had I been in such a storm." Needless to say, Crawford was glad to make it safely back to Port Moresby.[9]

That same day, seven planes from the 63rd BS took off at 3:00 A.M. to bomb a small Japanese convoy spotted in Hansa Bay, New Guinea. Wise to the skip bombing tactics of the Americans, the Japanese had lowered the aim of their searchlights to water top level. Still, the B-17s were able to set fire to two large cargo ships and one smaller vessel, and leave a destroyer listing badly. However, the heavy antiaircraft fire badly damaged Capt. Denault's B-17 and seriously wounded two crewmen. In addition to having a shell pass through his stabilizer and explode inside his rudder, the throttle cables to the No. 3 and No. 4 engines were severed, making it impossible to control the speed of the engines. By skill-ful piloting however, Denault managed to fly his injured plane through a thick storm and land safely at Seven Mile Strip.[10]

On April 16, Gen. Kenney gave the 43rd BG the day off and held another medal ceremony. After decorating everyone that had earned a medal, Kenney announced that Col. Roger Ramey was taking command of 5th Bomber Command. That evening, since the Japanese were now running small convoys into Wewak and moving their supplies and reinforcements overland to Lae, six B-17s from the 65th BS set out to punish the Japanese ships in Wewak harbor. Capt. Crawford, B-17F (41-24403, *The Old Man*), sank an 8,000-ton transport, and 2nd Lts. Robert B. Corrie and Raymond W. Baldwin Jr., each sank a smaller ship. Upon landing in the darkness and a thick fog, Capt. Crawford almost collided with the B-17 of Lt. Baldwin, which had blown a tire and was stuck in the mid-dle of the runway. "I landed on the extreme end of the runway at about 120 miles an hour," Crawford recorded. "About fifty yards from the crippled bomber I swung off the runway completely and went around the plane . . . It was a mira-cle we made it."[11]

Although Capt. Crawford was able to avoid a collision on April 16, two other pilots were not so lucky the next day. While on a compass swing flight 30 miles southeast of Port Moresby, Capt. Giddings, B-17F (41-24355, *Dinah Might*), was involved in a midair collision with Capt. Charles N. McArthur Jr. (64th BS), B-17F (41-24425). The top one-third of Giddings' tail and rudder were chewed off but he somehow managed to land the *Dinah Might* safely at Seven Mile Strip. However, Capt. McArthur and six crewmen died when B-17F (41-24425) plummeted into the sea.[12]

By the middle of April the Japanese were running fewer and fewer convoys into New Guinea. With the lack of Japanese offensive moves in the Southwest Pacific, the B-17s began flying individual reconnaissance missions and attacking targets of opportunity, usually along the coast of New Guinea. When a target did present itself, there was often a spirited fight to see who could hit it first. Reported the 63rd BS historian, "To make matters worse shipping was getting so scarce that the boys were attempting to cut each other out on sightings. On April 19th [Lt.] O'Brien and [Capt.] Sogaard went after the same tanker in a nip and tuck match. The sinking was credited to Sogaard's crew."[13]

During the beginning of April, the 403rd BS, the reconnaissance squadron of the 43rd BG, which had moved from Milne Bay to Mareeba in January, was finally informed that it was to join the parent group at Port Moresby. By now, the 403rd BS was equipped with both B-17s and B-24s. On April 24, an advance echelon of the 403rd BS left Mareeba for New Guinea with the rest of the squadron personnel and equipment leaving on May 13. Wrote the squadron historian, "Upon their arrival there the history of the 403rd Squadron merges with that of the 43rd Group as a whole."[14]

As April came to a close Admiral Halsey came to Brisbane for a conference with Gen. MacArthur. Halsey was making preparations for an invasion of Rendova Island and New Georgia, with the ultimate objective of seizing the Japanese airfield at Munda and using it as a base of operations for the next move to isolate Rabaul. At the same time, MacArthur was planning to seize the Trobriand and Woodlark Islands off the northeast tip of New Guinea, and to force an amphibious landing at Nassau Bay, about twenty miles southeast of Salamaua. All of the operations were to take place around June 30. With air bases in the Trobriand and Woodlark Islands, Gen. Kenney would be able to send out fighters to escort his bombers on their raids against Rabaul. "When that time came," Kenney wrote, "I could smash Rabaul, make it untenable for both aircraft and shipping, and isolate the place with an air blockade. Then if we wanted to, we could bypass Rabaul and start moving west."[15]

The month of May started with one week of bad weather obstructing movements by both the Americans and the Japanese. On May 7, Capt. Heichel, B-17F (41-24518, *The Reckless Mountain Boys*), took off at 6:50 A.M. for a routine patrol towards Kavieng and Rabaul. Upon reaching Kavieng, the B-17 was jumped by several Zeros. While Heichel was trying to reach the safety of clouds, the Zeros set the No. 2 engine on fire, knocked out the ball turret and wounded the gunner. As the plane filled with gas fumes, Heichel dropped low to the water, hoping to keep his plane airborne but when the fighters knocked out his No. 1 engine, he was forced to make a water landing 50 yards off the New Britain shore. Unfortunately, as *The Reckless Mountain Boys* skidded across the surface of the water, the ball turret snagged a coral reef and the B-17 jerked to a halt, throwing the top turret out of place and trapping Capt. Heichel. After a few anxious moments, the others were able to free Heichel and scramble out of the plane. Out of the 11 people on *The Reckless Mountain Boys*, three were killed either in the crash or from enemy gunfire, and two were wounded. Wading to shore, the eight survivors were eventually captured by the Japanese and taken to Rabaul. Only Capt. Heichel, the copilot, and one other crewman survived to tell of their experience.[16]

That same day, seven B-17s from the 65th BS, along with six B-24s, staged a coordinated attack on the Madang airfield. A number of fires were started on the field but four bombers were shot up and three crewmen were slightly wounded. Capt. Zeamer had an oxygen tank explode under his seat and came away shaken but unhurt.[17]

On May 8, the 63rd BS lost another plane and crew. Capt. Robert N. Keatts, B-17F (41-24520, *Fightin' Swede*), was on a routine reconnaissance mission along the north coast of New Guinea when his plane suddenly disappeared somewhere north of Madang. Search planes went out almost immediately but nothing was ever found. B-17F (41-24520, *The Fightin' Swede*) and nine crewmen had simply ceased to exist. Commented the 63rd BS historian on the loss of Capts. Heichel and Keatts, "These were the first signs of combat fatigue in the 63rd."[18]

The Japanese introduced the 43rd BG to a new type of antiaircraft shell on May 11. Eight B-17s from the 65th BS set off to bomb Vunakanau but only six were able to reach the target. As the B-17s unloaded 25,000 pounds of bombs on the airfield, a couple of Japanese "Firework" bombs shot through the formation. Wrote Capt. Crawford, "As we pressed home the attack a huge red ball about the size of a basketball shot past my plane . . . The shell burst into about fifty fragments which sprayed out in fantastic colors. As they fell, each fragment exploded into two or three more and these in turn burst into two." Nobody ever figured out just what the new shells were supposed to do. Commenting on the shells, the 65th BS historian wrote, "Most beautiful, all colors, just like the 4th of July."[19]

Daily reconnaissance flights showed that the Japanese were building up their airpower around Rabaul and by May 14 there were 116 fighters and 84 bombers in the area. Since the Americans were planning to unload a number of cargo ships opposite Dobodura the next day, six B-17s and four B-24s visited Vunakanau airdrome during the night and dropped incendiary and fragmentation bombs on the field. Although the crews were uncertain of the amount of damage they had caused, they started a number of fires and the next day, only 22 Japanese bombers and 20 fighter planes came out to attack the American ships. In the ensuing air battle eight bombers and eight fighters were destroyed and the American ships were unloaded without interruption.[20]

During the middle of April a number of veteran pilots and crews from the 43rd BG reached the maximum number of rotation points and were shipped back to the United States. Among the men sent home was Col. Roberts, the CO of the 43rd BG, who was quickly replaced by Harry Hawthorne, now a major and late-CO of the 65th BS. In the 63rd BS, three crews were replaced on May 16 by men from the 380th BG, a B-24 unit new to the area, and on May 20, three crews from the 403rd BS, which had only recently moved up to Port Moresby, joined the 63rd BS "on assignment for training." Subsequently, three more veteran crews from the 63rd BS went home.[21]

On May 17, Capt. Crawford, B-17E (41-2609, *Loose Goose*), was on a "routine milk run" reconnaissance mission towards the Bismarck Archipelago when he passed over Gasmata and dropped three bombs on the crowded runway. Unfortunately, a fourth bomb got hung up in the racks and before he could unload it, the enemy antiaircraft fire knocked out the No. 4 engine and hit the *Loose Goose* in the nose, setting the plane on fire. "We were in a tough spot," Crawford wrote, ". . . fire in the nose, one engine out and a live bomb in the rack."

While his bombardier and navigator fought the fire in the nose compartment, another antiaircraft shell tore a foot-wide hole through the right wing of the *Loose Goose*. "Now we had a new hazard," Crawford said. "At our speed the pressure of the wind shrieking through the torn wing might rip the skin completely off." While Crawford was worried about the right wing and the fire in the nose, another antiaircraft shell hit the B-17 just behind the flight deck, peppering Crawford in the back with shrapnel and setting fire to the bomb bay gas tank, which in turn threatened to detonate the remaining bomb. Fortunately, after some anxious moments in which the copilot and another crewmen received serious burns, the flaming bomb bay tank and the live bomb were salvoed.

With his crewmen still battling the fire in the nose and eventually getting it extinguished, Crawford headed for the Owen Stanley Mountains but suddenly ran into a flight of Zeros. Although he managed to reach friendly cloud cover, the *Loose Goose* took a couple of strafing runs and Capt. Crawford took a bullet in the left leg. With his copilot badly burned, Crawford was forced to ignore the shrapnel wounds to his back and the bullet in his leg and guide his plane safely back to Port Moresby. When he finally landed, he discovered that his left wheel had been shot out. "The 'Loose Goose' wobbled crazily along the runway, her left wing dragging in the dirt," Crawford reported, ". . . a poor crippled bird on its last legs." Eventually the dragging wing stopped the plane, after which Capt. Crawford passed out. The entire crew was awarded a Silver Star for their actions on May 17 but B-17E (41-2609, *Loose Goose*) was too badly damaged to be repaired. She was eventually taken apart and used for spare parts.[22]

With the Japanese build-up at Gasmata and Rabaul, both bases became targets for Ken's Men during the second half of May. Although most raids were by individual planes, five planes from the 64th BS attacked Vunakanau airfield during the early morning hours of May 21. When the flight returned to base, however, two planes were missing. A remark on the 64th BS Weekly Status and Operations Report states, "Two planes missing [B-17E] 41-9244 [*Honikuu Okole*] and [B-17E] 41-9011 possibly collided near target."[23] In actuality, both were shot down by Japanese night fighters.

B-17E (41-9244, *Honikuu Okole*), piloted by Paul Williams, now a major, was passing over Vunakanau when it was caught in the enemy searchlights. CPO Shigetoshi Kudo maneuvered underneath it in a twin-engine Irving night fighter, specially equipped with two fixed 20-mm cannon, and opened fire. Suffering severe damage, the B-17 fell from the sky and crashed into St. George's Channel at 3:37 A.M. Two men, the copilot and bombardier, managed to parachute out before the plane hit the water but the copilot was eventually captured and executed. The bombardier, M/Sgt. Gordon Manuel, despite having one broken leg and shrapnel injuries in the other, managed to reach shore and contact friendly natives. For the next several months he remained on New Britain, organizing the natives to help rescue downed American airmen.[24]

Less than an hour later, at 4:28 A.M., CPO Satoru Ono, piloting another specially equipped Irving night fighter, caught B-17E (41-9011) in his sights and blasted it out of the sky. Nothing was ever seen of the Fortress again.[25]

On May 24, Lt. Col. Roberts returned to the United States and Maj. Hawthorne, the CO of the 65th BS, took the helm of the 43rd BG. Around that same date, reconnaissance planes counted 102 Japanese fighters and 130 bombers based around Rabaul, with another 107 based around Kavieng. Additionally, the observation planes noticed a large number of enemy barges, heavily protected by Zero fighters, moving along the coast of New Guinea from Madang to Finschhaven. The 5th AF airplanes attacked almost immediately and by May 29, the number of planes at Rabaul had been reduced to 59 fighters and 85 bombers and daylight barge movement had stopped completely. Unknown to Gen. Kenney, he was shattering another one of Admiral Yamamoto's master plans.[26]

During the first week in April, Admiral Yamamoto had devised a plan to halt the Americans in their tracks. Having suffered innumerable losses to his ships, Yamamoto had concluded that the only way to halt the American advance was through airpower. Realizing that the Americans were pushing up through the Northern Solomons, and across New Guinea with the ultimate objective of taking Rabaul, the admiral set out to build up his air strength in the South and Southwest Pacific and hit the Americans with a massive air attack that would "weaken the claws of the American eagle." Stripping planes from his carriers and from the interior of the Empire, Yamamoto began building up his fighter and bomber strength at Rabaul and Kavieng in the Southwest Pacific, and at Buin in the South Pacific. However, almost as quickly as the planes arrived, Gen. Kenney's 5th AF and Gen. Twining's 13th AF put them out of commission.[27]

During April 1943, the 13th AF B-17s continued to fly almost nightly harassing missions over Kahili, Ballale, and Munda. Still based out of Espiritu Santo but flying out of the forward airfield on Guadalcanal, the planes harassed the Japanese whenever and wherever possible. Continual rotation of the 5th BG ground crews and aircrews between Guadalcanal and Espiritu Santo kept the strike crews alert and fresh and gave the personnel at Espiritu Santo a bit of relaxation from the shooting war and allowed for better maintenance on the planes.[28]

During the first three weeks of April, the 23rd BS was stationed at Guadalcanal and flew almost all of the combat missions. On April 6, three Fortresses hit Kahili. On the initial bomb run the planes were able to drop some bombs without trouble but when they doubled back for a second run, a dozen enemy searchlights converged on the planes and antiaircraft fire filled the sky. Although the B-17s suffered only minor damage, two of the planes developed engine trouble and had to limp back to Guadalcanal. "These crates have been flying so long," commented reporter Mack Morriss, "they're ready to come apart . . . Somehow I can't see why these people should fly patched-together airplanes."[29]

The following night five more planes started back towards Kahili. However, because of a few new inexperienced navigators, who had little training in over-water flight, one plane ended up over Buka, and the others ended up "at Kahili or somewhere else on the line." The inexperience was a result of the arrival of about 200 replacement personnel in early April, and the loss of a like number of veterans who had been selected to go home. Sorely in need of personnel, the new recruits were thrown into combat almost immediately, without the proper training.[30]

The inexperience of the navigators proved harmful again on April 10. Six Fortresses from the 23rd BS took off from Guadalcanal at 12:30 A.M. and headed for Kahili. Along for the ride on B-17E (41-9214, *The Skipper*) was Mack Morriss. ". . . I think we were lost from the time we cleared the island until we got back," he wrote. Unable to locate the target because of heavy clouds, the planes were forced to bring their bombs back to Henderson Field.[31]

Although the rumors about returning to the United States had persisted for some time, orders finally came through for the veterans of the 72nd BS on April 11. "Today was a big day for the 72nd," recorded the squadron historian, "for the original Squadron . . . received their justly earned awards and citations, followed by receiving orders to board ship to return to the United States." Within the next week, 40 officers and 131 enlisted men, left Espiritu Santo and headed back to Hawaii for eventual return to the United States. For the remainder of the 72nd BS, the transition to B-24s continued. On April 12, the 72nd BS flew its last mission with a B-17 when a crew took a Fortress on an 800 mile search from Espiritu Santo. Two days later, B-17F (41-24446, *Jezabel*) was transferred to the 23rd BS and B-17E (41-9093, *Spook!*) was given to the 31st BS. All of the 72nd BS B-17s were gone. The 72nd BS/5th BG was now a B-24 unit.[32]

April 12 was a bad day for the 23rd BS. "On 12 April two (2) of our planes got lost and were forced to land at sea," noted the squadron historian. "One officer and one enlisted man were lost." After a dusk raid on Kahili, the navigators on both planes became lost and the pilots were forced to set down at sea. Lt. Sesso ditched B-17E (41-2613, *Lucky-13*) at 1:00 A.M. off San Isabel Island but the entire crew was able to reach shore and was rescued a short time later by a PBY. The other B-17, flown by Capt. Flavel Sabin, was ditched off the eastern tip of San Isabel at 2:45 A.M. Unfortunately, the bombardier broke his neck and the flight engineer broke his back in the landing. Neither man survived.[33]

In spite of their losses, the 23rd BS kept the pressure on Kahili, hitting the enemy airfield on April 16 and 17. On April 18, acting on information obtained from the broken Japanese codes, the Allies achieved one of the biggest victories of the Pacific War when a P-38 fighter shot down the bomber carrying Admiral Yamamoto on an inspection tour of the Northern Solomons. Japan's highest ranking naval officer and one of her greatest military minds, the strategist behind the war in the Pacific, was dead. It was a crushing blow to Japan.[34]

The 5th BG lost another Fortress on April 23 when Capt. Leon Rockwell (31st

BS) suffered brake failure while landing B-17F (41-24457, *The Aztec's Curse*) and was forced to ground loop the plane. Still, Rockwell stated there was "no damage until the tug knocked off the tail stinger [tail guns]." Damaged beyond repair, *The Aztec's Curse* was relegated to salvage. Commented reporter Morriss, "It is absolutely a crying shame that these men should have to fly airplanes which should have been scrapped months ago." Yet, the 5th BG continued to attack.[35]

During the last week in April the 23rd BS was relieved from combat duties at Guadalcanal and sent back to Espiritu Santo. Replacing the unit at Carney Field, the new bomber airstrip to the east of Henderson Field, was the air echelon of the 394th BS, which was still based out of Nandi Field in Fiji and flying the old 19th BG B-17s. "It may be noted," wrote the 394th BS historian, "that despite the increasing age and hours of the Squadron Ships [i.e. planes] and the shortage of spare parts, especially new or reconditioned engines, eleven of the twelve airplanes were ready to fly and in combat condition..." The twelfth plane had been stripped of its engines to keep the other planes in the air.[36]

The 394th BS started combat operations almost immediately, sending two planes out on search operations on April 27 and again on April 28, and then dispatching two planes to Kahili airfield on April 29. Although the B-17s ran into heavy weather, they managed to reach the target and drop their bombs, "encountering active searchlights and ack-ack fire." On the last day of April three planes set out to hit Kahili again. While the first plane took the Japanese completely by surprise, scoring a number of good hits on the airdrome, the enemy was fully alerted by the time the next two planes arrived. Although both planes were able to unload their bombs, one plane was slightly damaged by the Japanese antiaircraft fire.[37]

Bad weather hampered all flying operations during the first two weeks of May. "Although missions were planned every night," wrote the 394th BS historian, "the weather continued unsafe for flying operations." Still, on May 4 three B-17s tried to bomb Kahili Field but ran into a heavy overcast. Somehow, two planes found an opening above Rekata Bay and bombed the Japanese installations there, while another bombed Munda. On May 8, in spite of the bad weather, six Fortresses, escorted by American fighter planes, took off from Guadalcanal to find two damaged enemy destroyers that were reported to be in the Munda area. "In one vain attempt to finish the enemy vessels," noted the squadron historian, "the B-17s flew as low as 500 feet in the bad weather trying to locate their target." When the fighter escorts ran low on fuel, the B-17s returned to Carney Field.[38]

The bad weather continued but on the night of May 11–12, five B-17s from the 394th BS followed two specially equipped "snooper" B-24s to Bougainville. Equipped with airborne radar for bombing at night or in bad weather, the B-24s dropped their bombs around the airfields at Kahili and Ballale, marking the way for the B-17s. Meeting only sporadic antiaircraft fire and searchlights, some of the B-17s stayed over the area for more than an hour and 45 minutes, dropping their 500-lb. bombs one at a time. "It was generally agreed that the Japanese received absolutely no sleep on that night," wrote the 394th BS historian.[39]

The 394th BS tried to hit the Ballale airfield on May 12 but found it socked in and bombed the Japanese troops on Treasury Island instead. On the 13th, two snooper B-24s led six Fortresses over Shortland Harbor. "The raid was notable," wrote the 394th BS historian, "in that the raid was made carrying six M26 flares in each ship in addition to the bombs, a device new to the enemy and the squadron. Following closely worked out time tables each ship was able to bomb by the light from the flares released by a sister ship and in turn release for the other ship." Proving highly successful, the B-17s ignited a number of large fires that were still visible 60 miles away.[40]

A few more two- and three-plane missions were flown against Kahili and Ballale airfields before four planes from the 394th BS took off on May 19 to fly a mission in conjunction with the United Sates Navy. While a flight of Navy TBF Avengers laid mines in Shortland Harbor, the four B-17s dropped 100-lb. bombs on the searchlights and antiaircraft guns. A follow-up mission the next night by both the B-17s and the TBFs, was also highly successful. "Both enemy searchlights and gun positions were hit hard," reported the squadron historian.[41]

On the night of May 22–23 five B-24s hit Kahili and Ballale Island but 10 B-17s that attempted a follow-up strike were forced to abort because of the weather. That night however, the 394th BS was engaged in another joint mine-laying operation with the United States Navy. Eight Fortresses, led by Maj. McLyle G. Zumwalt, and 11 B-24s dropped almost 30 tons of bombs on the Buin-Kahili-Tonolai shoreline. Wrote the squadron historian, "Enemy searchlight installations and antiaircraft guns were blasted to the extent that all Navy TBFs accomplished their mission and returned safely. Gun fire and searchlight activity, [although] heavy at first, became very light. After the bombs were dropped, the latter only flashing on occasionally, unwilling to be the target of a bomb run."[42]

By the end of May, the aircrews and airplanes of the 394th BS were worn out from the constant missions and the consistently bad weather. On May 28, the squadron was relieved from combat by the air echelon of the 31st BS, which moved up from Espiritu Santo. While the 394th BS personnel returned to Fiji, the 31st BS, still flying the B-17s given to them by the 72nd BS, continued the attacks on Kahili, and to carry on the isolation of Rabaul.[43]

XXIX

Here Come the Liberators

By June, Operation Cartwheel, the isolation of Rabaul, was in full swing. Plans were being made for the invasion and capture of a number of islands in the Northern Solomons and the capture of a number of points along the northern coast of New Guinea that would bring the Americans within easy striking distance of Rabaul. At the same time however, the new American bases would be within easy range of the Japanese forces at Rabaul. Intending to keep the enemy strength at a minimum, Gen. Kenney's 5th AF continued to strike the Japanese stronghold whenever possible.[1]

The rainy month of June started with B-24s and B-17s from the 403rd BS hitting Wewak on the night of June 2. Two days later, and again on June 7, the planes returned to hit the enemy held town and airfield. In the early morning hours of June 10, six planes from the 403rd BS dropped incendiary and fragmentation bombs on Vunakanau, "starting six good fires," while seven planes from the 63rd BS hit Rabaul. Five of the planes hit the town, causing a diversion while Lt. Murphy and one other pilot skip bombed ships in Simpson Harbor.[2]

As Murphy was about to enter the harbor area, his crew spotted a large Japanese night fighter trailing them. Murphy was piloting one of only two aircraft in the 63rd BS equipped with an anti-radar device and the radar operator, a sergeant from the RAAF, quickly confirmed the sighting. Before long, several twin-engine Japanese night fighters appeared. Although Murphy successfully eluded the fighters, he was unable to avoid the bright searchlights. Caught in their illuminating beam, he made a quick skip run against a Japanese transport and then headed for Port Moresby.[3]

Although Murphy had successfully evaded the Japanese night fighters, a Lt. Ensberg was not so lucky. Picked up by the searchlights while bombing the town, Ensberg's B-17 suffered hits from both the enemy antiaircraft guns and the twin-engine night fighters. His bomber received six hits across the wings and one hit in the camera well, beneath the radio compartment, which seriously injured the radio operator. "The dimensions of the holes were different enough to positively identify both a 20-mm shell [from the night fighter] that exploded on contact and the antiaircraft shell," Murphy wrote. "That was the first time any of our aircraft had been followed by or hit by two-engine night fighters."[4] More than likely, the 63rd BS was encountering the same specially-equipped, twin-engine Irving night fighters that the 5th BG had encountered at the end of May.

When Lt. Murphy, who turned 23 that day, returned to Port Moresby he was met by a small group of airmen singing "Happy Birthday." As surprised and overjoyed as he was by the reception, it paled in comparison to the news that he had finally accumulated enough service points and was being relieved from combat and sent back home. He could not have asked for a better birthday present.[5]

The next day, June 11, following Admiral Yamamoto's plan to protect Rabaul, the Japanese moved 100 airplanes to their airfields around the town, bringing their total in the area to 271. That night, Gen. Whitehead sent seven B-17s from the 65th BS, along with 16 B-24s, to hit the enemy airfields. In the B-17 attack on Vunakanau, the 65th BS ran into a ton of trouble. Although the planes set a number of fires and ignited the Japanese bomb dump, they were hit hard by the antiaircraft fire and Irving night fighters.[6]

Antiaircraft fire accounted for many light and medium size holes in one aircraft, and wounded one crewman above the left eye. The night fighters hit one B-17 in the tail compartment with a 20-mm shell that severed the rudder trim tab controls, started a fire, and severely wounded the tail gunner about the neck and head. "His life was saved by the flak helmet he wore," wrote the 65th BS historian. Night fighters also caused damage to B-17F (41-24403, *The Old Man*), flown by Maj. William A. Smith. Tracked by the searchlights for at least five minutes, *The Old Man* was hit repeatedly by the night fighters but refused to go down. Cannon shells tore holes in the left wing, in the radio compartment, through the waist area, and through the tail section. A spent shell hit the tail gunner, tearing his new flying suit and "scratching his tail . . ."[7]

Caught in the sweeping searchlights B-17F (41-24454, *Georgia Peach*), piloted by Lt. John Woodard, became a perfect target for the night fighters. At 3:14 A.M., the Japanese planes set fire to the *Georgia Peach*. Only the two men in the nose were able to parachute from the burning plane, bombardier Lt. Jack Wisener and navigator Lt. Philip Bek. Both men were captured but only Lt. Wisener survived the war. Lt. Bek was executed by his captors.[8]

In spite of the damage, the rest of the planes returned safely to Port Moresby. Then, in the early morning of April 14, the men were shown another example of how fickle fate could be. While taking off on a routine reconnaissance mission Lt. James A. Pickard (64th BS), B-17E (41-2664, *The Jersey Skeeter*), crashed. The bomb bay gas tank, oxygen tanks, and one of four bombs exploded. Miraculously, two men in the back of the plane survived.

Navigator Lt. Sutton, who saw the explosion, commented:

A horrible accident and most of us believe it was due to these worn out old B-17s we have to fly. It is nothing less than a crime to have to fly those old ships. How long can we continue to take this kicking is beyond me. Phenomenal results are expected of a few battered crews and still fewer B-17s.[9]

In spite of the continual bombings by the Americans, the Japanese refused to abandon Admiral Yamamoto's plan to stop the Allies with massive air strikes. On April 14 American reconnaissance planes found that another 80 to 100 Japanese bombers and fighters had been flown into the Rabaul area, increasing the total number of airplanes back up to 281. At the same time, search planes spotted another 120 enemy planes around the Bougainville area. The Japanese now had approximately 400 planes ready to stop the Allied advances.[10]

Wanting to get fresh, reliable information on the Japanese build-up at Buka airstrip in the Northern Solomons, headquarters tried to locate a plane and crew that was ready for the mission. Since the 63rd BS was preparing their planes for another night attack on Rabaul, and the 64th BS had no crews available, the call went out to the 65th BS. Since Capt. Zeamer was scheduled for an early morning flight to the Northern Solomons for a photo-mapping mission to Bougainville, in preparation for an American invasion scheduled for November 1, he was given the assignment. Zeamer recalled the midnight phone call that informed him of the added mission to recon Buka airstrip. "I told [the operations officer], 'Hell no,' that we were going to do an important mapping mission, and that was it," he wrote. "He never did tell me about the 400 Jap planes because he knew damn well I wouldn't go to Buka."[11]

At 4:00 A.M., April 16, Capt. Zeamer was about to take off in B-17E (41-2666, *Lucy*) when he was handed a written order to recon Buka. "I passed the order around to the crew and told them to read it and forget it," Zeamer wrote, "that we weren't going to do it." A bit of an eccentric, Zeamer had a crew that was made up of men that had been unwanted in other crews. All eight men had volunteered to fly with Zeamer and they had melded themselves into an effective and efficient crew, earning the nickname "Eager Beavers." When Zeamer took off from Seven Mile Strip on April 16, he took along Sgt. George Kendrick, a trained photographer.[12]

Flying through clear weather, the B-17 reached Bougainville at 7:30 A.M., a half hour ahead of schedule. Having to wait for the sun to get high enough for the camera to get the right exposure, Zeamer asked the crew if they should fly the reconnaissance mission of Buka. "Their response was unanimous," Zeamer recalled, "'What the hell, let's do the God-damned recce!'" Having flown a similar mission on June 2, Zeamer had seen only six Japanese fighters at Buka. "At this point we still had no idea that additional Jap planes had come into the area," he said. "We figured we could handle the six we had encountered two weeks before."

While passing over Buka at 25,000 feet, Sgt. Kendrick took the reconnaissance photos and noticed 22 enemy planes coming up to intercept them. "There was no question about postponing the mapping," Zeamer remembered, "it had to be done that day." While the Zeros rose to altitude, Zeamer started the mapping run and Sgt. Kendrick started taking the pictures. "We had done twenty-one minutes and 15 seconds of the mapping run and were right over Empress Augusta Bay where charts of the coral reefs would be critical for the landing craft [when the Zeros attacked]," Zeamer wrote. Deciding to finish the mapping mission, Zeamer held the plane steady while his gunners fought off the swarming fighters.

"It was a bad decision," Zeamer admitted. With the *Lucy* holding firm and steady, five Zeros attacked from head-on. Four 20-mm cannon shells and numerous machine-gun bullets tore into the nose of the bomber. Bombardier 2nd Lt. Joseph R. Sarnoski was hit in the neck but managed to shoot down one of the planes with two specially mounted .50 caliber nose guns.[13]

At almost the same time, 20-mm shells tore into the left wing root and crashed into the instrument panel, knocking out all of the instruments except the airspeed indicator and the magnetic compass. Both Zeamer and his copilot, Lt. John T. Britton, were wounded and Britton lost consciousness. Wrote Zeamer, ". . . I had been hit in my upper left arm and in both wrists. Blood was squirting into my lap and running down my hands, making my grip on the controls slippery." A cannon shell exploded under Zeamer's rudder pedals, smashing the pedals, shattering his left knee, and sending more than 125 pieces of shrapnel into both legs.[14]

Navigator 2nd Lt. Ruby E. Johnston was trying to staunch the flow of blood from Lt. Sarnoski's neck wound when the bombardier suddenly broke away. "Forget it," Sarnoski said. "Where the hell's my gun?" The second coordinated attack was coming in as Sarnoski and the other gunners opened up. Sgt. John J. Able, the engineer, shot down an attacker with the top turret guns but was in turn hit in the knee by the incoming enemy fire.[15]

In spite of his grievous injuries Capt. Zeamer kept the B-17 level until the photo mission was over. "[Then,] I immediately rolled the ship hard to the right and pushed the nose down into a steep dive," he recalled. "Oxygen and hydraulic lines behind my seat had been hit and were blazing." At one point Lt. Johnston came up from the nose and offered to help fly the plane but Zeamer sent him back to his position, refusing to relinquish control of the bomber until the fight was over. When Johnston returned to the nose, another cannon shell exploded in the compartment and tossed both him and Sarnoski onto the small catwalk leading up to the flight deck. Once again Lt. Sarnoski was hit, receiving a deadly wound to his side, and Lt. Johnston was hit in the forehead and left eye, temporarily blinding him. Although mortally wounded, Sarnoski crawled back to his gun and managed to bring down another enemy plane.[16]

After going into the dive and hitting 275 mph, Capt. Zeamer began pulling his plane out when he spotted a Zero directly in front of him. Having a specially built forward firing machine gun attached to the nose of the plane, triggered by a button on his control column, Zeamer fired two quick bursts and sent the Zero spinning out of the sky. Leveling off at 10,000 feet, Zeamer took evasive action whenever the Zeros lined up for an attack. "Just before they were ready to fire and when it was too late for them to make a correction," he remembered, "I cut the throttles and rolled our plane hard to the right or left and pulled back on the controls for all I was worth to side step and let them go by. As soon as they went by, I rolled our plane back toward the west, opened the throttles, and watched as they lined up again. I must have repeated this maneuver eight to 10 times over a period of forty minutes."[17]

Bleeding profusely from his shattered left knee, Zeamer tried to put a tourniquet above the wound with his belt but every time he nearly had it accomplished, the Zeros attacked and he had to grab the controls. By now the airplane and crew were in serious trouble. Copilot Britton was unconscious and seriously injured in both arms, bombardier Sarnoski was mortally wounded and slumped unconscious over his gun, navigator Johnston was temporarily blinded, engineer Able was wounded in the knee, radio operator Sgt. William Vaughan was hit in the neck, and Capt. Zeamer was a mess. The nose of the bomber looked like a sieve and the flight deck was in shambles. At some time, however, somebody extinguished the fire behind Zeamer's seat and eliminated one problem.[18]

After 40 minutes, the Zeros finally gave up. Unable to shoot down the B-17, and having lost at least five of their friends, the Zero pilots finally headed back towards Buka. With the Zeros gone, Capt. Zeamer finally gave control of the B-17 to Sgt. Able. Although wounded himself and having never flown a B-17 before, Able pulled the unconscious copilot out of his seat and took over the B-17. Unbelievably, two of the ten crewmen aboard the *Lucy*, Sgt. Kendrick and tail gunner Sgt. Herbert Pugh, had survived the fight with nary a scratch. While Kendrick tended to the wounded on the flight deck, Pugh climbed into the nose to tend to Sarnoski and Johnston. Found slumped over his guns in a pool of blood, Sarnoski died in Pugh's arms five minutes later.[19]

Having lost almost 50 percent of his blood, Zeamer lapsed in and out of consciousness as Able flew the plane back towards New Guinea. Whenever conscious, Zeamer told Able what to do, correcting his heading and his air speed, giving advice and encouragement. For three hours, and 580 miles, Sgt. Able flew the plane with occasional guidance from Capt. Zeamer. At 12:15 P.M., as they neared New Guinea, everyone knew that Able would never be able to get the plane safely over the Owen Stanley Mountains so the decision was made to land at the emergency field at Dobodura.[20]

With the hydraulic system shot out and no brakes or flaps, and with almost the entire instrument panel gone, Capt. Zeamer realized that Sgt. Able would never be able to safely land the plane. By this time Lt. Britton had regained consciousness so he climbed back into the copilot seat and worked the rudder pedals with his two good legs while Zeamer worked the control column with his one good arm. Somehow, the two wounded pilots managed to bring B-17E (41-2666, *Lucy*) down without further mishap and the wounded men were quickly hustled off to the hospital.[21]

Having lost so much blood, Capt. Zeamer was not expected to live. The doctors amputated his shattered left leg, but were afraid of giving him a transfusion from 43rd BG donors whose blood might be tainted with malaria. Instead, they elected to give him plasma only. However, when Zeamer lived through the night, a call went out for blood donors. "The [65th] squadron was at lunch when the word came in," wrote a reporter. "Ten seconds later the mess hall was deserted, and in five minutes a cavalcade of jeeps was churning up the dust to the hospital."[22]

Capt. Jay Zeamer Jr. eventually pulled through. He and Lt. Sarnoski were awarded the Medal of Honor, and everyone on the flight, including photographer Kendrick, were awarded the Distinguished Service Cross, thereby earning the reconnaissance flight to Buka the distinction of being the most decorated flight in AAF history. Although B-17E (41-2666, *Lucy*) had been left with a shattered nose, a broken instrument panel, five huge cannon holes, and 178 machine-gun holes, she would be repaired and fly again. As the Japanese from Buka had learned, it took a great deal of punishment to eliminate a B-17.[23]

Still trying to eliminate the strength of the enemy air force in preparation for the June 30 invasions of the Trobriand and Woodlark Islands, three B-17s and three B-24s from the 403rd BS attacked Rabaul on the night of June 19. Although one B-24 turned back with engine trouble, four of the bombers dropped 1,000-lb. bombs on Vunakanau airdrome and one dropped incendiaries on the town of Rabaul. All five planes returned safely to Port Moresby. One week later, however, when the 65th and 403rd BSs hit Rabaul again, the results were disastrous.[24]

While bombing Vunakanau, B-17E (41-2430, *Naughty But Nice*), flown by Lt. Charles Trimingham (65th BS), was caught in the Japanese searchlights. When the No. 3 engine was set on fire by an antiaircraft hit, an Irving night fighter, piloted by Chief Petty Officer Kodo, swooped in from below and peppered the B-17 with 20-mm shells. With the plane ablaze, the crew attempted to bail out but only the navigator, 1st Lt. Jose L. "Joe" Holguin, made it. Already wounded in the chin and left leg, Holguin hit a tree and then slammed his back into the ground. Although suffering from a broken back and his other wounds, Holguin eluded capture for 27 days before meeting a group of natives who eventually turned him over to the Japanese. Lt. Holguin was the only survivor of B-17E (41-2430, *Naughty But Nice*).[25]

Having already lost one Fortress, the attack force was returning to New Guinea when Officer Kudo scored another kill, shooting down Lt. Donald McEachern, B-17F (41-24448, *Taxpayer's Pride*). Only the tail gunner, Sgt. Joel Griffin, survived.[26]

On June 21, American Raiders stormed ashore unopposed on New Georgia Island in the Northern Solomons. The next day, American troops landed unopposed on Woodlark Island. During the night of June 23–24 American units landed on Kriwina Island, the largest island in the Trobriand Island Group. Again, because of the success of Gen. Kenney's constant air attacks on enemy shipping and airfields, the landing went unopposed.[27]

On the night of June 29–30, eight B-17s from the 63rd and 403rd BSs, and three B-24s from the 403rd BS hit Vunakanau as a preliminary strike to the Allied invasions in the Papua New Guinea area. 1st Lt. Harold S. Barnett, (63rd BS), B-17F (41-24543, *Pluto*), was shot down and crashed near the village of Kulit on the Gazelle Peninsula of New Britain. "This mission was significant," noted the 403rd BS historian, "in that it was the last strike in which B-17's of this squadron participated." After the June 30 mission, all 403rd BS B-17s were transferred to the other squadrons of the 43rd BG and the 403rd solely used B-24s.[28]

Operation Cartwheel began flawlessly on June 30 when American troops landed unopposed at Nassau Bay and immediately began pushing north towards Salamaua. More troops were poured into Woodlark and Kriwina Islands, along with a detachment of Seabees that immediately began work on twin airfields. In the Northern Solomons, American soldiers landed at Rendova Island and at other points around New Georgia, with the eventual objective of capturing Munda Airfield. Reported Gen. Kenney, "No Jap aircraft paid any attention to our landings [in the Southwest Pacific] all day, but during the afternoon over in SOPAC, a series of attacks were launched against the landing operations by bombers, dive-bombers, fighters, and even floatplanes." One American ship was lost after unloading its cargo, and two ships were damaged. Seventeen American fighters were shot down in exchange for 101 for the Japanese. Yamamoto's plan to stop the Americans from advancing any further with Japanese airpower was quickly unraveling.[29]

Clear weather during the first few days of July gave Gen. Kenney the opportunity to strike hard at Rabaul. Ten B-24s hit Lakunai and Rapopo on July 1. The following night, 11 B-17s from the 64th and 65th BSs, and seven B-24s bombed Vunakanau and Rapopo. On the July 2 mission, the 64th BS used a B-24 for the first time. Noted the squadron historian, "The months lazied by until July when the lid blew off—the 64th became a B-24 Squadron. Six of the B-17's crews and five B-17s were transferred to the 63rd and 65th Squadrons and the 64th received three more B-24's in addition to those already brought in by newly arrived crews." On July 13, the 64th BS sent two B-17Es, (41-2408) and (41-2464, *Queenie*), two B-17Fs, (41-24355, *Dinah Might*) and (41-24548, *War Horse*), and one B-24 to bomb Lae. This was the last B-17 mission flown by the 64th BS. During the week of July 18-24, the four B-17s were transferred to the 65th BS and the 64th BS became a B-24 unit.[30]

By the second week in July, the only units in the Southwest Pacific still flying B-17s were the 63rd and 65th BSs/43rd BG. On July 11, three planes from the 65th BS and four from the 63rd BS set out to hit Vunakanau. About one and a half hours from Rabaul, while passing through a severe tropical storm, Lt. Ralph De Loach (63rd BS), B-17F (41-24521, *Black Jack*), developed problems with engines No. 3 and 4. Both engines began to shake violently so De Loach feathered No. 4 and hoped for the best with No. 3. Able to make his bomb run, De Loach turned back toward New Guinea and tried to keep the plane airborne.[31]

Passing back through the storm, the *Black Jack* was tossed about furiously. "At 0500 our altitude was approximately 5,000 ft and we were in the midst of heavy weather," De Loach wrote. "It was impossible to climb to altitude to get above the storm, so we were forced to stay in it which resulted in our becoming completely lost." Finally breaking out of the storm along the New Guinea coast, De Loach and his navigator figured that they were close to Japanese-held Lae and turned south. In fact, they were close to the emergency landing field at Dobodura but had no way of knowing this.

Low on fuel, De Loach decided to put the *Black Jack* down on a coral reef. When he hit the water however, the Fortress shot forward and slammed into the deep water beyond the reef. Three of the ten crewmen aboard B-17F (41-24521, *Black Jack*) were badly injured but the others rescued them and helped them to shore. As they watched, the *Black Jack* sank nose first into the clear tropical water and settled upright on the ocean floor. The 10-man crew was eventually rescued and brought back to Port Moresby.[32]

By mid-July Rabaul had been thoroughly pounded and Gen. Kenney decided to switch objectives. He wrote, "With the Jap air strength around Rabaul pretty well beaten down and no attempts being made to build it up, we switched to heavy support of the Aussie drive towards Salamaua and to interfering with the Jap road-construction work from Madang . . ." At almost the same time, Kenney realized that his beat-up B-17s had had enough. Although Washington had promised to keep his heavy bomber strength near 200, two postponements of the scheduled due date had severely handicapped him. Figuring that he was losing an average of seven B-17s a month, Kenney warned Washington that he would have less than a dozen B-17s in commission by September if his usual rate of attrition continued. Knowing that all of the newly produced B-17s were going to Europe, Kenney asked for more B-24s, an aircraft he had compromised in accepting.[33]

While Gen. Kenney waited for his answer and his aircraft, his heavy bombers continued to strike. On July 23 the B-17s from the 63rd and 65th BSs joined the B-24s of the other squadrons to bomb Bogadjim, 15 miles south of Madang. Three days later, a combined force of more than 40 B-24s and B-17s dropped 125 tons of explosives on the Lae-Salamaua area. On July 29, another combined raid by B-17s, B-24s and B-25s pounded the Salamaua area.[34]

By the end of July, the Australian troops were slogging their way through the rain and the mud towards the Japanese position at Lae. Gen. Kenney's 5th AF was doing whatever it could to assist while at the same time keeping a wary eye on Rabaul and Kavieng. By the same time, in the South Pacific Area, the 13th AF had thoroughly pounded Kahili and American ground troops were on the verge of capturing Munda.

At the end of May, the air echelon of the 31st BS/5th BG had rotated to Guadalcanal to continue operations against the Japanese airfields in the Northern Solomons in conjunction with the upcoming American invasions. "[T]he air echelon moved to the 'Canal from the New Hebrides for the last strike period with B-17's," wrote the 31st BS historian. "Strikes were flown against Kahili, Munda, Shortland-Faisi, [and] Ballale . . . All strikes except one were night missions." During the night of June 3–4 the 31st BS B-17s hit Kahili airfield and the nearby

Moliko River area. Hampered by continuous bad weather, the next raid did not take place until June 9 when a flight of B-17s, escorted by P-40s and P-38s, hit Munda.[35]

Early on the morning of June 10, the 31st BS B-17s took off from Carney Field to bomb Kahili again. "Halfway to the target Lt. [Richard] Snoddy called Capt. Smith, the flight leader, and told him his artificial horizon was out and wanted to return to base," wrote Lt. Russell Knox, lead navigator with Capt. Smith. "He was told to continue on needle, ball and airspeed but replied that he was not that good at it." Ordered to continue the mission, Lt. Snoddy in B-17E (41-2525, *Madame-X*) pressed on.

"We were supposed to fly over the target at exactly dusk, however the briefing navigator had forgotten that, although it was dusk on the ground, it was bright sunshine at 20,000 feet and we were like sitting ducks," recalled Lt. Knox. "Furthermore, each crew plotted its own bomb run, so we were flying in all directions over the target." When the Fortresses finally returned to Guadalcanal, Lt. Snoddy and his crew were nowhere to be found. "We were flying in a very loose spread formation and it was very easy to lose contact with the rest of the flight," Knox wrote. "So I don't know whether he was shot down or lost control." B-17E (41-2525, *Madame-X*) and its crew were never seen again.[36]

At dusk on June 13, the B-17s from the 31st BS, accompanied by a flight of B-24s hit Kahili again, and the next day, June 14, eleven B-17s and B-24s returned to bomb the Kahili airfield and nearby Shortland Island. Upon returning to Carney Field, the 31st BS personnel were informed that they were to pack their belongings for a return to Espiritu Santo, the 394th BS was coming to take their place.[37]

On June 12, the 394th BS at Nandi Field in Fiji, had been informed that it was going to Guadalcanal. Fifty members of an advance echelon left immediately to set up the new base camp. "Plans were formulated by which the complete combat squadron would be moved to 'Cactus' by air," noted the squadron historian. "This necessitated taking only the most vital equipment and records in order to meet weight restrictions." The next day, seven planes, each carrying 15 men and their baggage, departed Fiji and flew to Espiritu Santo. For the next two weeks the 14 B-17s of the 394th BS engaged in numerous search patrols and training missions, trying to hone their skills to a fine edge. "The daily training program was increased and practice bombing and gunnery missions were scheduled daily," noted the historian. Since the squadron was moving into the shooting war, the new officers and men were "given instructions in the care and use of sidearms and machine guns."[38]

The air echelon of the 31st BS rotated out of Guadalcanal on June 15 and flew to Espiritu Santo. Once there, a drastic change took place. Explained the 31st BS historian, "The air echelon returned to the New Hebrides on 15 June 1943 and on that day all B-17's and crew were transferred to the 23rd Squadron."[39] As was happening in the Southwest Pacific, the B-17 units were slowly being phased out. By the middle of June there was only two B-17 squadrons in the South Pacific, the 23rd and 394th BSs/5th BG, both presently at Espiritu Santo.

For a period of almost two weeks there were no B-17s operating out of Guadalcanal. Instead, B-24s continued the bombing of Kahili. On June 21 the American troops stormed ashore on New Georgia and started their drive towards Munda airfield. The constant bombings of Munda and Kahili paid off. The Japanese air force at Munda had been rendered almost useless, while the force at Kahili had suffered fearfully. Although token Japanese air resistance appeared from Rabaul, the American landings were successful. Slowly but surely the Americans were moving up the Solomon Island chain.[40]

In spite of continuing bad weather, on June 28, the 394th BS moved up to Carney Field, Guadalcanal. Commented the squadron historian, "A camp area was set up in the middle of the jungle on the banks of the muddy Malimbu; and life without women began." The rain continued but on July 6, the B-17s of the 394th BS, accompanied by B-24s, bombed Ballale, covering about 95 percent of the airfield with fragmentation bombs. In a commendation from Gen. Twining, he wrote, "This successful attack with return to base during hours of darkness shows the high degree of training attained in high level bombardment technique, the excellent performance of your navigators and is a splendid tribute to the ground echelons for their many hours of conscientious work in maintaining your aircraft at a high standard in order that such missions may be possible."[41] Oddly, only a few weeks earlier there had been general criticism about the training, navigators, and condition of the airplanes.

After a few more combined B-17 and B-24 strikes on Kahili, the inexperienced 394th BS rotated off Guadalcanal, being replaced on July 14 by the B-17s of the 23rd BS. Thrown into the fray almost immediately, eight 23rd BS Fortresses hit Kahili on the night of July 15 and again on July 16 when more than 30 B-17s and B-24s hit the airfield. In an attempt to keep the Japanese at Kahili away from the American infantry driving towards Munda, the B-17s of the 23rd BS returned to Kahili on the night of July 18. Unfortunately, B-17E (41-9153, *Tokyo Taxi*), flown by Lt. Rex Echles, received a direct hit from the enemy antiaircraft fire and exploded, killing the entire crew.[42]

After a few more raids to knock out Kahili, the 23rd BS B-17s joined the other aircraft from the 13th AF for one massive strike against Munda as the ground troops started their final push. Noted the 23rd BS historian:

> On July 25, ten (10) of our B-17s loaded to capacity with 20 pound fragmentation clusters took part in the 'greatest show on earth'—the bombing of Munda, New Georgia, in support of ground troops. The crews of the planes participating plus all ground officers who had been able to talk themselves into a ride on the mission were thrilled at the sight of B-24's, B-25's, TBF's, SBD's, P-38's, P-39's, P-40's, F4F's and F4U's milling around over the target in coordinated attacks while destroyers stood off shore lobbing shells into the Jap positions.

While seven American destroyers shelled Munda, more than 170 bombers, escorted by more than 70 fighters, dropped roughly 145 tons of bombs on the Japanese in a little over half an hour. The July 25 pounding of Munda constituted the heaviest air attack in the South Pacific to date.[43]

That same day, Gen. Twining was promoted to air commander in the Solomons so on July 27, Brig. Gen. Ray L. Owens was given command of the 13th AF. Unfortunately, his appointment was greeted with another loss from the 23rd BS. On an early morning mission over Kahili, two planes planned to go over the target and attract the searchlights and antiaircraft fire, while two more made the actual bomb run. Lt. Berton Burns, B-17E (41-2520, *Jap Happy*), and Lt. Karl Stubberfield, B-17E (41-9128), flew the bombing aircraft and had just finished their bomb run when they were caught in the enemy searchlights. Japanese night fighters went after the two Fortresses and raked them with 20-mm cannon fire. B-17E (41-2520, *Jap Happy*) was hit six times and two men were wounded but the plane stayed airborne. However, B-17E (41-9128) was set on fire, exploded and went down in a ball of flame. Unknown to anyone at the time, the fiery death of B-17E (41-9128) was the last combat loss of a B-17 in the South Pacific Area.[44]

On July 27, six B-17s participated with nine B-24s in a strike on Tarawa Atoll in the Gilbert Islands in preparation for an invasion there in November. Having less range than the B-24s, the B-17s first flew from Espiritu Santo to Funafuti in the Ellice Islands and after refueling flew 700 miles to bomb Tarawa. "The mission was a success in more ways than one," commented the 5th BG historian. "The target was successfully bombed, and a difficult navigational feat was performed." Unfortunately, on the return to Funafuti, one B-17 ran out of fuel and ditched about 100 miles short of the base. When the other five landed, it was found that two of the planes did not have enough gas left to taxi to the revetment area.[45]

Although the bombing of Tarawa was a success, the loss of one B-17 due to a lack of fuel and the fact that the Fortresses had to stage through Funafuti while the B-24s flew directly to the target showed one of the major inadequacies for the B-17 in the Pacific. Although a rugged, tough plane, the limited range of the B-17 contributed to the decision to pull the Flying Fortress from the Pacific and replace it with the longer-range B-24. As the war in the Pacific progressed, the Americans hip-hopped past certain Japanese islands and invaded others. Unable to reach the far flung targets, by the end of July 1943 the days of the B-17 in the Pacific were numbered.

XXX

The Swan Song

"DURING THE MONTH of August," Gen. Kenney recalled, "the Air Force would continue the air blockade of Lae and Salamaua and support the drive of the Aussies and the regiment of the American 41st Division toward Salamaua." Utilizing their fighters and medium bombers, the Allies began flying "barge hunting" patrols along the New Guinea coast, strafing and bombing enemy barges found moving between Wewak and the Salamaua area. In accordance with the plan to punish Salamaua, the 65th BS/43rd BG opened the month by bombing the area on August 2 and 3. On both occasions the bombing results were listed as "good," with several fires started and all B-17s returning.[1]

On August 4, the 65th BS B-17s set out to bomb a construction camp at the southern end of the road running from the mouth of the Ramu River, about 70 miles southeast of Wewak, to Bogadjim, at the base of Astrolabe Bay on the New Guinea coast. Unfortunately, the weather turned sour and the planes were forced to bomb Bogadjim itself. Four enemy fighters intercepted the Fortresses, and shot down 1st Lt. Walter K. Brenneman, B-17E (41-2634, *Red Moose Express*). Seen crashing into the sea, there were no survivors.[2]

On August 8, the 65th BS lost another plane when B-17E (41-2481, *Old Topper*) was taking off from Port Moresby and crashed due to structural failure. Deemed unworthy for further combat, the plane was shipped to the 481st Service Squadron and was eventually written off on October 30.[3] In spite of the best efforts of the ground crews, the old, battered B-17s had had enough. They had been repeatedly patched, repatched, and patched again. They had taken all that they could and were beginning to show it. Yet, they continued to carry the war to the enemy.

Gen. Kenney staged a maximum effort on August 9, hitting Salamaua and Lae, and the bridges along the Bogadjim-Ramu Road in an attempt to stop the Japanese from sending reinforcements to the Salamaua area. Besides air strikes by

362

B-25s, a total of 33 B-24s and seven B-17s dropped 140 tons of bombs on the Salamaua pocket. Four days later, after six 65th BS Fortresses failed to bomb their primary target along the Bogadjim-Ramu Road because of heavy cloud cover, they joined the rest of the bombers from the 5th AF in dropping 175 tons of bombs around Salamaua in the heaviest single-day strike by the 5th AF to date.[4]

For the next two days the 5th AF continued to pound Salamaua. On August 14, more than 50 bombers, including seven Fortresses from the 65th BS, hit the Japanese position. The next day, eight B-17s from the 65th BS took off to bomb the Salamaua airdrome but ran into a strong front. Only one plane managed to penetrate the weather and drop its bombs.[5]

The Japanese, in an attempt to protect their barge traffic, and stop the Allied advance towards Salamaua, moved over 200 planes into Wewak during the first two weeks of August. Having prior knowledge of the move because of the broken Japanese codes, and realizing that the Australians were planning an amphibious landing near Lae on September 4, Gen. Kenney decided to stage a massive strike and knock out the planes at Wewak with one mighty blow. Near 3:00 A.M. on August 17, 38 B-24s and 12 B-17s pasted the Wewak airdrome and the nearby smaller airfields with 200 tons of bombs. While the B-17s came through unscathed, two B-24s were shot down by antiaircraft fire and another came home with four dead airmen.[6]

Two hours after the attack, the 5th AF fighters and medium bombers struck. On what Japan called "the Black Day of August 17," the American planes bombed and strafed the parked enemy aircraft and shot down any that ventured into the air. Having met with much success, the 5th AF returned the next day. Forty-nine heavy bombers set out from Port Moresby but after running into bad weather, only nine B-17s and seventeen B-24s reached the target. Dropping 100 tons of bombs and incendiaries, the heavies hit the airfield, the big supply installations and the antiaircraft defenses at Wewak, and one of the nearby smaller airfields. As the big bombers left, 53 B-25s and 74 P-38s arrived to strafe the parked enemy planes.[7]

When the raid was over, Gen. Kenney was ecstatic. He wrote:

> During the two day's operation we had destroyed on the ground and in the air practically the entire Japanese air force in the Wewak area, had burned up thousands of drums of gasoline and oil, destroyed a number of large supply dumps, and knocked out the greater part of the antiaircraft gun defenses around Wewak. It was doubtful if the Nips could have put over a half dozen aircraft in the air from all four airdromes combined.[8]

The 5th AF B-24s continued to hit the Wewak area, while the B-17s turned their attention back to the isolation of Lae and Salamaua. On August 21, five 65th BS B-17s went out to bomb two large bridges on the Bogadjim-Ramu road. Sadly, no hits were scored on either structure.[9]

On August 23, six B-17s from the 65th BS took off from Seven Mile Strip for a raid on a Japanese supply and troop concentration along Hansa Bay. "The bombs were dropped through the target [area] with excellent results," wrote the 65th BS historian. "Smoke was still visible thirty minutes after leaving the target." Two days later, perhaps based on observations made by the crews of the B-17s, almost 100 B-24s, B-25s and B-17s carried out an hour-long bombing of the Hansa Bay installations. Again, the results were considered "excellent."[10]

The preparation for the seizure of Lae was in full progress by the end of August so the B-17s of the 5th BG changed targets again and began hitting the Lae area. Since the Australia forces were already within sight of Salamaua, every effort was made to convince the Japanese that Salamaua was the next Allied objective. In reality, however, the Allies wanted Lae. Swallowing the bait completely, the Japanese shifted most of their men from Lae to Salamaua, and left only a small, almost ineffective force behind.[11]

On August 28, seven 65th BS B-17s bombed the dock area of Lae harbor and a few days later, on September 1, the 43rd BG B-17s began a week-long bombing of the Lae area to coincide with an Allied amphibious invasion at Hopoi, 20 miles above Lae, and an American parachute drop at Nadzab, 15 miles northwest of Lae. On the September 1 raid, five B-17s from the 65th BS, accompanied by a few B-17s from the 63rd BS, hit Labu Island, a strategically situated warning point just off the coast from Lae.[12]

The next day, the 63rd BS B-17s returned to Labu Island, "effectively" bombing the area, while seven 65th BS B-17s hit the enemy airfield on Cape Gloucester, on the southwestern tip of New Britain Island. Faced with "intense" antiaircraft fire that put four holes in one plane, the formation reported that the bombing "was fair." Attacked by at least eight twin-engine and several single-engine fighters, the Fortress crews shot down three planes and returned to base safely.[13]

The air assault continued on September 3 when the 5th AF heavy and medium bombers hit the Lae gun emplacements and defensive lines. In the early morning of September 4, the largest amphibious force yet to see action in the Southwest Pacific Area began putting the first Australian troops, and a regiment of the U.S. 41st Infantry Division, ashore at Hopoi. Although the B-17s did not participate, a dozen 43rd BG B-24s unloaded 96 tons of bombs on the enemy positions as the Australians stormed ashore. At the same time, Gen. Kenney's medium bombers and fighter planes struck at enemy airfields in the area to protect the Allied invasion fleet.[14]

On September 5, as the Australians and Americans pushed towards Lae, the U.S. 503rd Parachute Regiment was air dropped on Nadzab. When Gen. MacArthur learned that Gen. Kenney had decided to circle over the drop zone in a B-17 to watch the action, he naturally insisted on doing the same. Although Gen. Kenney was afraid that some "five-dollar a month Jap aviator" would shoot a hole in MacArthur, he contacted the 43rd BG. Three 63rd BS B-17s were selected for what Kenney called the "brass-hat flight." The 43rd BG CO, Harry Hawthorne, now a colonel, decided to take Gen. MacArthur in B-17F (41-24537,

Talisman) and take Gen. Ramey along as his copilot. Capt. John Van Trigt would take Gen. Kenney in B-17F (41-24353, *Cap'n & the Kids*) and Lt. William E. Crawford would carry Gen. Sutherland in B-17F (41-24554, *The Mustang*).[15]

At 10:22 A.M., after a preliminary bombing and strafing run by B-25s and A-20s, the first paratroopers jumped out of the C-47 transports and descended on Nadzab. From their ringside seats in the circling B-17s, Gen. MacArthur and the others watched the operation unfold "like clockwork." Caught completely by surprise, the Japanese at Nadzab were quickly overrun and work began immediately to repair the Nadzab landing strip for a division of Australian infantry scheduled to be airlifted to the area in a few days.[16]

Once again Gen. Kenney was overjoyed by the activities of his 5th AF. In a letter to Gen. Arnold he wrote, "You already know by this time the news on the preliminary moves to take out Lae, but I will tell you about the show on the 5th September, when we took Nadzab with 1700 paratroops and with Gen. MacArthur in a B-17 over the area watching the show and jumping up and down like a kid." After explaining the activities of the other planes, Kenney chronicled the activities of his B-17s:

> Following the transports came five B-17s, racks loaded with 300-pound [supply] packages with parachutes, to be dropped to the paratroopers . . . as they needed them. This mobile supply unit stayed over Nadzab practically all day serving the paratroops below, dropping a total of 15 tons of supplies in this manner. Following the echelon to the right and just behind the five supply B-17s was a group of twenty-four B-24s and four B-17s, which left the column [of C-47 transports] . . . to take out the Jap defensive position . . . halfway between Nadzab and Lae.[17]

The next day, September 6, the Australian troops were ferried into the quickly repaired airstrip while 24 heavy bombers, including three B-17s of the 65th BS, dropped 82 tons of 1000-lb. bombs on Lae. Two days later, six 65th BS B-17s bombed "Chinatown," a concentration of buildings and supplies at Lae, while the 43rd BG B-24s hit other targets. Encountering no antiaircraft fire or enemy fighter opposition, the 65th BS historian wrote, "Bombing was excellent. The mission was uneventful."[18]

Fearing the annihilation of their weak garrison at Lae, the Japanese at Salamaua began a withdrawal towards Lae on September 8. However, the move was too little too late. With Allied troops driving in from the east and west, and with Gen. Kenney's airplanes attacking almost hourly, the loss of Lae and Salamaua was a foregone conclusion. On September 12, Australian troops captured Salamaua and the nearby airfield and began pressing northward towards Lae, trapping the Japanese defenders in an ever-shrinking pocket.[19]

Hoping to inflict further injury on the remaining Japanese, the 65th BS B-17s struck at Lae again on September 15. On the way home to Port Moresby, the small formation of Fortresses entered a large thunderhead. For some unknown reason, Lt. Howard G. Eberly, B-17F (41-24552, *Listen Here, Tojo!*), was far to the left of the other planes when they entered the storm. Although the other crews tried to contact Eberly by radio, nothing was ever heard from him and it was assumed that the *Listen Here, Tojo!* had hit a cloud-covered mountain peak. B-17F (41-24552, *Listen Here, Tojo!*) holds the unenviable distinction of being the last B-17 lost in combat in the Pacific.[20]

After a thorough pounding of the Lae area by 5th AF airplanes on September 16, which included a few B-17s from the 65th BS, the 7,500 Japanese defenders pulled out of the town and the adjacent airfields and retired to the northwest, in the general direction of Wewak. Almost immediately the Australian infantry moved into the hard-won area. With Lae and Salamaua now in Allied hands, Gen. MacArthur began looking towards his next objective in Operation Cartwheel: the occupation of Finschhaven.[21]

That same day, the 43rd BG lost another Flying Fortress. After having already survived a mid-air collision on April 17, B-17F (41-24355, *Dinah Might*) was taxied into a ditch and wrecked beyond repair. Another bomber had met an inglorious death.[22]

On September 19, the 43rd BG historian wrote, "An historic day in the 43rd Bomb Group. Another squadron of our fast diminishing famed Flying Fortresses flew its last mission and was farmed out to pasture like a good old fire horse. The 65th Squadron flew its last mission with B-17's. . . ." Flying in formation with the 63rd BS B-17s, the flight of Fortresses, ceremoniously led by the CO of the 65th BS, Daniel Cromer, now a major, bombed the "stores and personnel area" at Cape Gloucester. Upon return from the raid, the 65th BS personnel gave up their B-17s. Noted the group historian, "There was no mistake about it, the boys of Maj. Cromer's outfit hated to see their beloved Fortresses go. Like all boys who trained on them, they loved them." The 65th BS had received their first B-24 during the week of September 5-11. On September 21, the 65th BS flew its last mission with a Flying Fortress when a B-17E was taken on an uneventful photo-reconnaissance mission of the Buka area.[23]

The 43rd BG historian wrote of the disposition of the Southwest Pacific Area Flying Fortresses. "Part of the retired B-17's were turned over to the 63rd Squadron, [while] a number were given to the air service command for use as troop and supply carriers in their 'old age'." While the 63rd BS got the best planes, the 481st Service Squadron got the remainder for supply service.[24]

In addition, a number of B-17s were grabbed by general officers to be used as personal airplanes. Gen. MacArthur selected B-17E (41-2593) and outfitted it for his special needs. The armor plating and all of the guns, except the nose and tail guns, were removed. An electric stove, an icebox, and two Pullman-type bunks were installed in the bomb bay, while the radio compartment was reconfigured into an office area, equipped with a desk and chairs. The plane was quickly named *Bataan*.[25]

B-17F (41-24537, *Talisman*) became the personal transport of Maj. Gen. James L.

Frink, the Services and Supply commander in the Southwest Pacific, and was quickly renamed *USASOS War-Horse*, and B-17F (41-24403, *The Old Man*) was chosen by Gen. Whitehead. The old 19th BG B-17E (41-2462, *Tojo's Jinx*) was taken by Lt. Gen. Walter Krueger of the Sixth Army and renamed *Billy*, while Gen. Kenney continued to fly his old 19th BG B-17E (41-2633, *Sally*).[26] The combat era of the B-17 in the Pacific was quickly coming to a close.

In the South Pacific Area, the month of August started with the 394th BS being selected as a 5th BG "snooper" unit to be equipped with radar-equipped B-24 Snoopers. All of the 394th BS B-17s were transferred to the 23rd BS, making that unit the last B-17-equipped squadron in the South Pacific. On August 4, Munda airfield was captured by the Americans and the following day, the town of Munda itself fell. On August 6, the 23rd BS B-17s participated with the 5th BG B-24s, B-25s and more than 50 Navy and Marine fighters and dive-bombers on a raid against Rekata Bay on the northwest coast of Santa Isabel Island.[27]

For some unknown reason, B-17E (41-2463, *Yankee Doodle*) was lost on the ground on August 13. The *Yankee Doodle* became the last B-17 of the 5th BG lost in the South Pacific.[28] As the 5th BG B-24s began to dominate the air strikes, nine B-17s from the 23rd BS staged one last mission on August 14 and hit the Rekata Bay area with everything they had. Two days later, the 23rd BS ceased combat operations. Twenty-four officers and enlisted men were awarded decorations on August 22 and by August 24, the air echelon had been moved from Guadalcanal back to Espiritu Santo for "a period of rest, training, and searches . . ."[29]

By the middle of September, the 23rd BS began receiving brand new B-24 bombers and crews from the States. Noted the squadron historian, "These were the first crews to arrive to relieve old B-17 crews." Slowly but surely the B-17s and their crews were being replaced. On October 9, after enough new bombers had arrived, the 23rd BS CO, Berton Burns, now a major, was relieved of his duties and led three other crews in their old B-17s from Espiritu Santo towards Oklahoma City. Among the B-17s making the trip were B-17Es (41-2444), (41-2467), and (41-9222, *Knucklehead*). Led to believe that they were to take their planes with them on bond selling tours once they got home, the men soon found otherwise. When the stateside authorities got a look at the battle-worn B-17s of the 5th BG, they pronounced them "Unfit to Fly" and quickly shelved them.[30]

A few days after the departure of Maj. Burns and the others, the last Flying Fortress of the 23rd BS and the 5th BG, B-17E (41-2611), was taken away and flown to Tontouta Field on New Caledonia. Eventually, the plane was returned to the United States in January 1944.[31] The era of the B-17 as a combat aircraft in the South Pacific Area was over.

With the demise of the 5th BG B-17s there remained only one unit in the entire Pacific Theater still flying B-17s in combat—the 63rd BS/43rd BG in the Southwest Pacific. Near the end of September, Australian forces had made an amphibious landing near Finschhaven. Instead of meeting light resistance they ran into over 5,000 Japanese defenders determined to hold out to the last man. Fighting fiercely, the Australians pushed steadily forward and on October 2, captured Finschhaven. Having taken complete control of the entire Huon Peninsula, the Allied armies were now in a position to make the jump to invade New Britain and threaten Rabaul.[32]

While the Australians were settling in at Finschhaven, word reached the Allies that an entire division of Japanese troops was coming down from the Wewak area to regain the vital peninsula. In response, the B-17s of the 63rd BS bombed portions of the Bogadjim-Ramu Road on October 5. Fortunately, the Japanese division never materialized and by the second week in October the Huon Peninsula was firmly in Allied Hands and Gen. MacArthur was looking across the Vitiaz Strait towards New Britain.[33]

The rapid movements by the Allied forces in New Guinea and by the Americans in the Northern Solomons caused great concern among the Japanese commanders at Rabaul. Fearing an invasion of Bougainville and New Britain, the Japanese set about to fortify Bougainville with 35,000 soldiers and stop both invasions with airpower from Rabaul. Unfortunately, Rabaul was now within easy reach of not only the American heavy bombers, but all of the Allied planes.[34]

On October 12 a total of 349 5th AF aircraft raided Rabaul with "the biggest attack so far in the Pacific." However, none of the planes were B-17s. Bad weather interfered with follow-up strikes until October 18 when nearly 80 heavy bombers and their fighter escorts took off from New Guinea. Out in the lead, Flight Officer Halbert Miller was flying B-17F (41-24353, *Cap'n & The Kids*) as a "weather ship," while two more Flying Fortresses, B-17F (41-24536) and B-17F (41-24554, *The Mustang*), flew along with the B-24s. Near Gasmata the weather shut down to a ceiling of only 200 feet and the bombers and fighters turned back.[35]

During the third week in October, the 63rd BS historian reported, "Edward Scott, now a Lt. Col., and the new CO [of the squadron], returned to Moresby with several new crews and B-24s. By the 20th of the month all 12 of the new crews were on hand and the 63rd had suddenly become a B-24 outfit. The last B-17 combat missions were flown on this date and then the war-weary bombers were placed on the retired list."[36] It was an inglorious way for a glorious airplane to end a storied career in the Pacific Theater.

Beginning with the first week in November several B-17s from the Southwest Pacific Area were returned to the United States. Among those sent home were B-17Es (41-2637) and (41-2638, *Chico*), and B-17Fs (41-24401, *Lak-A-Nookie*), (41-24455, *Old Baldy*), (41-24554, *The Mustang*), and (41-24574, *Tuffy*). Also in November, 12 of the best B-17s were transferred to the 54th Troop Carrier Wing (TCW) to act as armed transports, capable of carrying supplies and equipment into a contested area that would be too volatile for a C-47. The 12 aircraft were B-17Es (41-2408), (41-2432, *The Last Straw*), (41-2657, *Old Faithful*), (41-2662, *Spawn of Hell*), (41-2665, *Lulu*), and (41-2458, *Yankee Didd'ler—Wouldn't It Root Ya*), and B-17Fs (41-24353, *Cap'n & The Kids*), (41-24357, *Tojo's Nightmare*), (41-24358, *Lulu Belle*), (41-24381, *Panama Hattie*), (41-24420, *Super Snooper*), and (41-24548, *War Horse*).[37]

Once assigned to the 54th TCW the planes were sent to the 4th Air Depot at Garbutt Field, Townsville, for modification. Typifying the changes that took place on the old B-17s was the modifications made on B-17F (41-24353, *Cap'n & The Kids*). Being an armed transport, all of the gun positions were retained with the exception of the ball turret. The bomb racks and shackles were removed from the bomb bay and replaced with steel bins having hinged doors on the bottom that could be opened electrically by a switch controlled by the pilot.[38]

When the modifications on the airplanes were complete, the 12 bombers were sent to one of three different Troop Carrier Groups (TCG) within the wing. Furthermore, it appears as though each Fortress was sent to a different Troop Carrier Squadron (TGS) within each group. And, while the modified B-17s acted alone or in conjunction with their squadron C-47s on numerous occasions, ferrying ammunition and supplies to the rapidly moving Allied front, several of the Flying Fortresses banded together on a couple of occasions to deliver supplies into an especially hot drop zone.

By February 1944, the Americans had been able to capture Bougainville and had a firm foothold on New Britain. Instead of capturing the Japanese strongholds at Rabaul and nearby Kavieng, which might cost too many lives, the commanders agreed to isolate both positions and effectively neutralize the area. On February 29, American troops landed opposite the Momote Airfield on Los Negros Island in the Admiralty Islands, to the northwest of New Britain. Predicting that the landings would be hotly contested, and knowing that the troops were not scheduled to receive reinforcements until March 2, Gen. Whitehead had ordered eight B-17s from the 54th TCW to stand by at Finschhaven in case they were needed.[39]

Although the American landing was successful and Momote Airfield was captured by 10:00 A.M., the Japanese attacked after dark and encircled the American position. The next morning, while both sides fought over possession of the airstrip, B-17E (41-2458, *Yankee Didd'ler*), from the 317th TCG, made two supply drops. A short time later, B-17E (41-2662, *Spawn of Hell*), B-17F (41-24420, *Super Snooper*), B-17F (41-24548, *War Horse*), and one other B-17, all from the 375th TCG, dropped 12 tons of plasma, ammunition, barbed wire, and weapons to the American troops. Then, before the day was over, B-17E (41-2432, *The Last Straw*) and B-17F (41-24353, *Cap'n & The Kids*), both from the 433rd TCG, made three supply runs over the American position and followed up with three strafing runs along the Japanese lines.[40]

The next day, the B-17s were back. B-17E (41-2458, *Yankee Didd'ler*), B-17F (41-24353, *Cap'n & The Kids*), and at least one other B-17 flew over the American lines in the afternoon and unloaded their precious supplies. While Capt. A. J. Beck in the *Cap'n & The Kids* was making one of his supply runs, he was jumped by four Japanese fighters. As Beck raced for the safety of the antiaircraft fire of some American destroyers stationed offshore, one of the fighters, a single-engine Tony, came in a bit too close. Wrote the left waist gunner, Sgt. A. C. Crossen, "A . . . Tony, passed over and behind us from four o'clock; he flew straight out level and made a right turn and headed back towards us . . . I put several bursts into him in the engine and right wing, and as he came on I put more bursts in him . . . he suddenly turned right . . . he was smoking as he turned." The Tony was seen to crash into the water, creating a huge ball of flame and smoke.[41] Thus, Sgt. Crossen earned the distinction for the last recorded destruction of a Japanese aircraft by a B-17 crewman.

After the fire from the destroyer chased the other three enemy fighters away, Capt. Beck went back to Momote field to finish his supply runs. The Japanese were holding the western edge of the strip and the Americans were holding the eastern edge as Beck flew down the center dropping his supplies. Once his supply bins were empty, Beck made a number of strafing passes along the length of the Japanese line while the American troops ran out and retrieved the much-needed supplies. After 55 minutes of strafing, Capt. Beck flew back to Finschhaven where it was noted that B-17F (41-24353, *Cap'n & The Kids*) had two bullet holes in the tail and an antenna shot away.[42]

For the next few months the 54th TCW B-17s carried on routine supply drops. Then, on April 22, 1944, five B-17s, including B-17E (41-2432, *The Last Straw*) and B-17F (41-24353, *Cap'n & The Kids*) from the 433rd TCG, and B-17E (41-2458, *Yankee Didd'ler*) and B-17F (41-24357, *Super Chief*) from the 317th TCG, went on a "special operation" to support the amphibious invasion of Hollandia, on the northern coast of Netherlands New Guinea. When the Japanese abandoned the beaches and pulled back into the interior, the American troops gave chase and quickly outdistanced their supply lines. On April 26, the five B-17s began dropping tons of supplies to the rapidly advancing American infantrymen. Two days later, when the airstrip at Hollandia was made operational for C-47s, the emergency supply drop was discontinued.[43]

On May 4, Lt. Robert Kennedy, B-17F (41-24548, *War Horse*), delivered more supplies to the troops at Hollandia. On the way back to Port Moresby he ran out of gas and made an emergency landing at Tadji, New Guinea. When the left landing gear collapsed, the plane spun off the runway, mangling the right wing tip and damaging the entire underbelly beyond repair.[44]

By the fall of 1944 and the early part of 1945, the old B-17s had just about played themselves out. Most of them were scrapped, salvaged or written off but B-17F (41-24353, *Cap'n & The Kids*) continued to lead a long, charmed life. In September 1944, the plane was chosen by Lt. Gen. Robert L. Eichelberger, CO of the Eighth Army, as his personal transport and was quickly rechristened *Miss Em* in honor of his wife, Emaline. In spite of its age, B-17F (41-24353) continued to impress the crews that flew it. M/Sgt. Charles Cole, the radio operator, recalled, "*Miss Em* was a very reliable aircraft. Never once did it ever abort a flight in its almost daily schedule."

In October, Gen. MacArthur fulfilled his promise of returning to the Philippines when elements of Gen. Eichelberger's Eighth Army invaded Leyte Island on October 20. By November most of Leyte was in U.S. hands and B-17F (41-24353, *Miss Em*), piloted by Maj. Charles Downer, a veteran of the 403rd BS/43rd BG, carried Eichelberger to the island, becoming the first B-17 to touch down in the Philippines since May 1942.[45]

On December 15, American troops increased their activities in the Philippines and invaded Mindoro Island and on January 9, 1945, nearly 100,000 American troops landed at Lingayen Bay on the main island of Luzon. On February 16, the Americans executed a surprise parachute and amphibious invasion of Corregidor Island. Watching the invasion from a ringside seat in the *Miss Em* was Gen. Eichelberger. Noted Maj. Downer, "Circling overhead, we were high enough to take in the entire scene at once and low enough to see the individual participants."[46]

Three days later, Gen. MacArthur increased his activities in the Philippines by invading the northwest corner of Samar Island. Once again, Gen. Eichelberger was present but instead of just watching, he decided to add a little firepower to the invasion. Maj. Downer wrote, "[On] 19 February on the island of Samar, the general asked me to make a low pass just offshore from the landing beach. Then he grabbed one of our waist guns and added to the suppressive fire against possible targets hidden by trees."[47]

Months later, in August 1945, B-17F (41-24353, *Miss Em*) took her last flight with Gen. Eichelberger, a two-hour trip to Manila. After that, the aging B-17 was replaced by a brand-new B-17G. "The former *Cap'n & The Kids* had been kept busy in the 11 months since joining the Eighth Army," wrote Maj. Downer, "making 160 flights on 141 days. Eastern Air Defense Force Headquarters had classified 63 of them as combat missions." In April 1946, B-17F (41-24353, *Cap'n & The Kids* aka *Miss Em*) was scrapped at Tacloban, Leyte.[48] The last of the old warriors had finally been put to rest.

Although the old B-17Ds, Es, and Fs had been phased out of the Pacific, six new B-17Gs made their way to the Pacific Theater in early 1945, not as combat aircraft but as air-sea rescue planes. Fitted with special radar equipment and carrying a huge lifeboat under their belly, the planes were assigned the task of searching for and rescuing downed B-29 crews returning from raids on Japan. Known as SB-17Gs, and based out of Okinawa and Iwo Jima, the modified Fortresses helped save many a downed crew from disappearing in the vast Pacific.[49]

By the end of 1943 the B-17 Flying Fortress was gone from the Pacific as a combat aircraft. For almost two years the B-17 had flown through the Pacific skies, initiating many changes and going through many changes itself. At first employed as a high altitude bomber, it was soon found that such a tactic was highly ineffective in the mobile character of the first year of the war when many of the bombing missions were staged against moving enemy warships and transports. In the second year, when a majority of the bombing raids were staged against enemy airfields and harbors, high level bombing was a bit more effective. Still, it wasn't until the B-17s perfected skip bombing that the Flying Fortress crews began scoring numerous hits. However, the size and slow speed of the big Fortresses doomed their continued use as skip bombers from the start. In the end, it was the lighter, swifter B-25 and B-26 medium bombers that claimed fame throughout the world as deadly skip bombers.

Against enemy fighter planes, there was no better airplane than the B-17. Japanese pilots gained an early respect for the B-17 that lasted throughout the war. From the first time that a swarm of Zeros pumped numerous cannon and machine gun shells into the B-17C of Colin Kelly, to the very last round fired at a B-17 in the Pacific, the Japanese found it almost impossible to shoot down a Flying Fortress. With the appearance of the B-17Es and Fs, with their lethal tail guns, the Japanese soon learned to fear the Flying Fortress. Japanese ace Sakai wrote, ". . . In 1942, the Flying Fortress was the most formidable opponent among Allied planes."[50] Although the Japanese changed their tactics from tail end to frontal attacks, the results remained practically the same, few B-17s were ever brought down by Japanese fighter plane gunfire alone.

From the very beginning of the war, when the United States Navy was crippled by the disaster at Pearl Harbor and the Army was retreating through the Philippines, the B-17 was one of only a handful of offensive weapons that America possessed to try and slow down the fast-moving Japanese war machine. Although it eventually proved futile, the Flying Fortress crews dutifully bombed enemy warships, transports and landing parties. With the fall of the Philippines, the B-17s moved south to help defend the Netherlands East Indies and when the Indies fell, the Fortresses moved down to Australia and New Guinea. Here, strengthened by new planes and new crews from the United States, the B-17 airmen took their stand. By constantly bombing Japanese beachheads, harassing enemy shipping and airfields, and flying long range reconnaissance patrols, the B-17 Flying Fortress played a vital role in finally halting and turning back the onrushing Japanese tide in the Southwest Pacific.

At the same time, when fear existed that Japan might invade Hawaii, the B-17 was primarily utilized as a long-range search plane in the Central and South Pacific. In this capacity it played a crucial role in the battle of Midway, the turning point of the Pacific War, and later in the drawn-out battle for Guadalcanal. Although constantly harassing the enemy build-up on their island bastions, the B-17 proved its real worth in the South Pacific as an aerial reconnaissance plane. Rugged and sturdy, the B-17 was capable of taking massive amounts of punishment from enemy fighters or antiaircraft fire while doggedly clinging to an enemy convoy and relaying information back to headquarters.

When the B-17 was phased out of the Pacific it was not because of a lack of satisfactory performance. On the contrary, the B-17 had gained the respect of both the Allies and enemy alike. A lack of replacement B-17s, and the small bomb bay and limited range of the bomber caused the demise of the Flying Fortress in the Pacific. Unable to reach enemy targets spread far across the Pacific, the B-17 was slowly replaced by the B-24, and later, the B-29 bombers.

Although the B-17 was phased out of the Pacific, it went on to have an illustrious career in the European Theater. Many of the tactics and improvements employed against Nazi Germany first saw light in the Pacific. Troubles with the oxygen system, the remote-controlled Bendix belly turret, the improved Sperry ball turret, and the lack of forward firepower first appeared in the Pacific and had been ironed out or were being improved by the time the B-17 became a staple fixture in Europe. The Pacific was the proving grounds for the improved performance of the B-17 in Europe.

Although gone from the Pacific, the B-17 was never forgotten by the men that had flown or serviced it. None of the Pacific B-17 pilots, crewmen, or mechanics would ever forget their experiences with the Flying Fortress. Many men were forced to convert to B-24s, where they performed admirably, but in their hearts, most remained loyal to the B-17. From their first sight of the B-17, until long after the war-weary bombers were taken away, the Flying Fortress remained their bomber of choice.

The first plane to challenge the dominance of the Flying Fortress was the LB-30, the export version of the B-24. When the plane first appeared in Java, the B-17 crewmen were enthusiastic since the LB-30 sported twin .50 caliber tail guns and, at the time, the Japanese were still making tail-end attacks. However, it was soon found that the LB-30 lacked the ruggedness of the B-17 and being without superchargers, could not fly above 20,000 feet, leaving it well within reach of the Japanese Zeros.[51]

"An LB-30 was a B-24 that didn't have any turbo-superchargers," remembered Lt. Fields. "The disadvantage of not having turbo-superchargers was that it only had an operating ceiling of about 11 to 12 thousand feet, and it was not very maneuverable at that altitude . . . I didn't care too much for the LB-30 for the reasons that I just named."[52]

Mechanic Roy Davenport worked on both the B-17 and the B-24, the successor to the LB-30, and had a heartfelt love for the Flying Fortress. "To me, it was the pin-up plane of my era in looks and performance. When we were down under in 1942, it came through for us and saved us . . . Battle scars didn't seem to slow it down and when in this condition, brought our crews back to fight another day . . . She would fly faster than the B-24 at high altitudes and much higher. They could go further on one engine which saved many ditch jobs and lives." Summing up his war experiences with the B-17 and the B-24, Davenport wrote, "It took some time for me to see the worth in the B-24 that replaced it."[53]

Maj. Edmundson had flown the B-24, B-25 and B-26 but preferred the B-17. "I have flown them all and they were all fine birds," he wrote, "but the B-17 was the airplane of that era in a way that no other aircraft can ever be." To Maj. Edmundson, the Flying Fortress ". . . was a real treat to fly." Additionally, he found the plane to be "very forgiving." He commented, "In those days we knew nothing about weight and balance. Later, when I was faced with computing weight and balance for B-29s, B-47s, B-52s, and B-58s, I wondered how we ever avoided serious trouble with the B-17s. The answer, of course, is that it was a very forgiving airplane."[54]

To other men, their love for the B-17 was more simplistic. Lt. Minahan wrote, "In my opinion the B-17 was the finest combat airplane the Air Force has ever had." Technician Sgt. Green lovingly called the Flying Fortress, "that Ole rugged B-17." He remembered, "It was a great airplane and could withstand a lot of damage before it quit." Equally impressed with the ruggedness of the B-17 was Capt. Crawford. He remarked, ". . . a Boeing Fortress can take anything the Japs have to hand out."[55]

Overall, most of the B-17 veterans adored the ruggedness of the B-17 over any other airplane of the era. Lt. Fields recalled, "All those who flew the B-17 had great confidence in the plane to get them there and back . . . This was a pilots plane and after first flying it a pilot remembered it as his first love no matter how many other great planes he flew. I experienced the B-17 first then the B-24, then the B-29 and B-32 and liked the B-17 as first choice."[56]

Trying to explain why the B-17 had such a cherished reputation, Maj. Edmundson noted:

> A very few airplanes are of such special character, so outstanding in design and performance, and so much a part of a particular era that they have a great impact on human awareness, extending far beyond the pilots who flew them. These aircraft can come to represent to a nation, and sometimes to the world, the very essence of the years during which they were dominant in the sky.
> Such an airplane was the B-17, Flying Fortress.[57]

On August 25, 1945, two weeks after the explosion of the second atomic bomb forced Japan to surrender, but long before any American troops had set foot on any of the main Japanese islands, two P-38 pilots, Col. Clay Tice and Flight Off. Hall, were out on routine surveillance flight when Hall ran out of fuel and the two headed for Kyushu Island. Col. Tice wrote, "I called Jukebox 36 [a B-17G of the 6th Air-Sea Rescue Squadron], and informed him of my intentions and requested assistance. I landed at Nittagahara [airdrome], four hundred and fifty miles from base, at 1205 [P.M.]." After about an hour, Japanese officers finally appeared and although there was a problem with language, the two sides remained cordial. Col. Clay continued, "Jukebox 36 landed at approximately 1315 [1:15 P.M.] and with a fuel pump and hose furnished by the Japanese, we transferred approximately two hundred and sixty gallons from the B-17 to the P-38. . . . Flight Officer Hall and I were airborne behind the B-17 at 1445 [2:45 P.M.] . . ."[58]

It is almost fitting that the first American bomber to land on one of the main Japanese islands after the fall of Japan should be a B-17 Flying Fortress. Having flown into Pearl Harbor on December 7, 1941, the B-17 was in the war in the Pacific from the start to the finish.

XXXI

Beyond the Pacific

B-17s WERE USED in every theater in World War II; in the Pacific, in the Aleutians, in China-Burma-India, in the Zone of the Interior, and especially in Europe. The B-17 was pulled from the Pacific in late 1943 but went on to have an illustrious career in Europe where it was finally able to function in the capacity that it had been designed for—as a high altitude heavy bomber. The first B-17Es arrived in England and were assigned to the fledgling Eighth AF in July 1942. Beginning with only a dozen planes on a raid on Rouen, France, in August of 1942, the Eighth AF ended with thousand-plane raids against targets deep within Nazi Germany. The Eighth AF B-17s were at their best when flying in large, tight formations using their interlocking fields of defensive firepower to stave off enemy fighter planes while unloading a carpet of bombs upon designated targets. Like their brethren in the Pacific, the European crewmen soon learned that the B-17's rugged, sturdy construction made it capable of taking unusually high amounts of punishment from enemy fighters and antiaircraft guns. Although sometimes losing one, two or even three engines, more often than not, the B-17 stayed airborne and brought its crew home. Such ruggedness earned the B-17 undying respect.[1]

In November 1942, two Eighth AF bomb groups, the 97th and 301st, were shifted to North Africa immediately after the Allied invasion and became the backbone of the Twelfth Air Force (Twelfth AF). Much like the Pacific B-17 groups, the two North African groups operated out of primitive landing fields and were used to keep constant pressure on enemy troop and supply concentrations, airfields, and ships. Also similar to the Pacific units, the 97th and 301st BGs were subjected to devastating air raids from enemy fighter and bomber planes.

When North Africa was secured by the Allies in early 1943, the Twelfth AF, now joined by the 2nd and 99th BGs, began targeting airfields in Sicily, Sardinia, and Italy. Numerous attacks were carried out against the Italian docks and ships, and against airfields and coastal gun emplacements. During the ensuing invasions of Sicily and Italy, the four North African bomb groups continued to fly tactical support for the Allied troops and bomb enemy troop concentrations and strategic bridges.[2]

By late 1943, enough of Italy was in Allied hands so that it was deemed safe to establish an air force based on the Italian mainland. On October 30, the four North African bomb groups were combined with two B-24 and two fighter groups to form the Fifteenth Air Force (Fifteenth AF), flying out of Foggia, Italy. For the next year and a half the Fifteenth AF B-17s were engaged primarily in strategic bombing of targets in northern Italy, Southern France, Germany, Poland, Czechoslovakia, Austria, Hungary, and the Balkans. In February 1944, the Fifteenth AF cooperated with the Eighth AF and the Royal Air Force (RAF) in a week long bombing of German fighter production. While the Fifteenth, flying out of Italy, and the Eighth, flying from England, bombed the enemy manufacturing plants and oil refineries during the day, the RAF struck at night. In what would later become known as "Big Week," the Fifteenth AF B-17s continually ran into bad weather as they tried to get over the Italian Alps. By the time Big Week was over, the four bomb groups had lost a combined total of more than 30 planes. Two more B-17 BGs, the 463rd and the 483rd, joined the Fifteenth AF in the spring of 1944, allowing the Fifteenth to continue to strike at strategic targets in force.[3]

In June 1944, planes from the Fifteenth AF began flying shuttle missions to Russia, bombing strategic targets deep within German-controlled territory en route and on the way back. Throughout the remainder of 1944 the Fifteenth AF Fortresses targeted German airfields and factories, supported the Allied invasion of Southern France, and repeatedly bombed the oil refinery complex at Ploesti, Romania.[4]

As the Russian Army gobbled up territory in the east and the bad winter of 1944 came on, the B-17s of the Fifteenth AF were forced to concentrate on small tactical raids against targets in Italy. In March 1945 the strategic missions started again as the bombers flew to Austria, Hungary, and Germany. On March 24, 1945, Fifteenth AF B-17s flew all the way to Berlin, escorted by long-range P-51 Mustang fighters.[5]

By the end of the war the Fifteenth AF had just about run out of targets, flying tactical missions against Italian strong points in support of the advancing Allied units. Although looked on as bastard stepchildren to the Eighth AF, the Twelfth and Fifteenth AFs played fundamental roles in bringing Germany to its knees. Their early attacks against North Africa, and later Southern France and the vital oil fields in Romania caused Germany to keep an eye on the Mediterranean. Flying against some of the same targets as the Eighth AF B-17s, the Fortresses from the Fifteenth AF battled some of the same German fighter units and antiaircraft concentrations as the planes from England. The job they accomplished was just as successful as the Eighth AF airmen yet, like their brethren in the Pacific, the airmen and ground crew mechanics in the Mediterranean had to take a back seat to the Fortresses flying out of England.[6]

Following the first raid by the Eighth AF B-17s on August 17, 1942, the number of Fortresses in England continued to increase until it reached its peak of twenty-six bomb groups. High-altitude strategic bombing became the mainstay of the Eighth AF. Bombing in daylight, when the Norden bombsight was most effective, the B-17s and B-24s of the Eighth AF suffered terrible losses from both the German fighter planes and antiaircraft guns but continued to bring the war to the people of Germany.[7]

On October 9, 1942 the Eighth AF managed to put over 100 B-17s and B-24s into the air for the first time in the European Theater. Targets in France and along the French coast continued to draw the attention of the Eighth AF throughout the end of the year. Through trial and error, and the ingenuity of Col. Curtis LeMay, commander of the 305th BG, the Eighth AF groups began flying in a new, staggered box formation and eliminated evasive action from antiaircraft guns on bomb runs. In just a short time the bomb patterns improved and the German fighter pilots were kept further at bay.[8]

On January 27, 1943 the Eighth AF flew its first mission to Germany, bombing the naval base at Wilhelmshaven. Most of the Fortresses were B-17Fs, a new model of Fortress equipped with new "Tokyo tank" fuel cells in the outer wing tips to give them extra range. Lacking long-range friendly fighter cover, and having run up against spirited German head-on attacks, many of the B-17 groups, like those in the Pacific, began making field modifications to their planes. Forward firing single or double machine guns were quickly installed in the nose and cheeks. Throughout the spring and summer of 1943 the Eighth AF continued to bomb targets in France and Germany.[9]

In September 1943, a new model of B-17, the G-model, arrived in England sporting factory-installed cheek guns and a powered, remote-controlled chin turret with twin .50-caliber machine guns. At about the same time the Eighth AF began using Fortresses equipped with radar to pinpoint targets through clouds or German created smoke screens, and developed "window" and "carpet." Window were strips of thin tinfoil dropped from designated bombers to confuse German radar equipment, while carpet was a radar jamming device that played havoc with enemy ground radar.

Using their new planes and techniques, the Eighth AF continued to strike at targets deep within German territory. On August 17, 1943 the Eighth sent over 300 Fortresses against the German ball bearing plant at Schweinfurt, Germany. In an attempt to minimize losses, the planes shuttled from England to the target and then on to bases in North Africa, avoiding flying back through the same airspace as before. Still, the raid on Schweinfurt cost the Eighth AF 60 B-17s. To give an idea of the magnitude of the loss, more Fortresses were lost on the Schweinfurt raid than were available in all areas of the Pacific in August 1943.

In September another 45 B-17s were lost on a raid of Stuttgart, and on October 14, during another attack on Schweinfurt, the Eighth AF lost another 60 B-17s with an additional 17 damaged beyond repair and another 121 in need of repair.

October 14, 1943 was nicknamed "Black Thursday." Morale among the Eighth AF crews hit an all time low and those in command began questioning the continuance of daylight bombing, wondering if the heavy losses were worth the damage being inflicted upon the enemy. Although the bomber crews had been able to shoot down a large number of Luftwaffe pilots, the Eighth AF had lost a total of 176 B-17s in October alone. The perpetuation of daylight bombing depended on long range American fighters. If the bombers could get adequate protection, daylight bombing would continue.[10]

Fortunately for the Americans, P-47 Thunderbolt fighters, carrying long-range drop tanks, began to accompany the bombers on raids of France and western Germany. By December, the appearance of the long-range P-38 Lightning and P-51 Mustang fighters meant that daylight precision bombing would continue. Although the Eighth AF had suffered terrible losses in 1943, it had taken the war to the heart of Germany. And, in spite of all of their losses, the Eighth AF continued to grow. The Eighth had started 1943 with four bomb groups and about 100 Fortresses. It ended the year with 18 bomb groups and over 600 B-17s.[11]

Throughout January and February 1944, weather permitting, the Eighth AF continued to bomb German factories and air fields, and the new V-1 bomb sights in France. On February 20, the Eighth AF, in conjunction with the Fifteenth AF in Italy, took part in "Big Week." When it was all over, the Eighth AF had lost 105 B-17s and 53 B-24s. However, more and more bomb groups continued to arrive in England so that by the end of February, the Eighth AF consisted of 30 bomb groups. The Eighth now had more airmen and more airplanes than the entire RAF.[12]

On March 4, 1944, Eighth AF B-17s bombed Berlin for the first time, losing five Fortresses. Two days later, the Eighth returned, this time losing 53 B-17s and 16 B-24s. Berlin was the target again on March 8 when the strike force lost 28 more B-17s and 9 B-24s. Although the losses were high, the Allied commanders considered them acceptable. By striking deep into the heart of Germany and bombing Berlin, Hitler was forced to pull a large number of fighter units away from the French coast to protect his capital. In doing so, he left the coast open for invasion.[13]

In May the B-17s began flying tactical missions in northern France against airfields, railroad marshaling yards, and bridges in preparation for the scheduled landings at Normandy. On D-day, June 6, 1944, the Eighth AF heavy bombers flew over 1,600 sorties. Because of the Eighth AF's effective campaign against German air power, and by their constant attacks against Berlin, the Luftwaffe put up only minor resistance to the Allied invasion. D-day, the long awaited invasion of northern Europe, had been a success.[14]

The vital German synthetic oil refineries became the target of the Eighth AF during the summer of 1944. During four such missions the B-17s dropped their bombs and continued on to Russia. Although the planes increased their range by using bomb-bay gas tanks, which had proved so dangerous in the Pacific, they were escorted the entire way by long-range P-51 fighter planes.[15]

During the fall of 1944 the Eighth AF finally managed to put more than 1,000 bombers into the air. On October 2, 836 B-17s and 296 B-24s bombed industrial targets at Cologne and Kassel. By this time the Eighth consisted of twenty-six B-17 groups with more than 1,000 B-17s at the ready. It was the largest Army air force in existence, far outnumbering all the others by a wide margin.[16]

By the end of 1944 and the beginning of 1945, the German Luftwaffe was almost nonexistent. Only on rare occasions did the German fighter planes rise up in numbers great enough to threaten the large formations of American heavy bombers. Near the end of the war in Europe the biggest threat to the American bombers came from the massed installations of German antiaircraft guns. On April 25, 1944, 307 Flying Fortresses set out to bomb enemy airfields in Czechoslovakia. Six planes were shot down by flak. Unknown to everyone, this would be the last combat mission of the Eighth AF B-17s.

Having started with only a handful of B-17s and a small group of brave, dedicated men, the Eighth AF went on to become the largest Army air unit in existence by the end of World War II. Due to the size of the air force, and the publicity afforded the war in Europe, exploits of the Eighth AF B-17 aircrews became legendary, completely overshadowing the roles played by the smaller air forces. Although the other B-17 units around the world fought equally as valiant as the Eighth AF units, in conditions just as strained as those in Europe, and against an enemy equally, if not more aggressive, the large size of the Eighth AF, the steadfast valor of the aircrews, and the grand publicity afforded the European B-17s gave the Eighth AF a step up on all her sister air forces. While the Eighth AF received most of the attention, and much of the glory, the other units were mostly ignored. Yet, when it came to the love of the B-17, the feeling was universal throughout. The B-17 was the most rugged bomber flown in any theater in World War II and would always be regarded with awe and admiration as the rightful "Queen of the Sky."

Appendix A

B-17 Flying Fortress Combat Units in World War II[1]

Pacific Theater
South Pacific Area:
Seventh and Thirteenth Air Force
>> 5th BG - 23rd, 31st, 72nd, 394th (4th RS) BSs
>> 11th BG - 26th, 42nd, 98th, 431st (50th RS) BSs

Southwest Pacific Area:
Far East Air Force/China-Burma-India
>> 7th BG - 9th, 11th, 22, 436th (88th RS) BSs

Fifth Air Force
>> 19th BG - 14th, 28th, 30th, 32nd, 93rd, 435th
>> (40th RS) BSs
>> 43rd BG - 63rd, 64th, 65th, 403rd (13 RS) BSs

Mediterranean Theater
Eighth, Twelfth and Fifteenth Air Force
>> 97th BG - 340th, 341st, 342nd, 414th BSs
>> 301st BG - 32nd, 352nd, 353rd, 419th BSs

Twelfth and Fifteenth Air Force
>> 2nd BG - 11th, 49th, 91st, 429th BSs
>> 99th BG - 346th, 347th, 348th, 416th Bss

Fifteenth Air Force
>> 463rd BG - 772nd, 773rd, 774th, 775th BSs
>> 483rd BG - 815th, 816th, 817th, 840th Bss

European Theater
Eighth Air Force
>> 34th BG*- 4th, 7th, 18th, 391st BSs
>> 91st BG - 322nd, 323rd, 324th, 401st BSs
>> 92nd BG - 325th, 326th, 327th, 407th BSs
>> 94th BG - 331st, 332nd, 333rd, 410th BSs
>> 95th BG - 334th, 335th, 336th, 412th BSs

---

[1]   Hess, *B-17 Flying Fortress*, Appendix III; Freeman, *The Mighty Eighth*, 286-90; Thompson, *The Boeing B-17E & F Flying Fortress*, 16.

96th BG - 337th, 338th, 339th, 413th BSs
100th BG - 349th, 350th, 351st, 418th BSs
303rd BG - 358th, 359th, 360th, 427th BSs
305th BG - 364th, 365th, 366th, 422nd BSs
306th BG - 267th, 368th, 369th, 423rd BSs
351st BG - 408th, 409th, 410th, 411th BSs
379th BG - 524th, 525th, 526th, 527th BSs
381st BG - 532nd, 533rd, 534th, 535th BSs
384th BG - 544th, 545th, 546th, 547th BSs
385th BG - 548th, 549th, 550th, 551st BSs
388th BG - 560th, 561st, 562nd, 563rd BSs
390th BG - 568th, 569th, 570th, 571st BSs
398th BG - 600th, 601st, 602nd, 603rd BSs
401st BG - 612th, 613th, 614th, 615th BSs
447th BG - 708th, 709th, 710th, 711th BSs
452nd BG - 728th, 729th, 730th, 731st BSs
457th BG - 748th, 749th, 750th, 751st BSs
482nd BG - 812th, 813th BSs
486th BG*- 832nd, 833rd, 834th, 835th Bss
487th BG*- 836th, 837th, 838th, 839th BSs
490th BG*- 848th, 849th, 850th, 851st BSs
493rd BG*- 860th, 861st, 862nd, 863rd BSs

* These were originally B-24 units that switched to B-17s.

Other Eighth Air Force B-17 units:
36th BS (radio countermeasures squadron)
5th Air Sea Rescue Squadron
1st Air Division Headquarters Flight
3rd Air Division Headquarters Flight

Appendix B

The Pacific B-17s

Model	Serial #	Squad	Grp	Name	Comments
B-17C	40-2045	30	19		Shot down 10 Dec 41 at Luzon. Pilot: Capt. Colin P. Kelly, Jr.
B-17C	40-2048		19		Destroyed at Clark Field, 8 Dec 41.
B-17C	40-2049	38R/431	11	*Skipper*	Arrived Pearl Harbor, 7 Dec 41. Heavily damaged during attack. Salvaged. Pilot: 1st Lt. Robert Richards.
B-17C	40-2054	38R	11		Unknown fate.
B-17C	40-2059				Returned to U.S., 25 Oct. 42.
B-17C	40-2062	93	19		Shot down over Java 3 Feb 42. Pilot: 1st Lt Ray L. Cox.
B-17C	40-2063	38R	11		Written off, 29 May 43.
B-17C	40-2067		19		Destroyed at Clark Field, 8 Dec 41.
B-17C	40-2072		19		Heavily damaged on Davao mission, 25 Dec 41. Pilot: Alvin V. H. Mueller. Repaired and used for transport. Ultimate fate unknown.
B-17C	40-2074	38R	11		Arrived Pearl Harbor, 7 Dec 41. Destroyed during attack. Pilot: Capt. Raymond T. Swenson.
B-17C	40-2077		19		Destroyed at Clark Field, 8 Dec 41.
B-17D	40-3059		19		Destroyed at Clark Field, 8 Dec 41.
B-17D	40-3060	26	11		Unknown fate.
B-17D	40-3061	14	19		Destroyed 28 Feb 42 at evacuation of Malang.
B-17D	40-3062	93	19	*Old "62"*	Destroyed by strafing at Pasirian, 22 Feb 42.
B-17D	40-3063		19		Destroyed when hit by P-40 at Clark Field, 10 Dec 41.
B-17D	40-3064		19		Destroyed in ground accident, Malang, 16 Jan 42. Pilot: 1st Lt. William J. Bohnaker
B-17D	40-3066	14	19	*Old "66"*	Destroyed by strafing at Pasirian, 22 Feb 42.
B-17D	40-3067		19		Crackup during take off at Darwin, 28 Jan 42, Pilot: 1st Lt. Edward C. Teats.
B-17D	40-3068		19		Destroyed at Clark Field, 8 Dec 41.
B-17D	40-3069		19		Destroyed at Clark Field, 8 Dec 41. Part used by Japanese to reconstruct a B-17D.
B-17D	40-3070		19		Destroyed by strafing at Pasirian, 22 Feb 42.
B-17D	40-3071	4RS	5		Destroyed at Hickam Field, 7 Dec 41.
B-17D	40-3072		19		Destroyed by strafing at Pasirian, 22 Feb 42.

B-17D	40-3073	93	19		Badly damaged on raid to Masbate, 14 Dec 41. Pilot: 1st Lt. Jack Adams.
B-17D	40-3075		19		Destroyed at Clark Field, 8 Dec 41.
B-17D	40-3076		19		Destroyed at Clark Field, 8 Dec 41.
B-17D	40-3077		11		Destroyed at Hickam Field, 7 Dec 41.
B-17D	40-3078		19		Destroyed by strafing at Malang, 3 Feb 42.
B-17D	40-3079		19	*The Gazelle*	Crashed at Daly Waters, Aust., 14 March 42. Pilot: 1st Lt. Duane H. Skiles.
B-17D	40-3080		5		Destroyed at Hickam Field, 7 Dec 41.
B-17D	40-3081		11		Destroyed at Hickam Field, 7 Dec 41.
B-17D	40-3082		5		Written off, 19 July 43.
B-17D	40-3083		11		Destroyed at Hickam Field, 7 Dec 41.
B-17D	40-3084		11		Written off, 16 Oct 43.
B-17D	40-3085		5		Returned to U.S., 23 Oct. 42.
B-17D	40-3086		19		Ditched off Zamboanga, 10 Dec 41. Pilot: 1st Lt. Guilford R. Montgomery.
B-17D	40-3087		19		Destroyed by ground accident at Del Monte, 12 Dec 41.
B-17D	40-3088		19		Destroyed at Clark Field, 8 Dec 41.
B-17D	40-3089	26/ 431	11/5		Unknown fate.
B-17D	40-3090	20	11		Unknown fate.
B-17D	40-3091		19		Scrapped at Darwin because of battle damage, 27 Dec 41. Tail used on *The Swoose*.
B-17D	40-3092		5		Returned to U.S., 22 Oct. 42.
B-17D	40-3093		19		Destroyed by strafing at Del Monte, 19 Dec 41.
B-17D	40-3094		19		Destroyed at Clark Field, 8 Dec 41.
B-17D	40-3095	14	19		Destroyed at Clark Field, 8 Dec 41. Found damaged on Clark Field by Japanese after U.S. evacuation. Repaired and flown to Japan.
B-17D	40-3096	30	19		Heavily damaged on mission and crash landed at Cagayan, 14 Dec 41. Pilot: 1st Lt. Hewett T. "Shorty" Wheless.
B-17D	40-3097	14	19	*The Swoose*	Returned to U.S., 17 Nov 44.
B-17D	40-3098		19		Destroyed by take-off accident at Del Monte, 12 Dec 41. Pilot: 1st Lt. Jack Adams.
B-17D	40-3099		19	*Old "99"*	Destroyed at Clark Field, 8 Dec 41
B-17D	40-3100		19		Destroyed when hit by P-40 at Clark Field, 9 Dec. 41.
B-17E	41-2396	72	5		Ditched off San Cristobal after suffering engine failure, 7 Jan 43. Pilot: Capt. Jack Thornhill.
B-17E	41-2397	431/ 26	11	*Joe Bftsplk*	Written off, 31 Oct 44.
B-17E	41-2402	50RS	11		Water landing 40 miles south of Kauai, 27 Dec. 41. Pilot: 1st Lt. Earl J. Cooper.
B-17E	41-2403	26/ 42	11		Ditched south of Guadalcanal with Gen. Nathan Twining aboard, 26 Jan 43. Pilot: Capt. Woodruff.

B-17E	41-2404	431	11	*The Spider*	Ditched in sea, 12 Sept 42. Pilot: Lt. John Van Haur.
B-17E	41-2406	22	7		Destroyed by crash landing at Madera Is., 25 Jan 42. Pilot: Maj. Kenneth B. Hobson.
B-17E	41-2408	38R/ 40/65	19/43		Trfd 54 Troop Carrier Wing, Nov 43. Salvaged in Brisbane, 14 Oct. 44.
B-17E	41-2409	431	11	*Old Maid*	Crash landed Guadalcanal, 25 Nov. 42. Pilot: Lt. William B. Kyes. Written off, 20 Sept. 43.
B-17E	41-2413	38R/ 42	11		Written off, 11 June 44.
B-17E	41-2415	26/ 31	11/5	*City of San Francisco*	Shot down 5 June 42. Battle of Midway. Pilot: 1st Lt. Robert Porter.
B-17E	41-2416	40/ 88R	19	*San Antonio Rose*	Damaged Townsville, Aust., 22 Feb 42. Written off in Brisbane, 31 Jan 44. Scrapped Oct. 44.
B-17E	41-2417	28/ 63	19/43	*Monkey Bizz-Ness*	Unknown fate.
B-17E	41-2419	22	7		Destroyed by crash landing at Palembang, 22 Jan 42. Pilot: 1st Lt. Jack W. Hughes.
B-17E	41-2420	42	11	*Bessie the Jap Basher*	Ditched Doma Cove, Guadalcanal, 24 Sept 42. Pilot: Capt. Charles E. Norton.
B-17E	41-2421	40	19		Crashed landing and burned at Horn Is., 16 July 42. Pilot: Maj. Clarence E. "Sandy" McPherson.
B-17E	41-2424		19		Shot down. Date unknown.
B-17E	41-2426	431	11		Missing on reconnaissance mission of Northern Solomons. 7 Aug 42. Pilot: Maj. Marion Pharr.
B-17E	41-2427	9	7		Destroyed by strafing at Malang, 3 Feb 42.
B-17E	41-2428	98/42	11	*Ole Sh'asta*	Lost 28 Dec. 42. Pilot: 1st Lt. James R. Harp.
B-17E	41-2429	88R/ 40/ 93	19	*Why Don't We Do This More Often*	Shot down Rabaul, 8 Aug 42. Pilot: Capt. Harl Pease Jr., Medal of Honor recipient.
B-17E	41-2430	88R/ 40/ 65	7/19/ 43	*Naughty But Nice*	Shot down over Vunakanau, 23 June 43. Pilot: Lt. Charles Trimingham.
B-17E	41-2431	26/ 42	11		Returned to U.S., 11 Jan 44.
B-17E	41-2432	88R/ 40/ 65	7/19/ 43	*The Last Straw*	Trfd 54 Troop Carrier Wing, 433 TCG. Nov 43. Written off, 12 Jan 45.
B-17E	41-2433	88R/ 26	11		Returned to U.S., 1 Sept 44.
B-17E	41-2434	88R/ 40/ 65	19/43		Crashed near shore Yorkey Knob, Cairns en route to Aust., 17 Aug 42. Pilot: 2nd Lt. Paul M. Lindsey. 12 KIA including Maj. Dean C. "Pinky" Hoevet, CO 30th BS.
B-17E	41-2435	30	19		Shot down off Buna, 2 Aug 42. Pilot: Lt. Watson.
B-17E	41-2437	98	11		Written off, 15 June 44.
B-17E	41-2438	40	19		Returned to U.S., November 42.
B-17E	41-2440	40/ 98/ 394	19/11/ 5	*Calamity Jane*	Returned to U.S., 7 March 44.

B-17E	41-2442	42	11	*Yokohama Express*	Crashed Shortland Bay, 1 Feb 43. Pilot: Capt. Harold P. Hensley.
B-17E	41-2443	42	11		Crashed into Keaheakahoe Peak on Oahu, 5 April 42. Pilot: Lt. Charles O. Allen.
B-17E	41-2444	42	11		Returned to U.S., 17 Oct 43.
B-17E	41-2445	42	11	*So Solly Please*	Tore off tail in taxi accident, 9 Dec 42. Pilot: Unknown. Written off, 15 June 44.
B-17E	41-2446	22/ 14RS	7/19	*Swamp Ghost*	Crash landed in Agaiambo Swamp, New Guinea, 23 March 42. Pilot: 1st Lt. Frederick C. Eaton, Jr. Returned to U.S. Restored. (Oldest E in world.)
B-17E	41-2447	40	19	*San Antonio Rose II*	Destroyed at Del Monte on Royce Mission, 13 April 42. Pilot: 1st Lt. Frank P. Bostrom.
B-17E	41-2449		19		Destroyed by strafing at Broome, 3 March 42.
B-17E	41-2452	93	19/7		Landed on beach, Malapla Is., near New Guinea, 9 Aug 42. Pilot: Capt. Harry J. Hawthorne.
B-17E	41-2453	30	19		Returned to U.S., after Oct 42.
B-17E	41-2454		19/7	*Craps For The Japs*	Destroyed by strafing at Broome, 3 March 42.
B-17E	41-2455		19/7		Destroyed by strafing at Malang, 20 Feb 42.
B-17E	41-2456		7		Shot down at sea, 8 Feb 42. Pilot: Capt. John L."Duke" Dufrane.
B-17E	41-2457	26/ 63	11/43		Returned to U.S., 2 Aug 44.
B-17E	41-2458	28/ 65	19/43	*Yankee Diddl'er— Wouldn't It Root Ya*	Trfd 54 Troop Carrier Wing, 317 TCG, Nov. 43. Written off, 27 Jan 45.
B-17E	41-2459		7		Strafed on ground, Kendari. Damaged beyond repair. Burned by U.S. 16 Jan 42.
B-17E	41-2460	93	19		Crash landed at Horn Island, 27 July 42. Salvaged. Pilot: Lt. Edward J. Bechtold. Hit B-17E (41-2640).
B-17E	41-2461	30/11	19/7	*El Toro*	Destroyed by strafing Port Moresby, 25 Apr 42.
B-17E	41-2462	93	19	*Tojo's Jinx/Billy*	Gen. Kruger's plane. Written off 3 June 45. Scrapped New Guinea, 1945.
B-17E	41-2463	26	11	*Yankee Doodle*	Written off, 13 Aug 43.
B-17E	41-2464	--/ 28/64	7/ 19/ 43	*Queenie*	Lost with no trace, Nadzab/Biak area with 19 on board, 8 July 44. Pilot: Unknown.
B-17E	41-2466		19		Destroyed by strafing at Bandoeng, 19 Feb 42.
B-17E	41-2467				Returned to U.S., 21 Oct 43.
B-17E	41-2468	9	7		Destroyed by crash landing at Madera Is., 25 Jan 42. Pilot: 1st Lt. Robert E. Northcutt.
B-17E	41-2469	9	7		Destroyed by crash landing at Selembo, 3 Feb 42. Pilot: 1st Lt. Theodore B. Swanson.
B-17E	41-2470	9	7		Destroyed by strafing at Malang, 3 Feb 42.

B-17E	41-2471	9	7		Partially destroyed by burning at Djogjakarta 28 Feb 42. Found by Japanese after U.S. evacuation. Repaired and flown to Japan.
B-17E	41-2472	28/ 30	19/ 43	*Guinea Pig*	Written off, 31 Aug 44.
B-17E	41-2476	9	7		Shot down at sea, 29 Jan 42. Pilot: Capt. Walter W. Sparks.
B-17E	41-2478	Hq	7		Destroyed by strafing at Malang, 20 Feb 42.
B-17E	41-2481	30/ 63/ 431S	19/43	*Topper* aka *Old Topper*	Crashed on take off due to structural failure, Port Moresby, 8 Aug 43. Pilot: Unknown. Sent to 481 Service Sq. Written off, 30 Oct 43.
B-17E	41-2483	9	7		Blown up at evacuation of Madioen, 28 Feb 42.
B-17E	41-2484	9	7		Destroyed by strafing at Malang, 20 Feb 42.
B-17E	41-2486	30/ 9/ 64	19/7/ 43	*Lady Lou*	Returned to U.S., Oct. 42.
B-17E	41-2487	26/ 42	11		Written off, 11 June 44.
B-17E	41-2488	30	19		Destroyed by strafing at Malang, 20 Feb 42.
B-17E	41-2489	93	19	*Suzy-Q*	Returned to U.S., 23 Oct. 42.
B-17E	41-2492	9	7		Shot down at sea, 8 Feb 42. Pilot: 1st Lt. William J. Pritchard.
B-17E	41-2493	-	-		Destroyed by strafing at Bandoeng, 19 Feb 42.
B-17E	41-2494	32	19		Destroyed by crash landing at Malang, 8 Feb 42. Pilot: 2nd Lt. William A. Lorance Jr.
B-17E	41-2497	Hq/ 30	19/43	*Tojo's Nightmare* aka *MacMac*	Salvaged Horn Island, Sept 43.
B-17E	41-2498	20	19		Destroyed by strafing at Malang, 20 Feb 42.
B-17E	41-2500	9	7		Destroyed by bombing at Bandoeng, 19 Feb 42.
B-17E	41-2503	-	-		Destroyed by burning at Bandoeng, 19 Feb 42.
B-17E	41-2505	9/ 30	7/19		First B-17E with Sperry Ball Turret. (B-17E production #113) Crashed Tufi side Mt. Obree at 9,000 feet, New Guinea, 25 Apr 42. Pilot: 2nd Lt. Daniel W. Fagan.
B-17E	41-2506		19		Scrapped at Brisbane, October 44.
B-17E	41-2507	30	19		Crashed in Iligan Bay, Mindanao, 12 Mar 42. Pilot: Capt. Henry C. Godman.
B-17E	41-2520	23/ 26	5/11	*Jap Happy*	Returned to U.S., 2 Sept 44.
B-17E	41-2521	72	5	*GI Angel*	Unknown fate after 15 June 44.
B-17E	41-2523	98/ 72	11/5	*Goonie*	Shot down off Russell Is., 20 Mar 43. Pilot: Lt. Col. Marion Unruh.
B-17E	41-2524	26	11		Returned to U.S., 8 Dec 43.
B-17E	41-2525	98/ 31	11/5	*Madame-X*	Shot down on Kahili mission, 10 June 43. Pilot: Lt. Richard Snoddy.
B-17E	41-2527	431/ 26	11		Hit by AA fire off eastern Solomons. Lost, 14 Sept. 42. Pilot: 1st Lt. Hugh W. Owens.

B-17E	41-2529	72	5		Ditched near Midway, 5 June 42. Battle of Midway. Pilot: Capt. Glenn Kramer.
B-17E	41-2536	28	19/43		Missing in action, 12 Nov 42. Pilot: Unknown.
B-17E	41-2593			*Bataan*	Personal plane of Gen. MacArthur, 18 Sept 43. Scrapped at Reclamation Finance Center, U.S., 30 Oct 45.
B-17E	41-2599	93/ 65	19/43	*Tugboat Annie*	Ditched north of Buna after running out of fuel, 16 Jan. 43. Pilot: Lt. Lien.
B-17E	41-2603		43		Unknown fate.
B-17E	41-2609	64/ 65	43	*Loose-Goose*	Badly damaged on Reconnaissance mission of Bismarck Archipelago,17 May 43. Relegated to salvage. Pilot: Capt. William Crawford Jr.
B-17E	41-2610	23/ 26	5/11		Crash landing in jungle at Esprito Santos, 24 Aug 42. Pilot: 1st Lt. Robert D. Guenther.
B-17E	41-2611	31/ 26	5/11		Returned to U.S., 17 Jan 44.
B-17E	41-2612	72	5		Written off, 15 June 44.
B-17E	41-2613	72	5	*Lucky 13*	Ditched off San Isabel, 13 April 43. Pilot: 1st Lt. Mario Sesso.
B-17E	41-2616	98	7/11	*Blue Goose*	Direct hit by AA over Guadalcanal, 29 Sept 42. Pilot: Lt. Frank T. "Fritz" Waskowitz.
B-17E	41-2617	435/ 30	19		Crashed on take-off at Port Morseby, 7 Aug 42. Pilot: 1st Lt. Charles H. Hillhouse.
B-17E	41-2620	26	11		Unknown fate.
B-17E	41-2621	93	19	*The Daylight Ltd.*	Crash landing at Mareeba, after attacking convoy Milne Bay, 26 Aug 42. Pilot: Capt. Kenneth Casper.
B-17E	41-2627	63/8PRS	19/43/ 6	*RFD Tojo*	Crashed Schwimmer Airdrome, Laloki, New Guinea, 26 Dec 43. Pilot: Hutchinson
B-17E	41-2630		19/7 AF		Returned to U.S., date unknown. Scrapped Reclamation Finance Center, U.S., 10 Sept. 45
B-17E	41-2631		19		Crash landing at Charters Towers, 26 May 42. Pilot: 1st Lt. Pierre D. Jacques.
B-17E	41-2632	394	5	*Crock-o-crap*	Returned to U.S., 21 Dec 43.
B-17E	41-2633		19	*Sally*	Gen. Kenney's personal plane. April 45, damaged in severe thunderstorm. Written off and scrapped in Brisbane, 3 May 45.
B-17E	41-2634	435/65	19/43	*Red Moose Express*	Shot down over Bogadjim, NG, 3 Aug 43. Pilot: Lt. Walter K. Brenneman
B-17E	41-2635	28	19		Shot down over Solomons, Buin/Faisi area, 1 Nov 42. Last combat loss of 19th BG. Pilot: Lt. John S. Hancock.
B-17E	41-2636	30	19		Ditched 500 meters off Horn Is., 13 Jul 42. Pilot: Lt. Curtis J. Holdridge.
B-17E	41-2637	65	19/43		Returned to U.S., 6 Nov 43.
B-17E	41-2638	435/ 63	19/43	*Chico* aka *I'm Willing*	Returned to U.S., 24 Nov 43.

B-17E	41-2639	435	19		Written off, 19 Jan 43.
B-17E	41-2640	93	19	*Tojo's Physic*	Crack-up, collision, Horn Is., 27 Jul 42. Pilot: Capt. Carey O'Bryan.
B-17E	41-2641		19		Missing after raid on Buna, 31 July 42. Possibly shot down over Huon Gulf. Pilot: Unknown.
B-17E	41-2642	93	19/5 AF		Returned to U.S., 10 June 44.
B-17E	41-2643	93/ 64	19/43		Shot down by fighter, Lakunai. Crashed Rondahls Plantation., Mokurapaua, New Britain, 9 Aug 42. Pilot: 1st Lt. Hugh S. Grundman
B-17E	41-2644	28	19		Returned to U.S., 31 Aug 44.
B-17E	41-2645	28	19/43	*Miss Carriage*	Relegated to salvage around 11 Nov. 42. Written off, 6 Dec. 42.
B-17E	41-2648	63	43	*Little Buster Upper /Fat Cat*	Returned to U.S., date unknown. Scrapped Reclamation Finance Center, U.S., 8 Nov 46.
B-17E	41-2649	28/64	19/43		Trfd 5AF, 20 Jan 45. Salvaged N. Africa, 23 Aug 45.
B-17E	41-2650	93	19		Crashed at New Guinea, 17 Sept 42. Crew bailed out. Pilot: Lt. Claude N. Burcky.
B-17E	41-2652		19		Crashed at Ewan, Aust., 7 May 42. Pilot: 1st Lt. Edward C. Habberstad.
B-17E	41-2653		19/43	*Craps For The Japs*	Unknown fate.
B-17E	41-2655	30	19		Crashed into mud flat on take-off from Horn Is., 13 Jul 42. Pilot: 2nd Lt. Paul M. Lindsey.
B-17E	41-2656	435	43	*'Chief Seattle' from the Pacific Northwest*	Shot down 14 Aug 42 on reconnaissance mission to Rabaul. Pilot: Lt. Wilson L. Cook.
B-17E	41-2657	30	19/43	*Old Faithful*	Trfd 54 Troop Carrier Wing, Nov 43. Salvaged 21 June 45.
B-17E	41-2658	435	19		Trfd to 13th AF. Returned to U.S., after Oct. 42.
B-17E	41-2659	30/ 28/ --	19/43/ 11	*Tojo's Jinx* aka *Frank Buck*	Scrapped Port Moresby. Written off, 31 Oct 44.
B-17E	41-2660	28	19		Unknown fate.
B-17E	41-2661		5AF		Written off, 31 Oct 44.
B-17E	41-2662	26/ 30/ 64	11/19 43	*Spawn of Hell*	Trfd 54 Troop Carrier Wing, 375 TCG, Nov 43. Scrapped at Reclamation Finance Center, U.S., 4 April 45.
B-17E	41-2663	28/ 435	19		Direct hit by AA. Ditched 50 yds offshore, 20 miles south of Buna, 12 Sept 42. Pilot: Lt. Gilbert E. Erb.
B-17E	41-2664	30/ 64	19/43	*The Jersey Skeeter*	Crashed and exploded on take-off from Port Moresby, 14 June 43. Pilot: Lt. James A. Pickard.
B-17E	41-2665	93	19/43	*Lulu*	Trfd 54 Troop Carrier Wing, New Guinea, Nov 43. Trfd to 6 SR at Clark Field.
B-17E	41-2666	435/ 65	19/43	*Lucy*	Returned to U.S., 22 March 44.

Type	Serial	Sqdn	Group	Name	Fate
B-17E	41-2667	435	19		Exploded during take-off Whenuapi, near Auckland, New Zealand, 9 June 42. Pilot: Unknown.
B-17E	41-2668	93	19		Returned to U.S., 21 Oct 44.
B-17E	41-2669				Returned to U.S., 28 Nov 42.
B-17E	41-9011	64	19/43		Shot out of sky at 4:28 a.m., 21 May 43 by Japanese night fighter. Pilot: Unknown.
B-17E	41-9012	30	19		Burned on ground at Mareeba, Aust., 5 Nov 42.
B-17E	41-9014		19		Crashed near Hughes, Aust., 30 June 42. Pilot: Capt. Weldon Smith.
B-17E	41-9015	435/ 30	19/43		Written off, 19 Feb 43.
B-17E	41-9054	72/26	5/11		Returned to U.S., 18 July 45.
B-17E	41-9055		7/19	*Nippon Miss*	Crashed, 17 Oct. 42. Pilot: Unknown.
B-17E	41-9056	72	5		Written off, 15 June 44.
B-17E	41-9059	72	5	*Boomerang*	Written off, 11 June 44.
B-17E	41-9060	72/ 26	5/11	*Zero-Six-Zero*	Destroyed by Japanese bombing of Henderson Field, 23 March 43.
B-17E	41-9071	42	11		Missing in action off Rendowa Is., 8 Sept. 42. Pilot: Capt. Robert Richards.
B-17E	41-9076	26	11		Written off, 15 June 44.
B-17E	41-9093	431/ 72/ 31	11/5	*Spook!*	Returned to U.S., 27 Dec 43.
B-17E	41-9118	72	5		Rammed by Zero, near New Georgia, 4 Oct. 42. Pilot: Lt. David C. Everitt Jr.
B-17E	41-9122	72/26/42	5/11	*Eager Beavers*	Hit by AA in bomb bay over Bougainville, 1 Feb 43. Pilot: Capt. Frank L. Houx.
B-17E	41-9124	98/ 31	11/5	*Buzz King*	Destroyed by "Washing Machine Charlie," Henderson Field, 23 March 43.
B-17E	41-9128	72/26/23	5/11		Shot down over Kahili, 27 July 43. Pilot: Lt. Karl Stubberfield.
B-17E	41-9145	26	11		Written off, 31 Oct 44.
B-17E	41-9151	42	11		Shot down by Zeros over Bougainville, 1 Feb 43. Pilot: Capt. Earl O. Hall.
B-17E	41-9153	431/ 23	11/5	*Tokyo Taxi*	Shot down by AA over Kahili, 18 July 43. Pilot: Lt. Rex Echles.
B-17E	41-9155	42	11		Hit in taxi accident by another plane on Efate. Complete wreck, 2 Aug. 42.
B-17E	41-9156	431/ 72	11/5	*Uncle Biff*	Written off, 11 June 44.
B-17E	41-9157	42	11	*Hel-En-Wings*	Unknown fate.
B-17E	41-9193	435/ 65	19/43		Written off, 26 May 43.
B-17E	41-9194		43		Crashed into Port Moresby hillside, 2 Dec 42. Pilot: 1st Lt. Robert K. Freeman.
B-17E	41-9196	30/93	19		Shot down over New Britain on Vunakanau mission, 5 Oct 42. Pilot: 1st Lt. Earl L. Hareman.
B-17E	41-9206	435	19		Forced landing Orangerie Bay, New Guinea, 24 Sept 42. Pilot: Newton.
B-17E	41-9207	435	19/43	*Texas #6*	Shot down, 12 April 43. Crashed into the top of Hong Kong Mtn. Pilot: Unknown.
B-17E	41-9208	435/63	19/43		Unknown fate.

B-17E	41-9209	64	19/43	*Blues in the Night*	Hit a wallaby on night take-off from Seven Mile Strip, crashed, 12 April 43. Pilot: Maj. Ken McCullar.
B-17E	41-9211	98	11	*Typhoon McGoon II*	Returned to U.S., 14 Dec 45.
B-17E	41-9212		7AF		Written off, 8 Aug 42.
B-17E	41-9213	42	11		Unknown fate.
B-17E	41-9214	431/ 98/ 23	11/5	*The Skipper*	Returned to U.S., 27 Dec 43.
B-17E	41-9215	98	11	*Galloping Gus*	Written off, 15 June 44.
B-17E	41-9216	42/ 31/ 23	11/5	*Alley-Oop*	Written off, 15 June 44.
B-17E	41-9217	26/431	11	*Fiji Foo*	Lost in action February 19, 1943. Pilot: Capt. Smith.
B-17E	41-9218	26	11		Rammed by flaming Japanese Zero at Tulagi, 4 Aug. 42. Pilot: 1st Lt. Rush E. McDonald.
B-17E	41-9219	98	11	*Hellzapoppin*	Crash landed at sea, 13 Sept 42. Pilot: Maj. Philip M. Rasmussen.
B-17E	41-9220	26/431	11		Written off, 15 June 44.
B-17E	41-9221	42	11		Crash landed north end Espiritu Santo, 6 Aug 42. Pilot: Capt. Rolle W. Stone.
B-17E	41-9222	26/431	11	*Knuckle-Head*	Returned to U.S., 21 Oct 43.
B-17E	41-9223	72	5		Written off, 4 Nov 42.
B-17E	41-9224	30/ 72/ 98	19/5/ 11	*Kai-O-Keleiwa*	Missing on reconnaissance mission, 7 Aug 42. May have crashed in mountains on New Caledonia. Pilot: 1st Lt. Robert B. Loder.
B-17E	41-9226	431	11		Ditched in sea, 12 Sept. 42. Pilot: Lt. Willard G. Woodbury.
B-17E	41-9227	431	11	*Yankee Doodle Jr.*	Crashed at Espiritu Santo, 31 Dec 42. Pilot: Lt. Andrews. (Out to get more booze.)
B-17E	41-9234		19/43		Crashed New Guinea, 8 Jan 43. Pilot: Lt. Ray Dau.
B-17E	41-9235	30/ 93	19	*Clown House*	Ditched off Cooktown, Aust., 29 Oct 42. Pilot: Maj. Allen Lindberg.
B-17E	41-9244	72/64	5/43	*Honikuu Okole*	Shot down over Rabaul by night fighter at 3:37 a.m., 21 May 43. Pilot: Maj. Paul Williams.
B-17F	41-24353	63	43	*Cap'n & The Kids,* aka *Miss Em*	Trfd 54 Troop Carrier Wing, 69, TCS, 433 TCG, Nov. 43. Scrapped 31 April 45.
B-17F	41-24354	93	19		Shot down by AA, Milne Bay, 26 Aug 42. Pilot: Capt. Clyde Webb.
B-17F	41-24355	435/63	19/43	*Dinah Might*	Taxied into ditch, 16 Sept. 43. Destroyed. Pilot: Unknown.
B-17F	41-24356	63	43	*Ka-Puhio-Wela,* aka *Double Trouble*	Shot down Battle of Bismarck Sea, 3 March 43. Pilot: Lt. Woodrow W. Moore.
B-17F	41-24357	65	43	*Tojo's Nightmare* aka *The Super Chief*	Trfd 54 Troop Carrier Wing, 41 TCS, 317 TCG, Nov. 43. Written off, 7 Dec 45.

B-17F	41-24358	63	43	*Lulu Belle*	Trfd 54 Troop Carrier Wing, Nov 43. Salvaged, 13 Sept. 45.
B-17F	41-24381	63	43	*Panama Hattie*	Trfd 54 Troop Carrier Wing, Nov 43. Scrapped, 10 April 47.
B-17F	41-24383	63/ 64	43		Ditched in Gulf of Papua after running out of fuel after being lost. 6 Jan 43. Pilot: 2/Lt Guyton M. Christopher.
B-17F	41-24384	63	19/43	*Pluto*	Disappeared on mission, 26 March 43 with Brig. Gen. Howard Ramey. Pilot: Lt. Herbert Derr.
B-17F	41-24391	93/ 63	19/43	*Hoomalimali*	Destroyed in take-off crash (fire), Mareeba, Aust., 14 Sept. 42. Pilot: Capt. Herschall R. Henson
B-17F	41-24401	63/ 65	43	*Lak-A-Nookie*	Returned to U.S., Nov 43.
B-17F	41-24402	63	43	*E-Z Mary 4th*	Destroyed landing accident, Aust. 16 Nov 42. Pilot: Unknown.
B-17F	41-24403	30/ 65/ 63	19/43	*Blitz Buggy* aka *The Old Man*	Personal plane of Gen. Whitehead after Aug. 43.
B-17F	41-24420	28/ 64/ 65	19/43	*Super Snooper*	Trfd 54 Troop Carrier Wing, 58 TCS, 375 TCG, Nov 43. Written off, 23 July 46.
B-17F	41-24424	28/ 64	19/43	*Hell From Heaven Men*	Ditched off Wewak, 15 March 43. Pilot: Lt. Arthur McMullen
B-17F	41-24425	30/ 64	19/43		Crashed after midair collision with B-17E (24355, *Dinah Might*) over Port Moresby, 17 April 43. Pilot: Capt. Charles McArthur, Jr.
B-17F	41-24426	42	11		Returned to U.S., 28 July 44.
B-17F	41-24427	30	19		Missing from mission, 15 Sept. 42. Pilot: Capt. Robert. Williams.
B-17F	41-24428	30	19		Crack-up at Mareeba, 5 Sept 42. Written off. Pilot: Lt. William R. Humrichouse.
B-17F	41-24429	63	43	*Dumbo*	Missing near Finschaven, NG, 2 Dec 42. Pilot: Lt. Lewis A. Anderson.
B-17F	41-24430				Missing, unknown date. Assigned to S. Pac., Sept. 42. Got as far as New Zealand. Disappeared. Written off, 31 Oct 44.
B-17F	41-24446	42/ 72/ 23	11/5	*Jezebel*	Returned to U.S., 8 Nov 44.
B-17F	41-24448	64	19/43	*Taxpayer's Pride*	Shot down by Japanese night fighter near Rabaul, 26 June 43. Pilot: Lt. Donald McEachran.
B-17F	41-24450	72	5	*My Lovin' Dove*	Ditched near Nauru Is., 9 Feb. 43. Pilot: Capt. Thomas J. Classen.
B-17F	41-24454	28/ 65	19/43	*Georgia Peach*	Shot down by night fighter at Vunakanau Airdrome, 13 June 43. Pilot: Lt. John Woodard.
B-17F	41-24455	63	43	*Old Baldy*	Returned to U.S., 12 Nov 43.
B-17F	41-24457	26/ 31	11/5	*The Aztec's Curse*	Damaged on landing, 23 April 43. Salvaged. Written off, 30 April 45. Pilot: Capt. Leon Rockwell.

B-17F	41-24458	64	19/43	*San Antonio Rose*	Shot down over Rabaul, 5 Jan 43 with Gen. Walker. Pilot: Maj. Allen Lindberg.
B-17F	41-24513	403	43		Written off, 31 Oct. 44.
B-17F	41-24518	403/ 63	43	*The Reckless Mountain Boys*	Shot down over Kavieng, New Ireland, 7 May 43. Pilot: Capt. Byron Heichel.
B-17F	41-24520	403/ 63	43	*Fightin' Swede*	Lost between Finschaven and Wewak, 8 May 43. Pilot: Capt. Bob Keatts.
B-17F	41-24521	63	43	*Black Jack aka The Joker's Wild*	Ditched off New Guinea coast, 11 July 43. Pilot: Lt. Ralph De Loach.
B-17F	41-24522	403	43		Damaged by explosion of B-24 at Iron Range, Aust., 17 Aug 43. Written off, 31 Oct. 44.
B-17F	41-24528	431	11		Damaged by gunfire from battleship while at Guadalcanal, 13 Oct 42. Abandoned. Written off, 31 Oct. 44.
B-17F	41-24531	26	11		Shot down and ditched Baga Is., Vella Lavella, 18 Nov. 42. Pilot:: Maj. Alan J. Sewart.
B-17F	41-24534	98/403	11/43	*Omar Khayyam, The Plastered Bastard*	Rammed by Zero over New Georgia, 1 Dec 42. Pilot: Capt. Willis E. Jacobs.
B-17F	41-24535	431	11		Returned to U.S., 12 Sept. 43.
B-17F	41-24536	403/ 65	43		Returned to U.S., June 44.
B-17F	41-24537	63	43	*Talisman aka USASOS War-Horse*	Trfd to Brig. Gen. Frink, U.S. Services & Supplies, 8 Sept 43. Salvaged 9 Sept 45.
B-17F	41-24538	403	43		Ditched off Urasi Is., 5 Jan 43. Pilot: Lt. Jean Jack.
B-17F	41-24540	403/ 63	43		Destroyed by strafing at Milne Bay, New Guinea, 17 Jan 43.
B-17F	41-24543	403/ 63	43	*Pluto*	Crashed near Kulit, New Britain, 30 June 43. Pilot: 1st Lt. Harold S. Barnett.
B-17F	41-24546	403	43		Lost in Vitiaz Strait, 29 Nov. 42. Pilot: 2nd Lt. John E. Titus.
B-17F	41-24548	403/ 65	43	*War Horse*	Trfd 54 Troop Carrier Wing, Nov 43. Crash landing at Tadji, NG, 4 May 44. Damaged beyond repair. Pilot: Lt. Robert Kennedy.
B-17F	41-24550	403/ 63	43		Crashed on take-off due to engine failure. Ditched in Bootless Bay, Port Moresby, N.G., 14 Dec 42. Pilot: Lt. Ealon Hocutt.
B-17F	41-24551	403/ 63	43	*Fire Ball Mail*	Destroyed by strafing at Milne Bay, New Guinea, 17 Jan 43.
B-17F	41-24552	65	43	*Listen Here, Tojo*	Lost in storm after attack on Lae, NG, 15 Sept 43. Last B-17 lost in combat in Pacific. Pilot: Lt. Howard G. Eberly.
B-17F	41-24554	403/ 63	43	*The Mustang aka Lady Luck*	Returned to U.S., 2 Dec 43.
B-17F	41-24574	63/ 403	43	*Tuffy*	Returned to U.S., 9 Nov 43.

CHAPTER NOTES

Chapter 1
1. Arakaki, *7 December 1941*, 157, 158; Dorr, *7th Bombardment Group/Wing* [hereafter cited as Dorr, *7th BG*], 253.
2. Prange, *At Dawn We Slept*, 480-1; *Hearings Before the Joint Committee on the Investigation of the Pearl Harbor Attack, Congress of the United States, Seventy-Ninth Congress*, Part 30, 2472 [hereafter cited as Congressional Report]; Dorr, 7th BG, 49.
3. Arakaki, *7 December 1941*, 158, 159.
4. Dorr, *7th BG*, 48.
5. Prange, *At Dawn We Slept*, 476.
6. Prange, *December 7, 1941*, 34.
7. Ibid.; Arakaki, *7 December 1941*, 72-3.
8. Interview with Angelini, December 7, 1997.
9. Ibid.; Reid, "Shot Down at Pearl Harbor," *Air Force Magazine*, December 1991, 73; Congressional Report, Part 30, 2516 and Part 24, 1961.
10. Weintraub, *Long Day's Journey Into War*, 101; Prange, *At Dawn We Slept*, 476; Prange, *December 7, 1941*, 34; Congressional Report, Part 30, 2516.
11. Arakaki, *7 December 1941*, 157-160. Included in the book is a complete roster of the 16 crews scheduled to leave Hamilton Field on 6 December 1941; Reid, "Shot Down at Pearl Harbor," *Air Force Magazine*, December 1991, 72; Interview with Angelini, December 7, 1997
12. "Squadron Diary - Eighty-Eighth Reconnaissance, (H), AFCC," *Bomb Squadron History, 435th Bombardment Squadron* [hereafter cited as "Diary - 88th RS"], 6
13. Prange, *December 7, 1941*, 34.
14. Goldstein, *The Way it Was: Pearl Harbor*, 83, 84.
15. Perret, *Winged Victory*, 53.
16. Interview with Angelini, December 7, 1997.
17. Ibid.; "Diary - 88th RS," 6; Arakaki, *7 December 1941*, 158-9.
18. Carmichael statement in "Diary - 88th RS," 9.
19. Thacker statement in Ibid., 12.
20. "Diary - 88th RS," 7.
21. Arakaki, *7 December 1941*, 73; Interview with Angelini, December 7, 1997.
22. Thacker and Rawls statements in "Diary - 88th RS," 12, 15.
23. "Diary - 88th RS," 8.
24. Lord, *Day of Infamy*, 109.
25. Prange, *December 7, 1941*, 183.

26. McNalty, *Pearl Harbor and the War in the Pacific,* 32.
27. Interview with Angelini, December 7, 1997; Hammack biography in Turner Publishing Company, pub., *11th Bomb Group* (H) [hereafter cited as Turner, pub., *11th BG*], 89.
28. Goldstein, *The Way it Was,* 62-3, 178; Lord, *Day of Infamy,* 68.
29. Interview with Angelini, December 7, 1997.
30. Ibid. and December 8, 1997.
31. Lord, *Day of Infamy,* 110, 111.
32. Reid, "Shot Down at Pearl Harbor," *Air Force Magazine,* December 1991, 74 -5.
33. Ibid., 72, 74.
34. Goldstein, *The Way It Was,* 82.
35. Prange, *December 7, 1941,* 192.
36. Ibid., 190, 192; Reid, "Shot Down at Pearl Harbor", *Air Force Magazine,* December 1991, 75.
37. Ibid., 83.
38. Goldstein, *The Way It Was,* 82.
39. Lord, *Day of Infamy,* 110.
40. Prange, *December 7, 1941,* 192.
41. Interview with Angelini, December 7, 1997.
42. Arakaki, *7 December 1941,* 131.
43. Interview with Angelini, December 7, 1997.
44. Ibid.; Arakaki, *7 December 1941,* 131.
45. Ibid.
46. Carmichael statement in "Diary - 88th RS," 9-10.
47. Chaffin statement in Ibid., 11.
48. Carmichael statement in Ibid., 10
49. Bostrom statement in Ibid., 13-4.
50. Rawls statement in Ibid., 15-6.
51. Thacker statement in Ibid., 12.
52. Brandon statement in Ibid., 13; Lord, *Day of Infamy,* 110-1.
53. Carmichael statement in "Diary - 88th RS," 10.
54. Arakaki, *7 December 1941,* 158. Richard's B-17C (40-2049, *Skipper*) was found to be beyond repair. It was later used for spare parts.
55. Ibid., 119.
56. Lord, *Day of Infamy,* 151.
57. Ibid.; Arakaki, *7 December 1941,* 157n.
58. Arakaki, *7 December 1941,* 146, 153, 154. The 98th BS/11th BG was constituted on 2 December 1941 but not activated until 16 December 1941. The planes belonging to the two BGs were: 5th BG - (40-3071), (40-3080), (40-3082), (40-3085), (40-3089), and (40-3092). The 11th BG - (40-3060), (40-3077), (40-3081), (40-3083), (40-3084), and (40-3090).
59. Schaeffer, "December 7th 1941," 1; Hillsborough House, pub., *The Story of the Fifth Bombardment Group (Heavy)* [hereafter cited as Hillsborough, pub., *Fifth BG*], 29; Klingensmith to author, Nov. 10, 1996, 1; "394th Bombardment Squadron (H), Historical Officer, Squadron Historical Report," *Bomb Squadron History, 394th Bombardment Squadron (H)* [hereafter cited as "394th BS Report"], 6.
60. Kimmett, *The Attack on Pearl Harbor,* 55; Arakaki, *7 December 1941,* 83; Goldstein, *The Way It Was,* 62-4; La Forte, *Remembering Pearl Harbor,* 219.
61. Jenkins account in Ibid., 11; Arakaki, *7 December 1941,* 92.

62. Blutt account in Turner, pub., *11th BG*, 68; Arakaki, *7 December 1941*, 92.
63. Bradshaw, "Unlucky Thirteen," in Turner, pub., *11th BG*, 62.
64. Schaeffer, "December 7th 1941," 1-2.
65. Klingensmith to author, Nov. 10, 1996, 1; Clark, *Remember Pearl Harbor*, 115-6.
66. Prange, *December 7, 1941*, 191.
67. Latham account in Turner, pub., *11th BG*, 12.
68. Edmundson to Klingensmith, Oct. 19, 1991, 1.
69. Klingensmith to author, Dec. 15, 1996, 2, 4.
70. La Forte, *Remembering Pearl Harbor*, 219.
71. Belz, "Unusual Events with the 431st Bomb Squadron," in Turner, pub., *11th BG*, 68.
72. Prange, *December 7, 1941*, 243, 293.
73. Bradshaw, "Unlucky Thirteen," in Turner, pub., *11th BG*, 62.
74. Jenkins account in Ibid., 11.
75. Schaeffer, "December 7th 1941," 3.
76. La Forte, *Remembering Pearl Harbor*, 219-20; Jenkins account in Turner, pub., *11th BG*, 11.
77. Arakaki, *7 December 1941*, 100.
78. Latham account in Turner, pub., *11th BG*, 12; Arakaki, *7 December 1941*, 154.
79. Prange, *December 7, 1941*, 329; Arakaki, *7 December 1941*, 153. The only two 5th BG B-17's still in flying condition after the attack were (40-3082) and (40-3089). These were undoubtedly the two planes taken by Maj. Saunders and Capt. Allen, however, it is uncertain who piloted which plane.
80. Ibid., 243.
81. Ibid., 329-30.
82. Ibid., 340-1.
83. Ibid., 153, 154, 179-84. The status of the 5th BG B-17D's was as follows: In commission: (40-3082) and (40-3089); repairable: (40-3085) and (40-3092); and destroyed: (40-3071) and (40-3080). The status of the 11th BG B-17D's was as follows: In commission but awaiting repairs: (40-3084); In commission but with bent propellers: (40-3060); repairable: (40-3090); and destroyed: (40-3077), (40-3081) and (40-3083).

Chapter 2
1. Perret, *Winged Victory*, 70.
2. Mitchell, *In Alis Vicimus: On Wings We Conquer* [hereafter cited as Mitchell, *In Alis Vicimus*], 21, 165-6. The pilots and planes, all B-17Ds, were: Majs O'Donnell (40-3061), and William P. Fisher (40-3093), Capt. Colin P. Kelly, Jr., (40-3095), and 1st Lts. Henry C. Godman (40-3097, Ole Betsy), Edward C. Teats (40-3078), Guilford R. Montgomery (40-3086), George E. Schaetzel (40-3091), Donald M. Keiser (40-3091), and Weldon H. Smith (40-3079).
3. Teats, "Turn of the Tide," *Philadelphia Inquirer* [hereafter cited as Teats, "Tide"], Inst. III, Jan. 2, 1943, 1; Godman, *Supreme Commander*, 27; Brownstein, *The Swoose*, 22-6.
4. Teats, "Tide," Inst. III, Jan. 2, 1943, 1.
5. Ibid., 4; Godman, *Supreme Commander*, 28.
6. Godman, *Supreme Commander*, 29; Edmunds, *They Fought With What They Had* [hereafter cited as Edmunds, *They Fought*], 44n; Brownstein, *The Swoose*, 24.
7. Edmunds, *They Fought*, 3-13. The 19th BG left the 32nd BS and the 38th RS behind at Albuquerque, NM. The 38th RS arrived at Pearl Harbor during the Japanese attack. The 32nd BS, as a whole, never rejoined the group. Individual crews were ferried to Java one at a time and added to squadrons affected by wartime attrition.

8. Mitchell, *In Alis Vicimus*, 166-169. The pilots and planes, all B-17Ds, where known, were: Lt. Col. Eubank (40-3100), Majs Birrell Walsh, and David R. Gibbs, Capts. Edwin B. Broadhurst, Cecil E. Combs, and William E. McDonald (40-3062), 1st Lts. Arthur W. Schmitt, Patrick W. McIntyre, Edwin S. Green (40-3068), Raymond V. Schwanbeck, Jack Adams, Ray L. Cox, Lee B. Coats, Hewitt T. "Shorty" Wheless (40-3070), Frank A. Kurtz (40-3099), Sam Maddux, Jr., Alvin V. H. Mueller (40-2072), James Connally (40-3069), Morris H. Shedd, Dean C. Hoevet (40-3072), William J. Bohnaker (40-3073), Walter R. Ford (40-3087), Clyde Box, Fred T. Crimmins, Jr., and Elmer L. Parsel (40-3074), and 2nd Lt. William A. Cocke, Jr.,

9. Log entitled "Trans-Pacific Flight," and attached to Kimmerle, *Dec. '41 Personal Narrative of M. Sgt. B.F. Kimmerle* [hereafter cited as Kimmerle, *Personal Narrative*]; Jacquet, "Flight Into History," *Daedalian Flyer* [hereafter cited as Jacquet, "Flight"], Winter, 1985, 14-7; Edmunds, *They Fought*, 3-13.

10. Edmunds, *They Fought*, 12, 12n.

11. Mitchell, *In Alis Vicimus*, 18, 21-2, 26, 28, 30.

12. Ibid., 70; Brownstein, *The Swoose*, 27, 29; Whitcomb, *Escape From Corregidor*, 3-4, 13-4; White, *Queens Die Proudly* [hereafter cited as White, *Queens*], 7, 12, 22; Jacquet, "Flight," Winter, 1985, 17-8.

13. Edmunds, *They Fought*, 68; Kimmerle, *Personal Narrative*, 2.

14. Edmunds, *They Fought*, 23-4, 59, 59n.

15. Whitcomb, *Escape From Corregidor*, 13.

16. Kimmerle, *Personal Narrative*, 3; Godman, *Supreme Commander*, 27; Teats, "Tide," Inst. I, Dec. 31, 1942, 4; Edmunds, *They Fought*, 22.

17. Rutherford, *Fall of the Philippines*, 15, 18, 21.

18. Edmunds, *They Fought*, 37; Brereton, *The Brereton Diaries*, 5.

19. Edmunds, *They Fought*, 43; Brereton, *The Brereton Diaries*, 23.

20. Jacquet, "Flight," Winter, 1985, 18; Edmunds, *They Fought*, 45.

21. Brereton, *The Brereton Diaries*, 23.

22. Edmunds, *They Fought*, 18, 52, 57;

23. Ibid., 43.

24. Ibid.; Nicholas' statement in "History of the 28th Bombardment Squadron (H)," *Bomb Squadron History, 28th Bombardment Squadron (H)* [hereafter cited as "History of 28th BS"], 1; Mitchell, *In Alis Vicimus*, 26.

25. Brereton, *The Brereton Diaries*, 31; Whitcomb, *Escape From Corregidor*, 12-3.

26. Brereton, *The Brereton Diaries*, 34-5.

27. Kurtz quoted in White, *Queens*, 13-4.

28. Tash interview in Emmett, *Interviews of Men Who Fought in the Philippines, 1941-42*, 1. [hereafter cited as Emmett, *Interviews*]

29. Sakai, *Samurai!*, 59.

30. Jacquet, "Flight," Winter, 1985, 18; White, *Queens*, 14.

31. Brereton, *The Brereton Diaries*, 32, 35, 36. Sutherland claimed that he wanted all 35 of the B-17s sent to Del Monte, to get them out of the reach of the Japanese on Formosa. He claimed that he did not know that only 16 planes had been sent to Mindanao until after the Japanese attack.

32. Ibid., 36.

33. Jacquet, "Flight," Winter, 1985, 19; Teats, "Tide," Inst. I, Dec. 31, 1942, 4.

34. Jacquet, "Flight," Winter, 1985, 19; Tash interview in Emmett, *Interviews*, 1.

35. Carpenter and Tash interviews in Emmett, *Interviews*, 1, 2; Edmunds, *They Fought*, 55n.

36. Teats, "Tide," Inst. I, Dec. 31, 1942, 4; Jacquet, "Flight," Winter, 1985, 19.
37. "Air Services in the Visayan-Mindanao Area, Dec. 1941 - May 1942", *Fifth Air Force Operations, 1940-45,* Document 30a [hereafter cited as "Air Services Visayan-Mindanao Area"], 3; Dorr, *7th Bomb Group,* 69.
38. "Col. Elsmore on 'Queens'," *Fifth Air Force Operations, 1940-45,* Document 31, 2.
39. Brereton, *The Brereton Diaries,* 38.
40. Edmunds, *They Fought,* 75.
41. Brereton, *The Brereton Diaries,* 38.
42. Edmunds, *They Fought,* 79.
43. Carpenter interview in Emmett, *Interviews,* 1.
44. Kurtz quoted in White, *Queens,* 15.
45. Whitcomb, *Escape From Corregidor,* 15-7.
46. Tash interview in Emmett, *Interviews,* 2.
47. Freeman, B-17 *Fortress at War,* 48.
48. "Diary of the 19th Bombardment Group," *19th Bombardment Group (H) History* [hereafter cited as "Diary of the 19th BG], 1.
49. Tash interview in Emmett, *Interviews,* 3.
50. Edmunds, *They Fought,* 80; Eads interview in "6-8th December 1941 in the Philippines," *Fifth Air Force Operations, 1940-45,* 2.
51. Brereton, *The Brereton Diaries,* 38-9.
52. Costello, *The Pacific War,* 141-2.
53. Edmunds, *They Fought,* 88-90.
54. Brereton, *The Brereton Diaries,* 39.
55. Sakai, *Samurai!,* 61-3.
56. Costello, *The Pacific War,* 144.
57. Sakai, *Samurai!,* 61-3.
58. Costello, *The Pacific War,* 144-5.
59. Edmunds, *They Fought,* 80, 82n; McClendon, *The Legend of Colin Kelly,* 20. Many authors claim that Maj. Gibbs ordered the planes off the ground at 8:00 a.m. but eyewitness reports by a number of pilots put the time closer to 10:00 a.m. The radar at Iba Field did not detect enemy aircraft until 9:30 a.m.
60. White, *Queens,* 17-8; Carpenter interview in Emmett, *Interviews,* 1.
61. Brereton, *The Brereton Diaries,* 41.
62. Whitcomb, *Escape from Corregidor,* 19; Carlisle interview in Emmett, *Interviews,* 1; Kimmerle, *Personal Narrative,* 5.
63. Kurtz quoted in White, *Queens,* 20-1; Carlisle interview in Emmett, *Interviews,* 1.
64. Kurtz quoted in White, *Queens,* 22-3.
65. Edmunds, *They Fought,* 93-4, 97, 99.
66. White, *Queens,* 23.
67. Crimmins and Tash interview in Emmett, *Interviews,* 1, 4; Edmunds, *They Fought,* 102, 102n.
68. Sakai, *Samurai!,* 65-6.
69. Edmunds, *They Fought,* 85, 102; Maddox, "Bandits Over Clark," *American History Illustrated,* June 1974, 26.
70. Tash interview in Emmett, *Interviews,* 3-4.
71. Kimmerle, *Personal Narrative,* 5, 7; Edmunds, *They Fought,* 101.
72. Carlisle interview in Emmett, *Interviews,* 3.
73. Whitcomb, *Escape from Corregidor,* 20; Kurtz quoted in White, *Queens,* 25.
74. Sakai, *Samurai!,* 66.

75. Kimmerle, *Personal Narrative*, 5; Edmunds, *They Fought*, 100-1
76. Whitcomb, *Escape from Corregidor*, 20; Crimmins interview in Emmett, *Interviews*, 1-2.
77. Kurtz quoted in White, *Queens*, 27; Whitcomb, *Escape from Corregidor*, 21.
78. Crimmins interview in Emmett, *Interviews*, 2; Crimmins citation, "Awards to Members of USAFFE in Phillipine [sic] & Java," *Fifth Air Force Operations, 1940-45*, Document 19 [hereafter cited as "Philippine and Java Awards"], 1.
79. Edmunds, *They Fought*, 107, 107n.
80. Kurtz quoted in White, *Queens*, 30-1.
81. Holub citation in "Philippine and Java Awards," 1; Holub citation in "Roll of Honor," *Life*, March 16, 1942, 45. Both citations state that Holub fired the "top turret guns of his airplane" but the B-17C and D, the only models then in the Philippines, did not have top turrets. It is my belief that he was firing the twin guns in the radio compartment.
82. Carpenter interview in Emmett, *Interviews*, 3.
83. Tash interview in Ibid., 5-6.
84. Carpenter interview in Ibid., 1.
85. Edmunds, *They Fought*, 108; Kimmerle, *Personal Narrative*, 6.
86. Whitcomb, *Escape from Corregidor*, 21.
87. Kurtz quoted in White, *Queens*, 6-10, 32.
88. Kimmerle, *Personal Narrative*, 7; Edmunds, *They Fought*, 109.
89. Teats, "Tide," Inst. I, Dec. 31, 1942, 4.
90. Brereton, *The Brereton Diaries*, 43.
91. Ibid.; Jacquet, "Flight," Winter, 1985, 20; "Diary of the 19th BG," 1.
92. Whitcomb, *Escape from Corregidor*, 23; Mitchell, *In Alis Vicimus*, 164. In actuality, only 12 B-17s were totally destroyed on December 8, 1941, five were damaged but thought repairable. The destroyed planes were: B-17Cs (40-2048), (40-2067) and (40-2077); and B-17Ds (40-3059), (40-3068), (40-3069), (40-3075), (40-3076), (40-3088), (40-3094), (40-3095) and (40-3099).

Chapter 3

1. Collison, *Flying Fortress*, 4; Birdsall, *B-17 in Action*, 4.
2. Hess, *B-17 Flying Fortress*, 12; O'Leary, ed., *Air Combat Special - Flying Fortress* [hereafter cited as O'Leary, ed., *Air Combat Special*], 6, 9; Bowers, *50th Anniversary Boeing B-17 Flying Fortress*, 10.
3. O'Leary, ed., *Air Combat Special*, 11, 12; Collison, *Flying Fortress*, 13-6; Lloyd, *B-17 Flying Fortress in Detail and Scale*, 12.
4. Collison, *Flying Fortress*, 16.
5. Hess, *B-17 Flying Fortress*, 12; O'Leary, ed., *Air Combat Special*, 12.
6. Caidin, *Flying Forts*, 84n.
7. Hess, *B-17 Flying Fortress*, 13; O'Leary, ed., *Air Combat Special*, 13.
8. Caidin, *Flying Forts*, 69-78.
9. Ibid, 18; Davis, *B-17 in Action*, 5, 7.
10. Bowers, *50th Anniversary Boeing B-17 Flying Fortress*, 12-3; Davis, *B-17 in Action*, 5; O'Leary, ed., *Air Combat Special*, 15.
11. Bowers, *50th Anniversary Boeing B-17 Flying Fortress*, 13; Davis, *B-17 in Action*, 5; Birdsall, *B-17 in Action*, 4.
12. O'Leary, ed., *Air Combat Special*, 16; Perret, *Winged Victory*, 26.
13. Caidin, *Flying Forts*, 87-100; O'Leary, ed., *Air Combat Special*, 16, 19-20; Collison, *Flying Fortress*, 23-4.
14. Caidin, *Flying Forts*, 99-102.

15. Ibid., 105-6; O'Leary, ed., *Air Combat Special,* 21-2.
16. Davis, *B-17 in Action,* 7; O'Leary, ed., *Air Combat Special,* 22; Collison, *Flying Fortress,* 29
17. Davis, *B-17 in Action,* 9; O'Leary, ed., *Air Combat Special,* 27.
18. Davis, *B-17 in Action,* 9; O'Leary, ed., *Air Combat Special,* 31; Collison, *Flying Fortress,* 32-4.
19. Caidin, *Flying Forts,* 117-8; O'Leary, ed., *Air Combat Special,* 31; Davis, *B-17 in Action,* 9.
20. Davis, *B-17 in Action,* 7; Perret, *Winged Victory,* 129-30. Although the "top secret" Norden bombsight was safely guarded, the Germans had possessed knowledge of the sight since 1937. They even had a copy of their own.
21. Caidin, *Flying Forts,* 119; Collison, *Flying Fortress,* 34.
22. O'Leary, ed., *Air Combat Special,* 34-6; Davis, *B-17 in Action,* 11.
23. O'Leary, ed., *Air Combat Special,* 36.
24. Ibid., 29; Caidin, *Flying Forts,* 109-13; Hess, *B-17 Flying Fortress,* 25.
25. O'Leary, ed., *Air Combat Special,* 34, 36; Caidin, *Flying Forts,* 122.
26. O'Leary, ed., *Air Combat Special,* 36.
27. Birdsall, *B-17 in Action,* 5; Freeman, *B-17 Fortress at War,* 14-25; Caidin, *Flying Forts,* 128-42.
28. Davis, *B-17 in Action,* 11; O'Leary, ed., *Air Combat Special,* 36-7; Caidin, *Flying Forts,* 144.
29. Davis, *B-17 in Action,* 14; O'Leary, ed., *Air Combat Special,* 51,56.
30. Bowers, *50th Anniversary Boeing B-17 Flying Fortress,* 15; O'Leary, ed., *Air Combat Special,* 50, 53, 56, 59; Davis, *B-17 in Action,* 14-6; Turner, pub., *7th BG,* 43.
31. Freeman, *B-17 Fortress at War,* 32.
32. O'Leary, ed., *Air Combat Special,* 40, 59, 65; Davis, *B-17 in Action,* 14; Bowman, *USAAF Handbook 1939-45,* 12.
33. Caidin, *Flying Forts,* 143.
34. Bowers, *50th Anniversary Boeing B-17 Flying Fortress,* 15, 63; Davis, *B-17 in Action,* 14.
35. Aviations Publications, pub., *Pilot's Flight Operating Instructions for Army Models B-17F and G,* 70-3; Davis, *B-17 in Action,* 14.
36. Davis, *B-17 in Action,* 15-6; O'Leary, ed., *Air Combat Special,* 64; Birdsall, *B-17 in Action,* 11, 12; Freeman, *Combat Profile, B-17G Flying Fortress in World War 2,* 60-1.
37. O'Leary, ed., *Air Combat Special,* 67; Davis, *B-17 in Action,* 20.
38. Thompson, *The Boeing B-17E & F Flying Fortress,* 14; Davis, *B-17 in Action,* 20.
39. Ibid.
40. Bowers, *50th Anniversary Boeing B-17 Flying Fortress,* 16; Thompson, *The Boeing B-17E & F Flying Fortress,* 13-4; Birdsall, *Pride of Seattle,* 6-15. See also Appendix B.
41. Freeman, *Combat Profile: B-17G Flying Fortress in World War 2,* 80; Johnsen, ed., *Winged Majesty,* 11.
42. Patterson, *The Lady,* 22-49.
43. Edmundson to author, July 19, 1988; "19th BG Diary," 1 , 31.

Chapter 4
1. "History of the 26th Bombardment Squadron (H)," *Bomb Squadron History, 26th Bombardment Squadron (H)* [hereafter cited as "History of 26th BS"], 13.
2. Turner, pub., *11th Bomb Group,* 13.
3. Schaeffer, "December 7th 1941," 5.
4. "History of the 42nd Bombardment Squadron, 11th Bombardment Group, Seventh Air Force," *11th Bombardment Group (H) History* [hereafter cited as "42nd BS History"],

3 "Historical Data and History of the 23rd Bombardment Squadron (H), APO 324," *Bomb Squadron History, 23rd Bombardment Squadron (H)* [hereafter cited as "23rd BS History"], 4; Bradlyn account in Turner, pub., *11th Bomb Group*, 69.

5. Carmichael statement in "Diary - 88th RS," 10-11.
6. Ramsey, "Me Too," in Johnson, ed., *435th Overseas*, 22.
7. Latham accounts in Turner, pub., *11th Bomb Group*, 11, 12.
8. Belz, "Unusual Events with the 431st Bomb Squadron," in Ibid., 68.
9. Hillsborough, pub., *Fifth Bomb Group*, 30.
10. Arakaki, *7 December 1941*, 137.
11. Hillsborough, pub., *Fifth Bomb Group*, 30.
12. Jenkins account in Turner, pub., *11th Bomb Group*, 11.
13. Schaeffer, "December 7th 1941," 5-6.
14. Goldstein, *The Way it Was*, 153.
15. Schaeffer, "December 7th 1941," 6; Blutt account in Turner, pub., *11th Bomb Group*, 68; "Organizational History, 431st Bombardment Squadron (H), 11th Bombardment Group (H), VII Bomber Command, Seventh Air Force," *Bomb Squadron History, 431st Bombardment Squadron (H)* [hereafter cited as, "Organizational History, 431st BS"], 5.
16. Goldstein, *The Way it Was*, 153.
17. "Diary - 88th RS," 17.
18. "History of the Seventh Bombardment Group (H)," *7th Bombardment Group (H) History* [hereafter cited as "History of Seventh BG"], 2-3; Payne to author, Sept. 9, 1996, 1; Green to author, July 14, 1996; Dorr, *7th Bomb Group*, 46.
19. Ibid.; Payne to author, Sept. 9, 1996, 1.
20. Dorr, *7th Bomb Group*, 101.
21. Ibid.; "History of the Seventh BG," 2-3.
22. Ibid.; "History of the Seventh BG," 2-3.
23. "394th BS Report," 6.
24. Johnson quoted in Dorr, *7th Bomb Group*, 53.
25. Ibid.
26. Carmichael statement in "Diary - 88th RS," 11; "Diary - 88th RS," 17.
27. Interview with Angelini, December 7, 1997.
28. Ibid., 30.
29. "394th BS Report," 6; "History of the 42nd BS," 4; "23rd BS History," 4; Hillsborough, pub., *Fifth Bomb Group*, 31; "Seventy-Second Bombardment Squadron (H) History," in Cleveland, ed., *Grey Geese Calling*, 383-5.
30. "23rd BS History," 4.
31. "Organizational History, 431st BS,", 5.
32. Dorr, *7th Bomb Group*, 55. The pilots and planes, all B-17Es, where known, were: Maj. Hobson (41-2406), Capt. William Lewis, Jr., and 1st Lts. Frederick C. Eaton, Jr. (41-2446, *Swamp Ghost*), Jack W. Hughes (41-2419), John A. Roberts, and Harry E. Spieth (41-2440, *Calamity Jane*,). 1st Lts. James R. DuBose, and Clarence McPherson (41-2417) departed Hamilton Field for Hawaii with the others but aborted for unspecified reasons.
33. Fields, *Kangaroo Squadron*, 29.
34. Ibid.
35. Dorr, *7th Bomb Group*, 56.
36. "A Brief History of the 435th Bombardment Squadron, (H)," *Bomb Squadron History, 435th Bombardment Squadron (H)* [hereafter cited as "Brief History of 435th BS"], 1.
37. Fields, *Kangaroo Squadron*, 32-3.

38. "History of the 42nd BS," 5.
39. "Operational History of the Seventh Air Force," 48, 49.
40. Saunders statement in Cleveland, ed., *Grey Geese Calling*, 9. Saunders was officially put in charge of the 5th BG on January 12, 1942. Hillsborough, pub., *Fifth Bomb Group*, 31.
41. Ibid., 14; Turner, pub., *11th Bomb Group*, 12-3.
42. "394th BS Report," 6.
43. "Operational History of the Seventh Air Force," 50
44. Howard, *One Damned Island After Another* [hereafter cited as Howard, *One Damned Island*], 55-7; Freeman, *The B-17 Flying Fortress Story*, 73. Freeman erroneously reports that the crew of B-17E (41-2402) were "all killed."
45. Howard, *One Damned Island*, 51.

Chapter 5
1. Edmunds, *They Fought*, 108.
2. Crimmins interview in Emmett, *Interviews*, 3.
3. White, *Queens*, 33; Edmunds, *They Fought*, 112.
4. Carpenter interview in Emmett, *Interviews*, 2.
5. Edmunds, *They Fought*, 113; Kimmerle, *Personal Narrative*, 11; Bartsch, *Doomed at the Start*, 130-1.
6. Jacquet, "Flight," Winter, 1985, 20; Mitchell, *In Alis Vicimus*, 36; "Diary of the 19th BG," 2.
7. Mitchell, *In Alis Vicimus*, 36; "Diary of the 19th BG," 2.
8. Ibid.
9. Jacquet, "Flight," Winter, 1985, 20
10. Ibid., 20-1.
11. Shores, *Bloody Shambles*, Vol. 1, 176; Sakai, *Samurai!*, 68.
12. Teats, "Tide," Inst. I, Dec. 31, 1942, 4; "Diary of the 19th BG," 2-3; Edmunds, *They Fought*, 119.
13. Teats, "Tide," Inst. I, Dec. 31, 1942, 4.
14. Ibid.; "Diary of the 19th BG," 3.
15. Edmunds, *They Fought*, 119-20.
16. Brownstein, *The Swoose*, 39; Edmunds, *They Fought*, 154-5.
17. Jacquet, "Flight," Winter, 1985, 21-2.
18. Perret, *Winged Victory*, 80.
19. Edmunds, *They Fought*, 121n; "Diary of the 19th BG," 4.
20. Mitchell, *In Alis Vicimus*, 39; Haugland, *The AAF Against Japan*, 36; Edmunds, *They Fought*, 121-2; "Diary of the 19th BG," 3.
21. Ibid.; Vandevanter statement in, *Interviews of the 19th Bombardment Group, 9 December 1942* [hereafter cited as *Interviews, 9 Dec. 1942*], 1.
22. Mitchell, *In Alis Vicimus*, 40; Edmunds, *They Fought*, 121-2.
23. Teats, "Tide," Inst. II, Jan. 1, 1943, 1.
24. Edmunds, *They Fought*, 125; Mitchell, *In Alis Vicimus*, 40.
25. Mitchell, *In Alis Vicimus*, 40; Teats, "Tide," Inst. II, Jan. 1, 1943, 1.
26. Mitchell, *In Alis Vicimus*, 40-1; "Diary of the 19th BG," 3.
27. "Diary of the 19th BG," 3; Teats, "Tide," Inst. II, Jan. 1, 1943, 1.
28. Sakai, *Samurai!*, 69.
29. McClendon, *The Legend of Colin Kelly*, 23-4.
30. Ibid., 24.
31. Ibid., 56-7.

32. Ibid., 27. Japanese fighter pilot Saburo Sakai vehemently denies the reports that any Japanese Zeros strafed the men in their parachutes.
33. Ibid., 27, 59.
34. Shores, *Bloody Shambles*, Vol. 1, 182; Chesneau, ed., *Conway's All the World's Fighting Ships*, 1922-1946, 188, 210.
35. McClendon, *The Legend of Colin Kelly*, 33.
36. "Diary of the 19th BG," 3, 4.
37. Ibid., 5; Teats, "Tide," Inst. II, Jan. 1, 1943, 1.
38. Mitchell, *In Alis Vicimus*, 40; Bartsch, *Doomed at the Start*, 143.
39. Sakai, *Samurai!*, 69; Jacquet, "Flight," Winter, 1985, 23.
40. "Diary of the 19th BG," 5.
41. Ibid., 4;
42. Ibid.
43. Ibid., 3; Mitchell, *In Alis Vicimus*, 40.
44. Vandevanter statement in, *Interviews*, 9 Dec. 1942, 1-2.
45. "Diary of the 19th BG," 5; Teats, "Tide," Inst. III, Jan. 2, 1943, 4.
46. Ibid.
47. "Diary of the 19th BG," 5.
48. Ibid., 4, 5.
49. Teats, "Tide," Inst. II, Jan. 1, 1943, 4; Edmunds, *They Fought*, 129-30; Mitchell, *In Alis Vicimus*, 42.
50. Sakai, *Samurai!*, 70.

Chapter 6
1. "Diary of the 19th BG," 5; Vandevanter statement in, *Interviews 9 Dec. 1942*, 2.
2. "Diary of the 19th BG," 5.
3. Ibid.; Jacquet, "Flight," Winter, 1985, 23.
4. Teats, "Tide," Inst. II, Jan. 1, 1943, 1, 4.
5. White, *Queens*, 73; Shores, *Bloody Shambles*, Vol. 1, 183; Edmunds, *They Fought*, 152.
6. "Diary of the 19th BG," 5; Edmunds, *They Fought*, 153.
7. Edmunds, *They Fought*, 153.
8. Ibid., 153, 198; Teats, "Tide," Inst. IV, Jan. 4, 1943, 4; "Answers to Request for Historical Information Concerning 19th Bombardment Group (H)," in Fields, *Kangaroo Squadron*, 141. Much has been written about why O'Donnell was transferred to Clark Field. Many authors believe that the transfer was punishment because O'Donnell had requested that the B-17s be moved to Australia for repair and maintenance. Teats' reason that Eubank was injured and needed O'Donnell, written only one year after the event, is much more plausible. O'Donnell was much too important of an officer to bury.
9. Edmunds, *They Fought*, 153-4.
10. Ibid., 154-5; White, *Queens*, 51.
11. Edmunds, *They Fought*, 155; "Diary of the 19th BG," 5.
12. Edmunds, *They Fought*, 155
13. "Diary of the 19th BG," 5, 6.
14. Fesmire statement in Freeman, *B-17 Fortress at War*, 49; *Statement by Capt. H. T. Wheless*, A. C., 1; Brown, Cecil, ed., "War Pilot's Story," *Life*, May 11, 1942, 35; White, *Queens*, 55. Take-off times vary. Wheless said 9:00 a.m., navigator Harry Schrieber remembered 10:00 and the 19th BG reported 11:40 a.m.
15. Schrieber quoted in White, *Queens*, 59, 60, 63; Edmunds, *They Fought*, 156.

16. Schrieber quoted in White, *Queens,* 59-61, 69; Edmunds, *They Fought,* 156.
17. Schrieber quoted in White, *Queens,* 56-7; Edmunds, *They Fought,* 155-6; "Diary of the 19th BG," 6.
18. *Statement by Capt. H. T. Wheless, A. C.,* 1-4; Brown, "War Pilot's Story," *Life,* May 11, 1942, 35-6.
19. *Statement by Capt. H. T. Wheless, A. C.,* 2-3.
20. *Statement by Capt. H. T. Wheless, A. C.,* 1-4; Brown, "War Pilot's Story," *Life,* May 11, 1942, 35-6.
21. *Statement by Capt. H. T. Wheless, A. C.,* 1; Edmunds, *They Fought,* 160n. The DFC citation for Vandevanter claims that one transport was sunk and two were damaged, and the citation for a DSC for Adams states that one transport was destroyed. Additionally, Wheless thought he "probably destroyed one" transport. *Statement by Capt. H. T. Wheless, A. C.,* 1; Edmunds, *They Fought,* 160n.
22. Edmunds, *They Fought,* 160n.
23. Ibid., 160.
24. Teats, "Tide," Inst. IV, Jan. 4, 1943, 4.
25. Shores, *Bloody Shambles,* Vol. 1, 187; Kurtz quoted in White, *Queens,* 49; Carpenter interview in Emmett, *Interviews,* 3.
26. Brereton, *The Brereton Diaries,* 55.
27. Teats, "Tide," Inst. IV, Jan. 4, 1943, 4.
28. Edmunds, *They Fought,* 160; Mitchell, *In Alis Vicimus,* 171-2; "Diary of the 19th BG," 6.
29. Mitchell, *In Alis Vicimus,* 172; Teats, "Tide," Inst. V, Jan. 5, 1943, 4.
30. Teats, "Tide," Inst. V, Jan. 5, 1943, 4 and Inst. VII, Jan. 7, 1943, 4.; Brownstein, *The Swoose,* 45, 46.
31. Teats, "Tide," Inst. V, Jan. 5, 1943, 4.
32. White, *Queens,* 73.
33. Bartsch, *Doomed at the Start,* 178.
34. "Air Services Visayan-Mindanao Area," 9; Mitchell, *In Alis Vicimus,* 50.
35. Shores, *Bloody Shambles,* Vol. 1, 191.
36. Mitchell, *In Alis Vicimus,* 50, 165.
37. "Diary of the 19th BG," 8-9; Edmunds, *They Fought,* 178.
38. Ibid.
39. Rutherford, *Fall of the Philippines,* 59; Edmunds, *They Fought,* 180.
40. Teats, "Tide," Inst. VI, Jan. 6, 1943, 4.
41. Brownstein, *The Swoose,* 48.
42. Teats, "Tide," Inst. VI, Jan. 6, 1943, 4; Vandevanter statement in, *Interviews of the 19th Bombardment Group,* 9 December 1942, 2; Edmunds, *They Fought,* 180. Haugland, *The AAF Against Japan,* 39.
43. Mingos, *American Heroes of the War in the Air* [hereafter cited as Mingos, *American Heroes*], Vol. One, 41.
44. Teats, "Tide," Inst. VI, Jan. 6, 1943, 4; Vandevanter statement in, *Interviews,* 9 Dec. 1942, 2; Rutherford, *Fall of the Philippines,* 67.
45. Teats, "Tide," Inst. VI, Jan. 6, 1943, 4; Edmunds, *They Fought,* 182; "Diary of the 19th BG," 10.
46. Ibid.
47. Vandevanter statement in, *Interviews,* 9 Dec. 1942, 2-3.
48. Ibid.; "Diary of the 19th BG," 10.
49. "Diary of the 19th BG," 10; Teats, "Tide," Inst. VI, Jan. 6, 1943, 4.
50. Rutherford, *Fall of the Philippines,* 67.

51. Edmunds, *They Fought*, 185; Mitchell, *In Alis Vicimus*, 52. Edmunds reports that Combs flew straight to Australia after finding nothing at Cotabato while Mitchell states that Combs repaired his plane and hit Davao. Mitchell says nothing about the side trip to Cotabato. Combs' combative character would never have let him leave Mindanao without taking one last swipe at the Japanese. I am convinced that Combs first flew to Cotabato, found nothing, and then bombed Davao on his way south.

52. "Diary of the 19th BG," 10; Mingos, *American Heroes*, 41.

53. Rutherford, *Fall of the Philippines*, 71.

54. Teats, "Tide," Inst. VI, Jan. 6, 1943, 4.

55. Rutherford, *Fall of the Philippines*, 79.

56. Edmunds, *They Fought*, 214-5.

57. Ibid.; Jacquet, "Flight," Winter, 1985, 23.

58. Whitcomb, *Escape From Corregidor*, 30; "Answers to Request for Historical Information Concerning 19th Bombardment Group (H)," in Fields, *Kangaroo Squadron*, 147.

59. Teats, "Tide," Inst. VI, Jan. 6, 1943, 4; "Diary of the 19th BG," 11.

60. "Diary of the 19th BG," 11; Mingos, *American Heroes*, Vol. One, 50, 52.

61. Fesmire statement in Freeman, *B-17 Fortress at War*, 51; Kurtz quoted in White, *Queens*, 103.

62. "Diary of the 19th BG," 11-2; Mingos, *American Heroes*, Vol. One, 50, 52; White, *Queens*, 79.

63. "Diary of the 19th BG," 12-3; Edmunds, *They Fought*, 186n.

64. "Diary of the 19th BG," 11-3; Teats, "Tide," Inst. VI, Jan. 6, 1943, 4; Mingos, *American Heroes*, Vol. One, 50, 52.

65. Mitchell, *In Alis Vicimus*, 54; "Diary of the 19th BG," 12.

66. Mitchell, *In Alis Vicimus*, 54, 74, 164; Shores, *Bloody Shambles*, Vol. 1, 196.

67. Teats, "Tide," Inst. VII, Jan. 7, 1943, 4.

68. Brereton, *The Brereton Diaries*, 71-73.

69. Haugland, *The AAF Against Japan*, 49.

70. Kurtz quoted in White, *Queens*, 86-7.

71. Ibid., 88; Haugland, *The AAF Against Japan*, 49.

72. Teats, "Tide," Inst. IV, Jan. 4, 1943, 4; Edmunds, *They Fought*, 255.

73. "Diary of the 19th BG," 14. The pilots and planes were: Walsh B-17D (40-3061), Bohnaker B-17D (40-3064), Kurtz B-17D (40-3067), Parsel B-17D (40-3074), Smith B-17D (40-3079), Combs B-17D (40-3097, *Ole Betsy*) and Connally B-17C (40-2062).

74. Kurtz quoted in White, *Queens*, 90; "Diary of the 19th BG," 14.

75. Kurtz quoted in White, *Queens*, 91; Edmunds, *They Fought*, 258-9.

76. "Diary of the 19th BG," 14. The pilots and planes were: Keiser B-17D (40-3066), Schaetzel B-17D (40-3070) and Teats B-17D (40-3078).

77. "Answers to Request for Historical Information Concerning 19th Bombardment Group (H)," in Fields, *Kangaroo Squadron*, 147

78. Mitchell, *In Alis Vicimus*, 74, 164, 174; Edmunds, *They Fought*, 256n.

79. Mitchell, *In Alis Vicimus*, 55.

80. White, *Queens*, 87, 88.

81. Kurtz quoted in Ibid., 88-89.

Chapter 7

1. "History of the 5th Bombardment Group (H)," *5th Bombardment Group (H) History* [hereafter cited as "History of the 5th BG"], 2.

2. Howard, *One Damned Island*, 51-54.

3. Belz, "Unusual Events with the 431st Bomb Squadron," in Turner, pub., *11th Bomb Group*, 58.
4. "History of the 5th BG," 2; "394th BS Report," 7.
5. "Diary of the 19th BG," 27; Dorr, *7th Bomb Group*, 56. The other pilots and planes were Hughes B-17E (41-2419) and 1st Lt. Clarence E. McPherson B-17E (41-2417, *Monkey Bizz-Ness*).
6. Lambert, *The Pineapple Air Force*, 37; Fields, *Kangaroo Squadron*, 37-8.
7. "The AAF in Australia to the Summer of 1942," *Army Air Forces Historical Studies: No. 9* [hereafter cited as "AAF in Australia"], 8, 151-2; Lambert, *The Pineapple Air Force*, 37, 51; Fields, *Kangaroo Squadron*, 38-9
8. Fields, *Kangaroo Squadron*, 38-9.
9. "AAF in Australia," 8, 151-2; Fields, *Kangaroo Squadron*, 39-40.
10. "AAF in Australia," 8, 151-2; "Diary of the 19th BG," 26, 27.
11. Ibid.; Dorr, *7th Bomb Group*, 56.
12. "History of the 26th BS," 13; Turner, pub., *11th Bomb Group*, 12.
13. Haugland, *The AAF Against Japan*, 117; Howard, *One Damned Island*, 65, 67; "Operational History of the Seventh Air Force," 51.
14. Howard, *One Damned Island*, 67-68.
15. Ibid.; "Operational History of the Seventh Air Force," 51.
16. Howard, *One Damned Island*, 68; Carter, *Combat Chronology*, 6-7.
17. Maurer, ed., *Air Force Combat Units of World War II*, 444-5; Bonanza Books, pub., *AAF: The Official World War II Guide to the Army Air Forces*, 66.
18. Carter, *Combat Chronology*, 8; Maurer, *Air Force Combat Units of World War II*, 454, 463.
19. Craven, ed., *The Army Air Forces in World War II* [hereafter cited as Craven ed., *Army Air Forces*], Vol. I, 454.
20. "History of the 11th Bombardment Group,(H), February 1940 - March 1944," *11th Bombardment Group (H) History* [hereafter cited as "History of the 11th BG"], 3; "History of the 98th Bombardment Squadron, (H), 16 December 1941 to 1 April 1944," *Bomb Squadron History, 98th Bombardment Squadron (H)* [hereafter cited as "History of the 98th BS"], 2.
21. Teats, "Tide," Inst. VII, Jan. 7, 1943, 4.
22. "Diary of the 19th BG," 15, 16; Edmunds, *They Fought*, 255.
23. "Diary of the 19th BG," 15-16. The pilots and planes were Combs B-17D (40-3097, *Ole Betsy*), Keiser B-17D (40-3066), Parsel B-17D (40-3074), Connally B-17C (40-2062), Schaetzel B-17D (40-3070), Teats B-17D (40-3061), Smith B-17D (40-3079) and Kurtz B-17D (40-3067).
24. Kurtz quoted in White, *Queens*, 98.
25. Teats, "Tide," Inst. VII, Jan. 7, 1943, 4; "Diary of the 19th BG," 15. The additional pilot and plane was Bohnaker B-17D (40-3064.)
26. Kurtz quoted in White, *Queens*, 100-101; "Diary of the 19th BG," 18.
27. "Diary of the 19th BG," 17, 18; Teats, "Tide," Inst. VII, Jan. 7, 1943, 4.
28. Teats, "Tide," Inst. VII, Jan. 7, 1943, 4; Payne to author, July 12, 1996, 2.
29. "Diary of the 19th BG," 18; Teats, "Tide," Inst. VII, Jan. 7, 1943, 4.
30. Teats, "Tide," Inst. VII, Jan. 7, 1943, 4.
31. Shores, *Bloody Shambles*, Vol. 1, 211.
32. "Diary of the 19th BG," 18; Teats, "Tide," Inst. VII, Jan. 7, 1943, 4.
33. "Diary of the 19th BG," 18, 19.
34. Teats, "Tide," Inst. VII, Jan. 7, 1943, 4.
35. Kurtz quoted in White, *Queens*, 103-4.

36. "Diary of the 19th BG," 20.
37. "Gasoline," *Fifth Air Force Operations, 1940-45;* "Aromatic Action," *Fifth Air Force Operations, 1940-45;* "Aromatic Gasoline," *Fifth Air Force Operations, 1940-45;* "Damage to Rubber by Aromatic Gas," *Fifth Air Force Operations, 1940-45.*
38. Boone quoted in White, *Queens,* 195; Knudson, *Diary of Capt. Cecil C. Knudson* [hereafter cited as Knudson, *Diary*], 9.
39. Boone quoted in White, *Queens,* 196.
40. Payne to author, Sept. 9, 1996, 2.
41. Ibid., September 9, 1996; Green to author, July 14, 1996; Wyatt statement in "History of the 28th BS," 1.
42. Payne to author, September 9, 1996, 2.
43. "Historical Data of the 19th Bombardment Group," *19th Bombardment Group (H) History* [hereafter cited as "Historical Data, 19th BG"], 4; "Consolidated History of the Seventh Bombardment Group," *7th Bombardment Group (H) History,* 6.
44. "Diary of the 19th BG," 21. The pilots and planes were: Combs B-17D (40-3097, *Ole Betsy*), Bohnaker B-17D (40-3064), Keiser B-17D (40-3066), Parsel B-17D (40-3074), Teats B-17D (40-3078), Smith B-17D (40-3079), Connally B-17C (40-2062), Kurtz B-17D (40-3067) and Broadhurst B-17D (40-3061).
45. "Diary of the 19th BG," 21; Mitchell, *In Alis Vicimus,* 77; Edmunds, *They Fought,* 264.
46. "Diary of the 19th BG," 22.
47. Mitchell, *In Alis Vicimus,* 79; Edmunds, *They Fought,* 264; Kurtz quoted in White, *Queens,* 106.
48. Edmunds, *They Fought,* 265; White, *Queens,* 106-7.
49. "Diary of the 19th BG," 22; Mitchell, *In Alis Vicimus,* 79.
50. Ibid.; Edmunds, *They Fought,* 265.
51. Shores, *Bloody Shambles,* Vol. 1, 212.
52. Mingos, *American Heroes,* Vol. One, 39.
53. Edmunds, *They Fought,* 268-9; Costello, *The Pacific War,* 180-1.
54. Costello, *The Pacific War,* 63, 73-5, 182, 186.
55. Edmunds, *They Fought,* 238; Crimmins interview in Emmett, *Interviews,* 3.
56. Carpenter interview in Emmett, *Interviews,* 3.
57. Ibid.; "History of the 30th Bombardment Squadron, 19th Bomb Group," *Bomb Squadron History, 30th Bombardment Squadron (H),* [hereafter cited as "History of the 30th BS"], 2.
58. "History of the 30th BS," 2.
59. "Answers to Request for Historical Information Concerning 19th Bombardment Group (H),"in Fields, *Kangaroo Squadron,* 147; Crimmins interview in Emmett, *Interviews,* 4.
60. Crimmins interview in Emmett, *Interviews,* 4-5.
61. Ibid.
62. "History of the 30th BS," 2.
63. Crimmins interview in Emmett, *Interviews,* 5.
64. Edmunds, *They Fought,* 265; Mitchell, *In Alis Vicimus,* 79.
65. Edmunds, *They Fought,* 265-6; Shores, *Bloody Shambles,* Vol. 1, 212-3; "Diary of the 19th BG," 24. Pilots and planes were: Combs B-17D (40-3097, *Ole Betsy*), Bohnaker B-17D (40-3064), Keiser B-17D (40-3066), Connally B-17C (40-2062), Kurtz B-17D (40-3067), Broadhurst B-17D (40-3061) and Teats B-17D (40-3078).
66. Kurtz quoted in White, *Queens,* 127-37.
67. "Diary of the 19th BG," 25.

68. Ibid.; Kurtz quoted in White, *Queens*, 142.
69. "Diary of the 19th BG," 25-6.
70. Shores, *Bloody Shambles*, Vol. 1, 214.

Chapter 8
1. "Diary of the 19th BG," 23-4; Edmunds, *They Fought*, 294-6; Hardison, *The Suzy-Q*, 9-11.
2. Dorr, *7th Bomb Group*, 57.
3. "Diary of the 19th BG," 23-4; Edmunds, *They Fought*, 294-6; Hardison, *The Suzy-Q*, 9-11.
4. Reeves quoted in White, *Queens*, 149-50; Knudson, *Diary*, 8.
5. Hardison, *The Suzy-Q*, 11-14; Edmunds, *They Fought*, 296-300; White, *Queens*, 152-3.
6. "Diary of the 19th BG," 26, 27; Kurtz quoted in White, *Queens*, 144.
7. "Consolidated History of the Seventh Bombardment Group," *7th Bombardment Group (H) History*, 1; Dorr, *7th Bomb Group*, 253.
8. "Diary of the 19th BG," 30; Dorr, *7th Bomb Group*, 253.
9. Boone and Reeves quoted in White, *Queens*, 152-3.
10. "Diary of the 19th BG," 26, 31-2. The pilots and planes, all B-17Ds, were: Combs (40-3061), Bohnaker (40-3064), Vandevanter (40-3072), Parsel (40-3074), Schaetzel (40-3067), Smith (40-3066) and Teats (40-3078).
11. Ibid., 32; Vandevanter statement in *Interviews, 9 Dec. 1942*, 3.
12. Ibid., 32.
13. Teats, "Tide," Inst. VII, Jan. 9, 1943, 4.
14. "Diary of the 19th BG," 32-3; Mitchell, *In Alis Vicimus*, 80.
15. Brereton, *The Brereton Diaries*, 83; Gooch to author, September 2, 1996, 1.
16. Teats, "Tide," Inst. IX, Jan. 9, 1943, 4; Hardison, *The Suzy-Q*, 17.
17. White, *Queens*, 195.
18. Rouse, *Diary of Lt. Col. John A. Rouse* [hereafter cited as Rouse, *Diary*], 9; Payne to author, July 12, 1996, 1, and September 9, 1996,1.
19. Gooch to author, September 2, 1996, 2.
20. Edmundson to author, July 19, 1988, 3; Fields to author, July, 1996; Schaeffer, "A Few Missions Out of Guadalcanal," 3
21. Ibid.
22. Edmundson, "B-17 Flying Fortress," in Higham, *Flying Combat Aircraft of the USAAF - USAF*, Vol. 2, 39.
23. Edmundson to author, July 19, 1988, 3.
24. Fields to author, July, 1996
25. Godman, *Supreme Commander*, 25.
26. Minahan statement in Freeman, *B-17 Fortress at War*, 121.
27. Godman, *Supreme Commander*, 25; Kurtz statement in Edmunds, *Queens*, 80.
28. Minahan statement in Freeman, *B-17 Fortress at War*, 120; Fields to author, July 1996.
29. "Diary of the 19th BG," 33; Mitchell, *In Alis Vicimus*, 81; "Diary - 7th Bombardment GP (H)," *7th Bombardment Group (H) History* [hereafter cited as "Diary - 7th BG"], 1.
30. "Diary of the 19th BG," 33; Mingos, *American Heroes*, Vol. One, 48; Shores, *Bloody Shambles*, Vol. 1, 219; "Diary - 7th BG," 1; Taggart, *My Fighting Congregation*, 100.
31. Edmunds, *They Fought*, 306; Shores, *Bloody Shambles*, Vol. 1, 219.
32. Shores, *Bloody Shambles*, Vol. 1, 220; Mitchell, *In Alis Vicimus*, 81; "Diary - 7th BG," 1; Mingos, *American Heroes*, Vol. One, 49, 251.
33. Minahan statement in Freeman, *B-17 Fortress at War*, 124-5.

34. Boone quoted in White, *Queens*, 155.

35. O'Leary, *Air Combat Special*, 56.

36. Sakai, *Samurai!*, 75.

37. Fesmire statement in Freeman, *B-17 Fortress at War*, 51; Edmundson to author, July 19, 1988, 3.

38. Reeves quoted in White, *Queens*, 198.

39. Freeman, *B-17 Fortress at War*, 121; Freeman, *The B-17 Flying Fortress Story*, 39-40.

40. Minahan statement in Freeman, *B-17 Fortress at War*, 123-4.

41. Freeman, *The B-17 Flying Fortress Story*, 40.

42. Gooch to author, April 10, 1996, 5.

43. Minahan statement in Freeman, *B-17 Fortress at War*, 124.

44. Edmundson to author, July 19, 1988, 1; Davis, *B-17 in Action*, 14.

45. Knudson, *Diary*, 1.

46. Edmunds, *They Fought*, 298; Fesmire statement in Freeman, *B-17 Fortress at War*, 51.

47. Freeman, *The B-17 Flying Fortress Story*, 41.

48. "Report on Gun Turrets," *Fifth Air Force Operations, 1940-45*, Document 1078.

49. Ibid.; Edmunds, *They Fought*, 298; Freeman, *The B-17 Flying Fortress Story*, 41.

50. Reeves quoted in White, *Queens*, 164; Freeman, *The B-17 Flying Fortress Story*, 41; Mingos, *American Heroes*, Vol. One, 48.

51. Dunnigan, *Victory at Sea*, 514, 516; Teats, "Tide," Inst. VIII, Jan. 8, 1943, 4; "Diary of the 19th BG," 34.

52. "Diary of the 19th BG," 34. The "Diary" lists only eight pilots and planes. They were: 19th BG - Connally B-17C (40-2062), Tash (unknown), Keiser B-17D (40-3066) and Schaetzel B-17D (40-3070). 7th BG - Hobson B-17E (41-2406), Hughes B-17E (41-2419), F.M. Key B-17E (41-2472, *Guinea Pig*) and Hillhouse B-17E (41-2460). The fifth pilot from the 19th BG was unequivocally Lt. Teats, though the number of his plane is unknown. The "Diary" also notes that Tash flew B-17E (41-2419) but this plane was flown by Hughes. The number of Tash's plane is therefore, unknown.

53. Mitchell, *In Alis Vicimus*, 82; Teats, "Tide," Inst. VIII, Jan. 8, 1943, 4.

54. "Diary of the 19th BG," 34, 35. Connally citation in "Philippine and Java Awards," 3.

55. Teats, "Tide," Inst. VIII, Jan. 8, 1943, 4.

56. Fesmire account in Freeman, *B-17 Fortress at War*, 49.

57. Ibid.; Teats, "Tide," Inst. VIII, Jan. 8, 1943, 4.

58. Ibid.

59. Teats, "Tide," Inst. VIII, Jan. 8, 1943, 4.

60. Crimmins interview in Emmett, *Interviews*, 5.

61. Ibid.; Teats, "Tide," Inst. VIII, Jan. 8, 1943, 4.

62. Ibid.; "Diary of the 19th BG," 36; Connally citation in "Philippine and Java Awards," 3.

63. "Diary of the 19th BG," 34, 35, 36, 37; Dorr, *7th Bomb Group*, 253.

64. Edmunds, *They Fought*, 302; Mitchell, *In Alis Vicimus*, 81.

65. Edmunds, *They Fought*, 302, 302n; Mitchell, *In Alis Vicimus*, 81.

66. Edmunds, *They Fought*, 302-3.

67. "Diary of the 19th BG," 35, 36, 37; Edmunds, *They Fought*, 301-2; White, *Queens*, 192; "Historical Data, 19th BG," 4.

Chapter 9

1. "Diary of the 19th BG," 37-8. The pilots and planes were; 7th BG: Robinson B-17E (41-2456), Strother B-17E (41-2471), Hobson B-17E (41-2406), Hughes B-17E (41-2419), Skiles B-17E (41-2454, *Craps for the Japs*) and Northcutt B-17E (41-2468). 19th BG:

Parsel B-17D (40-3067), Hillhouse B-17E (41-2460), and F.M. Key B-17E (41-2472, *Guinea Pig*).

2. Ibid., 37, 38.
3. Ibid., 38; Teats, "Tide," Inst. VIII, Jan. 8, 1943, 4.
4. Shores, *Bloody Shambles*, Vol. 1, 224; "Diary of the 19th BG," 37. The pilots and planes were; 7th BG: Robinson B-17E (41-2456), Strother B-17E (41-2471), Hobson B-17E (41-2406) and Northcutt B-17E (41-2468). 19th BG: Capt. Ray V. Schwanbeck B-17D (40-3067), Hillhouse B-17E (41-2460), F.M. Key B-17E (41-2472, *Guinea Pig*), and Cox B-17D (40-3070).
5. "Diary of the 19th BG," 39; Sakai, *Samurai!*, 76. "The Sea Battle of Macassar Strait," *Life*, February 9, 1942, 34.
6. Sakai, *Samurai!*, 75-6.
7. "Diary of the 19th BG," 39, 40.
8. Costello, *The Pacific War*, 191. This action has also been called "The Battle of Balikpapan."
9. "Diary of the 19th BG," 39. The pilots and planes were: 7th BG: Hobson B-17E (41-2406), and Northcutt B-17E (41-2468). 19th BG: Bohnaker B-17E (41-2472, *Guinea Pig*), Hillhouse B-17E (41-2460), Crimmins B-17E (41-2469), Tash B-17D (40-3072), Parsel B-17D (40-3074) and Teats B-17D (40-3070).
10. Gooch to author, April 10, 1996, 1-2.
11. "Diary of the 19th BG," 40; Mitchell, *In Alis Vicimus*, 82; White, *Queens*, 191.
12. White, Queens, 191-2; Mitchell, *In Alis Vicimus*, 82.
13. Shores, *Bloody Shambles*, Vol. 1, 225.
14. "Diary of the 19th BG," 40, 41. Dorr, *7th Bomb Group*, 253.
15. Ibid. The pilots and planes were; 7th BG: Robinson B-17E (41-2456), Strother B-17E (41-2471), and Preston B-17E (41-2466). 19th BG: Schwanbeck B-17E (41-2472, *Guinea Pig*), Mathewson B-17E (41-2455), and Cox B-17D (40-3074).
16. "Diary of the 19th BG," 43; Shores, *Bloody Shambles*, Vol. 1, 229.
17. "Diary of the 19th BG," 43; Mitchell, *In Alis Vicimus*, 82-3.
18. Robinson citation, "Philippine and Java Awards," 5.
19. "The Sea Battle of Macassar Strait," *Life*, February 9, 1942, 34; Mingos, *American Heroes*, Vol. One, 32.
20. Teats, "Tide," Inst. IX, Jan. 9, 1943, 4; "Diary of the 19th BG," 38, 39, 40. The pilots and planes, all B-17Ds, that flew to Laverton Repair Depot were: Jan. 23, Schaetzel (40-3066); Jan. 25, Smith (40-3079); Jan. 27, Keiser (40-3097, *Ole Betsy*) and Teats (40-3067).
21. Day quoted in Morehead, *In My Sights - Memoirs of a P-40 Ace*, 42; Teats, "Tide," Inst. IX, Jan. 9, 1943, 4; Mitchell, *In Alis Vicimus*, 83.
22. Brownstein, *The Swoose*, 61-2.
23. "Consolidated History of the Seventh Bombardment Group (H)," *7th Bombardment Group (H) History*, 6; Edmunds, *They Fought*, 309n, 310n; Dalley, "Saga of the 22nd Ground Men," in Johnson, ed., *435th Overseas*, 24; "Gasoline," *Fifth Air Force Operations*, 1940-45.
24. Dalley, "Saga of the 22nd Ground Men," in Johnson, ed., *435th Overseas*, 24.
25. Payne to author, July 12, 1996, 1, and September 9, 1996,1.
26. Edmunds, *They Fought*, 304; "Diary of the 19th BG," 43. The pilots and planes were; 7th BG: Bleasdale B-17E (41-2464, *Queenie*) and Preston B-17E (41-2466). 19th BG: Combs B-17E (41-2472, *Guinea Pig*), Tash B-17E (41-2471) and Bohnaker B-17D (40-3074).
27. "Diary of the 19th BG," 43, 44. Bohnaker B-17D (40-3074) returned to Malang on Jan. 29; Edmunds, *They Fought*, 304n.

28. "Diary of the 19th BG," 43.
29. Ibid. The pilots and planes, all B-17Es, were; 7th BG: Sparks (41-2476), Habberstad (41-2427) and Skiles (41-2454, *Craps for the Japs*). 19th BG: Mathewson (41-2455), and Cox (41-2478).
30. Edmunds, *They Fought*, 308-9, 309n; Mitchell, *In Alis Vicimus*, 83-4; Robinson citation, "Philippine and Java Awards," 6.
31. Dufrane quoted in Taggart, *My Fighting Congregation*, 90.
32. Reeves quoted in White, *Queens*, 161, 162.
33. Dufrane quoted in Taggart, *My Fighting Congregation*, 90; Shores, *Bloody Shambles*, Vol. 1, 230.
34. White, *Queens*, 163; Dufrane quoted in Taggart, *My Fighting Congregation*, 90.
35. White, *Queens*, 163-4; Dufrane quoted in Taggart, *My Fighting Congregation*, 90.
36. "Diary - 7th BG," 2; Robinson citation, "Philippine and Java Awards," 6; Maurer, ed., *Air Force Combat Units of World War II*, 44.
37. Dorr, *7th Bomb Group*, 254; "Diary of the 19th BG," 44-6.
38. Ibid.
39. "Diary of the 19th BG," 47. The pilots and planes, all B-17Es, were: Hobson (41-2472, *Guinea Pig*), Strother (41-2471), Sargent (41-2458, *Yankee Diddl'er*), Swanson (41-2469), Dufrane (41-2456), Habberstad (41-2455), Bleasdale (41-2464, *Queenie*), Northcutt (41-2483) and Preston (41-2453).
40. Ibid., 48, 50; Edmunds, *They Fought*, 313; "Diary - 7th BG," 2.
41. Mingos, *American Heroes*, Vol. One, 47; "Diary - 7th BG," 2.
42. Payne to author, September 9, 1996, 1.
43. Teats, "Tide," Inst. VIII, Jan. 8, 1943, 4.
44. Ibid.; "Diary of the 19th BG," 47-8; Dalley, "Saga of the 22nd Ground Men," in Johnson, ed., *435th Overseas*, 24.
45. Teats, "Tide," Inst. VIII, Jan. 8, 1943, 4.
46. "Diary of the 19th BG," 48.
47. Ibid.; White, *Queens*, 192-3. Rouse, *Diary*, 9;
48. The planes used for transport and supply were: B-17C (40-2072) and B-17Ds (40-3062), (40-3072), (40-3079), and (40-3097, *Ole Betsy*). B-17D (40-3066) had been taken down to Laverton Field on Jan. 23 but was returned to combat at an unknown date.
49. The fifteen planes were: B-17Ds (40-3061), (40-3066) and (40-3070), and B17Es (41-2453), (41-2454, *Craps for the Japs*), (41-2455), (41-2456), (41-2458, *Yankee Diddl'er*), (41-2460), (41-2461, *El Toro*), (41-2464, *Queenie*), (41-2466), (41-2471), (41-2472, *Guinea Pig*), and (41-2483).
50. "Diary of the 19th BG," 47, 48, 49; Taggart, *My Fighting Congregation*, 88-9; Edmunds, *They Fought*, 311-2; Brereton, *The Brereton Diaries*, 86.
51. "Diary of the 19th BG," 48, 49; Knudson, *Diary*, 9.
52. Dalley, "Saga of the 22nd Ground Men," in Johnson, ed., *435th Overseas*, 25.
53. "Diary of the 19th BG," 48, 49; Brereton, *The Brereton Diaries*, 87; Dorr, *7th Bomb Group*, 254.
54. "Diary of the 19th BG," 49. The pilots and planes, all B-17Es, were: 7th BG: Hillhouse (41-2471) and Green (41-2483). 19th BG: Schwanbeck (41-2458, *Yankee Diddl'er*), Bohnaker (41-2455), Tash (41-2464, *Queenie*) and 1st Lt. M. A. McKenzie (41-2453).
55. Rouse, *Diary*, 10; "Diary of the 19th BG," 50; "Diary of Operations of the 19th Bomb Group in Java," *19th Bombardment Group (H) History* [hereafter cited as "*Diary*, 19th BG in Java"], 1.
56. Rouse, *Diary*, 11; "Diary, 19th BG in Java," 2; Dorr, *7th Bomb Group*, 254.

57. Dorr, *7th Bomb Group*, 254.
58. "Diary of the 19th BG," 52. The pilots and planes, all B-17Es, were: Dufrane (41-2456), Swanson (41-2458, *Yankee Diddl'er*), Pritchard (41-2492), Strother (41-2471), Preston (41-2455), Lindsey (41-2483), Habberstad (41-2488), Northcutt (41-2453), Bleasdale (41-2464, *Queenie*).
59. Ibid.; Worley quoted in Taggart, *My Fighting Congregation*, 104.
60. Boone quoted in White, *Queens*, 185.
61. Ibid.; Worley quoted in Taggart, *My Fighting Congregation*, 104.
62. "Diary of the 19th BG," 52-3; Knudson, *Diary*, 10.
63. Boone quoted in White, *Queens*, 185-6; Teats, "Tide," Inst. IX, Jan. 9, 1943, 4.
64. Knudson, *Diary*, 10.
65. Ibid.; Boone quoted in White, *Queens*, 186-8.
66. Boone quoted in White, *Queens*, 187; "Diary of the 19th BG," 53.
67. Worley statement in Taggart, *My Fighting Congregation*, 104; Edmunds, *They Fought*, 332; Knudson, *Diary*, 10; Mingos, *American Heroes*, Vol. One, 50.
68. "Diary of the 19th BG," 53
69. Boone quoted in White, *Queens*, 189-90; Worley statement in Taggart, *My Fighting Congregation*, 105.
70. Boone quoted in White, *Queens*, 189.
71. Edmunds, *They Fought*, 333; Lindsey quoted in Hardison, *The Suzy-Q*, 18-9.
72. Edmunds, *They Fought*, 333; Mingos, *American Heroes*, Vol. One, 46, 48.
73. "Diary, 19th BG in Java," 3; "Diary of the 19th BG," 53; Knudson, *Diary*, 10.
74. "Diary of the 19th BG," 53.
75. Payne to author, Sept. 9, 1996; White, *Queens*, 185n. Although some aircrews began whitewashing over the red disc in the center of their insignia after the February 8 mission, apparently, this practice was not fully implemented. A photo taken on February 20, of B-17E (41-2484) burning after an air raid on Singosari, distinctly shows the red center ball still in place.
76. Ibid., 334; Kurtz quoted in White, *Queens*, 86.
77. "Diary of the 19th BG," 53; Edmunds, *They Fought*, 334; Kurtz quoted in White, *Queens*, 86; "Diary, 19th BG in Java," 3.

Chapter 10

1. "Diary, 19th BG in Java," 4; "Diary of the 19th BG," 54. The pilots and planes, all B-17Es, were: Schwanbeck (41-2464, *Queenie*), Hillhouse (41-2489, *Suzy-Q*), Mathewson (41-2455), McKenzie (41-2466) and A. E. Key (41-2472, *Guinea Pig*).
2. "Diary, 19th BG in Java," 4-5.
3. Ibid., 5; Dorr, *7th Bomb Group*, 254.
4. Dorr, *7th Bomb Group*, 91; "Diary of the 19th BG," 54-6.
5. Ibid.
6. Dorr, *7th Bomb Group*, 91.
7. "Diary of the 19th BG," 54-6
8. Mitchell, *In Alis Vicimus*, 85; "Diary of the 19th BG," 56-7; "Diary, 19th BG in Java," 6-7; Dorr, *7th Bomb Group*, 91. The pilots and planes, all B-17Es, were: 7th BG: Strother (41-2454), Habberstad (41-2466), Beck (41-2488), Northcutt (41-2478), Swanson (41-2458, *Yankee Diddl'er*), Hardison (41-2489, *Suzy-Q*), Casper (41-2462, *Tojo's Jinx*), and Preston (41-2455). 19th BG: Key, F. M. (41-2486, *Lady Lou*), Key, A. E. (41-2472, *Guinea Pig*) and Mathewson (41-2449).
9. Dorr, *7th Bomb Group*, 92. The pilots and planes, all B-17Es, were: 19th BG: Schaetzel

(41-2486, *Lady Lou*), Adams (41-2455), Teats (41-2472, *Guinea Pig*), Vandevanter (41-2498), Rouse (41-2488), and Pease (41-2453). 7th BG: Unknown.

10. Brereton, *The Brereton Diaries,* 91; Costello, *The Pacific War,* 197.

11. Dorr, *7th Bomb Group,* 92; "Diary, 19th BG in Java," 9. Pilots and planes, all B-17Es, were: Parsel (41-2458, *Yankee Diddl'er*), Key, A. E. (41-2486, *Lady Lou*), Hoevet (41-2455), Jacques (41-2478), and Keiser (41-2472, *Guinea Pig*).

12. Dorr, *7th Bomb Group,* 92. The pilots were: Beck, Smelser and Bleasdale. The planes are unknown.

13. Ibid., 254.

14. Costello, *The Pacific War,* 197.

15. Goralski, *World War II Almanac: 1931-1945,* 203

16. "Diary of the 19th BG," 59. The pilots and planes, all B-17Es, were: Schwanbeck (41-2486, *Lady Lou*), Bridges (41-2481, *Topper*), Hillhouse (41-2453), Key, F. M. (41-2484), Green (41-2488), and Mathewson (41-2455).

17. Ibid. Pilots and planes, all B-17Es, where known, were: 7th BG: Lindsey (41-2452), Hardison (41-2489, *Suzy-Q*), and Northcutt. 19th BG: Keiser (41-2472, *Guinea Pig*).

18. Ibid.; Hardison, *The Suzy-Q,* 39.

19. "Diary of the 19th BG," 59-60; "Diary, 19th BG in Java," 10-1. Dorr, *7th Bomb Group,* 254. Pilots and planes, all B-17Es, for the February 17, 19th BG mission were: Schwanbeck (41-2478), Shedd (41-2498), McKenzie (41-2486, *Lady Lou*), Pease (41-2488), Hillhouse (41-2455), Adams (41-2458, *Yankee Diddl'er*) and Rouse (41-2484).

20. "Diary of the 19th BG," 59-60; "Diary, 19th BG in Java," 10-1. Dorr, *7th Bomb Group,* 254. Pilots and planes, all B-17Es, for the February 18, 19th BG mission were: Parsel (41-2498), Hoevet (41-2478), Key, A. E. (41-2484), Jacques (41-2486, *Lady Lou*), Adams (41-2458, *Yankee Diddl'er*), and Carpenter (41-2488). Pilots and planes for the February 18, 7th BG mission are not known.

21. Edmunds, *They Fought,* 340, 340n. Edmunds states that 55 B-17s took part in the nine missions. This author counts only 53.

22. Brereton, *The Brereton Diaries,* 92.

23. Edmunds, *They Fought,* 342; Dorr, *7th Bomb Group,* 93.

24. Teats, "Tide," Inst. X, Jan. 11, 1943, 4.

25. Godman, *Supreme Commander,* 34.

26. Hardison, *Suzy-Q,* 32-3.

27. "AAF in Australia," 2; "Document #846," *19th Bombardment Group (H) History*; "Document #1005," *19th Bombardment Group (H) History*.

28. Crimmins interview in Emmett, *Interviews,* 6.

29. Dalley, "Saga of the 22nd Ground Men," in Johnson, ed., *435th Overseas,* 25; Green to author, July 14, 1996.

30. Payne to author, Sept. 9, 1996.

31. Fesmire statement in Freeman, *B-17 Fortress at War,* 50; Vandevanter statement in, *Interviews, 9 December 1942,* 5.

32. Hardison, *The Suzy-Q,* 141-2.

33. Green to author, Sept. 10, 1996, 2.

34. Brereton, *The Brereton Diaries,* 93; "Diary - 7th BG," 3; Dorr, *7th Bomb Group,* 93.

35. "Diary, 19th BG in Java," 12, 13.

36. Ibid., 13.

37. Ibid.; Godman, *Supreme Commander,* 34-5

38. "Diary, 19th BG in Java," 13; Fesmire statement in Freeman, *B-17 Fortress at War,* 50; Vandevanter statement in, *Interviews, 9 December 1942,* 4.

39. "Diary, 19th BG in Java," 13; "Diary of the 19th BG," 61; Knudson, *Diary,* 12. The pilots and planes, all B-17Es, were: 19th BG: Schwanbeck (41-2458, *Yankee Diddl'er*), Tash (41-2486, *Lady Lou*), and Green (41-2488). 7th BG: Lindsey (41-2452).

40. "Diary of the 19th BG," 61. The pilots and planes are not known.

41. Ibid.; Edmunds, *They Fought,* 364, 364n. The serial number of Casper's B-17 is not known.

42. Fesmire statement in Freeman, *B-17 Fortress at War,* 50; Vandevanter statement in, *Interviews, 9 December 1942,* 4.

43. "Diary, 19th BG in Java," 14.

44. Dorr, *7th Bomb Group,* 94, 254; Shores, *Bloody Shambles,* Vol. 2, 208; Mitchell, *In Alis Vicimus,* 86, 176.

45. Ibid.; "Diary, 19th BG in Java," 17.

46. Dorr, *7th Bomb Group,* 94.

47. Ibid., 93-4.

48. Sakai, *Samurai,* 87-8.

49. Dorr, *7th Bomb Group,* 94; Hardison, *The Suzy-Q,* 38.

50. Edmunds, *They Fought,* 355-9.

51. Dorr, *7th Bomb Group,* 57, 253-4.

52. "Diary, 19th BG in Java," 15; "Diary of the 19th BG," 62; Reeves quoted in White, *Queens,* 199-200. Pilots and planes, all B-17Es, were: 19th BG: Parsel (41-2458, *Yankee Diddl'er*), McKenzie (41-2486, *Lady Lou*), Pease (41-2455), Keiser (41-2498), Bridges (41-2478), Adams (41-2484), and Rouse (41-2488). 7th BG: Unknown.

53. "Diary of the 19th BG," 62; Rouse, *Diary,* 13.

54. "Diary, 19th BG in Java," 16; Rouse, *Diary,* 13-4.

55. Hansen, "Jap Bombing," in Johnson, ed., *435th Overseas,* 30.

56. "Diary, 19th BG in Java," 17; "Diary of the 19th BG," 62-3; Rouse, *Diary,* 14.

57. "Diary, 19th BG in Java," 17-8.

58. "Diary of the 19th BG," 63.

59. "Diary, 19th BG in Java," 19.

60. Ibid.; Vandevanter statement in, *Interviews, 9 December 1942,* 4; Shores, *Bloody Shambles,* Vol. 2, 219.

61. Shores, *Bloody Shambles,* Vol. 2, 219; Mitchell, *In Alis Vicimus,* 86, 164. B-17D (40-3062) had arrived in Java on February 14, piloted by Capt. Godman, carrying a load of much needed parts for the P-40s and A-24s.

62. Rouse, *Diary,* 14; Brereton, *The Brereton Diaries,* 97-8; Edmunds, *They Fought,* 367.

63. Brereton, *The Brereton Diaries,* 98-9; Edmunds, *They Fought,* 370.

Chapter 11

1. "Diary of the 19th BG," 64; Knudson, *Diary,* 13.

2. Rouse, *Diary,* 14-5; "Diary, 19th BG in Java," 20.

3. Dorr, *7th Bomb Group,* 95. Pilots and planes, all B-17Es, were: Habberstad (41-2452), Beck (41-2489, *Suzy-Q*), Smelser (41-2454, *Craps for the Japs*), Hardison (41-2464, Queenie), Swanson (41-2462, *Tojo's Jinx*), and Beran (41-2449).

4. Dorr, *7th Bomb Group,* 96; "Diary, 19th BG in Java," 20; Dalley, "Saga of the 22nd Ground Men," in Johnson, ed., *435th Overseas,* 25.

5. Edmunds, *They Fought,* 367.

6. Payne to author, Sept. 9, 1996, 2.

7. Edmunds, *They Fought,* 408-9.

8. Ibid., 410-2; Dorr, *7th Bomb Group,* 98.

9. Taggart, *My Fighting Congregation*, 128-30; Dalley, "Saga of the 22nd Ground Men," in Johnson, ed., *435th Overseas*, 25; Edmunds, *They Fought*, 414.

10. Paine to author, Sept. 9, 1996, 2;

11. Dorr, *7th Bomb Group*, 96; Knudson, *Diary*, 14; "Diary, 19th BG in Java," 20-1

12. "Diary, 19th BG in Java," 21-2; Knudson, *Diary*, 14. The pilots and planes were: F.M. Key B-17E (41-2497), Teats B-17E (41-2453), and Godman (Unknown).

13. Shores, *Bloody Shambles*, Vol. 2, 231-3.

14. Dorr, *7th Bomb Group*, 96.

15. Teats, "Tide," Inst. IX, Jan. 9, 1943, 4. The pilots for this mission were: Teats, Hoevet, F.M. Key and Mathewson. The planes are unknown.

16. Dorr, *7th Bomb Group*, 96.

17. Ibid., 96-7; Shores, *Bloody Shambles*, Vol. 2, 238.

18. Teats, "Tide," Inst. IX, Jan. 9, 1943, 4.

19. Ibid., 424; Dorr, *7th Bomb Group*, 96; Teats, "Tide," Inst. X, Jan. 11, 1943, 4.

20. Nalty, ed., *Pearl Harbor and the War in the Pacific*, 76-7; Zich, *The Rising Sun*, 127.

21. "Journal, 5th Bomber Command," *Fifth Air Force Operations, 1940-45* [hereafter cited as "Journal, 5th Bomber Command"], 67.

22. White, *Queens*, 215.

23. Ibid., 216.

24. "Journal, 5th Bomber Command,", 67; Teats, "Tide," Inst. X, Jan. 11, 1943, 4.

25. "Journal, 5th Bomber Command," 67; Hardison, *The Suzy-Q*, 51.

26. "Journal, 5th Bomber Command,", 67.

27. Ibid., 68; Vandevanter statement in, *Interviews, 9 Dec. 1942*, 5.

28. Hardison, *The Suzy-Q*, 52-4.

29. Dorr, *7th Bomb Group*, 97; "Journal, 5th Bomber Command," 68.

30. Mitchell, *In Alis Vicimus*, 87; Shores, *Bloody Shambles*, Vol. 2, 305; "Journal, 5th Bomber Command,", 67. (The "Journal" erroneously records the date of the last bombing raid from Java as February 28, 1942.)

31. "Journal, 5th Bomber Command,", 68.

32. Yerington, "The Evacuation of Java," in Johnson, ed., *435th Overseas*, 27; Vandevanter statement in, *Interviews, 9 Dec. 1942*, 5; Teats, "Tide," Inst. X, Jan. 11, 1943, 4.

33. "Journal, 5th Bomber Command,", 68; Dorr, *7th Bomb Group*, 98; White, *Queens*, 217.

34. White, *Queens*, 217-8.

35. Edmunds, *They Fought*, 430-1n.

36. Teats, "Tide," Inst. X, Jan. 11, 1943, 4; Hardison, *The Suzy-Q*, 54.

37. Edmunds, *They Fought*, 432-3.

38. The sixteen B-17Es were: (41-2417, *Monkey Bizz-Ness*), (41-2449), (41-2452), (41-2453), (41-2454, *Craps for the Japs*), (41-2458, *Yankee Diddl'er*), (41-2461, *El Toro*), (41-2462, *Tojo's Jinx*), (41-2464, *Queenie*), (41-2472, *Guinea Pig*), (41-2481, *Topper*), (41-2486, *Lady Lou*), (41-2489, *Suzy-Q*), (41-2497), (41-2505), and (41-2507).

39. Maurer, ed., *Air Force Combat Units of World War II*, 44, 66.

40. Mikesh, "Japan's Little Fleet of Big American Bombers," *Air Force/Space Digest*, August 1969, 83-5, 87-8; Sakai, *Samurai!*, 224.

41. "AAF in Australia," 21; Carter, *Combat Chronology*, 8; Gillison, *Royal Australian Air Force, 1939-1942*, 451-2; "Brief History of the 435th BS," 1; Dorr, *7th Bomb Group*, 254-5. The pilots and planes, all B-17Es, were: 88th RS: Carmichael (41-2429, *Why Don't We Do This More Often*), Bostrom (41-2416, *San Antonio Rose*), Chaffin (41-2430, *Naughty But Nice*), Rawls (41-2434), Brandon (41-2433), and Thacker (41-2432, *The Last Straw*). 22nd BS: Eaton (41-2446, *Swamp Ghost*), Spieth (41-2440, *Calamity Jane*), Roberts

(Unknown), Lewis (Unknown), and Dubose (Unknown). 38th RS: Swenson (41-2408). The following B-17Es (41-2421), (41-2438) and (41-2447, *San Antonio Rose II*) were all part of this flight but can not be matched to any specific pilot.

42. "AAF in Australia," 21; Fields, *Kangaroo Squadron*, 41-2.

43. Fields, *Lt. Col. John Wallace Fields*, 3; Fields, *Kangaroo Squadron*, 43-4; Freeman, *The B-17 Flying Fortress Story*, 73; Fields to author, September 10, 1996, 2.

44. Dorr, *7th Bomb Group*, 106.

45. Ibid.

46. Ibid.; Lewis, "Narrative Report of Mission of February 23, 1942," *435th Bombardment Squadron (H) USAAFIA.*

47. Ibid.; Fields, *Lt. Col. John Wallace Fields*, 2; Fields, *Kangaroo Squadron*, 49-52; Gillson, *Royal Australian Air Force, 1939-1942*, 452; Johnson, "The 435th Short History," in Johnson, ed., *435th Overseas*, 6; Goralski, *World War II Almanac: 1931-1945*, 204.

48. Dorr, *7th Bomb Group*, 106; Johnson, "The 435th Short History," in Johnson, ed., *435th Overseas*, 6; Fields, *Kangaroo Squadron*, 49-50; "AAF in Australia," 22; Gillson, *Royal Australian Air Force*, 452; Lewis, "Narrative Report of Mission of February 23, 1942," *435th Bombardment Squadron (H) USAAFIA.*

49. Fields, *Kangaroo Squadron*, 165; Dorr, *7th Bomb Group*, 106.

50. "AAF in Australia," 21-2; Fields to Mooney, 1-2; Johnson, "The 435th Short History," in Johnson, ed., *435th Overseas*, 11; Lewis, "Narrative Report of Mission of February 23, 1942," *435th Bombardment Squadron (H) USAAFIA*; "Another Roll of Honor," in "435th Daily Bulletin," *435th Bombardment Squadron, 19th Bombardment Group (H)*, October 27, 1942. B-17E (41-2446, *Swamp Ghost*) was located by a Royal Australian Air Force helicopter in 1972. Over twenty years later the incredibly preserved bomber was taken to Travis Air Force Base, California, where it was restored and stands as the oldest E-model in the world.

51. Lewis, "Narrative Report of Mission of February 23, 1942," *435th Bombardment Squadron (H) USAAFIA*; Dorr, *7th Bomb Group*, 107.

52. Lillback to Mooney, August 15, 1996; Fields to author, April 15, 1996 and July 8, 1996.

53. Fields, *Kangaroo Squadron*, 53, 117; Johnson, "The 435th Short History," in Johnson, ed., *435th Overseas*, 6.

54. "Missions of the 435th BS," in *Bomb Squadron History 435th BS*, 1941-43, 1; "Destruction of Enemy Aircraft," *435th Bombardment Squadron, 19th Bombardment Group (H)* [hereafter cited as "Destruction of Aircraft by 435th BS"], 1-2.

55. Fields, *Kangaroo Squadron*, 53-4.

56. Murphy, *Skip Bombing*, 14-5.

57. Ibid.; Green to author, September 10, 1996, 1.

58. Murphy, *Skip Bombing*, 7, 14-5.

59. Green to author, September 10, 1996, 1-2.

60. Johnson, "The 435th Short History," in Johnson, ed., *435th Overseas*, 2; Lewis, "Narrative Report of Mission of March, 13, 1942," *435th Bombardment Squadron (H) USAAFIA*; "Another Roll of Honor," in "435th Daily Bulletin," *435th Bombardment Squadron, 19th Bombardment Group (H)*, October 27, 1942; "Missions of the 435th BS," in *Bomb Squadron History 435th BS, 1941-43*, 1; Mingos, *American Heroes*, Vol. One, 315; "Destruction of Aircraft by 435th BS," 2.

61. "Brief History of the 435th BS," 1.

62. Knudson, *Diary*, 15; Teats, "Tide," Inst. X, Jan. 11, 1943, 4; "Journal, 5th Bomber Command,", 68.

63. Rouse, *Diary*, 16; Teats, "Tide," Inst. X, Jan. 11, 1943, 4.

64. Shores, *Bloody Shambles*, Vol. 2, 312-4; "Journal, 5th Bomber Command,", 68; Dorr, *7th Bomb Group*, 99.
65. Teats, "Tide," Inst. X, Jan. 11, 1943, 4.
66. "A Short History of the 43rd Bombardment Group and the 63rd, 64th, 65th, and 403rd Bomb Squadron," *43rd Bombardment Group (H) History, 12 February 1942 to August 1945*, 1; "History of the 43rd Bombardment Group," *43rd Bombardment Group (H) History, 15 January 1941 to February 1944* [hereafter cited as "History of the 43rd BG"], 318.
67. Edmunds, *They Fought*, 444; Mitchell, *In Alis Vicimus*, 98, 100; Rouse, *Diary*, 19.
68. Taggart, *My Fighting Congregation*, 132; Payne to author, Sept. 9, 1996, 2.
69. Mitchell, *In Alis Vicimus*, 90-1.
70. Ibid., 93; Edmunds, *They Fought*, 432n, 433n; Shores, *Bloody Shambles*, Vol. 2, 323.

Chapter 12
1. Costello, *The Pacific War*, 212-3; Zich, *The Rising Sun*, 95.
2. "Answers to Request for Historical Information Concerning 19th Bombardment Group (H),"in Fields, *Kangaroo Squadron*, 146.
3. "Army Air Services in the Philippines, November 1941 - 29 April 1942," *Fifth Air Force Operations, 1940-45*, Document 8, 2.
4. Carpenter interview in Emmett, *Interviews*, 4; Edmunds, *They Fought*, 324n.
5. "History of the 28th BS," 5.
6. Zich, *The Rising Sun*, 93; Kimmerle, *Personal Narrative*, 31.
7. "Answers to Request for Historical Information Concerning 19th Bombardment Group (H),"in Fields, *Kangaroo Squadron*, 145.
8. Kimmerle, *Personal Narrative*, 31.
9. "Air Services Visayan-Mindanao Area," 10
10. "Diary of the 19th BG," 36-7, 42-3, 51; Dorr, *7th Bomb Group*, 70.
11. "Journal, 5th Bomber Command," 37-8.
12. Ibid., 69; Dorr, *7th Bomb Group*, 109.
13. Godman, *Supreme Commander*, 40.
14. Ibid., 41-2.
15. Epperson quoted in Ibid., 42.
16. Godman, *Supreme Commander*, 42-4; General Order No. 37, Part 2 in Fields, *Kangaroo Squadron*, 189.
17. General Order No. 37, Part 1 in Fields, *Kangaroo Squadron*, 188; Dorr, *7th Bomb Group*, 109.
18. Dorr, *7th Bomb Group*, 109; Mitchell, *In Alis Vicimus*, 106-7.
19. "Journal, 5th Bomber Command," 71; "History of the 28th BS," 10; "AAF in Australia," 49.
20. Mitchell, *In Alis Vicimus*, 22; Edmundson to author, September 6, 1988, 2-3.
21. "Journal, 5th Bomber Command," 70.
22. Dorr, *7th Bomb Group*, 109; Teats, "Tide," Inst. XI, Jan. 12, 1943, 4.
23. Ibid.
24. Godman, *Supreme Commander*, 46.
25. Teats, "Tide," Inst. XI, Jan. 12, 1943, 4; Dorr, *7th Bomb Group*, 109.
26. Ind, *Bataan: The Judgment Seat*, 351.
27. Godman, *Supreme Commander*, 47.
28. Dorr, *7th Bomb Group*, 109-10; Carruthers, "The MacArthur and Quezon Evacuation," in Johnson, ed., *435th Overseas*, 33.

29. Teats, "Tide," Inst. XI, Jan. 12, 1943, 4; Dorr, *7th Bomb Group*, 110.
30. Godman, *Supreme Commander*, 49.
31. Ind, *Bataan: The Judgment Seat*, 351-2; General Order No. 37, Part 5 in Fields, *Kangaroo Squadron*, 192.
32. Ind, *Bataan: The Judgment Seat*, 354-64.
33. General Order No. 37, Parts 3 and 4 in Fields, *Kangaroo Squadron*, 190, 191.
34. General Order No. 37, Parts 1-5 in Fields, *Kangaroo Squadron*, 188-92; Carruthers, "The MacArthur and Quezon Evacuation," in Johnson, ed., *435th Overseas*, 32
35. Costello, *The Pacific War*, 225.
36. Fields, *Kangaroo Squadron*, 57-8; "Brief History of the 435th BS" 1. A number of books covering the Fall of the Philippines have erroneously stated that President Quezon and his family were evacuated from the Philippines by submarine. Although Quezon was evacuated from Corregidor aboard a submarine, he was taken only as far as Mindanao. He evacuated Mindanao and the Philippines aboard a B-17.
37. Carruthers, "The MacArthur and Quezon Evacuation," in Johnson, ed., *435th Overseas*, 34; General Order No. 37, Part 6 in Fields, *Kangaroo Squadron*, 193.
38. Fields, *Kangaroo Squadron*, 57-9.
39. Ibid., 61.
40. Ibid.; Godman, *Supreme Commander*, 50.
41. General Order No. 37, Part 5, in Fields, *Kangaroo Squadron*, 193; Fields, *Kangaroo Squadron*, 60-1; Carruthers, "The MacArthur and Quezon Evacuation," in Johnson, ed., *435th Overseas*, 34.
42. "History of the 43rd BG," 214, 261, 283.
43. Ibid., 214, 283.
44. Ibid., 214-5.
45. Payne to author, September 9, 1996, 2, and July 12, 1996, 3.
46. "History of the 43rd BG," 214-5.

Chapter 13
1. Johnson, "Kangaroo Squadron," in Fields, *Kangaroo Squadron*, 176.
2. Fields, *Kangaroo Squadron*, 55-6; "Missions Flown by 435th BS" attached to "Brief History of the 435th BS," 1; Newspaper clipping from *Shamrock* (Texas) *Texan*, May 15, 1942, in Fields, *Kangaroo Squadron*, 156.
3. "Missions Flown by 435th BS" attached to "Brief History of the 435th BS," 1; Dalley, "Saga of the 22nd Ground Men," in Johnson, ed., *435th Overseas*, 25; Craven, ed., *Army Air Forces*, Vol. I, 414.
4. "History of the 30th BS," 4; "History of the 93rd Bombardment Squadron, (H), 19th Bomb Group, from December 8, 1941 to January 31, 1943," *Bomb Squadron History, 93rd Bombardment Squadron (H)* [hereafter cited as "History of the 93rd BS"], 3; "Historical Data, 19th BG," 3; Payne to author, September 9, 1996, 2.
5. Knudson, *Diary*, 21; Rouse, *Diary*, 21; "History of the 30th BS," 4.
6. Green to author, September 10, 1996, 1.
7. "History of the 28th BS," 10-1; Gooch to author, April 10, 1996, 2.
8. "AAF in Australia," 50.
9. "History of the 28th BS," 11.
10. Knudson, *Diary*, 21; Rouse, *Diary*, 21.
11. "History of the 30th BS," 4; "History of the 28th BS," 11; Rutherford, *Fall of the Philippines*, 133-4.
12. Mitchell, *In Alis Vicimus*, 108; Teats, "Tide," Inst. XII, Jan. 13, 1943, 4.

13. Mitchell, *In Alis Vicimus*, 108-9; MacAfee, "For the Boys on Bataan," *Time*, April 27, 1942, 21; Jones, "Royce's Raid," in Johnson, ed., *435th Overseas*, 40-1.

14. Mitchell, *In Alis Vicimus*, 108-9; MacAfee, "For the Boys on Bataan," *Time*, April 27, 1942, 21; Teats, "Tide," Inst. XII, Jan. 13, 1943, 4.

15. Teats, "Tide," Inst. XII, Jan. 13, 1943, 4.

16. Ibid.; Kimmerle, *Personal Narrative*, 32.

17. Mitchell, *In Alis Vicimus*, 109; Jones, "Royce's Raid," in Johnson, ed., *435th Overseas*, 41.

18. Teats, "Tide," Inst. XIII, Jan. 14, 1943, 4.

19. Ibid.; Jones, "Royce's Raid," in Johnson, ed., *435th Overseas*, 41.

20. Teats, "Tide," Inst. XIII, Jan. 14, 1943, 4.

21. Mitchell, *In Alis Vicimus*, 109; "AAF in Australia," 64.

22. Rutherford, *Fall of the Philippines*, 136-7; Salmaggi, *2194 Days of War*, 233-6.

23. Salmaggi, *2194 Days of War*, 237; Mitchell, *In Alis Vicimus*, 109.

24. Dorr, *7th Bomb Group*, 71; "Army Air Services in the Philippines, November 1941 - 29 April 1942," *Fifth Air Force Operations, 1940-45*, Document 8, 4.

25. Ibid.; Salmaggi, *2194 Days of War*, 238-9; Cool, "Excerpts from Maj. Paul E. Cool Personal Diary," *19th Bombardment Group (H) History* [hereafter cited as Cool, "Excerpts from Diary"], 1-2; "AAF in Australia," 119.

26. Rutherford, *Fall of the Philippines*, 150-1; Salmaggi, *2194 Days of War*, 239, 243; Mitchell, *In Alis Vicimus*, 110.

27. Dorr, *7th Bomb Group*, 71.

28. "Missions Flown by 435th BS" attached to "Brief History of the 435th BS," 1; Mitchell, *In Alis Vicimus*, 111; United States Strategic Bombing Survey, *The Fifth Air Force in the War Against Japan*, 100.

29. Willmott, *The Barrier and the Javelin*, 192-3.

30. "Missions Flown by 435th BS" attached to "Brief History of the 435th BS," 1; Fields, "Overseas Diary of Lt. John Wallace Fields," in Fields, *Kangaroo Squadron*, 121; Johnson, "The 435th Short History," in Johnson, ed., *435th Overseas*, 2.

31. "History of the 93rd BS," 3; "Aircraft Ferried from U.S.A.," *Fifth Air Force Operations, 1940-45*, 1.

32. Ibid.; "History of the 28th BS," 11-2; Maurer, *Air Force Combat Units of World War II*, 67; "AAF in Australia," 126.

33. "History of the 93rd BS," 3; Mitchell, *In Alis Vicimus*, 179; Freeman, *B-17 Flying Fortress Story*, 74, 75.

34. "Aircraft Ferried from U.S.A.," *Fifth Air Force Operations, 1940-45*, 1. The arrival dates and planes were: April 22: B-17Es (41-2630), (41-2437), (41-2437), and (41-2652). April 26: B-17E (41-9012). April 28: B-17Es (41-2627, RFD *Tojo*), (41-2633, *Sally*), (41-2640, *Tojo's Physic*), (41-2642), and (41-2644). April 30: B-17E (41-2638, *Chico*). The arrival dates of B-17E (41-2424) and (41-2433) are unknown but they were in Australia by May 1942.

35. Craven, ed., *Army Air Forces*, Vol. I., 421; "History of the 93rd BS," 3. Two of the three pilots sent to help the 40th RS were the Key brothers, Algene and Fred. The third pilot is unknown.

36. "AAF in Australia," 118; Salmaggi, *2194 Days of War*, 238; Steinberg, *Island Fighting*, 20.

37. Dunnigan, *Victory at Sea*, 21-2; Salmaggi, *2194 Days of War*, 240; Rouse, *Diary*, 25.

38. Greenwood Press, pub., *The Campaigns of the Pacific War: United States Strategic Bombing Survey*, 52; Fields, *Lt. Col. John Wallace Fields*, 6; Fields, "Overseas Diary of Lt. John Wallace Fields," in Fields, *Kangaroo Squadron*, 121.

39. Rouse, *Diary*, 25.

40. Dunnigan, *Victory at Sea*, 22; Costello, *The Pacific War*, 254-5.
41. Ibid.
42. Teats, "Tide," Inst. XV, Jan. 16, 1943, 4.
43. Ibid.; Johnson, "The 435th Short History," in Johnson, ed., *435th Overseas*, 2; Fields, "Overseas Diary of Lt. John Wallace Fields," in Fields, *Kangaroo Squadron*, 122.
44. Fields, *Kangaroo Squadron*, 65; Dunnigan, *Victory at Sea*, 23; Costello, *The Pacific War*, 256. Costello erroneously reports that it was three B-26 medium bombers that bombed the battleship *Australia*.
45. Fields, *Kangaroo Squadron*, 65; Costello, *The Pacific War*, 256.
46. Mitchell, *In Alis Vicimus*, 180; Hardison, *The Suzy-Q*, 86-7.
47. Dunnigan, *Victory at Sea*, 23; Costello, *The Pacific War*, 256-7.
48. Costello, *The Pacific War*, 258-60; Dunnigan, *Victory at Sea*, 23-4.
49. Costello, *The Pacific War*, 262.
50. Fields, "Overseas Diary of Lt. John Wallace Fields," in Fields, *Kangaroo Squadron*, 122.
51. Ibid.; Willmott, *The Barrier and the Javelin*, 286.
52. Rouse, *Diary*, 26.
53. Ibid.; Gooch to author, April 10, 1996, 3, and June 21, 1996, 1.
54. Rouse, *Diary*, 26; Teats, "Tide," Inst. XV, Jan. 16, 1943, 4.
55. Rouse, *Diary*, 26.
56. Willmott, *The Barrier and the Javelin*, 286-7; Dunnigan, *Victory at Sea*, 21; Costello, *The Pacific War*, 263.
57. Costello, *The Pacific War*, 263.

Chapter 14

1. Handrow diary in Cleveland, ed., *Grey Geese Calling*, 206.
2. "Operational History of the Seventh Air Force," 52; "War Diary," in Cleveland, ed., *Grey Geese Calling*, 217; Stage, "Second Raid on Pearl Harbor," *World War II*, January 1999, 31-35.
3. "War Diary," in Cleveland, ed., *Grey Geese Calling*, 217.
4. Craven, ed., *Army Air Forces*, Vol. I, 454.
5. Turner, pub., *11th Bomb Group*, 12;
6. "Planes and Missions," in Cleveland, ed., *Grey Geese Calling*, 12.
7. Hillsborough, pub., *Fifth Bomb Group*, 31; "394th BS Report," 7.
8. Crothers, "42nd Bombardment Squadron (H) History," in Cleveland, ed., *Grey Geese Calling*, 123.
9. "394th BS Report," 7.
10. Davenport to author, December 16, 1996.
11. Ibid.; "War Diary" and Gartland, "History of the 98th Bombardment Squadron (H)," in Cleveland, ed., *Grey Geese Calling*, 217, 311.
12. "Operational History of the Seventh Air Force," 52; Craven, ed., *Army Air Forces*, Vol. I, 455; Howard, *One Damned Island*, 72-3.
13. Goralski, *World War II Almanac: 1939-1945*, 212-3; Zich, *The Rising Sun*, 108; Dunnigan, *Victory at Sea*, 25; Costello, *The Pacific War*, 233-6.
14. Nalty, Bernard C., ed., *Pearl Harbor and the War in the Pacific*, 81.
15. Costello, *The Pacific War*, 268.
16. Ibid., 269-70; Nalty, Bernard C., ed., *Pearl Harbor and the War in the Pacific*, 82.
17. Willmott, *The Barrier and the Javelin*, 297-8; Dunnigan, *Victory at Sea*, 25-7; Costello, *The Pacific War*, 270-1; Nalty, ed., *Pearl Harbor and the War in the Pacific*, 82.
18. Nalty, ed., *Pearl Harbor and the War in the Pacific*, 82; Dunnigan, *Victory at Sea*, 26.

19. "394th BS Report," 7; Hillsborough, pub., *Fifth Bomb Group*, 33.
20. Craven, ed., *Army Air Forces*, Vol. I, 454-5.
21. Davenport to author, December 16, 1996, 1.
22. Craven, ed., *Army Air Forces*, Vol. I, 454-5.
23. "History of the 26th BS (H)," 14. The exchange included the following planes: B-17Es (41-2403) and (41-2431) were given to the 42nd BS. B-17E (41-2415, *City of San Francisco*) was given to the 31st BS. B-17D (40-3089) went to the 431st BS. In exchange, the 26th BS got B-17Es (41-2611) from the 31st BS, (41-2610) and (41-2659, *Frank Buck*) from the 23rd BS, and (41-2527) from the 431st BS.
24. Ibid., 14; Lord, *Incredible Victory*, 47; Prange, *Miracle at Midway*, 134; "Operational History of the Seventh Air Force," 52.
25. "Operational History of the Seventh Air Force," 52; Craven, ed., *Army Air Forces*, Vol. I, 454-5; Gregory narrative in "War Diary," in Cleveland, ed., *Grey Geese Calling*, 217. The pilots and planes were; 431st BS: Sweeney B-17E (41-2409, *Old Maid*), Capts. Charles E. Gregory (Unknown), Willard G. Woodbury (Unknown), Clarence P. Tokarz B-17E (41-2404, *The Spider*), Robert Sullivan (Unknown), and 1st Lts. Paul Payne B-17E (41-2463, *Yankee Doodle*) and Van Haur (Unknown). 72nd BS: Faulkner (Unknown) and 1st Lt. Robert B. Andrews (Unknown). 31st BS: Edward A. Steedman B-17E (41-2523, *Goonie*).
26. Schaeffer, "Battle of Midway," 1; Lord, *Incredible Victory*, 53; "Operational History of the Seventh Air Force," 52.
27. Prange, *Miracle at Midway*, 134.
28. Handrow diary in Cleveland, ed., *Grey Geese Calling*, 207.
29. Dunnigan, *Victory at Sea*, 27.
30. Prange, *Miracle at Midway*, 134-5; Willmott, *The Barrier and the Javelin*, 360; "Operational History of the Seventh Air Force," 52.
31. "War Diary," in Cleveland, ed., *Grey Geese Calling*, 217; "Operational History of the Seventh Air Force," 52.
32. "History of the 26th BS," 14; "Operational History of the Seventh Air Force," 52; Prange, *Miracle at Midway*, 134n.
33. "War Diary," in Cleveland, ed., *Grey Geese Calling*, 217; Lord, *Incredible Victory*, 65; Prange, *Miracle at Midway*, 167.
34. "Combat Operations, MIDWAY Area, 3-4 June 1942," Bomb Squadron Supplement, *431st Bombardment Squadron (H)* [hereafter cited as "Combat Operations, MIDWAY," *431st BS*], 1.
35. Prange, *Miracle at Midway*, 167; Hillsborough, pub., *Fifth Bomb Group*, 32. The bomb group history erroneously states that Smith located this small Japanese task force on May 26.
36. Lord, *Incredible Victory*, 68; Schaeffer, "Battle of Midway," 1; "War Diary," in Cleveland, ed., *Grey Geese Calling*, 217.
37. Handrow diary in Cleveland, ed., *Grey Geese Calling*, 207.
38. Payne account in Cleveland, ed., *Grey Geese Calling*, 222; Schaeffer, "The Battle of Midway," 1; "Combat Operations, MIDWAY," *431st BS*, 1.
39. Handrow diary in Cleveland, ed., *Grey Geese Calling*, 207; Howard, *One Damned Island*, 75; "Combat Operations, MIDWAY," *431st BS*, 1.
40. Payne account in Cleveland, ed., *Grey Geese Calling*, 222-3; Howard, *One Damned Island*, 75-6; Bowman, *Flying to Glory*, 51-2.
41. Schaeffer, "The Battle of Midway," 2; Howard, *One Damned Island*, 76; "Combat Operations, MIDWAY," *431st BS*, 1-2; Prange, *Miracle at Midway*, 173.

42. Lord, *Incredible Victory,* 69-70.
43. Schaeffer, "The Battle of Midway," 2.
44. Lord, *Incredible Victory,* 70.
45. Sorenson account in Cleveland, ed., *Grey Geese Calling,* 152.
46. "Operational History of the Seventh Air Force," 53; Handrow diary in Cleveland, ed., *Grey Geese Calling,* 207.
47. Prange, *Miracle at Midway,* 173-4; Edmundson, "B-17 Flying Fortress" in Higham, *Flying Combat Aircraft of the USAAF - USAF,* Vol. 2, 40.
48. Prange, *Miracle at Midway,* 183, 439; "Combat Operations, MIDWAY," *431st BS,* 2. Prange claims 16 B-17s took off on the morning of June 4, while Col. Sweeney, in his report on the Midway operations, reported that only 15 B-17s took to the air. The author has gone with Sweeney's number.
49. Prange, *Miracle at Midway,* 189; Bradshaw, "Lucky Thirteen," in Turner, *11th Bomb Group,* 62.
50. "Combat Operations, MIDWAY," *431st BS,* 2.
51. Lord, *Incredible Victory,* 103-110; Bradshaw, "Lucky Thirteen," in Turner, *11th Bomb Group,* 62.
52. Bradshaw, "Lucky Thirteen," in Turner, *11th Bomb Group,* 62.
53. Howard, *One Damned Island,* 77-8.
54. Lord, *Incredible Victory,* 103-110; Bradshaw, "Lucky Thirteen," in Turner, *11th Bomb Group,* 62. Bradshaw lists only two airmen killed in the attack, but the author has found another in "War Diary," in Cleveland, ed., *Grey Geese Calling,* 218.
55. Prange, *Miracle at Midway,* 190; Lord, *Incredible Victory,* 94-5; Costello, *The Pacific War,* 287.
56. Dunnigan, *Victory at Sea,* 27; Campbell, *Air War Pacific,* 69; Lord, *Incredible Victory,* 112-118; Prange, *Miracle at Midway,* 209-215.
57. Lord, *Incredible Victory,* 118-9; Dunnigan, *Victory at Sea,* 27-8.
58. "Operational History of the Seventh Air Force," 53. For unknown reasons one plane returned to Midway. This may have been piloted by Lt. Smith, who dropped no bombs during the entire Battle of Midway.
59. Prange, *Miracle at Midway,* 224-5; Sweeney account in Cleveland, ed., *Grey Geese Calling,* 225.
60. Prange, *Miracle at Midway,* 218-22; Costello, *The Pacific War,* 291; Lord, *Incredible Victory,* 120-3; Campbell, *Air War Pacific,* 69-70.
61. Prange, *Miracle at Midway,* 225-6.
62. Ibid., 226; Lord, *Incredible Victory,* 126; Howard, *One Damned Island,* 82.
63. Prange, *Miracle at Midway,* 226; Howard, *One Damned Island,* 82.
64. Sweeney and Payne accounts in Cleveland, ed., *Grey Geese Calling,* 223, 225.
65. Handrow and Payne accounts in Ibid., 207, 223.
66. Handrow, Payne and Bargdill accounts in Ibid., 207, 223.
67. Schaeffer, "Battle of Midway," 2.
68. Prange, *Miracle at Midway,* 226; Schaeffer, "Battle of Midway," 2.
69. Prange, *Miracle at Midway,* 226.
70. Ibid., 226-7; Lord, *Incredible Victory,* 127.
71. Schaeffer, "Battle of Midway," 3.
72. Sweeney account in Cleveland, ed., *Grey Geese Calling,* 225; Lord, *Incredible Victory,* 126.
73. Sweeney account in Cleveland, ed., *Grey Geese Calling,* 225; Prange, *Miracle at Midway,* 227; "Combat Operations, MIDWAY," *431st BS,* 2.
74. Lord, *Incredible Victory,* 127; Gregory account in Cleveland, ed., *Grey Geese Calling,* 152, 218; "Combat Operations, MIDWAY," *431st BS,* 2;

75. Costello, *The Pacific War*, 291-8; Prange, *Miracle at Midway*, 228-75; Campbell, *Air War Pacific*, 72-5; Lord, *Incredible Victory*, 132-87.

Chapter 15
1. "23rd BS History," 4; "Operational History of the Seventh Air Force," 53; "Narrative of Squadron History from Activation 18 February 1918 to 28 February 1944, Incl.," *Bomb Squadron History, 431st BS Bombardment Squadron (H)* [Hereafter cited as "Narrative History, 431st BS BS"], 16.
2. Campbell, *Air War Pacific*, 75; Prange, *Miracle at Midway*, 288-91; Lord, *Incredible Victory*, 234-7; Costello, *The Pacific War*, 299-302.
3. "Combat Operations, MIDWAY," *431st BS*, 2.
4. Ibid., 2-3
5. "Operational History of the Seventh Air Force," 54; "Operational History of the Seventh Air Force, 7 December 1941 to 6 November 1943, Appendix 10," *Army Air Force Historical Studies: No. 41* [hereafter cited as "Seventh Air Force, Appendix 10"], 263, 264; "War Diary," in Cleveland, ed., *Grey Geese Calling*, 152, 218; "Combat Operations, MIDWAY," *431st BS*, 3; Bradshaw, "Unlucky Thirteen," in Turner, pub., *11th Bomb Group*, 62.
6. Sweeney account in Cleveland, ed., *Grey Geese Calling*, 226; "Combat Operations, MIDWAY," *431st BS*, 2.
7. "Operational History of the Seventh Air Force," 54; Lord, *Incredible Victory*, 239.
8. Sorenson account in Cleveland, ed., *Grey Geese Calling*, 152.
9. Blakey statement in Hillsborough, pub., *Fifth Bomb Group*, 33.
10. Ibid.; Lord, *Incredible Victory*, 237; Howard, *One Damned Island*, 84; "Seventh Air Force, Appendix 10," 263.
11. Lord, *Incredible Victory*, 238; Blakey statement in Hillsborough, pub., *Fifth Bomb Group*, 33; Howard, *One Damned Island*, 84.
12. Howard, *One Damned Island*, 84-5.
13. Ibid., 85; "Operational History of the Seventh Air Force," 53.
14. Henckell and Fischencord statements in Hillsborough, pub., *Fifth Bomb Group*, 33-4.
15. Howard, *One Damned Island*, 85-6.
16. Lord, *Incredible Victory*, 238.
17. "Operational History of the Seventh Air Force," 54; "Combat Operations, MIDWAY," *431st BS*, 3; Sweeney account in Cleveland, ed., *Grey Geese Calling*, 226.
18. Howard, *One Damned Island*, 86.
19. Ibid.; Gregory and Payne accounts in Cleveland, ed., *Grey Geese Calling*, 152, 218, 224; Lord, *Incredible Victory*, 253. Lt. Wuertele undoubtedly flew back to Hawaii with Col. Sweeney since he does not appear on any further bomb runs, and Sweeney reported that only eight B-17s remained at Midway.
20. "Combat Operations, MIDWAY," *431st BS*, 3; Bradshaw, "Unlucky Thirteen," in Turner, pub., *11th Bomb Group*, 63.
21. Prange, *Miracle at Midway*, 325; Lord, *Incredible Victory*, 261.
22. Campbell, *Air War Pacific*, 75; Costello, *The Pacific War*, 306; Willmott, *The Barrier and the Javelin*, 507-9.
23. "Operational History of the Seventh Air Force," 54; "Seventh Air Force, Appendix 10," 263; Blakey statement in Hillsborough, pub., *Fifth Bomb Group*, 34; Prange, *Miracle at Midway*, 323-4.
24. Ibid., 325; Blakey statement in Hillsborough, pub., *Fifth Bomb Group*, 34; "Operational

History of the Seventh Air Force," 54; "Seventh Air Force, Appendix 10," 263; Howard, *One Damned Island*, 87.

25. Prange, *Miracle at Midway*, 330, 444; Willmott, *The Barrier and the Javelin*, 492; Howard, *One Damned Island*, 87. The seven B-17s were flown by Allen, Grundman, Williams, Haney, Blakey, Seeburger and Whitaker. The serial numbers of the individual planes are unknown.

26. Ibid., 87; Prange, *Miracle at Midway*, 330; Willmott, *The Barrier and the Javelin*, 493-4; "Operational History of the Seventh Air Force," 54; "Seventh Air Force, Appendix 10," 263. The First Echelon was led by Allen with Grundman, Williams and Haney. The Second Echelon was led by Blakey, with Seeburger and Whitaker. The serial numbers of the individual planes are unknown.

27. "Narrative History, 431st BS BS," 16-7; Willmott, *The Barrier and the Javelin*, 493; Prange, *Miracle at Midway*, 388.

28. "Narrative History, 431st BS BS," 17; Howard, *One Damned Island*, 88; Willmott, *The Barrier and the Javelin*, 494.

29. "Narrative History, 431st BS BS," 17; Howard, *One Damned Island*, 88.

30. "Operational History of the Seventh Air Force," 54-5; "History of the 26th BS," 4. The 24 B-17's belonged to the 23rd BS (five), the 26th BS (six), the 31st BS (six), the 42nd BS (three), the 431st BS BS (three), and the 394th BS (one).

31. Willmott, *The Barrier and the Javelin*, 498-500.

32. Prange, *Miracle at Midway*, 340; Lord, *Incredible Victory*, 279; "Operational History of the Seventh Air Force," 55.

33. Campbell, *Air War Pacific*, 75; Nalty, Bernard C., ed., *Pearl Harbor and the War in the Pacific*, 87, 89; Prange, *Miracle at Midway*, 396.

34. "Organizational History, 431st BS," 6; Handrow diary in Cleveland, ed., *Grey Geese Calling*, 208.

35. Howard, *One Damned Island*, 89.

36. Craven, ed., *Army Air Forces*, Vol. I, 460-1.

37. Sweeney statements in Cleveland, ed., *Grey Geese Calling*, 208, 226

38. "Seventh Air Force, Appendix 10," 264.

39. Craven, ed., *Army Air Forces*, Vol. I, 459-61; Edmundson to author, July 19, 1988, p. 2.

40. Craven, ed., *Army Air Forces*, Vol. I, 461-2.

41. "23rd BS History," 4.

42. Howard, *One Damned Island*, 91-7; "Operational History of the Seventh Air Force," 55.

Chapter 16

1. Craven, ed., *Army Air Forces*, Vol. I, 471.

2. United States Strategic Bombing Survey, *The Fifth Air Force in the War Against Japan*, 58.

3. Craven, ed., *Army Air Forces*, Vol. IV, 7-8.

4. "Historical Data of 19th Bombardment Group," *19th Bombardment Group (H) History*, 4.

5. Payne to author, July 12, 1996, 3, and September 9, 1996, 2; Rouse, *Diary*, 27.

6. Payne to author, July 12, 1996, 3, and September 9, 1996, 2.

7. Craven, ed., *Army Air Forces*, Vol. IV, 8-9.

8. Johnson, "The 435th Short History," in Johnson, ed., *435th Overseas*, 3; "Daily Summary on A/C Combats," Miscellaneous Data, *Southwest Pacific Theater* [hereafter cited as "Daily Summary"], May, 1942; "Destruction of Aircraft by 435th BS," 2.

9. Ibid.

10. "AAF in Australia," 78-9; Perry, "Our Aussie Co-Pilots," in Johnson, ed., *435th Overseas*, 43.

11. Perry, "Nose Guns," in Johnson, ed., *435th Overseas*, 60.
12. Birdsall, *Claims to Fame*, 23; Hardison, *The Suzy-Q*, 88-9; Fesmire statement in Freeman, *B-17 Fortress at War*, 51; "Daily Summary," May, 1942.
13. "History of the 93rd BS," 3.
14. "History of the 28th BS," 12; Sakai, *Samurai!*, 139.
15. "Daily Summary," May, 1942; Birdsall, *Claims to Fame*, 23; "History of the 28th BS," 12; Rouse, *Diary*, 28-9.
16. Hardison, *The Suzy-Q*, 96-7; Birdsall, *Claims to Fame*, 23; "Daily Summary," May, 1942; "History of the 93rd BS," 4; "History of the 28th BS," 12-3.
17. Hardison, *The Suzy-Q*, 97; Birdsall, *Claims to Fame*, 23.
18. Hardison, *The Suzy-Q*, 97-8.
19. Johnson, "The 435th Short History," in Johnson, ed., *435th Overseas*, 8.
20. Hardison, *The Suzy-Q*, 97-8.
21. Ibid., 98-100.
22. Ibid., 104-5; Birdsall, *Claims to Fame*, 23.
23. Birdsall, *Claims to Fame*, 23; Rouse, *Diary*, 29; Freeman, *The B-17 Flying Fortress Story*, 76; "Aircraft Ferried from U.S.A.," *Fifth Air Force Operations, 1940-45*, 1. The planes that arrived in May, 1942 were: (41-2633, *Sally*), (41-2637), (41-2638, *Chico*), (41-2640, *Tojo's Physic*), (41-2642), (41-2644), (41-2664, *The Jersey Skeeter*), (41-2666, *Lucy*) and (41-2668).
24. Knudson, *Diary*, 28; Rouse, *Diary*, 30; "Daily Summary," May and June, 1942.
25. "History of the 28th BS," 13.
26. Craven, ed., *Army Air Forces*, Vol IV, 9-10; Johnson, "The 435th Short History," Overseas, Johnson, ed., *435th Overseas*, 3; "Brief History of the 435th Bomb Squadron," 1; "Destruction of Aircraft by 435th BS," 3.
27. "Daily Summary," June, 1942; Fields, *Kangaroo Squadron*, 70-2.
28. Edmunds, *They Fought*, 10; Kurtz quoted in White, *Queens*, 260.
29. Mitchell, *In Alis Vicimus*, 114.
30. Ibid.
31. Hardison, *The Suzy-Q*, 83-4.
32. "History of the 93rd BS," 4; "Daily Summary," June, 1942; Carter, *Combat Chronology*, 20.
33. Brownstein, *The Swoose*, 92-7.
34. "History of the 93rd Bomb," 4; Knudson, *Diary*, 35; Rouse, *Diary*, 31.
35. "Missions Flown by 435th BS" attached to "Brief History of the 435th BS," 1; Johnson, "The 435th Short History," in Johnson, ed., *435th Overseas*, 3.
36. Johnson, "The 435th Short History," in Johnson, ed., *435th Overseas*, 7; "Daily Summary," June, 1942; Fields, *Kangaroo Squadron*, 72, 125. Pilots on this mission were Lts. Fields, Eaton, and Ted Faulkner. The serial numbers of the individual planes are unknown.
37. "History of the 93rd BS," 4; Gooch to author, April 10, 1996, 4, and June 21, 1996, 1.
38. Rouse, *Diary*, 32.
39. "Daily Summary," June, 1942; Fields, *Kangaroo Squadron*, 73.
40. Fields, *Kangaroo Squadron*, 73.
41. "Daily Summary," June, 1942; "Missions Flown by 435th BS" attached to "Brief History of the 435th BS," 2; Rawls, "Celebes Flank," in Johnson, ed., *435th Overseas*, 37-8; Fields, *Kangaroo Squadron*, 72; Gibb, "Most Interesting Mission," in Johnson, ed., *435th Overseas*, 73.
42. Pascoe, "Itchy Fingers," in Johnson, ed., *435th Overseas*, 53-4.

43. "Daily Summary," June, 1942; Carter, *Combat Chronology*, 22; "History of the 28th BS," 13-4; "History of the 93rd BS," 4; "Daily Summary," June, 1942; Knudson, *Diary*, 44-6.

44. Teats, "Tide," Conclusion, Jan. 18, 1943, 4; Rouse, *Diary*, 34. Pilots, where known, were: 28th BS - Teats. 93rd BS - Rouse, Weldon Smith and Bridges. The serial numbers of individual planes are unknown.

45. Teats, "Tide," Conclusion, Jan. 18, 1943, 4; Rouse, *Diary*, 35.

46. "History of the 93rd BS," 4; Rouse, *Diary*, 34.

47. Rouse, *Diary*, 34-5, 37; Teats, "Tide," Conclusion, Jan. 18, 1943, 4; Walker, "American Bombers Attacking From Australia," *National Geographic Magazine*, Vol. LXXXIII, No. 1, Jan. 1943, 67.

48. "History of the 93rd BS," 4.

49. Freeman, *The B-17 Flying Fortress Story*, 77; List of B-17s of the 19th BG assembled at a reunion of the 19th BG and supplied to the author by Wallace Fields.

50. "Daily Summary," July, 1942; "History of the 28th BS," 14; Knudson, *Diary*, 47-8. Pilots were: Knudson B-17E (41-2640, *Tojo's Physic*), Beck (Unknown), and Sargent (Unknown).

51. Carter, *Combat Chronology*, 24; Rouse, *Diary*, 35-6.

52. "Daily Summary," July, 1942; Walker, "American Bombers Attacking From Australia," *National Geographic Magazine*, Vol. LXXXIII, No. 1, Jan. 1943, 50-62.

53. Ibid., 61-2; Birdsall, *Claims to Fame*, 25-6; "History of the 93rd BS," 4.

54. "Daily Summary," July, 1942; "History of the 28th BS," 14.

55. Miller, *The Cactus Air Force*, 14; Steinberg, *Island Fighting*, 20.

56. "History of the 28th BS," 14.

57. Ibid., Appendix A, Narrative Report of Mission flown July 10 to July 12, 1942, 2; Tower, "Reconnaissance Mission," in Johnson, ed., *435th Overseas*, 70.

58. Tower, "Reconnaissance Mission," in Johnson, ed., *435th Overseas*, 70-2; "Destruction of Aircraft by 435th BS," 4.

59. Freeman, *The B-17 Flying Fortress Story*, 76, 77; "Aircraft Ferried from U.S.A.," *Fifth Air Force Operations, 1940-45*, 1.

60. Craven, ed., *Army Air Forces*, Vol. IV, 20-1; Costello, *The Pacific War*, 314; Salmaggi, *2194 Days of War*, 273-4.

61. Freeman, *The B-17 Flying Fortress Story*, 73; Fields, *Kangaroo Squadron*, 69.

62. Taggart, *My Fighting Congregation*, 148.

63. "Daily Summary," July, 1942; "History of the 28th BS," 15; "History of the 93rd BS," 4. The 93rd BS historian erroneously reports this attack taking place on July 18, 1942.

64. Carter, *Combat Chronology*, 27; Johnson, "The 435th Short History," in Johnson, ed., *435th Overseas*, 3; Nalty, Bernard C., *With Courage: the U.S. Army Air Force in World War II*, 128; "Destruction of Aircraft by 435th BS," 4; "History of the 93rd BS," 5. The 93rd BS historian erroneously stated that this attack occurred on July 18, 1942.

65. Craven, ed., *Army Air Forces*, Vol. IV, 27.

66. "History of the 93rd BS," 5; "History of the 28th BS," 15; "Historical Data, 19th BG," 4.

67. Rouse, *Diary*, 40; Hardison, *The Suzy-Q*, 110-1.

68. Gooch to author, September 2, 1996, 2; Payne to author, September 9, 1996, 3.

69. Hardison, *The Suzy-Q*, 111.

70. Payne to author, July 12, 1996, 3, and September 9, 1996, 3.

71. Salmaggi, *2194 Days of War*, 274.

72. "Daily Summary," July, 1942; Rouse, *Diary*, 39; "History of the 28th BS," 15.

73. "Daily Summary," July, 1942; Rouse, *Diary*, 39; "History of the 93rd BS," 5; Carter, *Combat Chronology*, 28.

74. Costello, *The Pacific War*, 316-7; Carter, *Combat Chronology*, 28-9; Rouse, *Diary*, 39.
75. Costello, *The Pacific War*, 318.

Chapter 17
1. "Operational History of the Seventh Air Force," 55.
2. "Narrative History, 72nd BS," 18; Howard, *One Damned Island*, 97-8.
3. Craven, ed., *Army Air Forces*, Vol. IV, 28.
4. Crothers, "42nd Bombardment Squadron (H) History," in Cleveland, ed., *Grey Geese Calling*, 123.
5. "History of the 98th BS," 3.
6. Edmundson account in Cleveland, ed., *Grey Geese Calling*, 37; Edmundson to author, July 19, 1988, p. 2.
7. Cleveland, ed., *Grey Geese Calling*, 20.
8. Ibid.; Handrow diary in Cleveland, ed., *Grey Geese Calling*, 208; "History of the 98th BS," 3, 4.
9. "History of the 98th BS," 5.
10. "Daily Diary, 4 May 1942 to 20 December 1942, Inclusive, Author Unknown," *Bomb Squadron History, 26th Bombardment Squadron (H)* [hereafter cited as "Daily Diary, 26th BS"], July 28, 1942 entry. The pilots and planes, all B-17Es, where known, were: Maj.'s Sewart (41-9076) and Edmundson (41-2611), Capt. Jack Thornhill (41-2527), Lt. William Kinney (41-9060), (41-2524), (41-2610), (41-9145), (41-2520, *Jap Happy*), and (41-9218).
11. "History of the 26th BS," 15; Craven, ed., *Army Air Forces*, Vol. IV, 11; "Daily Diary, 26th BS," July 19 - 26, 1942 entries.
12. Mansfield, "26th Bombardment Squadron (H) History," in Cleveland, ed., *Grey Geese Calling*, 64; Edmundson account in Cleveland, ed., *Grey Geese Calling*, 37.
13. "History of the 42nd BS," 7; Crothers, "42nd Bombardment Squadron (H) History," in Cleveland, ed., *Grey Geese Calling*, 123; "Organizational History, 431st BS," 7; "History of the 11th BG," 4.
14. "History of the 5th BG," 3.
15. "History of the 11th BG," 3-4.
16. Craven, ed., *Army Air Forces*, Vol. IV, 28-29; "History of the 98th BS," 4. The pilots were Maj.'s Philip M. Rasmussen and Karl T. Barthelmess, and Capt. Walter Y. Lucas. The serial numbers of the individual planes are unknown.
17. "Daily Diary, 26th BS," July 29, 1942 entry; Craven, ed., *Army Air Forces*, Vol. IV, 29.
18. Cleveland, ed., *Grey Geese Calling*, 20.
19. Ibid.; Bradshaw, "Unlucky Thirteen," in Turner, pub., *11th Bomb Group (H)*, 63.
20. Howard, *One Damned Island*, 101; "Daily Diary, 26th BS," July 30 and 31, 1942 entries. The pilots and planes, all B-17Es, were: 98th BS - Lts. John H. Buie (Unknown) and Frank T. Waskowitz (41-2616, *The Blue Goose*). 26th BS - Maj.'s Sewart (41-2527) and Edmundson (41-2610), and 1st Lts. Edwin A. Loberg (41-9218), James W. Lancaster (41-2524), John W. Livingston (41-2520, *Jap Happy*), and Hugh W. Owens (41-9145). A number of authors have claimed that all the B-17s on the 11th BG's first bombing mission of Guadalcanal took off from Efate but the highly accurate 26th BS Diary clearly states that the planes from that squadron took off from Espiritu Santo.
21. Howard, *One Damned Island*, 101-2.
22. "Daily Diary, 26th BS," July 31, 1942 entry; Cleveland, ed., *Grey Geese Calling*, 18.
23. Bowman, *Flying to Glory*, 58; McDowell, *Flying Fortress, The Boeing B-17*, 20.
24. Cleveland, ed., *Grey Geese Calling*, 18; "Daily Diary, 26th BS," July 31, 1942 entry.

25. Gartland, "History of the 98th Bombardment Squadron (H)," in Cleveland, ed., *Grey Geese Calling*, 311-2.

26. Crothers, "42nd Bombardment Squadron (H) History," in Cleveland, ed., *Grey Geese Calling*, 124; "Organizational History, 431st BS," 7-8.

27. Crothers, "42nd Bombardment Squadron (H) History," and Gartland, "History of the 98th Bombardment Squadron (H)," in Cleveland, ed., *Grey Geese Calling*, 124, 312; "Daily Diary, 26th BS," August 5, 1942 entry.

28. Crothers, "42nd Bombardment Squadron (H) History," in Cleveland, ed., *Grey Geese Calling*, 124.

29. "History of the 98th BS," 4, 6-7

30. Craven, ed., *Army Air Forces*, Vol. IV, 29; Costello, *The Pacific War*, 319-20.

31. "History of the 98th BS," 5; Wilkinson account in Cleveland, ed., *Grey Geese Calling*, 254; "Daily Diary, 26th BS," August 1, 1942 entry. Pilots and planes were: 98th BS - Lt. Waskowitz (41-2616, *The Blue Goose*). 26th BS - Maj. Sewart (41-9076), Capt. Thornhill (41-2527), and Lts. Loberg (41-9218), Livingston (41-2520, *Jap Happy*), Lancaster (41-2524), Robert D. Guenther (41-2610), and Owens (41-9145). 431st BS - Lts. John Van Haur (Unknown), and Manford K. Wagnon (Unknown).

32. Craven, ed., *Army Air Forces*, Vol. IV, 29; "History of the 98th BS," 5; Cleveland, ed., *Grey Geese Calling*, 18; "Daily Diary, 26th BS," August 1, 1942 entry.

33. "Daily Diary, 26th BS," August 2, 1942 entry.

34. Howard, *One Damned Island*, 102.

35. "History of the 98th BS," 5.

36. "Daily Diary, 26th BS," August 3, 1942 entry.

37. Howard, *One Damned Island*, 104.

38. Cleveland, ed., *Grey Geese Calling*, 20; Handrow diary in Cleveland, ed., *Grey Geese Calling*, 209.

39. "Daily Diary, 26th BS," August 4, 1942 entry; McDonald's DFC citation in "11th Bombardment Group Citations," *11th Bombardment Group (H) History;* "Performance, Results and Attrition of B-17, Heavy Bombers in Solomon Islands Operations - August and September, 1942," *11th Bombardment Group (H) History,* 1. It was reported that a captured Japanese diary indicated that two of McDonald's crewmen safely parachuted out of the burning aircraft and were taken prisoners.

40. Edmundson's DFC citation in "11th Bombardment Group Citations," *11th Bombardment Group (H) History;* "Daily Diary, 26th BS," August 4, 1942 entry.

41. "Daily Diary, 26th BS," August 4, 1942 entry.

42. Ibid.

43. Ibid., August 5, 1942 entry; Wilkinson account in Cleveland, ed., *Grey Geese Calling*, 254

44. Handrow diary in Ibid., 209.

45. "Daily Diary, 26th BS," August 5, 1942 entry.

46. Cleveland, ed., *Grey Geese Calling*, 20.

47. Handrow diary in Cleveland, ed., *Grey Geese Calling*, 254.

48. Miller account in Cleveland, ed., *Grey Geese Calling*, 341-2.

49. "Daily Diary, 26th BS," August 7, 1942 entry; "Performance, Results and Attrition of B-17, Heavy Bombers in Solomon Islands Operations - August and September, 1942," *11th Bombardment Group (H) History,* 1; Crothers, "42nd Bombardment Squadron (H) History," and Wilkinson account in Cleveland, ed., *Grey Geese Calling*, 125, 254; "History of the 42nd BS," 7.

50. MacDonald, *Great Battles of World War II*, 73-4; Costello, *The Pacific War*, 322-3.

51. "Daily Diary, 26th BS," August 7, 1942 entry; Handrow diary and Wilkinson account in Cleveland, ed., *Grey Geese Calling*, 209, 254.
52. Wilkinson account and "Losses 431st" in Cleveland, ed., *Grey Geese Calling*, 255, 310; Caidin, *Flying Forts*, 236; "Performance, Results and Attrition of B-17, Heavy Bombers in Solomon Islands Operations - August and September, 1942," *11th Bombardment Group (H) History*, 1.
53. "History of the 98th BS," 3; "Performance, Results and Attrition of B-17, Heavy Bombers in Solomon Islands Operations - August and September, 1942," *11th Bombardment Group (H) History*, 1.
54. Horgan, "Our battle," in Johnson, *435th Overseas*, 74; "Destruction of Aircraft by 435th BS," 4-5.
55. Rouse, *Diary*, 40; Birdsall, *Claims to Fame*, 26.
56. Kenney, *General Kenney Reports*, 29-33.
57. Ibid., 35-7, 42-4.
58. "Daily Summary," July, 1942; "A-3 Airplane Status Section Folder," *Fifth Air Force Operations*, 1940-45; "Historical Data, 19th BG," 6; Freeman, *The B-17 Flying Fortress Story*, 77.
59. History of the 28th BS," 17; Cool, "Excerpts from Diary," 2; Mitchell, *In Alis Vicimus*, 116. Mitchell erroneously states that B-17E (41-2435) was lost on August 12, 1942.
60. Kenney, *General Kenney Reports*, 51; Brownstein, *The Swoose*, 100-1. B-17D (40-3097, *The Swoose*) would make it back to the United States and become the only heavy bomber from the Philippines Campaign to survive the war. It is currently owned by the Smithsonian Institution and is awaiting restoration at the Paul E. Garber Preservation, Restoration, and Storage Facility in Suitland, Maryland.
61. "Daily Summary," August, 1942; Kenney, *General Kenney Reports*, 45. Kenney stated that he sent 20 bombers to Port Moresby and that 18 went on the bomb run. However, Air Force records show only 16 bombers participated in this raid.
62. Birdsall, *Claims to Fame*, 31; Mitchell, *In Alis Vicimus*, 129, 180-4; Hardison, *The Suzy-Q*, 117. Pilots and planes, all B-17Es, were: 28th BS - Capts. Dougherty (41-2536) and Zubko (41-2434), and Lts. Fletcher (41-2432, *The Last Straw*), P. Williams (41-2644), and Sargent (41-9015). 30th BS - Capts. Carpenter (41-2659, *Tojo's Jinx*) and Charles H. Giddings (41-2664, *The Jersey Skeeter*), and Lts. Fred Wesche (41-2657, *Old Faithful*), Hillhouse (41-2617), and Holdridge (41-2662, *Spawn of Hell*). 93rd BS - Maj. Hardison (41-2643), and Capts. Bridges (41-2665, Lulu), Pease (41-2429, *Why Don't We Do This More Often*), and Jacquet (41-2462, *Tojo's Jinx*), and Lts. Snyder (41-2464, *Queenie*), and Claude N. Burcky (41-2452).
63. Birdsall, *Claims to Fame*, 32; Mitchell, *In Alis Vicimus*, 130.
64. Mitchell, *In Alis Vicimus*, 130; Gooch to author, April 10, 1996, 3, and undated letter.
65. Birdsall, *Claims to Fame*, 32; Mitchell, *In Alis Vicimus*, 181-5.
66. Ibid.
67. Mingos, *American Heroes*, Vol. One, 283.
68. Kenney, *General Kenney Reports*, 59; Mitchell, *In Alis Vicimus*, 130.
69. Hardison, *The Suzy-Q*, 119-20.
70. Birdsall, *Claims to Fame*, 32-3.
71. Ibid.; Gooch to author, undated letter.
72. Birdsall, *Claims to Fame*, 33-5; Mitchell, *In Alis Vicimus*, 133-5.
73. Hardison, *The Suzy-Q*, 120.
74. Kenney, *General Kenney Reports*, 60; Mitchell, *In Alis Vicimus*, 131.
75. Craven, ed., *Army Air Forces*, Vol. IV, 35-6.

Chapter 18

1. Salmaggi, *2194 Days of War*, 280; Ballard, *The Lost Ships of Guadalcanal*, 40-1; Morison, *History of the United States Naval Operations in World War II* [hereafter cited as Morison, *Naval Operations*], Vol. V, 18, 23-4; Costello, *The Pacific War*, 324-6; Salmaggi, *2194 Days of War*, 280-1

2. Cleveland, ed., *Grey Geese Calling*, 19, 21.

3. Ibid., 6, 19, 21, 314; "Daily Diary, 26th BS," August 9, 1942 entry.

4. Cleveland, ed., *Grey Geese Calling*, 21.

5. Ibid., 314; Morison, *Naval Operations*, Vol. V, 70; Handrow diary in Cleveland, ed., *Grey Geese Calling*, 210; Salmaggi, *2194 Days of War*, 286-7.

6. Edmundson account and Handrow diary in Cleveland, ed., *Grey Geese Calling*, 38, 210; Cleveland, "431st Bombardment Squadron (H) History," in Cleveland, ed., *Grey Geese Calling*, 250.

7. Edmundson account and Handrow diary in Cleveland, ed., *Grey Geese Calling*, 38, 210; Morison, *Naval Operations*, Vol. V, 70.

8. Edmundson account in Cleveland, ed., *Grey Geese Calling*, 38, 210; Morison, *Naval Operations*, Vol. V, 70; Tregaskis, *Guadalcanal Diary*, 122-3.

9. Gartland, "History of the 98th Bombardment Squadron," in Cleveland, ed., *Grey Geese Calling*, 314-5.

10. Birdsall, *Claims to Fame*, 36; Birdsall, *Pride of Seattle*, 9, 11; Morton, *United States Army in World War II*, Vol. 2, Pt. 15, 327.

11. "Daily Diary, 26th BS," August 20 and 21, 1942 entries.

12. Costello, *The Pacific War*, 330-1.

13. Ibid., 331; Morison, *Naval Operations*, Vol. V, 82.

14. Cleveland, ed., *Grey Geese Calling*, 21; "Daily Diary, 26th BS," August 24, 1942 entry. Pilots and planes, all B-17Es, where known, were: 1st Flight - Maj. Manierre (42nd BS), Capt. Wuertele (42nd BS), and Lt. Guenther (26th BS)(41-2610); 2nd Flight - Maj. Sewart (26th BS)(41-9076), Capt. Thornhill (26th BS)(41-2527), Lt. Kinney (26th BS)(41-9060), and Capt. Sullivan (431st BS).

15. Morison, *Naval Operations*, Vol. V, 89-90; Cleveland, ed., *Grey Geese Calling*, p. 21

16. Cleveland, ed., *Grey Geese Calling*, p. 21; "Daily Diary, 26th BS," August 24, 1942 entry; Howard, *One Damned Island*, 112-3. It was believed that Sewart's flight might have damaged the seaplane carrier *Chitose* but Japanese, and American Naval records, claim that the *Chitose* was damaged by two bombs from Navy dive-bombers.

17. "Daily Diary, 26th BS," August 24, 1942 entry.

18. Ibid.; "Update," in Cleveland, ed., *Grey Geese Calling*, p. 118; and Cleveland, ed., *Grey Geese Calling*, p. 21.

19. Dunnigan, *Victory at Sea*, 36.

20. Morison, *Naval Operations*, Vol. V, 89-90; Cleveland, ed., *Grey Geese Calling*, p. 22.

21. Craven, ed., *Army Air Forces*, Vol. IV, 40; Morison, *Naval Operations*, Vol. V, 104-5; Cleveland, ed., *Grey Geese Calling*, p. 22; Miller, *The Cactus Air Force*, 56.

22. Craven, ed., *Army Air Forces*, Vol. IV, 40; Costello, *The Pacific War*, 333-4.

23. Costello, *The Pacific War*, p. 335.

24. "History of the 28th BS," 17; "Daily Summary,", August, 1942; Carter, *Combat Chronology*, 31.

25. "History of the 93rd BS," 3; Birdsall, *Claims to Fame*, 26.

26. "History of the 93rd BS," 3; Kenney, *General Kenney Reports*, 62-3.

27. Kenney, *General Kenney Reports*, 11-2, 63; Birdsall, *Flying Buccaneers*, 13

28. Ibid., 61; Birdsall, *Claims to Fame*, 36-7; "History of the 43rd BG," 76.

29. "History of the 43rd BG," 216-220; Birdsall, *Pride of Seattle,* 6-7. The pilots and planes, all B-17Fs, that arrived on August 6 were: Capts. Ken McCullar (41-24355, *Dinah Might*), James T. Barnett (41-24384, *Pluto*), and Edward W. Scott, Jr. (41-24357, *Tojo's Nightmare*), and Lt. Folmer J. Sogaard (41-24381, *Panama Hattie*). The pilots and planes, all B-17Fs, that arrived on August 11 were: Capts. Franklyn T. Green (41-24358, *Lulu Belle*), James O. Ellis (41-24429, *Dumbo*), and David W. Hassemer (41-24391, *Hoomalimali*) and Lts. James T. Murphy (41-24353, *Cap'n & The Kids*), Edwin C. Reeder (41-24402), and William M. Thompson (41-24401, *Lak-A-Nookie*). Lt. Lewis A. Anderson (41-24383) developed engine trouble near Christmas Island and was delayed a short time.
30. "History of the 43rd BG," 221.
31. Murphy, *Skip Bombing,* 3-4.
32. Kenney, *General Kenney Reports,* 64.
33. Statistical information taken from Appendix B. Total production of B-17s can be found in Freeman, *The B-17 Flying Fortress Story.*
34. "History of the 43rd BG," 15, 220.
35. Murphy, *Skip Bombing,* 43.
36. "History of the 28th BS," 17; "Daily Summary," August, 1942; Carter, *Combat Chronology,* 31; "History of the 93rd BS," 5; Hillhouse citation in Mingos, *American Heroes,* Vol. One, 269.
37. Salmaggi, *2194 Days of War,* 283-4; Dunnigan, *Victory at Sea,* 529.
38. Price "Shadowing Mission," in Johnson, ed., *435th Overseas,* 65; Carter, *Combat Chronology,* 32;
39. Cool, "Excerpts from Diary," 2; Rouse, *Diary,* 43; Price, "Shadowing Mission," in Johnson, ed., *435th Overseas,* 65-6; "Daily Summary," August, 1942. Known pilots on this mission were: Maj. Rouse, and Capts. Cool, Hillhouse, and Hoevet.
40. Cool, "Excerpts from Diary," 2; Rouse, *Diary,* 43; Carter, *Combat Chronology,* 32; "Daily Summary," August, 1942.
41. Spieth, *"Chief Seattle" from the Pacific Northwest, Missing in Action,* 4-6.
42. Rouse, *Diary,* 43; "Daily Summary," August, 1942.
43. Haugland, *The AAF Against Japan,* 155-6; Kenney, *General Kenney Reports,* 69.
44. Taggart, *My Fighting Congregation,* 151-2; Rouse, *Diary,* 44; List of B-17s of the 19th BG assembled at a reunion of the 19th BG and supplied to the author by Wallace Fields.
45. "History of the 28th BS," 18; "History of the 93rd BS," 6; "Daily Summary," August, 1942; Carter, *Combat Chronology,* 33.
46. "History of the 43rd BG," 321; Kenney, *General Kenney Reports,* 81-2. The 403rd BS arrived at Torrens Creek on August 27, 1942.
47. Carter, *Combat Chronology,* 34; Costello, *The Pacific War,* 335.
48. Ibid.; Kenney, *General Kenney Reports,* 82.
49. Rouse, *Diary,* 45; "Daily Summary," August, 1942.
50. Carter, *Combat Chronology,* 35; Salmaggi, *2194 Days of War,* 289; Kenney, *General Kenney Reports,* 83-4; Bergerud, *Touched With Fire,* 256.
51. Birdsall, *Claims to Fame,* 26-7; Hardison, *The Suzy-Q,* 133. The planes and pilots, where known, were: Maj. Hardison B-17F (41-24391, *Hoomalimali*), Capts. John Chiles B-17E (41-9234), Clyde Webb B-17F (41-24354) and Kenneth Casper B-17F (41-2621, *The Daylight Ltd.*), and Lts. Stripling (Unknown), Bruce Gibson B-17E (41-2663) and Percy Hinton B-17E (41-2668). It is unknown who piloted B-17E (41-2599, *Tugboat Annie*).
52. Birdsall, *Claims to Fame,* 26-7, 48-9; Hardison, *The Suzy-Q,* 133; Taggart, *My fighting*

Congregation, 153; Mingos, *American Heroes*, Vol. One, 266. Sgt. Cody received a Silver Star for his actions on August 26, 1942.
53. Birdsall, *Claims to Fame*, 26-7; Birdsall, *Pride of Seattle*, 6.
54. Birdsall, *Claims to Fame*, 27; Hardison, *The Suzy-Q*, 133; "Daily Summary,", August, 1942.
55. Hardison, *The Suzy-Q*, 133; Kenney, *General Kenney Reports*, 84; Carter, *Combat Chronology*, 35; Taggart, *My Fighting Congregation*, 153-4.
56. Rouse, *Diary*, 45-6; "Daily Summary," August, 1942; "History of the 28th BS," 18.
57. Bergerud, *Touched With Fire*, 261-2.
58. Fields, *Kangaroo Squadron*, 79-80; Salmaggi, *2194 Days of War*, 289.
59. "History of the 28th BS," 18; "Daily Summary," August, 1942; Rouse, *Diary*, 46; Carter, *Combat Chronology*, 36.

Chapter 19

1. Kenney, *General Kenney Reports*, 79-80.
2. Green to author, July 14, 1996, 2, and September 10, 1996, 1-2.
3. Rouse, *Diary*, 47; "Daily Summary," August, 1942.
4. Rouse, *Diary*, 48; Birdsall, Steve, *Pride of Seattle*, 8.
5. Salmaggi, *2194 Days of War*, 290-2; Bergerud, *Touched with Fire*, 266-7.
6. "History of the 28th BS," 19.
7. Steinberg, *Island Fighting*, 50-1; Bergerud, *Touched with Fire*, 267.
8. Steinberg, *Island Fighting*, 51; Salmaggi, *2194 Days of War*, 291-2.
9. Salmaggi, *2194 Days of War*, 291-2; Carter, *Combat Chronology*, 39.
10. Crawford, *Gore and Glory*, 65-6; "History of the 28th BS," 19; Birdsall, *Claims to Fame*, 49.
11. Crawford, *Gore and Glory*, 66-7; Birdsall, *Claims to Fame*, 49.
12. Crawford, *Gore and Glory*, 67-9; Craven, ed., *Army Air Forces*, Vol. IV, 715, n. 136.
13. Ibid., 71, 73-4; Kenney, *General Kenney Reports*, 93-4; "Daily Summary," September, 1942.
14. Crawford, *Gore and Glory*, 74-77; Erb citation in Mingos, *American Heroes*, 299.
15. Carter, *Combat Chronology*, 40; Rouse, *Diary*, 47-8; "Daily Summary," September, 1942.
16. Birdsall, *Pride of Seattle*, 7. Known pilots and planes were: Capts. Edward W. Scott, Jr. B-17F (41-24353, *Cap'n & The Kids*), and Hershell R. Henson B-17F (41-24391, *Hoomalimali*), and Lts. Folmer J. Sogaard B-17F (41-24520, *Fightin' Swede*), William M. Thompson B-17F (41-24356, *Ka-Puhio-Wela*), and Ray Holsey B-17E (41-2659, *Frank Buck*).
17. "History of the 43rd BG," 321. Birdsall, *Pride of Seattle*, 9, 11, 13-14. The 12 B-17Fs were: (41-24518, *The Reckless Mountain Boys*), (41-24520, *Fightin' Swede*), (41-24522), (41-24536), (41-24538), (41-24540), (41-24543, *Pluto*), (41-24546), (41-24548, *War Horse*), (41-24550), (41-24551, *Fire Ball Mail*), and (41-24554, *The Mustang*).
18. Birdsall, *Claims to Fame*, 38-9; Birdsall, *Pride of Seattle*, 13; Kenney, *General Kenney Reports*, 132-3.
19. "History of the 43rd BG," 221; Carter, *Combat Chronology*, 40.
20. Casualty Report found in "History of the 43rd BG," 191; Taggart, *My Fighting Congregation*, 155-6; Birdsall, *Pride of Seattle*, 7.
21. Birdsall, *Claims to Fame*, 61; "Daily Summary," September, 1942; "History of the 43rd BG," 221.
22. Kenney, *General Kenney Reports*, 98-9.
23. "Daily Summary," September, 1942.

24. "Mission Report for September 15/16, 1942," and Recommendation for Citation in Knudson, *Diary,* 49-51, 64-5.
25. Crawford, *Gore and Glory,* 59; Rouse, *Diary,* 48; Birdsall, *Pride of Seattle,* 8.
26. Crawford, *Gore and Glory,* 59; Rouse, *Diary,* 48-9; "Adventure in New Guinea," *Life,* January 4, 1943, 27-8, 30; List of B-17s of the 19th BG assembled at a reunion of the 19th BG and supplied to the author by Wallace Fields. Many authors, including General Kenney, have incorrectly reported that this incident occurred on August 26, 1942.
27. Rouse, *Diary,* 49; Freeman, *The B-17 Flying Fortress Story,* 77; List of B-17s of the 19th BG assembled at a reunion of the 19th BG and supplied to the author by Wallace Fields.
28. Salmaggi, *2194 Days of War,* 294-5; Steinberg, *Island Fighting,* 51.
29. Kenney, *General Kenney Reports,* 101; Carter, *Combat Chronology,* 41-2.
30. "History of the 43rd BG," 221.
31. Kenney, *General Kenney Reports,* 21-2.
32. Ibid., 64, 105; Murphy, *Skip-Bombing,* 22-4; Extract dated 21 November 1944 in "History of the 43rd BG," 70.
33. Murphy, *Skip-Bombing,* 23-4; "History of the 43rd BG," 243.
34. Ibid.
35. Extract entitled, "Skip Bombing," dated 21 November 1944 in "History of the 43rd BG," 70; Kenney, *General Kenney Reports,* 105.
36. Kenney, *General Kenney Reports,* 108; Fields, *Kangaroo Squadron,* 84.
37. Rouse, *Diary,* 49.
38. Ibid., 50; Fields, *Kangaroo Squadron,* 84.
39. List of B-17's of the 19th BG assembled at a reunion of the 19th BG and supplied to the author by Wallace Fields; Freeman, *The B-17 Flying Fortress Story,* 81.
40. Rouse, *Diary,* 51.
41. Kenney, *General Kenney Reports,* 112-3.
42. Rouse, *Diary,* 51; Murphy, *Skip Bombing,* 27.
43. Murphy, *Skip Bombing,* 27.
44. Ibid., 36-7.
45. Steinberg, *Island Fighting,* 51; Salmaggi, *2194 Days of War,* 296-7.

Chapter 20

1. "Daily Diary, 26th BS," September 2, 1942 entry; Gartland, "History of the 98th Bombardment Squadron," in Cleveland, ed., *Grey Geese Calling,* 315.
2. Costello, *The Pacific War,* 344; Salmaggi, *2194 Days of War,* 291-2.
3. Crothers, "42nd Bombardment Squadron (H) History," in Cleveland, ed., *Grey Geese Calling,* 125; Birdsall, *Claims to Fame,* 39.
4. Craven, ed., *Army Air Forces,* Vol. IV, 42-3.
5. "War Diary," and Storey biography in Cleveland, ed., *Grey Geese Calling,* 218, 231-2.
6. Murray biography in Cleveland, ed., *Grey Geese Calling,* 236-7.
7. Gartland, "History of the 98th Bombardment Squadron (H)," in Cleveland, ed., *Grey Geese Calling,* 316, 341; Interview with Joseph Angelini, December 7, 1997. The puppy Skipper flew a total of 54 missions with Sgt. Angelini and eventually returned to the U.S. with him. He went on to enjoy the life of an average dog in America.
8. Costello, *The Pacific War,* 345-6.
9. "Daily Diary, 26th BS," September 14, 1942 entry. Known pilots and planes, all B-17Es, were: 98th BS - Capt. Walter Lucas (41-9214, *Skipper*) and Lt. Eugene Thompson (41-9124, *Buzz King*), and 26th BS - Lts. Lancaster (41-2524) and Owens (41-2527).

10. Ibid.; Gartland, "History of the 98th Bombardment Squadron (H)," in Cleveland, ed., *Grey Geese Calling*, 316; Morison, *Naval Operations*, Vol. V, 180.
11. "Daily Diary, 26th BS," September 14, 1942 entry.
12. Morison, *Naval Operations*, Vol. V, 131-6; Costello, *The Pacific War*, 347.
13. Costello, *The Pacific War*, 347.
14. "Brief History of 5th Bombardment Group, 1918 - 1952," *5th Bombardment Group (H) History*, 5.
15. "Daily Diary, 26th BS," September 24, 26, and 28, 1942 entries; Craven, ed., *Army Air Forces*, Vol. IV, 53.
16. "Narrative History, 72nd BS,"19-20; Hillsborough, pub., *Fifth Bomb Group*, 78; "History of the 5th Bomb Group," 5. The pilots and planes, all B-17Es, were: Maj. Ridings (41-9223), Capts. Glenn H. Kramer (41-9122, *Eager Beavers*), George C. Darby, Jr. (41-9056), Whitaker (41-2613, *Lucky 13*), and Latham (41-2396), and Lts. Thomas J. Classen (41-9093, *Spook!*), David C. Everitt, Jr. (41-9118), Trent (41-9128), Healy (41-9059, *Boomerang*), and Hawes (41-2521, *G.I. Angel*). Lt. Thompson (41-2612) was delayed at Christmas Island for ten days.
17. Morton, *United States Army in World War II*, Vol. 2, Pt. 15, 327.
18. "History of the 5th Bomb Group," 5-6; "History of the 31st Bombardment Squadron, 5th Bomb Group," *Bomb Squadron History, 31st Bombardment Squadron (H)* [hereafter cited as "History of the 31st BS"], 1.
19. Gartland, "History of the 98th Bombardment Squadron," in Cleveland, ed., *Grey Geese Calling*, 316; Crothers, "42nd Bombardment Squadron (H) History," in Cleveland, ed., *Grey Geese Calling*, 125, 192. Pilots and planes, all B-17Es, were: 98th BS: Capt. Lucas (41-9215, *Gallopin' Gus*), and Lts. Durbin (41-2523, *Goonie*) and Waskowitz (41-2616, *Blue Goose*). 42nd BS: Capt. Charles E. Norton (41-2420, *Bessie the Jap Basher*).
20. Mingos, *American Heroes*, Vol. One, 252, 254, 258, 260, 261, 263, 268, 269, 271; "History of the 42nd BS," 8. In late 1943, the wreckage of B-17E (41-2420, *Bessie the Jap Basher*) was found in an isolated section of Guadalcanal. Identification was established through several dogtags of the dead crewmen and from a section of the fuselage bearing the name, "Bessie the Jap Basher."
21. Gartland, "History of the 98th Bombardment Squadron," in Cleveland, ed., *Grey Geese Calling*, 316.
22. Ibid.; Morison, *Naval Operations*, Vol. V, 138.
23. "Narrative History, 72nd BS," 20-1; "Daily Diary, 26th BS," September 26, 1942 entry. Pilots and planes, all B-17Es, where known, were: 72nd BS: Maj. Ridings (41-9223), Capt. Kramer (41-9122, *Eager Beavers*), and Lts. Classen (41-9093, *Spook*), Trent (41-9128), and Raphael Bloch (41-9059, *Boomerang*). 26th BS: Maj. Sewart (41-2611), Capt. Thornhill (41-9145), and Lt. Kinney (41-9060).
24. "Narrative History, 72nd BS,"20-1; "Daily Diary, 26th BS," September 27, 1942 entry.
25. Graham to author, May 9, 1997.
26. "Daily Diary, 26th BS," September 29, 1942 entry; Handrow diary in Cleveland, ed., *Grey Geese Calling*, 212-3; "History of the 98th BS Report," 12. Pilots and planes, where known, were: 26th BS: Maj. Sewart B-17E (41-2611), Lts. Kinney B-17F (41-24457, *The Aztec's Curse*), and Livingston B-17F (41-24531). 98th BS: Maj. Rasmussen B-17E (41-9214, *The Skipper*), Lts. Waskowitz B-17E (41-2616, *Blue Goose*), Durbin (41-2523, *Goonie*), and Cope B-17E (41-2525, *Madame-X*). 431st BS: Capt. White B-17E (41-9156, *Uncle Biff*).
27. "History of the 98th BS," 12.
28. "Daily Diary, 26th BS," September 29, 1942 entry; Handrow diary in Cleveland, ed., *Grey Geese Calling*, 213.

29. Handrow diary in Cleveland, ed., *Grey Geese Calling*, 213.

30. Miller, *The Cactus Air Force*, 106; Howard, *One Damned Island*, 117.

31. Schaeffer, "A Few Missions Out of Guadalcanal," 1.

32. "Daily Diary, 26th BS," October 3 and 4, 1942 entries. Pilot and planes, all B-17Es, were: 26th BS - Maj. Sewart (41-2611), Capts. Thornhill (41-24531), and Chambers (41-2457), and Lt. Livingston (41-24531). 72nd BS - Lt. Everitt (41-9118).

33. Ibid.; "Narrative History, 72nd BS," 22; Mingos, *American Heros*, 250, 252, 254, 257, 260, 262, 268.

34. Miller, *The Cactus Air Force*, 109; "Daily Diary, 26th BS," October 5, 1942 entry; "Narrative History, 72nd BS," 21-2; Mingos, *American Heroes*, 273. Pilots and planes, all B-17Es, where known, were: 26th BS - Maj. Sewart (41-2611), and Capts. Thornhill (41-9145), and Chambers (41-2457). 72nd BS - Maj. Ridings (41-9223), and Lts. Creech (41-2396), and Hawes (41-2531, *G.I. Angel*). 98th BS: Capt. Lucas (?).

35. Mingos, *American Heroes*, 273.

36. "Narrative History, 72nd BS," 22.

37. Costello, *The Pacific War*, 348-9.

38. Craven, ed., *Army Air Forces*, Vol. IV, 55; Morison, *Naval Operations*, Vol. V, 150; "Daily Diary, 26th BS," October 11, 1942 entry. Pilots and planes where known, were: 26th BS: Maj. Sewart B-17E (41-2611), 1st Lt. John C. Nissen B-17E (41-2524), and Lts. Kinney B-17E (41-9060) and Livingston B-17F (41-24531). 431st BS: Maj. Edmundson B-17E (41-9217, *Fiji Foo*), and Capt. Payne B-17F (41-24528).

39. Costello, *The Pacific War*, 351; Morison, *Naval Operations*, Vol. V, 151; Salmaggi, *2194 Days of War*, 298.

40. "Daily Diary, 26th BS," October 12, 1942 entry.

41. Ibid., October 13, 1942 entry; Edmundson account and Handrow diary in Cleveland, ed., *Grey Geese Calling*, 38-9, 213.

42. Edmundson account and Handrow diary in Cleveland, ed., *Grey Geese Calling*, 39, 213.

43. "Daily Diary, 26th BS," October 13, 1942 entry; "431st Bomb Sq in Action," in Cleveland, ed., *Grey Geese Calling*, 239.

44. Edmundson account, and "431st Bomb Sq in Action," in Cleveland, ed., *Grey Geese Calling*, 39, 239-40.

45. "Daily Diary, 26th BS," October 13, 1942 entry; "431st Bomb Sq in Action," in Cleveland, ed., *Grey Geese Calling*, 240.

46. Cleveland, ed., *Grey Geese Calling*, 24; Edmundson account, and "431st Bomb Sq in Action," in Cleveland, ed., *Grey Geese Calling*, 240; Carter, *Combat Chronology*, 48; Birdsall, *Pride of Seattle*, 12.

47. Craven, ed., *Army Air Force*, Vol. IV, 55-6; Cleveland, ed., *Grey Geese Calling*, 24; "Daily Diary, 26th BS," October 14, 1942 entry.

48. Handrow diary in Cleveland, ed., *Grey Geese Calling*, 213-4; "Daily Diary, 26th BS," October 15, 1942 entry.

49. Bowman, *Flying to Glory*, 64.

50. Costello, *The Pacific War*, 354; Craven, *Army Air Forces*, Vol. IV, 57.

51. Crothers, "42nd Bombardment Squadron (H) History," in Cleveland, ed., *Grey Geese Calling*, 125-6.

52. "Daily Diary, 26th BS," October 23, 1942 entry; Wolfert, *Battle for the Solomons*, 74-7.

53. Salmaggi, *2194 Days of War*, 303.

54. "Narrative History, 72nd BS," 19, 23.

55. Salmaggi, *2194 Days of War*, 303; Craven, *Army Air Forces*, Vol. IV, 57-8.

56. "Daily Diary, 26th BS," October 25, 1942 entry; Wolfert, *Battle for the Solomons*, 108-10.

57. Morison, *Naval Operations,* Vol. V, 194-7; Miller, *The Cactus Air Force,* 144-5.
58. Ibid.; "Daily Diary, 26th BS," October 25, 1942 entry; Mingos, *American Heroes,* 277, 278, 281. Pilots and planes, where known, were: 431st BS: Capts. Payne, Manford K. Wagnon, and Willis E. Jacobs. 26th BS: Lt. Loberg B-17E (41-2433).
59. "Daily Diary, 26th BS," October 25, 1942 entry; Craven, *Army Air Forces,* Vol IV, 58.
60. Costello, *The Pacific War,* 361-4; Dunnigan, *Victory at Sea,* 37-9; Salmaggi, *2194 Days of War,* 309.

Chapter 21
1. Murphy, *Skip Bombing,* 40; "History of the 43rd BG," 75, 221.
2. Murphy, *Skip Bombing,* 40, 42.
3. Rouse, *Diary,* 51.
4. Ibid., 52; Kenney, *General Kenney Reports,* 118.
5. Rouse, *Diary,* 52; Gooch to author, April 10, 1996, 3-4. Pilots and planes, where known, were: Maj. Rouse, Capt. Giddings, and Lts. Wesche B-17F (41-24403, *Blitz Buggy*), Hageman B-17E (41-9196), and McKenzie.
6. Birdsall, *Claims to Fame,* 81.
7. Rouse, *Diary,* 52-3.
8. Rouse, *Diary,* 53; Gooch to author, April 10, 1996, 4, and August 12, 1996, 1.
9. Birdsall, *Claims to Fame,* 49.
10. Kenney, *General Kenney Reports,* 120; Crawford, *Gore and Glory,* 84-5; Rouse, *Diary,* 53; Birdsall, *Claims to Fame,* 49; Wyatt statement in "History of the 28th BS," 2; "History of the 43rd BG," 222.
11. Kenney, *General Kenney Reports,* 121; Crawford, *Gore and Glory,* 85.
12. Murphy, *Skip Bombing,* 46.
13. Ibid., 46-7; Crawford, *Gore and Glory,* 86; United States Strategic Bombing Survey, *The Fifth Air Force in the War Against Japan,* 101.
14. Johnson, "Narrative Report of Mission of October 9, 1942," *435th Bombardment Squadron (H) USAAFIA;* "Destruction of Aircraft by 435th BS," 6; "Narrative History of the 435th Bombardment Squadron, 6 December 1941 to 20 December 1942," *Bomb Squadron History, 435th Bombardment Squadron (H),* 10.
15. Kenney, *General Kenney Reports,* 121; Wyatt statement in "History of the 28th BS," 2; "History of the 43rd BG," 222;
16. Murphy, *Skip Bombing,* 47; Kenney, *General Kenney Reports,* 121.
17. Murphy, *Skip Bombing,* 47.
18. Johnson, "The 435th Short History," in Johnson, ed., *435th Overseas,* 9.
19. Ibid., 6; Fields, *Kangaroo Squadron,* 81; "435th Daily Bulletin," *435th Bombardment Squadron, 19th Bombardment Group (H),* unknown date.
20. "History of the 43rd BG," 323.
21. Cool, "Excerpts from Diary," 3; "History of the 28th BS," 21; Knudson, *Diary,* 57-9; Rouse, *Diary,* 54.
22. Kenney, *General Kenney Reports,* 122; Taggart, *My Fighting Congregation,* 162.
23. "History of the 43rd BG," 16, 222; Carter, *Combat Chronology,* 49.
24. "History of the 43rd BG," 222; Murphy, *Skip Bombing,* 49, 51.
25. "History of the 43rd BG," 16, 222; Murphy, *Skip Bombing,* 51; Kenney, *General Kenney Reports,* 124-5; Cool, "Excerpts from Diary," 3; "History of the 28th BS," 21; Rouse, *Diary,* 54.
26. Kenney, *General Kenney Reports,* 125.
27. Taggart, *My Fighting Congregation,* 168-9 Rouse, *Diary,* 55.

28. "Eddie Rickenbacker's Own Story," *Life*, January 25, 1943, 19, 21-4, 26.
29. "Historical Data and History of the 23rd Bombardment Squadron (H), APO 324," *Bomb Squadron History, 23rd Bombardment Squadron (H)*, 4.
30. Kenney, *General Kenney Reports*, 126-7; "Extract" found in "History of the 43rd BG," 71.
31. Ibid.
32. Ibid.
33. Taggart, *My Fighting Congregation*, 169-70; Mitchell, *In Alis Vicimus*, 159, 186. The planes, all B-17Es, where known, were: (41-2438), (41-2453), (41-2462, *Tojo's Jinx*), (41-2486, *Lady Lou*), (41-2489, *Suzy-Q*), (41-2642), (41-2644), (41-2658), (41-2668), and (41-2669).
34. Hardison, *The Suzy-Q*, 160-1; "History of the 93rd BS," 6.
35. Ibid.
36. Kenney, *General Kenney Reports*, 126.
37. Ibid., 129; "History of the 43rd BG," 222; Birdsall, *Pride of Seattle*, 14.
38. Kenney, *General Kenney Reports*, 130.
39. Rouse, *Diary*, 56-7.
40. Rouse, *Diary*, 56-7; Taggart, *My Fighting Congregation*, 159-61.
41. Rouse, *Diary*, 56; "History of the 28th BS," 21; "History of the 43rd BG," 16, 222; Kenney, *General Kenney Reports*, 130.
42. Fields, *Kangaroo Squadron*, 86; "Narrative Report of Mission of October 31, 1942," *435th Bombardment Squadron (H) USAAFIA*.
43. Kenney, *General Kenney Reports*, 130; Rouse, *Diary*, 56.
44. Kenney, *General Kenney Reports*, 130-1; Rouse, *Diary*, 57.
45. Rouse, *Diary*, 57; Taggart, *My Fighting Congregation*, 171; Mitchell, *In Alis Vicimus*, 116, 185.
46. Kenney, *General Kenney Reports*, 131; "History of the 43rd BG," 223; Murphy, *Skip Bombing*, 52.
47. Kenney, *General Kenney Reports*, 131; "History of the 43rd BG," 223.
48. Kenney, *General Kenney Reports*, 131; Taggart, *My Fighting Congregation*, 171-2; "Deaths of Members of this Organization," attached to "Historical Data, 19th BG," 6; Rouse, *Diary*, 57.

Chapter 22
1. "History of the 403rd Bombardment Squadron (H) in Australia," *Bomb Squadron History, 403rd Bombardment Squadron (H)*, 1; "History of the 43rd BG," 323, 325.
2. Fields, *Kangaroo Squadron*, 85, 86-7.
3. Ibid., 87.
4. "History of the 28th BS," 21-2.
5. Kenney, *General Kenney Reports*, 129, 131.
6. "History of the 28th BS," 22; Carter, *Combat Chronology*, 55.
7. Freeman, *The B-17 Flying Fortress Story*, 77.
8. Kenney, *General Kenney Reports*, 135-9.
9. "History of the 43rd BG," 264; Maurer, *Air Force Combat Squadrons of World War II*, 243-4, 245-6.
10. Rouse, *Diary*, 58; Fields, *Kangaroo Squadron*, 137.
11. "History of the 43rd BG," 325.
12. Ibid., 264.
13. Murphy, *Skip Bombing*, 53-5.
14. Carter, *Combat Chronology*, 58; Freeman, *The B-17 Flying Fortress Story*, 75.

15. Ibid., 55, 57-8, 73. The dog "Pluto" flew with Lt. Murphy's crew until he developed an incurable case of ringworm and was taken off flying status. The author does not know the ultimate fate of the dog.
16. Ibid., 55, 57-8.
17. Knudson, *Diary*, 67-71, 75.
18. Fields, *Kangaroo Squadron*, 88, 137-8.
19. Ibid., 138; Knudson, *Diary*, 75.
20. Hardison, *The Suzy-Q*, 162; Fields, *Kangaroo Squadron*, 91-99; Jacquet, "Flight," Winter, 1985, 23; Gooch to author, October 22, 1997, 1.
21. Kenney, *General Kenney Reports*, 140.
22. Ibid., 141; Murphy, *Skip Bombing*, 60-1.
23. Murphy, *Skip Bombing*, 28; Carter, *Combat Chronology*, 59. The four pilots were Capts. Kenneth McCullar and William M. Thompson, and Lts. Lewis A. Anderson and James Dewolf.
24. "History of the 43rd BG," 264.
25. Kenney, *General Kenney Reports*, 140-1.
26. Ibid., 143-4; "History of the 43rd BG," 223; Carter, *Combat Chronology*, 60; Murphy, *Skip Bombing*, 68. Murphy wrote that this action took place on November 16, 1942 at Simpson Harbor, Rabaul.
27. "History of the 28th BS," 22; Wyatt statement in "History of the 28th BS," 3; Cool, "Excerpts from Diary," 3.
28. "History of the 43rd BG," 325.
29. Ibid., 192; Carter, *Combat Chronology*, 61. Unfortunately, this author could not determine the serial number of the B-17E lost on November 22, 1942 with Lt. Frost and crew.
30. Crawford, *Gore and Glory*, 94-5; "History of the 43rd BG," 18, 22, 224.
31. Murphy, *Skip Bombing*, 69; Crawford, *Gore and Glory*, 96-7; Kenney, *General Kenney Reports*, 147.
32. "History of the 43rd BG," 224; Crawford, *Gore and Glory*, 97-8; Birdsall, *Claims to Fame*, 67, 92. The pilots and planes, all B-17Fs, where known, were: Capts. McCullar (41-24521, *Black Jack*), Scott (41-24353, *Cap'n & The Kids*), James L. Harcrow, and Lts. Crawford and O'Brien.
33. Murphy, *Skip Bombing*, 69-70; Crawford, *Gore and Glory*, 98; Kenney, *General Kenney Reports*, 148-9.
34. Crawford, *Gore and Glory*, 98-9.
35. Kenney, *General Kenney Reports*, 148-9.
36. "History of the 43rd BG," 224; Crawford, *Gore and Glory*, 97-8; Birdsall, *Claims to Fame*, 67, 92.
37. "History of the 43rd BG," 224.
38. Ibid., 192; Birdsall, *Pride of Seattle*, 14.
39. "History of the 43rd Bomb Group," 18-19, 22; Kenney, *General Kenney Reports*, 155. The pilots from the 64th BS were: Capts. Marshall E. Nelson and Denton H. Daniel, and Lts. Wesche, Charles N. McArthur, and William P. Thorington. The pilots from the 65th BS were: Capts. Fletcher and Daniel T. Roberts, Jr.,and Lts. Harcrow, Daniel H. Cromer, Melville V. Ehlers, (?) Williams, and (?) Freeman.
40. Kenney, *General Kenney Reports*, 155-6.
41. Dalley, "Saga of the 22nd Ground Men," in Johnson, ed., *435th Overseas*, 24; Taggart, *My Fighting Congregation*, 173; Payne to author, September 9, 1996, 3.

Chapter 23

1. Salmaggi, *2194 Days of War*, 310.
2. "History of the 98th BS," 14; "Daily Diary, 26th BS," Nov. 1, 1942 entry. Pilots and planes, where known, were: 98th BS - Capt. Lucas B-17E (41-2523, *Goonie*), and Lts. Durbin B-17F (41-24534, *Omar Khayam*), (?) Charters B-17E (41-9214, *The Skipper*), Samuel J. Brewer, and Robert L. Gill B-17E (41-2428, *Ole Sh'asta*). 26th BS - Lts. Loberg B-17E (41-9060), Keyes B-17E (41-2433), and Sesso B-17E (41-2409, *Old Maid*).
3. Hillsborough, pub., *Fifth Bomb Group*, 78; "Organizational History, 431st BS," 9.
4. Salmaggi, *2194 Days of War*, 310-19.
5. Johnston, *Follow Me! The Story of the Second Marine Division in World War II*, 55-6.
6. Carter, *Combat Chronology*, 58; Costello, *The Pacific War*, 66.
7. Craven, ed., *Army Air Forces*, Vol. I, 705, n31.
8. Costello, *The Pacific War*, 366-8; Morison, *Naval Operations*, Vol. V, 231-5.
9. Howard, *One Damned Island*, 120-1; Miller, *The Cactus Air Force*, 186-7. The *Hiei* was eventually scuttled by the Japanese.
10. Gartland, "History of the 98th Bombardment Squadron (H)," in Cleveland, ed., *Grey Geese Calling*, 343-4; Kurzman, *Left to Die*, 157-9, 167-8, 170, 172, 173-5
11. Costello, *The Pacific War*, 369.
12. Carter, *Combat Chronology*, 58; Gartland, "History of the 98th Bombardment Squadron (H)," in Cleveland, ed., *Grey Geese Calling*, 318.
13. Costello, *The Pacific War*, 369-70; Morison, *Naval Operations*, Vol. V, 267.
14. Craven, ed., *Army Air Forces*, Vol. I, 59; Center for Air Force History, pub., *Pacific Counterblow*, 53; Miller, *The Cactus Air Force*, 196.
15. Costello, *The Pacific War*, 369-70; Morison, *Naval Operations*, Vol. V, 271-81.
16. Costello, *The Pacific War*, 372; "Daily Diary, 26th BS," Nov. 15, 1942 entry.
17. "Daily Diary, 26th BS," Nov. 15, 1942 entry.
18. Kurzman, *Left to Die*, 189-90.
19. Ibid., 192, 205; "Daily Diary, 26th BS," Nov. 17, 1942 entry.
20. "Daily Diary, 26th BS," Nov. 18, 1942 entry; Turner, pub., *11th Bomb Group*, 19.
21. "Daily Diary, 26th BS," Nov. 18, 1942 entry; Birdsall, *Claims to Fame*, 41. Pilots and planes, where known, were; First Echelon: 26th BS - Maj. Sewart B-17F (41-24531) and Capt. Thornhill B-17E (41-2524), and 42nd BS - Maj. Manierre B-17E (41-9213), and Capts. Donald Hyland B-17E (41-2442, *Yokohama Express*), and Philip Sprawls B-17E (41-9216, *Alley-Oop*). Second Echelon: 72nd BS - Maj. Whitaker, and Lt. Classen, and 98th BS - Capt. Lucas B-17E (41-9124, *Buzz King*), and Lts. Durbin B-17F (41-24534, *Omar Khayam*), and Roy Morgan B-17E (41-9215, *Gallopin' Gus*).
22. Ibid.
23. Ibid.
24. Birdsall, *Claims to Fame*, 41-2.
25. Ibid., 42; Birdsall, *Pride of Seattle*, 12.
26. Howard, *One Damned Island*, 124; "Daily Diary, 26th BS," Nov. 20, 1942 entry.
27. Saunders statement in Cleveland, ed., *Grey Geese Calling*, 34; "Daily Diary, 26th BS," Nov. 18, 1942 entry.
28. "Daily Diary, 26th BS," Nov. 18, 1942 entry.
29. Saunders statement in Cleveland, ed., *Grey Geese Calling*, 34; Birdsall, *Pride of Seattle*, 12; Howard, *One Damned Island*, 124; "Daily Diary, 26th BS," Nov. 19, 1942 entry.
30. Craven, ed., *Army Air Forces*, Vol. IV, 62.
31. "Daily Diary, 26th BS," Nov. 19, 1942 entry; Kurzman, *Left to Die*, 238-9. In addition to the unknown debriefing officer, Capt. Gilbert C. Hoover, leading the retreating

American vessels from the Battle of Guadalcanal, was deprived of his command by Admiral Halsey for abandoning the *Juneau.*
32. "Daily Diary, 26th BS," Nov. 21-23 and 25, 1942 entries.
33. "History of the 5th BG," 5-6.
34. Ibid., 6.
35. "History of the 31st BS," 5; "Data and History of the 23rd BS," 5.
36. "394th BS Report," 7.
37. Klingensmith to author, November 10, 1996, 1-2.
38. Ibid., 4; "394th BS Report," 7.
39. Klingensmith to author, November 10, 1996, 3, 4.
40. Ibid., 5.
41. Morison, *Naval Operations,* Vol. V, 288-315.
42. Craven, ed., *Army Air Forces,* Vol. IV, 61-3.
43. Ibid., 64-7.
44. Ibid., 67-9.
45. Ibid., 69-70.

Chapter 24
1. Howard, *One Damned Island,* 124.
2. Ibid., 127.
3. Edmundson account in Cleveland, ed., *Grey Geese Calling,* 40; "History of the 11th BG," 9.
4. "History of the 31st BS," 5.
5. Brady letter in *5th Bomb Group (H) Association, Inc. Newsletter,* December 5, 1994, 5.
6. Gartland, "History of the 98th Bombardment Squadron (H)," in Cleveland, ed., *Grey Geese Calling,* 322; "Narrative History, 72nd BS," 27; "Organizational History, 431st BS," 9.
7. "History of the 98th BS," 23-4.
8. Handrow diary in Cleveland, ed., *Grey Geese Calling,* 215.
9. Ibid.; Morriss, *South Pacific Diary,* 1942-1943, 49; "Narrative History, 72nd BS," 27.
10. Handrow diary, and "War Diary," in Cleveland, ed., *Grey Geese Calling,* 215, 219.
11. "History of the 98th BS," 24-5.
12. Hillsborough, pub., *Fifth BG,* 37; Davenport to author, December 16, 1996, 1.
13. Klingensmith to author, November 10, 1996, 6.
14. Turner, pub., *11th Bomb Group,* 19; Bowman, *Flying to Glory,* 69.
15. "History of the 98th BS," 25.
16. Ibid.; Crothers, "42nd Bombardment Squadron (H) History," "War Diary," and Handrow Statement in Cleveland, ed., *Grey Geese Calling,* 126, 215, 230.
17. Casualty Report found in "History of the 43rd BG," 191.
18. Ibid.; Murphy, *Skip Bombing,* 70-1.
19. "History of the 43rd BG," 225; Murphy, *Skip Bombing,* 73-4.
20. "History of the 43rd BG," 225; Murphy, *Skip Bombing,* 74-6;
21. Murphy, *Skip Bombing,* 76; Kenney, *General Kenney Reports,* 162; Birdsall, *Claims to Fame,* 92.
22. "History of the 43rd BG," 284; Birdsall, *Claims to Fame,* 50.
23. Kenney, *General Kenney Reports,* 163.
24. Ibid., 163, 168; Carter, *Combat Chronology,* 68-9; "History of the 43rd BG," 284.
25. "History of the 43rd BG," 284.
26. Birdsall, *Pride of Seattle,* 14, 17.
27. Carter, *Combat Chronology,* 68-9; "History of the 43rd BG," 225; Salmaggi, *2194 Days of War,* 238; Kenney, *General Kenney Reports,* 165.

28. Murphy, *Skip Bombing*, 77-8.
29. Kenney, *General Kenney Reports*, 169-70; Craven ed., *Army Air Forces*, Vol. IV, 715, 136n. General Kenney mistakenly reports McCullar's attack taking place at Lae.
30. "History of the 43rd BG," 284; Carter, *Combat Chronology*, 71.
31. "History of the 43rd BG," 284-5; Kenney, *General Kenney Reports*, 170; Craven ed., *Army Air Forces*, Vol. IV, 715, 136n.
32. Kenney, *General Kenney Reports*, 170; Crawford, *Gore and Glory*, 104.
33. Murphy, *Skip Bombing*, 79; "History of the 43rd BG," 225; Craven ed., *Army Air Forces*, Vol. IV, 715, 136n.
34. Murphy, *Skip Bombing*, 79-81; "History of the 43rd BG," 225-6; Craven ed., *Army Air Forces*, Vol. IV, 715, 136n.
35. Murphy, *Skip Bombing*, 81.

Chapter 25
1. Craven, ed., *Army Air Forces*, Vol. IV, 139.
2. "Daily Diary, 26th BS," January 1, 1943 entry.
3. Salmaggi, *2194 Days of War*, 338; Kenney, *General Kenney Reports*, 175.
4. Crawford, *Gore and Glory*, 105, 111-4.
5. Morton, *United States Army in World War II*, Vol. 2, Pt. 15, 624-9.
6. "Daily Diary, 26th BS," January 3, 1943 entry; Kenney, *General Kenney Reports*, 175-6; Birdsall, *Flying Buccaneers*, 45.
7. "History of the 43rd BG," 265, 328; Birdsall, *Pride of Seattle*, 14; Craven ed., *Army Air Forces*, Vol. IV, 715, 136n.
8. Kenney, *General Kenney Reports*, 176; Birdsall, *Pride of Seattle*, 9; Sharp & Dunnigan, *The Congressional Medal of Honor*, 472-3.
9. "History of the 43rd BG," 328; Birdsall, *Pride of Seattle*, 13-4.
10. Ibid., 177; "History of the 43rd BG," 98-100; Birdsall, *Pride of Seattle*, 7; Casualty Report found in "History of the 43rd BG," 195.
11. Kenney, *General Kenney Reports*, 177; Craven ed., *Army Air Forces*, Vol. IV, 136.
12. "History of the 43rd BG," 20; Craven ed., *Army Air Forces*, Vol. IV, 136.
13. Birdsall, *Claims to Fame*, 50-1; Casualty Report found in "History of the 43rd BG," 195-6.
14. "History of the 43rd BG," 285; Carter, *Combat Chronology*, 79-80.
15. Kenney, *General Kenney Reports*, 181, 182,
16. Murphy, *Skip Bombing*, 89; "History of the 43rd BG," 265.
17. "History of the 43rd BG," 89, 285.
18. Ibid., 21-2, 326-7; Birdsall, *Pride of Seattle*, 14, 17.
19. "History of the 43rd BG," 327.
20. Kenney, *General Kenney Reports*, 182-3.
21. Carter, *Combat Chronology*, 85-92; Kenney, *General Kenney Reports*, 184.
22. Murphy, *Skip Bombing*, 92; Birdsall, *Claims to Fame*, 68.
23. Murphy, *Skip Bombing*, 94-5.
24. "Organizational History, 431st BS," 9; "Brief History of 5th Bombardment Group, 1918-1952," *5th Bombardment Group (H) History*, 7.
25. "Daily Diary, 26th BS," January 4 and 5, 1943 entries.
26. Ibid., January 6, 1943 entry.
27. Ibid., January 7, 1943 entry.
28. "Brief History of 5th Bombardment Group, 1918-1952," *5th Bombardment Group (H) History*, 6; Bonanza Books, pub., *AAF: The Official World War II Guide to the Army Air Forces*, 291; Carter, *Combat Chronology*, 81.

29. "Brief History of 5th Bombardment Group, 1918-1952," *5th Bombardment Group (H) History,* 6-7; "History of the 5th BG," 7.

30. "History of the 31st BS," 5; Hillsborough, pub., *Fifth BG,* 38, 80; "History of the 5th BG," 7.

31. Hillsborough, pub., *Fifth BG,* 80; Morriss, *South Pacific Diary,* 131.

32. "Narrative History, 72nd BS," 28.

33. Craven, ed., *Army Air Forces,* Vol. IV, 82; "History of the 42nd BS," 10.

34. "Narrative History, 72nd BS," 28; Carter, *Combat Chronology,* 83; Schaeffer, "A Few Missions Out of Guadalcanal," 2.

35. "Narrative History, 72nd BS," 28; Carter, *Combat Chronology,* 84-5.

36. "History of the 98th BS," 26-7; "Award of Decorations, 27 January 1943," in "History of the 98th BS."

37. Turner, pub., *11th BG,* 19-20; Edmundson, "B-17 Flying Fortress," in Higham, *Flying Combat Aircraft of the USAAF-USAF,* Vol. 2, 39.

38. "Daily Diary, 26th BS," January 25, 26 and 28, 1943 entries; "Organizational History, 431st BS," 9.

39. Carter, *Combat Chronology,* 89; Hillsborough, pub., *Fifth BG,* 40; "23rd BS History," 4; Cleveland, "431st Bombardment Squadron (H) History," in Cleveland, ed., *Grey Geese Calling,* 256.

40. "History of the 98th BS," 27.

41. Hillsborough, pub., Fifth BG, 40; "Narrative History, 72nd BS," 28; Crothers, "42nd Bombardment Squadron (H) History," in Cleveland, ed., *Grey Geese Calling,* 127.

42. Ibid.

43. "Narrative History, 72nd BS," 28.

44. Ibid.; Schaeffer, "A Few Missions Out of Guadalcanal," 2.

45. "Narrative History, 72nd BS," 28.

Chapter 26

1. Craven, ed., *Army Air Forces,* Vol. IV, 86.

2. Ibid., 86, 88; Bowman, *Flying to Glory,* 70.

3. Craven, ed., *Army Air Forces,* Vol. IV, 216.

4. Birdsall, *Claims to Fame,* 43-7; Morriss, *South Pacific Diary,* 234-5 n22, 237-8 n45.

5. "Organizational History, 431st BS," 9; "History of the 98th BS," 27; Handrow diary in Cleveland, ed., *Grey Geese Calling,* 216.

6. Ibid.; Handrow diary in Cleveland, ed., *Grey Geese Calling,* 216; Davenport to author, January 22, 1997, 1.

7. Hillsborough, pub., *Fifth BG,* 41.

8. Hillsborough, pub., *Fifth BG,* 41; Birdsall, *Claims to Fame,* 62.

9. Birdsall, *Claims to Fame,* 62.

10. Ibid.; Carter, *Combat Chronology,* 108, 109; "Brief History of 5th Bombardment Group, 1918-1952," *5th Bombardment Group (H) History,* 7.

11. Carter, *Combat Chronology,* 109; Birdsall, *Claims to Fame,* 62-6; Craven, ed., *Army Air Forces,* Vol. IV, 217; "Brief History of 5th Bombardment Group, 1918-1952," *5th Bombardment Group (H) History,* 7.

12. Carter, *Combat Chronology,* 109; "Brief History of 5th Bombardment Group, 1918-1952," *5th Bombardment Group (H) History,* 7.

13. Birdsall, *Claims to Fame,* 67; Morriss, *South Pacific Diary,* 127; "Aircraft Losses from the 5th BG (H) in the Solomon Area," in *5th Bomb Group (H) Association, Inc. Newsletter,* January 5, 1996, 4.

14. Hillsborough, pub., *Fifth BG*, 79.
15. Belz, "Unusual Events with the 431st Bomb Squadron," in Ibid., 58.
16. "Organizational History, 431st BS," 10.
17. "History of the 42nd BS," 7; "History of 26th BS," 20.
18. Turner, pub., *11th BG*, 79, 80, 92, 95; Edmundson to Klingensmith, Oct. 19, 1991, 1.
19. Kenney, *General Kenney Reports*, 246-7, 258; Birdsall, *Flying Buccaneers*, 48.
20. Kenney, *General Kenney Reports*, 191-2; Crawford, *Gore and Glory*, 106-7
21. Birdsall, *Claims to Fame*, 92.
22. Kenney, *General Kenney Reports*, 192; Crawford, *Gore and Glory*, 108.
23. Crawford, *Gore and Glory*, 109-10.
24. Kenney, *General Kenney Reports*, 191.
25. Murphy, *Skip Bombing*, 98-100.
26. Kenney, *General Kenney Reports*, 192; Carter, *Combat Chronology*, 97-8; "History of the 43rd BG," 286.
27. Salmaggi, *2194 Days of War*, 356.
28. Casualty Report found in "History of the 43rd BG," 196; "History of the 43rd BG," 286.
29. "History of the 43rd BG," 226.
30. Kenney, *General Kenney Reports*, 197-8.
31. Ibid., 200; Murphy, *Skip Bombing*, 105-6; "History of the 43rd BG," 286; Carter, *Combat Chronology*, 100.
32. Kenney, *General Kenney Reports*, 201.
33. Murphy, *Skip Bombing*, 106-7; Craven, ed., *Army Air Forces*, Vol. IV, 142.
34. Murphy, *Skip Bombing*, 107-8; Kenney, *General Kenney Reports*, 202.

Chapter 27
1. Crawford, *Gore and Glory*, 119-20; Craven, ed., *Army Air Forces*, Vol. IV, 143, 148.
2. Haugland, *The AAF Against Japan*, 162; Murphy, *Skip Bombing*, 108.
3. Craven, ed., *Army Air Forces*, Vol. IV, 143, 148; Murphy, *Skip Bombing*, 111; "History of the 43rd BG," 238.
4. Murphy, *Skip Bombing*, 108-10.
5. Ibid., 112.
6. Haugland, *The AAF Against Japan*, 162.
7. Murphy, *Skip Bombing*, 114; Birdsall, *Pride of Seattle*, 12; "History fo the 43rd BG," 236.
8. "History of the 43rd BG," 24, 266-7; Craven, ed., *Army Air Forces*, Vol. IV, 143; Haugland, *The AAF Against Japan*, 162.
9. Craven, ed., *Army Air Forces*, Vol. IV, 143; "History of the 43rd BG," 24; Kenney, *General Kenney Reports*, 202.
10. Kenney, *General Kenney Reports*, 202; Hastings, "No Survivors," in "History of the 43rd BG," 63-4; "History of the 43rd BG," 267.
11. Murphy, *Skip Bombing*, 112; Haugland, *The AAF Against Japan*, 162; Craven, ed., *Army Air Forces*, Vol. IV, 143.
12. Hastings, "No Survivors," in "History of the 43rd BG," 64; "History of the 43rd BG," 24, 267; Murphy, *Skip Bombing*, 113-4.
13. Craven, ed., *Army Air Forces*, Vol. IV, 143; "History of the 43rd BG," 25.
14. Craven, ed., *Army Air Forces*, Vol. IV, 143; Hastings, "No Survivors," in "History of the 43rd BG," 63-4. The official AAF history states that only thirteen B-17s attacked on the morning of March 3, however, this author has found fifteen.
15. "History of the 43rd BG," 287; Crawford, *Gore and Glory*, 128-9.
16. Crawford, *Gore and Glory*, 123-4.

17. Ibid., 124-7.
18. Murphy, *Skip Bombing*, 115-6; Birdsall, *Flying Buccaneers*, 56-7; Birdsall, *Pride of Seattle*, 6.
19. Hastings, "No Survivors," in "History of the 43rd BG," 64.
20. Craven, ed., *Army Air Forces*, Vol. IV, 144.
21. "History of the 43rd BG," 24-5; Murphy, *Skip Bombing*, 116-7.
22. Craven, ed., *Army Air Forces*, Vol. IV, 145.
23. "History of the 43rd BG," 26; Birdsall, *Flying Buccaneers*, 61-2.
24. Murphy, *Skip Bombing*, 119-20.
25. Craven, ed., *Army Air Forces*, Vol. IV, 146, 148-50.
26. Kenney, *General Kenney Reports*, 206.
27. Carter, *Combat Chronology*, 103-4; Birdsall, *Claims to Fame*, 84-5.
28. "History of the 43rd BG," 27.
29. Ibid.
30. Ibid., 26a, 237-8; Birdsall, *Claims to Fame*, 68; Murphy, *Skip Bombing*, 125-6.
31. "Weekly Status and Operations Report," found in *Bomb Squadron History, 64th Bombardment Squadron* (H); Birdsall, *Pride of Seattle*, 8; Casualty Report found in "History of the 43rd BG," 197-8.
32. "History of the 43rd BG," 228; Murphy, *Skip Bombing*, 130.
33. "History of the 43rd BG," 228; Murphy, *Skip Bombing*, 128; Birdsall, *Pride of Seattle*, 7; Kenney, *General Kenney Reports*, 217-8.

Chapter 28

1. Costello, *The Pacific War*, 390-1.
2. "History of the 43rd BG," 228; Murphy, *Skip Bombing*, 131-2; Craven, ed., *Army Air Forces*, Vol. IV, 162.
3. "History of the 43rd BG," 287-8; Carter, *Combat Chronology*, 116-8; Kenney, *General Kenney Reports*, 226.
4. "History of the 43rd BG," 27, 271; Crawford, *Gore and Glory*, 136.
5. Crawford, *Gore and Glory*, 136-7.
6. "History of the 43rd BG," 27.
7. Murphy, *Skip Bombing*, 136-7.
8. "History of the 43rd BG," 27-8; Kenney, *General Kenney Reports*, 226.
9. Crawford, *Gore and Glory*, 138-40.
10. Murphy, *Skip Bombing*, 141-3.
11. Crawford, *Gore and Glory*, 147-53; Carter, *Combat Chronology*, 122.
12. Birdsall, *Pride of Seattle*, 6, 7, 8; Casualty Report found in "History of the 43rd BG," 199.
13. "History of the 43rd BG," 228; Murphy, *Skip Bombing*, 144.
14. "History of the 43rd BG," 328.
15. Kenney, *General Kenney Reports*, 238.
16. Murphy, *Skip Bombing*, 146-7; Birdsall, *Pride of Seattle*, 11.
17. "History of the 43rd BG," 289.
18. Ibid., 228-9; Murphy, *Skip Bombing*, 147; Birdsall, *Pride of Seattle*, 11.
19. "History of the 43rd BG," 289; Crawford, *Gore and Glory*, 156.
20. Kenney, *General Kenney Reports*, 244-5.
21. "History of the 43rd BG," 29, 229, 289.
22. Ibid., 289; Crawford, *Gore and Glory*, 156-66.
23. "Weekly Status and Operations Report," found in *Bomb Squadron History, 64th Bombardment Squadron* (H).
24. Sakaida, *The Siege of Rabaul*, 40; Kenney, *General Kenney Reports*, 354-5; "Aircraft

Losses from the 5th BG (H) in the Solomon Area," in *5th Bomb Group (H) Association, Inc. Newsletter*, January 5, 1996, 4.

25. Sakaida, *The Siege of Rabaul*, 40.
26. "History of the 43rd BG," 29; Kenney, *General Kenney Reports*, 247.
27. Salmaggi, *2194 Days of War*, 367-8.
28. "History of the 5th BG," 14; Hillsborough, pub., *Fifth BG*, 41-2.
29. Morriss, *South Pacific Diary*, 133.
30. Ibid., 130, 133.
31. Ibid., 136-40.
32. "Narrative History, 72nd BS," 30, 31, 32; "Weekly Status and Operations Report," found in *Bomb Squadron History, 72nd Bombardment Squadron (H)*.
33. Recollections of Ray Smith and J. Burrell Hudgins in *5th Bomb Group (H) Association, Inc. Newsletter*, October 5, 1996, 11-2; Morriss, *South Pacific Diary*, 144, 236.
34. Carter, *Combat Chronology*, 122-3; Craven, ed., *Army Air Forces*, Vol. IV, 213-4.
35. Birdsall, *Pride of Seattle*, 9; Morriss, *South Pacific Diary*, 144.
36. "History of the 394th Bombardment Squadron," *Bomb Squadron History, 394th Bombardment Squadron (H)* [hereafter cited as "394th BS History"], 4.
37. Ibid.
38. Ibid., 5.
39. Ibid.; Carter, *Combat Chronology*, 134; Dorr, *B-24 Liberator Units of the Pacific War*, 67.
40. "394th BS History," 5-6.
41. Ibid., 6-7.
42. Ibid., 7; Carter, *Combat Chronology*, 138.
43. "394th BS History," 7; "History of the 31st BS," 7.

Chapter 29
1. Craven, ed., *Army Air Forces*, Vol. IV, 163, 208.
2. "History of the 43rd BG," 329; Murphy, *Skip Bombing*, 158.
3. Murphy, *Skip Bombing*, 158-9, 161.
4. Ibid., 161; "History of the 43rd BG," 229.
5. Murphy, *Skip Bombing*, 162-3.
6. Kenney, *General Kenney Reports*, 259; Birdsall, *Claims to Fame*, 85; "History of the 43rd BG," 291.
7. "History of the 43rd BG," 291-2; Birdsall, *Claims to Fame*, 85-6.
8. Birdsall, *Pride of Seattle*, 9.
9. Birdsall, *Claims to Fame*, 86.
10. Kenney, *General Kenney Reports*, 259.
11. Murphy, *Skip Bombing*, 167.
12. Ibid.; Cohn, "Z is for Zeamer," *Liberty*, January 15, 1944, 22.
13. Murphy, *Skip Bombing*, 168-9; Hess, *B-17 Flying Fortress*, 49.
14. Ibid., 169; Cohn, "Z is for Zeamer," *Liberty*, January 15, 1944, 23.
15. Cohn, "Z is for Zeamer," *Liberty*, January 15, 1944, 23.
16. Murphy, *Skip Bombing*, 169; Cohn, "Z is for Zeamer," *Liberty*, January 15, 1944, 23, 69.
17. Ibid.
18. Ibid.
19. Caidin, *Flying Forts*, 31; Cohn, "Z is for Zeamer," *Liberty*, January 15, 1944, 69.
20. Cohn, "Z is for Zeamer," *Liberty*, January 15, 1944, 69.
21. Ibid.
22. Ibid.

23. Ibid.
24. "History of the 43rd BS," 330.
25. Sakaida, *The Siege of Rabaul*, 40-1; Birdsall, *Claims to Fame*, 35; Blank, "Lt. Holguin's Final Mission," *Reader's Digest*, April 1987, 83-5.
26. Birdsall, *Pride of Seattle*, 9; Sakaida, *The Siege of Rabaul*, 40.
27. Salmaggi, *2194 Days of War*, 384-5.
28. "History of the 43rd BS," 229, 330; Birdsall, *Pride of Seattle*, 14.
29. Salmaggi, *2194 Days of War*, 385-6; Kenney, *General Kenney Reports*, 265-6.
30. "Weekly Status and Operations Report," found in *Bomb Squadron History, 64th Bombardment Squadron (H)*.
31. Birdsall, *Claims to Fame*, 93-4.
32. Ibid., 94-5; Birdsall, *Pride of Seattle*, 15.
33. Kenney, *General Kenney Reports*, 271; Birdsall, *Flying Buccaneers*, 82-3; Craven, ed., *Army Air Forces*, Vol. IV, 171-2.
34. Carter, *Combat Chronology*, 162; "History of the 43rd BG," 229, 292-3; Kenney, *General Kenney Reports*, 271.
35. Carter, *Combat Chronology*, 142, 144; "History of the 31st BS," 7.
36. "Aircraft Losses from the 5th BG (H) in the Solomon Area," in *5th Bomb Group (H) Association, Inc. Newsletter*, January 5, 1996, 3; Recollections of Russell Knox in *5th Bomb Group (H) Association, Inc. Newsletter*, October 5, 1996, 11.
37. Carter, *Combat Chronology*, 145, 146; "394th BS Report," 7; "394th BS History," 8.
38. "394th BS History," 8-9.
39. "History of the 31st BS," 7.
40. Carter, *Combat Chronology*, 147, 148, 149.
41. Ibid., 154; Hillsborough, pub., *Fifth BG*, 43.
42. "23rd BS History," 6; "Aircraft Losses from the 5th BG (H) in the Solomon Area," in *5th Bomb Group (H) Association, Inc. Newsletter*, January 5, 1996, 3.
43. Carter, *Combat Chronology*, 161, 162, 164; "23rd BS History," 6.
44. Carter, *Combat Chronology*, 164, 165; "23rd BS History," 6; "Aircraft Losses from the 5th BG (H) in the Solomon Area," in *5th Bomb Group (H) Association, Inc. Newsletter*, January 5, 1996, 3; Morriss, *South Pacific Diary*, 239, 50n.
45. Hillsborough, pub., *Fifth BG*, 44.

Chapter 30

1. Kenney, *General Kenney Reports*, 273; "History of the 43rd BG," 293; Costello, *The Pacific War*, 240.
2. "History of the 43rd BG," 293; Casualty Report found in "History of the 43rd BG," 203.
3. "Weekly Status and Operations Report," found in *Bomb Squadron History, 63rd Bombardment Squadron (H)*; Freeman, *The B-17 Flying Fortress Story*, 74.
4. Carter, *Combat Chronology*, 171-2, 174; "History of the 43rd BG," 294; United States Strategic Bombing Survey, *The Fifth Air Force in the War Against Japan*, 102.
5. Carter, *Combat Chronology*, 174, 175; "History of the 43rd BG," 294.
6. Costello, *The Pacific War*, 240; Kenney, *General Kenney Reports*, 276-7; Craven, ed., *Army Air Forces*, Vol. IV, 178-9.
7. United States Strategic Bombing Survey, *The Fifth Air Force in the War Against Japan*, 102; Kenney, *General Kenney Reports*, 277-9; Craven, ed., *Army Air Forces*, Vol. IV, 179-80.
8. Kenney, *General Kenney Reports*, 279.
9. Craven, ed., *Army Air Forces*, Vol. IV, 180; "History of the 43rd BG," 294.

10. "History of the 43rd BG," 294; Carter, *Combat Chronology,* 179.
11. Craven, ed., *Army Air Forces,* Vol. IV, 180-1.
12. "History of the 43rd BG," 230, 295; Carter, *Combat Chronology,* 182-186; Craven, ed., *Army Air Forces,* Vol. IV, 182.
13. "History of the 43rd BG," 230, 295.
14. Craven, ed., *Army Air Forces,* Vol. IV, 182-3.
15. Kenney, *General Kenney Reports,* 288-9; Birdsall, *Flying Buccaneer,* 100-1; Birdsall, *Claims to Fame,* 69.
16. Costello, *The Pacific War,* 420-1; Salmaggi, *2194 Days of War,* 418; Kenney, *General Kenney Reports,* 293.
17. Kenney, *General Kenney Reports,* 292-4.
18. Ibid., 294; "History of the 43rd BG," 295.
19. Salmaggi, *2194 Days of War,* 419, 424.
20. Casualty Report found in "History of the 43rd BG," 203; Birdsall, *Pride of Seattle,* 14.
21. Carter, *Combat Chronology,* 191; "History of the 43rd BG," 295; Salmaggi, *2194 Days of War,* 424, 427; Costello, *The Pacific War,* 421.
22. Birdsall, *Pride of Seattle,* 6.
23. "History of the 43rd BG," 33-4, 295.
24. Ibid., 34; "Weekly Status and Operations Report," found in *Bomb Squadron History, 65th Bombardment Squadron (H).*
25. Brownstein, *The Swoose,* 192n, 32.
26. Birdsall, *Pride of Seattle,* 8, 13; Birdsall, *Claims to Fame,* 87.
27. Hillsborough, pub., *Fifth BG,* 44-5; "23rd BS History," 6.
28. Cleveland, ed., *Grey Geese Calling,* 216.
29. Carter, *Combat Chronology,* 174; "23rd BS History," 6.
30. "23rd BS History," 7; Recollection of Ray Smith in *5th Bomb Group (H) Association, Inc. Newsletter,* October 5, 1996, 7. The four pilots were: Maj. Burns, and Capts. Sabin, Ned Stuart, and Phillip Hodges. Three of the four planes were B-17Es (41-2444), (41-2467), and (41-9222, *Knucklehead).*
31. "23rd BS History," 7; Freeman, *The B-17 Flying Fortress Story,* 76.
32. Costello, *The Pacific War,* 421.
33. Ibid.; Carter, *Combat Chronology,* 198.
34. Costello, *The Pacific War,* 421-2.
35. Carter, *Combat Chronology,* 201, 203; Birdsall, *Claims to Fame,* 69; Birdsall, *Pride of Seattle,* 6, 13, 18; Kenney, *Gen. Kenney Reports,* 313, 316.
36. "History of the 43rd BG," 231.
37. Birdsall, *Claims to Fame,* 69; Birdsall, *Pride of Seattle,* 7, 9, 14, 15; Freeman, *The B-17 Flying Fortress Story,* 77.
38. Birdsall, *Pride of Seattle,* 6.
39. Salmaggi, *2194 Days of War,* 436; Birdsall, *Flying Buccaneers,* 155-6.
40. Birdsall, *Claims to Fame,* 70; Birdsall, *Flying Buccaneers,* 156.
41. Birdsall, *Claims to Fame,* 70-1.
42. Ibid., 71; Birdsall, *Flying Buccaneers,* 157.
43. Salmaggi, *2194 Days of War,* 509; Birdsall, *Claims to Fame,* 71.
44. Birdsall, *Pride of Seattle,* 14, 17.
45. Birdsall, *Claims to Fame,* 71-3.
46. Dunnigan, *Victory at Sea,* 579, 581, 582; Birdsall, *Claims to Fame,* 73.
47. Birdsall, *Claims to Fame,* 73.
48. Ibid., 73-5.

49. Drendel, *B-17 Walk Around*, 31.
50. Sakai, *Samurai!*, 88.
51. Edmunds, *They Fought*, 303.
52. Fields, *Kangaroo Squadron*, 74.
53. Davenport to author, January 22, 1997, 1, and May 20, 1997, 1.
54. Edmundson, "B-17 Flying Fortress" in Higham, *Flying Combat Aircraft of the USAAF-USAF*, Vol. 2, 34-5, 37.
55. Minahan statement in Freeman, *B-17 Fortress at War*, 121; Green to author, July 14, 1996; Crawford, *Gore and Glory*, 148.
56. Fields to author, February 6, 1996, 1.
57. Edmundson, "B-17 Flying Fortress" in Higham, *Flying Combat Aircraft of the USAAF-USAF*, Vol. 2, 34.
58. Birdsall, *Flying Buccaneers*, 289-90.

Chapter 31
1 Ethell, *B-17 Flying Fortress*, 33; McDowell, *Flying Fortress*, 23.
2 Hess, *B-17 Flying Fortress*, 103-8; Bonanza Books, pub., *AAF: The Official World War II Guide to the Army Air Forces*, 286-7.
3 Hess, *B-17 Flying Fortress*, 108-114; Bowman, *USAAF Handbook 1939-45*, 75-6.
4 Hess, *B-17 Flying Fortress*, 117, 120, 124.
5 Ibid., 124.
6 Ibid.
7 Ibid., 36, 38; Ethell, *B-17 Flying Fortress*, 33.
8 Hess, *B-17 Flying Fortress*, 38-43.
9 Ibid., 43-60
10 Ibid., 56-60, 64-7; Freeman, *The Mighty Eighth*, 67-9, 71, 78-9.
11 Hess, *B-17 Flying Fortress*, 67.
12 Ibid., 71, 73, 76-8; Freeman, *The Mighty Eighth*, 106, 107-9, 112.
13 Hess, *B-17 Flying Fortress*, 79, 84; Freeman, *Mighty Eighth War Diary*, 193, 195, 196-7.
14 Hess, *B-17 Flying Fortress*, 93; Freeman, *Mighty Eighth War Diary*, 259; Freeman, *The Mighty Eighth*, 140-6.
15 Freeman, *The Mighty Eighth*, 158.
16 Freeman, *Mighty Eighth War Diary*, 357; Hess, *B-17 Flying Fortress*, 97.

Appendix A
1 Hess, *B-17 Flying Fortress*, Appendix III; Freeman, *The Mighty Eighth*, 286-90; Thompson, *The Boeing B-17E & F Flying Fortress*, 16.

Bibliography

Primary and Secondary Published Material

Arakaki, Leatrice R., and John R. Kuborn, *7 December 1941: The Air Force Story.*
Washington, DC: U.S. Government Printing Office, 1991.

Aviation Publications, pub., *Pilot's Flight Operating Instructions for Army Models B-17F and*
G. Appleton, WI: Aviation Publications, 1984.

Ballard, Robert D. with Rick Archbold, *The Lost Ships of Guadalcanal.* Toronto, Ontario,
Canada: Madison Press Books, 1993.

Bartsch, William H., *Doomed at the Start: American Pursuit Pilots in the Philippines, 1941-*
1942. College Station, Texas: Texas A & M University Press, 1995.

Bergerud, Eric, *Touched With Fire: The Land War in the South Pacific.* New York: Viking,
1996.

Birdsall, Steve, *B-17 in Action.* Carrollton, Texas: Squadron/Signal Publications, Inc., 1973.
_____. *Flying Buccaneers: The Illustrated Story of Kenney's Fifth Air Force.* Garden
City, New York: Doubleday & Company, Inc., 1977.
_____. *Pride of Seattle, The Story of the First 300 B-17Fs.* Carrollton, Texas:
Squadron/Signal Publications, Inc., 1998.

Birdsall, Steve and Roger A. Freeman, *Claims to Fame, the B- 17 Flying Fortress.* London:
Arms and Armour Press, 1994.

Bonanza Books, pub., *AAF: The Official World War II Guide to the Army Air Forces.* New
York: Bonanza Books, 1988.

Bowers, Peter M., *50th Anniversary Boeing B-17 Flying Fortress.* Seattle, WA: Museum of
Flight, 1985.

Bowman, Martin W., *Flying to Glory.* Somerset, England: Patrick Stephens Limited, 1992.
_____. *USAAF Handbook 1939-45.* Mechanicsburg, PA: Stackpole Books, 1997.

Brereton, Lewis H., *The Brereton Diaries.* New York: Da Capo Press, 1976.

Brownstein, Herbert S., *The Swoose.* Washington, DC: Smithsonian Institution Press, 1993.

Caidin, Martin, *Flying Forts.* New York: Ballantine Books, 1969.

Campbell, Christy, *Air War Pacific.* New York: Crescent Books, 1990.

Carter, Kit C. and Robert Mueller, compilers, *Combat Chronology, 1941-1945.* Washington,
DC: Center for Air Force History, 1991.

Center for Air Force History, pub., *Pacific Counterblow.* Washington, DC: Center for Air
Force History, 1992.

Chesneau, Roger, ed., *Conway's All the World's Fighting Ships, 1922-1946.* Annapolis, MD:
United States Naval Institute, 1980.

Clark, Blake, *Remember Pearl Harbor.* New York: Harper & Brothers Publishers, 1943.

Cleveland, W. M., ed., *Grey Geese Calling: A History of the 11th Bombardment Group Heavy (H) in the Pacific, 1940- 1945.* Portsmouth, NH: privately printed, 1992.

Collison, Tom, *Flying Fortress.* New York: Charles Scribner's Sons, 1943.

Costello, John, *The Pacific War.* New York: Quill, 1982.

Craven, Wesley Frank and James Lea Cate, eds., *The Army Air Forces in World War II.* Vol. 1, *Plans and Early Operations, January 1939 to August 1942.* Chicago: University of Chicago Press, 1958.

_____. *The Army Air Forces in World War II.* Vol. 4, *The Pacific: Guadalcanal to Saipan, August 1942 to July 1944.* Chiacgo: University of Chicago Press, 1950..

Crawford, Capt. William, Jr., as told to Ted Saucier, *Gore and Glory.* Philadelphia: David McKay Company, 1944.

Davis, Larry, *B-17 in Action.* Carrollton, Texas: Squadron/Signal Publications, Inc., 1984.

Dorr, Robert F., *B-24 Liberator Units of the Pacific War.* Oxford, England: Osprey Publishing Ltd., 1999.

_____. *7th Bombardment Group/Wing.* Paducah, Kentucky: Turner Publishing Company, 1996.

Drendal, Lou, *B-17 Walk Around.* Carrollton, Texas: Squadron/Signal Publications, Inc., 1998.

Dunnigan, James F., and Albert A. Nofi, *Victory At Sea.* New York: Quill, 1995.

Edmunds, Walter D., *They Fought With What They Had.* Boston: Little, Brown and Company, 1951.

Freeman, Roger A., with David Osborne, *The B-17 Flying Fortress Story.* London: Arms & Armour Press, 1998.

Freeman, Roger A., *B-17 Fortress at War.* London: Ian Allan Ltd., 1977.

_____. *Combat Profile: B-17G Flying Fortress in World War 2.* London: Ian Allan Ltd., 1990.

Gillison, Douglas, *Royal Australian Air Force, 1939-1942, Series Three, (Air)* Vol. 1. Canberra, Australia: Australian War Museum, 1962.

Godman, Henry C., with Cliff Dudley, *Supreme Commander.* Harrison, Ark.: New Leaf Press, 1980.

Goldstein, Donald M., Katharine V. Dillon and J. Michael Wenger, *The Way it Was: Pearl Harbor.* McLean, VA: Brassey's (US), Inc., 1991.

Goralski, Robert, *World War II Almanac: 1931-1945.* New York: G.P. Putnam's Sons, 1981.

Greenwood Press, pub., *The Campaigns of the Pacific War: United States Strategic Bombing Survey (Pacific).* New York: Greenwood Press, Publishers, 1969.

Hardison, Patricia, *The Suzy-Q.* Cambridge, Massachusetts: The Riverside Press, 1943.

Haugland, Vern, *The AAF Against Japan.* New York: Harper & Brothers Publishers, 1948.

Hearings Before the Joint Committee on the Investigation of the Pearl Harbor Attack, Congress of the United States, Seventy-Ninth Congress, Part 30. Washington, DC: U.S. Government Printing Office, 1946.

Hess, William, *B-17 Flying Fortress: Combat and Development History of the Flying Fortress.* Osceola, WI: Motorbooks, 1994.

Higham, *Flying Combat Aircraft of the USAAF - USAF: Vol. 2.* Ames, Iowa: Iowa State University Press, 1975.

Hillsborough House, pub., *The Story of the Fifth Bombardment Group (Heavy).* Raleigh, NC: Hillsborough House, 1946.

Howard, Clive and Joe Whitley, *One Damned Island After Another.* Chapel Hill, NC: The University of North Carolina Press, 1947.

Ind, Allison, *Bataan, The Judgment Seat.* New York: The MacMillan Company, 1944.

Johnsen, Frederick A., ed., *Winged Majesty*. Tacoma, WA: Bomber Books, 1980.

Johnston, Richard W., *Follow Me! The Story of the Second Marine Division in World War II*. New York: Random House, 1948.

Kenney, George C., *Gen. Kenney Reports*. Washington, DC: Office of Air Force History, 1987.

Kimmett, Larry and Margaret Regis, *The Attack on Pearl Harbor: An Illustrated History*. Seattle, WA: Navigator Publishing, 1992.

Kurzman, Dan, *Left to Die: The Tragedy of the USS Juneau*. New York: Pocket Books, 1994.

La Forte, Robert S., and Ronald E. Marcello, *Remembering Pearl Harbor*. New York: Ballantine Books, 1992.

Lambert, John W., *The Pineapple Air Force: Pearl Harbor to Tokyo*. St. Paul, MN: Phalanx Publishing Co., Ltd., 1990.

Lloyd, Alwyn T. and Terry D. Moore, *B-17 Flying Fortress in Detail and Scale*. Falbrook, CA: Aero Publishers, Inc., 1981.

Lord, Walter, *Day of Infamy*. New York: Bantam Books, 1957.

_____. *Incredible Victory*. New York: Harper & Row, Publishers, 1967.

MacDonald, John, *Great Battles of World War II*. Philadelphia: Courage Books, 1993.

Maurer, Maurer, ed., *Air Force Combat Squadrons of World War II*. Washington, DC: Office of Air Force History, 1961.

_____. *Air Force Combat Units of World War II*. Washington, DC: Office of Air Force History, 1961.

McClendon, Dennis E., and Wallace F. Richards, *The Legend of Colin Kelly*. Missoula, Montana: Pictorial Histories Publishing Company, Inc., 1994.

McDowell, Ernest R., *Flying Fortress: The Boeing B-17*. Carrollton, Texas: Squadron/Signal Publications, 1987.

Miller, Thomas G., Jr., *The Cactus Air Force*. New York: Harper, Row, Publishers, 1969.

Mingos, Howard, *American Heroes of the War in the Air*, Vol. One. New York: Lanciar Publishers, Inc., 1943.

Mitchell, John H., *In Alis Vicimus, On Wings We Conquer*. Springfield, MO: G.E.M. Publications, 1990.

Morehead, James, *In My Sights - Memoirs of a P-40 Ace*. Novato, CA: Presidio Press, 1998.

Morison, Samuel Eliot, *History of the United States Naval Operations in World War II: The Struggle for Guadalcanal, August 1942-February 1943*. Vol. 5. Boston: Little, Brown and Company, 1975.

Morriss, Mack, *South Pacific Diary, 1942-1943*. Lexinton, Kentucky: The University Press of Kentucky, 1996.

Morton, Louis, *United States Army in World War II: Strategy and Command - The First Two Years*. Washington, DC: Office of the Chief of Military History, Department of the Army, 1962.

Murphy, James T., with A.B. Feuer, *Skip Bombing*. Westport, Connecticut: Praeger Publishers, 1993.

Nalty, Bernard C., ed., *Pearl Harbor and the War in the Pacific*. New York: Smithmark, Publishers Inc., 1991.

Nalty, Bernard C., with J. Shiner & G. Watson, *With Courage: the U.S. Army Air Force in World War II*. Washington, DC: U.S. Government Printing Office, 1994.

O'Leary, Michael, ed., *Air Combat Special - Flying Fortress*. Canoga Park, CA: Challenge Publications, Inc., 1985.

Patterson, *The Lady*. Charlottsville, VA: Howell Press, Inc., 1993.

Perret, Geoffrey, *Winged Victory*. New York: Random Press, 1993.

Prange, Gordon W., *At Dawn We Slept*. New York: McGraw-Hill Book Company, 1988.

_____. *Miracle at Midway.* New York: Viking, 1983.

Prange, Gordon W., with Donald M. Goldstein and Katharine V. Dillon, *December 7, 1941.* New York: McGraw-Hill Book Company, 1988.

Rutherford, Ward, *Fall of the Philippines.* New York: Ballantine Books Inc., 1971.

Salmaggi, Cesare and Alfredo Pallavisini, compilers, *2194 Days of War.* New York: Windward, 1977.

Sakaida, Henry, *The Siege of Rabaul.* St. Paul, MN: Phalanx Publishing Co., Ltd., 1996.

Sakai, Saburo, with Martin Caidin and Fred Saito, *Samurai!* Garden City, New York: Nelson Doubleday, Inc., 1978.

Sharp & Dunnigan Publications, Incorporated, *The Congressional Medal of Honor.* Chico, CA: Sharp & Dunnigan Publications, Incorporated, 1988.

Shores, Christopher, and Brian Cull with Yasuho Izawa, *Bloody Shambles,* Vol. 1 and Vol. 2. London: Grub Street Books, 1993.

Steinberg, Rafael, *Island Fighting.* Alexandria, VA: Time- Life Books Inc., 1978.

Taggart, William C., *My Fighting Congregation.* Garden City, New York: Doubleday, Doran & Company, Inc., 1943.

Thompson, Charles D., *The Boeing B-17E & F Flying Fortress.* Surrey, England: Profile Publications Ltd., 1966.

Tregaskis, Richard, *Guadalcanal Diary.* New York: Random House, 1943.

Turner Publishing Company, pub., *11th Bomb Group (H).* Paducah, Kentucky: Turner Publishing Company, 1996.

United States Strategic Bombing Survey (Pacific), *The Fifth Air Force in the War Against Japan.* Washington, DC: U.S. Government Printing Office, 1947.

USAAF, *Handbook of Operation and Flight Instructions for the Model B-17D Bombardment Airplane.* St. Louis, MO: Ross- Gould Co., 1942.

Weintraub, Stanley, *Long Day's Journey Into War.* New York: Truman Talley Books, 1991.

Whitcomb, Edgar D., *Escape From Corregidor.* Chicago: Henry Regnery Company, 1958.

White, William L., *Queens Die Proudly.* New York: Harcourt, Brace and Company, 1943.

Willmott, H.P., *The Barrier and the Javelin: Japanese and Allied Pacific Struggles, February to June 1942.* Annapolis, MD: Naval Institute Press, 1983.

Wolfert, Ira, *Battle for the Solomons.* Boston: Houghton Mifflin Company, 1943.

Zich, Arthur, *The Rising Sun.* Alexandria, VA: Time-Life Books Inc., 1977.

Unpublished Government Documents

Emmett, E. R., and W. D. Emmons, *Interviews of Men Who Fought in the Philippines, 1941-42.*

Statement by Capt. H. T. Wheless, A. C.

"The AAF in Australia to the Summer of 1942," *Army Air Forces Historical Studies: No. 9.*

Unpublished Bombardment Squadron Histories and Documents

"Historical Data and History of the 23rd Bombardment Squadron (H), APO 324," *Bomb Squadron History, 23rd Bombardment Squadron (H).*

"Daily Diary, 4 May 1942 to 20 December 1942, Inclusive, Author Unknown," *Bomb Squadron History, 26th Bombardment Squadron (H).*

"History of the 26th Bombardment Squadron (H)," *Bomb Squadron History, 26th Bombardment Squadron (H).*

"History of the 28th Bombardment," *Bomb Squadron History, 28th Bombardment Squadron (H).*

"History of the 30th Bombardment Squadron, 19th Bomb Group," *Bomb Squadron History, 30th Bombardment Squadron (H).*

"History of the 31st Bombardment Squadron, 5th Bomb Group," *Bomb Squadron History, 31st Bombardment Squadron (H).*

"History of the 42nd Bombardment Squadron, 11th Bombardment Group, Seventh Air Force," *11th Bombardment Group (H) History.*

"Weekly Status and Operations Report," *Bomb Squadron History, 63rd Bombardment Squadron (H).*

"Weekly Status and Operations Report," *Bomb Squadron History, 64th Bombardment Squadron (H).*

"Weekly Status and Operations Report," *Bomb Squadron History, 65th Bombardment Squadron (H).*

"Narrative of Squadron History from Activation 18 February 1918 to 28 February 1944, Incl.," *Bomb Squadron History, 72nd Bombardment Squadron (H).*

"History of the 93rd Bombardment Squadron, (H), 19th Bomb Group, from December 8, 1941 to January 31, 1943," *Bomb Squadron History, 93rd Bombardment Squadron (H).*

"History of the 98th Bombardment Squadron, (H), 16 December 1941 to 1 April 1944," *Bomb Squadron History, 98th Bombardment Squadron (H).*

"History of the 394th Bombardment Squadron," *Bomb Squadron History, 394th Bombardment Squadron (H).*

"394th Bombardment Squadron (H), Historical Officer, Squadron Historical Report," *Bomb Squadron History, 394th Bombardment Squadron (H).*

"History of the 403rd Bombardment Squadron (H) in Australia," *Bomb Squadron History, 403rd Bombardment Squadron (H).*

"Combat Operations, MIDWAY Area, 3-4 June 1942," *Bomb Squadron Supplement, 431st Bombardment Squadron (H).*

"Organizational History, 431st Bombardment Squadron (H), 11th Bombardment Group (H), VII Bomber Command, Seventh Air Force," *Bomb Squadron History, 431st Bombardment Squadron (H).*

"A Brief History of the 435th Bombardment Squadron, (H)," *Bomb Squadron History, 435th Bombardment Squadron (H).*

"Destruction of Enemy Aircraft," *435th Bombardment Squadron, 19th Bombardment Group (H).*

Johnson, ed., "435th Overseas," *Bomb Squadron History, 435th Bombardment Squadron (H).*

"Missions of the 435th BS," *Bomb Squadron History, 435th BS, 1941-43.*

"Narrative History of the 435th Bombardment Squadron, 6 December 1941 to 20 December 1942," *Bomb Squadron History, 435th Bombardment Squadron (H).*

"Squadron Diary-Eighty-Eighth Reconnaissance, (H), AFCC," *Bomb Squadron History, 435th Bombardment Squadron.*

"435th Daily Bulletin," *435th Bombardment Squadron, 19th Bombardment Group (H).*

Unpublished Bombardment Group Histories and Documents

"Brief History of 5th Bombardment Group, 1918-1952," *5th Bombardment Group (H) History.*

"History of the 5th Bombardment Group (H)," *5th Bombardment Group (H) History.*

"Consolidated History of the Seventh Bombardment Group," *7th Bombardment Group (H) History.*

"Diary - 7th Bombardment GP (H)," *7th Bombardment Group (H) History.*

"History of the Seventh Bombardment Group (H)," *7th Bombardment Group (H) History.*

"11th Bombardment Group Citations," *11th Bombardment Group (H) History.*

"History of the 11th Bombardment Group,(H), February 1940 - March 1944," *11th Bombardment Group (H) History.*

"Performance, Results and Attrition of B-17, Heavy Bombers in Solomon Islands Operations - August and September, 1942," *11th Bombardment Group (H) History.*

"Answers to Request for Historical Information Concerning 19th Bombardment Group (H),"in Fields, *Kangaroo Squadron.*

"Diary of the 19th Bombardment Group," *19th Bombardment Group (H) History.*

"Diary of Operations of the 19th Bomb Group in Java, " *19th Bombardment Group (H) History.*

"Historical Data of 19th Bombardment Group," *19th Bombardment Group (H) History.*

Interviews of the 19th Bombardment Group, 9 December 1942.

"A Short History of the 43rd Bombardment Group and the 63rd, 64th, 65th, and 403rd Bomb Squadron," *43rd Bombardment Group (H) History.*

"History of the Forty-Third Bombardment Group (H)," *43rd Bombardment Group (H) History, 15 January 1941 to February 1944.*

Unpublished Air Force Documents and Reports

"Air Services in the Visayan-Mindanao Area, Dec. 1941 - May 1942," Document 30a, *Fifth Air Force Operations, 1940- 45.*

"Aircraft Ferried from U.S.A.," *Fifth Air Force Operations, 1940-45.*

"A-3 Airplane Status Section Folder," *Fifth Air Force Operations, 1940-45.*

"Army Air Services in the Philippines, November 1941 - 29 April 1942," Document 8, *Fifth Air Force Operations, 1940-45.*

"Aromatic Action," *Fifth Air Force Operations, 1940-45.*

"Aromatic Gasoline," *Fifth Air Force Operations, 1940-45.*

"Awards - Citation" Document 18, 1, 3, *Fifth Air Force Operations, 1940-45.*

"Awards to Members of USAFFE in Phillipine [sic] & Java," Document 19, 4, *Fifth Air Force Operations, 1940-1945.*

"Col. Elsmore on 'Queens Die Proudly'," Document 31, 2, *Fifth Air Force Operations, 1940-45.*

"Daily Summary on A/C Combats," *Miscellaneous Data, Southwest Pacific Theater.*

"Damage to Rubber by Aromatic Gas," *Fifth Air Force Operations, 1940-45.*

"Gasoline," *Fifth Air Force Operations, 1940-45.*

"Journal of the 5th Bomber Command," *Fifth Air Force Operations, 1940-45.*

"Operational History of the Seventh Air Force, 7 December 1941 to 6 November 1943," *Army Air Force Historical Studies: No. 41.*

"Report on Gun Turrets," Document 1078, *Fifth Air Force Operations, 1940-45.*

"6-8th December 1941 in the Philippines," *Fifth Air Force Operations, 1940-45.*

Journals and Periodicals

5th Bombardment Group (H) Association Newsletter. December 5, 1994, January 7, and October 5, 1996.

"Adventure in New Guinea, U.S. Pilots save Flying Fortress," *Life*, January 4, 1943.

Blank, Joseph P., "Lt. Holguin's Final Mission," *Reader's Digest*, April 1987.

Brown, Cecil, ed., "War Pilot's Story," *Life*, May 11, 1942.

Cohn, Art, "Z is for Zeamer," *Liberty*, January 15, 1944.

Jacquet, Edward M., Jr., "Flight Into History," *Daedalian Flyer*, Winter, 1985.

Larder, John, "The Japs Don't Like the Sting of the Fortress," *Newsweek*, April 6, 1942, 19.

MacAfee, James Byington, "For the Boys on Bataan," *Time*, April 27, 1942.

Maddox, Robert J., "Bandits Over Clark," *American History Illustrated*, June 1974.

McCoy, John J., "Our Planes and Their Record," *Vital Speeches of the Day*, Vol. 8, October 1, 1942.

Mikesh, Maj. Robert C., USAF, "Japan's Little Fleet of Big American Bombers," *Air Force/Space Digest*, August 1969.
Reid, Ernest L., "Shot Down at Pearl Harbor," *Air Force Magazine*, December 1991.
Rickenbacker, Eddie, "Eddie Rickenbacker's Own Story," *Life*, January 25, 1943.
"Roll of Honor," *Life*, March 16, 1942.
Stage, Anson H., "Second Raid on Pearl Harbor," *World War II*, January 1999.
"The Sea Battle of Macassar Strait," *Life*, February 9, 1942.
Vader, John, "Fall of the Philippines," *History of the Second World War*, Pt. 31.
Walker, "American Bombers Attacking From Australia," *National Geographic Magazine*, Vol. LXXXIII, No. 1, January 1943.

Unpublished Sources
Cool, Paul E., "Excerpts from Maj. Paul E. Cool Personal Diary," *19th Bombardment Group (H) History*.
Fields, John Wallace, *Lt. Col. John Wallace Fields*.
_____. "Overseas Diary of Lt. John Wallace Fields" in Fields, *Kangaroo Squadron*.
_____. *Kangaroo Squadron*.
Kimmerle, Benjamin F., *Dec. '41 Personal Narrative of M. Sgt. B.F. Kimmerle*.
Knudson, Cecil C., *Diary of Capt. Cecil C. Knudson*.
Log entitled "Trans-Pacific Flight," and attached to Kimmerle, Benjamin F., *Dec. '41 Personal Narrative of M. Sgt. B.F. Kimmerle*.
Rouse, John A., *Diary of Lt. Col. John A. Rouse*.
Schaeffer, Earl M., Jr., "December 7th 1941."
_____. "A Few Missions Out of Guadalcanal."
_____. "Battle of Midway."
Spieth, Glen E., *"Chief Seattle" from the Pacific Northwest, Missing in Action*, 1988.

Newspapers
Teats, Edward C., "Turn of the Tide," *Philadelphia Inquirer*, December 1942-January 1943.

Correspondence and Interviews
Angelini, Joseph S. Interviews by author. December 7, and 8, 1997.
Davenport, Roy A. Letters to author. December 16, 1996, January 22, and May 20, 1997.
Edmundson, James V. Letter to author. July 19, 1988.
_____. Letter to Phil Klingensmith. Oct. 19, 1991.
Fields, John Wallace. Letters to author. February 5, April 15, July 8, and September 10, 1996.
_____. Letter to Councillor Tony Mooney. August 14, 1995.
Gooch, Ritchie B. Letters to author. April 10, August, 12, and September 2, 1996; October 22, 1997.
Graham, Robert H. Letter to author. May 9, 1997
Green, John W. Letters to author. July 14, and September 10, 1996.
Klingensmith, Phil. Letters to author. Nov. 10, and December 15, 1996, and March 23, 1998.
Lilliback, John. Letter to Councillor Tony Mooney, August 15, 1995.
Payne, L.M. "Mike." Letters to author. July 12, and September 9, 1996.

Index